Philosophy of Psychology

Philosophy of Psychology

*Debates on Psychological
Explanation, Volume One*

Edited by

Cynthia Macdonald and Graham Macdonald

BLACKWELL
Oxford UK & Cambridge USA

Copyright © Basil Blackwell Limited 1995

First published 1995

Blackwell Publishers, the publishing imprint of
Basil Blackwell Ltd
108 Cowley Road
Oxford OX4 1JF
UK

Basil Blackwell Inc.
238 Main Street
Cambridge, Massachusetts 02142
USA

British Library Cataloguing in Publication Data

A CIP catalogue record for this book is available from
the British Library.

Library of Congress Cataloging-in-Publication Data

Philosophy of Psychology/edited by Cynthia Macdonald and
Graham Macdonald.
    p. cm.
    Includes bibliographical references and index.
    ISBN 0–631–18541–0. – ISBN 0–631–18542–9 (pbk.)
    1. Psychology – Philosophy. I. Macdonald, Cynthia, 1951–
II. Macdonald, Graham.
BF38.P474 1995
150'.1 – dc20   94–21502
                CIP

Typeset in 10½ pt on 12 pt Ehrhardt
by CentraCet Limited, Cambridge
Printed in Great Britain by
Hartnolls Ltd, Bodmin

This book is printed on acid-free paper

Contents

Contributors

Ned Block is Professor of Philosophy at the Massachusetts Institute of Technology. He is editor of *Readings in the Philosophy of Psychology* (2 vols) and of *Imagery*, as well as author of articles on the philosophy of mind and psychology.

Tyler Burge is Professor of Philosophy at UCLA. He has written extensively on the philosophy of language, the philosophy of mind, and epistemology.

Martin Davies is Wilde Reader in Mental Philosophy at the University of Oxford. He is author of *Meaning, Quantification and Necessity*, co-editor with Tony Stone of *Mental Simulation*, co-editor with Glyn Humphreys of *Consciousness*, and author of articles on the philosophy of psychology.

Frederick Dretske is Professor of Philosophy at Stanford University. He is author of *Seeing and Knowing, Knowledge and the Flow of Information, Explaining Behaviour: Reasons in a World of Causes*, and articles on epistemology, philosophy of science, and the philosophy of mind.

Jerry A. Fodor is Professor of Philosophy at Rutgers University and CUNY Graduate Center. He has written extensively on the philosophy of mind and the philosophy of psychology, and is author of *The Modularity of Mind, Psychosemantics, A Theory of Content*, and co-author with Ernest LePore of *Holism: A Shopper's Guide*.

James Hopkins is Lecturer in Philosophy at King's College London. He is co-editor with Richard Wollheim of *Philosophical Essays on Freud*, co-editor with Anthony Saville of *Psychoanalysis, Mind and Art*, and author of articles on Wittgenstein and on psychoanalysis.

Mark Johnston is Professor of Philosophy at Princeton University. He has written articles on metaphysics, epistemology, and the philosophy of mind.

Jaegwon Kim is William Herbert Perry Faunce Professor of Philosophy at

Brown University. He has written extensively on metaphysics, epistemology, and the philosophy of mind, and is author of *Supervenience and Mind*.

Cynthia Macdonald is Senior Lecturer in Philosophy at the University of Manchester. She is author of *Mind–Body Identity Theories*, and has written articles on metaphysics, the philosophy of mind, and the philosophy of psychology.

Graham Macdonald is Senior Lecturer in Philosophy at the University of Bradford. He has written articles on the philosophy of social science and the philosophy of mind. He is co-author with Philip Pettit of *Semantics and Social Science*, editor of *Perception and Identity*, and co-editor with Crispin Wright of *Fact, Science, and Morality*.

Ruth Garrett Millikan is Professor of Philosophy at the University of Connecticut and the University of Michigan. She is author of *Language, Thought, and Other Biological Categories* and *White Queen Psychology and Other Essays for Alice*, and has written articles on the philosophy of language and the philosophy of mind.

Christopher Peacocke is Waynflete Professor of Metaphysical Philosophy at the University of Oxford and a Fellow of Magdalen College, Oxford. He is author of *Holistic Explanation, Sense and Content, Thoughts: An Essay on Content*, and *A Study of Concepts*, and author of articles on the philosophy of language and the philosophy of mind.

John R. Searle is Professor of Philosophy at the University of California at Berkeley. He has written extensively on the philosophy of language and the philosophy of mind. His books include *Speech Acts: An Essay in the Philosophy of Language, Expression and Meaning, Studies in the Theory of Speech Acts, Intentionality, Mind, Brain, and Science*, and *The Rediscovery of the Mind*.

Acknowledgements

The editors and the publisher wish to acknowledge with thanks permission to reprint the following material, previously published elsewhere, in this volume.

Ned Block, 'Can the Mind Change the World?', in G. Boolos (ed.), *Meaning and Method: Essays in Honor of Hilary Putnam* (Cambridge, Cambridge University Press, 1990), copyright © Cambridge University Press, reprinted by permission of the author and Cambridge University Press.

Tyler Burge, 'Individualism and Psychology', *Philosophical Review* **95**, 1986. Copyright © 1991 Cornell University. Reprinted by permission of the publisher and the author.

Martin Davies, 'Tacit Knowledge and Subdoxastic States', in A. George (ed.), *Reflections on Chomsky* (Oxford, Basil Blackwell, 1989), copyright © 1989 Basil Blackwell, reprinted by permission of the author and Basil Blackwell.

Frederick Dretske, 'Does Meaning Matter?', in E. Villanueva (ed.), *Information, Semantics, and Epistemology* (Oxford, Oxford University Press, 1990), copyright © Oxford University Press, reprinted by permission of the author and Oxford University Press.

Jerry A. Fodor, 'A Modal Argument for Narrow Content', *Journal of Philosophy* **88**, 1991, reprinted by permission of the author and *The Journal of Philosophy*.

James Hopkins, a selection from the Introduction to R. Wollheim and J. Hopkins (eds), *Philosophical Essays on Freud* (Cambridge, Cambridge University Press, 1982), copyright © Cambridge University Press, reprinted by permission of the author and Cambridge University Press.

Mark Johnston, 'Self-deception and the Nature of Mind', in B. McLaughlin and A. Rorty (eds), *Perspectives on Self-deception* (California, the University of California Press, 1988), copyright © The Regents of the University of

California, reprinted by permission of the author and the University of California Press.

Jaegwon Kim, 'Explanatory Exclusion and the Problem of Mental Causation', in E. Villanueva (ed.), *Information, Semantics, and Epistemology* (Oxford, Oxford University Press, 1990), copyright © 1990 Oxford University Press, reprinted by permission of the author and Oxford University Press.

Ruth Garrett Millikan, 'Biosemantics', *Journal of Philosophy* **86**, 1989, reprinted by permission of the author and *The Journal of Philosophy*.

Ruth Garrett Millikan, a selection from 'Explanation in Biopsychology', in J. Heil and A. Mele (eds), *Mental Causation* (Oxford, Clarendon Press, 1993), copyright © Oxford University Press, reprinted by permission of the author and Oxford University Press.

Christopher Peacocke, a selection from *A Study of Concepts* (Massachusetts, MIT Press, 1992), copyright © Massachusetts Institute of Technology, reprinted by permission of the author and The MIT Press.

John R. Searle, 'Consciousness, Explanatory Inversion and Cognitive Science', *Behavioral and Brain Sciences* **13**, 1990, reprinted by permission of the author and Cambridge University Press.

Preface

The philosophy of psychology has burgeoned in the past twenty years. The causes of the expanding interest in this area are varied, but among them must be counted the reaction to a positivist philosophy of science within both philosophy and psychology. Positivism had insisted on the unification of science, which in essence required that all science should conform to the model of physics. The effect of this requirement was to restrict science, including psychology, to the ontology, methodology and explanatory practice of physics. These restrictions made themselves felt in different ways within psychology, including a suspicion of theory and theoretical entities, an emphasis on laboratory-style experimentation and an insistence on the deductive-nomological conception of explanation.

This last proved particularly troublesome for psychology, as its subject matter – the mental – is naturally described and explained using intentional terminology. Actions are usually explained by describing the mental states of the agent, citing relevant beliefs, desires and emotions in order to make the resultant action intelligible. The nomological aspect of the deductive-nomological conception of explanation stipulated that the laws used must be *empirical* laws, where this meant that the antecedent and consequent of the conditional must be independently identifiable. This condition on laws was required, so it was thought, in order to ensure that the laws were confirmable or falsifiable, and to conform to the Humean conception of causation, where it is deemed essential to the existence of a cause-effect relation that its two terms be independently identifiable. The problem is that when intentional terminology is used in order to make an action intelligible, the mental state is described in ways which link it in a not merely empirical way to the action. An intention is an intention to do p, or a desire is a desire for p, where p is the action explained by the presence of the intention or desire. This conceptual link between antecedent and consequent was seen to cast doubt both on the empirical character of the explanations and on the status of the antecedent as describing a cause of the action it purported to explain. As a consequence of this non-conformity to the explanatory paradigm of physics, the positivist philosopher of science or psychologist was faced with a dilemma: either give up hope that psychology could be a *bona fide* science, or re-mould its explanations, getting rid of the intentionalist vocabulary.

As positivism loosened its grip on the philosophy of science, different options emerged, one of the most important being that introduced by Donald Davidson (1963) in his seminal paper, 'Actions, reasons, and causes'. Davidson insisted on the significance of the difference between descriptions and what is described. The mental state of the agent may be described using intentional terminology (and so in a manner linking it to the action), but what is described, the mental state, may well be independently identifiable using different terminology, and so could pass the test of being a genuine cause of the action. In subsequent papers Davidson elaborated on this option, further loosening positivist restrictions by allowing psychological explanations to be autonomous and so different from explanations in physics, while still requiring that the ontology – of events explained – be physicalist.

Within psychology, a similar destination was being reached by a different route. The appeal of behaviourism declined, partly as a consequence of the influence of computer-based models of cognition. These revealed the significance of the distinction between software and hardware descriptions of computational processes, such a distinction reinforcing the claim that intentional (software) explanations were viable independently of detailed knowledge concerning the nature of the hardware implementing the software. The importance of distinguishing levels of description and explanation is seen in the work of David Marr (1982) on the visual system. These trends have led to a renewed interest in the development of a cognitive psychology which uses intentional explanations and which relates the intentional domain to sub-intentional processes. Such a development has produced both new philosophical problems and reproduced some of the older problems in a new guise.

Each section of this two-volume collection presents a debate on a central issue relating to these problems. The debates consist of seminal articles, previously published elsewhere, which present differing solutions to some of the foundational problems generated by the developments, as well as entirely new contributions from some of the authors which further the debate. Substantial introductions to each section help set the debates in context. The introductions aim to provide assistance to the reader in focusing on the central points in dispute and also make the volumes valuable as the basis for upper level courses in the philosophy of mind/psychology, whether these be in second or third year undergraduate classes or postgraduate level. Both philosophy and psychology students will stand to benefit from such a course.

The present volume focuses on issues surrounding mental causation and intentional explanation. The two debates in Part I concern problems relating to the *autonomy* of the intentional domain. The first deals with the autonomy of intentional causation, the second with the autonomy of intentional explanation. The Davidsonian solution to the problem of mental causation, briefly outlined above, has appeared to some to be unsatisfactory. The complaint is that the solution makes the mental causally efficacious only in so far as mental events are identified with physical events; and this makes the causal powers of the mental reside only in the causal powers of the physical. The question addressed by the first debate is whether the mental can be causally efficacious while at the same time being dependent upon physical processes. The second debate deals with a similar problem at the level of explanation: given the dependence of the mental on the physical, can intentional explanations be anything more than instrumentally useful? Can they avoid being replaceable, in principle, by more basic physical explanations?

Arguments about causality and explanation recur in a different form in the first debate of Part II. Here the main question is how intentional mental states ought to be taxonomized or categorized for the purposes of causal explanation in psychology. The issue concerns the relation between two aspects of intentional content. The content of, say, a belief state is used in causal–explanatory contexts, but it is also semantically evaluable, capable of being true or false. Given that the truth or falsity of an intentional state appears to depend on some fact or facts that exist beyond the body of a person, the obtaining of which is independent of the belief itself, the question arises as to what role the semantic aspect of content plays in causal explanations in psychology. How can the obtaining (or not) of a state of the world extrinsic to a person's body play a part in the causal explanation of that person's action? Individualists say that, so far as the science of psychology is concerned, it cannot; all that is relevant are those occurrences that take place within the confines of the person's body. As a consequence they maintain that a scientific psychology should use a type of content, 'narrow content', in its explanations, whose possession by persons does not depend on factors beyond their bodies. Anti-individualists argue against this recommendation.

In all three debates – intentional causation, intentional explanation, and individualist versus anti-individualist explanation – the example of biology is often used to support points on the nature of psychological causation and explanation. This is unsurprising; its status as a science is not disputed, so if it can be shown that biological explanations have certain of the 'suspect' characteristics of intentional explanation, then this will lend support to those defending the scientific legitimacy of such explanation. Biopsychologists go one step further. They claim that psychology is a branch of biology, and as such psychological explanation should be seen as a species of biological explanation. Support for this comes from the consideration that what distinguishes both psychology and biology from physics and chemistry is the goal-oriented nature of the processes they seek to explain. This suggests that both biology and psychology should use functional explanation, where the explanation of the behaviour of a trait is in terms of what it has been selected to do. The second debate in Part II concerns whether psychological purposes can be so assimilated to biological purposes; whether concentrating on the biological-functional can provide the appropriate content for psychological states.

Part III departs from the terrain of intentional explanation to inspect the sub-terrain of tacit knowledge and the unconscious. Most of the psychological states referred to in everyday accounts of our actions are either conscious or easily accessible to consciousness. There is, however, a significant class of actions that give rise to the postulation of psychological states or processes which are not so easily accessed. When we speak grammatically, or correct the ungrammatical utterances of a child, we display a mastery of a grammar whose rules, if we were asked, we could not describe. The knowledge we have of the rules of our grammar is clearly not explicit or fully conscious, so it is said that we have implicit or tacit knowledge of these rules. The challenge is to defend the existence of such knowledge in the absence of what many see as the defining characteristic of the mental, its capturing of the distinctive point of view of the conscious agent. The first debate in Part III addresses this challenge.

The situation with respect to the unconscious states postulated by psychoanalytic theory, the subject matter of the second debate in Part III, is somewhat different. Here the point of view of the agent can be respected by attributing contents to the states which were, once upon a time, available to the aware subject. It is this awareness which produces repression, the subject recoiling from the knowledge and pushing it into the unconscious. Again, however, the controversy concerns how we are to understand the processes as intentional. If we see the repression as a deliberate act we seem to be saying that the subject does know, *qua* repressor, the contents of the states which at the same time they are deemed not to know, given that they have been expunged from consciousness. Both debates end on a fitting note, as what is at stake in these exchanges is the rationalistic model of the mental which has been our starting point, that proposed by Davidson.

One large and important area of the 'sub-terrain' of psychological explanation remains to be explored, and this is done in Volume Two. Here the debates centre on the controversies introduced into psychology by the connectionist architectures of some computers. Two crucial areas are explored. The first revolves around the question of whether classical architectures are better suited to modelling the intentional mental processes, given that these processes are related to one another in a systematic manner. The question is whether a connectionist architecture can represent the relevant notion of systematicity. The second area centres on the question of whether the processes exploited in connectionist models of mental processes are inconsistent with the intentional processes exploited in intentional explanations. Here the debate concerns whether connectionist explanations can recapture, at some level, certain features of intentional processes thought to be essential to the explanation of action by intentional psychology.

By focusing on the question of how explanations in terms of classical and connectionist architectures relate to intentional explanations, the connectionist debates in Volume Two integrate with the debates in Volume One to form a cohesive whole. Together the two volumes cover a wide area of types of psychological explanation and large number of issues that arise concerning their nature and relations to one another.

We would like to thank all the contributors to these volumes for their cooperation; it has been a great pleasure working with them. We would also like to express our gratitude to those who have read and commented on our contributions to the volume, and especially to Graham Bird, Stephen Laurence, Eve Garrard, Roger Fellows and Lawrence Lombard; and we are grateful to Sue Ashton for her careful work on the manuscript. Our children, Ian and Julia, have certainly taken a beating from our involvement in this project, and we heartily thank them for their patience and sense of humour. Our greatest debt of thanks we owe to one another.

C. A. M.
G. F. M.

References

Davidson, D. (1963) Actions, reasons and causes. *Journal of Philosophy* 60, 685–700.
Marr, D. (1982) *Vision*. New York, W.H. Freeman.

PART I

Causal Relevance

1

Introduction: Supervenient Causation

Cynthia Macdonald and Graham Macdonald

We take it as obvious that our minds make a difference to what happens in the physical world. We act in different ways *because* we have varied beliefs, desires, hopes, emotions and the like, and in so far as our actions involve our bodies, those beliefs etc. make a difference to what our bodies *do*. We also take it as obvious that this 'because' is to be understood causally: our minds cause us to act as we do. My switching on the light was caused by my belief that it was getting dark and my desire to read the newspaper. Although this much appears self-evident, there are difficulties in seeing how these obvious 'facts' can be true.

These difficulties concern the role of physical events in causal matters. We believe, for example, that our minds cannot cause us to act in ways which breach the laws of physics. Thus, if we are responsible for a physical effect, then this causal interaction must at least be in accordance with physical law. We also know that a good many of our psychological processes, for example, those involved in vision, memory and the like, are 'underwritten' by processes that are physical. We have every reason to believe that the underlying internal causes of the bodily movements which constitute human behaviour are physical, and that a completed physical theory will in principle be capable of providing complete causal explanations of such behaviour. That is to say, we believe that every physical event, if it has a cause, has a sufficient physical cause, i.e. a cause whose efficacy is due to its physical properties (this is the belief in the causal closedness of the physical domain).

This seems to present us with a dilemma, both horns of which are incompatible with the belief that minds make a distinctive causal contribution to the physical world. Either mental states are physical states, in which case minds may matter, but they matter in just the way that physical events and states matter (a way which accords no special status to the mental). It seems as though the mental power to change the world is just a physical power, that our minds do not have the causal powers that we assumed they did. That they appeared to cause physical changes is, on inspection, seen to be a mistake. Or mental states are not physical states, in which case, although they may have powers distinct from those of physical states, they do not matter to what happens in the physical world, i.e. they are mere epiphenomena.[1] In short, it looks as though, if mental states *are* physical states, then, since physical states effect change in the physical world by means of their physical properties, the mental makes no *distinctive* difference to the world; and if mental states are *not* physical states, then, for the same reason, the mental is epiphenomenal. How, given the causal closedness of the physical domain, can minds make a *distinctive* contribution to the world?

The problem here is partly, but not wholly, explicable in terms of the fact that there is evident causal competition between the mental and the physical. It is true that our intuitive understanding of causality is one according to which there is only one cause – *the* cause – for any given effect. So the presence of two candidates for *the* cause of a given piece of behaviour creates a kind of epistemic predicament, as Kim has pointed out (see chapter 7): one wants to know which one really brought about the effect. This predicament can occur within a single theory or explanatory scheme, and there are various ways of attempting to resolve it (Kim mentions at least five, of which the overdetermination option and the causal chain option are two).

However, this doesn't really get to the heart of the problem here. Identifying mental events with physical events will resolve the epistemic predicament that arises from there being two candidates for causes of a given behavioural effect, but it leaves the issue of which *properties* of the event make a difference to behaviour. The problem is that we believe that mental events and states make a difference to behaviour because of their *contents*: my switching on the light was caused by my desire *to read the newspaper* and my belief *that it was getting dark*; states which jointly caused my behaviour and did so because of their contents. But now the question arises, does the physical/mental event produce the effects it does because of its physical properties? Or does it produce the effects it does because of its mental properties?[2] Did I, or did I not, move toward the light switch because of the *content* of my desire, viz. to read the newspaper? Eliminating one of two physical properties of a given physical event as relevant to a given effect may be a loss, but it is a loss in number and not in kind. Eliminating intentional content is a loss, not in number but in kind. To eliminate this is to accept the view that our minds do not make a difference to the world, and we are not prepared to accept this view without a fight.

The above is a brief account of a complex story, much of which is developed in more detail by the contributors to this section. But there is sufficient in the brief account alone to make one pause and perhaps argue with some of its assumptions. In what follows we give some of the background to the recent emergence of the epiphenomenalist debate.

Background

The threat of epiphenomenalism, like most philosophical problems, arises against a background of assumptions. In this case, the assumptions concern what it is to be physical. It has seemed to many that the appropriate way to characterize the physical is by reference to the very sciences which take themselves to be the study of what is physical. If there is one such fundamental science, then physics is it – or so it has appeared since the Newtonian Revolution. But the bald assertion of 'fundamentality' raises questions: what is it that is fundamental (i.e. what is 'physics')? And what in this context does 'fundamental' mean?

There seem to be two ways of characterizing physics. One is to characterize it in a functional rather than substantive way. According to this, physics is concerned with those particles and their properties, such as forces, *which constitute all the elements out of which other objects are made*, and it studies properties of space-time. Intuitively, then, physics studies those lowest level elements out of which all else is constituted, and physical elements just are those that play the role of being mereological simples. This way of characterizing physics attempts to avoid the question of what, substantially, the physical is. Is it that set of elements and properties characterized in contemporary physics (whatever *that* is)? Or is it the set which is referred to in some future, 'true', physical theory? The former answer makes the discovery of new particles the discovery of non-physical elements, and the latter leaves us with no present idea of what the physical is.[3]

While it may avoid certain problems, it courts controversy in other respects, as even this characterization of physics includes a type of way in which it is fundamental: it is mereologically fundamental. Everything will have physical parts. It also suggests that nothing will have non-physical parts – that there will be no elementary object which is non-physical. To say this much might seem already to rule out Cartesian minds and Driesch's entelechies, since these were conceived of as non-physical elements of the universe. However, it does not. *If* it had turned out that they were required as fundamental elements in the best theory, then they would have been physical. Why not? Many of the fundamental particles and forces of current physical theory (substantially characterized) may well have been deemed non-physical by the lights of previous theories (substantially characterized), especially if those judgements had been made on the lines of a criterion such as: 'Whatever is physical must be similar in such-and-such respects to what is currently posited as being physical.' According to the functional strategy, it is better to avoid such criteria, and the functional characterization is designed to do just that.

While the functional characterization avoids too tight a specification of the physical, it looks as though 'physical' will be so flexible a term that traditional problems in the philosophy of science will be simply finessed. One such problem is the relation between the physical and purportedly non-physical features of the universe, especially the relation of causal interaction between the two. The all-purpose 'physical' threatens just to swallow up the non-physical, so no interaction problems remain.

We think that this is correct: against the background of a functional characterization of physics, the problem of how minds can change the world is not really a problem. The causal interaction problems of Cartesian dualism, say, exist, not in relation to physics, functionally characterized as above, but in relation to the development of physics at a particular time, i.e. physics, *substantially characterized*.

At a certain time in the history of science certain fundamental elements are recognized by physical theory, general features of which form the substantial conception of the physical for that time. In addition to these elements, it may appear that there are other features or processes operating in the universe which these particular physical posits cannot explain, and this failure may lead to the idea that there are elements which are non-physical, where this will mean that they do not fit into the best physical theory going at that time. They might not even share the *general* features possessed by the other physical elements, what could be called the categorial features of the physical (such as spatial position), and so there could be some bafflement as to how they could ever fit into the physical scheme of things. (We take it that this is the way that Descartes' test of 'having extension' worked to set the limits to what was physical.) However, there is no *a priori* constraint on what can count as a substantial physical element. Even the categorial physical features are subject to change.

If we combine these two ways of characterizing physics, what results is a vague 'functional role' model of the physical which is given substance at particular times in the development of the discipline, such substantial fillings generating a tension between the physical (substantially characterized) and the apparently non-physical. An example of such tensions occurs in the nineteenth century, when it appeared to many that physics was incapable of explaining chemical bonding, vital activity or mental processes. Two responses were made. The first invoked non-physical entities to do the explanatory work, such as 'entelechies', which were designed to explain life. The central difficulties with this response were (a) whether the non-physical elements were genuinely explanatory; and (b) what the nature of their relation to the physical was. Given their 'categorial' difference from the physical, their suitability for interacting causally with the physical was always in question.

The second response did away with special elements in favour of new forces: it was thought that at a certain level of complexity of physical organization new forces emerged. The 'newness' of the forces was due to their being not just sums of the forces of the physical elements making up the complex structure. At this level of complexity, it was asserted, some force which was not just the resultant of the antecedently given forces (i.e. the lower-level ones) was discernible. As a consequence, the total forces operating were not just physical;

from the complexity of physical structures vital and mental forces emerged. These new, non-physical, forces would do the job of causally explaining the features of the world which could not be captured by current physical theory. The general doctrine was suitably known as 'emergentism', and with it there developed a hierarchical conception of the relation between the sciences. The idea was that physics was fundamental ontologically, with the rest of the sciences stacking up in layers above it, each having its own laws describing the new forces that arose at the relevant level of complexity.[4]

Emergentism suffered two main empirical blows: chemical bonding and laws were seen to involve no essentially new forces, and Darwinian accounts of design and specification did much to alleviate the need for entelechies. In addition, there was some unease at the idea of independent, non-physical, causal forces operating 'downwards', threatening the pattern of purely physical causation of physical changes. Downward causation results from emergentism because the new forces were presumed to have effects in the physical world. Philosophers responded to these developments by retaining the hierarchical conception of science, but replacing emergentism with reduction as the favoured relation between the levels.

Very briefly, reduction requires *at least* that there be laws in the higher-level science which are connected to laws in the lower-level science via two-way 'bridge laws', such laws relating the terms of the separate scientific laws to each other in a manner which suggests that the higher-level law is just a stylistic variant of the lower-level law. (Although the bridge laws are bi-conditionals, the preference accorded the lower-level, physical, law in the reduction is justified in terms of the greater generality of the physical.) A stronger view holds that the properties of the different levels are merged by a reduction, that the higher-level property just is (i.e. is identical with) the lower-level property.[5] On this view, by reducing we discover that one type of phenomenon, or property, is identical with another type of phenomenon, or property. Arguably, this picture has been further supported by developments in microbiology, with the discovery of the nature of genes, how they are transmitted and how they work in organisms to programme for individual development. The use of chemical theory in all these developments has been crucial, suggesting that biology was reducible to chemistry, which in turn was reducible to physics.

Reductionism looked to be an eminently suitable research strategy. The postulation of supplementary non-physical forces seemed to be simply a reaction to our ignorance of the physical processes involved. The promise was that further physical knowledge would dispel the need for such special forces. In addition the difficulty of downward causation was solved, since reduction would place all such causation at the level of the physical. 'Fundamental' now meant that physics was seen to be both ontologically and explanatorily all-encompassing. The reductionist's treatment of higher-level properties (of which mental properties are a special case) would be to endorse their causal efficacy, but at a cost, robbing them of any causal autonomy. Any higher-level property which is a causal property is so becuase it is, really, a physical property. Or so the reductionist would have us believe.

It is easy to see the attractions of the reductionist picture. However, even if reduction worked in chemistry and biology, one large area of tension would remain, and that concerns the relation of the mental to the physical. The hope for a reduction here seems to have faded rather than strengthened, as it looks as though different types of neurophysiological/physiological processes can under-write, or be the basis of, the same type of mental phenomenon. If this is so, then the bi-conditional bridge laws are not available for a reduction to be effected. Empirically, it is an open question whether any reduction is available, and the prospects for psychological reduction are not good. Moreover, many believe that there is an *a priori* reason blocking any such reduction.[6] Mental states, such as belief states, have normative connections with each other: if one believes that $2+2=4$, and that $1+1+1+1=4$, then one *ought* to believe that $2+2=1+1+1+1$. If one wants to be a good chess player and believes that studying chess openings will improve one's game, then one ought to study chess openings. This would be rational, given this belief and desire. The argument is that the normativity involved in these connections is essential to the mental and is not to be found in the physical domain. No purely physical property has *rational* connections to other physical properties, so a reduction is in principle impossible.

The tension between the physical and the mental is exacerbated by the advances in physical theory. In the light of these advances, we have come to think that an ontology of physical elements is fundamental in the following way: the physical *determines* what there is. Two worlds physically identical, sharing all physical properties, would be identical in all other respects – they would share all non-physical properties. This is understood by many as the relation of *supervenience*. If mental properties are supervenient on physical ones, then a constraint is placed on what happens in the mental domain. There can be no change in the mental (where change involves the acquisition or loss of property) no change of mind, without a change in the physical domain. However, construing mental properties as causally autonomous would make it impossible to understand this constraint. These properties would be constrained in their occurrence (instantiation), and in the effects their instantiations bring about, by the physical properties upon which they supervene.

In sum, reduction looks to be too strong a relation between the mental and the physical. Supervenience is considered by many to be more promising. Supervenience theorists hope that supervenience will provide us with a relation which falls short of reduction but which still yields a plausible physicalism, one which leaves us with the idea that the physical is fundamental. The 'fundamental' here is ontological both with respect to events/states and with respect to properties: each mental event will be a physical event, but also physical properties will be the basic (subvenient) properties. Since, it is argued, supervenience is not a reductive relation, it leaves open the possibility that the special sciences can be explanatorily autonomous. However, supervenience appears to rule out the causal autonomy of mental properties for the reasons just given. Many have thought that explanatory autonomy of the mental requires causal autonomy, where this means that unless the causal powers of mental proeprties are to some extent independent of those of physical properties, then there cannot be explanatory autonomy. The idea is that without *some* such causal independence there will be nothing new for the mental hypotheses to explain. Everything that happens, if it is explainable, will be explainable by physics. Mental epiphenomalism will lead to explanatory impotence, and the physical again threatens to overwhelm the psychological. The question now is, can supervenience allow for mental properties to be causally potent, to have distinctive causal powers with regard to the physical world?

Supervenience

In order to assess the various claims made for and against supervenience, it is worth being clear about what supervenience amounts to. In our intuitive rendition of the supervenience relation we made use of the notion of one set of properties being dependent upon, in the sense of being determined by, another set of properties. Supervenience is in fact a term for a family of doctrines or claims, some of which are stronger than others. In order to be a bit more precise about what is involved it is useful to express the different strengths of the supervenience relation relevant to the present discussion in the following way, with x and y being objects/events and A and B being two non-empty families of properties:[7]

> *Weak supervenience*: A weakly supervenes on B if and only if necessarily for any x and y if x and y share all properties in B then x and y share all properties in A.
> *Strong supervenience*: A strongly supervenes on B if and only if necessarily, for each x and each property F in A, if x has F then there is a property G in B such that x has G, and necessarily if any y has G, it has F.

If the mental weakly supervenes on the physical, then the dependency on the physical is restricted to this world. In other worlds the properties involved may have different relations. Specifically, for the purposes of the present discussion, in another world a different set of mental properties from those in this world may supervene on the same set of physical properties as those in this world. Strong supervenience rules this out. However, it is vulnerable to the reductionist charge that there is now little to differentiate reduction from strong supervenience (Kim, 1978, 1984). Suppose that the properties (say, G_1, G_2 ... G_n) of the base science (physics) form a finite set B, and that this set is closed under Boolean (property-forming) operations of conjunction, disjunction and complementation. Then B will contain all those properties constructable by means of Boolean operations on members of B, upon which the mental property depends. Assuming, for example, that B contains just G_1, G_2, and G_3, it will contain eight such properties: $G_1\&G_2\&G_3$, $G_1\&G_2\&-G_3$, $G_1\&-G_2\&-G_3 \ldots - G_1-G_2\&-G_3$. (Kim, 1978, 1984 calls these B-*maximal* properties, since they are the strongest consistent properties constructable by means of Boolean operations on members of B.) Now, form the disjunction of all of these conjunctions, and call this disjunctive property B*. Then, for any mental property, say F_1, in A, a bi-conditional of the following form will be necessarily true:

$$(x)\ (B^*(x)\longleftrightarrow F_1(x))$$

This will be necessarily true becuse it will be necessarily true, for each F_1 in A, that any x that has it has some B-maximal property in B*. So it looks as though one has necessary co-extension, and thus reduction. With reduction, the problem of the causal dependence, and explanatory poverty, of the psychological looms again.

One way of avoiding this problem is to accept the weaker-strength supervenience, and so avoid the necessary co-extension between the base set of properties and the supervening property. Another way is to endorse the stronger conception of reduction. The argument above presupposes that necessary co-extension is sufficient for reduction, and as we can prove that strong supervenience leads to the necessary co-extension of mental and physical properties, reduction seems guaranteed. However, the stronger conception of reduction requires property identity, and it is open to a defender of the autonomy of the mental to claim that necessary co-extension does not yield property identity. The disjunctive property B* is formed in a fairly arbitrary way; it just is the disjunction of all the B-maximal properties upon which members of A supervene. There is no *a priori* reason to assume that the disjunctive property is a natural property. On the face of it its gerrymandered construction gives it a pretty artificial appearance. In general, there is no *a priori* reason to assume that if one property (say, *blueness*) is disjoined with another (say, *right-angledness*) then another genuine property is formed. So the disjoined property, B*, may not be a property. Unless one can make a special case for thinking that it is, no property identity can be asserted and reduction is avoided.

On the face of it this is a reasonable rejoinder. However, it leaves the situation fairly fluid. It is true that there is no *a priori* reason to suppose that the disjunction of properties will yield another property, but it is also true, given just the definition of strong supervenience, that there is no *a priori* reason to suppose that it will not. What looks like a supervenience relation may well turn out to be a reductive one. On this view, nothing in the formal characterizations of the supervenience relation will give us arguments *either* for *or* against reduction. So we are left with the possibility of a non-reductive physicalism which takes the fundamental character of physics to lie in its properties forming the supervenience base of others. We are also still left pondering whether even this non-reductive physicalism is going to rescue psychological causality.

Supervenience and Causality

The move from reduction to supervenience has been thought by some to solve the problem of the explanatory role of the special sciences. In particular, it has been thought that supervenience can allow that all the sciences use causal explanation, but they simply cross-classify the events which are invoked in the causal explanations. The interests of the physicist in the micro-particles will give rise to one causal-power taxonomy, while the interest of biologists in survival and reproduction will provide a different causal-power taxonomy. This cross-classification reflects different properties in nature, and so is thought to prevent reduction, while the use of causal explanation provides the special sciences with genuine causal powers and *bona fide* explanations.

This comfortable picture is disturbed if we look at the kind of supervenience which we have introduced; a supervenience of event-*properties* combined with a monism of *events/states*. The monism, or token event identity, suggests that the causal power of a mental *event* must be just that of the physical event with which it is identical. This equi-potency seems to be mandated by Leibniz's Principle of the Indiscernibility of Identicals: for any objects (events) x and y, if x is identical with y then x and y share all properties. The physical event and the mental event, for example, cannot be different in terms of what they are apt to, or what they tend to, cause. So *at token-event level* there can be no causal independence from the physical. Can we recover any independence by concentrating on the *mental* property or properties of mental/physical event?

The possibility of there being a non-reductive relation between the mental and the physical relies upon there being a plurality of properties, with the higher-order, or supervening, ones being irreducible to the basic, or subvening, physical ones. The physicalism that is allowed is one according to which physical events can be (i.e. be identical with) instantiations of a variety of properties, so ontological monism at the level of events is bought at the price of recognizing irreducible non-physical properties.

It is precisely this property dualism which leads some to wonder whether there really is any hope for supervenient, or higher-order, causal powers. The use of Leibniz's Principle to ensure sameness of causal efficacy at the level of events only works if we rest content with a 'brute' notion of events, one which construes them as 'unstructured' particulars. However, if we construe events as structured particulars, along the lines of the property exemplification account, sameness of causal efficacy is not automatically ensured. According to the property exemplification account, events are exemplifications (or, more accurately, exemplifyings) of act- or event-properties at (or during intervals) of times in objects (Kim, 1976; Lombard, 1986; Macdonald, 1989).[8] Water's coming to the boil just is water's exemplifying first one, then another, temperature-property during an interval of time. Once the focus is turned on these properties, whose instancings just *are* events, the causal picture seems to change.

If the supervening sciences are to deal with causes, it seems evident that we must attribute causal efficacy to the *properties* which are the particular concern of the special science. Now, this requirement is often taken to mean that these properties must have *autonomous* causal power: their potency must not just derive from that of the base properties. That is to say, it is often thought that these properties must be capable of exercising their causal powers through their instances independently of others, even ones upon which they supervene. Their force must not be what the emergentists would have called a mere resultant force, one *exhausted* by the forces of the base (physical) properties. However, if *this* kind of causal autonomy is what is required for special sciences to deal with causes, the requirement of supervenience rules it out. So if one thinks that being causally efficacious requires such autonomy, one has either to reject supervenience or to deny causal efficacy.

Why does supervenience require rejection of the type of causal autonomy described above? If properties from supervenient domains were to exercise causal powers independently of the physical, it would be plausible to think that they could produce changes in the supervenient domain independently of any change in the physical domain. This is surely what the *autonomy* of their causal power means. But this flouts their supervenient status: we would have a change in the supervening domain unaccompanied by any change in the base. So the supervenience of a set of properties plausibly precludes that set possessing autonomous causal powers.[9] Supervenience begets epiphenomeinalism, or so it seems.

Causal Efficacy of Events and Causal Relevance of Properties

The puzzle about psychological causation has taken us through various proposed ways of relating the mental to the physical, from substance dualism and emergentism to reduction and supervenience. The above historical sketch of this development takes us more or less to the present. It is important to see that in at least some respects psychological causation is an example of a general problem, that of the causal powers of higher-order properties.[10] If we can see how in certain cases the higher-order property, say, a biolgoical property, can be causally efficacious, then this could be helpful in the other cases. This will be especially useful in countering arguments which purport to show that *no* higher-order properties can be causally powerful.

In chapter 2, Ned Block produces just such an argument. He argues that the types of higher-order properties that interest us, those of the special sciences, are, for the most part, causally inert; their apparent power stems only from the lower-order properties that produce the effects which are consequent on the instantiation of the higher-order properties. The argument has a direct bearing on the question of whether the mind can change the world, since Block's concern is with functionalism as a theory of mind.

Briefly, functionalism as a view about the mind, broadly construed, is the view that mental states have natures that are determined by their causal roles; by their aptness to enter into causal relations with stimuli, other mental states, and behavioural output. Block's favoured version of functionalism seems to be what is known as a *functional state identity theory* (Block, 1980).[11] According to this, mental states are identical with states that are causal roles; and mental properties are identical with higher-order (specifically, second-order) properties, functional ones. That is to say, mental properties such as *pain* are functional properties, properties which, like having or fulfilling a given causal role, are possessed by lower-order properties (which may or may not be physical), and so are *second-order* properties of such properties. According to Block, 'Functional properties are properties that consist in the having or some properties or other (say, non-functional properties) that have certain causal relations to one another and to inputs and outputs.' (chapter 2, p. 45). Block's view is that functional properties, like many other higher-order properties, are causally inert; and they are causally inert because the production of outputs is due to the causal work done by the lower-order, non-functional properties.[12] With computational properties (i.e. mental properties, on the functionalist view Block is considering), the causal work is done by the properties which implement the computational properties. Similarly with properties like *dormitivity*, which are defined in terms of the effects they cause. Here again it is the lower-order chemical properties which are deemed to be really causally efficacious, the higher-order *dormitivity* being causally inert.

Part of what concerns Block here is whether there is a test that we might bring to bear to settle the question of whether a property is causally efficacious. One such test is whether the property figures in a causal law, the test of causal nomologicality. Block argues that properties defined in terms of the effects they bring about are not fit for causal laws relating them to *those* effects. The reason is that they are logically related to these effects. Given this, it would require some special reason to think that they are *also* nomologically related to those effects.[13] He also argues in a general way against causal nomologicality as a test for the causal efficacy of a property.

Block is also concerned with the problem of overdetermination. If both base and supervening properties are causally efficacious in bringing about the (same) effect, then it appears as though the effect is produced in virtue of two properties, either of which would have been sufficient to bring about the effect. This makes the causal explanations of the special sciences depend upon systematic massive overdetermination, an unsettling result.

So Block is concerned with two issues: (a) whether there is a test for causal efficacy (and, in particular, whether a nomological test is satisfactory); and (b) whether, given that special science properties pass that test, massive overdeter-mination in the special sciences is avoidable. With regard to both of these issues what worries him is not whether mental *events or states* are causally efficacious, but whether mental *properties* are causally efficacious. Block thinks that mental states are causes of the behaviour they produce, but this may be so, not in virtue of the contentful properties possessed by those states, but in virtue of other properties of those states. So what worries Block is just the problem set out at the very beginning of this discussion. If content properties were identified with, say, neurophysiological properties, then the causal efficacy of the neural would guarantee the causal efficacy of the content properties. What generates the accusation of epiphenomenalism is the view that such properties are *distinct*.

It seems clear that Block is operating with something like the structured view of events/states that we have already mentioned. In chapter 3, we also make use of this framework. However, we arrive at a different conclusion. In order to separate different issues, we distinguish between causal powers of properties (for which we reserve the term 'causal relevance') and the causal efficacy of *instances* (or, more accurately, of instancings, since events imply change) of properties.[14] Against the background of the property exemplification account of events, it is instances of properties that figure in causal relations, since causal relations hold between events, not properties. When it is said that mental event/state A causes event/state B *in virtue of* its possessing property M, we take this to mean that it is because A is (i.e. is identical with) an instance of M that B comes about.

One way the epiphenomenalist worry can emerge is by concentrating on properties rather than their instances, and so mislocating the *locus* of causality. If one concentrates on properties then it is pertinent to note that, given token event identity, the mental state or event is an instance of at least two properties, and to wonder which of the two is doing the causal work. A may cause B in virtue of its being an instance of physical property P, on this view, leaving the mental state causally efficacious, but not in virtue of M. Concentrating on *instances* of the properties allows us to formulate the question of the causal efficacy of *events* in terms of which *instance* is causally efficacious, and to argue that, given token event identity, although there are two properties there is only one instance, so there is no epiphenomenalist problem here to solve. If the instance of M, M_i, is identical with the instance of P, P_i, then at the level of causal efficacy we do not have two items contending for causal status. This also alleviates the worry about overdetermination, but as Block was not particularly concerned about this, we will not pursue the matter here.

In chapter 3 we expand on this solution, since, given the connection between instancings of properties (i.e. events), and properties instanced, we take causal efficacy of events to be a central feature of causal relevance. The main point involves making the case for the one-instance solution plausible, and we do so by analogy with other cases where there appear to be two properties instanced but only one instancing. Of particular interest is the biological case, because if it can be made credible there then we will at least have provided an answer to the epiphenomenalist threat for one special science.[15] However, this answer leaves Block's two issues unresolved, viz. that of the relation between causal efficacy of special science properties and nomologicality, and that of the causal powers of special science properties.

Causal Efficacy of Properties and Nomologicality

What is the relation between causality and nomologicality? On one view (a view which we endorse), if two *events* are causally related, then there is a (causal) nomological connection between them.[16] This allows that there can be a causal connection between two events even though there are descriptions of those events which logically relate them. These descriptions need not rule out the possibility of nomological ties between the events as well. At this level, logical relations do not preclude causal relations.[17] (This is just as well, since, for any two events related as cause and effect, there will be a description of the cause which logically relates them: if A causes B, there will be a description of A as 'the cause of B'.) If we use the language of properties rather than descriptions, we can say that two events may have properties in virtue of which they are logically related, and properties in virtue of which they are causally related.[18] Using this terminology, one can give a slightly more complex account of the connection between causality and nomologicality: if *properties* are causally potent (causally relevant, as we say) then they figure in causal laws.

This seems to be the kind of view that Block has in mind by the nomological view, since his worry is that if a property is logically related to the effects it supposedly brings about, there must be a special reason to think that it is also nomologically related to those effects. If there is no such reason and so no nomological relation between the properties, then Block is correct that on the nomological conception of causality just described, the property is not causally relevant to those effects. One event may be the instancing of the property, *taking a dormitive potion*, and also the instancing of the property, *taking Seconal*. The property, *taking a dormitive potion*, is defined in terms of its effects, and so is, in the loose sense used here, 'logically' connected to its effects. *Taking Seconal* is not so related, but it is (at least for the sake of argument) nomologically related to *falling asleep*. So far as the nomological criterion of causal power (relevance) of a property is concerned, only the nomological property is causally relevant.

It seems that the importance of this point, from Block's point of view, is that we may have rescued causal efficacy for instances of mental properties, but have not entitled ourselves to think of any causal powers pertaining to mental properties. If the psychological is related to the neurophysiological as is dormitivity to its various chemical bases, then the psychological may still be causally irrelevant.

Our own view is a bit more complicated, however. Although we have distinguished the problem of the causal relevance of the property from the problem of the causal efficacy of the instance of the property, we do think there is a connection between the two. We maintain that a property cannot be causally relevant unless it has causally efficacious instances.[19] The property can thus be said to have derivative causal efficacy, derivative because we take it that the causal relations are relations between events (which are instances of properties). So a property is causally efficacious in a certain transaction if and only if its instance, in that transaction, is causally efficacious. It follows, trivially, that *taking a dormitive potion* will be causally efficacious if it has an instance which is causally efficacious. And a mental property will likewise be causally efficacious if it has a causally efficacious instance.

Where does nomologicality fit in here? In the simplest version of the connection between nomologicality and causality outlined above, nomologicality relates events *simpliciter*. Nomologicality enters into our version in a similar way, by relating instancings of properties (note that these are *not* to be construed as tropes).[20] If an instancing of a property is causally efficacious, then it is covered by a causal law. So if a mental property is causally efficacious, then its instancings are covered by a causal law, *even if that law mentions only physical (or neurophysiological) properties*. This serves to emphasize that the property of being causally efficacious is extensional, and the consequences of the view are set out below, in the two following sections.

Causal Powers of Special Science Properties

There remains Block's second concern, about the causal relevance of the higher-order properties. The source of this concern is twofold. First, there is a worry that the causal efficacy of the higher-order properties will be *just* derivative, their causal powers exhausted by those of the physical properties with which they are co-instanced. The second, related, concern pertains to explanation, and hence to what would happen in other cases. It connects directly to Block's question: would the behaviour have been the same if the mental state had had a different content?[21] In the context of discussing causal powers, we need to ask, 'same' in what *respect*? What about *that* behavioural state must change in order to satisfy the thought that unless the change in the mental property instanced produces a change in behaviour, then the mental property is causally irrelevant? Our claim is that the action property of the 'behaviour' state would change if the mental property were different, and this is necessary for there to be any explanatory potential in the citing of the mental property.

We also suggest that, for there to be interesting counterfactuals of the sort required in the special sciences, there must be a discernible *pattern* in the instancing of the special science properties. In the case of biology, the pattern is that produced by design. The biological properties are, in the first instance, recognized as significantly different from the physico-chemical properties upon which they supervene because they are so well adapted to each other and to the environment. The adaptedness of such properties serves to provide us with a pattern, something significant to explain, and biological functional explanation works because of this. The general idea is not dissimilar to that of the emergentists, without their extra-physical forces. The physical interactions provide a different pattern from that just given by causal laws; higher-order properties do emerge. Natural selection produces functional properties, so functional explanation works, but it does not work as a form of nomological explanation, or so we say. Similarly, with the psychological: the relevant pattern here is that of rationality, and we again do not conceive rationalistic explanations to be a form of, nor even an extension of, causal nomological explanation. The normativity implicit in biological and psychological explanation precludes this.

So our account of causal relevance requires causal efficacy plus explanatory potential of the cause property. This latter notion is intensional, and we take it to require two things: first, that there be a pattern of relations between the properties whose instancings give rise to causal interactions (for reasons just given); and, secondly, that the cause property be nomological (or functional, or a reason, etc., these differences having to do with differences in patterns) *for* a certain *type* of effect. (These are conditions 2 and 3 of our account of causal relevance set out in the next and final section of this chapter.)

The rationale for condition 3 has to do with the fact that the two conditions of causal efficacy plus nomologicality (or a pattern) allows too *many* properties to be causally relevant to a given effect (see final section below). Suppose that the rising velocity of the same free elections is responsible both for the rising thermal conductivity and the rising electrical conductivity of, say, a bomb. Intuitively, it is the rising thermal conductivity rather than the rising electrical conductivity that is causally relevant to the heating effect, the explosion, of the bomb. However, nothing in the causal efficacy plus nomologicality/pattern requirement on causal relevance rules out rising electrical conductivity being causally relevant, since, as Block points out (see chapter 4) the mechanisms involved in causing the bomb to go off might be such that the detonator is triggered by electrical means. Condition 3 is meant to rule out the intuitively causally irrelevant cause properties in cases like these. It does so by requiring that the cause property bear the relevant pattern relation (nomological etc.) to a certain *type* of effect. Explanation is interest relative, and effects, like causes, are instancings of many properties. So, depending on which *type* of effect it is that we are out to explain, one rather than another cause property will be causally relevant.

We are left with the question: do physical properties exhaust the causal powers of the higher-order properties? In our discussion of emergentism above, we saw that if the relation between the mental and the physical is that of supervenience, then there could be no independent causal powers for the mental. To allow that there could be would be in effect to deny supervenience, and denying supervenience for this reason leads to the possibility of psycho-physical causal interaction in which the physical would be changed by the non-physical. Unless we are prepared to countenance this, we are stuck with some sense in which all causality is physical causality. However, this sense is not terribly damaging. It would be damaging if *no* sense could be made of an effect being caused *in virtue of* a mental property. But note that each mental property will have causal powers that are different from those of any physical property with which it may be co-instantiated. It could bring about the action while being co-instanced with different physical properties, each with its own distinctive causal powers.

This allows there to be interesting psychological explanation. If a psychological property's causal potential were to be exhausted by any of the physical properties with which it was co-instanced, taken singly, then there would be a strong case for a reduction of one to the other, and explanatory autonomy would be lost. However, while it is true that there could be cobbled together a base property which may well causally exhaust the potential of the mental property, it would be a very peculiar sort of physical property. The comments made above about the possibilities of a reduction given strong supervenience are relevant here. For each psychological property, we could construct a disjunctive property on which it supervened, but it might not itself be a property. Moreover, even if it were, it would hardly be of any explanatory significance on an occasion when any of its members was instanced.

The Debate

In this section we respond to Block's invitation to reply to his 'Causation and Two Kinds of Laws' (chapter 4).[22] As the previous section indicates, our conception of causal relevance for a given property P requires the following three conditions:

1   Instancings of P are causally efficacious.[23]
2   P participates in a pattern of relations among properties whose instancings are causally efficacious (a typical example of which is the nomological pattern).
3   P is nomological (or functional, or a reason, etc.) for a certain *type* of effect.

In his response to this account Block (chapter 4) rejects the idea that a notion of causal relevance can be buttressed by nomologicality (condition 2), and so he rejects our position completely. He objects to the account on two main grounds. The first is that the account is circular. His main charge of circularity, which concerns condition 2, is that causal relevance requires causal laws, and it seems that causal laws can only be defined in terms of causal relevance. However, he also seems to be concerned with the threat of a second kind of circularity involved, not in condition 2, but in condition 3. We address both of these charges below. Block's second main objection relates to the types of laws we may be thinking of: 'general' laws, or 'apparatus' laws. If we are connecting causal relevance to perfectly general laws, such as the ideal gas laws, then there will be no causal relevance, since there are no *general* laws relating, say, deaths of victims to firings of revolvers. Or, to take the example cited earlier of an explosion caused by rising thermal conductivity, there is no general law connecting rising thermal conductivity with explosions. So, Block argues, general laws do not give us *enough* causal relevance. 'Apparatus laws', on the other hand, give us too *much* causal relevance. Depending on how a particular bomb is constructed and what mechanisms are involved in triggering it, there will be apparatus laws connecting both *rising thermal conductivity* and *rising electrical conductivity* to particular explosions. So, if we are connecting causal relevance to this type of law, both properties (*rising thermal conductivity* and *rising electrical conductivity*) will be causally relevant to a given explosion, where intuitively we would say only one (*rising thermal conductivity*) is.

The problem being addressed in these chapters is that of the causal powers of higher-order properties, with special attention paid to the properties of the special sciences. (On Block's view, these pose a particular problem because they are functional properties: properties defined partly in terms of their effects.) One way of proceeding would be to attempt a wholesale reduction of the notion of causal efficacy, construct an account of causal relevance out of it, and apply the results to the special science difficulty. We do not see ourselves as doing this, partly because we are not optimistic about the success of that enterprise. Most attempts at such reductive analyses seem to smuggle in the notiong being analysed, 'cause', at some stage in the analysis. Reductions that depend on the causes and effects being 'constantly conjoined' (i.e. Humean reductions) have notorious trouble attempting to restrict the regularities which form the basis for attributions of causality to the right kind of regularities, and then have even more trouble convincing us that, by giving us the right regularities, they have *thereby* provided us with sufficient for causation. Stronger conceptions of causality, invoking some notion of nomologicality, have to distinguish which kind of law they intend to figure in the analysans, and what type or degree of necessity is involved in the nomological relation.[24]

Our view is that the proposed reductions are unilluminating, often resting on some other notion which is as much of a mystery as is that of causation. At some stage some property or relation will be taken as primitive, and the best one can hope for is to use that primitive to build the rest. Nomological analyses of causality which purport to be reductive will have to circumscribe the relevant type of law using non-causal vocabulary. But even to characterize the general notion of law non-reductively and illuminatingly is difficult enough. Michael Tooley's (1987, s. 3.1.2) account, for example, takes the truth-makers for law-statements to be *contingent* external relations between universals. Now the idea of there being such a type of relation is troubling; most contingent relations we can think of relate particulars, such as this cup's being on the table, or the door's being to the left of the chair. Relations between universals which immediately come to mind are non-contingent relations, such as determinate/determinable relations like that between *red* and *colour* (or *being red/being coloured*). As Tooley notes, it would be helpful if one could say more about this strange contingent relation, but it is irreducible, and also the only one of its kind: there is no other external relation between universals. This seems to us to relocate rather than to solve the puzzle of what makes for nomologicality.

Block himself seems to prefer a counterfactual approach to the question of causal relevance; he does not elaborate on how the usual problems of non-causal counterfactuals will be eliminated. We suggest that if he can make that discrimination without taking some causal notion as a primitive then he will also have provided the material for adumbrating a notion of causal law which is reductive, and thus eliminate the need for the otherwise cautious 'causal' attached to 'nomological' in our outline of causal efficacy. If it can be done, we would clearly welcome this addition. We do think that counterfactuals are important, since we take them to provide a 'test' for causal relevance (we take it as true, for example, that the action would not have occurred if the mental property had not been instantiated). However, we do not take counterfactuality as primitive. We think that its acceptability relies upon some generality, or pattern, existing in nature.

So what we are saying is that our 'nomological' account will, we think, inevitably presume some causal notion or other. However, we do *not* think that it will presume a notion of causal relevance (so there is no circularity involved in condition 2). Perhaps this can be made clearer by distinguishing between what appear to be two different conceptions of causal relevance implicit in Block's discussion. On one conception, for a property to be causally relevant is for it to figure in a causal law. This clearly is not our conception. Certainly, it follows from our account of causal relevance that if a property is causally relevant, then it figures in a pattern, and the pattern *may* be a nomological one. But this is not all there is to causal relevance for us. On another conception of 'causally relevant', the one that interests us, to be causally relevant is to be capable of *explanatory* potency for a particular effect. It follows from our conception that if a causal law is used in the explanation of a particular effect, the cause property cited in that law is causally relevant to that effect. But, as this makes clear, causal relevance is now context-relative. Given two 'apparatus' laws, citing different cause properties, the question of whether either of these properties is causally relevant cannot be answered simply by reference to the fact that they are cited in the laws.

When condition 2 is satisfied by the nomological pattern, the laws we have in mind are Block's 'apparatus' laws. Now there is a problem here, as Block points out, and that is that there are many generalizations (and so many counterfactuals), many 'apparatus' laws, and so causal relevance threatens to come in too much abundance. But relevance has always been cheap: it depends on what you are interested in. Causal relevance will similarly be context (interest)-relative, something we were trying to capture in condition 3 above when we say that for relevance the nomological property must be nomological 'for a certain type of effect'. Block notes the circularity threatening here: the type of effect will be that for which the causal property is relevant. The mistake, as suggested above, is to try to give conditions for causal relevance *tout court*; it would be better to give an account of causal relevance for X_i, where X_i is a placeholder for an instanced property.

Even given context relativity of effect, there may be problems leading to an 'anything goes' account of causal relevance, something we wish to avoid. So, in the example of thermal conductivity and electrical conductivity that concerns both Block and us, how do we avoid the conclusion that, since both properties will figure in 'apparatus' laws connecting them to a given explosion, both properties are causally relevant to the explosion? Block thinks our account cannot avoid this conclusion. In one example he gives, the Hot Bomb case, the bomb is connected, via a metal bar, to source of heat. So rising thermal conductivity is here causally relevant to the increase in the heat of the bomb and so to its exploding. However, given the Wiedemann–Franz law connecting electrical conductivity with thermal conductivity, rising electrical conductivity is also causally relevant to the explosion. In another example he gives, the Eletrical Bomb case, the bomb is attached to an electrical detonator (an electrical heater) which heats the bomb, thereby causing the explosion. Thus, he claims, rising electrical conductivity of the wires in the heater is here causally relevant to the increase in heat (a heating effect) in the heater (the detonator), and so is causally relevant to the explosion. But again, given the Wiedemann–Franz law, rising thermal conductivity is causally relevant to the explosion also. Do we think that rising electrical conductivity was causally relevant to the explosion in the first example, when the bomb is connected to a source of heat? Do we think that rising thermal conductivity was causally relevant to the explosion in the second example, when it was an electrical apparatus that was instrumental in bringing the explosion about? Condition 3 by itself will not help us here. Given the story that it is the rising velocity of free electrons that is responsible for *both* rising thermal conductivity *and* rising electrical conductivity, the requirment that the cause properties that participate in the laws must be nomological for certain types of effect will not by itself determine which of the two properties is causally relevant in these examples, since here the type of effect is the same in both. (Note, however, that these cases differ from the case of mental properties, where condition 3 does suffice by itself: mental properties are *reasons for* action-type effects, whereas neurophysiological properties are nomological for physical behaviour-type effects.)

This may make it look as though our three conditions on causal relevance are not sufficient. But we think that they are. Consider the Hot Bomb case. Suppose that there is a heating effect which we explain using the thermal conductivity laws; can we explain that type of effect using the electrical conductivity laws? Well, we could make use of the Wiedemann–Franz correlation law and construct an explanation which will have laws plus initial conditions as input and the heating effect as output. We *could* do this, yes. But why should we? And why should we think that the mere fact that we can use a property-correlation law to connect a second property of the cause (rising electrical conductivity) to the heating effect thereby makes that property causally relevant? The crucial phrase here is 'plus initial conditions'. Given a statement of the initial conditions (the bomb is connected to a source of heat) and the type of effect, rising thermal conductivity will be causally relevant to that type of effect. But then, as this makes clear, which explanation we go for depends, not just on the 'apparatus' law, but also on the statement of initial conditions. The applicability of a particular law is context-relative: it depends on the initial conditions. So same conditions, same law; different conditions, different law.

This does not show that causally relevant properties are not type-effect sensitive, nor that our conditions do not suffice for causal relevance. For it is no part of our view that a property can be causally relevant independently of the wider context of initial conditions. If the causal relevance of a property depends on its participation in laws (or, more generally, in patterns), and the applicability of a law depends on context, then the causal relevance (and so the explanatory potential) of that property depends on the wider context of initial conditions. But to think that because of this context-dependence, the three conditions we specify do not suffice for a property to be causally relevant is like thinking that because a cause's being efficacious depends on background conditions, these conditions are part of what is involved in being a cause. A cause is a cause against a background of conditions. Similarly a property's being causally relevant is its being causally relevant against a background of conditions. Relativity to initial conditions is presumed as given. Our problem was, *given* initial conditions and hence the applicability of particular patterns (nomological for the neurophysiological properties of a given event, and rationalistic for the mental properties of that same event), which of the two properties is causally relevant. Our answer was, it depends on what type of effect is involved.

To recognize that causal relevance is causal relevance relative to initial conditions is to see that one, *rather than* another law (or set of laws) will be called for in generating an explanation of a particular type of effect. The relevant laws will be the *simplest* ones available *given initial conditions and type of effect*. In the Hot Bomb case, where the initial condition is that the bomb is connected, via a metal bar, to a source of heat, the simplest 'apparatus' law will be that concerning thermal conductivity. The fact that we can connect thermal conductivity to electrical conductivity via the Wiedemann–Franz correlation law is irrelevant. The initial conditions rule out rising electrical conductivity as a candidate, on a par with rising thermal conductivity, for being the causally relevant property; and they do so by circumscribing the simplest relevant laws connecting initial conditions to the type of effect. (Electrical conductivity may be 'causally relevant' in the sense, earlier described, that the property figures in a law; but that sense, as we have made clear, is not the sense that concerns us.) In the Electrical Bomb case, on the other hand, where the initial conditions include the fact that the detonator is an electrical heater, the simplest set of laws will be ones concerning electrical conductivity. Here, although it is the increase in the heat of the bomb that causes it to explode, that increase is generated by a source which is electrical. Given that it is initial conditions that dictate what the simplest laws will be, and given that an 'appropriate' description of the apparatus in question (the heater) will reveal that it is responsible for heating effects, it is rising electrical conductivity that is causally relevant. As in the Hot Bomb case, the fact that we can connect electrical conductivity to thermal conductivity via the Wiedemann–Franz correlation law is irrelevant.

Block tells us that 'the property of rising electrical conductivity is causally relevant to the increase of heat in the detonator, and also to the resulting explosion.' (Chapter 4, p. 79). We are not too sure what he means by this (see note 25), but we think that recognizing that causal relevance is causal relevance *relative* to initial conditions, and that the set of 'apparatus' laws that are applicable, in a given case, to the explanation of a given type of effect given those conditions will be the *simplest* set, defuses his objection that 'apparatus' laws give us too much causal relevance. In both the Hot Bomb case and the Electrical Bomb case only one of the two candidates emerges as causally relevant. No doubt there is a lot more to be said, but we do not think a nomologically based account is effectively buried.[26] Given that there is such a feature as causal relevance to be characterized, and Block allows for this in the base properties for which the nomological condition is meant to hold, the account we offer deserves to be buried only if a better alternative is forthcoming, and Block provides no real alternative.

Is there agreement between Block and us about the causal efficacy of property instances? We do not know. Block takes it as uncontoversial that an instancing of rising thermal conductivity is an event that is causally efficacious in producing the explosion (when this was triggered by an increase in temperature). He then asks why we think that the rising electrical conductivity is co-instanced with the rising thermal conductivity. Well, bcause they share the same base property (rising velocity of free electrons). Block thinks this won't work, and provides another example to say why it will have counter-intuitive consequences. As Block suggests, we think the counter-intuitiveness arises only whe one thinks that a property whose instance is causally efficacious must also be *relevant* to the effect it causes, and this is precisely what we deny. Now Block says we cannot explain away the counter-intuitiveness in this way, because nomologicality will either make both properties irrelevant, or both properties relevant. As a consequence he thinks we may have to reconsider our identity conditions for events, presumably because it will lead to the more plausible (to Block) result of having the irrelevant property instanced in a separate event from that of the relevant property.

Well, if nomologicality will not work in these cases (and we are not convinced it cannot be made to work), something else will, because we are not here in the sceptical business of denying that any properties are causally relevant. *Whatever* account of causal relevance of properties is given, it seems to us that one will have the 'problem' of a property being irrelevant to some effects which that property's instance nevertheless causes. This much is guaranteed by the extensionality of the causal relation plus some independently plausible assumptions, one of which is that an instance can be an instance of more than one property. We spend some time defending this possibility, and think that the case of biological properties provides a good reason for the co-instantiation hypothesis. This is an important test case, as biological properties are supervenient on a suitable set of physico-chemical properties. In general, supervenient properties are good candidates for co-instantiation with their base properties. Moreover, there is nothing in the identity conditions for events which leads us to think otherwise.[27]

Notes

1   Strictly speaking, epiphenomenalism is the view that mental phenomena, i.e. events and states, are causally inert with regard to the physical world. Here we depart from the traditional view by focusing on a modern variant of the view, where mental events are taken to be identical with physical events, but mental properties are taken to be causally inert (i.e. to have no causal powers) with regard to the physical world. This also seems to be Block's interpretation of the view (see chapter 2).

2   One might attempt to resolve this causal tension by distinguishing between the effects of mental and internal physical causes, actions and bodily movements. We make use of this distinction at the level of properties in our account of causal relevance.

3   We have by-passed many tricky questions here, in particular a problem raised as to *which* elements and properties are physical. For discussion of these matters see Crane and Mellor (1990), Crane (1993), Pettit (1993) and the papers referred to by Pettit and Crane.

4   Emergentism is illuminatingly discussed in McLaughlin (1992).

5   The bridge-law conception of reduction is that of Ernest Nagel (1961). The stronger conception requiring property identity for reduction is developed by Robert Causey (1977).

6   The *locus classicus* for this argument is Donald Davidson's highly influential 'Mental events' (Davidson, 1970).

7   These formalizations are those given in Kim (1984). For further bibliographical material and discussion, see Horgan (1984). We restrict ourselves here to property formulations of supervenience.

8   'Object' here is to be construed in the broadest possible sense, to include oceans and winds, as well as cabbages and kings.

9   Only 'plausibly' because it may be held that the causally induced supervenient change 'produces' a corresponding change in the physical base, thus respecting the thesis of no supervenient change without supervened upon change. The implausibility here lies in the mysterious nature of this (non-causally mediated) 'production' relation. It also reverses the direction of the dependence; in this case we would have a change in the supervening properties inducing a change in the

supervened upon properties, just the kind of downward causation supervenience theorists want to avoid.

10   'In at least some respects' because there may be an argument that the problem of *mental* causation has an extra dimension, that associated with our thinking that our minds matter causally in a way that is more important than, and different from, say, economic forces, which are also examples of higher-level causal powers'. Whatever the answer to this is, it is clear that if *no* higher-level property can be causally efficacious, then if mental properties are higher-order ones, they are not causally efficacious. So the general problem requires a solution.

11   This is to be distinguished from the view known as the *functional specification theory*, a view held by David Lewis 1970, 1972; see Block, 1980. In chapter 4, Block notes the difference between the two views, but argues that the functional specification theory will not avoid the problem of epiphenomenalism either.

12   As noted, Block is specifically interested in what he terms *second-order* properties, a species of higher-order properties, which he takes functional properties to be. Nothing in our exposition or discussion here depends on this distinction between second-order and higher-order properties.

13   Block thinks they can be nomologically connected to effects other than those to which they are logically related. See chapter 2, p. 47.

14   Block, in chapter 2, talks of causal efficacy and causal relevance interchangeably. We introduce a distinction in order to keep different problems separated. Causal relevance of properties is, on our account, linked to explanatory interests, and relates to the 'in virtue of' relation between cause and property. Our causal efficacy connects to what Block calls 'event causation'. For the purposes of the present discussion, 'instance', 'instancing', 'exemplification, 'exemplifying' and 'instantiation' will be used interchangeably: such metaphysical differences as may underlie distinctions between these terms will not play a role in the discussion. Note, however, that ours is not a trope account of events.

15   It also provides the material to deal with the worries about explanatory competition that arise below. We postpone discussion of that issue to the end of the section headed 'The Debate' in this introduction.

16   Obviously no reduction is intended here, given the qualifier *causal*. See the discussion below of the prospects for a reduction of the notion of causality to nomologicality.

17   See Donald Davidson's (1963) seminal paper 'Actions, reasons and causes'.

18   Strictly speaking, descriptions, or conceptions, of properties enter into logical relations, so our formulation in terms of properties being logically related is shorthand for something like 'canonical conceptions of the properties being logically related'. See Burge (chapter 12) for the same point.

19   This does give the causal relevance of properties an Aristotelian rather than Platonic interpretation: there can be no uninstantiated causally relevant properties. We do not think that much hangs on this here, particularly as the question of the causal relevance of a property only arises when it is presumed to have causally efficacious instances.

20   For more on this, see Macdonald and Macdonald (1991).

21   There are tricky questions here concerning the identity of the mental state. Can the state, which is mental, be the same if it has a different content? On one theory, the answer is yes, and we shall assume that theory here (see Macdonald, 1989). Note that this is not to say that this mental state might have been the same mental

state with a different content. It is to say that this state, which happens to be a mental state with a given content, might have been a (different) mental state with a different content. Our justification for assuming this view is that our discussion takes place against the background of a physicalism that is a token event identity theory, where events are construed as property exemplifications. This physicalism is committed to the view that the essences of mental events are physical, not mental. For an alternative view, see Yablo (1992).

22 Readers may find it more useful to read this section after they have read the contributions to the debate.

23 Block notes that this condition assumes that a cause can be an instance of P and also have P. We agree: as we see it, in the case of events at least, an instancing of P *is* the thing that has it.

24 It was this issue, that of contingency versus necessity, that was the topic of our comment about 'causal-nomological' being given 'whatever strength is required for physical cause-effect relations', so that the tight circle of definition we are accused of by Block on p. 81 of chapter 4 is not applicable.

25 There is a difficulty with Block's description of the Electrical Bomb case. Block seems to assume that, given an appropriate description of the electrical heater, one will not need the Wiedemann-Franz law to connect rising electrical conductivity with the heating effect (in the detonator). This is evident from his comments on p. 80, and so we take this to be the correct interpretation of the Electrical Bomb case. But, on another interpretation of the case, the Wiedemann-Franz law might be seen to be necessary to connect rising electrical conductivity with the heating effect. If so, then that law as well as the appropriate 'apparatus' law will be the simplest set of laws needed to explain the explosion. This would make both rising electrical conductivity (of the detonator) of the cause, and the heating effect (i.e. rising thermal conductivity of the detonator) causally relevant to the explosion. But what is wrong with this? What is wrong with there being two causally relevant properties in a given case? The case that worried us was one where a *single* event that has *both* the property of being a rising in electrical conductivity *and* the property of being a rising in thermal conductivity, might be one where *both* properties are causally relevant, when intuitively it is only the latter property that is causally relevant. Interpreted in this second way, Block's Electrical Bomb example is not such a case, as this quotation makes clear. Here there is a chain of events, where an event which is a rising in electrical conductivity causes an event which is a heating *effect*, the increase of heat in the detonator, which in turn heats the bomb, causing an explosion. This is a case where the property, being a rising in electrical conductivity, of *one* event is causally relevant to another event, a type of *effect* – a rising in thermal conductivity – which in turn is causally relevant to the bomb's exploding. It is not a case where, in one and the same event, two properties are candidates for being causally relevant to the *same* type of effect. So it is not a case where we are concerned to show that only one of two properties of the cause is causally relevant to a certain type of effect. (This difficulty in Block's description of the Electrical Bomb case may be explained by the fact that Block, unlike us, sees no reason to assume that rising electrical conductivity and rising thermal and conductivity are properties that are co-instanced in a single event. Thus, in the quotation here he seems to treat rising electrical conductivity (in the detonator) as causally relevant to the heating *effect* of the detonator), i.e. to an instancing of rising thermal conductivity.)

26   Remember that nomologicality figured here for us twice: once in characterizing causal efficacy, and once when it was suggested that there could be nomological patterns, lawful generalities, which would generate causal relevance for some effects. In its second role it was not necessary for causal relevance; for the special sciences, nomologicality drops out to be replaced by other patterns, and so plays only the subsidiary role defined in the notion of causal efficacy. So there is *this* agreement between Block and ourselves: we both think that a nomological requirement on causal relevance for the special sciences is not going to work. Block goes further in denying its usefulness *tout court*.

27   There is a lot more on the identity conditions of events and how this pertains to the mental-physical divide in Cynthia Macdonald (1989).

References

Block, N. (1980) What is functionalism? In *Readings in the Philosophy of Psychology*, vol. 1, pp. 171–84. Cambridge, Mass., Harvard University Press.

Causey, R. (1977) *Unity of Science*. Dordrecht, D. Reidel.

Crane, T. (1993) Reply to Pettit. *Analysis* 53 (4), 224–7.

Crane, T. and Mellor, D.H. (1990) There is no question of physicialism. *Mind* 99, 185–206.

Davidson, D. (1963) Actions, reasons and causes. *Journal of Philosophy* 60, 685–700. Reprinted in *Essays on Actions and Events*, pp. 3–19. Oxford, Oxford University Press, 1980.

Davidson, D. 1970 Mental events. In L. Foster and J.W. Swanson (eds), *Experience and Theory*, pp. 79–101. Amherst, University of Massachusetts Press. Reprinted in *Essays on Actions and Events*, pp. 207–25. Oxford, Oxford University Press, 1980.

Horgan, T. (ed.), (1984) *The Southern Journal of Philosophy* 22, supplement (Spindel Conference on Supervenience).

Kim, J. (1976) Events as property exemplifications. In M. Brand and D. Walton (eds), *Action Theory*, pp. 159–77. Dordrecht, D. Reidel.

Kim, J. (1978) Supervenience and nomological incommensurables. *American Philosophical Quarterly* 15 (2), 149–56.

Kim, J. (1984) Concepts of supervenience. *Philosophy and Phenomenological Research* 45 (2), 153–76.

Lewis, D. (1970) How to define theoretical terms. *Journal of Philosophy* 67, 427–46.

Lewis, D. (1972) Psychophysical and theoretical identifications. *Australasian Journal of Philosophy* 50, 249–58.

Lombard, L. (1986) *Events: a Metaphysical Study*. London, Routledge and Kegan Paul.

Macdonald, C. (1989) *Mind-Body Identity Theories*. London, Routledge.

Macdonald, C. and Macdonald, G. (1991) Mental causation and non-reductive monism. *Analysis* 51 (1), 23–32.

McLaughlin, B. (1992) The rise and fall of British emergentism. In A. Beckermann, H. Flohe and J. Kim (eds), *Emergence or Reduction?*, pp. 49–93. Berlin, de Gruyter.

Nagel, E. (1961) *The Structure of Science*. New York, Harcourt, Brace and World.

Pettit, P. (1993) A definition of physicalism. *Analysis* 53 (4), 211–23.

Tooley, M. (1987) *Causation: a Realist Approach*. Oxford, Clarendon Press.

Yablo, S. (1992) Mental causation. *Philosophical Review* 101, 245–80.

2

Can the Mind Change the World?

Ned Block

Hilary Putnam originated the idea that mental states are computational states. At first (Putnam, 1960), his view was that although mental states are not *identical* with computational states (or 'logical states', as he then called them), there are useful analogies between them. Later (Putnam, 1967), he argued in favor of the identity on the grounds that it was more plausible to suppose mental states are functional states (as he then called them) than that they are behavioral or physical states. This doctrine – functionalism – has dominated the philosophy of mind for over twenty years. Shortly after proposing functionalism, Putnam rejected it again (1973), and he has maintained this position ever since (Putnam, 1988).

Putnam was my teacher during both my undergraduate and graduate days, and I fear I have absorbed his ambivalence toward functionalism. My teacher has had a habit of changing his mind, but never has he done so within a single essay, and so in this chapter I have surpassed him. My chapter starts out as an argument for functionalism, but it ends up suggesting an argument against it. The issue is whether we can avoid epiphenomenalism, which I here understand as the doctrine that what we think or want has no causal relevance to what we do. I propose functionalism as a way of warding off arguments for epiphenomenalism, but then I argue that functionalism may bring epiphenomenalism in its wake.

The orientation of the chapter is toward the sciences of the mind, and their relation to intentional content, that is, what is shared by the belief that grass grows and the desire that grass grows, the *that grass grows* that both states are directed toward. The question at hand is whether the sciences of the mind preclude intentional content from causal relevance to behavior. One argument that the intentional contents of our beliefs, thoughts, and the like have no effects on our behavior could be put this way: the processors in the head are not sensitive to content, so how could content have any effect on the outputs or changes of state of the system of processors? And if content can't affect the operation of this system of processors, how could it play any role in producing behavior? This argument seems formidable whether one thinks of the processors as neural devices reacting to neural inputs or, instead, from the cognitive science point of view, as computational devices processing representations.[1] In this chapter, I confine myself to the problem as it arises in the cognitive science approach that is dominated by the computer model of the mind. I assume a very specific picture of cognitive science and its relation to the common-sense conception of intentional content, namely, the view according to which there is an internal system of representation from whose meanings our intentional contents derive (Fodor, 1975; Pylyshyn, 1984). One of my reasons for couching the discussion in terms of this view is that, although those who adopt this view are *motivated* by the aim of showing how our common-sense beliefs about content (including our belief in content's causal efficacy) are vindicated by the computer model of the mind, the problem of the epiphenomenalism of content arises within this view in an extremely simple and straightforward (and poignant) way. The viewpoint assumed throughout the chapter is that of a supporter of the computer model in cognitive science who also would *like* to believe that the contents of our thoughts are indeed causally relevant to what we do.

The problem I have in mind might be put in terms of the 'Paradox of the Causal Efficacy of Content', namely, that the following claims all seem to be true, yet incompatible:

1   The intentional content of a thought (or other intentional state) is causally relevant to its behavioral (and other) effects.
2   Intentional content reduces to meanings of internal representations.
3   Internal processors are sensitive to the 'syntactic forms' of internal representations, not their meanings.

The first claim is meant to be part of the common-sense view of the mind. The third is plausibly taken to be a basic claim of the computer model of the mind, and the second is a useful and plausible way of thinking how common-sense psychology meshes with the computer model. This second claim is by far the most controversial, but I won't be questioning it here. My reasons are that I think it is true, that I see no useful purpose to dividing meaning and content in this context, and that I think the best bets for resolving the paradox are to question the third premise and whether the reasoning that leads to the paradox is right.

The reasoning behind the paradox goes something like this: any Turing machine can be constructed from simple primitive processors such as *and* gates, *or* gates, and the like (see Minsky, 1967). Gates are sensitive to the syntactic forms of representations, not their meanings. But if the meaning of a representation cannot infuence the behavior of a gate, how could it influence the behavior of a computer – a system of gates? Since intentional content reduces to meanings of internal representations, and since meanings of internal representations cannot influence behavior, content cannot influence behavior either. The reasoning assumes that at least as far as our thinking is concerned, we *are* computers. This idea – which is simply the computer model of the mind (our cognitive mind, that is) – may be wrong, but I will be assuming it to explore where it leads.

My plan for the chapter involves

1 Explaining each premise.
2 Examining and rejecting a putative solution based on a nomological conception of causal relevance.
3 Suggesting a solution based on a functionalist conception of content and meaning and a counterfactual theory of causal relevance.
4 Discussing a problem with the proposed solution, one that suggests that functionalism actually breeds epiphenomenalism.

A sub-theme of the chapter is that a nomological theory of causal relevance (a theory that explains causal relevance in terms of the notion of a law of nature) has more of a problem with epiphenomenalism than a counterfactual approach.

The Premises

The first premise uses the notion of a *causally relevant property*. Some properties of a cause are relevant to the production of an effect, and some are not. Hurricane Eliza broke my window. Eliza's wind speed and geographical path are causally relevant to the breaking, but its name and the location of its records in the United States Weather Bureau are not. According to the first premise, if my belief that the United States is a dangerous place causes me to leave the country, the content of the belief is causally relevant to the behavior; a property that is not causally relevant to the behavior is the last letter of the name of the city in which the belief was formed.

Note that the point is *not* that beliefs, thoughts, desires, and the like (mental states or events that have content) are *causes*, for example, of behavior. (I assume that they are.) Rather, the point is that when mental events have effects, they typically have those effects (rather than different effects) *because* the mental events have the contents that they have rather than some other contents. Typically, if the beliefs, thoughts, and so forth, had had contents that were appropriately different, they would have had quite different effects. For example, had I believed that everywhere except the United States is a dangerous place, then I wouldn't have left the country.

My metaphysical stance in this chapter is one in which mental events are the causes of behavior, and their contents are properties of those events that may or may not be causally relevant to the events' effects. I shall say that property P of event c is causally relevant to effect e and that c causes e in virtue of P more or less interchangeably. Also, I shall put the claim that content is causally relevant to something by saying that content is causally efficacious, and not epiphenomenal. Of course, my use of 'epiphenomenalism' is importantly different from the traditional one. I'm not raising any possibility of content being a property of a distinct mental substance, events in which are caused by events in the brain even though events in the mental substance never cause anything. And epiphenomenalism in my sense does not entail that content is itself caused by an underlying physical state that also causes behavior. The reason I use this old word ('epiphenomenalism') for this newer problem is that the problem I raise is the modern heir of the old problem.

The second premise – that content reduces to meanings of internal representations (symbols in the head) – is much more tendentious than the first, and is certainly not part of common-sense wisdom about the mind. But it is a straightforward way of making common-sense realism about content compatible with the view that the machinery of the mind is one of computations on internal representations. According to the computer model, the mind (or its cognitive aspect) can be thought of as a system of processors that take representations as inputs, transform them in various ways, and then send them to other processors, as in computers. One can think of the representations in such a system as being in certain computational relations to the whole system. These computational relations are determined by the ways the system would treat the representation given various different states of its component processors. A sample computational relation is that of storing a representation.

Of course, computers that you can buy don't currently think or remember. But if computers can be programmed to think, or if we are computers, this story can be extended to thinking things. Thus, remembering might consist in the storing of a representation in such a way that it can later be accessed. Remembering that grass grows would be storing a representation that means that grass grows. This is the doctrine of reduction of content to meaning stated in the second premise. More generally, as is argued in Fodor (1975), to have the thought that p is to be in a certain computational relation to an internal representation that means that p, and likewise for other propositional attitudes. The slogan – and it is only a slogan – is that thinking that grass grows is having 'Grass grows' in the thought box in the head.

Talk of the thought box in the head is (thinly) disguised *functional* talk. The sentences that are in the thought box share a computational situation, a role within the system – in other words, a function within the system. This functional theory of what a thought *is* (and how it differs from a desire) should be firmly distinguished from other functionalisms to be mentioned in this chapter, especially the much more controversial idea that the meaning of a representation is itself functional.

The third premise is that internal processors are sensitive to the syntactic form of the internal representations that they process, not their meanings. Consider the *and* gate of figure 2.1. What makes it an *and* gate is that it emits a '1' if and only if both inputs are '1's; all other inputs yield a 'O' as output.

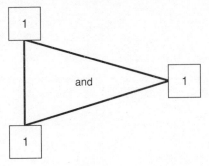

Figure 2.1

The *and* gate.

1 Is not sensitive to
2 Does not react to
3 Does not detect

whether the '1's represent truth or the number 1 or nothing at all. Rather, the *and* gate is sensitive to, reacts to, and detects only whether the inputs are both '1's or not. Thus it is sensitive to the syntax, not the meaning of its inputs, and likewise for the primitive processors postulated by cognitive science accounts of the mind. (The primitive processors of a system are the ones for which there is no explanation *within* cognitive science of how they work; their operation can be explained only in terms of a lower-level branch of science, physiology, in the case of human primitive processors, electronics in the case of standard computer primitives.)

Note that the sense of 'syntax' I am using here (somewhat misleadingly) means *form class*; '1' and '0' are different synactic objects in this sense. It is important to be aware that syntax in this sense of the term is another functional notion. English orthography is also functional, although this may be obscured by the rigidification of function by convention. For %xampl%, you will hav% littl% troubl% figuring out what l%ett%r of th% alphab%t is th% on% to which th% unusual symbol in this s%nt%nc% should b% tr%at%d as functionally %quival%nt.

Consider an input-output system whose input and output registers are bi-stable, and take on values of either 7 volts or 4 volts. Suppose that if both input registers are at 4 volts, then the output is 4 volts, and every other input yields the 7-volt output. Then (1) the system is an *and* gate, (2) the 4-volt value counts as a '1' for this *and* gate, and the 7-volt value counts as a '0'. A differently constructed *and* gate might be one for which 7 volts counts as a '1'. Conventionally, '1' is assigned to states of computer registers using this type of consideration. The functional roles of the bi-stable states of registers simultaneously determine our identifications of the devices in the system (e.g. as adders and gates) and our identifications of the states of the registers as

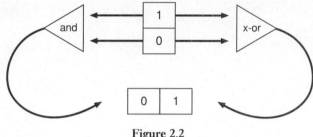

Figure 2.2

symbols. So it is having a certain functional role that makes a state satisfy a *syntactic* description, in the sense of syntax used here.

Note that it would be a mistake to say that 4 volts in the first gate mentioned has the same *meaning* as 7 volts in the second gate. We don't know *what* the meanings of the '1's in either gate are until we see other aspects of their function. These '1's could be used to mean one, or true, or green; the input-output function does not choose among these and other possibilities. The aspects of function relevant to syntax are different from, though overlapping with, the aspects of function relevant to meaning.

In the next section, I will explain the picture common in cognitive science of sensible or 'rational' relations among contents deriving from the correlation between rational relations among contents on the one hand, and processing relations among syntactic objects in the brain on the other. This idea will illustrate both the strength and weakness of the cognitive science picture I will be assuming. The strength lies in its potential for a mechanical account of thought and reason, but as we shall see, it does so in a way that relegates syntactic properties to 'going proxy' for semantic properties, and that opens it up to the worries about epiphenomenalism discussed here. My aim in the next section is to motivate premise 3 – that internal processors are sensitive to syntax, not meaning – since it will take the heat in my proposed solution.

The Brain as a Syntactic Engine Driving a Semantic Engine

The heading above can be understood by attention to a simple example, a common type of computer adder stripped down so as to handle only one-digit addenda. To understand the example, you need only know the following simple facts about binary notation: 0 and 1 are represented alike in binary and decimal, but the binary translation of decimal '2' is '10'. The adder pictured in figure 2.2 will solve the following four problems:

$$0 + 0 = 0$$
$$1 + 0 = 1$$

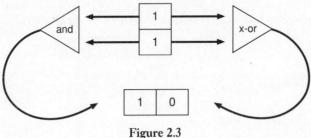

Figure 2.3

$$0 + 1 = 1$$
$$1 + 1 = 10$$

The first three equations are true in both binary and decimal, but the last is true only in binary.

Here is how the adder works. The two digits to be added, a '1' and a '0' in this case, are connected both to an *and* gate and an *exclusive-or* gate. The latter gate is a 'difference detector', i.e. it outputs a '1' if its inputs are different, and a '0' if they are the same. In the case illustrated in figure 2.2, the *exclusive-or* gate sees a difference, and so it outputs a '1' to the rightmost box of the answer register. The *and* gate outputs a '0', and so the device computes the answer. The *exclusive-or* gate does the 'work' in the first three problems, and is needed only for carrying, whch comes in only in the last problem as illustrated in figure 2.3. Both inputs are '1's, and so the *and* gate outputs a '1' to the leftmost box of the answer register. The other gate makes the rightmost box a '0', and so we have the answer.

Seeing the adder as a syntactic engine driving a semantic engine requires noting two functions: one maps numbers onto other numbers, and the other maps symbols onto other symbols. The latter function is concerned with the numerals as symbols, without attention to their meanings. Here is the symbol function:

'0', '0'→'0'
'0', '1'→'1'
'1', '0'→'1'
'1', '1'→'10'

This symbol function is mirrored by a function that maps the numbers represented by the numerals on the left onto the numbers represented by the numerals on the right. This function will thus map numbers onto numbers. We can speak of this function that maps numbers onto numbers as the *semantic* function, since it is concerned with the meanings of the symbols, not the symbols themselves. (It is important not to confuse the notion of a semantic function in this sense with a function that maps symbols onto what they refer to; I shall discuss this latter function shortly.) Here is the semantic function (in decimal notation – you must choose *some* notation to express any function):

0, 0→0
0, 1→1
1, 0→1
1, 1→2

The first function maps symbols onto symbols; the second function maps the numbers referred to by the arguments of the first function onto the numbers referred to by the values of the first function.

The key idea behind the adders is that of a correlation between these two functions. The designer has joined together

1 A meaningful notation (binary notation).
2 Symbolic manipulations in that notation.
3 Useful relations among the meanings of the symbols.

The symbolic manipulations correspond to useful relations among the meanings of the symbols – namely, the relations of addition. The useful relations among the meanings are captured by the semantic function above, and the corresponding symbolic relations are the ones described in the symbolic function above. It is the *correlation between these two functions* (which establishes a semantic function in the more usual sense of a function from words to their referents) that explains how it is that a device that manipulates symbols manages to add numbers. Now the idea of the brain as a syntactic engine driving a semantic engine is just a generalization of this picture to a wider class of symbolic activities, namely, the symbolic activities of human thought. The idea is that we have symbolic structures in our brains, and that nature has seen to it that there are correlations between causal interactions among these structures and sensible relations among the meanings of the symbolic structures. The primitive processors 'know' only the 'syntactic' form of the symbols they process (e.g. what strings of 0s and 1s they see), and not what the symbols mean. None the less, these meaning-blind primitive processors control processes that 'make sense' – processes of decision, problem-solving, and the like. In short, there is a correlation between the meanings of our internal representations and their forms. And this explains how it is that our syntactic engine can drive our semantic engine.[2]

Now the picture just sketched of the brain as a syntactic engine driving a semantic engine reveals how it is that a mechanistic theory of intentionality can invite the charge of epiphenomenalism. It seems that our cognitive processes exploit a *correlation* between the semantic and the syntactic. The syntactic propeties of the representations do the causal work, and the semantic properties come along for the ride.

The Appeal to Laws

In this section, I will examine a putative solution, that is, a way of making the cognitive science picture (premises 2 and 3) compatible with the causal relevance of content (to the behavioral and other effects of contentful mental states, of course – I'll be leaving the prepositional phrase out often, just speaking, elliptically, of the causal relevance of content). Actually, I shall start by briefly mentioning a reductionist proposal just to set it to one side. If content properties could be *identified* with, say, neurophysiological properties, then there would be no opening for epiphenomenalism. If content properties are simply identical to neurophysiological properties, then the causal efficacy of the neural would guarantee the causal efficacy of content. Whatever the merits of physiological reductionism, it is not available to the cognitive science point of view assumed here. According to cognitive science, the essence of the mental is computational, and any computational state is 'multiply realizable' by physiological or electronic states that are not identical with one another, and so content cannot be identified with any one of them.[3]

Note that in rejecting this putative solution, I am not rejecting a 'physicalistic' point of view. If all the nomologically possible things that can have computational properties are physical things, then the computational point of view, embracing this idea, is itself physicalistic. Even if the computational properties that characterize mentality are in this sense *physical*, that does not make them *physiological or electronic* (or syntactic, for that matter), and so physicalism in this sense does not lead to any suggestion that processors in the head can detect content or meaning.

There is another putative solution to which I will devote more attention, one that appeals to a nomological view of causation. The idea is that there are non-strict psychological laws involving content, and that law – even non-strict law – makes for causal relevance. Fodor (1987b, 1989) argues that intentional laws provide non-strict intentional sufficient conditions for behavior, and that is what makes content causally relevant to behavior. It will pay us to examine a simple version of this nomist perspective: F is causally relevant to an effect e if the instantiation of F is nomologically sufficient for e – even if the nomological sufficiency holds only *ceteris paribus*.

The trouble with this simple version of the nomist approach is familiar: there can be correlation without causation – even nomological correlation of F with G without a causal relevance relation between F and G. And nomological correlation can involve nomological sufficiency. Suppose C (for *c*ause) is nomologically sufficient for and uncontroversially causally relevant to E (for *e*ffect). Suppose X is nomologically correlated with C because X and C share a causal source, and so X is not causally relevant to C. Then, X is nomologically sufficient for E without being causally relevant to E (see figure 2.4, which pictures this 'fork' case).

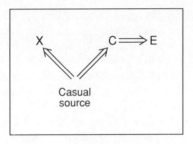

Figure 2.4

Here is an example. Consider a set-up in which a metal rod connects a fire to a bomb. So long as the thermal conductivity of the rod is low, not enough heat is transferred from the fire to the bomb to cause an explosion. But if the thermal conductivity of the rod is increased enough (say, by altering its composition), then the heat from the fire will explode the bomb.[4]

Now there is a law – the Wiedemann-Franz Law – linking thermal and electrical conductivity under normal conditions. (The same free electrons carry both charge and heat.) Hence for this set-up, rising electrical conductivity, together with other things being equal, is sufficient for an explosion. Hence by the nomist criterion, rising electrical conductivity is causally relevant to the explosion.

I take it that to the extent that we have a pretheoretical grasp on the notion of causal relevance, this consequence of the simple version of the nomist criterion is simply wrong. The electrical conductivity increase does not cause the explosion; certainly it does not cause the explosion *in virtue of being a rise in electrical conductivity*. Rather, the rising electrical conductivity is an inactive concomitant of the causally relevant rising thermal conductivity. It is the rising thermal conductivity that allows more heat to be conducted to the bomb, causing the bomb to explode.

The obvious nomist response would be to reformulate the thesis to avoid these fork cases. The idea would be to formulate what the fork cases have in common that distinguishes them from genuine causal cases, and use this result to produce a definition of causal relevance in terms of 'non-fork' nomological sufficiency. I think this is a promising way to go about characterizing causal relevance, but I have two doubts about whether the resulting nomist conception of causal relevance will be one that saves us from epiphenomenalism.

First, recall that the problem of epiphenomenalism arose to begin with because the cognitive science point of view held that nature had produced a correlation between syntax and semantics, only the former being directly causally related to behavior. What reason is there to think that an independently motivated definition of 'non-fork' nomological sufficiency would count semantics as any more causally relevant to behavior than rising electrical conductivity is to the explosion in the example considered earlier? Indeed, the correlation between semantics and syntax via a common cause is a good example of a fork.

Secondly, the issue of the epiphenomenalism of the semantic may simply resurface in a different form in an independently motivated account of causal relevance in terms of nomologicity. Horwich (1987) frames a definition of causation in terms of the idea of a basic law. A cause is linked to its effects by chains of *direct* nomological determination, and direct nomological determination is determination via basic law. 'A direct cause of some effect is an essential part of an antecedent condition whose intrinsic description entails, via basic laws of nature, that the effect will occur' (Horwich, 1987). Cause c causes effect e if there is a set of events, $e_1 \ldots e_n$ linked by basic laws, and if $c = e_1$, and $e = e_n$. The account concerns event causation, not the causal relevance of properties. But assuming that it could be supplemented to form an account of causal relevance using the notion of a basic law, we can see that although it shifts the terms of the discussion of epiphenomenalism, it does not solve the problem. Is content epiphenomenal? That depends on whether the laws that determine behavior in terms of content are basic. But one's decisions on whether these laws are basic – and, indeed, what basicness is – will be (and should be) conditioned by one's decisions on what is causally relevant to what. Of course, the fact that the nomist conception of causal relevance will not solve this problem all by itself is not a reason to reject the nomist conception.

Fodor (1989) says that if there is a *causal* law that F instantiations cause G instantiations (*ceteris paribus*), then F is causally relevant to the G instantiations that are caused by F instantiations. The appeal to causation in this sufficient condition is harmless for Fodor's purposes, but not for mine. For how are we supposed to know whether the laws that relate content to behavior are *causal* laws? For example, consider the (very low quality) law to the effect that instantiations of wanting G and believing that A is required for G cause instantiations of A, *ceteris paribus*. To know whether the content properties are causally relevant to the action, we must know if the law is causal. But if Fodor's sufficient condition is all we have to work with, the issue of whether the law is causal just *is* the epiphenomenalism issue we are discussing, so no progress has been made.

A Proposal

We have just been considering an approach to causal relevance in terms of nomologicity, and we have not succeeded in avoiding epiphenomenalism. I know of only one other remotely promising approach to causal relevance, namely, the approach in terms of counterfactuals. In this section, I will first give a version of the argument for epiphenomenalism – the 'counterfactual argument' I will call it – in which causal relevance is construed counterfactually. Then I will suggest a functionalist way of avoiding the conclusion.

Suppose we have a computational device (say, an *and* gate) to which a ('1',

'0') pair – representing the numbers 1 and 0 – is input, yielding a '0' output, representing 0. Now the ('1', '0') input pair would have had just the same effect, viz. the production of '0' as output, even if the '1' and '0' had represented truth and falsity instead of 1 and 0, or even if these symbols had represented black and white, or even if we hadn't been using them to represent anything at all. And what holds for a primitive processor also holds for any system of them. If a syntactic object (say, a string of '0's and '1's) is input to the whole system, and another string of zeros and ones is output, the input string would have caused the same output string no matter what it had meant. In common philosophical parlance, the syntax of the representation 'screens off' the meaning from having any causal relevance to the output. The conclusion is that since meanings of representations are epiphenomenal, so are the contents of the mental states that they ground.

I want to offer the claim that if the meanings of internal representations are their 'functional roles', then the counterfactual argument for epiphenomenalism can be vanquished.

The functional role of a representation is its causal role in reasoning, thinking, planning, and in general in the way the representation combines with and interacts with other representations so as to mediate between inputs and outputs. The functional roles of representations arise from the ways processors manipulate their syntactic forms. Some functionalists take inputs to be impingements on the surfaces of the body, others take inputs to be the things in the world that produce these impingements (and likewise for outputs). Thus some functionalists take functional role to be internal, whereas others take it to be partly internal, partly external. My use of the functionalist perspective requires no commitment on this matter. More specifically, nothing I say here should be construed as an endorsement of 'narrow content'.

A functional role theory of meaning is a theory of what meaning *is* that yields an account of what it is about representations that *gives* them their meanings, not a 'semantics' in the sense of a theory of particular constructions in particular langauges. Thus, it would not be the job of a functional role theory of meaning to explain why it is that 'The temperature is 70°', and 'The temperature is rising' do not entail '70° is rising'. Theories of the sort that would deal with such questions often address themselves to what meaning is, but they do not yield an account of what gives representations their meanings. Usually for their purposes any 'surrogate' of meaning – anything that acts like meaning in the way that set theoretic entities 'act like' numbers – will do (see Block, 1986, 1987, for more on this distinction). A functional role theory can be thought of as a 'use' theory of meaning, where the uses are at least partly inside the head.

One motivation for such an account can perhaps be seen more clearly if one reflects on a case in which one learns the meanings of words without anything approximating an eliminative definition for them. Consider, for example, the learning of a new scientific theory with its new theoretical terms, e.g. 'force', 'mass', 'momentum', 'energy'. These new terms are not definable in everyday language (or anything like an 'observation language'), though they are definable in terms of one another. The student learns these terms by coming to understand how to use them in thought, in experiment and observation, and in solving problems on quizzes. If meaning is functional role, then it is easy to see why learning new terms is acquiring their use. It is a plus for a theory of what meaning is if it also tells us what it is to know and learn meanings. That is all I will say here to motivate the functional role account.[5] Now on to the counterfactual argument.

You will recall that the counterfactual argument said that it appeared that a given syntactic object would have caused the same output even if it had meant something quite different from what it actually means or even if it had meant nothing at all, so the syntactic form of a representation screens off its meaning from having any causal relevance.[6]

Suppose, for example, that the sentence 'There is danger coming this way' is in the 'belief box' (with its normal meaning), causing one to flee. According to the counterfactual argument, the sentence would have caused the fleeing even if it had meant that my long-lost friend approaches, or that Empedocles leaped. But if functional role semantics is correct, then it is not at all guaranteed that 'There is danger coming this way' would have caused fleeing even if it had meant that Empedocles leaped. For if it had had a different meaning, or no meaning at all, its functional role would have been different, and since functional role is causal role, abstractly construed, a difference in functional role typically will include a difference in behavioral effects.

Perhaps the functional role of 'There is danger coming this way' includes an inference to sentences such as 'It would be best not to be here when the danger arrives' (with its normal functional role and hence its normal meaning), and perhaps this inference is part of the causal chain that led to fleeing. Then if the token of 'There is danger coming this way' that was in the belief box had meant that a long-lost friend approaches, the inference would not have taken place, and the fleeing would not have occurred. We would have approach instead of avoidance, and friendly words instead of fear. If the meaning of the sentence in the belief box had been different, its effects would have been different and required different semantic descriptions.

In sum, if meaning is functional role, then it is false that a representation would have had just the effects that it did have if its meaning had been different. Different meaning requires different functional role, and different functional role requires different causes and/or effects. So the counterfactual argument is unsound if meaning is functional role.

In terms of the original paradox, the point is that internal processors can be sensitive to *both* syntax and semantics. But how is this possible? Are the meanings of a *gate's* outputs dependent on the meanings of its inputs?

Of course not – and therein lies the fallacy of the original argument. Thinking of internal processors on the model of gates misleads. For a processor that *is a genuine intentional system* the difference between a representation's meaning one as opposed to truth or green, would involve differences in the internal part of the functional role of the representation. Not so for a gate. If we ask whether a representation would have had just the same behavioral effects had it had a different meaning, then for many differences in meaning, the answer will be yes for a genuine intentional system, though not for a simple primitive processor such as a gate. Indeed, the criterion of identity natural for a complex processor allows one to consider whether a given processor would have processed a representation differently had it had a different meaning. But the natural criterion of identity for a gate rules out the possibility of *its* processing differently (while remaining the same gate).

This point is easier to appreciate if we distinguish between autonomous and observer-relative meaning (Haugeland, 1980; Searle, 1980). Observer-relative meanings are inherited meanings, meanings that intentional systems assign (e.g. to linguistic items or states of a machine). Autonomous meanings are meanings of representations or representational states of an intentional system – *for* that system. They get their meanings from their function in the system. The representations of gates have *only* observer-relative meanings. (My representations have autonomous meanings for me, but they can also have a variety of observer-relative meanings for others.) We can decide, if we like, that a '1' that is input to a gate means one, whereas an output '1' means Richard Nixon. We have a free hand. But autonomous meanings are not subject to whim in this way. It is for autonomous meanings that the point I have been making applies. Had an input symbol had a different autonomous meaning (for a genuine intentional system), then it could have had a different functional role and thus different effects. The trick of the argument that originally got us into trouble is to concentrate on the example of a gate in which only observer-relative meaning is relevant, making us forget that we do not have a free hand in this way with autonomous meaning.

Of course, the autonomous meanings of my representations could have been different in *certain* ways without any change in the movements of my body. This is what is imagined in the famous 'twin earth' examples – referential changes without changes in internal functional roles. But of course twin earth cases are elaborately artificial, and one should not conclude from them that had a representation meant something else, the same behavioral effects would have occurred none the less. The misleading effect of the gate example is to trick us into treating *all* hypothetical differences in meanings of representations as if they are twin earth cases. If we compare *and* gates whose '1's mean one versus truth, we are considering an analog of a twin earth case for gates. But for gates, twin earth cases come cheap. To read this cheapness of twin earth cases back onto genuine intentional systems is in effect to suppose that any old counterfactual situation in whch references would be different is a twin earth case, and this is a bad mistake.

When I presented the 'Paradox of the Causal Efficacy of Content', I mentioned three premises: that intentional content is causally relevnt to behavior, that intentional content reduces to meanings of internal representations, and that internal processors are sensitive to syntax, not meaning.

Thinking of these as the premises, the argument is unsound because the third premise is false.

But when I spelled the argument out, I said that primitive processors are sensitive to syntax, not meaning. I then argued that the meaning of a representation cannot influence the behavior of a system of processors without influencing any of the particular processors themselves. So if meaning can't influence the behavior of a gate, it can't influence the behavior of a system of gates. This reasoning is mistaken (given the cognitive science assumption that a computer – a system of gates – can be an intentional system – an assumption that I am accepting for the purposes of this discussion) and so understood this way, the original argument is sound but invalid.

Internal Functional Role and External Content

Dretske (1988) has argued that the semantic content of a representation is causally relevant to behavior. This section will briefly note that his point has little to do with the problem of epiphenomenalism as I have been discussing it. I think of Dretske's considerations as counting in favor of the idea that the informational values of our representations – what they 'indicate' about the world – are causally relevant to the production of the purely 'internal' aspect of their functional roles. (In terms of the 'two factor' version of functional role semantics – see Block, 1986, and further references there – the external factor is causally relevant to the production of the internal factor.) But – and this is my point – informational value can be causally responsible for our representations' functional roles without being involved in the 'triggering' of any actual behavior (in the usual sense of 'behavior').

Consider whatever it is that the frog uses to represent flies – let's call it the frog's fly representer.[7] There is an aspect of the functional role of this representer that is completely internal – mainly a matter of its production by flashes of movement on the frog's retina and its role in controlling the aim of tongue launchings. In addition to its internal functional role, this representer has informational content regarding flies and their locations. The point is that the latter plausibly has been causally relevant to the former. More exactly, the informational value of ancestors of this representer – what they have been indicating about the world – have been involved, or so one might suppose, in the production of the representer's current functional role. Perhaps an ancestor of the frog had an internal state that had some informational content with respect to ancestors of flies or other food on the wing, and influence of this state on tongue launching conferred extra inclusive fitness on the frog ancestors whose fly-information state had the right sort of influence on tongue launchings. We may speculate that evolution recruited a primitive motion detector that provided a modicum of information about winged bugs to guide the pre-frog's tongue, thereby improving the pre-frog's chances of a meal. As the bugs evolved into (or were replaced by) flies, the detector was turned by evolution to flies. Then the fact that the frog's fly representer has been carrying information about flies has causally contributed to giving this representation the functional role that it has – being produced by retinal movement flashes and guiding zapping. More generally, the line of thought is that what our representations have been indicating about the world has had an influence – via evolution – on their having the functional roles that they have in our hands.

I do not wish to go into this reasoning in any detail, consider objections to it, or talk about the extrapolation from frogs to people. I want to point out only that even if the reasoning is entirely correct in its own terms, it does not show that the informational content of a representation is part of what is causally relevant to (in the sense of a 'triggering' cause) the behavioral output that the representation causes, and so Dretske's proposal is not a solution to the problem being considered in this chapter.

Suppose that the frog has a fly-word ('FLY'), the informational content of which has been causally relevant to the establishment of the internal functional role of 'FLY', including the guiding of the frog's tongue-zapping behavior. Is this informational content thereby causally relevant to the production of, i.e. involved in the causation of, any particular zapping? This is the epiphenomenalism issue of this chapter (applied to this case). The answer is obviously not. X can have causally promoted the pattern of Y→Z without in any way triggering the current token of Z. For X can have promoted Y→Z without now causing Y or enabling Y to cause Z. The informational content of 'FLY' does not causally contribute to the appearance of this token of 'FLY' in the frog's head. That is done by the fly that caused it. And once 'FLY' has appeared in the frog, the informational content does not enable or aid 'FLY' in producing a zapping. To dramatize the point, suppose that the current 'FLY' token is a *mis*representation caused, say, by a B-B. This fly token none the less indicates flies (a misrepresentation of a fly is still a representation of a fly). The history of correlation of 'FLY' tokens with flies has contributed to the functional role of 'FLY' tokens in the frog, but once that role is set, the past correlation is irrelevant to the process by which the B-B now produces the current 'FLY' token, which in turn produces the zapping that pops the B-B into the frog's gut. We can tell the whole mechanistic story about this causal process without saying anything about how the mechanisms that subserve it arose. And it is this former question that this chapter is about: is content part of the causal process by which behavior is produced?

Functional Properties

The plot so far is: functionalism meets arguments for epiphenomenalism and slays them. It would be nice to stop here, but alas, the story of the victory of functionalism over epiphenomenalism is fiction. I argued that functionalism does defeat the counterfactual argument, but you can win a battle and still lose the war. Functionalism loses the war in the end because functional properties are causally inert in certain crucial cases. Or, rather, I fear that all this is true. The point of this section is to raise a skeptical doubt. The issues are complex, and I do not have the space to explore them adequately. So my claims must be tentative.

In brief, my point is this. Functional properties are properties that consist in the having of some properties or other (say non-functional properties) that have certain causal relations to one another and to inputs and outputs. In the production of those outputs, it is the non-functional properties that are standardly the causally relevant ones, not the functional properties.

To get at the point, let's consider a slightly more general notion than that of a functional property, the notion of a second-order property, by which I mean a property that consists in the having of some properties or other (say first-order properties) thave have certain causal relations to one another. (The greater generality here is just that second-order properties needn't involve inputs and outputs, as with functional properties.) Consider the bullfighter's cape. The myth (which we will accept, ignoring the inconvenient color-blindness of bulls) is that its red color provokes the bull; that is, redness is causally relevant to the bull's anger. The cape also has the second-order property of being provocative, of having some property or other that provokes the bull, of having some property or other that is causally relevant to the bull's anger. But does the *provocativeness* of the cape provoke the bull? Is the provocativeness causally relevant to the bull's anger? It would seem not. The bull is too stupid for that. The provocativeness of the cape might provoke the ASPCA, but not the bull.

Another example: consider dormitivity construed as a second-order property, the possession of some property or other (for example, a first-order chemical property) that is causally relevant to sleep. That is, x is dormitive $= x$ has some property that is causally relevant to sleep (when x is ingested). If a dormitive pill is slipped into your food without your noticing, the property of the pill that is causally relevant to your falling asleep is a (presumably first-order) chemical property, not, it would seem, the dormitivity itself. Different dormitive potions will act via different chemical properties, one in the case of Valium, another in the case of Seconal. But unless you know about the dormitivity of the pill, how could the dormitivity itself be causally relevant to your falling asleep?

Of course, if you *do* know about the dormitivity, then it can be causally relevant to your sleep, just as the provocativeness of the cape can affect ASPCA. In fact, there is a well-known phenomenon in which dormitivity *does* cause sleep, namely, the placebo effect. If a dormitive pill is so labeled, thereby causing knowledge of its dormitivity, this knowledge can cause sleep (though the truth and justification of the knowledge are of course causally irrelevant). So dormitivity can be causally relevant to sleep. (Indeed, there can be a dormitive pill that works without any first-order effect, a pill whose dormitivity requires its own recognition. Suppose I market a sugar pill as a dormitive pill, and it becomes popular and works well. I make a fortune and close my plant. Years later, when all my pills have been used up, one of my customers who had had years of sound sleep as a result of taking my pills finds out that they worked via the placebo effect and sues me. Surely I can point out that he was not cheated – the pills were genuinely dormitive, there was no false advertising.)

My claim is that second-order properties are not *always* causally relevant to the effects in terms of which they are defined.[8] The only cases that I can think of in which second-order properties seem to be causally efficacious are those where an intelligent being recognizes them. That is why I keep mentioning 'standard' cases, cases where a second-order property is defined in terms of an effect and that effect is produced without any recognition of the second-order property by an intelligent being. I add to the claim of the first sentence of this paragraph the more tentative claim that in these standard cases, the second-order property is causally inefficacious.

But how can it be that second-order properties are inert in some cases, efficacious in others? Think (temporarily) in terms of a nomist theory of causal relevance. If dormitivity of a pill were nomologically sufficient for the ingester getting cancer (Jerry Fodor keeps trying to convince me that such a thing could happen without recognition of dormitivity by an intelligent being), then (let us suppose) dormitivity would be causally relevant to cancer. But such causal relevance to cancer would not show or even suggest that dormitivity is *nomolgoically* sufficient for *sleep*. Hence we might have causal relevance to cancer but not to sleep: non-standard causal relevance without standard causal relevance. (More on nomological sufficiency in a moment.)

Second-order properties involve having some properties or other, and though it is often helpful to think of the properties quantified over as first-order, actually they can be any properties at all. There is a general procedure (see Lewis, 1970) for defining a second-order property, given a theory in which the property plays a role so long as the theory allows some sort of a distinction between theoretical and observational terms. (In the case of a psychological theory, the distinction would be cashed as theoretical = mental, and observational = input/output.) If the theoretical terms are 'T_1'...'T_n', we can write the theory as $T(T_1 ... T_n)$, leaving out all mention of the observational entities. Then we can define 'T_1' as follows: x has $T_1 = EF_1 ... EF_n [T(F_1 ... F_n) \& x$ has $F_1]$.

So far, the case I've made for the limited causal inertness of second-order properties is based entirely on examples. But if the counter-intuitive consequences of this causal inertness are as bad as I will claim they are, a natural response will be simply to live with rejecting my way of taking such examples. That is, if I am convincing later when I say why the causal inertness of the second-order commits us to a view of the special sciences that is hard to swallow, the reasonable response would be that we should just suppose that dormitivity *is* causally relevant to sleep, and provocativeness does affect the bull. So I will try to get at the principles that underlie our reaction to the examples. I can think of two.

First, let us return to the nomist conception of causal relevance. On that conception, second-order properties are not causally relevant to the effects in terms of which they are defined because they are not nomologically sufficient for those effects. Consider dormitivity and sleep. The relation between the two is more like the relation between being a widow and having had a husband than that between, say, heat and expansion. If a pill is dormitive in the following sense: x is dormitive iff x has some property that causally *guarantees* (this is where this definition differs from the one offered earlier) sleep if x is ingested – and I take the pill, it follows that I sleep. The fact that dormitivity is sufficient for sleep is perfectly intelligible in terms of this logical relation. What reason is there to suppose that there must *also* be a nomological relation between dormivitity and sleep?

Now, I am very much not saying that a logical relation between properties *precludes* a nomological relation. This is as much a fallacy for properties as for Davidsonian token events. Suppose dormitivity is my aunt's favorite property, and sleep is my uncle's, and that my uncle tracks changes in my aunt's favorite property, changing his own so that his is always entailed by hers. Then dormitivity and sleep will be *both* nomologically and logically related. Logically related under one set of descriptions, nomologically under another. My point is not that a logical relation precludes a nomological relation, but rather that the logical relation between dormitivity and sleep tells us perfectly well why dormivitity involves sleep. There would have to be some *special* reason to postulate a nomological relation as well, and since the story about my aunt and uncle wasn't true, I don't see any such special reason. The point that this example is meant to make is that it would be amazing if there was *always* some special reason why a second-order property was nomologically related to the effects in terms of which it is defined.

This consideration is based on the fact that second-order properties are defined in terms of effects. A second argument is based on a different feature of second-order properties, the quantification involved in them.

Supposing that provocativeness provokes the bull would be supposing a strange sort of overdetermination of the bull's anger. Of course, overdetermination does sometimes happen. (The placebo effect is an example.) But to suppose that it always happens would be to suppose a bizarre systematic overdetermination. Whenever we have a first-order causal relation we can always define a second-order property on the model of provocativeness, and so every first-order causally relevant property would jointly determine its effect together with a second-order property. Indeed, the procedure iterates (for there is a third-order property that consists in the possession of a second-order property that is causally relevant to the effect), and so whenever there is one causally relevant property there would be an infinity of them. Even if the first-order property is causally sufficient for the effect, there would still be an unending series of other causally relevant properties. And we can define causally sufficient higher-order properties that would also be causally sufficient by the same reasoning.

The relation between second-order properties and the effects mentioned in their definitions is a 'fork' relation, a *bit* like the one discussed earlier in the selection on correlation and causation. Both heat and electricity are conducted by free electrons in metals. Rising velocity of free electrons:

1   Is responsible for rising thermal conductivity, and thus causally relevant to the explosion.
2   Is responsible for the epiphenomenal rising electrical conductivity.

Similarly, there is a first-order chemical property of Seconal that:

1   Is causally relevant to sleep.
2   'Generates' an epiphenomenal second-order property of possessing some property that is causally relevant to sleep.

In other words, just as the rising velocity of free electrons causes the explosion while engendering an epiphenomenal increase in electrical conductivity, so the chemical property causes the sleep while engendering an epiphenomenal second-order property of dormitivity.

The picture just sketched is attractive, but hardly compelling. The analogy just mentioned is far from perfect. The two engendering relations mentioned in the preceding paragraph are certainly very different, and besides the analogy only holds if I am right about the (limited) epiphenomenality of second-order properties, so it cannot be used to prove that epiphenomenality. (Incidentally, the fact that the chemical propety 'engenders' dormitivity rather than causing dormitivity illustrates the difference between what I am calling 'epiphenomen- alism' and traditional epiphenomenalism.) The overdetermination argument also is far from convincing. We are normally reluctant to accept overdetermi- nation because it is wrong, other things being equal, to postulate coincidences. If a man dies by drowning, we cannot suppose that there is always another cause of death as well, say, shooting. But no such coincidence would be involved in the series of higher-and-higher-order causally efficacious proper- ties I mentioned. If accepting such a series of causally efficacious properties is a price that must be paid for avoiding the problems to be mentioned, it can be paid.

In the end, the argument based on nomological theories of causal relevance is the best one. However, we can hardly expect those who favor counterfactual theories of causal relevance to be convinced. *Here, as earlier in the chapter, the lesson is that if you want to avoid epiphenomenalism, go for a counterfactual theory of causal relevance, not a nomological theory.* This is, I suppose, the main positive point of the paper, though its significance depends on the fate of the counterfactual approach.

Let me sum up the skeptical thesis. Suppose that a second-order property is instantiated, and the effect in terms of which it is defined occurs; my claim is that the second-order property needn't be causally relevant to the effect. I have

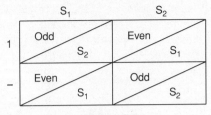

Figure 2.5

mentioned one type of case in which a second-order property can affect the effects in terms of which it is defined (and other things as well), namely, when intelligent recognition of them takes place, as in the placebo effect. Accepting other sorts of second-order effects (e.g. causal relevance of dormitivity to cancer) would not change my claim, since the arguments I gave for the limited epiphenomenality – the nomological argument and the overdetermination argument – were restricted to the causal relevance of a second-order property on the effects in terms of which it is defined, not other effects. The epiphenomenalism I am worried about is not total inertness of content properties, but whether, for example, the content of my desire for an ice cream cone is causally relevant to my going to the ice cream shop.[9]

At this point, I shall change gears abruptly. Although, as I've said, the case I've made for the (limited) inefficacy of the second-order property is far from conclusive, I think I have said enough for it to be taken seriously. What I now propose to do is simply *assume* that second-order properties are not always causally relevant to the effects in terms of which they are defined, and go on to discuss the consequences of this idea.

The skeptical point of this section depends on the fact that the mechanisms that manipulate genes and the mechanisms that manipulate the internal representations in the brain are not intelligent, and so cannot recognize second-order properties. Hence these are just the kinds of cases in which it would seem that the second-order properties are inefficacious with respect to the effects in terms of which they are defined. Likewise for other special sciences whose properties are plausibly second-hand.

By way of an example, consider a simple finite automaton, the one specified by the machine table of figure 2.5. What the table requires of any machine that it describes is that it have two states, S_1, and S_2, such that when the machine is in S_1 and sees a '1' it cries 'odd' and goes into S_2; and when the machine is in S_2 and sees a '1', it cries 'even' and goes back into S_1. And when the machine is in S_1/S_2 and sees no input ('-' symbolizes the null input), it cries 'even'/'odd' (respectively), staying in the same state. Thus the machine tells us whether it has seen an odd or even number of '1's (though not entirely sucessfully, since it is under the impression that 0 is an even number).

Now suppose we have a machine on the desk in front of us that satisfies figure 2.5 (i.e. is described by the table) and is in S_1; it sees a '1', and so it cries 'odd'. Let us ask: is the property of being in state S_1 (of a machine of the type of figure 2.5) causally relevant to the production of the cry of 'odd'? If the points made about dormitivity and provocativeness are right, it would seem not. If we think of S_1 as a property, it is the property that consists in having two other properties that are related to one another and to inputs and outputs as specified in figure 2.5. These other properties would be mechanical properties in the case of a gears-and-pulleys implementation, electronic properties in a usual computer implementation, and so on. If we are dealing with an electronic implementation, then it is the electronic properties that are causally relevant to the cry of 'odd', not the property of possessing some such implementation property.

The upshot is that *computational properties have no causal relevance to what computers do*, these effects being entirely the product of the implementations of the computational properties. This is, indeed, a strange conclusion, and if I am right about second-order properties, comparably strange conclusions could be reached about other functional sciences.

Consider the property of being a brown-hair gene. This property is plausibly functionally characterizable in terms of its patterns of inheritance and interaction with other genetic properties in determining actual characteristics, for example, in the fact that brown-hair genes are dominant over blond-hair genes. Such second-order properties are part of the distinctive conceptual apparatus of Mendelian genetics. But there are no genetic mechanisms that detect or are sensitive to the property of being a brown-hair gene. Genetic mechanisms detect biochemical properties, and the property of being a brown-hair gene arises via the processing based on biochemical properties. Similarly, computational properties such as S_1 mentioned above arise via the activity of processors that detect syntactic properties, not computational properties such as S_1. And semantic properties arise via the activity of processors that detect syntactic properties. All these second-order properties are epiphenomenal with respect to the effects in terms of which they are defined, such as brown hair in the case of the brown-hair gene.[10]

In sum, we want to maintain all of the following, but they are inconsistent:

1   Special science properties are causally relevant to the effects those sciences predict and explain.
2   Special science properties are often functional.
3   Functional properties are standardly causally irrelevant to the effects they are defined in terms of.

I have just argued for 3. If I am right, then we have what for many of us is a dilemma: we must either abandon functionalism or accept epiphenomenalism. But am I right about 3? Recall that the case for 3 depended mainly on the nomological approach to causation, and perhaps the way out is to reject that approach. Before accepting that conclusion, however, it would be best to examine another way out.

Because

The claim that second-order properties are standardly causally irrelevant to the effects in terms of which they are defined seems to fly in the face of a variety of common-sense and scientific facts, for example, true uses of the following:

I slept because I took a sleeping pill.
My muscle tension evaporated because I took a muscle relaxant.
The vase broke because it was fragile.
I have blue eyes because I have two blue-eye genes

I shall argue that such facts only seem incompatible with the (standard) causal inefficacy of the second order because of two ambiguities that easily escape notice.

Explanation and causation

One ambiguity is that between explanatory and causal uses of 'because'. It is easy to be unclear about whether a 'because' statement is true in an explanatory or causal sense of 'because'. If the dispositional/functional terms in the sentences listed above are understood to refer to second-order properties, then the sentences are only true on an explanatory, not a causal, reading of 'because' – if the line of thought of the last section is correct.

Audiences who have heard this chapter read as a paper have often objected that although there is a clear distinction between explanation and causation, the distinction between the *causal-explanatory relevance and causal relevance of properties* that I rely on here is a distinction without a difference. Here is the issue: the kind of explanation involved here is causal explanation, which is one of a number of species of explanation. So the kind of explanatory relevance of properties at issue is causal-explanatory relevance. And what is the distinction between causal-explanatory relevance of properties and causal relevance of properties?

Here is a way of seeing that there is a difference and what it is: notice that we can causally explain a case of sleep via appeal to the second-order property of dormitivity. I fell asleep because I took a pill that had the property of having some property or other that causes sleep. This is causal explanatory because it rules out alternative causal explanations of my falling asleep – for example, that I was grading papers. But second-order properties being (standardly) causally inefficacious, the appeal to dormitivity is not an appeal to a causally relevant property. Dormitivity is causal-explanatorily relevant to sleep without being causally relevant to sleep. Why? The appeal to dormitivity *involves* an appeal to a property that is genuinely causally relevant to the production of sleep, namely, the unnamed property (presumably a first-order chemical property) whose existence is mentioned in the analysis of the second-order property, the one that the dormitivity of the pill consists in the possession of. Dormitivity has causal-explanatory relevance because it involves a causally efficacious property. A causally inefficacious property can none the less be causal explanatory if it 'brings in' a causally efficacious property. But the causally relevant property is the first-order one, not the second-order one (assuming that my argument for the standard causal inertness of the second-order was right).

Ambiguity of functional terms

Functional terms are ambiguous. Let's take 'dormitivity' as an example. One construal is the second-order one much discussed here already – dormitivity = *possessing a property that causes sleep*. The other construal, one equally justified in ordinary usage, is *the property that causes sleep*. This is the natural reading of 'dormitive virtue' in the assertion that the dormitive virtue of Seconal is causally responsible for sleep. This latter construal is one in which 'dormitivity' is analyzed as a definite description that picks out the first-order property that is quantified over in the former construal. The two construals are very different in their relation to context. 'Dormitivity', on the former construal, always picks out the same second-order property. But on the latter construal, it picks out different first-order properties in the case of different types of sleeping potions. For the property that causes sleep in the case of Seconal is different from the property that causes sleep in the case of Valium. Similarly, 'the winning number' picks out different numbers in different lotteries (Lewis's example).

To sum up: in the second-order sense, dormitivity is not causally relevant to sleep; in the first-order sense, it is. And the plausibility of the 'because' claims mentioned at the outset of this section can be ascribed to the first-order interpretation.[11]

David Lewis has long advocated a form of functionalism based on Smart's idea of topic neutral analyses of mental terms (Lewis, 1972). Functional terms are defined by Lewis in the latter of the two manners mentioned above – in terms of definite descriptions. Many functionalists adopt a functional state identity thesis, one that identifies mental states with second-order properties. Lewis, by contrast, says that mental states are *functionally specified* brain states. Many functionalists take pain to be a second-order state, but Lewis takes pain to be the first-order brain state that plays the role characterized by the second-order state. Where some functionalists identify mental states with states that consist in causal roles, Lewis takes mental states to be the entities that have the causal roles. The issue is about how to regiment the language of the mental (and other theoretical languages).

Now some may embrace Lewis's first-order reading of functional terms of the special sciences as a way of having their cake and eating it too. On Lewis's construal, it is correct to say 'Dormitivity is causally relevant to sleep', 'Content is causally relevant to be behavior', and the like.[12] If we accept Lewis's reading, we can preserve the talk that would be appropriate if special science properties were causally efficacious. So it seems that we can avoid epiphenomenalism, and not have to give up functionalism. And there is no need to reject a nomological theory of causal relevance.

Unfortunately, the Lewis solution (as I shall call it) is only cosmetic. To construe the functional terms of a special science in Lewis's manner is to construe them as picking out 'lower-level' properties, properties of an *implementation* science. 'Believing that grass is green' on the Lewis construal picks out a *physiological* property. (In us, that is; in the case of a hypothetical intelligent computer, it would pick out an electronic property.) And in a certain sense, 'believing that grass is green' does not pick out a *psychological* property; that is, it does not pick out a property that is part of the distinctive conceptual apparatus of psychology. On Lewis's construal, 'brown-hair gene' (a term used by Mendelian geneticists long before the advent of molecular biology) picks out a piece of DNA, the concept of which would have been utterly alien to Mendel. Consider the computational state S_1 of figure 2.5. I said it was a computational state, and indeed the computational definition was given in the text. But on Lewis's construal, 'S_1' picks out an electronic state or a mechanical state, or some other implementation state, depending on the way the automaton is construed. 'S_1' would be defined by Lewis's method as *the (contextually relevant) state that has the role specified in the table of figure 2.5*. So 'S_1' does *not* pick out a computational state at all.

Of course, if a 'psychological property' is just a property picked out by a psychological term, then 'believing that grass is green' does pick out a psychological property, and likewise 'brown-hair gene' does pick out a Mendelian property and 'S_1' does pick out a computational property. But these construals of 'psychological property' etc. are Pickwickian. Psychological properties, on this construal, are not part of the conceptual apparatus of psychology; Mendelian properties are not part of the conceptual apparatus of Mendelian genetics; and computational properties are properties that a computer scientist may know nothing about, properties that are really part of the conceptual apparatus of electronics or mechanics or hydraulics.

My point is this: you do not vindicate the causal efficacy of the properties of a special science by construing its terms as referring to the properties of other sciences, implementation sciences. The Lewis construal does preserve a way of talking that we want. We can speak of the state S_1 being causally relevant to the production of the machine's cry of 'Even!' But the cost is that we no longer take S_1 to be a computational state (except in a Pickwickian sense). So a Lewis vindication of the causal efficacy of the computational is certainly Pickwickian. Similarly, since believing that grass is green is a physiological, not a psychological, state, the preservation of talk of the causal efficacy of believing that grass is green is no real vindication of the causal efficacy of the mental.

Construing terms of the special sciences in Lewis's manner does not make the second-order properties I have been talking about any less distinctive of their special sciences. Rather, it merely forces a different way of referring to them. 'Believing that grass grows', construed in Lewis's manner, picks out a physiological state, not a functional state. But 'having the belief that grass grows' picks out the functional state. 'S_1' picks out an electronic or mechanical or some other implementation state, but 'being in S_1' picks out a genuine computational state. Computational states are what are distinctive about the computational sciences, and Lewis's way of talking does not prevent us from referring to them or make them any less distinctive of the computational sciences. The same holds for the functional properties of all the special sciences for which functional properties are part of the distinctive conceptual apparatus. These properties remain distinctive of these special sciences even if we construe terms à la Lewis, and these properties remain causally inert (that is, causally inert with respect to effects in terms of which they are defined).

In sum, moving to the Lewis way of talking does not solve the epiphenomenalism problem, but only provides a way of talking that allows us to avoid facing it. The basic picture provided by the Lewis way of talking is the same as the one I have been trying to avoid: special sciences whose distinctive properties are causally inert but that can be used to pick out causally efficacious properties of lower-level sciences.

This brings me to a second objection to the Lewis solution. Second-order properties in the sense discussed here are properties that consist in the having of properties with such and such relations to one another. As I mentioned earlier, the properties quantified over need not be first-order. In the case of our mental properties construed as second-order properties, the quantified properties are physiological. Physiological properties are biological properties, and biological properties generally are prime candidates for functional analysis. Thus 'believing that grass grows' construed in the Lewis manner, since it picks out a physiological property, *may pick out another functionally individuated property*. Perhaps biological terms themselves pick out first-order properties, but perhaps not. Perhaps only the most fundamental of physical properties are genuinely first-order. In that case, even much of physics would be epiphenomenal! Or perhaps not even the most fundamental physical properties are first-order. (Maybe there isn't any most fundamental level.) Perhaps science is functional 'all the way down'. (Recall that there is a case made by Lewis himself for functional analysis of all theoretical terms.) This is not a matter that is easily resolved, but without a resolution that rules out the 'functional all the way down' option, we cannot rely on construing mental language in Lewis's manner to rescue us from epiphenomenalism.

Construing special science terms in Lewis's manner makes epiphenomenalism easier to stomach, but epiphenomenalism with controlled heartburn is still epiphenomenalism. Perhaps the solution is to reject functionalism, but if functionalism is rejected, we must begin anew to confront the arguments for epiphenomenalism in the computer model all over again. Functionalism at least has the virtue of disposing of epiphenomenalism on a counterfactual understanding of causal relevance. However, if we prefer the nomological approach to causal relevance, I am doubtful that there is any way of avoiding epiphenomenalism.

Acknowledgements

I am grateful for support to the American Council of Learned Societies and to the National Science Foundation, grant number DIR88 12559. I am also grateful to Jerry Fodor, Paul Horwich, Frank Jackson, Gabriel Segal, and Marianne Talbot for their comments on an earlier draft; to Thomas Nagel, who was the commentator on the paper on which this chapter is based at a conference at Columbia University in December 1988; to Simon Blackburn, who was the commentator on the paper at Oxford in February 1989; to Martin Davies, Dorothy Edgington, and Barry Smith for discussion of the issues while I was at Birkbeck College, University of London; and to the audiences at a number of philosophy colloquia.

Notes

1 There are, however, important differences that I don't have the space to go into. Briefly, it is more plausible that content supervenes on the neural level than that content supervenes on the 'syntactic' level. (More about the meaning of 'syntactic' here shortly.) An appeal to supervenience of content on lower levels can be used to attempt to avoid the epiphenomenalism argument.

2 The idea described here was, as far as I know, first articulated in Fodor (1975, 1980). See also Dennett (1981) in which the terms 'semantic engine' and 'syntactic engine' first appear, and Newell (1980) and Pylyshyn (1984). I spoke of a correlation between causal interactions among symbolic structures in our brains and sensible relations among the meanings of the symbol structures. This way of speaking can be misleading if it encourages the picture of the neuroscientist opening the brain, just *seeing* the symbols, and then figuring out what they mean. Since syntactic objects (and perhaps meanings as well) are functional entities (though different types of functional entities), identifying either of them in the brain will require considerable appreciation of neurological function.

3 This has long been a central dogma of the computational point of view, and has long been challenged by some philosophers. For arguments against the claim stated here, see Kim (1972), Richardson (1979), Enc (1983), and Patricia Churchland (1986). Block (1980a) argues against Kim, Patricia Kitcher (1980, 1982) argues against Richardson, and Blackburn (1991) argues against Enc and Churchland.

4 Alternatively, we could raise the thermal conductivity of the rod by raising its temperature, in which case part of the additional heat that causes the bomb to explode will come from the heat source that raises the temperature of the rod, and part will come from the fire via the increased thermal conductivity of the rod. I take it to be uncontroversial that rising thermal conductivity of the rod is causally relevant to the explosion. Further, this case fits the nomist model. For in this set-

up, rising thermal conductivity, *ceteris paribus*, is sufficient for an explosion (and the *ceteris paribus* condition is satisfied).

5   See Block (1986, 1987) for other reasons for taking functional role theories seriously. See Fodor (1987a), chapter 3, and Schiffer (1987), chapter 2, for opposing arguments.

6   LePore and Loewer (1987) give an objection (in effect) to Sosa's (1984) version of the counterfactual argument. Putting the matter in my terms, they agree that if a syntactic object with a certain meaning produces an output, the syntactic object would have caused the same output even if it had had a different meaning. But they add that meanings are lawfully related to behavior in some circumstances, so in such circumstances, the meaning would have caused the same output even if it had been carried by a different syntactic object. If the first counterfactual shows that syntactic forms screen off meanings from causal relevance, then the second shows the converse, that meanings screen off syntactic forms from causal relevance. But if both are true, both the syntactic form and the meaning of a representation are epiphenomenal, and since that is absurd, the obvious conclusion is that something is wrong with the form of the counterfactual argument. According to LePore and Loewer, semantics and syntax are *symmetrically* related to the production of behavior; if one is epiphenomenal, so is the other, so the counterfactual argument cannot use the causal relevance of syntax as a club against the causal relevance of semantics.

This issue deserves much more detailed treatment, but I can only summarize briefly. The LePore and Loewer argument fails to take into account the distinction between a particular event token, and *some* token of that type. Suppose I have a syntactic object in my head, Sally, with certain syntactic and semantic properties that produces behavior, Bruce. As I mentioned in the last paragraph, LePore and Loewer and I agree that Sally would have caused Bruce even if it had had a different meaning or no meaning at all. But can we make the *symmetrical claim* that Sally would have caused Bruce even if it had had a different syntactic identity or no syntactic identity at all? Certainly not! If Sally had had a difference syntactic identity or no syntactic identity at all, then it simply would not be the syntactic object I originally picked out as 'Sally'. Had the original meaning been 'carried' by a syntactic object not identical to Sally, we may suppose that the result would have been a Bruce-*like* behavior. But this Bruce-like behavior would not be identical to Bruce – given that events are individuated causally, as all good Davidsonians (such as LePore and Loewer) believe. Bruce's identity requires being caused by Sally. LePore and Loewer may feel that the way out is to talk not about the production of Bruce, but rather of Bruce-like events – types, not tokens. (There is some hint of this in their paper.) But the screening argument only works with tokens. What makes us want to say that the syntactic screens off the semantic is that the very same bit of behavior would have been produced even if the syntactic event that produced it had had a different meaning. (See Enc, 1986 for a dissection of another fallacy that falls foul of the type/token distinction together with causal individuation.) LePore and Loewer are right that there is a *nomological symmetry* between syntax and semantics. That is, there are circumstances in which both the semantic and syntactic properties of an event are nomologically sufficient for a certain type of behavior. But what is at issue here is counterfactual symmetry rather than a nomological symmetry, and this they have not argued for.

7   Note that it is no part of the 'Language of Thought' view to insist that the frog has a language of thought. The argument for a language of thought in humans depends

on the productivity and systematicity of human thought, and this argument will not apply to creatures whose thought is not at least as productive and systematic (see the epilogue of Fodor, 1987a).

8   My point differs from the usual skepticism about the causal efficacy of dispositional properties in this respect, and also in that it is about a category of properties – second-order properties – of which dispositional properties are only a special case.

9   After writing this chapter, I read Jackson and Pettit (1988), whch claimed that second-order properties are inefficacious before I did. However, Jackson and Pettit say that second-order properties are inert, not just with respect to the effects in terms of which they are defined, but all effects. They don't give any of the arguments used here, though Jackson tells me (in correspondence) that the overdetermination argument is essentially consonant with their way of looking at things. They go further, committing themselves, I think, to the claim that all 'multiply realizable' properties are causally inert. Thus if an increase in tempera-ture of a gas inside a sealed glass container results in the glass shattering, they take the fact that there are many configurations of molecules that could realize this process to show that the increase in temperature did not cause the shattering, but rather the cause was the specific molecular interactions. They do not note that the same point applies to the molecular interactions, which are themselves multiply realizable in terms of interactions among electrons, protons, neutrons, etc. And, of course, some of these particles are perhaps realizable in different ways by still smaller particles. The upshot of their position would be that the only genuine causality inheres at the level of basic physics. But what if there is no such level? This is a real physical possibility (see Dehmelt, 1989, 1990). *Their position dictates that we do not now know for sure whether there are any causally efficacious properties at all.* Jackson tells me that they are prepared to locate all genuine causality at the basic physics level, so long as one distinguishes between two types of causal relevance: the notion used here and the notion of causal relevance that corresponds to their idea of a causal programming explanation. The idea of causal programming can be illustrated by their example of an explanation of why trees grow faster in Melbourne than in Canberra: Why? Because there are more frosts in Canberra. There being more frosts in Canberra causally programs there being faster growth in Melbourne. They hold that second-order properties (and other multiply realizable properties) can be causally relevant to something in this causal program-ming sense, but not in the sense appropriate only to basic physics.

10   For the purposes of this example, I am ignoring the issue of whether there is anything at the molecular level that corresponds very well to the gene (see Philip Kitcher, 1982).

11   See Block (1980a) for a more detailed discussion of the difference between the first-and second-order interpretations.

12   Block (1986, pp. 668–9) takes this way out, as does Jackson and Pettit (1988).

References

Blackburn, S. (1991) Losing your mind: physics, identity and folk burglar prevention. In J.D. Greenwood (ed.), *The Future of Folk Psychology*, pp. 196–225. Cambridge, Cambridge University Press.

Block, N. (1980a) *Readings in the Philosophy of Psychology*, vol. 1. Cambridge, Mass., Harvard University Press.

Block, N. (1980b) What is functionalism? In *Readings in the Philosophy of Psychology*, vol. 1. Cambridge, Mass., Harvard University Press.

Block, N. (1986) Advertisement for a semantics for psychology. In P.A. French et al. (eds), *Midwest Studies in Philosophy*, vol. X, pp. 615–78. Minneapolis, University of Minnesota Press.

Block, N. (1987) Functional role and truth conditions. *Proceedings of the Aristotelian Society*, suppl. vol. 61, 157–81.

Churchland, P.S. (1986) *Neurophilosophy*. Cambridge, Mass., MIT Press.

Dehmelt, H. (1989) Triton ... electron,... cosmon,...: an infinite regression? *Proceedings of the National Academy of Sciences* 86, 8618.

Dehmett, H. (1990) Experiments on the structure of an individual elementary particle. *Science* 247, 539–45.

Dennett, D. (1981) Three kinds of intentional psychology. In R. Healy (ed.), *Reduction, Time and Reality*. Cambridge, Cambridge University Press.

Dretske, F. (1988) *Explaining Behavior: Reasons in a World of Causes*. Cambridge, Mass., MIT Press.

Enc, B. (1983) In defence of the identity theory. *Journal of Philosophy* 80, 279–98.

Enc, B. (1986) Essentialism with individual essences: causation, kinds, supervenience, and restricted identities. In P.A. French et al. (eds), *Midwest Studies in Philosophy*, vol. XI, pp. 403–26. Minneapolis, University of Minnesota Press.

Fodor, J. (1975) *The Language of Thought*. Cambridge, Mass., Harvard University Press.

Fodor, J. (1980) Methodological solipsism considered as a research stragey in cognitive psychology. *Behavioral and Brain Sciences* 3, 417–24.

Fodor, J. (1987a) *Psychosemantics*. Cambridge, Mass., MIT Press.

Fodor, J. (1987b) Making mind matter more. This is Fodor's reply to LePore and Loewer (1987). The abstract appeared in *Journal of Philosophy* 84, 642.

Fodor, J. (1989) Making mind matter more. *Philosophical Topics* 17, 59–79.

Haugeland, J. (1980) Programs, causal powers and intentionality. *Behavioral and Brain Sciences* 3, 432–3.

Haugeland, J. (1981) *Mind design*. Cambridge, Mass., MIT Press.

Horwich, P.(1987) *Asymmetries in Time*. Cambridge, Mass., MIT Press.

Jackson, F. and Pettit, P. (1988) Functionalism and broad content. *Mind* 97, 387, 381–400.

Kim, J. (1972) Phenomenal properties, psychophysical laws, and the identity theory. *Monist* 56, 177–92. Partially reprinted in Block (1980).

Kim, J. (1984) Epiphenomenal and supervenient causation. In P.A. French et al. (eds), *Midwest Studies in Philosophy*, vol. IX, pp. 257–70. Minneapolis, University of Minneasota Press.

Kitcher, Patricia (1980) How to reduce a functional psychology. *Philosophy of Science* 47, 134–40.

Kitcher, Patricia (1982) Genes, reduction and functional psychology. *Philosophy of Science* 49, 633–6.

Kitcher, Philip (1982) Genes. *British Journal for the Philosophy of Science* 33, 337–59.

LePore, E. and Loewer, B. (1987) Mind matters. *Journal of Philosophy* 84, 630–41.

Lewis, D. (1970) How to define theoretical terms. *Journal of Philosophy* 67, 427–46.

Lewis, D. (1972) Psychophysical and theoretical identifications. *Australasian Journal of Philosophy* 50, 249–58. Reprinted in Block (1980).

Minsky, M. (1967) *Computation*. Englewood Cliffs, N.J., Prentice-Hall.

Newell, A. (1980) Physical symbol systems. *Cognitive Science* 4, 135–83.

Putnam, H. (1960) Minds and machines. In S. Hook (ed.), *Dimensions of Mind*. New York, New York University Press.

Putnam, H. (1967) Psychological predicates. In W.H. Capitan and D.D. Merrill (eds), *Art, Mind, and Religion*. Pittsburgh, University of Pittsburgh Press. Retitled 'The nature of mental states' in Putnam's collected papers. Reprinted in Block (1980).

Putnam, H. (1973, 1975) Philosophy and our mental life. *Mind, Language and Reality: Philosophical Papers*, vol. 2. Cambridge, Cambridge University Press. Reprinted in Block (1980), and in somewhat different form, in Haugeland (1981). Originally published in *Cognition* 2 (1973), with a section on IQ that has been omitted from all of the reprinted versions.

Putnam, H. (1988) *Representation and Reality*. Cambridge, Mass., MIT Press.

Pylyshyn, Z. (1984) *Computation and Cognition: Issues in the Foundations of Cognitive Science*. Cambridge, Mass., MIT Press.

Richardson, R. (1979) Functionalism and reductionism. *Philosophy of Science* 46, 533–58.

Schiffer, S. (1987) *Remnants of Meaning*. Cambridge, Mass., MIT Press.

Searle, J. (1980) Searle's reply to critics of 'Minds, Brains and Programs'. *Behavioral and Brain Sciences* 3, 450–7.

Sosa, E. (1984) Mind-body interaction and supervenient causation. In P.A. French et al. (eds), *Midwest Studies in Philosophy*, vol. IX, pp. 271–82. Minneapolis, University of Minnesota Press.

3

How to be Psychologically Relevant

Cynthia Macdonald and Graham Macdonald

How did I raise my arm? The simple answer is that I raised it as a consequence of intending to raise it. A slightly more complicated response would mention the absence of any factors which would inhibit the execution of the intention; and a more complicated one still would specify the intention in terms of a goal (say, drinking a beer) which requires arm-raising as a means towards that end. Whatever the complications, the simple answer appears to be on the right track.

The complexities already mentioned, however, indicate that the original question admits of two different types of answer. The first complexity requires that certain causal conditions be satisfied; that there must be no circumstances which block the causal efficacy of the intention. This suggests that the type of explanation required is a causal explanation, and that the simple answer works by citing a causally efficacious feature of an event, one which was causally responsible for producing the result. Elaborating on this explanatory sketch would involve differentiating real from apparent causes, perhaps by delving deeper into the causally nomological features which underpin the causal citation of a causal state (the intention). The second complexity brings into play the goal of the action, and credits the agent with having a reason for the arm-raising. Here we are in the field of reason-giving explanations, an elaboration of which would yield yet further reasons for the particular action (the agent was thirsty or wanted to get drunk etc.). These explanations seem to compete, and one wants to know which is the correct one, the cause-citing one or the goal-citing one.

It has seemed obvious to many that the explanations need not conflict.[1] After all, the reason-giving explanation requires that the causal conditions be satisfied, so the reason must itself be a cause of the action, albeit one which specifies the cause in a reason-giving way. If reasons are causes, then the availability of the different explanations for the same effect need not trouble us. This resolution of the apparent clash fits neatly into a materialist ontology. Given that mental states are causes, identifying them with physical causes both avoids any problems of overdetermination and seems to be the best way of making their causal efficacy intelligible. The physical causal–nomological underpinnings, far from clashing with reason-giving, give respectability to the claim that the reasons are causes of the action. The position is further strenghtened by denying that the same reasons are always identical with the same physical causes. Reduction is avoided, and so one avoids the redundancy of the mentalistic explanation. It appears that we can have both a causal cake and an explanatory feast. (The biologist and the sociologist will also want their share of the cake: the beer drinking was caused by a functional–biological state selected because of its progeny-producing effects, and it was the outcome of a ritual in which group identities were being affirmed.)

This harmony on monistic causation and pluralistic explanation has recently been disturbed. The criticisms come from different sources, but one in particular singles out non-reductive monism as its target (Honderich, 1982; Macdonald and Macdonald, 1986).[2] Here the claim is that the three premises of the argument for that position, viz. (a) the Principle of Causal Interaction (PCI); (b) the Principle of the Nomological Character of Causality (PNCC); and (c) the Principle of the Causal Anomalism of the Mental (PAM), plus the conclusion that each individual (token) mental event is a physical event, leads either to inconsistency or to epiphenomenalism given a proper construal of (a) and (b). That construal connnects (a) and (b) by way of the claim that events interact causally in virtue of some but not all of their properties, the causally relevant ones, these being the properties that figure in causal laws governing the events causally related. Short of rejecting (c), it is claimed, non-reductive monism must accept mental epiphenomenalism.

We believe that non-reductive monism is the only viable position to be taken on the mind–body relation. We also agree with those who think that the problem of causal relevance is a real one that the non-reductive monist cannot sidestep by taking an instrumentalist or otherwise anti-realist attitude toward mental properties. Elsewhere we have argued that *the* problem of causal relevance concerns not one but two distinct issues (Macdonald and Macdonald, 1986). The first has to do with mental *causation*, a relation that holds between token mental and physical events. The second has to do with intentional *explanation*, which relates mental and physical types or properties. Since the argument for non-reductive monism trades on the distinction between causation, a relation which holds between events in extension, and explanation, which relates events but only by virtue of their possession of certain properties and not others, the charge of epiphenomenalism can only be made to stick if this distinction is respected.[3] The epiphenomenalist charge thus bifurcates into two distinct objections, responses to the first requiring work in the metaphysics of events, and responses to the second requiring work in the epistemology of explanation. Philosophers who have sought to solve the issue of mental *causation* by requiring it to be a four-place relation between two events and their respective 'causally relevant' properties simply confuse the one issue with the other (Horgan, 1989).[4] The problem of mental causation is no different from the problem of causation generally, and if causation is an extensional relation between events, it is an extensional relation between mental and physical events. To require that a relation holds between events *and* certain of their properties in order for mental events to be causally efficacious is to make the causal relation intensional *for mental events that interact with any other event*. Similarly, philosophers who believe that the question of whether mental events are *causally* efficacious reduces to the question of whether mental properties figure in causal–nomological explanations fail to appreciate the explanatory space which is opened up by the type-token distinction, and so confuse causal tokens with explanatory types (Fodor, 1987).

Our earlier solution to the two epiphenomenalist objections, which we briefly outline in the section 'Causal Efficacy' below, is relevant to the work we do in the remaining sections of the chapter. However, we now think that more needs to be said about mental epiphenomenalism if non-reductive monism is to be finally free of various charges of leading to causal or explanatory irrelevance of the mental. Recent literature suggests that 'causal relevance' is intended as elliptical for 'causal-explanatory relevance', and that, as such, the problem for non-reductive monism concerns the explanatory redundancy of mental *proper-ties* (Pettit and Jackson, 1988; Dretske, 1989; Fodor, 1989; Horgan, 1989; Kim, chapter 7 of this volume). However, the issue of explanatory relevance is intimately connected to the question of whether mental properties have some kind of causal autonomy; whether the (rationalistic) pattern, or network of relations between properties, they produce in virtue of having the causal powers they do is significantly different from the (causal) pattern produced by physical properties in virtue of their having the causal powers they do. If there is such a pattern to be discerned, then mental properties have causal powers distinct from any physical property or properties upon which they are generally assumed to supervene. If not, then non-reductive monism leads to the causal redundancy of mental properties. (That this is compatible with the causal efficacy, of mental *events* can be seen from the section 'Causal Efficacy' below.) This causal redundancy leads immediately to the explanatory redundancy of mental properties, since, if there is no distinctive patttern at the psychological level, then there is nothing for the psychological properties to explain. We shall argue that mental properties do have causal powers distinct from any physical property or properties, so that mental properties are explanatorily relevant, though not *causal*-explanatorily relevant.

There are thus three distinct claims that go under the name of 'the epiphenomenalist charge' that non-reductive monism must effectively deal with:

1   That mental *events* are causally inefficacious.
2   That mental *properties* are causally irrelevant.
3   That mental *properties* are *explanatorily* redundant.

We believe all three to be false. Our principal aim in what follows is to deal with (1) and (2), although what we have to say about these will have ramifications for (3). We can set out the problems before us and our position on them schematically in the following way.

Suppose that events are construed along the lines of the property exemplification account as instancings of act or event properties in objects at times, and suppose that, in a given case, an instance of a mental property (M_i) causes an instancing of an action property (A_i) (i.e. that a mental event causes an action). Suppose also that non-reductive monism is true and that M_i is identical with an instance of a physical property, P_i, and further, that A_i is identical with an instance of a behavioural property, B_i. Call this latter event E. Finally, suppose that P_i causes B_i. Since $M_i = P_i$, the causal *efficacy* of M_i is not at issue, for reasons which we briefly set out in the next section. However, there is still a question of the causal *relevance* of the mental property (MP), whose instancing is identical with the instancing of the physical property (PP). On a very intuitive test of causal relevance, a counterfactual test, it can be argued that the mental property in this case is causally irrelevant. Version One of the argument goes like this:

(a)   If MP hadn't been instanced, then E would still have occurred.
(b)   If PP hadn't been instanced, then E would not have occurred.
(c)   Therefore, PP is causally relevant whereas MP is not.

Our reply to this version is that (a) is false. E, by hypothesis, is an instance of *both* the action property (A) and the behavioural property (B). And if MP hadn't been instanced, A would not have been instanced. So E would not have occurred.

However, this response easily leads to a variant, Version Two, of the argument, which goes like this:

(a')   If PP hadn't been instanced, B would not have been instanced.
(b')   If MP hadn't been instanced, A would not have been instanced.
(c')   But (b') is true only because (a') is true, and PP is instanced, and B is instanced; and this, given the plausible assumption that MP supervenes on PP and A supervenes on B, is sufficient for the causal irrelevancue of MP.

Our reply to this is that, for (c') to be true, the following must be true:

(d)   If PP hadn't been instanced, A would not have been instanced.

But (d) is false because of the variable realizability of mental properties by physical events, an issue we address in the section 'Causal Relevance' below.[5] And if (d) is false, it is false that MP is causally irrelevant to A's being instanced.

In the next section on 'Causal Efficacy' we briefly outline our earlier solution to (1) and (3), partly to expose the reasoning that leads to (2) and partly to indicate where our response leaves work still to be done on (3). In the later section on 'Causal Relevance' we deal with (2). Although we do not consider (3) explicitly, our solution to (2) provides the resources for an effective response to it.

Causal Efficacy

The argument for non-reductive monism, if it works, works because of the extensionality of the causal relation and the intensionality of nomologicality. If two events are causally related, they are so irrespective of how they are described (or what properties they instance). Nomologicality, however, is another matter: whether a pair of events instantiates a (causal) law depends crucially on which properties they instantiate. Non-reductive monism reconciles the requirement that causality entail nomologicality with causal anomalism of the mental by adopting the further thesis that each event with a mental property has a physical property and so is a physical event. Mental events that interact causally with other events instantiate physical properties, properties in virtue of which they are covered by causal laws.

The issue of the *causal* efficacy of mental events can easily be confused with that of the *explanatory* efficacy of mentalistic explanations, and it is not surprising to find critics of non-reductive monism who begin their charge of epiphenomenalism by speaking of causal efficacy and finish by accusing that position of leading to explanatory inefficacy (Honderich, 1982; Horgan, 1989). One obvious source of such confusion can be traced to the dual function that the PNCC often plays with regard to causation and explanation. On the one hand, it figures in the nomological conception of causality, a conception which stands opposed to a singularist account (Armstrong, 1983; G. Macdonald, 1986; C. Macdonald, 1989). On the other hand, it figures in the familiar deductive-nomological account of causal explanation (Hempel, 1965). The fact that the PNCC plays this dual role makes it easy to suppose that, because mental properties (according to PAM) do not figure in causal laws, both the causal efficacy of mental events *and* the explanatory efficacy of mentalistic explanations are ruled out by non-reductive monism.[6] So the PNCC, in fact, provides two separate sources for two distinct charges of epiphenomenalism.

Since these charges *are* distinct, however, different strategies are needed to deal with them. Let us first look more closely at the issue of causal efficacy. Suppose that a cause–effect relation between events entails that those events have properties by which they are subsumed under a causal law.[7] It is then tempting to think that the only causally relevant properties of events are those which figure in the causal laws, and that the only causally efficacious instances are those which are instances of nomological properties, where this is taken to have the consequence that no instance of any non-nomological property can be causally efficacious. If we assume that all the nomological properties are 'lower-order' properties, then the conclusion will be that all higher-order properties are causally irrelevant, and so none of their properties is causally efficacious.[8]

Our position can be briefly stated: we agree that all instances which are causally efficacious are instances of nomological properties, and that properties which are causally relevant must have causally efficacious instances (this being a necessary condition for causal relevance). But it does not follow that there can be no instances of non-nomological properties which are casually efficacious. And so it does not follow that only nomological properties are causally relevant. The crux of our argument is that the claim, central to non-reductive monism, that each individual mental event is identical with a physical event, must be interpreted as the claim that two distinct properties, one mental and one physical, can be jointly instanced in a *single* instance (i.e. in an individual event). If, as seems evident from cases of determinate properties and their determinables, this is possible, then an instance of a non-nomological mental property (i.e. a mental event), M_i, can be co-instanced with (i.e. can be identical with) an instance of a nomological physical property (i.e. a physical event), P_i.[9] The mental property will then have an instance which *is* (i.e. is identical with) an instance of a nomological property. This single instance will be causally efficacious, and so the mental property will have met the necessary condition on causal relevance. (Whether it meets what we will call the pattern condition will be considered in the next section of this chapter).

That two properties *can* be jointly instanced in a single instance is well illustrated by cases of determinate properties and their associated determinables. Consider two such properties, one of which supervenes on the other, viz. the property of being red, and that of being coloured. No one would suppose that, in order for an object to possess both properties, it must first instance the former property, and *then*, in addition, instance the second. An object's instancing of the former property just *is* its instancing of the latter: nothing *further* is required, once the former is instanced, for the latter to be instanced, despite the distinctness of the properties themselves. But if this is so, then any case in which an instance of the property of being red is causally efficacious is one in which an instance of the property of being coloured is *also* causally efficacious, by the extensionality of the causal relation.

Similarly, we maintain, with mental and physical properties.[10] It is almost certain that non-reductive monism cannot escape commitment to some kind of supervenience thesis if it is to retain allegiance to its physicalist commitments. Given some such thesis, there is no *a priori* reason to assume that mental and physical properties of events *cannot* be jointly instanced in a single instance. To the objection that the mental/physical case is not like the colour/redness one, since in the latter but not in the former, the properties are logically related, our response is that the explanation of the nature of the supervenience relation may well vary from case to case (i.e. in some cases the relation will be best understood as logical, in others it will be best understood as metaphysical or physical), and that in the absence of an argument to the effect that properties that are logically or conceptually distinct *cannot* be jointly instanced, the move will not work.[11]

Such an argument will not be easy to come by. Consider a dispositional property such as that of dormitivity. The virtue of such a property is that it can be variably realized in different chemical bases. On some interpretations of this variable realizability claim, dormitivity is a higher-order property whose causal efficacy is usurped by its lower-order chemical properties.[12] But we claim that causal efficacy is a matter pertaining to property-instances, and when the lower-order property is instanced, so is the higher-order property. And if the base property-instance is causally efficacious, then so is the higher-order property-instance.

Is this simply a consequence of the pecularities of dispositional properties? We think not. Consider biological properties. A defensible, and in our opinion correct, view of how they arise or come into existence is that they result from the process of natural selection operating on instances of physico-chemical properties. The instances of some of these properties have effects which favour the reproductive capacity of those organisms which are the subjects of the instantiations. Given the transmission of the properties to descendants, the outcome of natural selection is a property, or set of properties, whose instances then proliferate among the species because of the favourable reproductive effects their instances have had in ancestors. This outcome just is the production of functional properties, and the view is that biological properties are these functional properties.[13] On this story, biological properties are physico-chemical properties whose instances have proliferated. More specifically, they are physico-chemical properties whose instances have a certain history and are biologically co-typed because of the types of effect those instances have.

Consider the property of having aposematic colouring, which is a distinctive colouring produced in order to warn predators that the putative prey is inedible, or at least unpalatable. Suppose that three butterflies have bottle-green wings. The first has the colouring because it warns the predator of its awful taste, so it has the property of being aposematic. The second has the colouring because it has enabled predecessors with that colouring to avoid predators, given the bottle-green environment they inhabited. The third just has the colouring, which has no biological effect either for it or its ancestors. The second will not instance the property of having aposematic colouring, but will instance the biological property of having a camouflaging colouring. The third will not instance any biological property simply by virtue of its having that colouring. The most plausible account of the metaphysics of the situation is to say that to instance the property of having aposematic colouring just is to instance the bottle-green property, given that this instance has the history it has. It seems simply perverse to deny that instances of biological properties are *at the same time* instances of physical properties. This is a particularly interesting case, for, like the mental/physical property relation, biological properties are logically distinct from physical ones.

There seems, then, to be no reasonable objection to the idea that instances of mental properties can be identical with instances of physical properties (i.e. that an event can be a single instance of both a mental and a physical property), and we stand by this response to the charge that mental events are causally efficacious. However, we no longer believe that it will suffice to dispel the charge of causal irrelevance of mental *properties*, an issue to which we now turn.

Causal Relevance

Why is the causal efficacy of property instances insufficient for the causal relevance of those properties? We have suggested that those who are suspicious of our view of causal efficacy have in mind objections which have more to do with explanation than with causation. On the other hand, we have conceded that causal relevance is intimately connected to explanation. There are two related objections which will reveal the connection and show what, in addition to the causal efficacy of instances of properties, is required for the causal relevance of the properties themselves.

First, consider an example used by Ned Block (in chapter 2).[14] Apparently the rising velocity of the same free electrons is the basis for both the rise in thermal conductivity and the rise in electrical conductivity of an object. Suppose that on a particular occasion the rise in thermal conductivity of an object causes an explosion. It is tempting and intuitive to say that the rise in electrical conductivity was epiphenomenal to the explosion. However, on the co-instantiation hypothesis, the rise in electrical conductivity (being identical with the rise in thermal conductivity) must be held to have caused the explosion. That is, this *instance* of a rise in electrical conductivity was causally efficacious.

Consider another example which has been used explicitly against the co-instantiation theory of causal efficacy. A piece of putty, resting on a metal mesh, changes shape and falls through the mesh. Suppose that, at a lower level, it is the change in the arrangement of its microphysical parts that is responsible for both the change in shape and for the change in the volume, or expansion, of the putty, with which the change in shape is co-temporaneous. On the co-instantiation model it looks as though the change in shape and the expansion in volume will be co-instanced, so that if the one is causally efficacious, then so is the other. But if this is so, then we are forced to the conclusion that the expansion of the putty must be held to be causally responsible for the putty's falling through the mesh. This has been deemed to be 'outlandish'.[15]

These two examples, though significantly different, have the same moral. The moral is that the co-instantiation view is committed to allowing intuitively causally inert properties to have causally efficacious instances. Note, however, that neither of the examples uses properties related to each other as higher to lower-order properties. And the significant difference between them is that the first example appears to exploit a type–type correlation between one kind of change, a change in electrical conductivity, and another, a change in thermal conductivity, which the second example lacks. In that example the change in shape and the expansion in volume are accidentally connected; there is no suggestion that every such change in shape must be accompanied by the same, or indeed any, expansion in volume.

Secondly, a slightly different objection to our model of causal efficacy insists that if we allow any property to be causally relevant because its instance is causally efficacious, then we are committed to the causal relevance of an infinite number of properties.[16] If a cricket ball instances the property of travelling at 20 miles per hour, then that ball also instances the property of travelling at less than 30 miles per hour, and instances the property of travelling at less than 35 miles per hour, and so on. All of these properties seem to be co-instanced with the ball's travelling at 20 miles an hour. Suppose that the cricket ball's travelling at 20 miles per hour is causally responsible for its smashing a window. If the property of travelling at 20 miles per hour is causally relevant because its instance is causally efficacious, then so too are all the other, infinite number, of properties causally relevant. Again, the conclusion is thought to be a *reductio* of the co-instantiation hypothesis.

We accept all the apparently counter-intuitive conclusions *which pertain to instances*, but deny that this tells against our model. The reason is that all of these examples equivocate between concerns about causation and concerns about explanation. The counter-intuitiveness of the conclusions results from the, in itself, *correct* view that many of the properties whose instances are causally efficacious would not be adequate to a *general* explanation of the effects produced.[17] But the examples themselves equivocate between the irrelevance of an explanatory 'because' and the irrelevance of a causal 'because'. This equivocation can be traced to the dual role that nomologicality is often viewed as playing with regard to both causation and explanation. Given this dual function, it is easy to reason that if a property fails to figure in a causal law, and so to figure as part of a causal explanation, it cannot be causally relevant because its instances are not causally efficacious.

We have already indicated that we reject this line of reasoning and the assumptions that lie behind it. In particular, we reject the *specific* connection between nomologicality and causality that the assumptions reveal, since we allow non-nomological properties to have causally efficacious instances. We also, as it happens, reject the connection btween nomologicality and explanation, since we believe that non-nomological properties can be explanatory, but we will return to this topic shortly. What is important in assessing the force of the counter-examples is whether non-explanatory properties can have causally efficacious instances, and for reasons previously stated it is clear to us that they can. What is driving the counter-examples is the thought that in a counterfactual situation the exemplification of the suspect property would not have the required effect, so that, on a counterfactual test of causal relevance, the suspect property would fail to be causally relevant. So, for example, the shape of the putty is causally relevant because, if that shape were to be re-instanced, the putty would fall through the mesh again. That is to say, *however the micro-particles arranged themselves*, as long as that shape recurred, the effect would follow. The claim must be that this need not happen with another expansion of the putty; *this* expansion just so happened to occur in a way that the micro-particle arrangement instantiating this expansion caused the putty to fall through the mesh. On another occasion this could not be expected to occur. Similarly with the cricket ball case: another instantiation of the property of travelling at under 30 miles per hour may be one of travelling at 1 mile per hour, and in that case the window would not have smashed.[18]

In both of these types of counter-example the failure of the effect of a certain type to occur in the counterfactual situation is held to be sufficient to deny the property instance causal efficacy in the actual situation. That is, the failure of the property to be *generally* efficacious (in the relevant respect of each of its instance's causing an instance of this type of effect) is thought to be sufficient to disqualify it from being *particularly* efficacious (in this instance). But there seems to us to be no good reason to disallow such particular efficacy. Why should what happens elsewhere, with other instances, be relevant to whether *this* instance is efficacious? The principle which the objectors seem to assume is one we will call 'supergen': whenever an instance is causally efficacious, every property of which it is an instance must be generally linked to any property co-instanced in the effect and caused by that instance.[19] This is an exceptionally strong claim, which few would wish to make. It has the consequence that if an instance of MP (a mental property) is causally efficacious and co-instanced with PP (a physical property), *both* MP and PP must be generally linked, not just to B (the behavioural property of the effect), but to A (an action property of that effect which, on our view and on non-reductive monism generally, is co-instanced with B). This will make an instance of PP inefficacious for an instance of A. One can reject an outright singularism with respect to causality (a view which claims that there need not be *any* general connection between cause and effect instances) without endorsing supergen. The position we have outlined above seems to be the best compromise. Causal connections do entail nomologicality, but it is not required that every property co-instanced with a nomological property must itself be nomological.[20] If the connection between efficacy and nomologicality is understood in this way, and if an instance can be an instance of both a nomological and non-nomological property, then the non-nomological property will have an efficacious instance in this case, but such efficacy *may* not hold in general. That is to say, there may be no general relation between the non-nomological property and the nomological property of the effect. When this happens the property-instance will be causally efficacious, but the property will not be causally relevant to the nomological *type* of effect.

This response makes it look as though the only way for a property to be causally relevant, and so meet what we earlier called the pattern condition on causal relevance, is for it to be nomological, where this means that it figures in causal laws. On this reading, a casually relevant property is one which (a) has causally efficacious instances; and (b) figures in causal laws. We have said that (a) is a necessary condition for causal relevance, and we agree that in general the combination of (a) and (b) will provide sufficiency (but not necessity, because we do not think that (b) is necessary for causal relevance).

However, even for those cases where the pattern condition is met by nomologicality, the *caveat*, 'in general', is required, in order to take into account counter-examples such as Block's. Here we have an effect – an explosion – which is best explained as due to the rising thermal conductivity, rather than as due to the rising electrical conductivity, of an object. But, according to our model, the rise in electrical conductivity satisfies both (a) and (b). It satisfies (a) because this instance of rising electrical conductivity, being identical with this instance of rising thermal conductivity, is causally efficacious. And it satisfies (b) because rising electrical conductivity figures in law-like explanations. Shock-type effects are thereby explained. However, it is evident that rising electrical conductivity is irrelevant to the explosion. The crucial lesson to be learned is that the causal relevance of a property is *type*-relevant: a given property will be causally relevant to some types of effects and not others. What is required, in addition to (a) and (b) is (c): the nomological property must be nomological *for a certain type of effect*. The generality which causally relevant properties display must be of the right type for a given type of effect: otherwise we will have electrical conduction causally relevant to, and so explaining, heating effects.

Is this the end of the story of causal relevance? Not quite. When we said that what was needed to be added to the causal efficacy condition to get causal relevance was a 'pattern' condition, we meant that the generality which the causal relevance of properties must capture depends upon there being a pattern, or network of relations between properties, in nature which the generality reflects. If there is no such pattern, then the connection between the properties instanced in the cause and effect will not be generalizable. In these cases there can be causal efficacy without causal relevance. In the cases where the properties are nomologically connected there will be the required pattern, and this is captured by (b) above. However, given our allegiance to causal anomalism of the mental, it is an essential part of our theory that this is not the only pattern to be found. If (b) were the only way in which generality could be purchased, then we would agree with the critics of non-reductive monism who say that it is committed to the causal irrelevance of mental properties. The pattern condition, if it is to be met by mental properties, must therefore be met in some other way than by meeting condition (b).

The validity of functional explanations in biology is a useful reminder that there can be other patterns in nature, in this case that of the design resulting from natural selection.[21] Here the operation of 'normal' (physical) causation has resulted in a new pattern emerging, one which is produced by, but which does not just replicate, the regularity of the physical causal connections. Natural selection, in producing the pattern, underwrites the causal relevance of biological properties to their effects. What selection requires is that in the world as we find it there are certain effects *reliably* produced by the instances of some physico-chemical properties, and the consequence of selection is the spread of instances of reproductively advantageous properties. What is crucial in this case is that the 'reliability' of the connections is relative to the reproductive advantage of the effects in comparsion with the reproductive effects of other properties, and so does not require the stricter reliability associated with nomologicality. For example, the fertilizing effect of sperm may be seldom realized, but it is so *often enough* (in comparison with other items) for fertilization to be its function. So here we can have the generality required for causal relevance, one which is dependent upon nomological connections but which does not just reflect those connections. If we were to provide only a statistical-cum-causal account of what sperm do, it would be impossible to see why one type of effect (fertilizing eggs), which only an incredibly small number of sperm cause, is singled out as being the function of sperm. In the case where a sperm fertilizes an egg, there will be an instance of both a nomological and a functional pattern. Our explanation of what is happening in any such case will depend on which aspect of the effect (what *type* of effect) we want explained.[22] This is why (b) must be relaxed to allow for patterns other than the nomological. The biological case also reinforces the need for (c), since it shows that any instance of a cause–effect relation can be an instance of more than one pattern.

The existence of two patterns here, the physical and the biological, accounts for the different explanations we can give for what is happening when functional behaviour is explained. One can explain what is happening when a particular chameleon changes colour by noting that it is responding to a difference in the colour of its environment, where this can in turn be explained in terms of a physico-chemical response to changes in light. We can also say that the chameleon is camouflaging itself in order to make itself less visible to predators. The important point is that one could not say this of another animal, a possible world twin chameleon, which may undergo exactly the same physico-chemical changes in response to the same environmental changes, but which lacked the relevant biological history of this chameleon. The twin's behaviour would be explained by the same physico-chemical laws as that of our actual chameleon; it would be an indiscernible twin from the perspective of the nomological pattern, but not from the biological perspective. Although subsumed under the same causal laws, the behaviour of only one of the chameleons exemplifies biological design. Of only that chameleon can be it said that its behaviour has a biological aspect, and it is because of this difference in the effect that one can say that the biological property instanced in the cause will have a causal relevance different from that of the co-instantiated physico-chemical property. It will have a different causal 'shape' as a consequence of the difference in the effects its instances produce.

In the above example we have a case of different causes, from the biological perspective, of behaviour which would be typed as identical from the physical perspective. In one case we have a biological cause of camouflaging behaviour (a biological effect), whereas in the other there is no biological cause, and no functional aspect to the effect. The behaviour is not camouflaging behaviour. (The animal may be camouflaged, but it does not exhibit camouflaging behaviour. Its being camouflaged is a biological, but not a physical, accident.) It is worth noting that the biological cause can also malfunction, producing effects rather different from those which nature intended. In such a case, the same biological cause (the same as in the functional case) will produce effects which are typed differently for the purposes of physics and chemistry.[23] The same biological cause will be invoked to explain behaviour which falls under different causal laws. Depending on the reason for the malfunction, the cause may also be physically type-different from the physical causes of functional behaviour.

The biological case illustrates nicely what is needed for mental properties to be causally relevant. First, they need to meet condition (a): they must have causally efficacious instances. We have argued that they can meet this condition without disturbing the pattern of physical causality (a point that was important to establish given our physicalism). They do not disturb the pattern of physical causality because they are co-instanced with physical properties. But, secondly, they need to meet some analogue of condition (b), since there must be a distinctive pattern in nature which secures the generality required for causal relevance. It is evident to us that the distinctive pattern exemplified, and which mental properties display, is that of rationality. The connections which provide the generality are, in the main, rational connections between mental properties.[24] What explains a particular effect *under its 'action' aspect* is a mental property; the instance of that property is causally efficacious and citing it under that aspect renders the action *intelligible* (this, of course, ensures that an analogue of condition (c) is met). If the effect were to be explained only via nomologicality, this intelligibility would vanish. It is the rational connections which underwrite the counterfactual which we endorsed earlier: if MP (the mental property) had not been instanced, then A (the action) would not have occurred.

A full justification of the existence of a rational pattern in nature is beyond the scope of this chapter. What is important for present purposes, however, is that connection between actions and the rational pattern be noted. The problem of mental causation arises if we look at the effect under only one aspect, its physical aspect, and ignore the fact that it is also an action. One consequence of overlooking action-properties is that mental and physical properties appear to compete for causal relevance; relevance to the same type of effect (see Kim, chapter 7). If they do so compete, the mental property will inevitably lose out. However, this appearance is misleading and fails to take seriously the occurrence of actions in nature.[25] The causal relevance of the mental property instanced in the antecedent cause must therefore be a relevance to the action aspect of the effect. The occurrence of actions in nature goes hand in hand with the existence of a rational pattern. Were there no instances of action-properties, there would be no rational pattern; but, equally, were there no rational pattern, there would be no actions. Because the rational pattern is distinctive – not just a mirror of the physical pattern described in physical causal laws – different counterfactuals involving mental properties will be licensed. In particular, the falsity of

(d) If PP (the physical property) had not been instanced, A (the action) would not have occurred

is due to the difference between the generality exemplified in physical property causal relevance and mental property causal relevance. This difference is dependent upon there being a mental aspect to the effects produced, *irrespective* of their physical 'realizers', so that the effects are not just bodily movements, but are also actions. The fact that action properties are variably realizable by different physical properties is explicable in terms of this difference in generality between physical property causal relevance and mental property causal relevance. The epiphenomenalist charge of causal irrelevance of mental properties will only get a foothold if one thinks that there are no actions, and that there is no rational pattern. But here the onus of argument lies with the epiphenomenalist.

Notes

1 The *locus classicus* for this response is Davidson (1963).
2 Another, very general, line of thought begins by assuming that meanings, or the contents of propositional attitudes, aren't in the head, but that the physical states that are causative of behaviour are in the head, and concludes that propositional content (or something in the head's having propositional content) is causally irrelevant to behaviour. This is discussed by Fred Dretske (1989).
3 Unless, of course, independent argument is forthcoming.
4 Ned Block agrees that mental states or events can be causes of behaviour, and says that the epiphenomenalist accusation is that they are not causes of their behavioural effects in virtue of their mental properties (see Block, chapter 2 of this volume). This is what we call the issue of the causal relevance of mental properties.
5 By 'mental properties' we mean both intentional properties of mental causes and intentional properties of action effects.
6 Of course, this assumes that all mentalistic explanation is causal explanation (Stich, 1983; Fodor, 1989). We take this issue up in the following section.
7 This need not involve any Humean reduction of causality to nomologicality. We

think that the nature of causality is such that it involves nomologicality, not that nomologicality is all that causality consists in.

8   This is the position partially defended by Block in chapter 2. ('Partially' because he allows that some second-order properties can be causally relevant, but only when special conditions obtain, and in most cases which concern us these conditions do not obtain. He allows mental events to be causes, but this leaves it unclear whether they are causes because instances of mental properties are efficacious.) The obvious rejoinder, that higher-order properties also figure in causal laws, is defended by Fodor (1987, 1989). Given our commitment to causal anomalism of the mental, this position is not open to us, but see also Block's criticism. The higher-order/lower-order property distinction can be explicated in a number of ways. On one account, a higher-order property is a property of having a lower-order property that stands in certain causal relations to other lower-order properties. (Block favours this characterization of the first-order/second-order property distinction.) On another account, a higher-order property is a determinable, of which lower-order properties are derterminates (so that, e.g. being coloured is a higher-order property and being red is lower-ordered). On still another account, a higher-order property is a property of a property (so that, e.g. being a colour is a higher-order property of being red). We do not think that the relation between mental and physical properties easily fits any of these characterizations. Rather, the relation between mental and physical properties seems best described as one of supervenience, where this relation is distinct from the three just characterized. In particular, it is a more general relation than the relation determinates bear to their determinables.

9   This should make it clear that, by 'instance of a property', we do not mean 'trope of that property'. The view of events being presumed here is a version of the property exemplification account (Kim, 1976; Lombard, 1986; Macdonald, 1989). This is not, on our reading, a trope view of events. Nor do we wish to endorse any such view. The crucial difference between the property exemplification account and a trope view for present purposes is that tropes, unlike mere property instances, are essentially typed. On the property exemplification account, events are exemplifications of act or event properties at (or during periods of) times in objects. The account is not committed to any particular view as to which properties are constitutive of events. Nor, for this reason, is it committed to any view as to which properties of events are essences of them. This makes it possible to hold that mental and physical properties (a) can be jointly instanced in a single instance, but (b) are distinct properties. And this is just what non-reductive monism requires: a dualism of properties combined with a monism of instances.

10   But only similarly. We do not believe that the mental property, M, is a determinable of a physical property, P (see n. 8). The analogy is intended to show that it is possible for the two properties to be co-instanced in a single instance. Stephen Yablo takes the stronger line, arguing that the mental/physical property relation is one of determinable to determinate (Yablo, 1992).

11   Stephen Yablo (1992) claims that the fact that many properties related as determinate to determinable are logically related doesn't tell against the view that mental and physical properties are literally related as determinate to determinable, since things that are conceptually related can also be metaphysically related, and it is the metaphysical relation that matters. We agree with his reason, but since we do not think that mental properties are examples of the determinate/determinable

property relation, but rather, of a more general supervenience relation, the lack of a logical relation between mental and physical properties does not worry us. For us, cases that satisfy the determinate/determinable property relation will also satisfy the supervenience relation, but not all cases that satisfy the supervenience relation will satisfy the determinate/determinable relation.

12 See Block's discussion of the causal inefficacy of dormitivity (chapter 2 of this volume).

13 This view is ably defended in a number of places: see especially Ruth Garrett Millikan's discussion (1984). It is a non-reductive conception of biological properties (G. Macdonald, 1992).

14 The same example is used by Pettit and Jackson (1990).

15 See Pettit (1992), especially pp. 257–8. (The argument was directed against Graham Macdonald's contribution to the same volume.)

16 Block (chapter 2) suggests this as an objection, but thinks that it is a price that can be paid for avoiding epiphenomenalism. Yablo (1992) uses it as an objection to our view. Yablo's position is quite close to ours, but he raises issues about the identity of events which go beyond the scope of the present discussion.

17 Block (chapter 2) notes that explanation and causation are often confused, but does so in order to draw a different conclusion from ours. He holds that one can mistakenly infer from the causal-explanatory relevance of second-order properties to the conclusion that they are causally efficacious (see the final section of chapter 2). In fact, our reasoning is the reverse: we hold that a property can only be causally explanatorily relevant if it is causally efficacious (i.e. that causal efficacy of the instance is a necessary condition of the causal relevance of the property instanced). The confusion we detect here is not in the move from causal relevance to causal efficacy, but in the slide from the causal irrelevance of the property to the inefficiency of its instance.

18 There is an aspect of this counter-example we do not directly address, and that is the profligacy attaching to there being an infinite number of properties which have a causally efficacious instance. But note that the counter-example appears to be even more profilgate. For us, there is only one instance. The objector seems unable to deny that these infinite number of properties are instanced. When the cricket ball travels at 20 miles per hour, it travels at under 30 miles per hour, and so on. So if co-instancing is denied, then the objector is committed to there being an infinite number of instances whenever there is one. We see no need for this profligacy.

19 An alternative would be to deny that an instance could be an instance of more than one property. We have already indicated why this is an unattractive option, but in any case this is not an alternative available here, since the counter-examples assume that (at least) two properties are co-instanced.

20 'Nomological' throughout this chapter is to be understood as 'causal–nomological', and is to be given whatever strength is required for physical cause–effect relations. This will allow for probabilistic laws. Commitment to the view that such (causal) law-like connections are involved in all cause–effect relations reflects both our understanding of causality and our physicalism, by which we hold that all causal connections involve physical events.

21 We are thus in agreement with Ruth Garrett Millikan's claim that biological explanation is non-nomological (Millikan, 1986, 1993). Where we disagree is with her further claim that the functional pattern is to be found in psychological matters.

22   The use of 'aspect' here is deliberate, as it connects our topic with that of constrastive explanation, where one explains why something happens rather than something else. Why did a purple fire occur? The choice of explanation (a choice of what is causally relevant to a type of effect) will depend upon whether we want to know why a fire occurred (rather than no fire), or whether we want to know why the fire was purple rather than red. Note that in these examples the fact that we have such a choice of explanation (of causally relevant properties) does not seem to force us to the conclusion that the effect, the purple fire, must have had two different causes (causally efficacious instances). Those who insist that a mental property can have causal relevance only if its instance has 'separate' causal efficacy, i.e. is not co-instanced with a physical property instance, must apply the same principle to the examples alluded to in the dicussions of contrastive explanation. The result is not appealing. For further discussion, see Peter Lipton's discussion (1990).

23   The causes in the functional and malfunctional cases will be biologically type identical because they share (enough of) the same history. We realize that we are here asserting what needs defence, but for this see the arguments and examples provided by Millikan (1984, 1986, 1993).

24   'In the main' because we are leaving it open wehther there can be non-rational mental connectivity. The obvious candidates would be causation by sentient (as opposed to sapient) properties, and mental causation which does not surface in consciousness. If there are these connections, then it may be that the first will be nomological, and the second functional. The query will then be: why are these mental properties? And the answer will have to be that they essentially interact with the central cases of mental properties.

25   Our strategy for solving the problem of causal (hence explanatory) exclusion (Kim, chapter 7), understood as a problem of how both mental and physical properties can be causally relevant, is thus a version of the 'two-explananda' strategy. Dretske (1988, 1989, chapter 6 of this volume) invokes a version of this strategy to solve a related problem (see n. 2 above). However, we do not intend here to be endorsing his version of the strategy.

References

Armstrong, D. (1983) *What is a Law of Nature?* Cambridge, Cambridge University Press.

Davidson, D. (1963) Actions, Reasons, and Causes. *Journal of Philosophy* 60, 685–700. Reprinted in *Essays on Actions and Events*. Oxford, Oxford University Press, 1980.

Dretske, F. (1988) *Explaining Behavior: Reasons in a World of Causes*. Cambridge, Mass., MIT Press.

Dretske, F. (1989) Reasons and causes. In J. Tomberlin (ed.), *Philosophical Perspectives*, vol. 3, pp. 1–16. California, Ridgeview.

Fodor, J. (1987) *Pyschosemantics*. Cambridge, Mass., MIT Press.

Fodor, J. (1989) Making mind matter more. *Philosophical Topics* 17, 59–79.

Hempel, C. (1965) *Aspects of Scientific Explanation*. New York, Free Press.

Honderich, T. (1982) The argument for anomalous monism. *Analysis* 42, 59–64.

Horgan, T. (1989) Mental quasation. In J. Tomberlin (ed.), *Philosophical Perspectives*, vol. 3, pp. 47–76. California, Ridgeview.

Kim, J. (1976) Events as property exemplifications. In M. Brand and D. Walton (eds), *Action Theory*, pp. 159–77. Dordrecht, D. Reidel.

Lipton, P. (1990) Contrastive explanation. In D. Knowles (ed.), *Explanation and its Limits*, pp. 247–66. Cambridge, Cambridge University Press.

Lombard, L. (1986) *Events: a Metaphysical Study*. London, Routledge and Kegan Paul.

Macdonald, C. (1989) *Mind–Body Identity Theories*. London, Routledge.

Macdonald, C. and Macdonald, G. (1986) Mental causation and explanation of action. *Philosophical Quarterly* 36, 145–58.

Macdonald, G. (1986) The possibility of the disunity of science. In G. Macdonald and C. Wright (eds), *Fact, Science, and Morality*, pp. 219–46. Oxford, Blackwell.

Macdonald, G. (1992) Reduction and evolutionary biology. In D. Charles and K. Lennon (eds), *Explanation, Reduction, and Realism*, pp. 69–96. Oxford, Oxford University Press.

Millikan, R. (1984) *Language, Thought, and Other Biological Categories*. Cambridge, Mass, MIT Press.

Millikan, R. (1986) Thoughts without laws: cognitive science with content. *Philosophical Review* 95, 47–80.

Millikan, R. (1993) Explanation in biopsychology. In J. Heil and A. Mele (eds), *Mental Causation*, pp. 211–32. Oxford, Oxford University Press.

Pettit, P. (1992) The nature of naturalism. *Proceedings of the Aristotelian Society* suppl. vol. 66, 245–66.

Pettit, P. and Jackson, F. (1988) Functionalism and broad content. *Mind* 97, 381–400.

Pettit, P. and Jackson, F. (1990) Causation in the philosophy of mind. *Philosophy and Phenomenological Research* suppl. vol. 50, 195–214.

Stich, S. (1983) *From Folk Psychology to Cognitive Science*. Cambridge, Mass, MIT Press.

Yablo, S. (1992) Mental causation. *Philosophical Review* 101, 245–80.

4

Reply: Causation and Two Kinds of Laws

Ned Block

The shooting caused the death, but not all the properties of the cause were relevant to the production of that effect. For example, the shooting had the property of involving a bullet of a certain mass, and that property was causally relevant to the effect, but the shooting also had the property of involving a loud noise, and that property was not causally relevant to the effect. The question at hand is: if one event causes another, which properties of the cause are causally relevant to the effect? More generally, what is causal relevance, and which properties have it?

I take the Macdonalds to give an account of causal relevance of properties in terms of three conditions. I will consider a simplified version of their account, ignoring the extension of the category of the nomological to cover non-nomological patterns in biology and psychology. I take their claim to be this: consider a pair of events, cause and effect. For a property P of the cause to be causally relevant to the effect is

1 For the cause to be an instantiation (they say 'instance' and 'instancing') of P,[1] and
2 For P to be a 'nomological property', to figure in laws (or analogous patterns – but recall that I am simplifying by ignoring the patterns), and
3 For P to be nomological for that 'type of effect'. I take their meaning here to be that causal relevance of a property to an effect requires the property to be nomologically sufficient for that type of effect.

In sum, they hope to characterize the causal relevance of properties in terms of events as property instantiations, causation of one event by another, and nomologicity.

Condition (3) is motivated in part by my bomb example. A metal bar connects a source of heat to a bomb. When we first see the bomb, the thermal conductivity of the bar is sufficiently low that not enough heat is conducted to the bomb to set it off. Then we raise the thermal conductivity of the bar (never mind how), and as a result, the bomb explodes. Call this the Hot Bomb case.

While the Hot Bomb case is occupying us in Cambridge, in San Francisco a cooperating thought experiment team is dealing with a different case, the Electrical Bomb case. When they first see the electrical bomb, it is attached to an electrical detonator. (I'll tell you how the detonator works later.) The switch is thrown on the electrical detonator, but the bomb doesn't explode because the electrical conductivity of the wires connecting the switch and the battery to the bomb is sufficiently low that not enough electricity is conducted to the detonator to set off the bomb. Then they raise the electrical conductivity of the wires (never mind how), and as a result the bomb explodes.

The Hot Bomb case troubles the Macdonalds. They start off characterizing causal relevance in terms of their first two conditions. The instantiation of the rising thermal conductivity is identical to the instantiation of the rising electrical conductivity, they say. That is, one event instantiates both rising magnitudes. Since the instantiation of rising thermal conductivity is uncontroversially causally efficacious in producing the explosion, the instantiation of rising electrical conductivity, being the same event, is causally efficacious in producing the explosion. Given the co-instantiation, the property of rising electrical conductivity passes the test of condition (1) for causal relevance to the explosion. Further, rising electrical conductivity figures in laws, and is in that sense, nomological, so it passes the test of condition (2) as well. Of course, the Macdonalds deny (and I agree) that the property of rising electrical conductivity is genuinely causally relevant to the explosion. What to do? They introduce requirement (3): 'the nomological property must be nomological *for a certain type of effect*. The generality which causally relevant properties display must be of the right type for a given type of effect: otherwise we will have electrical conduction causally relevant to, and so explaining, heating effects' (chapter 3, p. 70).

But, of course, electrical conduction *can* be causally relevant to and explain heating effects. Indeed, that's how the detonator in the Electrical Bomb case (the one whose workings I kept secret) works. The detonator is a little electric heater. The heater heats up the bomb enough to make it explode. So once the electrical conductivity of the wires is sufficiently increased, the result is an increase of heat in the bomb and hence an explosion. The property of rising electrical conductivity is causally relevant to the increase of heat in the detonator and also to the resulting explosion.

What to do? Let's think about relativizing to apparatus. Relative to the apparatus of the Hot Bomb case, one might say, the rising thermal but not electrical conductivity is nomologically sufficient for the explosion. And likewise: relative to the apparatus of the Electrical Bomb case, one might say, the rising electrical but not thermal conductivity is nomologically sufficient for the explosion. But if we look more carefully at what relativity to apparatus comes to, we can see that it will not serve the Macdonalds' purpose.

Let us distinguish between two types of nomological relations or laws:

General laws Laws that don't depend on any particular apparatus such as the law of universal gravitation (F = GM $_1$M$_2$/r^2) and the ideal gas law (PV = NRT).

Apparatus laws Consequences of general laws plus an appropriate description of the apparatus in question. For example, a sufficiently detailed description of the appropriate sort of coke machine and a handful of coins will entail that the coins going into one slot is nomologically sufficient for a can of coke (all under the relevant descriptions) to emerge from another slot.

You will recall that condition (3) (as I am understanding it) says that for a property P of a cause to be causally relevant to an effect, the property must be nomologically sufficient for that effect. Two types of laws, then, yield two versions of condition (3).

The Macdonalds' statement, quoted above, that rejects electrical conduction being causally relevant to heating effects may embody a suggestion that there is no such *general law* dictating that rising electrical conductivity is nomologically sufficient for heating effects. But there is also very likely no general law dictating that rising *thermal* conductivity is sufficient for heating effects. I only checked one textbook, but no matter, think of the effect as the explosion instead. Surely there is no general law relating either electrical or thermal conductivity to explosions. And there is no point in moving to *chains* of laws. There is no general law relating heating to explosions either. Indeed, there is no general law relating anything to explosions.

It is obvious that our claims of causal relevance of properties cannot in general depend on general laws. The jiggling of the earthquake causes the rear view mirror to fall off. The insertion of the coins causes a coke to pop out. But there are no general laws that have truck with properties like jiggling, coin insertion, mirror-falling and coke pop-out. The properties of causes and effects that interest us are often ones that have no place in general laws. Conclusion: there are too few general laws for the Macdonalds' purposes.

Well, what about apparatus laws then? Can the Macdonalds' claim be cashed out in terms of them? Given an appropriate description of the Hot Bomb case, there will be an apparatus law dictating that the property of rising thermal conductivity is nomologically sufficient for the explosion. And given an appropriate description of the Electrical Bomb case, there will be an apparatus law dictating that the property of rising electrical conductivity is nomologically sufficient for that explosion. Unfortunately, given the Wiedemann–Franz Law correlating electrical and thermal conductivity, there will *also* be an apparatus law dictating that the property of rising electrical conductivity is nomologically sufficient for the explosion in the Hot Bomb case, and also an apparatus law dictating that the rising thermal conductivity is nomologically sufficient for the explosion in the Electrical Bomb case. There are too many apparatus laws for the Macdonalds' purposes.

Indeed, the point doesn't depend on general nomological correlations such as that between electrical and thermal conductivity. *Local correlations* ground the same sort of point. There is a description of the gun and its surround that together with general laws entail that if the gun emits a certain noise a death will inevitably follow. *In that situation*, no such noise could occur without the gun being fired in such a way as to result in a death. That is, for a given described situation, a noise of a certain sort is nomologically sufficient for a death. Nomological sufficiency relative to description of a situation is *cheap*, perhaps even totally vacuous. Indeed, given familiar assumptions about time symmetry of laws of nature, the death is also nomologically sufficient for the noise relative to the description on which the noise is nomologically sufficient for the death. Thus, relative to appropriate descriptions, nomological correlations abound, and the problem posed by the Hot Bomb case appears everywhere, like a metastasizing tumour.

There are a few comments in chapter 3 that suggest that the Macdonalds will try to avoid the problem by insisting on a *special kind* of nomologicality, namely one for which the nomologically related properties are *also related by the relation of causal relevance*. That is, on this special kind of nomologicality, F is not nomologically sufficient for G unless F is causally relevant to G. At one point they state condition (2) saying that a causally relevant property is one which 'figures in causal laws'. And in note 20, they say '"Nomological" throughout this chapter is to be understood as "causal nomological", and is to be given whatever strength is required for physical cause–effect relations.' But the required strength would seem to be just that of causal relevance. If anything weaker will do, they don't hint at what it is. Of course, you can't characterize the causal relevance of properties in terms of nomological relations between properties if you use a notion of nomological relation that itself involves causal relevance. That would be to characterize causal relevance in terms of itself.

One could distinguish two senses of 'causal nomological'. The sense of the last paragraph is just *nomological* plus *causally relevant*. That is, for F to be causally nomologically sufficient for G is for F to be causally relevant to G and for F to be nomologically sufficient for G. With apologies, I will call this 'causal-relevance-nomologicity'. There is, however, another sense which uses the notion of causation in the Macdonalds' condition (1) which has to do with event causation rather than causal relevance of properties. This sense substitutes event causation ('causal efficacy') for causal relevance. Call it 'event-causation-nomologicity'. For F to be event-causation nomologically sufficient for G is for all instantiations of F to cause instantiations of G, and for F to be nomologically sufficient for G. On the first sense (causal-relevance-nomologicity), as I pointed out in the last paragraph, for the Macdonalds to insist on reading 'nomological' as causal nomological is circular and question begging. It is no surprise that if F is causal-relevance-nomologically sufficient for G, then F is causally relevant to G. But on the second sense (event-causation-nomologicity), to insist on reading 'nomological' as causal nomological would be useless. To see this, recall that in the Hot Bomb case, the Macdonalds agree that there is an event that is both an instantiation of rising thermal and also rising electrical conductivity that causes the explosion. Thus, *both* rising electrical and thermal conductivity are event-causation-nomologically sufficient for the explosion (in the Hot Bomb type of case). Both properties are nomologically sufficient and all instances of both properties (in the type of set-up envisaged) cause explosions. So the appeal to causal efficacy of events would be useless for the Macdonalds. I am sorry to have to bring up this event-caustion sense of 'causal nomological', since it clutters the discussion, and after the next paragraph I will drop the matter.

Returning to the first notion of causal nomological (causal-relevance-nomologicality), even if we were to allow appeal to causal *general* laws, that wouldn't help in the cases we have been talking about. General laws will not tell us which properties of the shooting are causally relevant to the death. And once we move to apparatus laws, it would seem as if the decision as to whether the apparatus laws are causal or not amounts to the same thing as the decision as to whether the properties adverted to in the laws are causally relevant to the indicated effects. The vacuity of the analysis construed in this way is most embarrassing when we look at the issue that is motivating the entire discussion, the issue of whether mental properties are causally relevant to the production of behavior. Talk of patterns replaces talk of laws, according to the Macdonalds, but the problem remains: are the patterns that connect mental properties to behavioral properties causal patterns or not? The disagreement we see among philosophers about whether mental properties are causally relevant to behavior will simply reappear as a disagreement as to whether these patterns are causal patterns. Of course, we can all agree that, for example, the pattern relating hunger and eating is causal in the sense that hunger-events cause eating-events (the event-causation sense of 'causal nomological' again). That isn't the issue. The issue is whether a hunger-event causes an eating-event *in virtue of* any of its mental properties, e.g. its experiential quality or in virtue of being a hunger-event. That is the issue of causal relevance of properties as applied here. To say that the pattern is causal is either to say that the hunger-events cause eating-events, in which case it is uncontroversial and irrelevant, or it is to say that hunger-events cause eating-events *in virtue of* being hunger events, in which case it is question begging.

The problem with (3) was that it appeals to nomologicality, but there are too few general laws and too many apparatus laws. So it looks as if their attempt to handle the Hot Bomb case founders. Actually, this is the tip of an iceberg, for the same point affects the notion of nomologicality in (2). The shooting had the properties of involving both a noise and a high-velocity bullet. On a notion of nomologicality tied to general law, neither property is nomological. On a notion of nomologicality tied to apparatus laws, both properties are nomological (relative to appropriate descriptions of the set-up). Thus the notion of nomologicality deployed in (2) and (3) is of no use.

I will conclude with a brief remark about the relation between the problems with nomologicality in conditions (2) and (3) and the notion of an event that is assumed in condition (1). Consider the question of whether condition (1) could be exploited to deal with the Hot Bomb case without the resource of appeal to nomologicality? I take it as uncontroversial that an instantiation of rising thermal conductivity is an event that is causally efficacious in producing the explosion (in the Hot Bomb case). But is that instantiation of rising thermal conductivity identical to an instantiation of rising electrical conductivity (as the Macdonalds suppose)? Are the nomologically correlated properties co-instantiated ('co-instanced', in their terminology)? The Macdonalds simply assume co-instantiation here without saying why. Indeed, they don't say what they take the identity conditions of these instantiations to be.

We find a clue in the discussion of the piece of putty that expands and changes shape at the same time. The Macdonalds say 'it looks as though the change in shape and the expansion in volume will be co-instanced' (chapter 3, p. 67), but without saying exactly why. They say that it is a change in arrangement of microphysical parts that is responsible both for the expansion and the change of shape, and this seems to be their justification for the co-instantiation claim. Similarly, the co-instantiation claim mentioned above seems to derive from the idea that it is the rising velocity of free electrons that is the basis for both the rise in electrical and thermal conductivity. So it would appear that if x and y are property instantiations that have the same microphysical basis, then $x = y$.

Now, this sufficient condition for event identity is famously counter-intuitive. Consider Davidson's example of the solid sphere that simultaneously rotates and increases in temperature. Suppose that the event of increasing temperature of the sphere causes the paint to craze. If the event of increasing temperature = the rotation event, then the rotation event causes the paint to craze. So there is a reason to take the rotation and the temperature increase to be distinct events despite their having a basis in the same particle trajectories.

But this reason would be undermined if we could see the intuition appealed to as really directed to causal relevance of properties. We could say that there is one event that instantiates both rising temperature and rotation, but only the first property is causally relevant to the paint crazing. The problem I have been talking about applied here is that nomologicality cannot be used to support the causal relevance of one property but not the other. There are *no general laws* relating either temperature or rotation to paint crazing, and there are apparatus laws relating *both* temperature and rotation to paint crazing, so nomologicality will not draw the distinction rightly. Without a way of justifying the desired result about causal relevance of properties, the Macdonalds may have to reconsider their identity conditions for events.

Acknowledgements

I am grateful to Paul Horwich and Judy Thomson for comments on this chapter.

Note

1 Note that this condition assumes that a cause can both be an instantiation of P and also have P. I will not discuss whether there is a real problem here.

Explanatory Relevance

5

Introduction: Causal Relevance and Explanatory Exclusion

Cynthia Macdonald and Graham Macdonald

It is a firmly entrenched thesis of common-sense psychology that people behave the way they do because of reasons – beliefs, desires and other contentful states – that they have, and these reasons rationalize behaviour by explaining why it came about. But exactly how do such explanations work to rationalize behaviour? One standard and familiar account involves two central claims. The first is that reasons rationalize behaviour by causing it, and that reasons-giving explanations are a species of causal explanation. This claim takes it to be a necessary condition of reasons-explaining behaviour that they cause it. The second claim is that the *way* reasons rationalize behaviour is by assigning a causal role to intentional content itself; by assigning a causal role to the *contents* of beliefs, desires and other contentful states that constitute those reasons. Thus, my moving toward the refrigerator is explained by my desire *for a coke* and my belief *that there is a coke in the refrigerator*: states which jointly cause my behaviour and do so because of their contents.

This account has proved to be problematic for those concerned to give naturalistic explanations of intentionality; explanations which attempt to show that mental states can be accounted for within the domain of natural science. (In the context of the present debate, this is taken to require that mentalistic explanation, or explanation by reasons, be a species of causal explanation.) If one assumes that behaviour is, or is at least partly constituted by, bodily processes or events, the problem is part of a wider one of showing how mental states can causally interact with physical ones; a problem that has dominated work in the philosophy of mind for centuries. Against the background of naturalism, this wider problem is solved in part by taking mental states, i.e. states with mental content, to be identical with internal physical states of their subject's bodies. However, two specific problems remain for the account.

First, there is a problem about how the content, or meaning, of an intentional state can *matter* to the effects that that state is capable of having with regard to behaviour. The problem arises because it is almost universally agreed that the content of an intentional state is a *relational*, or an *extrinsic*, rather than an intrinsic, feature of it. Beliefs may be within-the-head causes of behaviour, but one cannot discover what their contents are by poking around inside the head. What gives the belief that there is a coke in the refrigerator its meaning, or content, has to do with a subject's relation to things that lie outside the subject's body. In short, intentional content does not supervene on the intrinsic physical properties of internal states and processes of subjects alone. But if this is so, then how can intentional content be causally relevant to behaviour? This problem is particularly pressing for those concerned with naturalizing intentionality, since, in assuming that mental states can be accounted for within the domain of natural science, it is assumed that their causal powers are determined by the intrinsic physical properties of those internal states which are responsible for the bodily movements that constitute behaviour. How can content have a genuine causal-explanatory role unless it, and not just the states which have it, supervenes on the intrinsic physical properties of internal states that cause behaviour? Identifying mental states with those internal physical states that are causally responsible for behaviour will not solve this problem. For, in order for content itself to be causally relevant to those states' effects in behaviour, content itself must be seen to be implicated in the production of behaviour.

Suppose, however, that this problem can be solved. Then a second problem arises, again against the background of naturalism. The problem concerns explanatory *competition* between reasons-giving explanations and other explanations, ones that invoke only intrinsic physical properties of subjects' internal events and states. On the assumption that there is only one complete and independent explanation of a single explanandum, the question arises of whether reasons-giving explanations of behaviour do not now compete with these other explanations. How is this explanatory tension to be resolved? Is it to be resolved by showing that reasons-giving explanations are not really independent of other explanations which invoke only intrinsic physical properties of internal causes of behaviour? Or is it to be resolved by showing that the latter explanations are actually incomplete ones, and require completion by reasons-giving explanations? Or is it to be resolved in some other manner? And what are the implications of these different ways of resolving the explanatory tension?

Both of these problems threaten the explanatory efficacy of reasons *qua* reasons, but they do so in different ways. Following Dretske, we can call the first the problem of the *causal relevance* of the mental (a problem he refers to elsewhere as the soprano problem). This problem is one of seeing how content can have a causal role, and so an explanatory one, with respect to behaviour *at all*. The soprano whose voice shatters glass does so because of the physical properties of the sounds produced, not because of the meanings of those sounds. What those sounds mean is causally, and so explanatorily, irrelevant to their effects on the glass. Is the same true for intentional content in general? After all, behaviour is, or is constituted by, bodily states and processes: both the glass's shattering and a subject's behaviour are physical events or processes. If semantic content, or meaning, doesn't matter to the one because it is an extrinsic feature of the cause, why should intentional content, which gives intentional states their meaning and is also an extrinsic feature of the causes of behaviour, matter to the other?

The second problem only arises once one accepts that content or meaning *does* have a causal and so an explanatory role to play *vis à vis* behaviour. The problem here is in seeing how rationalizing explanations of behaviour can be accommodated alongside others which cite only intrinsic physical properties of their internal causes. The explanatory tension that results itself cries out for explanation, given the assumption (which Kim, chapter 7, labels 'the Principle of Explanatory Exclusion') that we may accept only one complete and independent explanation for a given explanandum event. Given this principle, if we are faced with a situation in which there appear to be two explanations of a single explanandum, we are entitled to ask whether these explanations are related, and if so, how. Since explanation sets out to resolve epistemic perplexity, we cannot rest content with two explanations for a single explanandum event. The perplexity has not been resolved until we know how these two explanations are related.

The debate in this section is concerned with these two closely related problems regarding the genuineness of reasons-giving explanations. Fred Dretske, in chapter 6, raises the problem of the causal relevance of intentional properties, and argues for an account that assigns a distinctive causal-explanatory role to content within a naturalistic framework. This account anchors the causal role of content in the natural function internal physical states have of indicating various factors external to an organism. Dretske's account of how the internal physical states of an organism represent factors in its environment builds on the account of indication, and his account of the causal relevance of content makes essential use of the account of representation in a sense described more fully in the next section.

Jaegwon Kim's interest, in chapter 7, is not so much with the question of how intentional content can be causally relevant, but with how its causal relevance can remain intact in a naturalistic framework. A guiding principle in a framework such as this is the Principle of Explanatory Exclusion (PEE). If, as naturalism states, all mental states, including their causes and effects, can be accounted for within the domain of natural science, then one can expect that it is in principle possible for natural science to provide complete causal explanations of all the physical states and processes that constitute human behaviour. Naturalism and its presumptions seem to exclude intentional content's having a genuine causal-explanatory role to play, not because content is an extrinsic feature of intentional states, but because it is causally *redundant*.

Dretske's final reply emphasizes the point that the problem of causal relevance and that of explanatory exclusion are distinct problems. Being distinct, they require distinct solutions. Dretske points out that his account may seem to be concerned with the problem of explanatory exclusion but is not. Its central concern is with the causal relevance of content. The solution to the problem of how content can be causally relevant will not do to solve the problem of explanatory exclusion. Nevertheless, Dretske makes clear that his account of how content is causally relevant has the resources to deal with the problem of explanatory exclusion. His solutions to both problems make use of the distinction between behaviour and bodily movement.

When I raise my arm, my arm moves. But the movement of my arm (M) is distinct (although not wholly distinct) from the behaviour (B) which is my raising my arm. Dretske takes the latter to be an internal state's *causing* the movement of my arm (C's causing M). Since the event, M, and the process, C's causing M, are distinct phenomena, to explain why M occurred is not the same thing as to explain why C's causing M occurred.

This distinction between movement and behaviour plays an important role both in Dretske's account of how content can be causally relevant and in Dretske's account of how explanations that invoke content do not compete with other explanations that invoke physical events or states with their intrinsic physical properties. Since so much of interest centres on the distinction, it is worth examining the role it plays in accounting for (a) the causal relevance/ explanatory relevance of content; and (b) the fact that reasons-giving explanations do not compete with others.

The Causal/Explanatory Relevance of Content

Dretske tells us, in both chapter 6 and in his reply to Kim in chapter 8, that his concern with intentional content has increasingly become a quest for an explanation, not of what meaning *is*, but of what meaning *does*. The sounds of the soprano, even though they may mean something, do not have the effects they do (shattering glass) *because* of what they mean. Even if the physical events which carry meaning (sounds) have physical effects, so that their presence or absence in the physical world matters, it is not *because* of the meaning of those events that they matter. Dretske's worry is that the same might be true for intentional content generally. Suppose that my beliefs and desires are (i.e. are identical with) internal physical causes, perhaps brain-events, of the movements of my body. Does my body move *because* of what my mental states mean? In a naturalistic framework, where all phenomena are causally explained in terms of events and properties that fall within the domain of natural science, it seems that if my beliefs and desires cause my body to move, this can be accounted for solely in terms of the intrinsic physical properties of those states. Just as the physical properties of the soprano's sounds account for the effects those sounds have on the glass, the purely physical intrinsic properties of my beliefs and desires seem necessary and sufficient to causally explain the movements of my body. So just as the soprano's sounds could have meant something different or nothing at all, and this would not have made a difference to the effects those sounds had on the glass, my beliefs and desires might have meant something different, or meant nothing at all, and this would not have made a difference to the movements of my body.

If one assumes, plausibly enough, that human behaviour just is, or is constituted by, bodily movements, this runs counter to one of the strongest intuitions we have about our intentional states. We think that they not only make a difference to human behaviour, but that they make a difference because their contents make a difference. If my belief and desire had concerned, not coke, but cigarettes, then I would have behaved differently. Rather than going to the refrigerator, I would have headed for my coat pocket. Dretske asks how this intuition can be accounted for in a naturalistic framework.

His answer involves distinguishing between bodily movements, on the one hand, and behaviour, on the other, and further, distinguishing between *structuring* causes, on the one hand, and *triggering* causes, on the other. Dretske's claim is that, whereas meaning, or content, does not matter to bodily movements, it *does* matter to behaviour; and it matters because it is a *structuring*, rather than a *triggering*, cause of behaviour (Dretske, 1988, 1991; see also Adams, 1991; Horgan, 1991; Kim, 1991).

Suppose that a certain belief/desire pair (call it C) of mine, say, my belief that there is a fly on my plate and my desire to be rid of the fly, causes me to flick my hand at the fly. There are not one but two things going on here, either or both of which we might wish to explain. First, there is the movement of my hand (call it M), a bodily movement. We might wish to know why or how this movement occurred. Secondly, there is the *process* (C's causing M) of my belief/desire's causing the movement of my hand. We might wish to know why or how this process occurred. Dretske's view is that the movement and the process are distinct phenomena and so require distinct explanations. The first, a movement, is *not* something that content needs to be called upon to explain. Although my belief and desire, internal physical states of mine, did cause this movement, they did not do so because of their content. So content is not causally relevant either to the explanation of how M occurred or to the explanation of why M occurred. What matters to the movement are only the intrinsic physical properties of the internal physical states which caused it. But the second, a piece of behaviour, *is* something that content needs to be called upon to explain. Specifically, *why* C caused M is something that content is needed to explain (although *how* C caused M also need only refer to the purely intrinsic properties of the cause). The reason, Dretske argues, is that an explanation of why C caused M requires an explanation of how C came to be *hooked up* with M. More specifically, in order to explain why *this* C-event caused *this* M-event, one needs an explanation of the *general* fact of why C-type events cause M-type events, and this requires an investigation into the mechanism responsible for the causal hook-up between C-type events and M-type events. Dretske argues that content is required for explanations of this type, and this is because what is required for these explanations are *structuring* rather than *triggering* causes. Reasons are structuring causes by virtue of their contents.

All of this requires a good deal of spelling out, and involves Dretske's accounts of indication and representation. Dretske's account of how content is causal-explanatorily relevant is rooted in his account of indication, of which only a brief summary can be given here (see Dretske, 1981, 1988). This account can be illustrated with the help of an example from biology. Suppose that an organism, say, a frog, has a need to produce a bodily movement of a certain type, say, a flicking of the tongue (call this M) only in the presence of a certain feature, say, the presence of a fly (F) in its immediate environment. This need, to be satisfied, requires a reliable 'head-world' connection between F and M (so that the frog flicks its tongue *only when* a fly is present).[1] In order to establish this connection, two things need to occur. First, a reliable connection needs to be secured between the presence of F and some internal state of the frog that can serve as an *indicator* of F. For this the frog needs an F-detector that can register the presence of Fs, on the basis of which it can enter into an internal physical state, say, a state of type C, reliably in the presence of Fs. When this happens, C-type states are *de facto* indicators of Fs.[2] Secondly, a reliable connection needs to be forged between Cs and movements of type M. Dretske argues that this connection is forged by C-type states being made into a 'switch' for Ms, in which case C-type states acquire the (natural) *function* of indicating Fs. How does this happen?

In the case of biological organisms, this functional connection is secured by the process of natural selection. Those frogs whose C states produce movements of type M are fit – the presence of this F-C-M connection in their ancestors has led to the proliferation of offspring. The connection was selected for because of its favourable progeny-producing effects.

Now we can ask two 'why' questions about the frog. The first is, why does its tongue flick (i.e. why does M occur)? The answer here need only mention the fact that a C occurs and causes an M. There is no need here to speak of the indicator function states of type C have in the frog: physical states with their intrinsic physical properties suffice to explain why M occurs. The second question is, why does the frog flick its tongue (i.e. why does C's causing M occur)? This is a question, not about why the frog's tongue moves, but about why the frog *behaves* as it does; why internal states of type C in the frog cause movements of type M. Dretske claims that what is called for here is an explanation of how the hook-up between Cs and Ms came about, of how C states came to be 'switches' for M states. The fact that C-type states are not only *de facto* indicators of Fs, but have the natural *function* of indicating the presence of Fs is relevant to this explanation. For, having the indicator *function*, Cs indicate Fs *in order to* produce Ms. C-type states occur in order to produce M-type states in the presence of Fs. It is in this way that purposeful behaviour – behaviour which does not just happen to occur, but which occurs for a purpose – can be explained.

Dretske thinks that this account can be applied to many types of case behaviour which is *designed*. It can be applied to hook-ups between light switches and lights, whose design is intentional, but not intrinsically so (the design originates in humans). It can be applied, as in the case just illustrated, to hook-ups between biological organisms' internal physical states and their bodily movements, whose design – Nature – is not intentional. And it can be applied to hook-ups between internal physical states of humans and their bodily movements, whose design – learning – *is* intrinsically intentional.

How does Dretske's account solve the problem of the causal relevance of content? We have seen that, in any explanation of human behaviour, we must distinguish between two questions: (1) why a given bodily movement occurs; and (2) why a given piece of behaviour occurs. Common sense tells us that the content of an agent's reason is relevant to the explanation of that agent's behaviour. If one were to assume that what content explains is the bodily movement itself – that content is causally relevant to the explanation of (1) – then one would be saddled with the soprano problem: one would not be able to show how meaning, or intentional content, matters. However, on Dretske's story, common sense is vindicated: content is causally relevant to behaviour, since content, being a feature of one of the constituents of behaviour, is intrinsically rather than extrinsically connected with it.

This raises a question. How can content be causally relevant to behaviour if content is a feature, not of the causes of behaviour, but of one of the constituents of behaviour *itself?* On Dretske's account, those events which bring behaviour about – that cause internal physical states (Cs) with content, which in turn cause bodily movements – are not ones where content plays a causal role. Content is therefore not only causal/explanatorily irrelevant to why and how bodily movement occurs, but *also*, in a certain sense, to the explanation of *why* (and not just how) behaviour occurs. For, just as it suffices for the explanation of why a given bodily movement occurs to cite intrinsic physical properties of its internal cause, it suffices for the explanation of why a given piece of behaviour occurs to cite intrinsic physical properties of *its* cause. Dretske's way of acknowledging this point while insisting on the causal relevance of content is to distinguish between *triggering* and *structuring* causes. Content is not a triggering cause of behaviour, of the process which is C's causing M. Content does not cause C, which causes M. But content is a structuring cause. Content is causally responsible for the C's-causing-M connection, since it is causally responsible for *forging* that connection, for 'wiring up' organisms in such a way that C-type states bring about M-type states (and so for *this* C's causing *this* M).

Suppose, now, that in a specific case we want an explanation of why a given subject, say Sue, is behaving as she is, say, why she is going to the refrigerator. Dretske tells us that, depending on the precise nature of this 'why' question, content will or will not be causally relevant. If what we want to know is what caused this C, *which* caused this M, to occur, then content will not be causally implicated, since this is a request for a triggering cause of C's causing M, for an explanation of what set the C-to-M process off. If, on the other hand, what we want to know is what caused this C *to cause* this M to occur, then content *will* be causally relevant, since this latter is a request for a structuring cause; a request for an explanation of the factors which were causally responsible for the causal hook-up between this C and this M.

A number of critics of Dretske's account have complained that content's being a structuring cause may show how it was *once* causally relevant to the hook-up between C-type events and M-type events, or to how C-type events got 'wired up' to M-type ones, but it is causally *irrelevant* to any explanation *now* of why a particular piece of behaviour occurs (Cummins, 1991; Dennett, 1991; Horgan, 1991; Kim, 1991). What Dretske's account shows, they have claimed, is how it came to be that there is now a nomological causal connection between C-type events and M-type events, and perhaps further, of how it came to be that C-type events occur *in order to produce* M-type events (of how C-type events came to have the *function* of indicating feature F in order to produce M-type events). But content doesn't explain why *this* C's causing this M occurs. In order for content to explain this particular process, one needs to show, not that reasons are *past* structuring causes of behaviour, but that they are (to use Horgan's terminology) *here-and-now* structuring causes of behaviour.

However, as Dretske argues, this objection seems misguided. Consider again the account given earlier of how the F-to-C-to-M connection in the frog is established. In particular, consider how C-type events come to *represent* (i.e. have the *function* of indicating) F, from being a *de facto* indicator of F. This is an account, not of how past Cs came to cause *past* Ms, but of how C-*type* events came to have the function – the causal role – of causing M-*type* events. Because in the past, earlier tokens of C-type events came to indicate F, subsequent tokens came to have the *function* of indicating F. That is to say, they came to represent F. This fact about what tokens of C *now* represent, or mean, is a historical fact about the role of C-type events in the causal re-structuring of the organism (the frog) so as to produce tokens of M-type events. This fact determines the causal role of C-type states, of which *this* C is a token. So this historical fact explains why this C has the causal role it does in producing this M. In explaining why C-*type* states were assigned the causal role of producing M-type states, it explains why this C is causing this M. It is in virtue of this that we can explain why this frog is flicking its tongue by saying that it is doing so *in order* to catch the fly, and why this chameleon is turning green by saying that it is doing so *in order to* camouflage itself. In all of these cases, human behaviour included, it is *purposiveness* of physical movements that is explained, and it is this that gives content a distinctive explanatory role to play.

In other words content is needed, not to explain *de facto* head-world causal/ nomological connections like that between C-type events and M-type events, i.e. *mere* behaviour, but *purposeful* behaviour, behaviour where Cs occur in order to bring about Ms. C-type events were designed to bring about M-type ones. So, if what we want to know is why this C occurs *in order to* cause this M, we need to find a feature *of this* C that explains this causal-*functional* connection between C and M. It is this that the content of C, what C represents, explains.

Some critics have suggested that Dretske's distinction between bodily movement and behaviour is a dispensable part of his account of how content is causally relevant to behaviour. (Dretske himself concurs with this, although he stands by the distinction for other reasons; see his reply in chapter 8.) The reason, as Adams (1991, p. 139) succinctly puts it, is that

> The real job is to explain how a state's having a content can cause anything, especially a bodily movement of the relevant sort (one made purposively). Also, the job of content may be to explain why I did *that* (shout obscenities) rather than something else (applaud). But that would still be the job of content even on the *product* view [where behaviour = bodily movement]. Whether we *locate* the behavior *in the causing* of one bodily product or another, or identify the behavior with *the product itself*, the job of content is to explain why we get *one product rather than another*. The answer is that the reason had one content rather than another.

Similarly, Kim (1991) points out that, whereas it is the job of triggering causes to explain why this C causes this M now rather than at some other time, it is the job of content to explain why C causes M rather than M*.

But will this suggestion work? Many of Dretske's critics (see, for example, Horgan, 1991) have claimed that behaviour just *is* bodily movement that is caused (in the right way) by intentional states. On this view, the soprano problem immediately arises unless an account can be given of the distinctive role content plays *vis à vis* behaviour; a role that intrinsic physical properties of internal states like C *cannot* play. The suggestion that Adams and Kim make is that content plays a *contrastive* role in the causal explanation of bodily movement (= behaviour): whereas the purely physical properties of C explain why M occurs, the content properties of C explain why M rather than M* occurs.

However, it is doubtful whether the notion of a contrastive explanatory role is strong enough by itself to mark out a distinctive explanatory job for content to do. As stated above, in order for content to be causally relevant on this account, there must be a causal/explanatory role that it plays which no purely intrinsic physical features of internal events like C can play. But if the purely intrinsic physical properties of events like C suffice to explain why M, a physical movement, occurs, why should we *not* think that purely intrinsic physical properties of C (and/or of some other internal event) also suffice to explain why M rather than M* occurs? After all, both M and M* are bodily movements. The problem here is not with the notion of a contrastive explanatory role, but with the fact that that notion is neutral on the kinds of properties that are called for in explaining why M rather than M* occurs. Given that, in both the case of explaining why M occurs and in the case of explaining why M rather than M* occurs, the product is a bodily movement, there is no clear motivation for an appeal to content properties of C in one case but not the other. Dretske (1991, p. 197) tell us that one doesn't *need* my view of behavior to provide, as it were, an explanatory role for reasons. Asking why S moved his finger, as oppposed to asking why his finger moved, may be merely asking for a different kind of explanation of why the finger moved. One is still looking for a *causal* explanation of the finger movement, but a causal explanation of this movement *with*, as it were, *a different set of contrasting alternatives*. The biologist (explaining finger movement) wants to know why the finger *moved* rather than remaining stationary; the psychologist, including the folk psychologist, on the other hand, wants to know why the *finger* (rather than the ear, the tongue, the toes, or perhaps nothing at all) moved.

This, he claims, will probably do, since it brings out the important point that, in the second explanation but not the first, one's interest is in the *process* by which the *finger* is moved. So the second explanation, unlike the first, brings out the importance of the hook-up between the internal state and its product.

But while Dretske's example may illustrate the need, in the second explanation, to refer not only to the cause of the finger movement but also to the details of the hook-up between that cause and the movement, there seems to be no additional need to explain *how* the hook-up came about. So there seems to be no need (even by Dretske's lights) to invoke content. Dretske, in fact, makes just this point in another context (Dretske, 1991, pp. 212–13), when discussing a situation in which a thermostat behaves (in the relational sense) strangely, opening the garage door whenever the room temperature goes below a certain level. One could give a structuring-cause explanation of why the thermostat behaves like this, citing the way the electrician wired it up. But one isn't required to give this explanation:

> Depending on the interests and knowlege of one's audience, one could explain the device's behaviour by simply saying that there are wires leading from the thermostat to a motor that opens the garage door, that these wires are supplied with electricity, that changes in room temperature cause a metal strip in the thermostat to bend, closing an electrical circuit, energizing the motor, etc., etc. With the right audience . . . this may be the *right* way to explain the thermostat's behavior. (Dretske, 1991, p. 212)

Still, Dretske argues, this doesn't show that the structuring cause *doesn't* explain the thermostat's behaviour.

However, on the contrastive explanatory role account of the causal relevance of content, given the *product* view of behaviour, one wants to know why. Sometimes we may wish to explain why a death occurred, other times why a sudden (rather than a slow) death occurred. In order to exlain the latter, there seems to be no special need to appeal to a structuring cause. In general, there appears to be nothing in the notion of a contrastive explanatory role *per se* that requires mention of structuring causes. Nor does there appear to be anything in the product view of behaviour that would seem to require it. If, on the other hand, behaviour is construed (as Dretske construes it in the thermostat example), not as movement (M), but as an (internal) event's causing movement

M, then the explicit reference to a C-to-M hook-up in the explanandum would provide some motivation for the view that a structuring cause – a feature of the cause that explains that hook-up – is called for in the explanation of behaviour. So the distinction between behaviour and bodily movement does seem to be central to Dretske's account of the causal relevance of content, inasmuch as it motivates the need for a structuring cause.

Does the account explain how content is causally relevant to behaviour? This is a large question that can only briefly be touched upon here. Some commentators (e.g. Horgan, 1991) have criticized Dretske's view on the grounds that it does not do justice to the strong intuition we have that reasons are triggering causes of behaviour (i.e. our intuition that reasons 'trigger' actions). Dretske denies that everyone has this intuition. While he is happy to accept that reasons (i.e. states that have content) trigger (cause) bodily movements, and happy to accept that reasons are structuring causes and so causally explain behaviour, his view is that reasons do not cause (trigger) what they explain. Anyone who insists that they do by assuming intuitions which contradict this position needs to provide independent support for the intuitions themselves. The support could be provided by the product view of behaviour, but then that view faces the soprano problem, which the distinction between bodily movement and behaviour was designed to avoid.

The question of whether Dretske's account explains the causal relevance of content really concerns whether the account of indication works to explain why the hook-up exists between certain types of internal states of an organism and certain types of bodily movements. The problem that Dretske's account of content sets out to solve is the *design* problem, the problem of why a certain type of internal state *functions* to produce a bodily movement of a certain kind. Dretske claims that it does this because of what it indicates (i.e. because it has the indicator function). Indication may not be all that is relevant to the explanation of the indicator function, but it plays a very large role in that explanation. However, in certain cases it seems not to be the most important, or even *an* important, part of the explanation of why a certain type of state gets recruited as a cause of a certain type of bodily movement. Consider again our frog, who has a need to produce a bodily movement of type M in the presence of Fs. Then whether C rather than some other type of internal state is recruited to cause M may depend on a number of factors, among them how easy and economical it is to produce M-type movements, whether C-type states take a longer time than C^*-type states do to produce M-type states, and so on. Peter Godfrey-Smith (1992, p. 299) puts the point succinctly:

> Consider a situation where M is a very cheap and easy movement for an organism to make, and production of M in response to F is greatly beneficial. Production of M when F does not obtain, when C misfires, is of negligible importance. In this case the organism simply does not need – and might not even want – an indicator of F. To make this point clearly, we need to distinguish between two kinds of mistakes the organism can make (Stich, 1990). There are, firstly, 'false

positives', tokens of C produced in the absence of F; and then there are 'false negatives', failures to produce C, when F does obtain. It is the asymmetry between the consequences of each kind of mistake that causes problems. For in these circumstances the organism can afford many false positive tokens of C; it is only concerned to avoid false negatives. It can make (perhaps literally) a hair-trigger response, with very low reliability. It may be that many prey-detectors used by predators are of this sort; it is more important that they fire whenever there is a chance of success, than have a high reliability. False negative tokens of C are much more harmful than false positives, if prey is scarce and M not too taxing.

Godfrey-Smith argues that much of the problem with Dretske's account of the importance of indication has to do with the fact that Dretske works with a certain construal of the design problem. According to this, we want a system that will produce movements of type M only when feature F is present, without concern for questions of the cost-effectiveness of recruiting one cause over another in terms of length of time and energy, the ease with which M can be produced, the chances of certain types of internal events' leading to error, the consequences of such error, and so forth. The main question for Dretske is only how the connection between F and M-type events is to be secured. However, the kinds of design problems that organisms typically face are not like Dretske's: they must take into account all of these other factors. When these factors are taken into account, that a state of type C indicates F not only may be less important to whether it gets recruited as a cause of M than these other factors: it may drop out altogether (along with the indicator function, which requires it) in the explanation of why C is recruited as a cause of M.

In general, Godfrey-Smith argues, the reliability of a 'head-world' dependency relationship (i.e. one where C-type events occur only when F is present) will matter when the consequences for the organism of false positives are much more costly than the consequences for the organism of false negatives. Thus, to use one of Dretske's examples, a plant whose chances of survival are slim if it buds too early in the spring and whose chances of survival are much greater if it buds too late will benefit from a 'spring' indicator. For then it will recruit as a cause of its budding an event that occurs *only if* it is spring. If, on the other hand, what matters for the organism is that it avoid false negatives, since the consequences of these are much more costly than the consequences of false positives, then the organism may well have no need for an indicator. In an environment where many predators are present and food is scarce, a chameleon's need may be to turn green *if* (but perhaps not only if) a predator is nearby. The consequences of a false negative here are so costly for the organism that they may outweigh entirely the importance of the reliability of the F-to-C connection. C may here be recruited as a cause of M simply because it produces M quickly and economically.

What does this show about Dretske's account of the causal relevance of content? In so far as the explanatory importance of content is derivative upon the indicator function of internal events like C, which in turn derives from the reliability of the *de facto* head-world (and not also world-head) relation between such events and features in the environment such as F, certain kinds of adaptive behaviour do not fit the model of the design problem that Dretske's account is tailor-made to address. Indicators, and indicator functions, matter when an organism's need is to produce behaviour that avoids false negatives; but they may not matter at all when an organism's need is to produce behaviour that avoids 'false positives'. Even in cases where indicators and indicator functions matter, they are not all that matters; and in certain cases (say, cases where the consequences of C's being recruited over C* as a cause of M may have disastrous consequences for the organism for reasons other than those having to do with the need to produce M, despite C's being a much better indicator of F than C*), their mattering may be 'cancelled out', as it were, by more pressing considerations.

If this is right, there are many cases of adaptive behaviours where indicator functions do not matter, when weighed against other factors that figure in the selection process. Inasmuch as the causal relevance of content depends on indicator functions mattering, this casts doubt on the causal relevance of content.

The Problem of Explanatory Exclusion

Dretske tells us in his reply (chapter 8) that the problem of the causal relevance of content is one thing, the problem of explanatory exclusion another. This being so, different strategies are required to deal with the two problems. The 'dual-explananda' strategy that Kim addresses in chapter 7 is not invoked to deal with the second problem but to deal with the first. That behaviour is a process, distinct from the bodily movement that is its product, matters to the causal-explanatory role of content. The distinction between bodily movement and behaviour was not invoked to solve, nor will it solve, the problem of explanatory exclusion.

This raises the question of whether the distinction between bodily movement and behaviour is relevant to Dretske's proposed solution to the problem of explanatory exclusion at all, and if so, how. In order to answer this, we need to know what exactly the problem of explanatory exclusion for mentalistic explanation is, and how one might mistakenly suppose Dretske's account of the causal relevance of content to be an account designed to deal with the problem of explanatory exclusion.

Kim (1987) tells us that explanation is an epistemological exercise, and that explanations are complexes of propositions that are divisible into two parts. The first is the *explanans* proposition, the one that does the explaining. The second is the *explanandum* proposition, the one that is to be explained. The Principle of Explanatory Exclusion (PEE) states that there can be only one complete and independent explanation of a given event, and that we may not accept more than one such explanation in a given case unless we have reason to believe that these explanations are related appropriately. The appropriate relation will be one which shows the explanations to be either (a) individually incomplete; or (b) not independent of one another. The principle is grounded in an assumption which Kim calls *explanatory realism*. This is the view that, in any given explanation, the explanans proposition (C) explains the explanandum proposition (E) in virtue of the fact that event c bears some determinate relation (R) to event e. In general, we expect there to be only one such c event, and that the explanans proposition explains the explanandum proposition precisely because there is only one such c (i.e. that only one c event bears the determinate relation R to event e). So we expect that there can be only one complete and independent causal explanation of a given event because we expect, given explanatory realism, that there can be only one complete and independent *cause* of a given event.

This principle poses clear problems for those concerned with the (causal) explanation of human behaviour, on a certain (Davidsonian) understanding of the relation between reasons and causes. According to this, reasons – the contents of intentional states – rationalize, or explain behaviour, only if they cause it. More precisely, for the purposes of the present discussion, reasons only explain behaviour, as Dretske points out, if content itself is causally relevant to behaviour. Suppose, as Davidson does, that intentional states are (i.e. are identical with) internal physical states of their subjects. Then content, to be capable of explaining behaviour, must be implicated in the causal processes that produce it. If the causes of behaviour do so, not in virtue of their content properties, but in virtue of their intrinsic physical ones, then it is hard to see how content can be *causal-explanatory* of behaviour.[3]

As mentioned in the introduction to the debate on causal relevance (chapter 1), we believe that every physical event, if it has a cause, has a sufficient physical cause, i.e. *a cause whose efficacy is due to its physical properties*, and that physical events that have causal explanations have physical causal explanations (i.e. *causal explanations that work at least in part by citing those physical properties whose efficacy is responsible for the explanandum event having occurred*). We believe, in short, that the physical domain is *closed* under causality, and that physical theory is *closed* under causal explanation. However, we also believe that mental phenomena play a role in the causation of those bodily movements that constitute human behaviour, and that they play an explanatory role with regard to behaviour. Such phenomena not only include the so-called sensations, but also the propositional attitudes, mental phenomena essentially characterized in terms of their propositional content, such as beliefs, desires, hopes, fears, and the like.

Given PEE, there is a problem reconciling these two beliefs. Why? Because distinct causal explanations of a single explanandum-event seems to exclude one another, in spite of the fact that their explanantia propositions are consistent with one another. Take Kim's example of George's desire for a beer and his belief that there is a beer in the fridge (call this pair of events c).

Suppose, as Dretske and others do, that these events, in virtue of their contents, cause the event which is George's rising from the couch. That is, suppose that

c (with content R) and c's having R, caused b (George's rising from the couch)

Now b, as a physical event, will in principle have a purely physical explanation citing purely physical causes, given the belief in the causal closedness of the physical domain and the closedness of physical theory under causal explanation. So, in the case of George's rising from the couch, we can also suppose that

c^* (with, say, neural property N) and c^*'s having N, caused b.

We now have two causal claims about a single event b. Given explanatory realism, we appear thus to have two causal explanations for the question: why did George rise from the couch?

Answer (1): because c occurred and had R.
Answer (2): because c^* occurred and had N.

Given PEE, we need an explanation of how these different explanatory stories relate.

Kim (chapter 7) briefly outlines a number of strategies that might be employed to resolve this epistemic predicament, only two of which he considers promising. These are the *identity option* and the *supervenience option*. The identity option attempts to resolve the explanatory tension between answer (1) and answer (2) by claiming that $c = c^*$. The idea here is that, if $c = c^*$, then there is only one causal chain, only one set of causal relations between events, to consider, so there is only one causal story to tell. Davidson's anomalous monism is a form of this. However, as Kim points out, identity can only be part of the story here. We need to deal with the question of how R and N, the two properties of c and c^*, are related to each other, since the causal-explanatory relevance of these *properties* is the central issue. Does it make sense to identify R with N? A variant of anomalous monism says no: mental and physical kinds, or properties, are irreducibly distinct from one another. (Even if we were to reject this reasoning to this conclusion, identifying R with N will in fact lead to the explanatory *redundancy or inefficiency* of mentalistic explanations; see the discussion below. This may solve the explanatory exclusion problem, but at too high a price for those who, like Dretske, are primarily concerned to establish the *causal-explanatory* relevance of content.) So, in the absence of some established relation between N and R, there are two stories to tell, one *via* R and one *via* N. The identity option by itself does not solve the explanatory exclusion problem.

The supervenience option attempts to resolve the explanatory tension between answers (1) and (2) by claiming that mental properties like R are in fact *dependent* on physical ones, so that the two explanations, and underlying causal relations, are not independent of one another. Kim points out that this is a name for a group of options, depending on how supervenience is understood: as (a) strong; (b) weak; or (c) global. Further, he claims that (a) implies psychophysical laws and hence reduction, and so solves the explanatory exclusion problem but at the (too high) price of giving no explanatory efficacy to the mental domain; (b) and (c), on the other hand, are too weak to solve the explanatory exclusion problem, even though they avoid reduction. The reason, it seems, is that they do not establish a sufficiently strong relation of dependency between mental and physical properties.

This brings us to what Kim takes Dretske's solution to be: the 'dual explananda' strategy. Kim notes that Dretske's concern is with a different problem than those concerned with anomalous monism. Whereas they are concerned with the *anomalous* nature of intentional properties, Dretske is concerned with the *extrinsic* nature of such properties. The contents of intentional states are essentially relational, involving reference to historical and ecological conditions external to the organism. This being so, they fail to supervene on internal physical properties of the organism. If whatever causes behaviour must be supervenient on the internal physical states of an organism, and content does not supervene only on the internal physical states of an organism, then how can content be causally, hence causal-explanatorily, relevant?

Dretske's solution, as we have seen, involves distinguishing behaviour from bodily movement, and further, distinguishing structuring from triggering causes of behaviour. Kim argues that these distinctions in themselves will not motivate the need to refer to content in explanations of behaviour. He points out that the claim that we need two types of explananda in explaining behaviour/bodily movement is consistent with a *monistic* explanatory theory, since it is possible that purely physical (or physical–biological) explanations can be given of both. What would prevent explanatory exclusion problems arising is the further claim, which Kim points out is essentially dualistic in nature, that there *are* no physical explanations for one type of explananda (behaviour). The problem is that Dretske's version of the two-explananda strategy provides us with no reason for thinking that that further claim is true (so it won't work to solve the explanatory exclusion problem). That it invokes *relational* rather than *intrinsic* properties of agent's internal states will not provide intentional explanation with a distinctive explanatory role. Neurobiology need not be limited to intrinsic properties in its explanantia. And even if it should turn out that it is, physical theory is not. But now the explanatory exclusion problem arises once again. Given that there *is* a physical causal explanation of C's causing M, how does the physical causal explanation relate to the intentional one?

Kim suggests that Dretske might complete the project he began in *Knowledge and the Flow of Information* (1981), a physicalistic reduction of intentional content. This would entitle Dretske to the identity or supervenience options (since reduction (identity) is a special case of supervenience). In his reply (chapter 8), Dretske confirms that this is the strategy he intends to employ. Specifically, his proposal is that content properties not only *supervene* on but *reduce to* (i.e. *are identical with*) both the intrinsic physical properties of organisms and their causal history.

> This is a *type-type* identity theory, but not the classic (Smart–Feigl) identity between a type of mental state (e.g. the belief that F) and a type of brain state, but, rather, an identity between intentional content and the set of external relations that give brain states their representational character. This is reductionism, yes, but (if you please) *wide* reductionism. (Dretske, chapter 8, pp. 147–8)

Dretske defends his reductionism by arguing that the key elements in the account of intentional content (of representation), indication and function, are natural ones. That the former is natural stems from its basis in the information relation, whose naturalness is defended at length and in great detail in *Knowledge and the Flow of Information* (Dretske, 1981). That the latter is natural, Dretske acknowledges may be more of a problem to establish; but assuming that organs have biological functions – functions that they acquired in their evolutionary history – there is no reason why perceptual systems cannot also have functions that are acquired in their evolutionary history. The main difference between these two is that in the latter case but not the biological one, the functions that make for intentional content are acquired through learning, and are acquired during the life of an individual organism.

But there is a problem here. If content is not just supervenient upon, but *reducible to*, intrinsic physical properties of organisms plus their causal histories, if, as Dretske says, 'an explanation in terms of reasons would *be* a physical explanation', then the explanatory exclusion problem may be solved, but at the cost of raising once again the problem of causal-explanatory relevance of content. Explaining how one physical fact can explain another physical fact will not help us with the problem of the causal-explanatory relevance of content, if that problem is the problem of seeing how content can do something that nothing else does (Kim, chapter 7).

The difficulty that faces a project such as Dretske's, in short, is how to effect a resolution to the problem of explanatory exclusion that leaves the account of the causal-explanatory relevance of content intact. Dretske's own proposed resolution solves the explanatory exclusion problem, but at the expense, it seems, of robbing content of its *distinctive* explanatory role. But does this resolution really need the commitment to fully fledged reduction? Suppose that Dretske were to go for the weaker option of supervenience. Suppose, more specifically, that he were to opt for the strongest version of that doctrine, so as to ensure a relation of dependency strong enough to justify (if any supervenience doctrine can justify) the claim that the account is naturalistic. How might one claim a distinctive causal-explanatory role for content (i.e. one which, while endorsing strong supervenience, is non-reductive) while denying that this role competes with the roles that physical, or physico-biological, properties have?

Here is one suggestion. Suppose that we construe supervenience as expressing a co-variance dependency relation between properties or sets of them, asymmetric dependency being an independent component characterizing certain cases of supervenience but not others. Then, in the case of psychophysical supervenience, the question is what might justify the *asymmetric* but *non-reductive* dependence of intentional upon physical properties. One justification might be found in the argument for anomalous monism, the non-reductive physicalist position originated by Donald Davidson. That argument moves from the claim that mental and physical events causally interact, the claim that such interactions are governed by strict causal laws, and the claim that there are no strict causal laws governing mental and physical events, to the conclusion that each mental event is a physical event (hence its causal interactions with physical events are governed by strict physical laws). The asymmetry between intentional mental and physical properties is implicit in the argument from the start, and arises from the fact that there are causal laws in which physical properties figure, but there are no causal laws in which intentional mental properties figure. The asymmetry concerns the causal powers of mental and physical properties. Specifically, the fact that physical properties enter into causal-nomological relations, whereas intentional mental ones do not, requires, given the nomological nature of causality, that intentional properties discharge or exercise their causal powers by being co-instanced with physical properties, whereas physical properties are not similarly required to exercise any of their causal powers through being jointly instanced with intentional properties.[4] This makes intentional properties dependent on physical ones in a way in which physical properties are not dependent on intentional ones.

This asymmetric dependency must fall short of reducibility if the intentional properties are to retain their distinctive explanatory role. Given that intentional properties must, in accordance with the nomological nature of causality, exercise their causal powers through being jointly instanced with physical properties that figure in causal laws, the question now is where the source of their irreducibility to physical properties lies. One suggestion might be that intentional properties have distinctive causal powers, ones that are not exhausted by the physical properties upon which they supervene. However, this is not an intuitively appealing strategy: given strong supervenience, it is difficult to avoid the conclusion that, even if the causal powers of intentional properties are not identical with the causal powers of their subvenient base properties, the causal powers of the base properties exhaust those of intentional properties.

Another, more promising, suggestion is that intentional properties have a contentful nature which is not exhausted by their causal powers. One might argue that it is in virtue of having this nature that such properties exhibit a rationalistic pattern, or network of relations among themselves, of the sort appealed to in the argument for anomalous monism in support of the anomalousness of the mental; and further, that this pattern is not only distinct from that which physical properties display, but irreducible to it for reasons appealed to in the argument for the anomalousness of the mental. In order to make this claim plausible, some explanation is needed of how, even though intentional mental events instantiate a causal-nomological pattern, intentional properties exhibit a (rationalistic) pattern that is irreducible to the causal-nomological.

Of some help in establishing this is an appeal to biological properties, an appeal which might satisfy Dretske's own predilections. Biology makes use of a species of explanation which exploits properties that are plausibly viewed as (a) co-instanced with physico-chemical properties; (b) (strongly) supervenient upon physico-chemical properties; but (c) generally acknowledged *not* to be reducible to their physico-chemical bases. Biological properties thus seem to present a clear case of a pattern, or network of relations, in nature which is underwritten by but is not reducible to the pattern exhibited by physico-chemical properties (see chapters 1 and 3 in the debate on causal relevance).

If the analogy with biological properties works, it establishes a degree of autonomy for mental properties. What the biological example shows is that some cases of strong supervenience are not ones where supervenience is sufficient for reduction. The interesting question in the biological case is why, and here the explanation seems to be that biological properties have a nature which is such as to produce a pattern of relations among themselves that is different from the causal-nomological pattern produced by physico-chemical properties, *despite the fact that the causal powers of biological properties seem to be exhausted by the causal powers of their physico-chemical bases*. What makes the pattern distinctive is that it is functional. The properties are individuated by their biological functions, and the claim is that this notion of function, being normative, has no role to play in physical theory. So the pattern is produced by properties whose individuation conditions are normative. This makes it not only different from, but irreducible to, the causal-nomological pattern exhibited by physical properties.

This might establish that intentional properties are like biological ones in participating in a distinctive pattern of relations among themselves that does not merely replicate the pattern of causal-nomological relations in the physical domain. But the fact (if it is a fact) that the biological pattern is irreducible to the physical causal-nomological one is not enough to establish a distinctive explanatory role for intentional properties. In order to establish this, *differences* as well as similarities between the biological and intentional patterns must be established, and this is where the second stage of the argument comes in (see chapter 13).

The strategy suggested here for establishing real autonomy for intentional properties assuming strong supervenience is very much in the spirit of Dretske's own commitments. Does it resolve the explanatory exclusion problem, however? We think it does. What the strategy brings out is that the distinctive explanatory role that intentional properties have derives from the kind of normativity that attaches to the pattern of relations in which they figure. In biology, too, the pattern of relations that holds between functional properties is normative. If the argument for mental anomalism is sound, the distinctive rationalistic pattern that intentional properties exhibit itself argues for such properties having a role to play that is not defined by their participation in causal-nomological relations. And it is this that enables us to say not only that reasons are causes, but that reasons rationalize behaviour.

Notes

1 There is some controversy about the direction of dependency involved in indication, but Dretske's original work seems clearly to require only that the dependency be one-way, of an internal state (C) on a feature (F) in the environment, so that the presence of such a feature is a necessary condition, but not a sufficient condition, for the occurrence of the inner state. This matters because requiring that the presence of such a feature be both necessary and sufficient (i.e. that C occurs *when and only when* feature F is present) is a much stronger, and problematic requirement (see Fodor, 1987, on the problematic nature of this aspect of indicator theories). I follow Peter Godfrey-Smith (1992) in interpreting Dretske's account as requiring only that F be a necessary condition for the occurrence of C. The 'head-world' and 'world-head' terminology is Field's (1990).

2 The question of what conditions must be met for an F-to-C connection to be reliable is also a controversial matter. For discussion of this, see Godfrey-Smith (1992).

3 Of course, Davidson himself denies that the connection between mental causation and intentional explanation of behaviour requires speaking, not just of events, but of properties of events. According to him, because causality is extensional, events (with all of their properties) *per se* are causes, and it makes no sense to speak of them being efficacious in virtue of certain of their causes and not others. See Davidson (1993) and McLaughlin (1993) for an illuminating discussion of the commitments of anomalous monism, and see the debate on the causal relevance of the mental (chapters 1–4) for further discussion of the general problem of mental causation and causal relevance of mental properties.

4 This just is the argument for anomalous monism on a reading of it which treats events as property exemplifications. Note, however, that this is not Davidson's formulation of anomalous monism. The property exemplification account of events is a 'fine-grained' account (see Goldman, 1970; Kim, 1976; Heil, 1992), and Davidson explicitly rejects such an account (see Davidson, 1980, 1993). The conclusion of anomalous monism for him is that each mental event is a physical event, where events are 'unstructured' particulars. So the claim made here is stronger than any claim that Davidson would wish to make. It is stronger even than the claim, which property exemplification theorists of events who are non-reductive monists are committed to, that mental events are identical with physical events in the sense that each event which is the exemplification of a mental property is identical with an event which is the exemplification of a physial property. This latter claim need not commit one to the view, implied here, that the property-

exemplifications are identical (i.e. that mental properties and physical properties are co-instanced in a *single* instance).

References

Adams, F. (1991) Causal contents. In B. McLaughlin (ed.), *Dretske and his Critics*, pp. 131–56. Oxford, Basil Blackwell.

Cummins, R. (1991) The role of mental meaning in psychological explanation. In B. McLaughlin (ed.), *Dretske and his Critics*, pp. 102–18. Oxford, Basil Blackwell.

Davidson, D. (1980) The material mind. In *Essays on Actions and Events*, pp. 245–59. Oxford, Clarendon Press.

Davidson, D. (1993) Thinking causes. In J. Heil and A. Mele (eds), *Mental Causation*, pp. 3–18. Oxford, Clarendon Press.

Dennett, D. (1991) Ways of establishing harmony. In B. McLaughlin (ed.), *Dretske and his Critics*, pp. 119–30. Oxford, Basil Blackwell.

Dretske, F. (1981) *Knowledge and the Flow of Information*. Cambridge, Mass., MIT Press.

Dretske, F. (1988) *Explaining Behavior: Reasons in a World of Causes*. Cambridge, Mass., MIT Press.

Dretske, F. (1991) Replies. In B. McLaughlin (ed.), *Dretske and his Critics*, pp. 180–221. Oxford, Basil Blackwell.

Field, H. (1990) Narrow aspects of intentionality and the information-theoretic approach to content. In E. Villanueva (ed.), *Information, Semantics, and Epistemology*, pp. 102–16. Oxford, Basil Blackwell.

Fodor, J. (1987) *Psychosemantics*. Cambridge, Mass., MIT Press.

Godfrey-Smith, P. (1992) Indication and adaptation. *Synthese* 92, 283–312.

Goldman, A. (1970) *A Theory of Human Action*. Princeton, NJ, Princeton University Press.

Heil, J. (1992) *The Nature of True Minds*. Cambridge, Cambridge University Press.

Horgan, T. (1991) Actions, reasons, and the explanatory role of content. In B. McLaughlin (ed.), *Dretske and his Critics*, pp. 73–101. Oxford, Basil Blackwell.

Kim, J. (1976) Events as property exemplifications. In M. Brand and D. Walton (eds), *Action Theory*, pp. 159–77. Dordrecht, D. Reidel.

Kim, J. (1987) Causal realism, explanatory realism, and explanatory exclusion. In P. French, T. Uehling and H. Wettstein (eds), *Midwest Studies in Philosophy*, vol. 12, pp. 225–39. Notre Dame, University of Notre Dame Press.

Kim, J. (1989) Mechanism, purpose, and explanatory exclusion. In J. Tomberlin (ed.), *Philosophical Perspectives*, vol. 3, pp. 77–108. California, Ridgeview.

Kim, J. (1991) Dretske on how reasons explain behavior. In B. McLaughlin (ed.), *Dretske and his Critics*, pp. 52–72. Oxford, Basil Blackwell.

McLaughlin, B. (1993) On Davidson's response to the charge of epiphenomenalism. In J. Heil and A. Mele (eds), *Mental Causation*, pp. 27–40. Oxford, Clarendon Press.

Stich, S. (1990) *The Fragmentation of Reason*. Cambridge, Mass., MIT Press.

6

Does Meaning Matter?

Frederick Dretske

The prevailing wisdom among materialists is that even if we can give an otherwise creditable account of intentionality, the properties that give a structure its intentional identity, the facts that underlie its content or meaning,[1] will (indeed, *must*) turn out to be explanatorily irrelevant. Even if some events will have a meaning, and even if, as physical events in good standing, they have an impact on their material surroundings, the fact that they mean what they do won't help explain why they do what they do.

This doctrine about what Dennett (1983) calls the *impotence* of meaning should not be taken to imply that the objects having meaning are causally inert. It only means that it is not their intentional properties, their content or meaning, from which they derive their causal powers. Though a brick was made in Hoboken, it gets its power to break windows from its velocity and mass, not from its having been made in Hoboken. By the same token, although events in the brain, those we might want to identify with a particular thought *about* Hoboken, are *about* Hoboken, their power to stimulate glands and regulate muscle tension – and thus to control behavior – derive not from what they mean, not from the fact that they are about Hoboken, but from their electrical and chemical properties. The brain is a syntactic, not a semantic, engine (Dennett, 1981).

Hence, in their efforts to avoid classical dualism and the attendant mysteries of interactionism, materialists – at least those willing to acknowledge the existence of intentional states – find themselves driven to embrace an equally troublesome form of *property*-dualism. Substance dualism is avoided by conceiving of thought, desire, hope and fear as *material* events, the same kind of event as are the bodily movements (the behavior) they are supposed to influence. Hence, causal interaction between mind and body is no longer a problem – at least no *more* of a problem than the causal action of brain on muscle. The pineal gland is no longer needed to engage *reasons* – beliefs, desires, purposes and plans – with the *behavior* for which they are the reasons. None the less, though the causal barriers separating mind and body are thus removed (thanks largely to Donald Davidson), *explanatory* barriers remain intact. The explanatory barriers remain intact because the properties of physical events and processes that give them their intentional character, those properties on which their meaning, content and aboutness supervene, are properties that remain explanatorily irrelevant to *how* (or even *whether*) these events and processes influence behavior. The explanatory gulf between those properties of events that make them mental and those properties (of the same events) that explain their causal impact on other material events – in particular motor output – constitutes a dualism, a property-dualism, that exists *within* a materialistic metaphysics. To understand *why* a system behaves the way it does, to understand why beliefs, desires and fears affect action the way they do, one need never know what the beliefs are beliefs *about*, what the desires are desires *for*, or what the fears are fears *of*. Though they cause me to do A, their *being* beliefs and desires, the *fact* that these material events have truth and satisfaction conditions, is as relevant (that is, totally *irrelevant*) to why I do A as is the fact that a brick was made in Hoboken to why it broke the window.[2]

This, it seems to me, is an unacceptable position for any theory of the mind to occupy.[3] If the mind – or, better, that set of facts that collectively constitutes the mind – is not good for something, and by 'good for something' I mean good for helping one understand why the system possessing it does what it does, then I don't see the point in having a mind. Why bother thinking if the fact that you think, and facts about what you think, do not – sometimes at least – explain why you behave the way you do? Even if we suppose that people, despite its making no difference to what they do, think none the less, I see no reason to make a great fuss about it. From a practical standpoint, it may be useful to know what a person is thinking if he generally does A whenever he thinks T, but if he doesn't do A, in part at least, *because* he thinks T, why, in our philosophical (not to mention scientific) efforts to understand why people do what they do, should we be interested in *what* (or even *that*) they think?

This is why, in my own efforts to naturalize the mental, to understand the material basis of intentionality, I have become increasingly preoccupied with the question, not of what meaning (or content) *is*, but what meaning (content) *does*. It is no good having a theory of meaning if the meaning in question doesn't *do* something, something that both needs to be done and will, without the help of meaning, not be done. Does the mind do something the brain can't do? Is there something that meaning does that a material bearer-of-meaning can't do? If there, for that matter, something that information (understood as a semantic commodity) does that a signal or event *carrying* this information can't do? If not, why are philosophers (some of us anyway) so interested in getting a theory of meaning or semantic information? People stopped talking about the soul when they realized there was nothing for the soul to do. Information and meaning deserve the same fate.

This problem – a problem about the causal role of meaning – arises from the fact that meaning, on any *plausible* theory of meaning, supervenes on a set of facts that are *different* from the facts that explain why a structure (with that meaning) has the effects it has. Let M be the set of properties and relations in virtue of which event E *means* what it does. Let C be the set of properties and relations in virtue of which E *causes* what it does. M is not identical to C. These sets don't even overlap. What gives sounds the meaning they have is not what confers on them the power to shatter glass and rattle eardrums; what makes a photograph represent another condition in the world, what makes it a picture *of*, and therefore able to carry information *about*, my Uncle Harold, is not what gives it the power to reflect light in the way it does. Pictures of Walter (Harold's twin) reflect light in exactly the same way. The same can be said about those physical events, processes and structures in the brain that are supposed to *be* a person's thoughts, hopes and desires. The fact that something in the head, a thought for instance, has truth conditions doesn't help explain the thought's effect on motor output. Thoughts, the things *with* content, make a difference, to be sure, but the fact that they are thoughts (much less their being the thoughts they are) is not relevant to the difference they make.

The problem of giving *meaning* some explanatory bite is, I think, the same as the problem of giving certain kinds of *value* an explanatory job to do. The value – at least the objective value – of some objects derives from *the way* they were produced, *when* or *where* they were produced, or *by whom* they were produced. The value of such objects devolves, in part at least, on certain historical and relational facts about the article. A genuine Picasso – one that was painted by that particular person – has greater value than an imitation. A real $100 bill – one produced by an authorized government agency – has greater monetary value than the counterfeit produced in someone's basement. As we all know, if the fakes are very good, physically indistinguishable (let us suppose) from the genuine article, then they will pass without detection. Since everyone will *take* them (mistakenly) to have real value, they will prove as commercially (and aesthetically?) *useful* (and, in *this* sense, as valuable) as the article of real value. On the objective conception of value, however, these imitations will not have the same value, the same worth, as the genuine Picasso or the real $100 bill. As we like to say, they aren't worth the paper they're printed on.

On this (objective) conception of value, the painting's or the paper's value supervenes on facts (call them V, primarily *historical* and *relational* facts, that (given the possibility of perfect forgeries) *do not* supervene on the intrinsic physical properties, C, of the canvas or paper that has this value, the properties that determine the object's causal powers. This is why inspection and analysis of the forgery need not be able to reveal its bogus character. For its being a forgery is a fact about its history, a fact in V, while the facts that determine the outcome of examination and inspection are facts relating to C, how an object (with this history) *affects* other objects (like chemicals and light). If objects having a different value can be indistinguishable, then facts about an object's objective value are explanatorily irrelevant to how that object affects another object. To borrow Schiffer's (1987) language (he was talking about meaning), an object's value is an excrescence; it does nothing and it explains nothing.

That, no doubt, is why some people regard objective value a scientifically useless notion.

The argument that meaning, as this is understood in the philosophy of mind, is epiphenomenal is, for many philosophers, exactly the same as the argument that value, as understood above, is epiphenomenal. The reason the arguments are the same is that for many philosophers meaning, like value, is a property that, if it supervenes on *any* cluster of material properties, supervenes on historical and relational properties of the event or structure having meaning. Meaning, on this view of things, has to do with the etiology of a structure type, with how (and perhaps why) it was developed to service an organism's needs, with the network of causal and informational relations in which it enters with other objects and conditions, with (according to others) its function (developmentally determined) of indicating when conditions are right for initiating behavior. These are all historical and relational (including causal) facts about a structure, facts that need *not* leave a trace in the structures that differ in this respect. There *can* be perfect forgeries – physically identical structures that are the results of much different historical and developmental processes. Since this is so, the historical and relational differences, the ones on which the structure's meaning (and value) supervene, are *screened off* (LePore and Loewer, 1987) from the explanation of the object's behavior. Even if those historical and relational differences that underlie differences in meaning and value *cause* intrinsic differences, differences that, because they persist up to the present moment, help explain an object's current behavior, those remote differences will not help *explain* (at one remove, as it were) the object's present behavior. For these temporarily remote differences in V or M are explanatorily relevant only in so far as they act *through* current differences in C, and if, as we are assuming, there *need* be no contemporary trace of these past differences (the possibility, that is, of perfect forgeries), it will be differences in C (*caused* by differences in V and M), not V or M themselves, that *explain* the different effects. The cashier accepts my $100 bill because she thinks it is genuine, and she thinks it is genuine, not because it *is* genuine (a fact V about the history of this paper), but because it *looks* genuine (a fact C about its intrinsic properties). Even if it was an authorized government agency that *caused* it to look this way, it is the fact that it looks this way, not the fact that an authorized agency made it look this way (the fact on which the value of the paper supervenes) that explains the cashier's coming to believe that it is genuine and, hence, her reaction to it.

Epiphenomenalism has always been a tempting response to the causal and explanatory problems of dualism – whether the dualism in question was a traditional substance dualism or the property dualism just described. I think we can see this temptation at work in Jerry Fodor's (1980, 1987) version of pre-established harmony between syntax and semantics in the language of thought. Just as programmers, via the software they create, coordinate the formal (C) and semantic (M) properties of a computer's internal states – thus allowing the formulation of useful generalizations about the machine's behavior in terms of the semantic properties of its internal processes – so, in the case of some animals, nature sets up a correspondence between the formal properties of the brain (the properties studied by neuroscientists) and the brain's semantic properties – those we describe in saying what a person believes and wants. Once this coordination is in place, we can explain (at least we can predict) an animal's behavior – a behavior that is in fact causally determined by the brain's possession of C (the properties studied by neuroscientists) – by appealing to M, the semantic properties, the meaning, of those neural structures controlling behavior. We thereby salvage the common view that we do things because of what we want, believe, and fear – *because* we occupy states with a certain intentional (semantic) character.

I don't think this works. Or, if it does work, it does so at a cost that I'm not prepared (unless forced) to pay. For I think this theory, like all forms of pre-established harmony (whether instituted by God, nature or computer program-mers) saves the appearances by sacrificing the substance. It substitutes the *predictability* (and, therefore, *control*) of behavior for the *explanation* (and, therefore, *understanding*) of behavior. There is, to be sure, nothing wrong with achieving predictability and control. These are legitimate scientific (and practical) goals. But they shouldn't be confused with explanation. Coordination between the facts on which an event's meaning devolves (M) and the facts on which its causal efficacy depends (C), however this correlation is instituted or maintained, does not enable one to *explain* anything by appealing to M. What explains why an event with meaning M has the effects it has are (by hypothesis) the facts C, the facts with which M is correlated. The correlation between M and C, assuming it is known, enables one to predict what will occur by appealing to M, but it is C, not M, that *explains* why these effects occur. Pre-established harmony allows one to say that Harold will do A *when* he thinks T; depending on the nature of the coordination, and just how one chooses to evaluate the counterfactual, one may even say that he *wouldn't* have done A *unless* he believed T.[4] It will not, however, support the claim that he did A *because* he thought T. And *that* is what it takes to vindicate belief-desire psychology or our ordinary view about the causal efficacy of thought – that we stopped, for example, *because* we thought the light was red.

Materialists have painted themselves into this corner – a corner in which epiphenomenalism (or skepticism)[5] is the only logical escape – by misidentify-ing what meaning and content, the what-it-is we believe, desire, fear and intend, are supposed to explain. A fact, of course, may be explanatorily irrelevant to one thing, not another. And what has been shown about meaning is that if meaning supervenes, at least in part, on the *extrinsic* properties of an event – historical and relational facts that *need not* be mirrored in the event's current (= the time at which it has its effects) physical constitution or structure – then, if A causes B, the fact, if it is a fact, that A means M will not – indeed, cannot – figure in a causal explanation of B. It cannot because, in similar circumstances, an event lacking this meaning, but otherwise the same, will have exactly the same effects. So it isn't A's having the meaning M that explains why B occurred. It is, rather, A's having C, a given set of intrinsic properties, that explains this. None the less, the fact that A means M, though it fails to explain why B occurred, may help explain a closely related fact: the fact that events of type A, when they occur, cause events of type B. Should this fact be explicable in terms of the meaning of A, then the meaning of A, though it will not explain why B occurred, will explain why A caused it. And this fact, especially when we are trying to explain the behavior of a system, is a fact eminently worth explaining.

To illustrate this important difference – the difference between explaining B, an event that A causes, on the one hand, and explaining A's causing B, an event (I prefer to think of it as a process) A doesn't cause, on the other – suppose switch S is wired to light L in such a way that one can turn on the light by closing the switch. If I now close the switch, causing the light to go on, an explanation of why the light went on will include, among other things, a description of the switch's being closed. A *full* explanation may involve mentioning other factors (such as the supply of electricity, the fact that the switch is wired to the light, and so on) that, collectively, more nearly approximate a sufficient condition for the light's going on, but, given the conditions that presently exist (in which closure of the switch is necessary) one fact that is relevant to – hence, part of the explanation of – the light's going on, is the fact that the switch was closed. So we causally explain B (the light's going on) by mentioning (perhaps among other things) A (the fact that the switch was closed).

Think, now, of explaining a different fact, a fact that, though different, is still intimately related to understanding why the system is behaving the way it is: the fact that closure of the switch *causes* the light to go on. A question about why one thing causes another – why, in this case, closure of the switch caused the light to go on – makes perfectly good sense with little or no special context. If, none the less, one wants a setting in which the question seems natural, imagine that the switch is *supposed* to be wired, and *was* formerly wired, to a bell. Someone, knowing all this, and expecting the bell to ring (when he closes the switch), is surprised to see the light come on when he closes the switch. Why, he might ask, did the *light* come on? This question might *sound* like our earlier question, a question in which we were seeking the cause of the light's going on, but it is, in fact, quite different. The present question has a different contrastive presupposition. What the person is really asking is why, when he threw the switch, the light came on *instead of the bell*? Understood in this way, the question is not answered in the way we formerly explained the light's coming on. The person asking the second question does not want to hear about the switch's being closed, about its being wired to the light, about the availability of electricity, and so on. He already *knows*, or should (by fiddling with the switch) be able to quickly discover, all these facts. He knows (or can easily be imagined as knowing) that *he* caused the light to come on by flipping the switch. No, what he wants to know is not (as before) what caused the light to come on, but how things *got this way*, why the switch (now) controls *the light*, why the switch (now) makes the light go on rather than the bell. What he wants to know, in other words, is not why B happened (he knows A caused it), but why A caused B.

An answer to this second question will take us backward in time, to the processes and circumstances that shaped the control circuits of the device whose behavior is in question. There may be a variety of different possible explanations of why the switch is (now) controlling the light, why the one event – a closure of the switch – caused another (a lighting of the bulb). Perhaps things were mistakenly wired in this way. Perhaps someone had a purpose (a practical joke?) in changing the wiring. Perhaps no one did anything; there was merely a short-circuit, the device got hit by lightning, or there was faulty design. Whatever the correct answer, it seems clear that in trying to understand, in this particular way, why the light came on, we are seeking to find out something about how the device came to be in its present condition, a condition in which one event causes another. If we have identical systems – both of which have a light wired to a switch – there may, none the less, be quite different answers to questions about why they are behaving the way they are. In the one case switch S causes the light L to go on. In the second case a similar (similar, if you please, down to the last molecule) switch, S*, causes a similar (also down to the last molecule) light, L*, to come on. We have an instance of physically indistinguishable systems, one an exact clone of the other, *behaving* (naturally enough) in the same way. None the less, *if* we identify a question about why the systems are behaving in this way as a question, not about why L and L*, the respective lights, came on (in which case the explanations would be the same: their respective switches, S and S*, were closed), but about why their respective switches caused their respective lights to go on, then the explanation for *why* they are behaving this way is much different. The first system, the one in which S is causing L, is behaving this way because its owner, preferring a light to a bell, deliberately rewired it this way. The second system's behavior is explained differently: S* is causing L* as the result of an accidental short-circuit.

I have argued elsewhere (Dretske, 1988) that the behavior of a system should not be identified with its bodily movements. What distinguishes the movement of my arm (an event) from my moving my arm (behavior), even when my arm moves because I move it, is the fact that the behavior, my moving my arm, consists in arm movements being caused by some internal event or process.[6] The behavior, let me repeat, is not a movement *which is caused* by some internal event or process; it is, rather, this movement's *being caused* by some internal event or process. Hence, on this conception of behavior, to explain a person's *behavior* (in contrast to explaining the bodily movements in which behavior typically culminates) one must explain, not why this or that event occurs (not why the arm moves) but why one event is causing another (why the arm is being caused to move). If this is so, then, just as with our two light systems described above, there can be *different* causal explanations for why systems that are otherwise identical are behaving in the same way. Both people are, say, moving their arms. The first may be doing it for reasons – because he wants W and believes B – while the second is doing it for quite different reasons or, possibly, for no reason at all (unintentionally). This is not to say that there may not be an explanation – and in *this* sense a reason – why the second person is moving his arm; only that the explanation for *why* he is moving it does not involve his purposes, beliefs and desires.

Were I able to convince you that this is the correct way of thinking about behavior, I would thereby convince you that an event's extrinsic properties – properties it has because of the way it is related, historically and otherwise, to other objects and events – *are*, or at least may be, relevant to explaining the behavior of the system in which those events occur. If, for example, A is an event in the brain of an animal, and B is a bodily movement resulting (in part) from A, then to explain the animal's behavior – not A, not B, but *A's causing B* – one can, indeed one may have to, advert to precisely those historial and relational facts about A on which its meaning supervenes. This, in turn, would mean that even though meaning does not supervene on the intrinsic physical properties of an event – even though, in other words, the psychological states, the beliefs and desires, of an organism do not supervene on the biological stuff of which it is composed – none the less, meaning, and therefore what the organism believes and desires, can figure in the explanation of its behavior. On this view of behavior and its explanation, it turns out that biologically indistinguishable organisms can not only be in psychologically different states, this psychological difference can help to explain their respective *bodily* behaviors. They are both moving their arm – moving it, in fact, in exactly the same way. Yet, they may have quite different reasons for moving their arms in this way: the one person is waving goodbye, the other brushing away a pesky fly. This means, in turn, that in so far as otherwise identical behaviors can qualify as different *actions* because the corresponding movements are produced with different intentions (i.e. however much the *movements* resemble one another, waving goodbye is not the same *action* as brushing away a fly) biologically identical organisms can *act* in much different ways. These results are achieved by identifying an organism's behavior, not with the surface changes – including bodily movements – that are internally produced, but with the *process* in which such changes are brought about.

But I do not have the time to convince you that this is, indeed, the correct way of thinking about behavior. So I must make do with something less. I propose, therefore, to forgo arguments in favor of illustrations. And what I would like to illustrate is the way meaning – or at least some of the relational facts on which the meaning of an event might plausibly be thought to supervene[7] – *can* figure in the explanation of why that event causes what it does. This, once again, is not an attempt to show that the meaning of A can be invoked to explain B, where B is one of A's effects. As I argued earlier, if the meaning of an event does not supervene on the event's intrinsic properties, as on most (plausible) accounts of meaning it does not, the meaning of this event is effectively screened off from explanations of its effects. The meaning of neural events *is*, I agree, epiphenomenal if all we are trying to explain is why bodily movements occur. It *is not* – or (depending on your view of meaning) it *may not be* – epiphenomenal if what we are trying to explain is something else, not why this or that bodily movement occurs, but why this or that movement is *being caused* to occur. *This*, then, is what I shall be trying to illustrate.

Suppose we have a network of neurons, A, that, *if* it were connected (to other neurons) in the right way, would serve as an electrical switch for certain efferent (outgoing) processes. Suppose, also, that this assembly of neurons, because of the particular way it is associated with sensory processes, has various states that are correlated with – and hence serve as an indication of – external condition F. Because F is a highly toxic condition (to the animal in which A occurs) there is a need for this animal to avoid condition F. It develops, therefore, that neural assembly A, a reliable sign of F, is made into a switch for effector processes, B, that result in the animal's withdrawal from condition F. A', the state of assembly A that signals the presence of condition F, causes movements to occur that bring the animal away from F. Suppose, finally, that the process in which A becomes a switch for B, and hence A' (the positive indication of F) a cause of withdrawal movements, is a process that takes place precisely *because* A is a reliable sign of those conditions the animal needs to avoid. In other words, the process mentioned above, the process in which A gets connected to effector circuits in such a way to make A' a cause of B, is a selectional process that is sensitive to A's semantic or intentional properties, not its intrinsic formal properties. A gets selected *as* a switch for B because of what it indicates about F. One can think of the process as natural selection over many generations: individuals whose F-indicator is more directly connected to the appropriate efferent circuits (so that A' more often results in withdrawal movements) enjoy a competitive edge. Or one can think of the process in which the animal's control circuits are reconfigured, thereby making A' a cause of B, as a process in which an individual learns to avoid F by conditioning. A few bouts of violent sickness and the bird no longer eats, in fact positively avoids, the bitter-tasting butterfly. In either event, the fact that A indicates what it does helps explain why it gets connected the way it does, why it now, after many generations (in the case of natural selection) or after many trials (in the case of individual learning) functions as a cause of movements that take the animal away from F.

According to this scenario – a scenario that I hope is not entirely unrealistic from the point of view of evolutionary biology and learning theory – an extrinsic property of A, the fact that it indicates condition F to exist, helps to explain why A comes to cause B, why it is, therefore, now causing B. If, then, we take the indicator relation – whatever, ultimately, its correct analysis is – as a plausible, at least a *possible*, partial basis for meaning, if it is (at least) *among* the relations on which mental content supervenes, then we have a illustration of how such relations, though epiphenominal from the point of view of bodily movement (i.e. B), may none the less be central components in the explanation of the processes (A's causing B) having bodily movements as their result. This,

I submit, is the basis for our (or *my*) conviction that though a physical duplicate of me, one that materializes – miraculously or randomly – out of some stray collection of molecules, may be physically the same as me, though he (it?) may (as a result) *behave* in exactly the same way as me (moving his arm, for example, in exactly the circumstances, and in exactly the same way, as I move my arm), such a being would *not* behave in this way for the same *reasons*.[8] I move my arm in this way *in order to* frighten away a pesky fly. With such a purpose I am, let us say, *shooing away a fly*. That is my *action*. My biological twin, though he moves his arm in the same way (with the same result), does not shoo away a fly. He doesn't have wants or beliefs, the kind of purposes I have in moving my arm. He isn't, therefore, performing the same action. Though there *is* a fly there, and it *is* frightened away by the movements of his arm, he isn't shooing it away. We saw earlier that two electric circuits, behaving in identical ways, could have quite different explanations for why they behaved in this way. Just so: though my twin and I behave in the same way (we both move our arm, we both frighten away the fly) the explanation of my twin's behavior is much different from the explanation of my behavior. This is why I perform an action – shooing away a fly – and he doesn't. The explanation of my behavior, my moving my arm, is much different from the explanation of his behavior. I did it *in order to* get the fly to move. He didn't. Hence, all he does is move his arm and frighten away a fly – things one can do without intentions, purposes, beliefs and desires (falling meteorites can frighten flies). At least this is so until the twin accumulates enough experience – until, that is, his internal processes acquire the requisite extrinsic relations – to give his control processes, the processes governing the movement of his hand, the same kind of explanation as mine. Until that occurs, my twin, though he may remain indistinguishable from me, cannot *do* many of the things I do.

Post-conference Note

A serious misunderstanding (mostly, I admit, my fault) occurred at the Tepoztlán conference during Dan Dennett's discussion of the paper that forms this chapter. In order to illustrate the way a meaning that does not supervene on the biological substrate (and is, therefore, a plausible candidate for the content of a belief) might play a direct role in the explanation of an organism's behavior, I spoke of the 'selection' of reliable signs for causal roles (causing, e.g. certain bodily movements) because of what they (the signs) meant or indicated about external affairs. I thereby conflated natural selection and the kind of selection (learning) that occurs during the life of an individual organism. Since I was merely illustrating a point, exploring (as it were) possibilities for meaning being causally active, I did not think this conflation would even be noticed, much less prove confusing. I was wrong. If I had known, before I wrote the paper, that Dan Dennett was going to be my commentator, I wouldn't have been so careless. He tends to notice things like that.

I do not think that natural selection is itself an instance of meaning being directly active in the causal production of behavior. You can't get intentionality, at least not the kind we associate with belief and desire, out of a process of biological selection. In order to get meaning itself (and not just the structures that have meaning) to play an important role in the explanation of an *individual's* behavior (as beliefs and desires do) one has to look at a meaning that was instrumental in shaping the behavior that is being explained. This occurs only during individual learning. Only then is the meaning of a structure type (the fact that it indicates such-and-such about the animal's surroundings) responsible for its recruitment as a control element in the production of appropriate action. It is at this point, and not before, that belief (and other intentional attitudes) enter the explanatory picture. Natural selection gives us something quite different: reflex, instinct, tropisms, fixed-action-patterns, and other forms of involuntary behavior – behavior that is (typically) *not* explained in terms of the actors beliefs and desires (if any). These genetically determined patterns of behavior often involve (as triggers for response) internal indicators (information-carrying elements), but unlike belief, it isn't *their* content that explains the way they affect output. That is determined by the genes.

I regret that I did not make my position on this point clear in the paper that forms this chapter. My apologies to Dan Dennett. The fact that it *is* my position (and *was* before the Tepoztlán conference) should be obvious from the chapters in Dretske (1988) devoted to its articulation and defense.

Acknowledgements

This chapter was written while I was a fellow at the Center for Advanced Study in the Behavioral Sciences at Stanford University. I am grateful for the financial support of the Center, the National Endowment for the Humanities, and the Andrew W. Mellon Foundation.

Notes

1 Throughout this chapter I will be primarily concerned with meaning in so far as it relates to issues in the philosophy of mind. I therefore use (interchangeably) the words *meaning* and *content* to refer to *what-it-is* that we believe, know, remember, judge, conclude and infer. On this usage, the meaning of a thought or memory is its propositional object, that which is expressed by the sentence occuring as factive complement of the verb 'to think' or 'to remember'. If Oscar thinks (remembers) that snow is white, the meaning or content of this thought (memory) is that snow is white.

2 By property-dualism I mean, of course, a dichotomy between two kinds of *material* properties – not (as is sometimes meant) a distinction between the material and

non-material properties of material events and objects. Those who think that an object's relational properties – being an *uncle* or a *virgin*, for instance – are irreducible to its intrinsic (monadic) properties likewise acknowledge a kind of dualism among the object's material properties. Materialists can (and typically *do*) recognize this kind of basic difference between types of properties without supposing that there is anything mysterious (non-material) in being an uncle or a virgin. Relational properties are just material properties of a special kind.

3 It also seems that way to a variety of other philosophers; see, for example, Stoutland (1976, 1980, 1982), Tuomela (1977), McGinn (1979), Mackie (1979), Honderich (1982), Robinson (1982), Sosa (1984), Skillen (1984) and Follesdal (1985). Many of these discussions focus on the explanatory irrelevance of the mind. See LePore and Loewer (1987) for a discussion of this point.

4 If A and B have common cause C, and neither A nor B has other causes, it may be true that A *will not* happen without B. Depending on just what circumstances are taken as fixed (in the evaluation of the counterfactual) it may also be true to say that A would not have happened without B, and this *despite* the absence of any explanatory relation between A and B. Given that we are tuned to the same channel, what appears on my TV screen wouldn't be there unless it also appeared on your TV screen. That doesn't mean it appears on my screen *because* it appears on yours.

   [*Note added after conference*: Jaegwon Kim, in conversation, has convinced me this is an extremely implausible reading of the counterfactual. It simply isn't true that the image wouldn't appear on my TV screen unless it was also on yours. There are countless ways it might fail: you can, after all, just turn your set off. If this is right, and I now think it is, so much the worse for theories attempting to account for the explanatory relevance of meaning by some kind of pre-established harmony between meaning and form. Not only do such pre-established correspondences (exhibiting a common cause pattern) fail to support an explanatory relation, they don't even imply the right sort of dependency – the sort we mean to be describing by saying that someone wouldn't have done this *unless* he thought that.]

5 By skepticism here I mean doubt, or outright denial, that there is a materialistically coherent – much less a scientifically workable – notion of mental content. For a materialist, of course, this is doubt, or open denial. that there is a coherent notion of mental content *at all*. Our ordinary descriptions of what people believe, want, intend and fear are either (at best) useful constructs, epistemologically convenient stances, that enable us to better organize and classify patterns of behavior for predictive purposes (e.g. Dennett, 1987) or (at worst) a kind of confused, albeit useful, heuristic (or – depending on who is talking – mythology) that is destined for replacement by neuroscience (Churchland, 1981; Stich, 1983).

6 This behavior need not be voluntary (i.e. an *action*) in order to qualify as behavior. Sometimes we move our arms (in sleep, for example) with no relevant intention or purpose. This is simply to say that the internal cause need not be an intention, a purpose or a reason in order for the causal process to qualify as behavior. Unless the process is intentional, deliberate or voluntary, though, the behavior will not have an intentional explanation – an explanation in terms of the agent's reasons or purposes.

7 I, personally, happen to think that the relations I shall be discussing, the relations in virtue of which one event or state indicates or means (in Grice's *natural* sense of meaning) that another event or condition obtains, is one of the most important relations for analyzing the meaning (in Grice's *non*-natural sense of meaning) or

content of mental states. To speak of what an event or condition *indicates* is, in fact, a way of describing the *information* carried by that event or condition. Since I happen to think the meaning or content of cognitive structures derives from their information-carrying role, from what it is their function (acquired in learning) to indicate, the indicator relation (and, hence, information) is important to my own (1981, 1986, 1988) account of meaning. I do not, however, have space to argue for this general view here.

8 I am here reacting to Stich's (1983) Replacement Argument and Davidson's (1987) 'Swampman' example.

References

Churchland, P.M. (1981) Eliminative materialism and propositional attitudes. *Journal of Philosophy* 78 (2), 67–90.

Davidson, D. (1987) Knowing one's own mind. *Proceedings and Addresses of the American Philosophical Association* 60 (3).

Dennett, D. (1981) Three kinds of intentional psychology. In R. Healy (ed.), *Reduction, Time and Reality*. Cambridge, Cambridge University Press.

Dennett, D. (1983) Intentional systems in cognitive ethology: the 'Panglossian paradigm' defended. *Behavioral and Brain Sciences* 6 (3).

Dennett, D. (1987) *The Intentional Stance*. Cambridge, Mass., MIT Press.

Dretske, F. (1981) *Knowledge and the Flow of Information*. Cambridge, Mass., MIT Press.

Dretske, F. (1986) Misrepresentation. In R. Bogdan (ed.), *Belief*. Oxford, Oxford University Press.

Dretske, F. (1988) *Explaining Behavior: Reasons in a World of Causes*. Cambridge, Mass., MIT Press.

Fodor, J. (1980) Methodological solipsism considered as a research strategy in cognitive psychology. *Behavioral and Brain Sciences* 3 (1), 63–110.

Fodor, J. (1987) *Psychosemantics*. Cambridge, Mass., MIT Press.

Follesdal, D. (1985) Causation and explanation: a problem in Davidson's view on action and mind. In E. LePore and B. McLaughlin (eds), *Actions and Events: Perspectives on the Philosophy of Donald Davidson*. New York, Basil Blackwell.

Honderich, T. (1982) The argument for anomalous monism. *Analysis* 42 (1), 192.

LePore, E. and Loewer, B. (1987) Mind matters. *Journal of Philosophy* 84 (11), 630–41.

Mackie, J.L. (1979) Mind, brain and causation. In P. French et al. (eds), *Midwest Studies in Philosophy*, vol. 4. Minneapolis, Minn., University of Minnesota Press.

McGinn, C. (1979) Action and its explanation. In N. Bolton (ed.), *Philosophical Problems in Psychology*, London, Methuen.

Robinson, H. (1982) *Matter and Sense*. Cambridge, Cambridge University Press.

Schiffer, S. (1987) *Remnants of Meaning*. Cambridge, Mass., MIT Press.

Skillen, A. (1984) Mind and matter: a problem that refuses dissolution. *Mind* 93 (372), 514–26.

Sosa, E. (1984) Mind-body interaction and supervenient causation. In P. French et al. (eds.), Minneapolis, Minn., University of Minnesota Press.

Stich, S. (1983) *From Folk Psychology to Cognitive Science*, Cambridge, Mass., MIT Press.

Stoutland, F. (1976) The causation of behavior. In *Essays on Wittgenstein in Honor of G.H. von Wright (Acta Philosophica Fennica 28)*. Amsterdam, North-Holland.

Stoutland, F. (1980) Oblique causation and reasons for action. *Synthese* 43, 351–67.
Stoutland, F. (1982) Philosophy of action: Davidson, von Wright, and the debate over causation. In G. Fløistad (ed.), *Contemporary Philosophy*, vol. 3, Philosophy of Action. The Hague, Martinus Nijhoff.
Tuomela, R. (1977) *Human Action and its Explanation. Synthese* Library, vol. 116. Dordrecht: Reidel.

7

Explanatory Exclusion and the Problem of Mental Causation

Jaegwon Kim

By 'mental causation' I mean causal relations involving mental events as causes or effects. Thus, such causal relations include not only cases in which a mental event causes a physical event but also those in which a physical event causes a mental event and those in which a mental event causes another mental event. That mental causation exists is not controversial; at least, it shouldn't be for those who reject radical irrealism or eliminativism about the mental. For it would be entirely pointless to insist on the reality of the mental and then withhold from it the capacity to be cause or effect. To deny the mental causal powers would seem tantamount to denying it the ability to explain anything, or to make a difference to anything; to be real and to have the power to enter into causal relations arguably go hand in hand, at least for concrete entities.

The problem philosophers have faced, since Descartes, is that of explaining *how mental causation is possible*. But why has this been thought to be a problem? What makes us think mental causation might *not* be possible? Philosophical problems do not arise in a vacuum, but against a backdrop of assumptions and constraints. In the case of mental causation the problem takes the form of the question 'How is mental causation possible, *given X?*', where X is an assumption we have some independent reason to respect which makes mental causation prima facie problematic. Different replacements for 'X' will in effect yield different problems. For Descartes, the trouble-making assumption was the dualist premise that the soul is radically non-spatial, perhaps not even in physical space at all.[1] How could such a thing causally interact with matter whose essence is to occupy a volume of space and for which spatially contiguous action was regarded as the sole mechanism of causal influence?

That, of course, is not *our* problem of mental causation: mental substance having entirely vanished from the scene, it is now difficult for us even to formulate the Cartesian problem. In fact, the rejection of mental substance was the simplest solution to that problem, although I don't know whether histori-cally this played a role in the demise of the Cartesian soul. Our problem stems from different concerns, and I begin with Donald Davidson's 'anomalism of the mental'.

The Problem of Mental Anomalism

Much of the current debate concerning mental causation has been initiated by Davidson's influential if not uncontroversial views on the mind–body relation. The distinctively Davidsonian problem of mental causation has arisen from his doctrine of mental anomalism,[2] the claim that mental phenomena are not governed by causal laws. The auxiliary metaphysical thesis which, together with mental anomalism, generates the initial puzzle is the widely accepted belief that causal relations must somehow instantiate general laws or regularities. So how can mental events, which do not fall under any laws, enter into causal relations, either with other mental events or with physical events?

Davidson's own answer is his 'anomalous monism'. He has held that mental events in causal relations do fall under laws – that is, under *physical* laws since these are the only laws that there are. From this it follows that mental events fall under physical kinds (or have true physical descriptions), from which it further follows, Davidson argued, that mental events are physical events. This was Davidson's argument for monism, a form of the so-called 'token physicalism'.

This is an elegantly simple solution. It gives us not only an account of mental causation but also a solution to the mind–body problem. As the example of Cartesian interactionism shows, the problem of psycho-physical causation is a major component of the mind–body problem, and no theory of the mind–body relation can be thought adequate unless it gives a satisfactory account of mental causation. So why has Davidson's elegant solution failed to satisfy?

The answer, in short, is because it fails, in the view of many commentators, to accord the mental its full due as cause.[3] According to Davidson, a mental event can enter into causal transactions only under a physical description – that is, only as a physical event kind or as an instantiation of a physical property. Suppose that George's desire for a beer and his belief that there is one in the refrigerator cause him to rise from the couch and proceed to the kitchen. Davidson's account has seemed to represent the situation as follows: it isn't George's belief as a belief with the content it has, or his desire as a desire for a particular sort of object, that underlie their causal powers; rather, it is George's belief and desire *qua* neural states or processes of appropriate sorts – that is, as instantiations of certain neurobiological properties – that cause, and causally explain, the consequent movement of his body. Thus, although mental events are allowed by Davidson to be terms of causal relations, the fact that they are mental events of a given kind is given no role play, and is seemingly irrelevant to what causal relations they enter into; the only fact that determines the causal role of an event is what physical properties it has or under what physical kinds it falls. In short, Davidson's anomalous monism has seemed a species of what Brian McLaughlin usefully calls 'type epiphenomenalism',[4] the view that mental events *qua mental event types* are causally inert.

Thus, the problem of mental causation that has arisen out of Davidson's work is that of providing an account of the causal powers of *mental properties* that respects mental anomalism. For example, Dretske describes the project of his *Explaining Behavior* as one of understanding 'how [certain mental events'] being reasons contributes to, or helps explain, their effects on motor output',[5] and says that he is looking for 'an account of the way reasons, in virtue of being reasons, in virtue of standing in semantically relevant relations to other situations, causally explain the behavior that they, in virtue of having this content, help to rationalize'.[6] In a similar vein, Horgan asks, 'Even if individual mental events and states are causally efficacious, are they efficacious *qua* mental?'[7] and asserts that a negative answer to this question would amount to epiphenomenalism. LePore and Loewer, in defense of Davidson on this issue, undertake to show that there is a sense of 'causal relevance' in which Davidson's anomalous monism is consistent with the causal relevance of mental events *qua* instantiations of mental properties in the production of behavior.[8]

The problem Dretske refers to above concerning rationalizing causes of behavior is an important special case of the problem of mental causation. It seems a deep and fundamental fact about the way we make sense of what we do, and what our fellow humans do, that we invoke *reasons for which* we do what we do. Davidson's influential thesis has been that reasons and the actions they rationalize must be related as cause to effect: reasons, to be efficacious as reasons, must cause the actions for which they serve as explanations. However, according to mental anomalism, there are no causal laws connecting reasons as such to actions as such; there are no causal laws connecting beliefs and desires as such to what bodily movement issues from the agent. But doesn't this mean that reasons *qua* reasons are, on Davidson's account, causally irrelevant? The problem, therefore, is how reasons can be efficacious as causes in virtue of being reasons of the kinds that they are, that is, in virtue of having the content that they have. The problem in other words is that of giving an account of the causal efficacy of 'content properties', an important sub-class of mental properties.

This, then, is 'the Davidsonian problem' of mental causation, to wit: how can mental properties be causally efficacious, given mental anomalism? There, however, is another important issue about mental causation that, in my view, has not been given due attention in recent discussions. This issue emerges from certain metaphysical and methodological reflections on the nature of *multiple causal and explanatory claims* about a given event, and has direct implications for theories of mental causation within a broadly physicalist picture of the world. As will become clear, the problem is closely related to a question discussed some years ago, concerning the compatibility between 'mechanistic' and 'purposive' explanations of actions – that is, the compatibility of 'mechanism' and 'purpose'.[9] I see this issue as arising from some very plausible general considerations concerning the phenomenon of 'explanatory exclusion', as I call it, namely the fact that distinct explanations (in particular, causal explanations) of a single explanandum seem to exclude one another, in spite of the fact that their explanatory premises are mutually consistent.

The purpose of this chapter is to show why the problem of causal–explanatory exclusion must be considered another important aspect of the problem of mental causation, and why it should be taken as imposing an overall constraint on theories of mental causation. In the sections to follow, I will first introduce the problem of exclusion in the context of mental causation, and then discuss some current approaches to mental causation in the light of this problem. I will conclude with some remarks on how the problem of mental causation is best approached.

Causal-explanatory Exclusion

Suppose that we have in hand a working account of mental causation; suppose, that is, we have managed to put together an account of causality and of the nature of the mental and the physical according to which George's desire for beer and his belief that beer can be found in the refrigerator can be seen to constitute, in virtue of their content properties, a cause of his rising from the couch. Schematically, there occurs in George an event c with a certain content property R and c's being an event of kind R (or c's having property R, as we will sometimes say) caused B (the rising of George from the couch). B, too, can be thought of as having a similar structure of an event being a certain kind; but for now this won't be necessary.

Now, event B, as a physical event, should be causally explainable in physical terms alone; that is, there must be a physical (presumably, neurobiological) explanation setting forth a sufficient physical cause of B, whether or not we now or ever will know it. (I assume we already know plenty about the physiology of simple limb movements.) Consider, in particular, the total physical state of the agent concurrent with the supposed mental cause of B; it is highly plausible that a sufficient cause of B is contained in that physical state. To deny this is to require a physical event to have a cause, or a causal explanation, outside the physical domain, effectively breaching the closedness of the physical domain.[10] That is, to explain why a physical event occurs, or why an event has a certain physical property, we would be forced to go outside the realm of physical events and their physical properties. That is exactly what Cartesian interactionism holds. Let us assume then that such physical causes of B exist, and, in particular, that there exists a certain event c^* in George such that c^*'s being a neural event of kind N was a cause of B.

Thus, we have two causal claims about a single event, B: (1) c's having content property R caused B; and (2) c^*'s having neural property N caused B.

(In line with Davidson's anomalism we may assume $c = c^*$, but this will not materially affect the discussion to follow.) When these two claims are viewed together, we should find the situation perplexing and somewhat unsettling. Why did George get up from the couch? What caused it? We are offered two causal explanations: 'Because c occurred and had R' and 'Because c^* occurred and had N.' But what is the relationship between c and c^*, or between c's having R and c^*'s having N? George's reason, his desire for beer and his belief about where he could find some, is offered as what made him get up; but then a certain neurophysiological event of kind N is also offered as what made him get up. We want to ask: 'Which *really* did it? What's the *real story*?' The premises of the two causal explanations are mutually consistent; however, there is something perplexing and perhaps even incoherent about accepting both as telling us what caused George's behavior, without an account of how the two accounts are related to each other. Each explanation specifies a cause of George's behavior. But how are the two supposed causes related to each other? Let us survey the possibilities.

Case 1 (the *partial cause* option): when two events are offered each as a cause for one and the same effect, it may be that each is only a *partial* cause; that is, each is only a part, perhaps an indispensable part, of a sufficient cause. (Why did Wilbur fall and break his nose? Because he was dizzy from the allergy medication and stumbled on the curb.) However, this is not an alternative we can take seriously, for the case of behavior causation; it's absurd to think that to bring about B, we need *both* an event of kind R and an event of kind N as *distinct* and *independent* causal conditions, and that they *together* make up a sufficient cause of the bodily movement that issued. Note that this alternative may involve a violation of the closedness of the physical domain.

Case 2 (the *overdetermination* option): could c's having R and c^*'s having N *each* be an independent sufficient cause of B? If we said yes, we would be saying that B is causally *overdetermined* by the two events, since either one singly would have been sufficient to bring about B. But again this seems like an absurd picture of the situation; it implies, for example, that every bit of rationalizable behavior is overdetermined by both a mental cause and a physical cause. This could also involve a violation of the closed character of the physical domain.

Case 3 (the *causal chain* option): two conditions can each be a sufficient cause of some single event by being different links in the same causal chain leading to the effect event. In this case, the later cause is causally dependent on the earlier one; and we may think of one explanation as causally dependent on the other. Could c's having R and c^*'s having N be related in this way with respect to the behavior they are assumed to cause? No, for two reasons: first, we can suppose the two events occur at the same time (as we do if, with Davidson, we assume $c = c^*$); secondly, to allow this could violate the closedness of the physical domain.

I hope you agree that when we are confronted with two proffered causes of a single event, an explanation of their relationship is called for; and that unless we know, or have a view about, how the two supposed causes are related to one another, we are faced by a new perplexity about the etiology of the event in question. Further, when we are offered two causal explanations of one and the same explanandum, each adducing a different event as an explanatory cause, we are back in the same sort of 'epistemic predicament' from which we sought escape by finding an explanation; we are in need of an account of how the two explanatory causes are related to each other. We have so far spoken indifferently of both events *simpliciter* and events' being a certain kind or having a certain property as causes and effects. This makes no difference: however we individuate causes and effects, when two things are proposed as causing a single effect, we face the same problem. The full 'principle of explanatory exclusion' that I have elaborated elsewhere says this: there can be at most one *complete* and *independent* explanation of a single explanandum.[11]

For the present case of intentional and neural causes of behavior, none of the three possibilities we have looked at offers a genuine option. Are there others that are more plausible? I believe there are two that we must consider:

Case 4 (the *identity* option): perhaps, the two supposed causes are in reality one, and there are not here two distinct causal relations, or two distinct causal stories to tell. If we were to identify the mental cause and the neural cause as one and the same, that would greatly simplify the picture, permitting us to avoid questions like those raised above, for example, whether we have here a case of causal overdetermination, whether each is only a partial cause, etc. This is the classic identity solution to the mind–body problem; the simplicity effected by psycho-neural identification is best appreciated in the context of mental causation, not in the abstract setting of 'ontological parsimony', 'Occam's Razor', etc. Davidson's anomalous monoism is a form of the identity solution. It may be recalled that Davidson's argument for the identity of mental with physical events is based principally on causal considerations. The present line of thought can be taken as constituting another causal argument for the identity solution.[12]

Case 5 (the *supervenience* option): for various reasons, we may shy away from an outright identification of the mental with the physical. We may nevertheless want to acknowledge the dependence, or supervenience, of the mental on the physical, and hence the dependence of mental causal relations upon more fundamental causal processes at the physical level. Thus, this solution would accept two (or more) causal explanations of one and the same event; however, the explanations, and the causal relations that underlie them, are not independent of each other. One of them is dependent, or supervenient, on the other; and, depending on how these terms are understood, it may even be possible to regard the higher-level causal story as *reducible* to the lower-level one.[13]

For the case of rationalizing versus biological explanation of behavior, identity and supervenience are the only alternatives that are not immediately ruled out; the rest are obvious non-starters. But is the identity option really viable, in the context of the Davidsonian problem? Here we have two events c and c^*, and their respective properties R and N whose causal powers are at issue. Davidson's anomalous monoism, embraced by many philosophers who reject reductionism, says that c and c^* are one and the same event. But this is only part of the story, and the easy part; we need to deal with the question of how R and N, the two properties, are related to each other; for the causal relevance to these properties is the central issue on hand. So does it make sense to identify R and N, and mental properties, in general, with neural properties? Davidson would say that there is not, and need not be, any significant connection, not even contingent co-extensiveness, between R and N, although one and the same event has them both. In fact, psycho-neural property identities seem entirely ruled out by his mental anomalism. Given this, the identification of R and N, and hence of the two causes, c's having R and c's having N (assuming $c = c^*$), is out of the question for Davidson, or as part of a defense of Davidson.

Many philosophers who are not sympathetic with Davidson's arguments for mental anomalism will go along with him in rejecting the identification of R and N. Conventional wisdom today is that such identifications have been shown to be untenable by the phenomenon of 'multiple realizability' of mental properties.[14] To identify R and N, and, more generally, mental properties with physical properties, is commonly regarded as embracing a cluster of discredited mind–body theories, such as the classic type-identity theory associated with Smart and Feigl, physical reductionism, and the illusion of a unified science based on an all-encompassing physics. It is true, I think, that even if we buy neither Davidson's mental anomalism nor arguments from multiple realization, property identities between the mental and the physical are fraught with difficulties, not the least of which is the fact that we seem to have no clear idea as to the conditions under which such identities are true, or can be reasonably affirmed.

It seems then that the supervenience alternative must be taken seriously. This, however, is not a single option but a group of options, depending on how supervenience is understood. Three principal supervenient relations have lately been distinguished, 'strong', 'weak', and 'global', each differing from the rest in the strength of connection or dependency it requires between what supervenes and its supervenience base.[15] Although there is some controversy about this, strong supervenience of the mental on the physical can be understood to imply the existence of psycho-physical laws and psycho-physical reduction. Weak and global supervenience, while neither implies the other, are weaker than strong supervenience, and neither implies reducibility or the presence of nomic correlations between the supervenient properties and their 'base' properties. However, the common core that ties all these relations together is the idea that supervenient properties are in some sense *dependent* on, and *determined* by, the properties upon which they supervene. I will say more about this later; however, for now this core idea of supervenience as a dependency or determinative relation will be sufficient for our limited purposes. All we need to note here is that the supervenience alternative is a weaker position than the identity solution but one that is consistent with both the multiple realizability of mental phenomena and the explanatory exclusion principle. It is weaker than the identity position because supervenient properties are not in general a subset of their base properties. And it is consistent with the exclusion principle because the principle only rules out more than one complete and *independent* explanation of a single explanandum. If the mental supervenes on the physical, a psychological explanation of a given event can be construed as supervenient, and hence dependent, on its physical explanations. That this approach is in harmony with multiple realization can be seen roughly as follows.[16] Let R be multiply realized in N_1, N_2 ... This means that whenever an event of kind R occurs in an organism, one of the Ns, says N_j, is realized in the organism, and that it is *in virtue of* the realization of N_j at the time in question that R is realized at the time. More, there is an implicit general claim to the effect that if any organism with a similar biological–physical structure were to realize N_j at any time, it too would instantiate R at that time. All this nicely fits the definition of 'strong supervenience': under these conditions, R 'strongly supervenes' on N_1, N_2 ... It follows that multiple realization is also consistent with weak and global supervenience since these relations are entailed by strong supervenience (which we may assume to be consistent).

But is supervenience consistent with mental anomalism? We will look into this question below.

Explanatory Exclusion and Recent Approaches to Mental Causation

It is my claim then that unless a definitive stand on the problem of exclusion between mental and physical causation is taken and defended, we do not have a full understanding of the possibility of mental causation. With this in mind, let us consider some of the recent attempts at an account of mental causation. None of the writers we will discuss below, with the possible exception of Dretske, are consciously concerned with the issue of explanatory exclusion, or how the relationship between rational and neural explanations of behavior is to be understood – or, indeed, whether there should be any signficant relationship between them at all.

Let us first look at the writers who are concerned with the Davidsonian problem of mental causation, namely the problem of anomalous mental properties. The approach that has been the most popular with these philosophers is to weaken the nomic subsumption requirement on causal relations, by focusing on Davidson's version of this requirement that causal relations must instantiate 'strict laws'. As far as I know, Davidson has never stated a fully explicit explanation of the term 'strict law', and I doubt that his writings can support a single robust sense to be attached to the term; however, most writers seem agreed on one point: a strict law is not hedged by a *ceteris paribus* clause. Philosophers who have chosen the route of relaxing the nomic subsumption requirement include Jerry Fodor,[17] who argues that singular causal statements are sufficiently backed by laws qualified by *ceteris paribus* conditions; McLaughlin,[18] who, somewhat like Fodor, entertains the possibility that a causal relation can hold in virtue of instantiating a 'non-strict' law as well as a strict law; and Horgan,[19] who explains causal relevance of properties directly in terms of counterfactuals, by-passing explicit consideration of laws, whether strict or non-strict. It should be clear that these writers must all confront the issue of explanatory exclusion. If, for example, as McLaughlin envisages, a physical event, B, is caused by c's having content property R, in virtue of an appropriate non-strict law being instantiated, and is *also* caused by c's having neural property N, in virtue of some strict physical law being instantiated, how are these two causes related to each other?[20] Could each be a sufficient cause of B? If so, is B causally overdetermined? If not, why? Perhaps because if c had not had N, it would not have had R either? Does this mean tht there is a kind of dependence between N and R, if so, what is its nature and ground, and is it consistent with mental anomalism? And so on.

LePore and Loewer use a similar strategy; however, they differ from the authors mentioned above in that they explicitly do what others have done implicitly, that is, to recognize two distinct relations of causation, or 'causal relevance'. They write:[21]

> Consider the following locutions:
> a) Properties F and G are relevant$_1$ to making it the case that c causes e and
> b) c's possessing property F is causally relevant$_2$ to e's possessing property G.
>   We will say that (a) holds if c has F and e has G, and there is a strict law that entails Fs cause Gs. It is in this sense that it is *c's having F and e's having G 'make it the case' that c causes e*. Relevance$_2$ is a relation among c, one of its properties F, e, and one of its properties G. It holds when *c's being F brings it about that e is G*.

Their defense of Davidson consists in the claim that while mental anomalism does entail causal irrelevance$_1$ of mental properties, it is consistent with their having causal relevance$_2$ in relation to physical events.

Can we avoid the issue of explanatory exclusion by positing two distinct types of causal relation, one holding between behavior and reasons and the other between behavior and neural states? Is there any reason for thinking that these two disparate relations cannot co-exist? LePore and Loewer do not explicitly discuss the relationship between these two causal relevance relations; for example, whether, as seems plausible, causal relevance$_1$ entails causal relevance$_2$.[22] For this reason, it is not clear what might be the most persuasive way of setting up the issue of exclusion for them. But let us try a couple of things. First, assume, as suggested above, that relevance$_1$ implies relevance$_2$, and consider the Davidsonian situation: event c has both physical–neural property N and content property R, and event e has behavioral property B, where we suppose that a causal relevance$_2$ relation holds between N and B; that is, c's having N and e's having B make it the case that c causes e. Given the entailment of relevance$_2$ by relevance$_1$, we also have it that c's having N is causally relevant$_2$ to e's having B. We further suppose, as part of the Davidsonian situation, that e's having B is rationalized by c's having content property R. On LePore and Loewer's view, this means that c's having R is causally relevant$_2$ to e's having B. Thus, we have both that (1) c's having N 'brings it about' that e has B, and that (2) c's having R 'brings it about' that e has B. We can ask how we are to understand the relationship between the two 'causes', c's having R and c's having N.

Secondly, suppose that causal relevance$_1$ does not entail causal relevance$_2$: we can still apply pressure on LePore and Loewer's account by appealing to a broad generic conception of cause. Stripped to its essentials, LePore and Loewer's point is that neural property N can be causally relevant$_1$ via a strict law, to behavioral property B, while at the same time content property R is relevant$_2$, via a *ceteris paribus* law, to the same behavioral property B. It seems to me that these two relevance relations must be assumed to be in some unified sense both 'causal' relations, if LePore and Loewer's theory is to be a theory of mental causation. If so, when we encounter an instance of B for which both an instance of N and an instance of R claim causal relevance, of *one sort or another*, we should be entitled to raise some questions, questions of the sort that lead us to the exclusion principle; such as this one, to start with, 'Given that c occurred and had N and that e occurred and had B, would e have had B if c had not had R also?' If the answer is no, would that mean that we must have a content property *in addition to* neural–physical properties to bring about a physical–behavioral state (e's having B)? Why isn't this a violation of the closedness of the physical realm? If the answer is yes, then in what sense is c's having R 'causally relevant', in any significant sense, to e's having B? It appears that LePore and Loewer are thinking of relevance$_1$ as in some sense a stronger causal relation than relevance$_2$. The basic question to raise against any such proposal is this: given that c's neural properties cause a certain behavior in the strong sense of causation, what *further* causal contribution can c's content properties make, properties that are only weakly causally related to the behavior? Is there any leftover causal work for them to do?

Thus, the problem I have with the proposals of LePore and Loewer, Horgan, McLaughlin, and others is not that they don't work. On the contrary: it seems to me eminently possible, even plausible, to support counterfactuals with *ceteris paribus* laws (whatever these really are); and it may be possible to analyze causal relations in terms of counterfactuals alone, largely independently of considerations of laws. While these are important matters to get clear about, there is, I think, a more fundamental issue here about mental causation; if the demonstration of the possibility of mental causation consisted merely in showing that there are true counterfactuals of the form 'If S hadn't thought that p, S wouldn't have done A', or some other related forms, who could disagree? What makes mental causation, especially mental-to-physical causation, a deep philosophical problem is, among other things, the issue of compatibility, or exclusion, between rationalizing causes of behavior and its neurobiological causes, and, more generally, how mental causation relations are to be understood in relation to physical causation. Given the basic physicalist assumptions, which all parties to the present debate accept, every physical occurrence must be assumed to have a physical cause (in so far as it has a cause) and, in principle, a physical explanation. So how are mental causes of physical events *also* possible? Where do they fit in? Why aren't they redundant at best? So these proposals, if they work, go only part way toward the solution of the problem of mental causation.

'Syntacticalism' and Dretske's Informational Approach

The writers we have thus far surveyed adopt a common approach: in trying to account for the possibility of mental causation, they all tinker with the concept of causation, trying to weaken Davidson's strict nomological requirement on causal relations. This, however, is not Dretske's approach; Dretske's strategy is entirely different as we shall see, and there is a simple explanation of why this is so.

As will be recalled, the problem of mental causation for our earlier authors arises out of mental anomalism – that is, worries about whether there are psychological laws, in enough numbers and of sufficient strength, to support mental causal relations. This is what we called the 'Davidsonian problem'. Although Dretske, too, sometimes sets up the problem of mental causation by reference to Davidson's anomalous monism,[23] his real concern about mental causation arises not from mental anomalism but from what might be called 'syntacticalism'[24] or 'psychological solipsism'.[25] Briefly, it is generated by the following set of considerations: (1) whatever causes behavior must be supervenient on the internal biological–physical state of the organism that emits the behavior, and (2) intentional states (or their content, or 'semantic', properties), in virtue of their representational character, are essentially *relational* states, involving reference to historical and ecological conditions *external* to the organism, and fail to supervene on the internal biological–physical facts about the organism.[26] Thus, content properties of neural states are necessarily relational, and extrinsic to the physical–physiological–anatomical conditions obtaining in the organism; since only the non-relational, or 'syntactic', properties (that is, physical properties) of neural states can be causally relevant in the production of motor output, this seems to exclude content properties from having a causal role in respect of behavior, at least the organism's motor output. To make this reasoning plausible, consider this line of thought: if the external conditions were altered in appropriate ways, the neural states could lose their content properties while retaining all of their intrinsic physical properties; but as long as their intrinsic physical properties remain the same, the neural states would cause exactly the same motor output. So how can intentional properties be causally involved in behavior causation?

To summarize: the problem of mental causation for LePore and Loewer, McLaughlin, Fodor,[27] Horgan et al. arises from the puzzle 'How can *anomalous properties* be causal properties?' For Dretske, it arises from the puzzle 'How can *extrinsic relational properties* be causal properties?' We should note, though, the common methodological assumption Dretske shares with these philosophers, and with Davidson: the explanatory efficacy of reasons depends on their causal efficacy.

Since my concern here is restricted to the metaphysical issue of causal–explanatory exclusion, I will sketch Dretske's account in the briefest outline. The starting point of Dretske's theory is his distinctive conception of the *explananda* of rationalizations. What we explain when we offer 'reasons' is behavior or action, something the agent 'does'. But what is a *doing?* Dretske holds that agent S does something A only if some *internal* state S_i of S *causes* a certain *result* R (typically, motor output) associated with A.[28] Thus, if I raise my arm, R is my arm's rising and S_i perhaps my desire or intention to raise my arm (Dretske assumes that S_i is a neural state with an intentional property). Dretske takes this relational causal structure, S_i's causing R, to be the distinctive characteristic of behavior, that is, of actions and doings. And to explain S's doing A, we must, on Dretske's view, explain S_i's causing R, that is, *why S_i causes R*.

Dretske stresses the crucial importance to his account of the distinction between doing A (that is, S_i's causing R) and R. To explain R, or specify the cause of R, is one thing; to explain why S_i caused R is quite another. Neurobiology can give an exhaustive account of the causal etiology of R, including a story of *how* S_i caused R – what sequence of causally connected states led to the occurrence of R – but it does not, and cannot, explain *why* S_i causes R. It is the distinctive and indispensable job of psychology to provide an explanation of why this causal relation obtains.

And it is this relational causal structure, S_i's causing R, that the representational character of intentional states is specifically fit for explaining. How does this work? Briefly, it works like this: to explain why S_i causes R is, on Dretske's construal, to explain why or how *S_i came to be 'hooked up' with R in agent S*, and the content property of S_i explains, and was the cause of, how this causal hook-up came about.

Let me flesh this a bit more, although the details will be unimportant and I will not discuss any of the many substantive questions that arise for Dretske's innovative and highly intriguing account.[29] Suppose that it is, for some reason, advantageous to the organism to emit R when F is present in its vicinity (e.g. press a bar when a red light flashes). How can this be secured? First of all, the organism needs an F-detector, a sub-system that reliably enters a certain state, S_i, when, and only when, F is present in its vicinity. Secondly, by conditioning and learning (or through natural selection, in the case of a population), this F-detector comes to be hooked up with the system's motor system in such a fashion that whenever the F-detector enters state S_i, the motor system is activated to produce R. That is what associative learning is, and instances of such learning, of course, are a commonplace, although we may still be largely in the dark about the exact neurobiological details. On Dretske's informational account of content, the nomological correlation between S_i and F makes it the case that S_i has F as its content property – that is, S_i has the content that F is present in the vicinity. So the fact that S_i represents F, or the fact that it has the content property it has, explains why S_i has been 'recruited' or 'promoted', as Dretske puts it, as a cause of R.

Dretske does not claim that this simple model, in its present form, is sufficient as an account of the way our beliefs, desires and other intentional states, with their highly complex and interanimating contents, rationalize our actions. The importance of the model for Dretske lies in the fact that it is a prototype that shows, in a concrete way, the possibility of how a relational representational property of a neural state can causally account for behavior. As I said, we are not here concerned with the substance of Dretske's account, but only in how it fares in relation to the problem of causal-explanatory exclusion.

Let us begin then by looking at Dretske's conception of 'doings'. Dretske's solution to the exclusion problem is an instance of what may be called the 'two explananda' strategy: rationalizations and biological explanations do not share the same explananda, and therefore there need be no explanatory competition between them, no excluding of explanations of one type by those of the other. It has been argued by some philosophers,[30] that whereas reasons rationalize actions in a fully fledged intentional sense, physiological explanations can only explain bodily movements described in purely physical terms, and that once the two types of explanations are seen to have different explananda, the potential for conflict vanishes. The strategy is appealing: resolve the explanatory rivalry by splitting the explanandum. Give each explanation a morsel of its own to chew on and we shall have peace. For Dretske, psychology is in charge of actions and doings, causal–relational structures of the form S_i-causing-R, and neurobiology and other physical sciences are in charge of events *simpliciter*, such as R. Although Dretske never explcitly mentions the issue of explanatory exclusion, it seems that this would be his answer if the problem were put to him.

First, I would like to point out one extremely important characteristic of the two explananda approach to the problem of explanatory exclusion: it is fundamentally dualistic, if it is to work. And by 'dualistic' I mean mind–body dualism. To hold that an action, or bit of behavior, has two or more distinguishable aspects that require explanation is one thing; it is quite another to insist that one of the distinguished aspects can be explained *only* by recourse to an intentional theory, or that it can have *only* content properties as causes. The claim that we need to contend with two types of explananda in explaining behavior is entirely consistent with keeping faith with a monistic explanatory theory; for *it is possible that explananda of both types are amenable to physical–biological explanations*. If this is admitted, it is obvious that the sundering of the explanandum by itself does not solve the explanatory exclusion problem:

for it may be that one or the other, perhaps both, of the splintered explananda are susceptible of both an intentional and a biological explanation, and the exclusion problem can arise all over again. What can prevent it from arising is the *further* claim, which is what introduces dualism into the picture, that there are no physical–biological explanations for the explananda of one type, that is, actions properly so-called – or, to put it in terms of cause, that there are no physical–biological causes for actions properly so-called.

More concretely, consider Dretske's causings, the supposed explananda of psychological explanations. We can put the issue in a simple and stark way: are these causings physical entities or are they not? If they are not, we have an overt dualism. If they are in the physical domain, are they susceptible of physical causal explanations or are they not? If they are, then these explananda, special though they might be, cannot serve to separate psychology from physical theory, and the exclusion problem arises again. If they are not, we would again have a form of psycho–physical dualism: there are entities in the physical world for which there in principle are no physical causal explanations, but only intentional explanations. In fact, this looks very much like Cartesian interactionist dualism, violating as it does the closed character of the physical domain.

But Dretske is a committed naturalist and physicalist; he will not brook dualism in any form. What he has in mind in claiming a special psychological character for the explanations appropriate for his causings is, probably, not that psychological explanations are non-physical, but rather that these explanations invoke *relational* properties of the agent's internal states whereas neurobiological explanations of the 'results' of the causings refer only to their *intrinsic* physical properties. But this distinction surely cannot by itself confer a special character or status on psychology or psychological explanation. The distinction between explaining S_i's causing R and explaining R surely does not neatly line up with the distinction between having a relational explanans and having a non-relational explanans. For this depends on the kind of R we are interested in; Dretske's thought is not implausible when R is motor output, but not, it seems, when R involves conditions external to the agent (e.g. the window's being broken, Xanthippe's being widowed). In any case, even if Dretske is right about neurobiology being limited in the kind of explanandum it can handle, it still doesn't follow that physical theory, broadly construed, cannot handle these causings as explananda (physics, after all, is full of relations and relational properties). Unless this is so, nothing follows about a unique or special status of psychology or psychological explanation, and the problem of exclusion remains unresolved. Thus, Dretske's strategy may resolve a potential explanatory conflict between psychology and biology – perhaps for a limited range of behavior involving motor output – but not between psychology and physical theory.

So the dual explananda strategy by itself isn't going to solve the problem of exclusion for Dretske. What might do the job for him is not his theory of mental causation, but his program, in *Knowledge and the Flow of Information*,[31] of a physical reduction of intentionality. If that program works, he would be entitled to the identity or supervenience option earlier described. But if Dretske opts for identity, he would not be in a position to claim any distinctive status for psychological explanations. Whether the supervenience alternative supports the claim of a distinctive status for psychology *vis-à-vis* physical theory is much less clear; but this much is clear: the stronger the supervenience relation holding between the psychological and physical, the weaker the claim of the distinctiveness of psychological explanation.

How to Approach the Problem of Exclusion

How should we approach the problem of explanatory exclusion for biological and rationalizing explanations of behavior? My basic suggestions can be quickly stated: if you stand fast by the view (we may call this 'the causal thesis') that rationalizations are a species of causal explanations involving physical behavior as effect, your only option is the supervenience option – that is, to explain mental causal relations as supervenient on underlying physical causal relations. But what if we gave up the causal thesis? I believe that a partial rejection, or modification, of this assumption is called for; however, there appears to be no acceptable alternative to a broadly causal view of rationalization. And it seems to me that supervenience is the only viable solution to the exclusion problem as long as rationalizations are taken as causal explanations. Not all of these points will be argued or defended in any detail here, but I will try to make the flow of my thinking as natural and cogent as possible.

Why the supervenience option? Because identity and supervenience are the only alternatives available to us, as may be recalled, and unless mental anomalism is rejected, the identity alternative must be ruled out. As we saw, the resolution of the exclusion issue via the identity option requires the identification of mental with physical attrributes, and it would seem that such attribute identities in turn require strict and exceptionless correlations between the properties involved. It seems clear that if laws hedged with *ceteris paribus* clauses are all we can get, psycho-physical attribute identities are not in the cards. And few philosophers will now argue that strict and exceptionless correlations with a requisite modal force exist between mental and physical attributes across the board.

But might supervenience, too, commit us to exceptionless psycho-physical correlations? That is, if psychological properties are supervenient on physical–biological properties, wouldn't that require that there be strict correlation laws between the two sets of properties? Here, the answer is a bit complicated, since, as noted earlier, supervenience comes in varying strengths, and whether mind–body supervenience is compatible with mental anomalism depends on the kind of supervenience relation one favors for the psycho-physical case, and also on the particular concept of law deemed appropriate to our present concerns. The main problem is to find a supervenience relation that is strong enough to give us an appropriate sort of dependence of the mental on the physical and yet not strong enough to come into conflict with mental anomalism.

But that turns out to be a difficult bill to fill. As noted earlier, there are three principal supervenience relations currently on the scene: 'strong', 'weak' and 'global'. Strong supervenience is too strong; strong psycho-physical supervenience will give us psycho-physical dependence but will conflict with mental anomalism for it requires, as we saw in connection with multiple realizability of the mental, that for each supervenient property there be a condition in the base properties that is sufficient for it in all possible worlds, or at least all causally possible worlds. On the other hand, I believe that both weak and global supervenience are too weak. Neither entails the existence of necessary correlations between supervenient and base properties; therefore, they are both consistent with mental anomalism. However, for that very reason among others, it is doubtful that they can underwrite a strong enough dependency relation between the mental and the physical to resolve the exclusion issue. But there is here room for disagreement and further explorations.[32] For my part, I think the best hope lies in developing another supervenience relation that is designed to exploit *ceteris paribus* psycho-physical connections. This relation (call it '*ceteris paribus* supervenience') will have mental properties lawfully correlate, *ceteris paribus*, with their base physical properties. Thus, this will be a weaker form of strong supervenience, in the following sense: whereas strong psycho-physical supervenience requires each mental property to be strictly and exceptionlessly correlated with its physical base properties across possible worlds, *ceteris paribus* psycho-physical supervenience would qualify such correlations with an appropriate *ceteris paribus* clause.[33] This is, at this point, only a programmatic suggestion: whether or not such a supervenience relation makes sense will depend on whether we can make a coherent sense of *ceteris paribus* clauses, and it remains to be seen whether such a relation will yield a dependence relation of sufficient strength to resolve the exclusion problem.

Our discussion thus far has presupposed the causal thesis, that rationalizations are causal explanations of behavior – behavior involving bodily motion. This 'Davidsonian assumption' is widely accepted. Thus, rationalizations are assumed to involve mental-to-physical causation. But what if we rejected this assumption? There are two separate aspects to this assumption, either of which could be rejected independently of the other: (1) we might reject the view that rationalizations are *causal* explanations; and (2) we might reject the view that rationalizations rationalize *physical* behavior. I think (1) is not viable but (2) is. Let us begin with (2).

There are plausible considerations against the view that bodily movements are involved in rationalizations as explananda. What a rationalization rationalizes is naturally regarded as something that itself has content, for rationalization depends essentially on logical relations among contents, and it is widely accepted that an action, to be rationalized, must be viewed under an intentional description, perhaps as conceived by the agent, not under a purely physical–physiological description. Behavior as described in purely mechanistic or physiological terms simply is not a fit object of rationalization. If this is the case, we might as well take *intentions* as the objects, or explananda, of rationalizations. Another way of putting this is to say that we reconstrue actions as intentions, intentions that we usually think of as *underlying* the actions for which they are intentions.[34] In the paradigmatic case of a coordinated belief–desire pair rationalizing an action, the rationalizing relation holds in virtue of the logical relation between the contents of three intentional states, a desire, a belief and an intention (to do the action). If George gets up to go to the kitchen because he wants a beer and believes that he can get it in the kitchen, it would be proper to take his intention to go to the kitchen, rather than his going to the kitchen, as what can be, and needs to be, rationalized by his want and belief; that is what we need to make sense of and render intelligible, if we are to understand what 'George is doing'. Whether the intention is successfully executed in an appropriate physical motion depends on the vagaries of external environmental factors, such as there being an unobstructed path to the kitchen and George's having at the time a pair of functioning legs or other means of locomotion. Whether the intention is successfully implemented is important, of course; however, what requires rationalization, and what is a fit object of rationalization, is an intention (or decision, when an intention is formed deliberately), not the bodily movement that carries it out. The latter is perhaps also worthy of causal explanation; but the point is that rationalization need not reach it – at least, not as its proximate object. Rationalization may stop at intentions, as shown by cases of intentions that, for one reason or another, are not properly executed.

This, I think, is an appealing way of looking at rationalizations. But it in itself does not help us with any of the problems of mental causation. It begets new problems which threaten to take us right back to the old ones, including this: what is the nature of the relationship between an intention and the physical behavior that executes it – that is, the relation between my intention to raise my arm and my arm going up? This, according to the present approach, is not a rationalizing relation,[35] but it is a psycho-physical relation evidently in need of an explanation. Surely, it is no mere coincidence that when I intend to raise my arm, my arm (at least, quite often) rises. If we think of it as a causal relation, then we are back with the problem of mental causation, and with it, the problem of exclusion; if it isn't a causal relation, what is it? A second problem this approach must address is that of physical-to-mental causation. If intentions, our new explananda, have physical explanations, in terms of physical causal antecedents, as well as rationalizing explanations, the problem of exclusion arises all over again. So the present approach, if it is to avoid the exclusion issue, must, it seems, renounce psycho-physical causation altogether, both mental-to-physical and physical-to-mental. The upshot would be a sharp separation of the mental and the physical, allowing no causal transaction between the two domains.[36] This, I take it, is not an option that many philosophers will find appealing.

The sundering of the two domains and denial of psycho-physical causation, if we are willing to pay the price, may buy us a solution to the problem of exclusion, but not a full solution to the problem of mental causation. For there remains the intra-domain problem of giving an account of how reasons are related to the intentions they rationalize, and, more generally, an account of the possibility of causal relations among mental events. For it is difficult to believe that the rationalizing relation is entirely logical, a relation that can be fully captured in logical terms alone, or quasi-logical and epistemic terms, such as 'making sense', 'being appropriate', etc. It is difficult to believe that, by using these terms alone, we can capture the difference between *being a reason for* and *being the reason for which*, a distinction Davidson has rightly empha-sized.[37] The best bet is that some causal notions must be implicated in any satisfactory account of this distinction. Thus, although we may reject the view that rationalizations rationalize physical behavior, it is another thing to reject the view that rationalizations are causal explanations – or essentially involve causal relations in some way.

The computational viewpoint of the sort defended by many philosophers[38] seems to come very close to the claim that intra-psychological explanatory relations need not invoke any causal notions. According to this point of view, these relations are fully capturable in terms of such essentially logi-cal–normative–epistemic relations as 'cogency' and 'making sense', without the use of causal concepts. I believe this approach won't work; it will not be able to account for the distinction between reason for and reason for which, and is likely to collapse to syntacticalism.[39]

The approach I have been sketching, which takes the objects of rationaliza-tions themselves as intentional states, therefore, has one large unsolved problem on its agenda: how to make sense of mental-to-mental rationalizing relations. They are *ex hypothesi* explanatory relations, and must respect the distinction between reason for and reason for which. As noted, that seems to rule out accounts that are wholly non-causal. But if they are causal, can we explain them autonomously at the mental level, without recourse to causal–nomological processes at the physical level? This is a deep metaphysical question; my conjecture is that the answer has to be 'No'. I believe that this approach must be combined with the supervenience alternative earlier dis-cussed if it is to yield a coherent theory that is also consistent with a broadly physicalist outlook. For it seems to me that mental-to-mental causal relations, including rationalizations, must be explained as supervenient causal relations, supervenient upon fundamental physical processes.[40] And it is in psycho-physical supervenience that I believe we must seek a solution to the problem of syntacticalism as well. But an elaboration of this and other points goes far beyond the scope of this chapter.

Notes

1   For discussions of mental causation in Descartes see R.C. Richardson, 'The "scandal" of Cartesian interactionism', *Mind* 91 (1982), 20–37; M. Bedau, 'Cartesian interaction', *Midwest Studies in Philosophy* 10 (1986), 483–502.

2   See especially 'Mental events', reprinted in D. Davidson, *Essays on Actions and Events* (Oxford and New York, Oxford University Press, 1980).

3   There has been remarkable unanimity among the commentators (who appear to have reached their conclusions largely independently of each other) on how the difficulty arises. See, e.g., F. Stoutland, 'Oblique causation and reasons for action', *Synthese* 43 (1980), 351–67; T. Honderich, 'The argument for anomalous monism', *Analysis* 42 (1982), 59–64; E. Sosa, 'Mind–body interaction and supervenient causation', *Midwest Studies in Philosophy* 9 (1984), 271–82; J. Kim, 'Self-understanding and rationalizing explanations', *Philosophia Naturalis* 21 (1984), 309–20; J. Kim, 'Epiphenomenal and supervenient causation', *Midwest Studies in Philosophy* 9 (1984), 257–70; F. Dretske, 'The explanatory role of content', in R.H. Grimm and D.D. Merrill (eds), *Contents of Thought* (Tucson, University of Arizona Press, 1988); F. Dretske, *Explaining Behavior: Reasons in a World of Causes* (Cambridge, Mass., MIT Press, 1988). For further discussion see G. and C. Macdonald, 'Mental causes and the explanation of action', in L. Stevenson, R. Squires and J. Haldane (eds), *Mind, Causation and Action* (Oxford, Basil Blackwell, 1986).

4   B. McLaughlin, 'Type epiphenomenalism, type dualism, and the causal priority of the physical', in J. Tomberlin (ed.), *Philosophical Perspectives*, vol. 3, pp. 109–36 (California, Ridgeview, 1989).

5   Dretske, *Explaining Behavior*, p. 79.

6   Ibid., p. 83.

7   T. Horgan, 'Mental quasation', in J. Tomberlin (ed.), *Philosophical Perspectives*, vol. 3, pp. 47–76 (California, Ridgeview, 1989).

8   E. LePore and B. Loewer, 'Mind matters', *Journal of Philosophy* 84, (1987), 630–42.

9   See, e.g. N. Malcolm, 'The conceivability of mechanism', *Philosophical Review* 77 (1968), 45–72; and my 'Mechanism, purpose, and explanatory exclusion', in J. Tomberlin (ed.), *Philosophical Perspectives* vol. 3 (California, Ridgeview, 1989).

10 Compare John Pollock: 'We have good reason to believe that physical events constitute a closed causal system – insofar as physical events have a causal ancestry, that ancestry can be described in purely physical terms', in 'My brother, the machine', *Nous* 22 (1988), 173–212, p. 185. There are various ways of stating the principle that the physical domain is 'closed', and the principle that the physical is 'complete' or 'comprehensive'. See, e.g. McLaughlin's discussion in 'Type epiphenomenalism, type dualism, and the causal priority of the physical'. A precise statement is not needed for my present purposes. Nor do I need the general assumption that every physical event has a physical causal explanation.

11 In 'Mechanism, purpose, and explanatory exclusion'; see also 'Causal realism, explanatory realism, and explanatory exclusion', in P. French, T. Uehling and H. Wettstein (eds), *Midwest Studies in Philosophy* vol. 12, pp. 225–39 (Notre Dame, University of Notre Dame Press, 1987).

12   Pollock's 'causal nexus argument' in 'My brother, the machine', p. 185 is an argument for token physicalism based on essentially these considerations. In *Holistic Explanation*, pp. 134–9 (Oxford, Clarendon Press, 1979), Christopher Peacocke, too, presents considerations very much like mine as an argument for physicalism. Like Pollock, however, he is concerned with token identity and does not consider questions of mental properties or types in this context. And neither considers supervenience as an alternative account. I first discussed these issues in 'Identity, causality, and supervenience in the mind–body problem', *Midwest Studies in Philosophy* 4 (1979), 31–49.

13   According to the current usage, reducibility may be taken to entail supervenience. If we were to believe that mental properties are 'reducible' to physical properties but refuse, for some reason, to identify the former with the latter, our position would, according to the present taxonomy of options, fall under the supervenience option.

14   The classic source is H. Putnam, 'The nature of mental states', reprinted in N. Block (ed.), *Readings in Philosophy of Psychology*, vol. 1 (Cambridge, Mass., Harvard University Press, 1980); originally published in 1967. See for further development J. Fodor, *The Language of Thought* (New York, Thomas Y. Crowell, 1975), Introduction. I discuss some metaphysical and methodological issues concerning multiple realization in 'Multiple realization and the metaphysics of reduction', *Philosophy and Phenomenological Research* 53 (1992), 1–26.

15   For details see my 'Concepts of supervenience', *Philosophy and Phenomenological Research* 45 (1984), 153–76, and ' "Strong" and "global" supervenience revisited', *Philosophy and Phenomenological Research* 48 (1987), 315–26.

16   For more details see my 'Psychophysical supervenience as a mind–body theory', *Cognition and Brain Theory* 5 (1983), 129–47; and 'Concepts of supervenience'.

17   J. Fodor, 'Making mind matter more', *Journal of Philosophy* 84 (1987), 642.

18   McLaughlin, 'Type epiphenomenalism, type dualism, and the causal priority of the physical'.

19   Horgan, 'Mental quasation'.

20   McLaughlin discusses various issues involving supervenience. He might in fact favor the supervenience option as I described it above; however, I am not clear about this.

21   'Mind matters', pp. 634–5 (emphasis added).

22   Loewer has pointed out to me that the entailment does not hold under their formal definition of 'relevance$_2$'. Here I am going by the intuitive motivating considerations in the quoted passage above for the two relevance relations; this seems to me the appropriate thing to do, given my overall aims in this chapter.

23   As he calls it in 'The explanatory role of content'. However, the problem to which he offers a solution is not the Davidsonian problem of anomalism but the problem of syntacticalism.

24   After S.P. Stich's 'syntactic theory of the mind'; see his *From Folk Psychology to Cognitive Science* (Cambridge, Mass., MIT Press, 1983).

25   After Fodor, 'Methodological solipsism considered as a research strategy in cognitive science', reprinted in Fodor, *Representations* (Cambridge, Mass., MIT Press, 1981).

26   See H. Putnam, 'The meaning of "meaning"', *Mind, Language, and Reality: Philosophical Papers*, vol. 2 (Cambridge, Cambridge University Press, 1975); Stich, 'Autonomous psychology and the belief-desire thesis', *The Monist* 61 (1978),

571–91; T. Burge, 'Individualism and the mental', *Midwest Studies in Philosophy* 4 (1979), 73–121.

27   Here I am referring only to the problem Fodor tackles in the piece cited in n. 17. As the reference to him in n. 25 shows, Fodor has been very much concerned with the problem of syntacticalism or solipsism.

28   A similar idea was worked out in detail by some earlier writers, though Dretske develops it in a distinctive way; see, e.g. G.H. von Wright, *Explanation and Understanding* (Ithaca, Cornell University Press, 1971); R.M. Chisholm, *Person and Object* (LaSalle, Illinois, Open Court, 1976).

29   I take up some of them in 'Dretske on how reasons explain behavior', in B. McLaughlin (ed.), *Dretske and his Critics*, pp. 52–72 (Oxford, Basil Blackwell, 1991).

30   Compare, e.g. von Wright, *Explanation and Understanding*.

31   Cambridge, Mass., MIT Press, 1981. See also his 'Misrepresentation' in R. Bogdan (ed.), *Belief* (Oxford, Oxford University Press, 1986).

32   W.E. Seager argues that weak psycho-physical supervenience is strong enough in 'Weak supervenience and materialism', *Philosophy and Phenomenological Research* 48 (1988), 697–710.

33   Technical details need to be worked out. I believe Barry Loewer first mentioned to me the possibility of developing such a notion.

34   Compare L.H. Davis, *Theory of Action* (Englewood Cliffs, NJ, Prentice-Hall, 1979); J. Hornsby, *Actions* (London, Routledge & Kegan Paul, 1980).

35   At least, not in a direct way; it is possible to consider a belief–desire pair as indirectly rationalizing a physical behavior by rationalizing the intention that is executed by the behavior.

36   This is perhaps less drastic than it may sound; for the causal transactions being denied are those between mental and physical properties, not necessarily between 'token' mental events and 'token' physical events.

37   'Actions, reasons, and causes', reprinted in *Essays on Actions and Events*.

38   See, e.g. J. Haugeland, 'The nature and plausibility of cognitivism' and 'Semantic engines: an introduction to mind design', in J. Haugeland (ed.) *Mind Design* (Cambridge, Mass., MIT Press, 1981); and Cummins's 'Comments on Dretske', in Grimm and Merrill (eds.), *Contents of Thought*.

39   Compare Dretske's critique of certain views associated with AI and computer simulation of behavior, in *Explaining Behavior*, pp. 81–2.

40   I explore the possibility of such an account in 'Epiphenomenal and supervenient causation', *Midwest Studies in Philosophy* 9 (1984), 257–70.

8

Reply: Causal Relevance and Explanatory Exclusion

Frederick Dretske

Kim is right. As he often is. Adopting a dual explananda strategy solves some problems, not others. In particular, it does not solve the explanatory exclusion problem. For that one needs stronger medicine.

I agree with this diagnosis. In *Explaining Behavior* (1988), I took great pains to distinguish bodily movement from the behavior having that movement as its product. The purpose of this distinction was to identify the sort of thing that reasons are supposed to explain. Only if we know what behavior *is* can we hope to assess the chances of its being explained by what we believe and desire. None the less, even if one agrees that behavior is a process, not to be identified with the events (including bodily movement) that are its product, one still has the task of describing how rational explanations of this process, explanations in terms of what we believe and desire, comport with physical explanations of the same process. As long as what reasons are called upon to explain is a physical phenomenon of some sort – and thus (for a materialist) explicable (if explicable at all) in physical terms – we will have questions about explanatory exclusion. Insisting (as I do) that what reasons are called upon to explain in the case of bodily behavior is not the occurrence of bodily movement (M) but behavior, a causal process (C→M) having movement as its product, will not make these questions go away.[1]

Nevertheless, changing the explanandum, though it does not answer all questions, certainly helps answer some. One of the problems it helps with is something we might (following Kim's lead) call the 'explanatory relevance problem'. Since it is important to distinguish the problem of explanatory relevance from the problem of explanatory exclusion (lest a good solution to one be mistaken for a bad solution to the other), let me describe the problem of explanatory relevance and the way the distinction between behavior and movements helps with it. I will then return to the problem of explanatory exclusion.

Explanatory Relevance

There is a sense in which diaphragms (in microphones and ears, for example) obey us when we tell them to vibrate rapidly. But the sense in which they 'obey' us does not exhibit a causal relevance for meaning. It isn't *what* we tell the microphone to do (= content or meaning), but the sounds we produce in telling it to do it, that explains why it vibrates. The sounds we produce *have* a meaning, of course, but this meaning is not causally relevant to the result. The microphone does what we tell it to do, yes; it vibrates rapidly and that is what we tell it to do. There is even a sense in which it does this as a result of our telling it to do it. Telling it to vibrate (at least the sound one produces *in* telling it to vibrate) *causes* it to vibrate. This, however, does not make a microphone an obedient instrument. Obedience requires more; it requires doing A *because* one is told to do A. That is something the microphone does not do.

The same is true of thought. Even if an animal has thoughts and these thoughts cause it to do things, the animal may not do what it does because it thinks what it does. *What* it thinks, the content of its internal states, may be causally irrelevant to the behavior. If so, then from the point of view of understanding why the animal does what it does, the animal may just as well not think at all. This animal's behavior may no more be under the control of thought – hence, no more to be explained by *what* the animal thinks – than is the microphone's behavior to be understood in terms of *what* we tell it to do.

So it is not enough to have content-bearing events – whether they be words or thoughts – cause movement. That is easy. We can get microphones to do that. We want content itself – what we think and say – to be part of the explanation. Until we understand the part that content plays in these explanations, we will not really understand the way thought is related to action. This is not so easy.

The reason it is not so easy is because on almost everyone's conception of what content is, or where it comes from, the content of a thought is an extrinsic (relational) property of the thought. What makes event C in someone's brain *mean* (truly or falsely, as the case may be) that condition F exists (thereby qualifying for the belief or thought that F) is not something about its *intrinsic* character. It is not something one could discover by poking around *inside* the skull where the beliefs are. That would be like trying to discover what words mean by subjecting the sounds to acoustical analysis. No, what gives something its representational character, what makes it into a belief, is something *extrinsic* to whatever has this content, something about the way it is related to other things.

If this is, indeed, the right general approach to content (and I do not know of any serious alternatives) then, as Kim correctly notes, the explanatory role of content is jeopardized. The problem is not how anomalous properties can be relevant to behavior. That may be Davidson's problem, but it is not my problem. For I do not think content is anomalous. I think it is relational. So I have the problem of saying how *relational* properties can be relevant to behavior.

It is the threatened epiphenomenalism of relational content that the dual explananda strategy counters. It does so in the following way. Even if causality is local, even if:

(1)   the effects of C depend exclusively on the intrinsic properties of C;

and even if content is relational:

(2)   the content of C is an extrinsic property of C,

it does not follow that content is causally irrelevant to behavior. That depends on whether behavior is an effect of thought. (1) and (2) become a genuine threat to the causal relevance of content *only if* one accepts the (Davidsonian) idea that the way reasons explain behavior is by causing behavior. If, though, one does not accept this equation, if one distinguishes between behavior (what thought explains) and bodily movements (what thought causes), the threat evaporates.

There are, to be sure, strategies for neutralizing this threat without adopting the view that behavior is a process that is not caused by the reasons that explain it. But they all pay a price that I am not willing to bear. If they are not, like anomalous monism or methodological solipsism, driven to epiphenomenalism about (broad) content (which I take to be epiphenomenalism about content *period*), they must either reject (1) or (2). I regard (2) as obvious, *as* obvious as anything ever gets in philosophy. So rejecting it is not an option for me. Frankly, I don't see how it can be an option for anyone. Since (1) is less obvious, there is a temptation to fiddle with it. Kim describes some of the recent fiddling. It is, I admit, hard to formulate (1) in a crisp way. There are, I realize, counter-examples to my crude formulation. In particular, one has to be careful about specifying what is to count as an 'effect'. If one describes an effect in such a way as to require (logically) the cause to have a certain extrinsic property, then (1) may turn out false. Suppose, for example, that one only acquires legal ownership of an item if one purchases it with genuine (= non-counterfeit) currency. Then two events can be imagined to be the same in all intrinsic respects (the one event involves the transfer of genuine money, the other a transfer of perfect counterfeit) while having different effects. In the one case (where real money is used) the result is legal ownership. In the other case not. So different 'effects' are produced by events that are intrinsically the same. So, contrary to (1), extrinsic properties *are* causally relevant.

Examples like these have an obvious fishy quality to them. None the less, they point up the need to formulate (1) in a more careful way. I will not here make the effort.[2] Given reasonable and, I think, plausible restrictions on what is to count as the effects of an event (excluding descriptions that logically require the cause to have certain extrinsic properties), I think (1) is as acceptable as (2). At any rate, I accept both (1) and (2). That is my cake. The only way I know how to have this cake and eat it too is by distinguishing between the movements (M) reasons cause and the behavior (C→M) they explain.[3]

Incidentally, (1) is fully compatible with the transitivity of causality and, hence, with the existence of remote causes. If A causes B, and B causes C, then A is a cause, a more remote (than B) cause of C. But the causal relevance (to C) of A does not make *B's being caused by A* (an extrinsic property of B) a causally relevant (to C) property of B. For even if B did not have this property,[4] it would, assuming it retained all the same intrinsic properties, still cause C. The intrinsic properties of B 'screen off' all the (non-essential) extrinsic properties of B from causal relevance (to C). Thus, even if A, the cause of B, is causally relevant to C, A's being the cause of B (this extrinsic property of B) is not itself a causally relevant (to C) property of B.

The distinction between bodily movements and behavior does not imply that reasons are not causes. Of course they are. Why else have them? In the case of behavior having movement as its product, though, what they cause is not behavior but movement. The content of thought, being an extrinsic property of the thought, is thus causally irrelevant to what my arm does (moves) when I raise it, but it is not thereby causally irrelevant to what *I* do (move it) when I raise it. What I do, the behavior that reasons are called upon to explain, is distinct from the movement required for me to do it. What reasons (C) cause (i.e. M), and what the content of these reasons (the fact that C has the content F) explains (C→M), are two different things. By thus identifying behavior with a causal process having movement as its product, we satisfy both (1) and (2): only C's intrinsic properties are relevant to M, but its extrinsic properties (and, thus, its content) are relevant to its causing M.

In Dretske (1988) I tried to describe how content acquires an explanatory role in certain learning episodes. I will not repeat that story here. I will only review a few high points in order to emphasize some important explanatory benefits achieved by this way of understanding behavior.[5]

We have a system, S, that needs to produce movement M when condition F exists nearby. S has the 'sensory' powers to detect nearby occurrences of F. By this I mean, among other things (but these other things are not here relevant), that an internal state of S – call it C – is normally activated by (and only by) nearby Fs. The solution to S's coordination problem (making M occur when F exists) is thus solvable. C must be made into a switch for M. That is, C must be 'wired' to effector mechanisms in such a way that an active C (indicating the presence of condition F) causes M. If S is some artifact, we (designers and builders) can do this for S. We simply wire the C-detector to the M-effector so that an active C will produce M. If S is a living organism, capable of learning, the re-structuring of S can happen without anyone's help. Through a process of learning, S starts to produce M when it senses F. The only way such learning can occur (and it occurs every day) is if S's control circuits are re-structured by learning so that an active C becomes a cause of M.

All this is history. It is now Thursday morning. Condition F occurs. S senses it and promptly produces M. What causes M? An active C. M occurs because C is active. C's activity indicates the presence of F, to be sure, but it is C's activity, not its indication of F, that *explains* the occurrence of M. To convince yourself of this, try activating C (with a handy screwdriver or a micro-electrode) when C fails to indicate the existence of condition F (e.g. when F does not exist). M will occur anyway. It is the activation of C, an intrinsic condition of C, not C's extrinsic properties (its being, or its having been, an F indicator) that explains M's occurrence.[6] If C's content is bound up with its extrinsic properties, with (in this case) its indication (past or present) of condition F, then C's content is irrelevant to why M occurs.

But C's content, though irrelevant to why movement M occurs, is not irrelevant to why, on the present construal of behavior, S *behaves* the way it does. If S's behavior is not the M S produces, but S's *producing* it (i.e. C's activity causing M), then extrinsic facts about C – and in particular the indicational facts about C – are relevant to why S is behaving this way. They are relevant because, given the developmental history of the animal (see above), the fact that, when things are working right, an active C indicates F is part of the explanation of why C was wired in the way it was, thus making an active C into a cause of M. The fact that C is an F-indicator, this extrinsic fact about C, can be a legitimate part of the explanation of why C is causing M *without* being a part of the explanation of why M occurs. This is especially evident in the 'twin' systems I describe in chapter 6. Physically indistinguishable systems will have the same cause for their M's (outputs) but not for their C→M's (their behavior).

By distinguishing behavior from the bodily movements required for its occurrence, by distinguishing C's causing M from M, we make available for the explanation of behavior the extrinsic facts about our internal states (C) that underlie their content (that make C *of* or *about* condition F). This is one of the benefits of (but not the only reason for) adopting a dual explananda strategy: the strategy of distinguishing what reasons explain (behavior) but do not cause from what reasons cause (bodily movements) but do not (*qua* reasons) explain. We can let neurobiology explain bodily movements; content is available to explain a different set of facts.

Since the point has been cited as an objection to my account,[7] I cannot forbear a brief observation about the temporal aspects of behavior explanations. To say that the Duke rose from his chair when the Queen entered the room in order to show respect is to explain (in terms of the Duke's purposes) why he rose from his chair. He wanted to show respect for the Queen and he thought he could do so by rising. Such reasons explain why he then *rose*, not why he rose *then*. If you want to know why he rose *then*, at that particular time, the explanation will presumably be in terms of what caused him to believe, at that particular time, that the Queen was entering the room. What will explain this will be, let us suppose, some fact about the Queen's entrance or the Duke's perception of her entry. It will consist of an explanation of why the Duke thought *then* that the Queen was entering the room. This is quite a different explanation from the reasons given for his standing (when she entered the room).

This point is neatly captured on a process view of behavior. It is, in fact, the distinction between what I call a triggering and a structuring cause of behavior. In explaining why a process (C→M) is occurring, we can either be explaining what triggered the process (what caused the C *which* causes M) or what structured it (what caused C *to* cause M). Reasons are normally *structuring* explanations of behavior. They tell us why the Duke's belief that the Queen is entering the room causes the movements it does, not why he has that belief at that particular time.

Explanatory Exclusion

This, though, leaves me with Kim's question about explanatory exclusion. I have changed the explanandum – what reasons are called upon to explain – but I haven't eliminated it. So how does a reason-based explanation of behavior (C's causing M) comport with, say, a physical explanation of the same fact (process)?

Kim suggests that what might do the job for me is the program I started in *Knowledge and the Flow of Information*, the project of providing a physicalistic reduction of intentionality. If content can be reduced to (identified with), or at least made to supervene on (in some tight enough way) a type of physical condition, then there would be no competition, nothing to exclude. An explanation in terms of reasons would *be* a physical explanation.

Once again, Kim is right, not only about what is needed, but (if this was his intention) about the position I adopt in order to satisfy this need. I agree with Kim (p. 135) that as long as rationalizations are taken as causal explanations, supervenience (of which reduction is a special case) is the only viable solution to the exclusion problem. I said in *Explaining Behavior* that if my body and I are not to march off in different directions when I go to the kitchen in order to get a drink, my *reasons* for going to the kitchen must either *be*, or be intimately related to, those events in my central nervous system that cause my limbs to move so as to bring me into the kitchen. I think, in fact, that reasons (in the sense of those things that have content) *are* states of the central nervous system. But their content, what it is we want and believe, what it is that makes these internal states into the beliefs and desires they are, is not itself reducible to (nor does it supervene on) a state or condition of the nervous system. Content, after all, is extrinsic. If it reduces to anything, it reduces to some set of physical relations existing between what is inside the head and what is outside. This is a *type-type* identity theory, but not the classic (Smart–Feigl) identity between a type of mental state (e.g. the belief that F) and a type of brain state, but, rather, an identity between intentional content and the set of external relations that give brain states their representational character. This is reductionism, yes, but (if you please) *wide* reductionism. Wide reductionism does not (see Kim, p. 127) sacrifice the benefits of functionalism. Multiple realizability remains. Tokens of quite different types of brains state can possess the same *extrinsic* properties defining content. Hence, different brain states can be the same belief. Beliefs may be in the head, but (echoing Putnam) what makes them the beliefs they are isn't in there. *Any* internal state can serve as a representation of F, as a belief that F. As long as this internal state stands in the right physical relations to the right conditions, it will qualify as a representation of, and thus a belief that, F.

What are the 'right' relations, the ones that convert internal states into representations? According to the naturalized theory of representation I offered in Dretske (1988), an improvement (or so I think) of the one began in Dretske (1981), an active C represents an external object, x, as being F if it is C's function (acquired in learning) to indicate the F-condition of things and it is, in the present instance, performing its function, doing its job, with respect to x. When C does not do its job (sometimes even when it *is* doing its job – the fault may lie elsewhere) C will be active when x is not F. In this case C misrepresents x as being F. C has the job of 'reporting' on the F-condition of such objects and the way it does its job, the way it reports that they are F, is by becoming active. So an active C is C's way of representing x as F. This state of C *says* that x is F whether or not x is F, whether or not what it says is true. That x is F is, therefore, the content, the meaning (Grice's non-natural meaning), of an active C.

Is this a naturalized theory of representation? Is it really a physical reduction of intentionality? That depends, of course, on how 'natural' are the elements to which the reduction is made. The key ingredients in this recipe are *indication* and *function*: an element becomes an F representation (representing things *as* F) if it has the function of indicating that they are F. The idea of indication is, of course, merely another way of talking about the information an event or condition carries about another, and about this relation I have said all that I can usefully say. Information and indication are relations (between token events or states) that manifest (in the circumstances in which the tokens occur) objective (nomic) dependencies between the types of which they are tokens. If there are such objective dependencies (I do not think physics makes much sense if there isn't), then there must be information in my sense of the word. Information – and, hence, indication – in this purified sense, constitutes an acceptable basis for reductionistic theories of the mind. At least it presupposes no more about the world than does a materialistic picture of the world as governed, either wholly or in part, by natural laws.

The idea of *function* may be more problematic. I none the less assume (pending more convincing objections than I have yet heard) that organs can have functions independent of our explanatory and intentional stances towards them. If the heart and kidneys have a function that they acquired in their evolutionnary development, then I see no reason to think that the perceptual systems (for example) do not also have a function – an information supplying function – a function they acquired in their evolutionary history. I also see no reason to think that information providing (or using) functions, the sort of functions underlying representation (as defined above) might not also develop during the life of individual organisms – in those learning episodes wherein an organism acquires the capacity to use sensory information for the guidance of purposeful behavior. It is, in fact, the developed (during learning) functions – what I call the ontogenetic functions – that I take to be characteristic of conceptual phenomena, i.e. of reasons (both belief and desire).[8]

I do not argue for these claims. I have done that elsewhere. I merely state what the strategy is. My purpose is not to defend the naturalistic reduction, but to acknowledge that that, indeed, is what it is: a naturalistic reduction. Since both what a state indicates and what it has the function of indicating are construed as *bona fide* physical notions, explanations of behavior by appeal to content (what we believe) are explanations of behavior by *bona fide* physical facts, those constituting the indicator functions of our internal states. Explanatory exclusion, therefore, is not a problem. We do not risk (what Kim describes as) 'the closedness of the physical domain' by letting content explain behavior. Content is already *in* the physical domain.

Things are not quite that simple. They never are. I have identified intentional (at least representational) content with a structure's (natural) indicator function. And I have identified behavior (at least intentional behavior, the sort of behavior that reasons are supposed to explain) with a causal process having (in the first instance)[9] bodily movements as its product. But just how is this supposed to work? How is C's having an indicator function, the function of indicating F (say), supposed to explain C's causing bodily movement M: the person's (intentional) behavior? We may not have an *exclusion* problem anymore, but we seem to have developed an *explanatory* problem: how does one physical fact, the one with which belief is identified, explain the other, the one with which behavior is identified?

These are good questions, questions that deserve answers, but they are *different* questions from those I have undertaken to answer in this Reply. Kim (1991) and others[10] have pressed this question in other places. I have tried to answer in Dretske (1988, 1991a, b). I will not repeat myself here.

Notes

1 Since Kim and I use a number of different abbreviatory schemes, the notation can get confusing. In this reply, I choose to use the scheme that I used throughout *Explaining Behavior*. In the case of simple bodily behaviors (moving one's arm, winking), M stands for the bodily movement in question (the movement of one's arm or eye lid), C for an internal (to the behaver) event of some sort, and C→M (C's causing M) for a causal process having M as its product. When the behavior, C's causing M, is intentional (an action), C is a belief–desire complex. Since the

role of desire is being ignored in this exchange, C may be thought of (in the case of action) as a belief. In order to avoid unnecessary distractions I also ignore behavior that has events and conditions other than bodily movements as its product (e.g. closing the door, buying a car).

2   For a reasonable try, see Fodor in chapter 11 of this volume.

3   I hope it is clear that I am exploiting an ambiguity when I speak of reasons (beliefs and desires) causing movements on the one hand and explaining behavior on the other. In speaking of beliefs (S's belief that F, for example) we can be referring to either that which has content F (the believing, as it were) or the fact that it has that content (what it is that is believed). In speaking of beliefs as causes, I am speaking of the internal state that has content F. When I speak of reasons as explanations I am speaking of the *fact* that this state has content F, i.e. the fact that S believes that F.

4   Something that is always possible as long as being caused by A is not an *essential* property of B. In this case, though, we are back to the case discussed above: the case where the cause of C (namely, B) is understood to logically require its having a certain extrinsic property (being caused by A).

5   It has been argued by Fred Adams (1991) and others that I can achieve these benefits without distinguishing behavior from the movements (events) required for its occurrence. If one makes a distinction between explanatory sets (explaining why M occurred rather than not-M, on the one hand, and explaining why M occurred rather than Q or S on the other) a similar result can be achieved. I think this is probably true. I none the less continue to make the distinction. A solution to the problem of causal relevance (of content) is a benefit of, not my reason for, making the distinction between movement and behavior. See my response to Adams in Dretske (1991a).

6   The fact that C indicated (in the past) F is not even among the remote causes of M. The fact that C indicated F did not cause C to be active on this Thursday morning. F did.

7   See, for example, L. Baker (1991) and T. Horgan (1991).

8   I did not make this fact clear in the original appearance of 'Does Meaning Matter?' (Chapter 2) in Villanueva (1990). Dennett (1990) (my commentator at the Mexico conference) criticized me on this point. So did Fodor (1990). I thought my position was sufficiently clear from Dretske (1988) and did not bother to emphasize the critical importance I attach to learning. Beliefs are not merely internal representations. They are internal representations whose content helps explain behavior. Representations whose indicator function derives from natural selection (e.g. the senses) have a content, but the content does not help explain behavior (although the representations themselves may *cause* bodily movements). They do not, therefore, qualify as beliefs.

9   In the second instance, of course, there will be more remote effects (doors closing, windows opening, gears changing, etc). Of course, many behaviors do not require any specific bodily movement (or, perhaps, no bodily movement at all). I restrict myself to the simplest possible behaviors (what might be called basic actions) in this discussion. For details, see Dretske, 1988, chapters 1 and 2.

10 See, for example, Dennett (1990); Baker (1991); Cummins (1991); Horgan (1991).

References

Adams, F. (1991) Causal contents. In B. McLaughlin (ed.), *Dretske and his Critics*, pp. 131–56. Oxford, Basil Blackwell.

Baker, L.R. (1991) Dretske on the explanatory role of belief. *Philosophical Studies*, 63.

Cummins, R. (1991) The role of mental meaning in psychological explanation. In B. McLaughlin (ed.), *Dretske and his Critics*, pp. 102–18. Oxford, Basil Blackwell.

Dennett, D. (1990) Ways of establishing harmony. In E. Villanueva (ed.) *Information, Semantics and Epistemology*, pp. 119–30. Oxford, Basil Blackwell.

Dretske, F. (1981) *Knowledge and the Flow of Information*. Cambridge, Mass., MIT Press.

Dretske, F. (1988) *Explaining Behavior: Reasons on a World of Causes*. Cambridge, Mass., MIT Press.

Dretske, F. (1991a) Replies. In B. McLaughlin (ed.) *Dretske and his Critics*, pp. 180–221. Oxford, Basil Blackwell.

Dretske, F. (1991b) How beliefs explain: reply to Baker. *Philosophical Studies* 62, 1–5.

Fodor, J. (1990) Reply to Dretske's 'Does meaning matter?' In E. Villanueva (ed.), *Information, Semantics and Epistemology*, pp. 28–35. Oxford, Basil Blackwell.

Horgan, T. (1991) Actions, reasons, and the explanatory role of content. In B. McLaughlin (ed.), *Dretske and his Critics*, pp. 73–101. Oxford, Basil Blackwell.

Kim, J. (1991) Dretske on how reasons explain behavior. In B. McLaughlin (ed.), *Dretske and his Critics*, pp. 52–72. Oxford, Basil Blackwell.

McLaughlin, B. (ed.) (1991) *Dretske and his Critics*. Oxford, Basil Blackwell.

Villanueva, E. (ed.) (1990) *Information, Semantics and Epistemology*. Oxford, Basil Blackwell.

PART II

Anti-individualism and
Psychological Explanation

9

Introduction: Anti-individualism and Psychological Explanation

Cynthia Macdonald

How ought mental kinds to be individuated – to be determined and distinguished from one another – for the purposes of a scientific psychology? Ought they to be individuated, as are the kinds of other natural sciences such as physics, in terms of their causal powers? Or are other factors, distinctive to the kinds of psychology, relevant to how they ought to be individuated? In either case, will the individuation of intentional kinds, like the kind, *believes that water is wet*, depend on factors extrinsic to subjects' bodies, factors in the environment of those subjects, such as the presence of water? Or will the individuation of intentional kinds be independent of such factors? These questions lie at the heart of what is known as the individualism/anti-individualism debate.

Anti-individualism about the mind is a view about how certain mental kinds, intentional ones like the kind, *believes that water is wet*, are determined to be what they are for the purposes of a scientific psychology; how they are correctly individuated.[1] It is the view that these kinds have contentful natures that depend on and are in part determined by factors external to subjects' bodies (Burge, 1979, 1982). A subject's belief that water is wet has a content that depends on the existence, in the world of the subject, of water. Accordingly, a subject cannot have a belief about water in a world in which there is no water. Similarly for beliefs about aluminium, salt, tigers and other natural kinds of substances.[2]

The roots of anti-individualism about the mind stems from the work of Hilary Putnam, who was concerned to establish a claim, not specifically about the nature of intentional kinds, but about the nature of meaning (Putnam, 1975). Putnam argued that one's meaning what one does by a natural kind term, such as 'water', although intuitively a state of mind, is 'world-involving'.[3] This is because one's meaning what one does is determined in part by the actual, empirically discoverable, nature of something in the world (e.g. water) external to one's body. By saying that meanings 'ain't in the head', Putnam meant that a person's meaning something by a natural kind term cannot be determined independently of that person's relation to the physical world around her.

Putnam reinforced this claim by employing the now-familiar strategy of twin earth thought experiments. Consider a typical speaker of English who is ignorant of chemical theory. This person, S, correctly uses the term 'water' to apply to a substance with a certain nature, a substance that quenches thirst, fills lakes and rivers, is odourless, colourless, etc. In fact, S uses it to apply to water, which on earth is (although S does not know this) H_2O. Suppose now that there is another world which is physically just like earth except for this difference: in that world the substance that quenches thirst, fills lakes and rivers, and in fact has all of the phenomenological qualities of water, is a substance that has the chemical constitution XYZ and so is not water. This world – call it twin earth – is otherwise physically and superficially indistinguishable from earth. On twin earth there is a person, S*, who is physically indistinguishable (i.e. indistinguishable in all non-intentional behavioural, phenomenal and functional respects, individualistically specified) from S (except for the irrelevant fact that S*'s body contains XYZ where S's body contains H_2O). This is S's twin. Since, on twin earth, there is no water, S* does not mean by 'water' water: on twin earth S* uses 'water' to apply to XYZ. So S and S* mean different things by their indistinguishable utterances. When S utters the words, 'there is water in my glass', S says something that is true on earth and false on twin earth; and when S* utters the words, 'there is water in my glass', S* says something that is true on twin earth and false on earth.

Tyler Burge took the moral of the twin earth thought experiments a stage further. In a series of papers, he argued that since it is normally understood that when a speaker is sincere (i.e. she means what she says), what she says is what she believes, the Putnam conclusion about meaning carries over to intentional mental states such as beliefs, desires, and the like (see Burge, 1979, 1982, 1985a,b). Burge argued that the twin earth thought experiments not only showed that meaning is partly determined by factors external to subjects' bodies, but also that mental states like beliefs, desires, and the like, whose contents are typically specified using terms whose meanings depend on factors external to persons' bodies, are *also* world-involving in this way. So, just as S* on twin earth means something different by the use of 'water' from what S on earth means, S* on twin earth also *believes* something different from what S on earth believes (Burge, 1982). S believes that there is water in her glass, whereas S* believes that there is twater (a substance that behaves exactly like water but which has the chemical constitution XYZ) in her glass.

Anti-individualism poses a threat to a familiar understanding of the psychological. On that understanding, beliefs, desires and other intentional states, being states of mind, depend only on factors that exist within the confines of subjects' bodies. This view has a number of sources. One is the Cartesian belief that the world external to a subject's body might be varied at will without altering the contents of that subject's intentional states.[4] Another is a commitment to the view that mental states supervene on, or are determined by,

physical events and states of the body.[5] This commitment (which is incompatible with anti-individualism) may itself have a number of sources. One plausible
one is that the physical determinants of persons' behaviour (which is, or is
constituted by, bodily movements) appear to lie squarely within the body, in
the sense that these states are not individuation-dependent on factors external
to persons' bodies. Combined with the belief that intentional states cause
persons' bodies to behave as they do, it easily leads to the view that intentional
states are dependent on – are fixed, or determined by – only those within-the-
body physical processes that are involved in the production of behaviour. (One
may feel driven to accept this view irrespective of whether one believes that
mental states are identical with physical states of the body.)

This commitment to within-the-body or 'local' supervenience appears to be
a driving force behind arguments against anti-individualism (see, for example,
Fodor, 1987). Anti-individualism entails the falsity of any within-the-body
supervenience thesis: it has the consequence that two subjects could be
physically identical and yet their mental states might vary only because of
differences in the world external to their bodies. So those who accept local
supervenience are also bound to accept the view known as individualism. Burge
(chapter 10, p. 173) characterizes individualism about the mind as the view
that

> the mental natures of all a person's or animal's mental states (and events) are
> such that there is no necessary or deep individuative relation between the
> individual's being in states of those kinds and the nature of the individual's
> physical or social environments.

Burge and Fodor disagree fundamentally on whether psychology is, or
should be, individualistic. Fodor believes that psychology is committed to
individualism, and he defends this view in a number of his works, most recently
in 'A modal argument for narrow content' (chapter 11). According to Fodor,
all sciences, including psychology, are in the business of causal explanation.
This being so, taxonomy in psychology, as elsewhere, is taxonomy by causal
powers. Since, Fodor argues, differences in the relational properties of
intentional states (i.e. properties which relate subjects' states to factors external
to their bodies) do not affect the causal powers of those states, taxonomy by
causal powers respects local supervenience.[6] Hence psychology is
individualistic.

Burge thinks otherwise. In his view, the causal powers of intentional states
are affected by differences in the relational properties of those states. They are
affected in the sense that such differences affect the *individuation* of those
states. Fodor does not see this because he thinks that one can judge sameness
and differences of causal powers of intentional states independently of
assumptions concerning what intentional kinds they are. But Fodor, Burge
argues, is mistaken here: judgements about causal powers can only be made
against the background of assumptions concerning the kinds in question.

At the heart of the dispute between Burge and Fodor is the question of whether taxonomy by causal powers in psychology is individualistic or non-individualistic. Whereas Fodor maintains that taxonomy by causal powers is both necessary and sufficient to determine psychological kinds, Burge claims that taxonomy by causal powers is not independent of assumptions about the kinds in question. It is against this background that the dispute over the twin earth cases arises. Fodor argues that differences in intentional behaviour between, say, S, who reaches for water, and S*, who reaches for twater, are not *relevant* to psychological taxonomy, since these differences do not make for a difference in causal powers of S's water thoughts and S*'s twater thoughts (this despite the fact that sameness and difference of causal powers is to be judged by actual and potential behaviour across contexts). Burge, on the other hand, argues that since judgements as to the causal powers of S's intentional states and S*'s intentional states – what behaviour they are apt to produce – depend on what kinds of psychological states they are, and this depends on factors extrinsic to their bodies, S's and S*'s intentional states differ in their causal powers. That is to say, their intentional states are apt to produce different intentional behaviour *because* they are of different psychological kinds.

Both Burge and Fodor assume that the twin earth thought experiments are of critical importance to the individualism/anti-individualism debate. However, it is not entirely clear what role they play in the debate. To what extent is passing – or failing – a twin earth test of some kind decisive either for or against individualism? Fodor also assumes that, for the purposes of a scientific psychology, taxonomy of psychological kinds is taxonomy by causal powers. But as the brief discussion above of Burge's argument indicates, it is unclear whether this is all that matters to psychological taxonomy. Is taxonomy by causal powers necessary and sufficient for the determination of psychological kinds? This question is not independent of (a) whether psychological explanation is causal explanation; and further, (b) whether all sicences are in the business of causal explanation. Fodor's position on this issue is clear; Burge's is less so. Below I shall attempt to address some of these issues and questions.

The Role of Twin Earth Thought Experiments

Burge's arguments for anti-individualism rely heavily on the use of twin earth thought experiments. In Chapter 10 these experiments are employed as a test for whether psychology is, or should be, individualistic. Burge's purpose in this chapter is twofold. First, he aims to discredit certain arguments for the claim that all of psychology is, or should be, individualistic. Secondly, he aims to show, with specific reference to David Marr's computational theory of vision (Marr, 1982) and by means of a twin earth test, that some parts of psychology are anti-individualistic. With regard to both of these aims, his central claim is that

Questions of what exists, how things are individuated, and what reduces to what, are questions that arise by reference to going explanatory and descriptive practices. By themselves, proposed answers to these questions cannot be used to criticize an otherwise successful mode of explanation and description. (Chapter 10, p. 183)

Burge's reply to Fodor in the debate below (see Chapter 12) emphasizes the point that questions concerning the distinctive causal powers of psychological kinds must be answered against the background of existing explanatory and descriptive practices in psychology.

Burge discusses two main arguments for individualism, beginning with the following:

[1] The behavior of the physiologically and functionally identical protagonists in our thought experiments is identical. But [2] psychology is the science (only) of behavior. [3] Since the behavior of the protagonists is the same, a science of behavior should give the *same* explanations and descriptions of the two cases . . . [4] So there is no room in the discipline for explaining their behavior in terms of different mental states. (Chapter 10, p. 178)

Burge thinks that [1], [2] and [3] are problematic.

He claims that [1] either ignores actual psychological practice or simply begs the question against anti-individualism on one clear understanding of 'behaviour' that is relevant to the debate, viz. intentional behaviour or action. Many descriptions of behaviour in psychology are intentional and also non-individualistic. Subjects reach out for objects, point to them, and so on. It is true that there are many non-individualistic descriptions of behaviour that are not suitable for explanatory purposes in psychology (Burge's example is 'my friend's favourite bodily movement'), but these do not in general appear to figure in psychological descriptions and explanations. Again, [2] ignores actual psychological explanatory practice. Some parts of psychology, for example, cognitive psychology, appear not to have as their subject matter behaviour (even intentional behaviour) but rather certain cognitive capacities (such as those involved in memory and vision), which seem to involve intentional states, non-individualistically understood. And when certain theories in cognitive psychology, for example, theories of vision, *are* understood as being about behaviour, they seem to be concerned, at least in part, with relations between organisms and their environment. In short, [2] is doubtful for two reasons. First, the subject matter of psychology seems to include not only behaviour but also intentional states, non-individualistically understood; and secondly, even where it does involve behaviour, it seems to involve relations between organisms and their environment and so does not support individualism. Finally, [3] is dubious because it is unclear why a science such as psychology must offer the same explanations for the same behaviour, especially in cases where the behaviour arose in different circumstances.

This argument, and Burge's assessment of it, is important to the present debate because of its emphasis on the relevance of behaviour to the question of whether psychology is, or should be, individualistic. Whether the subject matter of psychology is behaviour (only) Burge thinks doubtful; but more important for his purposes is that, even where it is, such behaviour (intentional and also non-intentional) is in many parts of psychology understood relationally (i.e. non-individualistically). In so far as behaviour is relevant to the question of how mental kinds are or should be taxonomized for the purposes of a scientific psychology, Burge's criticisms here connect directly with Fodor's modal argument for individualism and with Burge's reply to it. I shall return to this issue in the next section.

Burge addresses a second argument which is similar to that referred to above as a general source of the motivation for individualism and which is also relevant to Fodor's position. It is that 'the determinants of behavior supervene on states of the brain . . . So if the propositional attitudes are to be treated as among the determinants of behavior, they must be taken to supervene on brain states. The alternative is to take propositional attitudes as behaviorally irrelevant (Chapter 10, pp. 179–80). Burge's response is that the argument can be 'turned on its head': since propositional attitudes are determinants of behaviour and propositional attitudes don't supervene on brain states, some determinants of behaviour do not supervene on brain states. It thus begs the question against anti-individualism. Burge also wishes to make some metaphysical and epistemological points about the argument.

The first point is that supervenience doesn't buy much in the way of ontological conclusions, since what supervenes on what depends on how things are individuated.[7] The second point is that the argument seems to purchase what plausibility it has by conflating issues concerning individuation with issues concerning causation. Causation is local; a person's intentional states and behaviour can only be affected by items in her environment in so far as those items affect her body. But this does not show that anti-individualism is false. One might think it does because, in the twin earth experiments, all physical and non-intentional facts about S and S* remain the same, while S*'s intentional states differ from S's in a way that makes for a difference in their intentional behaviour. This makes it look as though one's mental states can affect one's behaviour in a way that by-passes one's physiology entirely. But, argues Burge, this is not so. Objects and events in a subject's environment cannot affect – cause – her mental events or behaviour without causing events in her body. However, differences in those objects or events can affect – individuate – the information that is transmitted by those bodily events, and so can affect – individuate – intentional content. That is to say, such differences in information will make for an individuative difference in the intentional content of the subject's mental states and hence will make for differences in those states' causal powers. But they will not make for differences in the causal powers of the bodily events considered *as* physical events. *Their* (physical) causal-power taxonomy will remain unaffected by such informational differences.[8]

The third and final point is that the argument relies on a metaphysical conjecture – local supervenience – that is independent of, and ungrounded in, particular cases of actual explanatory and descriptive practices in psychology. It is, Burge argues, both revisionist (as Fodor, 1987, expressly concedes) and *aprioristic*. However, the questions of what psychological kinds there are and how they are to be individuated must be answered against the background of explanatory practices of psychology.

A central point that emerges from Burge's discussion of these two arguments for individualism is the importance of careful interpretation of actual explanatory and descriptive practices in psychology in adjudicating between individualism and anti-individualism. It is Burge's view that the interpretation of such practices reveals the taxonomy of behaviour (both intentional and non-intentional) and the taxonomy of intentional states in certain parts of psychology to be non-individualistic. The interpretation of such practices, in failing to respect local supervenience, is in keeping with the twin earth thought experiments.

Burge pushes this point home by reference to a specific example, Marr's computational theory of vision, where the twin earth thought experiments play a more prominent role in the argument for anti-individualism. Specifically, these experiments are employed as a test of whether psychology is individualistic. According to the test, a psychological theory is individualistic if and only if it fails to distinguish the types of intentional states that physically identical twins are capable of having in accordance with differences in their environments.[9] That is to say, it is both necessary and sufficient for a theory to be individualistic that it fails to discriminate between the types of intentional states of physically identical twins. Burge applies this test to Marr's theory and claims that, since the theory would distinguish the types of intentional states of physically identical twins, it is anti-individualistic.

We are now in a position to argue that the theory is not individualistic:

1 The theory is intentional.
2 The intentional primitives of the theory and the information they carry are individuated by reference to contingently existing physical items or conditions by which they are normally caused and to which they normally apply.
3 So if these physical conditions and, possibly, attendent physical laws were regularly different, the information conveyed to the subject and the intentional content of his or her visual representations would be different.
4 It is not incoherent to conceive of relevantly different physical conditions and perhaps relevantly different (say, optical) laws regularly causing the same non-intentionally, individualistically individuated physical regularities in the subject's eyes and nervous system. It is enough if the differences are small; they need not be wholesale.
5 In such a case (by (3)) the individual's visual representations would carry different information and have different representational content, though the person's whole non-intentional physical history (at least up to a certain time) might remain the same.

6 Assuming that some perceptual states are identified in terms of their informational or intentional content, it follows that individualism is not true for the theory of vision. (Chapter 10, pp. 194–5)

Here it seems that Burge is appealing to the fact that Marr's theory of vision fails the twin earth test for individualism to establish that the theory is non-individualistic.[10]

Later in Chapter 10, a more general argument for anti-individualism is given, again based on a twin earth thought experiment, this time involving cracks and shadows. Suppose that there are, in the actual environment of a subject P, objective features, cracks (Cs) and shadows (Os). Normally P sees instances of Os as Os, and we may suppose that P's perceptual states are intentionally typed as perceptions *of Os* (call this intentional type O'). Occasionally P sees instances of Cs as Os. In these cases P *mistakenly* perceives, or *mis*perceives, a C as an O (since P's perceptual type is intentionally typed with respect to Os, not Cs, and is therefore of type O').

Suppose now that, holding all non-intentional facts about P constant, including discriminative capacities (individualistically characterized), the environment were to differ from the actual one in lacking Os altogether. Then, Burge argues, assuming that the optical laws in this environment explain P's visual representations, not in terms of Os, but in terms of Cs (or some other objective feature), P's visual perceptions would not be of type O'.

Both arguments rely on the use of the twin earth thought experiments to establish their conclusion. However, these experiments are doing no real work in the two arguments (see Shapiro, 1993). Given Burge's characterization of individualism, the first argument simply states that Marr's theory is non-individualistic in premise (2). And the second, more general, argument contains a statement of anti-individualism in its supposition about how P's perceptual states are intentionally typed. So the arguments assume what they purport, by means of the twin earth experiments, to establish.

In a similar vein, Burge (in his reply in Chapter 12) effectively accuses Fodor's use of the twin earth examples of presuming individualism to be true. In 'A modal argument for narrow content' (Chapter 11) Fodor argues that, since whether or not twins have type-identical states depends on whether they have the same causal powers, and since sameness and difference of causal powers must be assessed across contexts rather than within them (causal power being a counterfactual notion), whether twins have type-identical intentional states depends on whether their states have the same causal powers across contexts. Burge agrees, but argues that twin earth considerations cannot determine and distinguish causal powers of intentional kinds because one cannot decide which contexts are relevant for determining and distinguishing causal powers without making assumptions about the kinds in question. To suppose that the actual environment external to subjects' bodies is not relevant to determining causal powers is already to assume individualism.[11]

The moral for the twin earth thought experiments is that they play a more peripheral role in adjudicating between individualism and anti-individualism than discussions would suggest. The reason is that their employment by both Burge and Fodor evidently is not independent of individualistic/anti-individualistic assumptions.

Causal Powers and Psychological Kinds

This leaves us with the question: what *is* decisive in establishing the truth or otherwise of individualism? Fodor and Burge both think that behaviour is decisive. Fodor's emphasis on the role of behaviour is not surprising. Psychological kinds are determined to be what they are by their causal powers and, in particular, by their aptness to produce distinctive types of behaviour. So, same type of behaviour, same causal powers; different types of behaviour, different causal powers. This emerges clearly in the modal argument for narrow content:

1 My twin and I are molecular duplicates.
2 Therefore our (actual and counterfactual) behaviors are identical in relevant respects.
3 Therefore the causal powers of our mental states are identical in relevant respects.
4 Therefore my twin and I belong to the same natural kind for purposes of psychological explanation and 'individualism' is true. (Fodor, Chapter 11, p. 206)

The connection between causal powers and behaviour makes Fodor's arguments vulnerable to the (anti-individualistic) criticism that, because twins' behaviour differs (in the relevant respects, i.e. S reaches for water, whereas S* reaches for twater), their intentional states differ in their causal powers. Differences in behaviour, non-intentionally described, do not matter for Fodor.[12] Consider S who utters the words 'Gimme water'. Being on earth, S gets water. S*, on the other hand, who utters the words 'Gimme water' on twin earth, gets twater. But this does not show that their behaviours, non-intentionally described, are not type-identical.

> The salient consideration is that, if twin-me had uttered 'Gimme water' here, he would have gotten water; and if I had uttered 'Gimme water' on twin earth, I would have gotten twater. To put it slightly differently, my 'Gimme water' does not get water *come what may*; at best it gets water *in certain circumstances*. But in *those* circumstances, his 'Gimme water' gets water too.
> The moral is that you have to judge identity and difference of causal powers in a way that bears the counterfactuals in mind, namely, *across* contexts rather than *within* contexts. (Fodor, Chapter 11, p. 208)

(This is Fodor's counterfactual 'cross-context' test for sameness and differences of causal powers.) However, Fodor sees that this will not work to block anti-individualistic arguments of the kind just mentioned, since when I utter the words 'Gimme water' on earth, I get what I ask for, but when I utter the words 'Gimme water' on twin earth, I do not get what I ask for. Similarly for my twin. Our behaviours, intentionally described as water/twater requests, do not have the same causal powers, even across contexts.

Fodor attempts to save the cross-context test by providing a general characterization of when differences in properties of causes are differences of causal powers. Suppose that we are able to identify certain properties of causes (token or type), *which may or may not be distinctive causal powers*, as ones that are 'responsible' for differences in properties of their effects (this is what Fodor's schema S enables us to do). So, for example, we are able to identify being a *water* thought and being a *twater* thought as properties of water thoughts and twater thoughts that are responsible for differences in properties of intentional behaviour – being *water* behaviour, and being *twater* behaviour, or being a *water* drinking, and being a *twater* drinking. Fodor's question is, when is the difference between causes' having such properties a difference in causal powers, in virtue of being responsible for the difference between properties of their effects (in short, when are these properties of causes causal powers?)[13] His answer is that it is only when these cause properties are *non-conceptually* connected to the effect properties for which they are responsible that they are causal powers. (This is Fodor's condition C on a property's being a distinctive causal power.)

This condition, Fodor tells us, is motivated both by our intuitions concerning certain examples and by considerations about causal powers' being powers to enter into contingent causal relations. Thus, for example, in virtue of my having siblings I am able to have sons that are nephews. People who do not have siblings are not capable of having sons that are nephews. But intuitively the difference between having siblings and not having siblings is not a causal power in virtue of its being responsible for the difference between the properties of sons (Chapter 11, p. 210).

Fodor acknowledges that some properties of causes *are* distinctive causal powers even though they are necessarily (or conceptually) connected to properties of their effects for which they are responsible. Being soluble is one such property; being a camshaft is another. So these properties fail to satisfy condition C despite being distintive causal powers. Fodor rules these examples out as ones that C is meant to apply to, however, on the grounds that they are *identical* with causal powers. It is trivially true for these causal powers that they are 'responsible' for their effect properties. What Fodor is interested in are properties that are contingently (i.e. not identical with) causal powers, since in these cases the question of whether causes that have such properties have causal powers in virtue of having those properties is not trivial. He thinks, moreover, that intentional properties are *not* identical with causal powers.

In short, what Fodor is interested in are properties of causes, all of which can be said to satisfy his schema S in that differences between them are responsible for differences in properties of their effects, and none of which is actually identical with a distinctive causal power, but only some of which, intuitively, are distinctive causal powers. Being a planet and being a meteor are distinctive causal powers, but being a sibling and being a meteor crater are not. Condition C is applicable to all of these properties, and to intentional ones too, because if they are causal powers, they are contingently so. However, intentional properties fail to satisfy the condition, along with being a sibling and being a meteor crater, and for the same reason. All are conceptually connected to the properties of the effects for which they are responsible. A sibling is conceptually related to being a nephew, since to be a nephew is to be a son of a parent that has siblings. Similarly, Fodor argues, being a *water* thought is conceptually related to being *water* behaviour (Chapter 11, p. 217). That is to say, although intentional properties are contingently causal powers, they do not satisfy condition C because differences in intentional properties of causes that are responsible for differences in intentional properties of their effects are conceptually related. That is to say, intentional properties are not distinctive causal powers.

It is important to note that Fodor is not arguing that intentional properties are not causal powers, but that they are not *distinctive* causal powers, since the issue of individualism for him turns on whether *differences* in twins' behaviour, intentionally described, are relevant to taxonomy of intentional kinds by causal powers:

> it is actually not in dispute whether water thoughts and twater thoughts are causal powers. On the contrary, *of course* they are: my water thoughts are causally responsible for my reaching for water, my twin's twater thoughts are causally responsible for his reaching for twater . . ., and so on. The question on which local supervenience – hence individualism – turns, however, is whether the difference between water thoughts and twater thoughts is a *difference* in causal powers. (Chapter 11, p. 214)

Burge agrees with Fodor on this (see Chapter 12). However, he disagrees with Fodor on whether differences in twins' behaviour mark a difference in causal powers. In his view, the fact that there are conceptual links between intentional properties and intentional–behavioural properties does not show that intentional properties are not distintive causal powers. That is to say, Burge *rejects* condition C as a test for whether differences in mental states' intentional properties are differences in causal powers in virtue of their being responsible for differences in the intentional properties of their effects. He rejects C because of its commitment to the 'Humean' view that, for a property to be a distinctive causal power, it must be contingently, or non-conceptually, related to its distinctive effect property.

Burge sees no reason why all sciences that are in the business of causal explanation must conform to this Humean requirement, and he emphasizes the point that how particular sciences develop cannot and ought not to be stipulated *a priori*. Moreover, he points out that even in the natural sciences, where this Humean requirement might be thought to apply, there are perfectly respectable properties (as Fodor acknowledges) that are in good explanatory standing, such as being soluble and being a camshaft, but fail to meet the Humean requirement. Intentional properties, Burge argues, are like these properties: 'They necessarily have causal implications as such. They are scientifically and causally relevant kinds. And many of them bear a conceptual relation to standard conceptions of the properties that are causally effected by them (Chapter 12, p. 231). Perhaps, Burge suggests, Fodor's worry with this is that if the Humean requirement is dropped, the explanatory generalizations of psychology will turn out to have a 'quasi-logical' status like the 'quasi-logical' status of 'if soluble, then dissolves' (Chapter 11, n. 22). However, the fact that there are *some* conceptual connections between intentional properties and intentional–behavioural properties does not show that they are logical truths: for example, it does not follow from the fact that 'water' turns up in the antecedent and the consequent of 'If you have water wants . . . then you drill for water' does not show that the antecedent conceptually implies the consequent (Chapter 12, n. 7). Nor does it show that there are not or cannot be interesting contingent generalizations connecting those properties under those descriptions. What prevents such generalizations being 'quasi-logical' truths is that they presuppose or make existential assumptions, and specify conditions under which antecedent and consequent apply.

Burge's emphasis on the role of behaviour in the determination of psychological kinds flows from his belief that intentional properties 'necessarily have causal implications' *vis à vis* behaviour, so that distinctive behaviour makes for distinctive causal powers (Chapter 12, p. 231). He believes with Fodor that taxonomy of psychological kinds is taxonomy by causal powers, and that psychology is in the business of causal explanation. Since he does not think that this prohibits conceptual connections holding between intentional properties and intentional–behavioural ones, he rejects the Humean requirement on causal powers. Despite disagreeing with Fodor on the Humean requirement, however, he agrees with Fodor that (a) intentional behaviour plays a crucial role in determining psychological kinds because distinctive behaviour makes for distinctive causal powers; (b) taxonomy of psychological kinds is taxonomy by causal powers; and (c) psychology is in the business of causal explanation.

Conclusion

Where does this leave us? The dispute between Fodor and Burge appears to be a complete stalemate, with each side begging the question as to whether taxonomy of intentional kinds in psychology is or should be individualistic against the other. Given that both agree that taxonomy of intentional kinds is taxonomy by causal powers, the argument seems to boil down to Burge claiming that such taxonomy must take into account specific relations to actual environmental context because psychology is like biology, and Fodor claiming that such taxonomy need not take into account these specific environmental relations because psychology is like physics. However, these claims presume, and do not establish, anti-individualism/individualism. The dispute seems question-begging precisely because now all of the focus is on whether biology is, or must be, individualistic, and exactly the same considerations that Burge and Fodor bring to bear on psychology will reappear here. Attention to actual explanatory practices alone does not seem likely to solve the dispute because what matters is how these practices are to be interpreted, and this is also up for dispute.[14] What is really needed here is a principled reason for thinking that biology is very unlike physics; and one promising way of proceeding is to forge a distinction between taxonomy by biological function and taxonomy by causal powers.

On one well-known view, the concept of biological function is not plausibly viewed as a statistical-cum-causal notion (Millikan, 1984 and Chapter 14, this volume; Neander, 1991a, b). One cannot, for instance, determine the biological function of the sperm by its causal tendency to fertilize ova, since so few sperm actually realize this 'power'. Still, the biological function of the sperm is to fertilize ova.[15] In short, the concept of biological function is a normative one, of how an organ ought, given normal conditions and normal circumstances (which are again normatively constrained) to behave: what effects it ought, given these conditions and environment, to have. But the notion of causal power is not normative in this way. A property's causal powers concern the causal tendency of instances of that property to produce a given effect, what those instances tend (not ought, in the normative sense) to do. The fact that causal power is a counterfactual notion does not alter this point.

Burge's emphasis on the similarities between psychological kinds and functional kinds in biology, an emphasis that appears to be crucial to Burge's defence of anti-individualism, seems consistent with such a view. For instance, when criticizing Fodor's counterfactual cross-context test for sameness and differences of causal powers on the grounds that deciding which contexts are relevant for determining and distinguishing causal powers is not independent of assumptions about psychological kinds, he cites as an example the difference between a heart and a physically indistinguishable organ that pumps waste. These two organs, he says, have different causal powers; but deciding what the causal powers of the heart are is not independent of its function, which is not independent of assumptions about its normal environment. So causal powers depend on biological function.

Burge's emphasis on the conceptual relations between intentional properties and their intentional–behavioural effect properties is also consistent with this view of functional properties. He notes that 'One could plausibly claim that it is a conceptual truth that hearts differ from twin waste-pumps in that they pump blood. One could plausibly claim that it is conceptually necessary that if something is a heart, then when functioning normally, it pumps blood' (Chapter 12, p. 233). This view of the connection between biological–functional properties and their 'normal' effect properties (instances of which it is their function to produce) is not uncommon among those who hold that the concept of biological function is not a statistical–causal notion (see, for example, Neander, 1991a, b).

However, supposing that the similarity between intentional properties and biological–functional ones is of this kind argues against, rather than for, the view that taxonomy of intentional properties is taxonomy by causal powers. In particular, it forces the rejection of (a), (b), and (c) cited above: that taxonomy of intentional properties in psychology is taxonomy by causal powers, that psychological explanation is causal explanation, and that actual and counterfactual behaviour plays a decisive role in the determination of psychological kinds. But what does it matter whether we call this taxonomy 'causal' and reject the Humean view, or reject the view that this taxonomy is 'causal'? The important point for Burge is that it need not be any part of the view that functional taxonomy is not taxonomy by causal powers that functional properties do *not* necessarily have causal implications *vis à vis* behaviour. In biology, behaviour matters, but what is crucial is *normal* behaviour, where 'normal' is understood as 'biologically normal', and this is not a statistical–causal notion. It is this point that seems to be crucial to Burge's position. Morever, it offers a way out of this particular stalemate.

Notes

1   Note that Fodor explicitly distinguishes this view from the view known as *externalism* (see Chapter 11). Externalism is a view about how the contents of intentional states, states with propositional content, are correctly individuated. Anti-individualism, on the other hand, is a view about how the contents of intentional states are, or should be, individuated *for the purposes of a scientific psychology*, i.e. for the purposes of (causal) explanation in psychology. Fodor does not deny the truth of externalism; but he does deny the truth of anti-individualism.

2   The view need not be restricted to natural kinds, however. See Fodor (1987, p. 29) and Pettit and McDowell (1986). Some of Burge's thought experiments include social factors that help to determine kinds such as *sofa* and *arthritis* (see, e.g. Burge, 1979), whereas others concentrate on natural kinds such as water (see, e.g. Burge, 1982).

3   The terminology here is Pettit and McDowell's (1986).

4   Thus Descartes says at the beginning of his *Second Meditation*: 'I suppose, then, that all the things that I see are false; I persuade myself that nothing has ever existed of all that my fallacious memory represents to me. I consider that I possess no senses; I imagine that body, figure, extension, movement and place are but fictions of my mind' (Descartes, 1969, p. 171).

5   Burge mentions this in 'Individualism and psychology' (Chapter 10). He suggests that some passages in Fodor's work seem to indicate that he holds this view (see n. 6, p. 202).

6   Note that Fodor has no objection to the view that *relational* properties may be causal powers that are relevant to scientific taxonomy (e.g. being a planet, and being meteor). See Fodor (1987) and Chapter 11.

7   Supervenience theses typically specify an asymmetric co-variance relation between

(sets of) properties, entities or kinds, whose individuation conditions are presumed as independently given (see Kim, 1984, 1990).

8 Fodor argues that this line of reasoning won't work if, as seems likely, local causation implies 'local supervenience of causal powers' (Fodor, 1987, p. 42), i.e. the supervenience of the causal powers of intentional states on the causal powers of physical states within subjects' bodies. As he puts it, 'But is Burge seriously prepared to give up the local supervenience of causal powers? How *could* differences of context affect the causal powers of one's mental states without affecting the states of one's brain?' (Fodor, 1987, pp. 41–2). To the first question, Burge's answer seems to be an unqualified *yes*: if individuation of intentional states is non-individualistic, local supervenience fails across the board. Differences in the environment external to subjects' bodies can make for a difference in the taxonomy of those subjects' states, and so can make for a difference in causal powers. (Moreover, to assume that local supervenience of causal powers of intentional states on causal powers of physical events/states of subjects' bodies holds seems no less question-begging against anti-individualism than to assume that local supervenience of mental kinds on physical events/states of subjects' bodies holds.) To the second question, Burge's answer seems to be that differences of context *cannot* affect the causal powers of one's mental states without affecting the states of one's brain, in the sense that such differences can only affect the contents of one's mental states by causing brain states to transmit different information from the environment to those mental states. However, differences of context do not affect the *individuation* of brain states, since they do not affect their physical causal powers.

9 This test is formulated by Lawrence Shapiro (1993). He makes the complaint that Burge's argument for the claim that Marr's theory is anti-individualistic is question-begging.

10 The twin earth experiment Burge employs here is specified, not in terms of twins or *doppelgängers*, but rather in terms of a single perceiver in actual and counterfactual environments. The more general argument concerning cracks and shadows is also specified in this way. Such differences in the way the twin earth thought experiments are set up are not, however, relevant for present purposes.

11 Shapiro (1993) also points out that critics of Burge's arguments rely on the use of twin earth thought experiments to establish that Marr's theory is *individualistic*. Gabriel Segal (1989), for example, argues that Marr's theory would fail to distinguish perceptual types concerning objects in subjects' environments that subjects themselves are unable to discriminate (as Burge concedes the differences between cracks and shadows are). Therefore, he argues, the theory would type-identify the perceptual states of actual-P and counterfactual-P, construing O' as a disjunctive content (as of cracks or shadows), including both Cs and Os in its extension. Shapiro claims that the appropriate conclusion to be drawn from this is that the twin earth thought experiments are not decisive for *or* against individualism, since passing the twin earth test for individualism does not suffice to determine whether a psychological theory is individualistic. If Burge is right, Marr's theory is non-individualistic. But also, if Segal is right, Marr's theory is (contrary to Segal's claims) non-individualistic. According to Shapiro, Burge and Segal disagree about whether actual-P and counterfactual-P have the same types of intentional states, holding all facts about P, non-intentionally specified, constant and given variations in the environment. However, both Burge and Segal take the intentional types in

question to be individuated relationally, by reference to objective features in the environment. And Segal accepts Burge's characterization of individualism as described above. By that criterion, Segal's arguments are no less anti-individualistic than Burge's. However, this seems to miscontrue Segal's argument. Segal certainly claims that cracks and shadows fall into the extension of both actual-P's and counterfactual-P's perceptual representations, but this claim is neutral as between individualism and anti-individualism. It is no part of the individualist position to deny the existence of broad or extrinsic content; what matters is whether extension *determines* content. Segal's argument is that since, in Marr's theory, the attribution of perceptual content is *accounted for* in a 'bottom-up' rather than a 'top-down' way (although its *motivation* may be 'top-down'), it is individualistically, rather than non-individualistically, contrained. Thus, he argues that 'Only if the subject could visually discriminate between [cracks and shadows] would it be correct to attribute crack or shadow representations, rather than crackdow representations. The system will represent crackdows as shadows, or as cracks, rather than merely as crackdows, only if it extracts this information from the retinal array, with the aid of additional cues, assumptions and computations. Whether or not the system is doing this depends upon it, not upon what normally causes the gray arrays' (Segal, 1989, pp. 210–11).

12 Burge criticizes this aspect of Fodor's position also: 'Fodor begins by assuming that differences in intentional properties are the only relevant differences between the behavior of a person and a twin earth twin. I think that this is a mistake. Non-intentional descriptions of behavioral relations between an individual and specific kinds in his/her environment seem to be a significant part of what psychology is interested in' (Chapter 12, p. 227). Even Fodor's 'cross-context' test for sameness and differences of causal powers, Burge argues, gives us no reason to suppose that psychology isn't or shouldn't be interested in explaining relational behaviour, non-intentionally described (see Chapter 12, p. 228).

13 This short-hand is apt to be misleading, since Fodor explicitly states that intentional properties *are* causal powers despite failing to satisfy condition C. But see Chapter 11, n. 14, where he repeats his position clearly.

14 This emerges clearly in the dispute between Burge and Segal. Both cite passages from Marr to support their claims concerning the individualistic/non-individualistic nature of Marr's theory. Here the actual explanatory practice is insufficient to resolve the dispute; what is needed is a way of adjudicating between rival theories of that practice.

15 See Millikan in Chapters 14 and 16. For further argument in support of this view, see Chapters 1 and 3.

References

Burge, T. (1979) Individualism and the mental. In P. French, T. Uehling and H. Wettstein (eds.), *Midwest Studies in Philosophy* vol. 4, pp. 73–122. Minnesota, University of Minnesota Press.

Burge, T. (1982) Other Bodies. In A. Woodfield (ed.), *Thought and Object*, pp. 97–120. Oxford, Clarendon Press.

Burge, T. (1985a) Cartesian error and the objectivity of perception. In R. Grimm and D. Merrill (eds.), *Contents of Thought*, pp. 62–76. Arizona, University of Arizona Press.

Burge, T. (1985b) Authoritative self-knowledge and perceptual individualism. In R. Grimm and D. Merrill (eds.), *Contents of Thought*, pp. 86–98. Arizona, University of Arizona Press.

Descartes, R. (1969) *Meditations*. In M.D. Wilson (ed.), *The Essential Descartes*. New York, The New American Library.

Fodor, J. (1987) *Psychosemantics*. Cambridge, Mass., MIT Press.

Kim, J. (1984) Concepts of supervenience. *Philosophy and Phenomenological Research* 45, 153–76.

Kim, J. (1990) Supervenience as a philosophical concept. *Metaphilosophy* 12, 1–27.

Marr, D. (1982) *Vision*. New York, Freeman and Co.

Millikan, R.G. (1984) *Language, Thought, and Other Biological Categories*. Cambridge, Mass., MIT Press.

Neander, K. (1991a) Functions as selected effects: the conceptual analyst's defense. *Philosophy of Science* 58, 168–84.

Neander, K. (1991b) The teleological notion of 'function'. *Australasian Journal of Philosophy* 69, 454–68.

Pettit, P. and McDowell, J. (1986) Introduction. In P. Pettit and J. McDowell (eds.), *Subject, Thought, and Context*. Oxford, Oxford University Press.

Putnam, H. (1975) The meaning of 'meaning'. In *Mind, Language and Reality*, vol. II, pp. 215–71.

Segal, G. (1989) Seeing what is not there. *Philosophical Review* 98, 189–214.

Shapiro, L. (1993) Content, kinds, and individualism in Marr's theory of vision. *Philosophical Review* 102, 489–513.

10

Individualism and Psychology

Tyler Burge

Recent years have seen in psychology – and overlapping parts of linguistics, artificial intelligence and the social sciences – the development of some semblance of agreement about an approach to the empirical study of human activity and ability. The approach is broadly mentalistic in that it involves the attribution of states, processes and events that are intentional, in the sense of 'representational'. Many of these events and states are unconscious and inaccessible to mere reflection. Computer jargon is prominent in labeling them. But they bear comparison to thoughts, wants, memories, perceptions, plans, mental sets and the like – ordinarily so-called. Like ordinary propositional attitudes, some are described by means of that-clauses and may be evaluated as true or false. All are involved in a system by means of which a person knows, represents and utilizes information about his or her surroundings.

In the first part of this chapter, I shall criticize some arguments that have been given for thinking that explanation in psychology is, and ought to be, purely 'individualistic'. In the second part of the chapter, I shall discuss in some detail a powerful psychological theory that is not individualistic. The point of this latter discussion will be to illustrate a non-individualistic conception of explanatory kinds. In a third section, I shall offer a general argument against individualism, that centers on visual perception. What I have to say, throughout the chapter, will bear on all parts of psychology that attribute intentional states. But I will make special reference to explanation in cognitive psychology.

Individualism is a view about how kinds are correctly individuated, how their natures are fixed. We shall be concerned primarily with individualism about the individuation of mental kinds. According to individualism about the mind, the mental natures of all a person's or animal's mental states (and events) are such that there is no necessary or deep individuative relation between the individual's being in states of those kinds and the nature of the individual's physical or social environments.

This view owes its prominence to Descartes. It was embraced by Locke,

Leibniz and Hume. And it has recently found a home in the phenomenological tradition and in the doctrines of twentieth-century behaviorists, functionalists and mind–brain identity theorists. There are various more specific versions of the doctrine. A number of fundamental issues in traditional philosophy are shaped by them. In this chapter, however, I shall concentrate on versions of the doctrine that have been prominent in recent philosophy of psychology.

Current individualistic views of intentional mental states and events have tended to take one or two forms. One form maintains that an individual's being in any given intentional state (or being the subject of such a state) can be *explicated* by reference to states and events of the individual that are specifiable without using intentional vocabulary and without presupposing anything about the individual subject's social or physical environments. The explication is supposed to specify – in non-intentional terms – stimulations, behavior and internal physical or functional states of the individual. The other form of individualism is implied by the first, but is weaker. It does not attempt to explicate anything. It simply makes a claim of *supervenience*: an individual's intentional states and events (types and tokens) could not be different from what they are, given the individual's physical, chemical, neural, or functional histories, where these histories are specified non-intentionally and in a way that is independent of physical or social conditions outside the individual's body.

In other papers I have argued that both forms of individualism are mistaken. A person's intentional states and events could (counterfactually) vary, even as the individual's physical, functional (and perhaps phenomenological) history, specified non-intentionally and individualistically, is held constant. I have offered several arguments for this conclusion. Appreciating the strength of these arguments, and discerning the philosophical potential of a non-individualist view of mind, depend heavily on reflecting on differences among these arguments. They both reinforce one another and help map the topography of a positive position.

For present purposes, however, I shall merely sketch a couple of the arguments to give their flavor. I shall not defend them or enter a variety of relevant qualifications. Consider a person A who thinks that aluminum is a light metal used in sailboat masts, and a person B who believes that he or she has arthritis in the thigh. We assume that A and B can pick out instances of aluminum and arthritis (respectively) and know many familiar general facts about aluminum and arthritis. A is, however, ignorant of aluminum's chemical structure and micro-properties. B is ignorant of the fact that arthritis cannot occur outside of joints. Now we can imagine counterfactual cases in which A and B's bodies have their same histories considered in isolation of their physical environments, but in which there are significant environmental differences from the actual situation. A's counterfactual environment lacks aluminum and has in its place a similar-looking light metal. B's counterfactual environment is such that no one has ever isolated arthritis as a specific disease, or syndrome of diseases. In these cases, A would lack 'aluminum thoughts' and B would lack 'arthritis thoughts'. Assuming natural developmental patterns, both would have different thoughts. Thus these differences from the actual situation show up not only in the protagonist's relations to their environments, but also in their intentional mental states and events, ordinarily so-called. The arguments bring out variations in obliquely (or intensionally) occurring expressions in literal mental state and event ascriptions, our primary means of identifying intentional mental states.[1]

I believe that these arguments use literal descriptions of mental events, and are independent of conversational devices that may affect the form of an ascription without bearing on the nature of the mental event described. The sort of argument that we have illustrated does not depend on special features of the notions of arthritis or aluminum. Such arguments go through for observational and theoretical notions, for percepts as well as concepts, for natural kind and non-natural kind notions, for notions that are the special preserve of experts, and for what are known in the psychological literature as 'basic categories'. Indeed, I think that, at a minimum, relevantly similar arguments can be shown to go through with any notion that applies to public types of objects, properties, or events that are typically known by empirical means.[2]

I shall not elaborate or defend the arguments here. In what follows, I shall presuppose that they are cogent. For our purposes, it will be enough if one bears firmly in mind their conclusion: mental states and events in principle vary with variations in the environment, even as an individual's physical (functional, phenomenological) history, specified non-intentionally and individualistically, remains constant.

A common reaction to these conclusions, often unsupported by argument, has been to concede their force, but to try to limit their effect. It is frequently held that they apply to common-sense attributions of attitudes, but have no application to analogous attributions in psychology. Non-individualistic aspects of mentalistic attribution have been held to be uncongenial with the purposes and requirements of psychological theory. Of course, there is a tradition of holding that ordinary intentional attributions are incapable of yielding any knowledge at all. Others have held the more modest view that mentalistic attributions are capable of yielding only knowledge that could not in principle be systematized in a theory.

I shall not be able to discuss all of these lines of thought. In particular I shall ignore generalized arguments that mentalistic ascriptions are deeply indeterminate, or otherwise incapable of yielding knowledge. Our focus will be on arguments that purport to show that non-individualistic mentalistic ascriptions cannot play a systematic role in psychological explanation – *because* of the fact that they are not individualistic.

There are indeed significant differences between theoretical discourse in psychology and the mentalistic discourse of common sense. The most obvious one is that the language of theoretical psychology requires refinements on ordinary discourse. It not only requires greater system and rigor, and a raft of unconscious states and events that are not ordinarily attributed (though they are, I think, ordinarily allowed for). It also must distill out descriptive–explanatory purposes of common attributions from uses that serve communication at the expense of description and explanation. Making this distinction is already common practice. Refinement for scientific purposes must, however, be systematic and meticulous, though it need not eliminate all vagueness. I think that there are no sound reasons to believe that such refinement cannot be effected through the development of psychological theory, or that effecting it will fundamentally change the nature of ordinary mentalistic attributions.

Differences between scientific and ordinary discourse survive even when ordinary discourse undergoes the refinements just mentioned. Although common-sense discourse – both about macrophysical objects and about mental events – yields knowledge, I believe that the principles governing justification for such discourse differ from those that are invoked in systematic scientific theorizing. So there is, prima facie, room for the view that psychology is or should be fully individualistic, even though ordinary descriptions of mental states are not. Nevertheless, the arguments for this view that have been offered do not seem to me cogent. Nor do I find the view independently persuasive.

Before considering such arguments, I must articulate some further background assumptions, this time about psychology itself. I shall be taking those parts of psychology that utilize mentalistic and information-processing discourse pretty much as they are. I assume that they employ standard scientific methodology, that they have produced interesting empirical results, and that they contain more than a smattering of genuine theory. I shall not prejudge what sort of science psychology is, or how it relates to the natural sciences. I do, however, assume that its cognitive claims and, more especially, its methods and presuppositions are to be taken seriously as the best we now have in this area of inquiry. I believe that there are no good reasons for thinking that the methods or findings of this body of work are radically misguided.

I shall not be assuming that psychology *must* continue to maintain touch with common-sense discourse. I believe that such touch will almost surely be maintained. But I think that empirical disciplines must find their own way according to standards that they set for themselves. Quasi-*a priori* strictures laid down by philosophers count for little. So our reflections concern psychology as it is, not as it will be or must be.

In taking psychology as it is, I am assuming that it seeks to refine, deepen, generalize and systematize some of the statements of informed common sense about people's mental activity. It accepts, for example, that people see objects with certain shapes, textures and hues, and in certain spatial relations, under certain specified conditions. And it attempts to explain in more depth what people do when they see such things, and how their doing it is done. Psychology accepts that people remember events and truths, that they categorize objects, that they draw inferences, that they act on beliefs and preferences. And it attempts to find deep regularities in these activities, to specify mechanisms that underly them, and to provide systematic accounts of how these activities relate to one another. In describing and, at least partly, in explaining these activities and abilities, psychology makes use of interpreted that-clauses and other intensional constructions – or what we might loosely call 'intentional content'.[3] I have seen no sound reason to believe that this use is merely heuristic, instrumentalistic or second class in any other sense.

I assume that intentional content has internal structure – something like grammatical or logical structure – and that the parts of this structure are individuated finely enough to correspond to certain individual abilities, procedures or perspectives. Since various abilities, procedures or perspectives may be associated with any given event, object, property, or relation, intentional content must be individuated more finely than the entities in the world with which the individual interacts. We must allow different ways (even, I think, different primitive ways) for the individual to conceive of, or represent, any given entity. This assumption about the fine-grainedness of content in psychology will play no explicit role in what follows. I note it here to indicate that my skepticism about individualism as an interpretation of psychology does not stem from a conception of content about which it is already clear that it does not play a dominant role in psychology.[4]

Finally, I shall assume that individualism is *prima facie wrong* about psychology, including cognitive psychology. Since the relevant parts of psychology frequently use attributions of intentional states that are subject to our thought experiments, the language actually used in psychology is not purely individualistic. That is, the generalizations with counterfactual force that appear in psychological theories, given their standard interpretations, are not all individualistic. For ordinary understanding of the truth conditions, or individuation conditions, of the relevant attributions suffices to verify the thought experiments. Moreover, there is at present no well-explained, well-understood, much less well-tested, individualistic language – or individualistic reinterpretation of the linguistic forms currently in use in psychology – that could serve as surrogate.

Thus individualism as applied to psychology must be revisionistic. It must be revisionistic at least about the language of psychological theory. I shall be developing the view that it is also revisionistic, without good reason, about the underlying presuppositions of the science. To justify itself, individualism must fulfill two tasks. It must show that the language of psychology should be revised by demonstrating that the presuppositions of the science are or should be *purely* individualistic. And it must explain a new individualistic language (attributing what is sometimes called 'narrow content') that captures genuine theoretical commitments of the science.

These tasks are independent. If the second were accomplished, but the first remained unaccomplishable, individualism would be wrong; but it would have engendered a new level of explanation. For reasons I will mention later, I am skeptical about such wholesale supplementation of current theory. But psychology is not a monolith. Different explanatory tasks and types of explanation co-exist within it. In questioning the view that psychology is individualistic, I am not *thereby* doubting whether there are some sub-parts of psychology that conform to the strictures of individualism. I am doubting whether all of psychology as it is currently practiced is or should be individualistic. Thus I shall concentrate on attempts to fulfill the first of the two tasks that face someone bent on revising psychology along individualistic lines. So much for preliminaries.

I

Let us begin by discussing a general argument against non-individualistic accounts. It goes as follows. The behavior of the physiologically and function-ally identical protagonists in our thought experiments is identical. But psychol-ogy is the science (only) of behavior. Since the behavior of the protagonists is the same, a science of behavior should give the *same* explanations and descriptions of the two cases (by some Ockhamesque principle of parsimony). So there is no room in the discipline for explaining their behavior in terms of different mental states.[5]

The two initial premises are problematic. To begin with the first: it is not to be assumed that the protagonists are behaviorally identical in the thought experiments. I believe that the only clear, general interpretation of 'behavior' that is available and that would verify the first premise is 'bodily motion'. But this construal has almost no relevance to psychology as it is actually practiced. 'Behavior' has become a catch-all term in psychology for observable activity on whose description and character psychologists can reach quick 'pre-theoretical' agreement. Apart from methodological bias, it is just not true that all descriptions that would count as 'behavioral' in cognitive (social, develop-mental) psychology would apply to both the protagonists. Much behavior is intentional action; many action specifications are non-individualistic. Thought experiments relevantly similar to those which we have already developed will apply to them.

For example, much 'behavioral' evidence in psychology is drawn from what people say or how they answer questions. Subjects' utterances (and the questions asked them) must be taken to be interpreted in order to be of any use in the experiments; and it is often assumed that theories may be checked by experiments carried out in different languages. Since the protagonists' sayings in the thought experiments are different, even in non-transparent or oblique occurrences, it is prima facie mistaken to count the protagonists as 'behaviorally' identical. Many attributions of non-verbal behavior are also intentional and non-individualistic, or even relational: she picked up the apple, pointed to the square block, tracked the moving ball, smiled at the familiar face, took the money instead of the risk. These attributions can be elaborated to produce non-individualist thought experiments. The general point is that many relevant specifications of behavior in psychology are intentional, or relational, or both. The thought experiments indicate that these specifications ground non-individualist mental attributions. An argument for individualism cannot reasonably *assume* that these specifications are individualistic or ought to be.

Of course, there are non-individualistic specifications of behavior that are unsuitable for any scientific enterprise ('my friend's favorite bodily movement'). But most of these do not even appear to occur in psychology. The problem of providing reasonable specifications of behavior cannot be solved from an armchair. Sanitizing the notion of behavior to meet some antecedently held methodological principle is an old game, never won. One must look at what psychology actually takes as 'behavioral' evidence. It is the responsibility of the argument to show that non-individualistic notions have no place in psychology. In so far as the argument assumes that intentional, non-individualistic specifications of behavior are illegitimate, it either ignores obvious aspects of psychological practice or begs the question at issue.

The second step of the argument also limps. One cannot assume without serious discussion that psychology is correctly characterized as a science (only) of behavior. This is, of course, particularly so if behavior is construed in a restrictive way. But even disregarding how behavior is construed, the premise is doubtful. One reason is that it is hardly to be assumed that a putative science is to be characterized in terms of its evidence as opposed to its subject matter. Of course, the subject matter is to some extent under dispute. But cognitive psychology appears to be about certain molar abilities and activities some of which are propositional attitudes. Since the propositional attitudes attributed do not seem to be fully individuable in individualistic terms, we need a direct argument that cognitive psychology is not a science of what it appears to be a science of.

A second reason for doubting the premise is that psychology seems to be partly about relations between people, or animals, and their environment. It is hard to see how to provide a natural description of a theory of vision, for example, as a science of behavior. The point of the theory is to figure out how people do what they obviously succeed in doing – how they see objects in their environment. We are trying to explain relations between a subject and a physical world that we take ourselves to know something about. Theories of memory, of certain sorts of learning, of linguistic understanding, of belief formation, of categorization, do the same. It is certainly not obvious that these references to relations between subject and environment are somehow inessential to (all parts of) psychological theory. They seem, in fact, to be a large part of the point of such theory. In my view, these relations help motivate non-individualistic principles of individuation (see the next section). In sum, I think that the argument we have so far considered begs significant questions at almost every step.

There is a kindred argument worth considering: the determinants of behavior supervene on states of the brain. (If one is a materialist, one might take this to be a triviality: 'brain states supervene on brain states.') So if propositional attitudes are to be treated as among the determinants of behavior, they must be taken to supervene on brain states. The alternative is to take propositional attitudes as behaviorally irrelevant.[6]

This argument can, I think, be turned on its head. Since propositional attitudes are among the determinants of our 'behavior' (where this expression is as open-ended as ever), and since propositional attitudes do not supervene on our brain states, not all determinants of our 'behavior' supervene on our brain states. I want to make three points against the original argument, two metaphysical and one epistemic or methodological. Metaphysics first.

The ontological stakes that ride on the supervenience doctrine are far less substantial than one might think. It is simply not a 'trivial consequence' of materialism about mental states and events that the determinants of our behavior supervene on the states of our brains. This is because what supervenes on what has at least as much to do with how the relevant entities are individuated as with what they are made of. If a mental event m is individuated partly by reference to normal conditions outside a person's body, then, regardless of whether m has material composition, m might vary even as the body remains the same.

Since intentional phenomena form such a large special case, it is probably misleading to seek analogies from other domains to illustrate the point. To loosen up the imagination, however, consider the Battle of Hastings. Suppose that we preserve every human body, every piece of turf, every weapon, every physical structure and all the physical interactions among them, from the first confrontation to the last death or withdrawal on the day of the battle. Suppose that, counterfactually, we imagine all these physical events and props placed in California (perhaps at the same time in 1066). Suppose that the physical activity is artifically induced by brilliant scientists transported to earth by Martian film producers. The distal causes of the battle have nothing to do with the causes of the Battle of Hastings. I think it plausible (and certainly coherent) to say that in such circumstances, not the Battle of Hastings, but only a physical facsimile would have taken place. I think that even if the location in Hastings were maintained, sufficiently different counterfactual causal antecedents would suffice to vary the identity of the battle. The battle is individuated partly in terms of its causes. Though the battle does not supervene on its physical constituents, we have little hesitation about counting it a physical event.

Our individuation of historical battles is probably wrapped up with intentional states of the participants. The point can also be made by reference to cases that are clearly independent of intentional considerations. Consider the emergence of North America from the ocean. Suppose that we delimit what count as constituent (say, micro-) physical events of this larger event. It seems that if the surrounding physical conditions and laws are artfully enough contrived, we can counterfactually conceive these same constituent events (or the constituent physical objects' undergoing physically identical changes in the same places) in such a way that they are embedded in a much larger land mass, so that the physical constituents of North America do not make up any salient part of this larger mass. The emergence of North America would not have occurred in such a case, even though its 'constituent' physical events were, in isolation, physically identical with the actual events. We individuate the emergence of continents or other land masses in such a way that they are not supervenient on their physical constituents. But such events are none the less physical.

In fact, I think that materialism does not provide reasonable restrictions on theories of the role of mentalistic attributions in psychology. The relation of physical composition presently plays no significant role in any established scientific theory of mental events, or of their relations to brain events. The restrictions that physiological considerations place on psychological theorizing, though substantial, are weaker than those of any of the articulated materialisms, even the weak compositional variety I am alluding to. My point is just that rejecting individualistic supervenience does not entail rejecting a materialistic standpoint. So materialism *per se* does nothing to support individualism.[7]

The second 'metaphysical' point concerns causation. The argument we are considering in effect simply assumes that propositional attitudes (type and token) supervene on physico-chemical events in the body. But many philosophers appear to think that this assumption is rendered obvious by bland observations about the etiology of mental events and behavior. It is plausible that events in the external world causally affect the mental events of a subject only by affecting the subject's bodily surfaces; and that nothing (not excluding mental events) causally affects behavior except by affecting (causing or being a causal antecedent of causes of) local states of the subject's body. One might reason that in the anti-individualistic thought experiments these principles are violated in so far as events in the environment are alleged to differentially 'affect' a person's mental events and behavior without differentially 'affecting' his or her body: only if mental events (and states) supervene on the individual's body can the causal principles be maintained.

The reasoning is confused. The confusion is abetted by careless use of the term 'affect', conflating causation with individuation. Variations in the environment that do not vary the impacts that causally 'affect' the subject's body may 'affect' the individuation of the information that the subject is receiving, of the intentional processes he or she is undergoing, or of the way the subject is acting. It does not follow that the environment causally affects the subject in any way that circumvents its having effects on the subject's body.

Once the conflation is avoided, it becomes clear that there is no simple argument from the causal principles just enunciated to individualism. The example from geology provides a useful counter-model. It shows that one can accept the causal principles and thereby experience no bewilderment whatsoever in rejecting individualism. A continent moves and is moved by local impacts from rocks, waves, molecules. Yet we can conceive of holding constant the continent's peripheral impacts and chemically constituent events and objects, without holding identical the continent or certain of its macro-changes – because the continent's spatial relations to other land masses affect the way we individuate it. Or take an example from biology. Let us accept the plausible principle that nothing causally affects breathing except as it causally affects local states of the lungs. It does not follow, and indeed is not true, that we individuate lungs and the various sub-events of respiration in such a way as to treat those objects and events as supervenient on the chemically described objects and events that compose them. If the same chemical process (same from the surfaces of the lungs inside, and back to the surfaces) were embedded in a different sort of body and had an entirely different function (say, digestive, immunological or regulatory), we would not be dealing with the same biological states and events. Local causation does not make more plausible local individuation, or individualistic supervenience.

The intended analogy to mental events should be evident. We may agree that a person's mental events and behavior are causally affected by the person's environment only through local causal effects on the person's body. Without the slightest conceptual discomfort we may individuate mental events so as to allow distinct events (types or tokens) with indistinguishable chemistries, or even physiologies, for the subject's body. Information from and about the environment is transmitted only through proximal stimulations, but the information is individuated partly by reference to the nature of normal distal stimuli. Causation is local. Individuation may presuppose facts about the specific nature of a subject's environment.

Where intentional psychological explanation is itself causal, it may well presuppose that the causal transactions to which its generalizations apply bear some necessary relation to some underlying physical transactions (or other). Without a set of physical transactions, none of the intentional transactions would transpire. But it does not follow that the kinds invoked in explaining causal interactions among intentional states (or between physical states and intentional states – for example, in vision or in action) supervene on the underlying physiological transactions. The same physical transactions in a given person may in principle mediate, or underly, transactions involving different intentional states – if the environmental features that enter into the individuation of the intentional states and that are critical in the explanatory generalizations that invoke those states vary in appropriate ways.

Let us turn to our epistemic point. The view that propositional attitudes help determine behavior is well entrenched in common judgements and in the explanatory practices of psychology. Our arguments that a subject's propositional attitudes are not fixed purely by his or her brain states are based on widely shared judgments regarding *particular* cases that in relevant respects bring out familiar elements in our actual psychological and common-sense practices of attitude attribution. By contrast, the claim that none of an individual's propositional attitudes (or determinants of his or her behavior) could have been different unless some of his/her brain states were different is a metaphysical conjecture. It is a modal generalization that is not grounded in judgments about particular cases, or (so far) in careful interpretation of the actual explanatory and descriptive practices of psychology. Metaphysical ideology should either conform to and illuminate intellectual praxis, or produce strong reasons for revising it.

What we know about supervenience must be derived, partly, from what we know about individuation. What we know about individuation is derived from reflecting on explanations and descriptions of going cognitive practices. Individuative methods are bound up with the explanatory and descriptive needs of such practices. Thus justified judgments about what supervenes on what are *derivative* from reflection on the nature of explanation and description in psychological discourse and common attitude attributions. I think that such judgments cannot be reasonably invoked to restrict such discourse. It seems to me therefore that, apart from further argument, the individualistic supervenience thesis provides no reason for requiring (pan-) individualism in psychology. In fact, the argument from individualistic supervenience begs the question. It *presupposes* rather than establishes that *individuation – hence explanation and description –* in psychology should be fully individualistic. It is simply the wrong sort of consideration to invoke in a dispute about explanation and description.

This remark is, I think, quite general. Not just questions of supervenience, but questions of ontology, reduction and causation generally, are epistemically posterior to questions about the success of explanatory and descriptive practices.[8] One cannot reasonably criticize a purported explanatory or descriptive practice primarily by appeal to some prior conception of what a 'good entity' is, or of what individuation or reference should be like, or of what the overall structure of science (or knowledge) should turn out to look like. Questions of what exists, how things are individuated, and what reduces to what, are questions that arise by reference to going explanatory and descriptive practices. By themselves, proposed answers to these questions cannot be used to criticize an otherwise successful mode of explanation and description.[9]

Of course, one might purport to base the individualist supervenience principle on what we know about good explanation. Perhaps one might hope to argue from inference to the best explanation concerning the relations of higher-level to more basic theories in the natural sciences that the entities postulated by psychology should supervene on those of physiology. Or perhaps one might try to draw analogies between non-individualistic theories in psychology and past, unscuccessful theories. These two strategies might meet our methodological strictures on answering the question of whether non-individualistic explanations are viable in a way that an unalloyed appeal to a supervenience principle does not. But philosophical invocations of inference to the best explanation tend to conceal wild leaps supported primarily by ideology. Such considerations must be spelled out into arguments. So far they do not seem very promising.

Take the first strategy. Inductions from the natural sciences to the human sciences are problematic from the start. The problems of the two sorts of sciences look very different, in a multitude of ways. One can, of course, reasonably try to exploit analogies in a pragmatic spirit. But the fact that some given analogy does not hold hardly counts against an otherwise viable mode of explanation. Moreover, there are non-individualistic modes of explanation even in the natural sciences. Geology, physiology and other parts of biology appeal to entities that are not supervenient on their underlying physical make up. Kind notions in these sciences (plates, organs, species) presuppose individuative methods that make essential reference to the environment surrounding instances of those kinds.

The second strategy seems even less promising. As it stands, it is afflicted with a bad case of vagueness. Some authors have suggested similarities between vitalism in biology, or action-at-a-distance theories in physics, and non-individualist theories in psychology. The analogies are tenuous. Unlike vitalism, non-individualist psychology does not *ipso facto* appeal to a new sort of force. Unlike action-at-a-distance theories, it does not appeal to action at a distance. It is true that aspects of the environment that do not differentially affect the physical movement of the protagonists in the thought experiments do differentially affect the explanations and descriptions. This is not, however, because some special causal relation is postulated, but rather because environmental differences affect what kinds of laws obtain, and the way causes and effects are individuated.

Let us now consider a further type of objection to applying the thought experiments to psychology. Since the actual and counterfactual protagonists are so impressively *similar* in so many psychologically relevant ways, can a theoretical language that cuts across these similarities be empirically adequate? The physiological and non-intensional 'behavioral' similarities between the protagonists seem to demand similarity of explanation. In its stronger form this objection purports to indicate that non-individualistic mentalistic language has no place in psychology. In its weaker form it attempts to motivate a new theoretical language that attributes intensional content, yet is individualistic. Only the stronger form would establish individualism in psychology. I shall consider it first.

The objection is that the similarities between the protagonists render implausible any theory that treats them differently. This objection is vague or enthymemic. Filling it out tends to lead one back towards the arguments that we have already rejected. On any view, there are several means available (neurophysiology, parts of psychology) for explaining in similar fashion those similarities that are postulated between protagonists in the thought experiments. The argument is not even of the right form to produce a reason for thinking that the differences between the protagonists should not be reflected somewhere in psychological theory – precisely the point at issue.

The objection is often coupled with the remark that non-individualistic explanations would make the parallels between the behavior of the protagonists in the thought experiments 'miraculous': explaining the same behavioral phenomena as resulting from different propositional attitudes would be to invoke a 'miracle'. The rhetoric about miracles can be deflated by noting that the protagonists' 'behavior' is not straightforwardly identical, that non-individualistic explanations postulate no special forces, and that there are physical differences in the protagonists' environments that help motivate describing and explaining their activity, at least at one level, in different ways.

The rhetoric about miracles borders on a fundamental misunderstanding of the status of the non-individualistic thought experiments, and of the relation between philosophy and psychology. There is, of course, considerable empirical implausibility, which we might with some exaggeration call 'miraculousness', in two persons' having identical individualistic physical histories but different thoughts. Most of this implausibility is an artifact of the two-person version of the thought experiments, a feature that is quite inessential. (One may take a single person in two counterfactual circumstances.) This point raises a caution. It is important not to think of the thought experiments as if they were describing actual empirical cases. Let me articulate this remark.

The kinds of a theory, and its principles of individuation, evolve in response to the world as it actually is found to be. Our notions of similarity result from attempts to explain actual cases. They are not necessarily responsive to preconceived philosophical ideals.[10] The kind terms of propositional attitude discourse are responsive to broad, stable similarities in the actual environment that agents are taken to respond to, operate on, and represent. If theory had been frequently confronted with physically similar agents in different environments, it might have evolved different kind terms. But we are so far from being confronted by even rough approximations to global physical similarities between agents that there is little plausibility in imposing individual physical similarity by itself as an ideal sufficient condition for sameness of kind terms throughout psychology. Moreover, I think that local physical similarities between the psychologically relevant activities of agents are so frequently intertwined with environmental constancies that a psychological theory that insisted on entirely abstracting from the nature of the environment in choosing its kind terms would be empirically emasculate.

The correct use of counterfactuals in the thought experiments is to explore the scope and limits of the kind notions that have been antecedently developed in attempts to explain actual empirical cases. In counterfactual reasoning we assume an understanding of what our language expresses and explore its application conditions through considering non-actual applications. The counterfactuals in the philosophical thought experiments illumine individuative and theoretical principles to which we are already committed.

The empirical implausibility of the thought experiments is irrelevant to their philosophical point – which concerns possibility, not plausibility. Unlikely but limiting cases are sometimes needed to clarify the modal status of presuppositions that govern more mundane examples. Conversely, the highly counterfactual cases are largely irrelevant to *evaluating* an empirical theory, except in cases (not at issue here) where they present empirical possibilities that a theory counts impossible. To invoke a general philosophical principle, like the supervenience principle, or to insist in the face of the thought experiments that only certain sorts of similarity can be relevant to psychology – without criticizing psychological theory on empirical grounds or showing how the kind notions exhibited by the thought experiments are empirically inadequate – is either to treat counterfactual circumstances as if they were actual, or to fall into apriorism about empirical science.

Let us turn to the weaker form of the worry that we have been considering. The worry purports to motivate a new individualistic language of attitude attribution. As I have noted, accepting such a language is consistent with rejecting (pan-) individualism in psychology. There are various levels or kinds of explanation in psychology. Adding another will not alter the issues at stake here. But let us pursue the matter briefly.

There are in psychology levels of individualistic description above the physiological but below the attitudinal that play a role in systematic explanations. Formalistically described computational processes are appealed to in the attempt to specify an algorithm by which a person's propositional information is processed. I think that the protagonists in our thought experiments might, for some purposes, be said to go through identical algorithms formalistically described. Different information is processed in the 'same' ways, at least at this formal level of description. But then might we not want a whole level of description, between the formal algorithm and ordinary propositional attitude ascription, that counts 'information' everywhere the same between protagonists in the thought experiments? This is a difficult and complex question, which I shall not attempt to answer here. I do, however, want to mention grounds for caution about supplementing psychology wholesale.

In the first place, the motivation for demanding the relevant additions to psychological theory is empirically weak. In recent philosophical literature, the motivation rests largely on intuitions about Cartesian demons or brains in vats, whose relevance and even coherence have been repeatedly challenged; on preconceptions about the supervenience of the mental on the neural that have no generalized scientific warrant; on misapplications of ordinary observations about causation; and on a sketchy and unclear conception of behavior unsupported by scientific practice.[11] Of course, one may reasonably investigate any hypothesis on no more than an intuitively based hunch. What is questionable is the view that there are currently strong philosophical or scientific grounds for instituting a new type of indivudalistic explanation.

In the second place, it is easy to underestimate what is involved in creating a relevant individualistic language that would be of genuine use in psychology. Explications of such language have so far been pretty make-shift. It does not suffice to sketch a semantics that says in effect that a sentence comes out true in all worlds that chemically identical protagonists in relevant thought experiments cannot distinguish. Such an explanation gives no clear rules for the *use* of the language, much less a demonstration that it can do distinctive work in psychology. Moreover, explication of the individualistic language (or language component) only for the special case in which the language-user's physiological or (individualistically specified) functional states are held constant is psychologically useless since no two people are ever actually identical in their physical states.

To fashion an individualist language, it will not do to limit its reference to objective properties accessible to perception. For our language for ascribing notions of perceptually accessible physical properties is not individualistic. More generally, as I have argued elsewhere, any attitudes that contain notions for physical objects, events and properties are non-individualistic.[12] The assumptions about objective representation needed to generate the argument are very minimal. I think it questionable whether there is a coherent conception of objective representation that can support an individualistic language of intentional attitude attribution. Advocates of such a language must either explain such a conception in depth, or attribute intentional states that lack objective physical reference.

II

I have been criticizing arguments for revising the language of psychology to accord with individualism. I have not tried to argue for non-individualistic psychological theories from a standpoint outside psychology. The heart of my case is the observation that psychological theories, taken literally, are not purely individualistic, that there are no strong reasons for taking them non-literally, and that we currently have no superior standpoint for judging how psychology ought to be done than that of seeing how it *is* done. One can, of course, seek deeper understanding of non-individualistic aspects of psychological theory. Development of such understanding is a multi-faceted task. Here I shall develop only points that are crucial to my thesis, illustrating them in some detail by reference to one theory.

Ascription of intentional states and events in psychology constitutes a type of individuation and explanation that carries presuppositions about the specific nature of the person's or animal's surrounding environment. Moreover, states and events are individuated so as to set the terms for specific evaluations of them for truth or other types of success. We can judge directly whether conative states are practically successful and cognitive states are veridical. For example, by characterizing a subject as visually representing an X, and specifying whether the visual state appropriately derives from an X in the particular case, we can judge whether the subject's state is veridical. Theories of vision, of belief formation, of memory, learning, decision-making, categorization, and perhaps even reasoning all attribute states that are subject to practical and semantical evaluation *by reference to standards partly set by a wider environment*.

Psychological theories are not themselves evaluative theories. But they often individuate phenomena so as to make evaluation readily accessible *because* they are partly motivated by such judgments. Thus we judge that in certain delimitable contexts people get what they want, know what is the case, and perceive what is there. And we try to frame explanations that account for these successes, and correlative failures, in such a way as to illumine as specifically as possible the mechanisms that underly and make true our evaluations.

I want to illustrate and develop these points by considering at some length a theory of vision. I choose this example primarily because it is a very advanced and impressive theory, and admits to being treated in some depth. Its information-processing approach is congenial with mainstream work in cognitive psychology. Some of its intentional aspects are well understood – and indeed are sometimes conceptually and mathematically far ahead of its formal (or syntactical) and physiological aspects. Thus the theory provides an example of a mentalistic theory with solid achievements to its credit.

The theory of vision maintains a pivotal position in psychology. Since perceptual processes provide the input for many higher cognitive processes, it is reasonable to think that if the theory of vision treats intentional states non-individualistically, other central parts of cognitive psychology will do likewise. Information processed by more central capacities depends, to a large extent, on visual information.

Certain special aspects of the vision example must be noted at the outset. The arguments that I have previously published against individualism (cf. n. 1) have centered on 'higher' mental capacities, some of which essentially involve the use of language. This focus was motivated by an interest in the relation between thought and linguistic meaning and in certain sorts of intellectual responsibility. Early human vision makes use of a limited range of representations – representations of shape, texture, depth and other spatial relations, motion, color, and so forth. These representations (percepts) are formed by processes that are relatively immune to correction from other sources of information; and the representations of early vision appear to be fully independent of language. So the thought experiments that I have previously elaborated will not carry over simply to early human vision. (One would expect those thought experiments to be more relevant to social and developmental psychology, to concept learning, and to parts of 'higher' cognitive psychology.) But the case against individualism need not center on higher cognitive capacities or on the relation between thought and language. The anti-individualstic conclusions of our previous arguments can be shown to apply to early human vision. The abstract schema which those thought experiments articulate also applies.

The schema rests on three general facts. The first is that what entities in the objective world one intentionally interacts with in the employment of many representational (intentional) types affects the semantical properties of those representational types, what they are, and how we individuate them.[13] A near consequence of this first fact is that there can be slack between, on the one hand, the way a subject's representational types apply to the world, and on the other, what that person knows about, and how he or she can react to, the way they apply. It is possible for representational types to apply differently, without the person's physical reactions or discriminative powers being different. These facts, together with the fact that many fundamental mental states and events are individuated in terms of the relevant representational types, suffice to generate the conclusion that many paradigmatic mental states and events are not individualistically individuated: they may vary while a person's body and discriminative powers are conceived as constant. For by the second fact one can conceive of the way a person's representational types apply to the objective world as varying, while that person's history, non-intentionally and individualistically specified, is held constant. By the first fact, such variation may vary the individuation of the person's representational types. And by the third, such variation may affect the individuation of the person's mental states and events. I shall illustrate how instances of this schema are supported by Marr's theory of vision.[14]

Marr's theory subsumes three explanatory enterprises: (a) a theory of the computation of the information; (b) an account of the representations used and of the algorithms by which they are manipulated; and (c) a theory of the underlying physiology. Our primary interest is in the first level, and in that part of the second that deals with the individuation of representations. Both of these parts of the theory are fundamentally intentional.

The theory of the computation of information encompasses an account of what information is extracted from what antecedent resources, and an account of the reference-preserving 'logic' of the extraction. These accounts proceed against a set of biological background assumptions. It is assumed that visual systems have evolved to solve certain problems forced on them by the environment. Different species are set different problems and solve them differently. The theory of human vision specifies a general information-processing problem – that of generating reliable representations of certain objective, distal properties of the surrounding world on the basis of proximal stimulations.

The human visual system computes complex representations of certain visible properties, on the basis of light intensity values on retinal images. The primary visible properties that Marr's theory treats are the shapes and locations of things in the world. But various other properties – motion, texture, color, lightness, shading – are also dealt with in some detail. The overall computation is broken down into stages of increasing complexity, each containing modules that solve various sub-problems.

The theory of computation of information clearly treats the visual system as going through a serious of intentional or representational states. At an early stage, the visual system is counted as representing objective features of the physical world.[15] There is no other way to treat the visual system as solving the problem that the theory sees it as solving than by attributing intentional states that represent objective, physical properties.

More than half of Marr's book is concerned with developing the theory of the computation of information and with individuating representational primitives. These parts of the theory are more deeply developed, both conceptually and mathematically, than the account of the algorithms. This point is worth emphasizing because it serves to correct the impression, often conveyed in recent philosophy of psychology, that intentional theories are regressive and all of the development of genuine theory in psychology has been proceeding at the level of purely formal, 'syntactical' transformations (algorithms) that are used in cognitive systems.

I now want, by a series of examples, to give a fairly concrete sense of how the theory treats the relation between the visual system and the physical environment. Understanding this relation will form essential background for understanding the non-individualistic character of the theory. The reader may skip the detail and still follow the philosophical argument. But the detail is there to support the argument and to render the conception of explanation that the argument yields both concrete and vivid.

Initially, I will illustrate two broad points. The *first* is that the theory makes essential reference to the subject's distal stimuli and makes essential assumptions about contingent facts regarding the subject's physical environment. Not only do the basic questions of the theory refer to what one sees under normal conditions, but the computational theory and its theorems are derived from numerous explicit assumptions about the physical world.

The *second* point to be illustrated is that the theory is set up to explain the reliability of a great variety of processes and sub-processes for acquiring information, at least to the extent that they are reliable. Reliability is presupposed in the formulations of the theory's basic questions. It is also explained through a detailed account of how in certain specified, standard conditions, veridical information is derived from limited means. The theory explains not merely the reliability of the system as a whole, but the reliability of various stages in the visual process. It begins by assuming that we see certain objective properties and proceeds to explain particular successes by framing conditions under which success would be expected (where the conditions are in fact typical). Failures are explained primarily by reference to a failure of these conditions to obtain. To use a phrase of Bernie Kobes, the theory is not success-neutral. The explanations and, as we shall later see, the kinds of theory presuppose that perception and numerous sub-routines of perception are veridical in normal circumstances.

Example 1

In an early stage of the construction of visual representation, the outputs of channels or filters that are sensitive to spatial distributions of light intensities are combined to produce representations of local contours, edges, shadows, and so forth. The filters fall into groups of different sizes, in the sense that different groups are sensitive to different bands of spatial frequencies. The channels are primarily sensitive to sudden intensity changes, called 'zero-crossings', at their scales (within their frequency bands). The theoretical question arises: how do we combine the results of the different sized channels to construct representations with physical meaning – representations that indicate edge segments or local contours in the external physical world? There is no *a priori* reason why zero-crossings obtained from different sized filters should be related to some one physical phenomenon in the environment. There is, however, a physical basis for their being thus related. This basis is identified by *the constraint of spatial localization*. Things in the world that give rise to intensity changes in the image, such as changes of illumination (caused by shadows, light sources) or changes in surface reflectance (caused by contours, creases and surface boundaries), are spatially localized, not scattered and not made up of waves. Because of this fact, if a zero-crossing is present in a channel centered on a given frequency band, there should be a corresponding zero-crossing at the same spatial location in larger-scaled channels. If this ceases to be so at larger scales, it is because (a) two or more local intensity changes are being averaged together in the larger channel (for example, the edges of a thin bar may register radical frequency changes in small channels, but go undetected in larger ones); (b) because two independent physical phenomena are producing intensity changes in the same area but at different scales (for example, a shadow superimposed on a sudden reflectance change; if the shadow is located in a certain way, the positions of the zero-crossings may not make possible a separation of the two physical phenomena). Some of these exceptions are sufficiently rare that the visual system need not and does not account for them, thus allowing for possible illusions; others are reflected in complications of the basic assumption that follows. The spatial coincidence constraint yields *the spatial coincidence assumption*:

> If a zero-crossing segment is present in a set of independent channels over a contiguous range of sizes, and the segment has the same position and orientation in each channel, then the set of such zero-crossing segments indicates the presence of an intensity change in the image that is due to a single physical phenomenon (a change in reflectance, illumination, depth, or surface orientation).

Thus the theory starts with the observation that physical edges produce roughly coincident zero-crossings in channels of neighboring sizes. The spatial coincidence assumption asserts that the coincidence of zero-crossings of neighboring sizes is normally sufficient evidence of a real physical edge. Under such circumstances, according to the theory, a representation of an edge is formed.[16]

Example 2

Because of the laws of light and the way our eyes are made, positioned and controlled, our brains typically receive similar image signals originating from two points that are fairly similarly located in the respective eyes or images, at the same horizontal level. If two objects are separated in depth from the viewer, the relative positions of their image signals will differ in the two eyes. The visual system determines the distance of physical surfaces by measuring the angular discrepancy in position (disparity) of the image of an object in the two eyes. This process is called stereopsis. To solve the problem of determining distance, the visual system must select a location on a surface as represented by one image, identify the same location in the other image, and measure the disparity between the corresponding image points. There is, of course, no *a priori* means of matching points from the two images. The theory indicates how correct matches are produced by appealing to three '*physical constraints*' (actually the first is not made explicit, but is relied upon): (1) the two eyes produce similar representations of the same external items; (2) a given point on a physical surface has a unique position in space at any given time; (3) matter is cohesive – separated into objects, the surfaces of which are usually smooth in the sense that surface variation is small compared to overall distance from the observer. These three physical constraints are rewritten as three corresponding '*constraints on matching*': (1) two representational elements can match if and only if they normally could have arisen from the same physical item (for example, in stereograms, dots match dots rather than bars); (2) nearly always, each representational element can match only one element from the other image (exceptions occur when two markings lie along the line of sight of one eye but are separately visible by the other, causing illusions); (3) disparity varies smoothly almost everywhere (this derives from physical constraint (3) because that constraint implies that the distance to the visible surface varies, approximately continuously except at object boundaries, which occupy a small fraction of the area of an image). Given suitable precisifications, these matching constraints can be used to prove *the fundamental theorem of stereopsis*:

> If a correspondence is established between physically meaningful represen- tational primitives extracted from the left and right images of a scene that contains a sufficient amount of detail (roughly 2 per cent density for dot stereograms), and if the correspondence satisfies the three matching constraints, then that correspondence is physically correct – hence unique.

The method is again to identify general physical conditions that give rise to a visual process, then to use those conditions to motivate constraints on the form of the process that, when satisfied, will allow the process to be interpreted as providing reliable representations of the physical environment.[17]

These examples illustrate theories of the computation of information. The critical move is the formulation of general physical facts that limit the interpretation of a visual problem enough to allow one to interpret the machinations of the visual system as providing a unique and veridical solution, at least in typical cases. The primary aim of referring to contingent physical facts and properties is to enable the theory to explain the visual system's reliable acquisition of information about the physical world: to explain the success or veridicality of various types of visual representation. So much for the first two points that we set out to illustrate.

I now turn to a *third* that is a natural corollary of the second, and that will be critical for our argument that the theory is non-individualistic: the information carried by representations – their intentional content – is individuated in terms of the specific distal causal antecedents in the physical world that the information is about and that the representations normally apply to. The individuation of the intentional features of numerous representations depends on a variety of physical constraints that our knowledge of the external world gives us. Thus the individuation of intentional content of representational types presupposes the veridicality of perception. Not only the explanations, but the intentional kinds of the theory presuppose contingent facts about the subject's physical environment.

Example 3

In building up informational or representational primitives in primal sketch, Marr states six general physical assumptions that constrain the choice of primitives. I shall state some of these to give a sense of their character: (a) the visible world is composed of smooth surfaces having reflectance functions whose spatial structure may be complex; (b) markings generated on a surface by a single process are often arranged in continuous spatial structures: curves, lines, etc.; (c) if direction of motion is discontinuous at more than one point, for example, along a line, then an object boundary is present. These assumptions are used to identify the physical significance of – the objective information normally given by – certain types of patterns in the image. The computational theory states conditions under which these primitives form to carry information about items in the physical world.[18] The theory in Example 1 is a case in point: conditions are laid down under which certain patterns may be taken as representing an objective physical condition; as being edge, boundary, bar or blob detectors. Similar points apply for more advanced primitives.

Example 4

In answering the question 'what assumptions do we reasonably and actually employ when we interpret silhouettes as three-dimensional shapes?' Marr motivates a central representational primitive by stating physical constraints that lead to the proof of a theorem. *Physical constraints*: (1) each line of sight from the viewer to the object grazes the object's surface at exactly one point; (2) nearby points on the contour in an image arise from nearby points on the contour generator on the viewed object (that is, points that appear close together in the image actually are close together on the object's surface); (3) the contour generator lies wholly in a single plane. Obviously, these are conditions of perception that may fail, but they are conditions under which we seem to do best at solving the problem of deriving three-dimensional shape descriptions from representations of silhouettes. *Definition: a generalized cone* is a three-dimensional object generated by moving a cross-section along an axis; the cross-section may vary smoothly in size, but its shape remains the same. (For example, footballs, pyramids, legs, stalagmites are or approximate generalized cones.) *Theorem*: if the surface is smooth and if physical constraints (1)–(3) hold for all distant viewing positions in any one plane, then the viewed surface is a generalized cone. The theorem indicates a natural connection between generalized cones and the imaging process. Marr infers from this, and from certain psycho-physical evidence, that representations of generalized cones – that is, representations with intentional content concerning generalized cones – are likely to be fundamental among our visual representations of three-dimensional objects.[19]

Throughout the theory, representational primitives are selected and individuated by considering specific, contingent facts about the physical world that typically hold when we succeed in obtaining veridical visual information about that world. The information or content of the visual representations is always individuated by reference to the physical objects, properties or relations that are seen. In view of the success-orientation of the theory, this mode of individuation is grounded in its basic methods. If theory were confronted with a species of organism reliably and successfully interacting with a different set of objective visible properties, the representational types that the theory would attribute to the organism would be different, regardless of whether an individual organism's physical mechanisms were different.

We are now in a position to argue that the theory is not individualistic.

1   The theory is intentional.
2   The intentional primitives of the theory and the information they carry are individuated by reference to contingently existing phyiscal items or conditions by which they are normally caused and to which they normally apply.
3   So if these physical conditions and, possibly, attendant physical laws were regularly different, the information conveyed to the subject and the intentional content of his or her visual representations would be different.
4   It is not incoherent to conceive of relevantly different physical conditions and perhaps relevantly different (say, optical) laws regularly causing the same non-intentionally, individualistically individuated physical regularities in the subject's eyes and nervous system. It is enough if the differences are small; they need not be wholesale.
5   In such a case (by 3) the individual's visual representations would carry different information and have different representational content, though the person's whole non-intentional physical history (at least up to a certain time) might remain the same.
6   Assuming that some perceptual states are identified in the theory in terms

of their informational or intentional content, it follows that individualism is not true for the theory of vision.

I shall defend the argument stepwise. I take it that the claim that the theory is intentional is sufficiently evident. The top levels of the theory are explicitly formulated in intentional terms. And their method of explanation is to show how the problem of arriving at certain veridical representations is solved.

The second step of the argument was substantiated through Examples 3 and 4. The intentional content of representations of edges or generalized cones is individuated in terms of *specific* reference to those very contingently instantiated physical properties, on the assumption that those properties normally give rise to veridical representations of them.

The third step in our argument is supported both by the way the theory individuates intentional content (cf. the previous paragraph and Examples 3 and 4), and by the explanatory method of the theory (cf. the second point illustrated above, and Examples 1 and 2). The methods of individuation and explanation are governed by the assumption that the subject has adapted to his or her environment sufficiently to obtain veridical information from it under certain normal conditions. If the properties and relations that *normally* caused visual impressions were regularly different from what they are, the individual would obtain different information and have visual experiences with different intentional content. If the regular, law-like relations between perception and the environment were different, the visual system would be solving different information-processing problems; it would pass through different informational or intentional states; and the explanation of vision would be different. To reject this third step of our argument would be to reject the theory's basic methods and questions. But these methods and questions have already borne fruit, and there are presently no good reasons for rejecting them.

I take it that step four is a relatively unproblematic counterfactual. There is no metaphysically necessary relation between individualistically individuated processes in a person's body and the causal antecedents of those processes in the surrounding world.[20] (To reject this step would be self-defeating for the individualist.) If the environmental conditions were different, the same proximal *visual* stimulations could have regularly had different distal causes. In principle, we can conceive of some regular variation in the distal causes of perceptual impressions with no variation in a person's individualistically specified physical processes, even while conceiving the person as *well adapted* to the relevant environment – though, of course, not uniquely adapted.

Steps three and four, together with the unproblematic claim that the theory individuates some perceptual states in terms of their intentional content or representational types, entail that the theory is non-individualistic.

Steps two and three are incompatible with certain philosophical approaches that have no basis in psychological theory. One might claim that the information content of a visual representation would remain constant even if the physical conditions that lead to the representation were regularly different. It is common to motivate this claim by pointing out that one's visual representations remain the same, whether one is perceiving a black blob on a white surface or having an eidetic hallucination of such a blob. So, runs the reasoning, why should changing the distal causes of a perceptual representation affect its content? On this view, the content of a given perceptual representation is commonly given as that of 'the distal cause of *this* representation', or 'the property in the world that has *this* sort of visual appearance'. The content of these descriptions is intended to remain constant between possible situations in which the micro-physical events of a person's visual processes remain the same while distal causes of those processes are regularly and significantly different. For it is thought that the representations themselves (and our experiences of *them*) remain constant under these circumstances. So as the distal antecedents of one's perceptual representations vary, the reference of those representations will vary, but their intentional content will not.[21]

There is more wrong with this line than I have room to develop here. I will mention some of the more straightforward difficulties. In the first place, the motivation from perceptual illusion falls far short. One is indeed in the same perceptual state whether one is seeing or hallucinating. But that is because the intentional content of one's visual state (or representation) is individuated against a background in which the relelvant state is *normally* veridical. Thus the fact that one's percepts or perceptual states remain constant between normal perception and halluncinations does not even tend to show that the intentional visual state remains constant between circumstances in which different physical conditions are the normal antecedents of one's perceptions.

Let us consider the proposals for interpreting the content of our visual representations. In the first place both descriptions ('the distal cause of *this* representation' *et al.*) are insufficiently specific. There are lots of distal causes and lots of things that might be said to appear 'thus' (for example, the array of light striking the retina as well as the physical surface). We identify the relevant distal cause (and the thing that normally appears thus and so) as the thing that we actually see. To accurately pick out the 'correct' object with one of these descriptions would at the very least require a more complex specifi-cation. But filling out the descriptive content runs into one or both of two difficulties: either it includes kinds that are tied to a specific environ-ment ('the convex, rough-textured object that is causing this representation'). In such a case, the description is still subject to our argument. For these kinds are individuated by reference to the empirical environment. Or it complicates the constraints on the causal chain to the extent that the com-plications cannot plausibly be attributed to the content of processes in the early visual system.

Even in these unrevised forms, the descriptions are over-intellectualized philosophers' conceits. It is extremely implausible and empirically without warrant to think that packed into every perceptual representation is a distinction between distal cause and experiential effect, or between objective reality and perceptual appearance. These are distinctions developed by reflecting on the ups and downs of visual perception. They do not come in at the ground, animal level of early vision.

A further mistake is the view that the perceptual representations never purport to specify particular physical properties *as such*, but only via some relation they bear to inner occurrences, which are directly referred to. (Even the phrase 'the convex object causing this percept' invokes a specification of objective convexity as such.) The view will not serve the needs of psychological explanation as actually practiced. For the descriptions of information are too inspecific to account for specific successes in solving problems in retrieving information about the actual, objective world.

The best empirical theory that we have individuates the intentional content of visual representations by specific reference to specific physical characteristics of visible properties and relations. The theory does not utilize complicated, self-referential, attributively used role descriptions of those properties. It does not individuate content primarily by reference to phenomenological qualities. Nor does it use the notions of cause or appearance in specifying the intentional content of early visual representations.[22]

The second and third steps of our argument are incompatible with the claim that the intentional content of visual representations is determined by their 'functional role' in each person's system of dispositions, non-intentionally and individualistically specified. This claim lacks any warrant in the practice of the science. In the first place, the theory suggests no reduction of the intentional to the non-intentional. In the second, although what a person can do, non-visually, constitutes evidence for what he or she can see, there is little ground for thinking that either science or common sense takes an individual person's non-visual abilities fully to determine the content of his or her early visual experience. A person's dispositions and beliefs develop by adapting to what the person sees. As the person develops, the visual system (at least at its more advanced stages – those involving recognition) and the belief and language systems affect each other. But early vision seems relatively independent of these non-visual systems. A large part of learning is accommodating one's dispositions to the information carried by visual representations. Where there are failures of adaptation, the person does not know what the visual apparatus is presenting to him or her. Yet the presentations are there to be understood.

III

There is a general argument that seems to me to show that a person's non-intentional dispositions could not fix (individuate) the intentional content of the person's visual presentations. The argument begins with a conception of objectivity. As long as the person's visual presentations are of public, objective objects, properties, or relations, it is possible for the person to have mistaken presentations. Such mistakes usually arise for a single sensory modality, so that when dispositions associated with other modalities (for example, touch) are brought into play, the mistake is rectified. But as long as the represented object or property is objective and physical, it is in principle possible, however unlikely, that there be a confluence of illusions such that all an individual person's sensory modalities would be fooled and all of the person's non-intentional dispositions would fail to distinguish between the normal condition and the one producing the mistaken sensory representations. This is our first assumption. In the argument, we shall employ a corollary: our concept of objectivity is such that no one objective entity that we visually represent is such that it must vary with, or be typed so as necessarily to match exactly, an individual's proximal stimuli and discriminative abilities. The point follows from a realistic, and even from a non-subjectivistic, view of the objects of sight.[23]

We argued earlier that intentional representational types are not in general individuated purely in terms of an attributive role description of a causal relation, or a relation of appearance similarity, between external objects and qualitative perceptual representatives of them. For present purposes, this is our second assumption: some objective physical objects and properties are visually represented as such; they are specifically specified.

Thirdly, in order to be empirically informative, some visual representations that represent objective entities as such must have the representational characteristics that they have partly *because* instances regularly enter into certain relations with those objective entities.[24] Their carrying information, their having objective intentional content, consists partly in their being the normal causal products of objective entities. And their specific intentional content depends partly on their being the normal products of the specific objective entities that give rise to them. That is why we individuate intentional visual representations in terms of the objective entities that they normally apply to, for members of a given species. This is the core of truth in the slogan, sometimes misapplied I think, that mistakes presuppose a background of veridicality.

The assumptions in the three preceding paragraphs enable us to state a general argument against individualism regarding visual states. Consider a person P who normally correctly perceives instances of a particular objective visible property O. In such cases, let the intentional type of P's perceptual representation (or perceptual state) be O'. Such perceptual representations are normally the product of interaction with instances of O. But imagine that for P, perceptual representations typed O' are on some few occasions the product of instances of a different objective property C. On such occasions, P mistakenly sees an instance of C as an O; P's perceptual state is of type O'. We are assuming that O' represents any instance of O as such (as an O), in the sense of our second premise, not merely in terms of some attributive role description. Since O' represents an objective property, we may, by our first premise, conceive of P as lacking at his or her disposal (at every moment up to a given time) any means of discriminating the instance of C from instances of O.

Now hold fixed both P's physical states (up to the given time) and his or her discriminative abilities, non-intentionally and individualistically specified. But conceive of the world as lacking O altogether. Suppose that the optical laws in the counterfactual environment are such that the impressions on P's eyes and the normal causal processes that lead to P's visual representations are explained in terms of Cs (or at any rate, in terms of some objective, visible entities other than instances of O). Then, by our third premise, P's visual representation (or visual state) would not be of intentional type O'. At the time when in the actual situation P is misrepresenting a C as an O, P may counterfactually be perceiving something (say, a C) correctly (as a C) – if the processes that lead to that visual impression are normal and of a type that normally produces the visual impression that P has on that occasion. So the person's intentional visual states could vary while his or her physical states and non-intentionally specified discriminative abilities remained constant.

The first premise and the methodology of intentional–content individuation articulated in the third premise entail the existence of examples. Since examples usually involve shifts in optical laws, they are hard to fill out in great detail. But it is easiest to imagine concrete cases taken from early but still conscious vision. These limit the number of an individual's dispositions that might be reasonably thought to bear on the content of his or her visual states. Early vision is relatively independent of linguistic or other cognitive abilities. It appears to be relatively modular.

Suppose that the relevant visible entities are very small and not such as to bear heavily on adaptive success. An O may be a shadow of a certain small size and shape on a gently contoured surface. A C may be a similarly sized, shallow crack. In the actual situation P sees Os regularly and correctly as Os: P's visual representations are properly explained and specified as shadow representations of the relevant sort. We assume that P's visual and other discriminative abilities are fairly normal. P encounters Cs very rarely and on those few occasions not only misperceives them as Os, but has no dispositions that would enable him or her to discriminate those instances from Os. We may assume that given P's actual abilities and the actual laws of optics, P would be capable, in ideal circumstances, of visually discriminating some instances of Cs (relevantly similar cracks) from instances of O (the relevant sort of shadows). But our supposition is that in the actual cases where P is confronted by instances of Cs, the circumstances are not ideal. All P's abilities would not succeed in discriminating those instances of relevant cracks, in those circumstances, from instances of relevant shadows. P may not rely on touch in cases of such small objects; or touch may also be fooled. P's ability to have such mistaken visual states is argued for by the objectivity premise.

In the counterfactural case, the environment is different. There are no instances of the relevant shadows visible to P; and the laws of optics differ in a way that P's physical visual stimulations (and the rest of P's physical make-up) are unaffected. Suppose that the physical visual stimulations that in the actual case are derived from instances of O – at the relevant sort of shadows – are counterfactually caused by and explained in terms of Cs, relevantly sized cracks. Counterfactually, the cracks take the places of the shadows. On the few occasions where, in the actual case, P misperceives shadows as cracks, P is counterfactually confronted with cracks; and the optical circumstances that lead to the visual impressions on those occasions are, we may suppose, normal for the counterfactual environment.[25] On such counterfactual occasions, P would be visually representing small cracks as small cracks. P would never have visual representations of the relevant sort of shadows. One can suppose that even if there were the relevant sort of shadows in the counterfactual environment, the different laws of optics in that environment would not enable P ever to see them. But since P's visual states would be the normal products of normal processes and would provide as good an empirical basis for learning about the counterfactual environment as P has for learning about the actual environment, it would be absurd to hold that (counterfactually) P misperceives the prevalent cracks as shadows on gently contoured surfaces. Counterfactually, P correctly sees the cracks as cracks. So P's intentional perceptual states differ between actual and counterfactual situations. This general argument is independent of the theory of vision that we have been discussing. It supports and is further supported by that theory.

IV

Although the theory of vision is in various ways special, I see no reason why its non-individualistic methods will not find analogs in other parts of psychology. In fact, as we noted, since vision provides intentional input for other cognitive capacities, there is reason to think that the methods of the theory of vision are presupposed by other parts of psychology. These non-individualistic methods are grounded in two natural assumptions. One is that there are psychological states that represent, or are about, an objective world. The other is that there is a scientific account to be given that presupposes certain successes in our interaction with the world (vision, hearing, memory, decision, reasoning, empirical belief formation, communication, and so forth), and that explains specific successes and failures by reference to these states.

The two assumptions are, of course, inter-related. Although an intention to eat meat is 'conceptually' related to eating meat, the relation is not one of entailment in either direction, since the representation is about an objective matter. An individual may be, and often is, ignorant, deluded, misdirected or impotent. The very thing that makes the non-individualistic thought experiments possible – the possibility of certain sorts of ignorance, failure and misunderstanding – helps make it possible for explanations using non-individualistic language to be empirically informative. On the other hand, as I have argued above, some successful interaction with an objective world seems to be a precondition for the objectivity of some of our intentional representations.

Any attempt to produced detailed accounts of the relations between our attitudes and the surrounding world will confront a compendium of empirically interesting problems. Some of the most normal and mundane successes in our cognitive and conative relations to the world must be explained in terms of surprisingly complicated intervening processes, many of which are themselves partly described in terms of intentional states. Our failures may be explained by reference to *specific* abnormalities in operations or surrounding conditions. Accounting for environmentally specific successes (and failures) is one of the tasks that psychology has traditionally set itself.

An illuminating philosophy of psychology must do justice not only to the mechanistic elements in the science. It must also relate these to psychology's attempt to account for tasks that we succeed and fail at, *where these tasks are set by the environment and represented by the subject him- or herself.* The most salient and important of these tasks are those that arise through relations to the natural and social worlds. A theory that insists on describing the states of human beings *purely* in terms that abstract from their relations to any specific environment cannot hope to provide a completely satisfying explanation of our accomplishments. At present our best theories in many domains of psychology do not attempt such an abstraction. No sound reason has been given for thinking that the non-individualistic language that psychology now employs is not an appropriate language for explaining these matters, or that explanation of this sort is impossible.

Acknowledgements

A version of this chapter was given at the Sloan Conference at MIT in May 1984. I have benefited from commentaries by Ned Block, Fred Dretske and Stephen Stich. I have also made use of discussion with Jerry Fodor, David Israel, Bernie Kobes and Neil Stillings; and I am grateful to the editors of *The Philosophical Review* for several suggestions.

Notes

1 'Individualism and the Mental', *Midwest Studies in Philosophy* 4 (1979), 73–121 (Minnesota, University of Minnesota Press); 'Other bodies', in A. Woodfield (ed.), *Thought and Object* pp. 97–120 (Oxford, Oxford University Press, 1982); 'Two thought experiments reviewed', *Notre Dame Journal of Formal Logic* 23 (1982), 284–93; 'Cartesian error and the obectivity of perception', R. Grimm and D. Merrill (eds), *Contents of Thought*, pp. 62–76 (Arizona, University of Arizona Press); 'Intellectual norms and foundations of mind', *Journal of Philosophy* 83 (1986), 697–720. The aluminum argument is adpated from an argument in H. Putnam, 'The meaning of "meaning",' *Philosophical Papers*, vol. 2 (Cambridge, Cambridge University Press, 1975). What Putnam wrote in his paper was, strictly, not even compatible with this argument (cf. the first two cited papers in this note

for discussion). But the aluminum argument lies close to the surface of the argument he does give. The arthritis argument raises rather different issues, despite its parallel methodology.

2   On basic categories, cf., e.g., E. Rosch et al., 'Basic objects in natural categories', *Cognitive Psychology* 8 (1976), 382–439. On the general claim in the last sentence, cf. 'Intellectual norms', and the latter portion of this chapter.

3   Our talk of intentional 'content' will be ontologically colorless. It can be converted to talk about how that-clauses (or their components) are interpreted and differentiated – taken as equivalent or non-equivalent – for the cognitive purposes of psychology. Not all intentional states or structures that are attributed in psychology are explicitly propositional. My views in this chapter apply to intentional states generally.

4   Certain approaches to intensional logic featuring either 'direct reference' or some analogy between the attitudes and necessity have urged that this practice of fine-structuring attitudinal content be revised. I think that for purely philosophical reasons these approaches cannot account for the attitudes. For example, they do little to illumine the numerous variations on Frege's 'paradox of identity'. They seem to have even less to recommend them as prescriptions for the language of psychology. Some defenses of individualism have taken these approaches to propositional content to constitute the opposition to individualism. I think that these approaches are not serious contenders as accounts of propositional attitudes and thus should be left out of the discussion.

5   S. Stich, *From Folk Psychology to Cognitive Science* (Cambridge, Mass., MIT Press, 1983), ch. 8. Although I shall not discuss the unformulated Ockhamesque principle, I am skeptical of it. Apart from question-begging assumptions, it seems to me quite unclear why a science should be required to explain two instances of the same phenomenon in the same way, particularly if the surrounding conditions that led to the instances differ.

6   I have not been able to find a fully explicit statement to this argument in published work. It seems to inform some passages of Jerry Fodor's 'Methodological solipsism considered as a research strategy in cognitive psychology' in Fodor's *Representations* (Cambridge, Mass., MIT Press, 1981), e.g., pp. 228–32. It lies closer to the surface in much work influenced by Fodor's paper. Cf., e.g., C. McGinn, 'The structure of content' in A. Woodfield (ed.) *Thought and Object*, pp. 207–16 (Oxford, Oxford University Press, 1982). Many who, like McGinn, concede the force of the arguments against individualism utilize something like this argument to maintain that individualistic 'aspects' of intentional states are all that are relevant to psychological explanation.

7   In 'Individualism and the mental', pp. 109–13, I argue that token *identity* theories are rendered implausible by non-individualistic thought experiments. But token identity theories are not the last bastion for materialist defense policy. Composition is what is crucial. It is coherent, but I think mistaken, to hold that propositional attitude attributions non-rigidly pick out physical events: so the propositional attributions vary between the actual and counterfactual protagonists in the thought experiments, though the ontology of mental event tokens remains identical. This view is compatible with most of my opposition to individualism. But I think that there is no good reason to believe the very implausible thesis that mental events are not individuated ('essentially' or 'basically') in terms of the relevant propositional attitude attributions. So I reject the view that the same mental events

(types or tokens) are picked out under different descriptions in the thought experiments. These considerations stand behind my recommending, to the convinced materialist, composition rather than identity as a paradigm. (I remain unconvinced.)

8   The points about ontology and reference go back to Frege, *Foundations of Arithmetic*, trans. Austin (Northwestern University Press, Evanston, 1968). The point about reduction is relatively obvious, though a few philosophers have urged conceptions of the unity of science in a relatively aprioristic spirit. At least as applied to ontology, the point is also basic to Quine's pragmatism. There are, however, strands to Quine's work and in the work of most of his followers that seem to me to let a preoccupation with physicalism get in the way of the Fregean (and Quinean) pramatic insight. It is simply an illusion to think that metaphysical or even epistemic preconceptions provide a standard for judging the ontolgoies or explanatory efforts of particular sciences, deductive or inductive.

9   Even more generally, I think that epistemic power in philosophy derives largely from reflections on particular implementations of successful cognitive practices. By a cognitive practice, I mean a cognitive enterprise that is stable, that conforms to standard conditions of inter-subjective checkability, and that incorporates a substantial core of agreement among its practitioners. Revisionistic and philosophical hypotheses must not, of course, be rejected out of hand. Sometimes, but rarely nowadays, such hypotheses influence cognitive practices by expanding theoretical imagination so as to lead to new discoveries. The changed practice may vindicate the philosophical hypothesis. But the hypothesis waits on such vindication.

10   For an interesting elaboration of this theme in an experimental context, see A. Tversky, 'Features of similarity', *Psychological Review* 84 (1977), 327–52. Cf. also Rosch et al., 'Basic objects in natural categories'.

11   The most careful and plausible of several papers advocating a new language of individualist explanation is Stephen White, 'Partial character and the language of thought', *Pacific Philosophical Quarterly* 63 (1982), 347–65. It seems to me, however, that many of the problems mentioned in the text here and below, beset this advocacy. Moreover, the positive tasks set for the new language are already performed by the actual non-individualist language of psychology. The brain-in-vat intuitions raise very complex issues that I cannot pursue here. I discuss them further in 'Cartesian error and the objectivity of perception'.

12   See especially 'Intellectual norms and foundations of mind', but also 'Individualism and the mental', pp. 81–2.

13   'Representational type' (also 'intentional type') is a relatively theory-neutral term for intentional content, or even intentional state-kinds. Cf. n. 3. One could about as well speak of concepts, percepts, and the representational or intentional aspects of thought contents – or of the counterpart states.

14   In what follows I make use of the important book *Vision*, by David Marr, New York, W.H. Freeman, 1982). Marr writes: 'The purpose of these representations is to provide useful descriptions of aspects of the real world. The structure of the real world therefore plays an important role in determining both the nature of the representations that are used and the nature of the processes that derive and maintain them. An important part of the theoretical analysis is to make explicit the physical constraints and assumptions that have been used in the design of the representations and processes ... It is of critical importance that the tokens [representational particulars] one obtains [in the theoretical analysis] correspond

to real physical changes on the viewed surface; the blobs, lines, edges, groups, and so forth that we shall use must not be artifacts of the imaging process, or else inferences made from their structure backwards to the structures of the surface will be meaningless' (pp. 43–4). Marr's claim that the structure of the real world figures in determining the nature of the representations that are attributed in the theory is tantamount to the chief point about representation or reference that generates our non-individualist thought experiments – the first step in the schema. I shall show that these remarks constitute the central theoretical orientation of the book. Calling the theory Marr's is convenient but misleading. Very substantial contributions have been made by many others; and the approach has developed rapidly since Marr's death. Cf. for example, Ballard et al., 'Parallel vision computation', *Nature* 306 (1983), 21–6. What I say about Marr's book applies equally to more recent developments.

15   It is an interesting question when to count the visual system as having become intentional. I take it that information is, in a broad sense, carried by the intensity values in the retinal image; but I think that this is too early to count the system as intentional or symbolic. I'm inclined to agree with Marr that where zero-crossings from different sized filters are checked against one another (cf. Example 1), it is reasonable to count visual processes as representational of an external physical reality. Doing so, however, depends on seeing this stage as part of the larger system in which objective properties are often discriminated from subjective artifacts of the visual system.

16   Marr, *Vision*, pp. 68–70; cf. also D. Marr and B. Hildreth, 'Theory of edge detection', *Proceedings of the Royal Society of London* Series B 207 (1980), 187–217, where the account is substantially more detailed.

17   Marr *Vision*, pp. 111–16; D. Marr and Poggio, 'A computational theory of human stereo vision', *Proceedings of the Royal Society of London*, Series B 204 (1979), 301–28. Marr, *Vision* pp. 205–12; S. Ullman, *The Interpretation of Visual Motion* (Cambridge, Mass., MIT Press, 1979).

18   Marr, *Vision*, pp. 44–71.

19   Ibid., pp. 215–25.

20   As I have intimated above, I doubt that all biological, including physiological, processes and states in a person's body are individualistically individuated. The failures of individualism for these sciences involve different, but related considerations.

21   Descartes went further in the same direction. He thought that the perceptual system, and indeed the intellect, could not make a mistake. Mistakes derived from the will. The underlying view is that we primarily perceive or make perceptual reference to our own perceptions. This position fails to account plausibly for various visual illusions and errors that precede any activity of the will, or even intellect. And the idea that perceptions are in general what we make perceptual reference to has little to recommend it and, nowadays, little influence. The natural and, I think, plausible view is that we have visual representations that specify external properties specifically, that these representations are pre-doxastic in the sense they are not themselves objects of belief, and that they sometimes fail to represent correctly what is before the person's eyes: when they result from abnormal processes.

22   Of course, at least in the earliest stages of visual representation, there are analogies between qualitative features of representations in the experienced image and the

features that those representations represent. Representations that represent bar segments are bar-shaped, or have some phenomenological property that strongly tempts us to call them 'bar-shaped'. Similarly for blobs, dots, lines and so forth. (Marr and Hildreth, 'Theory of edge detection', p. 211, remark on this dual aspect of representations.) These 'analogies' are hardly fortuitous. Eventually they will probably receive rigorous psycho-physical explanations. But they should not tempt one into the idea that visual representations in general make reference to themselves, much less into the idea that the content of objective representation is independent of empirical relations between the representations and the objective entities that give rise to them. Perhaps these qualitative features are constant across all cases where one's bodily processes, non-intentionally specified, are held constant. But the information they carry, their intentional content, may vary with their causal antecedents and causal laws in the environment.

23   There is no need to assume that the abnormal condition is unverifiable. Another person with relevant background information might be able to infer that the abnormal condition is producing a perceptual illusion. In fact, another person with different dispositions might even be able to perceive the difference.

24   Not all perceptual representations that specify objective entities need have their representational characteristics determined in this way. The representational characters of *some* visual representations (or states) may depend on the subject's background theory or primarily on interaction among other representations. There are hallucinations of purple dragons. (Incidentally, few if any of the perceptual representations – even the conscious perceptual representations – discussed in Marr's theory depend in this way on the subject's conceptual background.) Here, I assume only that *some* visual representations acquire their representational characters through interaction. This amounts to the weak assumption that the formation of some perceptual representations is *empirical*. Some of the interaction that leads to the formation and representational characters of certain innate perceptual tendencies (or perhaps even representations) may occur in the making of the species, not in the learning histories of individuals. Clearly this complication could be incorporated into a generalization of this third premise, without affecting the anti-individualistic thrust of the argument.

25   What of the non-intentionally specified dispositions that in the actual environment (given the actual laws of optics) would have enabled P to discriminate Cs from Os in ideal circumstances? In the counterfactual environment, in view of the very different optical laws and different objects that confront P, one can suppose that these dispositions have almost any visual meaning that one likes. These dispositions would serve to discriminate Cs from some other sort of entity. In view of the objectivity premise, the non-intentional dispositions can always be correlated with different, normal antecedent laws and conditions, in terms of which their intentional content may be explained. The argument of this section is developed in parallel but different ways in 'Cartesian error and the objectivity of perception'.

11

A Modal Argument for Narrow Content

Jerry A. Fodor

Here is a modern antinomy. On the one hand, there is argument A:

Argument A:
1 My twin and I are molecular duplicates.
2 Therefore our (actual and counterfactual) behaviors are identical in relevant respects.
3 Therefore the causal powers of our mental states are identical in relevant respects.
4 Therefore my twin and I belong to the same natural kind for purposes of psychological explanation and 'individualism' is true.

But, on the other hand, there is argument B:

Argument B:
1′ My twin and I are molecular duplicates.
2′ Nevertheless, our (actual and counterfactual) behaviors are different in relevant respects.
3′ Therefore the causal powers of our mental states are different in relevant respects.
4′ Therefore my twin and I belong to different natural kinds for purposes of psychological explanation and 'individualism' is false.

At least one of these arguments must be unsound. Which one? And what is wrong with it?

In chapter 2 of *Psychosemantics*,[1] I offered some considerations intended to advance the cause of argument A. They were supposed to show that mental states that differ only in 'broad' intentional properties (the sorts of intentional properties that the mental states of molecular twins may fail to share) *ipso facto* do not differ in causal powers; hence that mere differences in broad intentional content do not determine differences in natural kinds for purposes of psychological explanation. The arguments I offered in *Psychosemantics* were not, however, greeted with unequivocal enthusiasm. Such was their subtlety, in fact, that I am not, myself, always quite sure how they were supposed to go. In the present chapter, I propose to have another try at bolstering argument A. I shall use many of the same materials that I did in *Psychosemantics*, but I shall put the pieces together somewhat differently. In passing, I shall have a word or two to say about some of the comments that the *Psychosemantics* arguments have provoked.

A preliminary remark, however, before we are under way. For most philosophical purposes, it may not really matter much how the individualism issue turns out. For example, I do not think that a resolution in favor of argument A (that is, in favor of individualism) would affect the status of 'externalism' in semantics. Externalism is independent of individualism because, whatever the *explanatory* status of broad content, it is not in dispute (anyhow, it is not in *this* dispute) that the content of my twin's *water* thoughts differ from the content of mine; or that 'water' means something different in my mouth and in his; or that these semantical differences derive from differences in our respective head–world relations. (Presumably they derive from the fact that, whereas the causal history of my *water* thoughts connects them to samples of H_2O, the causal history of his connects them to samples of XYZ. If, in short, the intuitions about twins make a case for content externalism at all, then that case stands whether or not broad intentional states determine natural kinds for the purposes of causal explanation in psychology.

Similarly – and *pace*, for example, Stephen Stich[2] – it is by no means obvious that the scientific vindication of intentional realism depends on how the issues about individualism are resolved. Suppose that there is some metaphysical argument to show that causal explanation in psychology requires the individuation of mental states to be individualistic (so that the mental states of molecular twins are *ipso facto* type-identical, as in argument A). It would follow that psychological explanation is not, strictly speaking, a species of belief–desire explanation since it is common ground that beliefs and desires are individuated broadly. But it would still be open whether psychological explanations are species of *intentional* explanations. That would depend on whether an individualistic notion of 'intentional state' suitable for the purposes of psychological explanation can be constructed. (For more on this, see *Psychosemantics*.)

In short, you can do quite a lot of business in semantics and the philosophy of mind while benignly neglecting the issues about individualism. Still, I think it is worth trying to get these issues straight. We are about to see that they raise some interesting questions about the family of notions that include causal explanation, causal power, type identity and natural kind. Getting some of this stuff sorted out may therefore be of use to metaphysics and the philosophy of science, even if it leaves things more or less unaltered in semantics and the philosophy of mind. So here we go.

Argument A says that, in virtue of our molecular identity, my twin's behavior and my behavior are identical *in all relevant respects*. Not, of course, that they are identical *tout court*. On the contrary, just as it is common ground in this discussion that the *mental states* of twins can differ in certain of their intentional properties, so it is common ground that twin *behaviors* can differ under some of their intentional descriptions. Indeed, it may be that the second concession is entailed by the first, since it is plausible that the intentional properties of behaviors are inherited from the intentional contents of their mental causes. Thus, it is plausibly because I can think about water and my twin cannot that I but not my twin can reach for water; drill for water, or recommend water to a thirsty friend. A committed individualist might wish to argue that none of these is really, *strictu dictu*, an example of *behavioral* description; but that is not a tack that I propose to take.

So then: twins can differ in the contents of their mental states; and, in consequence of these mental state differences, the behaviors of twins can differ in certain of their intentional properties. I shall take for granted (what is not, however, uncontested) that these differences in intentional properties are the *only* (relevant) differences between the twins' behaviors. That is, I am taking it for granted that the behaviors of twins are *ipso facto* identical in all non-intentional properties that are relevant to psychological taxonomy. That is, of course, stronger than assuming what, I think, literally everybody agrees about, namely, that our behaviors are identical under *physical* descriptions, i.e. identical *qua* motions.

Here is an apparent exception to the stronger claim: if I utter 'Gimme water', then, if all goes well, I get water; but if my twin utters 'Gimme water', then, if all goes well, he gets twater. So maybe there are non-intentional descriptions under which our behaviors are relevantly different after all. Second thoughts, however, make this difference go away; it is an artifact of the boring consideration that, whereas my utterance happened on earth, his happened on twin-earth. The salient consideration is that, if twin-me had uttered 'Gimme water' here, he would have gotten water; and if I had uttered 'Gimme water' on twin earth, I would have gotten twater. To put it slightly differently, my 'Gimme water' does not get water *come what may*; at best it gets water *in certain circumstances*. But in *those* circumstances, his 'Gimme water' gets water, too.[3]

The moral is that you have to judge identity and difference of causal powers in a way that bears the counterfactuals in mind, namely, *across* contexts rather than *within* contexts.[4] That does not get us out of the woods, however. For notice that, in the case where I utter 'Gimme water' on earth$_2$, and my twin utters it here, neither of us gets what he asks for. That is, whatever the context of utterance, my utterance is a water request and his utterance is a twater request. So our behaviors remain relevantly different under these intentional descriptions *even by the across-context test*. It is this residual difference between the behaviors – their cross-context difference under certain intentional descriptions – which is the challenge to individualism and local supervenience.

So then, the question about individualism is: do the twins' mental states belong to different natural kinds (do they have different causal powers) in virtue of differences in the intentional properties of the twins' behavior for which they are responsible? Since 'causal power', 'natural kind', and the like are, of course, technical terms, this question is not possessed of the highest degree of clarity. We shall see, however, that there are some clear intuitions about cases, and they will do for the purposes at hand.

It should be evident that the kind of question we are raising about the intentional states of twins can also arise in cases that have nothing in particular to do with intentionality. Suppose we have a pair of causes C1, C2, together with their respective effects E1, E2. Assume that:

C1 differs from C2 in that C1 has cause property CP1 where C2 has cause property CP2.
E1 differs from E2 in that E1 has effect property EP1 and E2 has effect property EP2.
The difference between C1 and C2 is responsible for the difference between E1 and E2 in the sense that, if C1 had had CP2 rather than CP1, then E1 would have EP2 rather than EP1; and if C2 had had CP1 rather than CP2, E2 would have had EP1 rather than EP2.[5]

Call this *schema* S.[6] And now, what we want to know is: which instances of schema S are cases where the difference between having CP1 and having CP2 is a difference in causal power in virtue of its responsibility for the difference between E1 and E2? (I shall often abbreviate this to 'When is having CP1 rather than CP2 a causal power?') If we knew the answer to this general question, then we would know whether, in particular, the difference between having water thoughts and having twater thoughts is a difference in causal power in virtue of its being responsible for the difference between my producing water behaviors and my twin's producing twater behaviors.[7] And, if we knew *that* we would know whether individualism is true; which is what we started out wanting to know, as the patient reader may recall.

Now, a plausible first reaction to this is that it is just not a philosophical issue. For, one might say, the question being raised is when the fact that a generalization supports counterfactuals shows that it has explanatory status. And the answer will depend, in the usual way, on systematic questions about the simplicity, plausibility, power and so forth of the explanation, and on whether alternative counterfactual supporting generalizations are available. Some of the things that Tyler Burge[8] says about the desirability of not apriorizing about the taxonomy that psychological explanation requires suggest that he would approve of this line of thought; for example: 'It is a mistake . . . to allow ontological preconceptions that have only philosophical underpinning to affect one's interpretation of scientific enterprises. It is a larger mistake to allow them to dictate the sorts of explanatory kinds that are deemed admissible for explanation.'

But though I would not have thought that apriorism is among my major methodological vices, still this does strike me as perhaps a little prim. It would be surprising if we could give interesting *a priori sufficient* conditions for when a difference in the properties of causes constitutes a difference in their causal powers. But it seems likely that we can give *a priori* arguments for some *necessary* conditions. After all, the commitment to causal explanation presumably has *some* methodological consequences *qua* commitment to causal explanation; and it ought to be possible to tease these out by refecting on what kinds of things causal explanations are.

And, in fact, it does seem reasonably clear, *a priori*, that some instances of schema S are not *bona fide*. Consider, for a thoroughly trivial example, the case where EP1 is the property of being the effect of C1, and EP2 is the property of being the effect of C2. There is, of course, a property of C1 in virtue of which its effects are effects of C1, namely, the property of being C1. Correspondingly, there is a property of C2 in virtue of which its effects are effects of C2, namely, the property of being C2. Counterfactual support goes through in the required way; if the cause of E1 had had the property of being C2 rather than C1, then E1 would have had the property EP2 rather than the property EP1. But it seems *a priori* obvious that this is not a case where having CP1 is a causal power of C's in the virtue of its responsibility for E's having EP1. One of the properties of my effects that your effects cannot have, however hard you try, is *the property of being caused by me*. But I take it to be simply obvious that this difference in our effects does not make the property of *being me rather than you* a causal power. I am not a unit natural kind in virtue of my unique power to cause effects that are effects of me.

It seems clear *a priori*, then, that not every case in which a difference between causes is responsible for a difference in effects is a case where the difference in causes is a difference in their causal powers. There are, in fact, plenty of examples. I can define a property *being an H-particle* that is satisifed by any *x* at time *t* iff [(*x* is a physical particle at *t*) & (the coin in my hand at *t* is heads up)]. And correspondingly for T-particles. So a difference between properties of coins in my hand (namely, the difference between being heads up and being tails up) is responsible for the difference between the state of affairs in which all the particles in the universe are H-particles and the state of affairs in which all the particles in the universe are T-particles. But, of course, the difference between being heads up and being tails up does not count as a causal power in virtue of its responsibility for this difference in the particles.

Or again: in virtue of my having siblings, I am able to have sons who are nephews. A molecular twin who did not have siblings would *ipso facto* fail to have nephews among his children. But I take it to be *a priori* obvious that the difference between having siblings and not having siblings does not constitute a difference in the causal powers of parents in virtue of its responsibility for this difference among the properties of their offspring.[9]

While we are on the topic of what is *a priori* obvious: the preceding three examples might suggest that the difference between CP1 and CP2 in instances of schema S does not constitute a difference of causal powers when CP1 and CP2 are *relational* properties. But a moment's reflection shows that this cannot be right (as, indeed, *Psychosemantics* was at some pains to point out). Taxonomy by relational properties is ubiquitous in the sciences, and it is not in dispute that properties like *being a meteor* or *being a planet* – properties which could, notice, distinguish molecularly identical chunks of rock – constitute causal powers. It is because *this* rock-twin is a planet and *that* rock-twin is not that this rock-twin has a Keplerian orbit and that rock-twin does not; it is because this rock-twin is a meteor and that rock-twin is not that this rock-twin's effects include craters and that rock-twin's effects do not. But, patently, *being a planet* and *being a meteor* are relational properties in good standing. To be a planet is to be a rock (or whatever) that is revolving around a star; to be a meteor is to be a rock (or whatever) that is falling, or has fallen, into collision with another rock.

Since the intuitions are pretty strong in all these cases, there is *prima facie* reason to suppose that there are some conditions on cause properties being causal powers which can be recognized from the armchair; not all cause properties are causal powers; not all relational properties fail to be, for two examples. I shall presently state a condition that, I claim, has to be satisifed if a property of a cause is a causal power in virtue of its responsibility for a certain property of an effect; and I shall claim that properties that distinguish twins (like being causally connected to water rather than twater; or having water thoughts rather than twater thoughts) do not satisfy this condition in virtue of their responsibility for differences between the intentional properties of the twins' behaviors. My evidence for the acceptability of this condition will be largely that it sorts examples like the ones I have just run through in an intuitively satisfactory way.

We need, however, some more ground clearing before we get down to it. (I solicit the reader's forbearance; once the ground is all clear, we shall be able to move very fast.) To begin with, I want to call your attention to what turns out to be a critical property of schema S: the question we are raising is not whether the difference between having CP1 and having CP2 is a difference in causal powers; rather, it is whether the difference between having CP1 and having CP2 is a difference in causal powers *in virtue of its being responsible for a certain difference between E1 and E2*, namely, in virtue of its being responsible for E1's having EP1 rather than EP2 and for E2's having EP2 rather than EP1. The point I am wanting to emphasize is that a cause property might fail to count as a causal power in virtue of its responsibility for one effect property, but still might constitute a causal power in virtue of its responsibility for some other effect property.

My coin's being heads up (rather than tails up) does not constitute a causal power in virtue of its responsibility for the universe being populated with H-particles; but it might constitute a causal power in virtue of its being responsible for my coin's reflecting light the way it does rather than some other way (e.g. rather than the way it would if it were tails up). Similarly, my having siblings does not constitute a causal power in virtue of its enabling me to have sons who are nephews. But suppose there is such a thing as sibling's disease; it causes people who have siblings to break out in a rash. Having a sibling might then be a causal power in virtue of being responsible for people coming down with sibling's disease. I stress this point because, if you do not relativize the issue about causal powers in this way, it turns out on a weak assumption that every contingent property is a causal power. The weak assumption is that it is (nomologically) possible to build a detector for any contingent property.

Consider, for example, the property of having had a Bulgarian grandmother who once plucked a daffodil as she went trippingly on her way to market. This is the sort of property that can distinguish between you and your molecular twin. And, no doubt, your effects have properties because of your having had such a grandmother which his do not have because he did not, e.g. your effects have one and all got the property of being the effects of someone who had a Bulgarian grandmother who . . ., etc. But, intuitively, that is not sufficient for making the possession of a Bulgarian G who . . . – or the lack of a Bulgarian G who . . . – a causal power. Indeed, you would not have that that *any* of the Bulgarian-grandmother-dependent properties of your effects – any of the properties that distinguish the effects of the molecular twin with the Bulgarian G . . . from the effects of the molecular twin without one – would be of the right kind to make having a Bulgarian grandmother a causal power.

And yet, it would surely be possible to build (more precisely, it would surely have been possible to have built) a machine which exhaustively examines the piece of space–time that starts with the birth of your grandmother and ends with your birth and which goes into one state if it detects somebody who was your grandmother and was Bulgarian and once plucked a daffodil as she went trippingly on her way to market, but which goes into a different state in case it detects no such person. I assume that it is possible (in principle) to build a machine that reliably detects this property. I am prepared to assume that it is possible (in principle) to build such a machine for any contingent property at all. If this assumption is true, then the Bulgarian grandmother detector can distinguish between you and your molecular twin, and having a Bulgarian grandmother is having a causal power *in virtue of the (actual or possible) effects that instantiations of this property have on Bulgarian G . . . detectors.* (Quite generally, if any contingent property can be detected then any contingent property is a causal power in virtue of the effects of its instantiations on its detectors.) What does not follow, however, is that having had a Bulgarian G . . . is a causal power *in virtue of its effects on your behavior*; or, indeed, in virtue of its responsibility for *any property of yours*.

I am going through this song and dance by way of replying to an argument that Burge suggested (but does *not* endorse) that might lead one to think that having a water thought (rather than a twater thought) *must* be a causal power. After all, this argument says, it must be possible, in principle, to build a machine which looks through the chunk of space–time that starts with my birth and ends up with now, and which goes into one state if I am connected (in the right way) to water but goes into another state if I am connected (in the right way) to twater. This machine responds differently to me and my molecular twin, and does so in virtue of the fact that I am connected with water in the way that my twin is connected to XYZ. So my twin and I differ in our power to effect the states of this machine. So having water thoughts rather than twater thoughts (namely, having the kind of thoughts that you have if you are connected with water rather than twater) is a causal power in virtue of its responsibility for the machine's being in the state it is. So, if individualism says that having water thoughts rather than twater thoughts is *not* a causal power, then individualism is false.

Individualism does *not* say, however, that having water thoughts rather than twater thoughts is not a causal power. What it says is that having water thoughts rather than twater thoughts is not a causal power *in virtue of its being responsible for your producing water behaviors rather than twater behaviors.* (And similarly, being connected to water than than twater is not a causal power in virtue of its being responsible for your having water thoughts rather than twater thoughts.) This is to say that the difference between having water thoughts and having twater thoughts is not a causal power in virtue of its responsibility for those of your properties *which are relevant to what psychological natural kinds your thoughts belong to*, e.g. it is not a causal power in virtue of its responsibility for the properties of your behavior.

That is all that an individualist has to show; to ask him to show more would be to make individualism false if there can be detectors for broad content properties. But that would be to trivialize the issue about individualism[10] since, as remarked above, it is plausible that there can be detectors for *any* contingent property (and, up to the limits of Turing machines, for quite a lot of non-contingent properties, too).

So now: two causes differ in a certain property, and their effects differ in a certain property in virtue of this difference in the causes, and we want to know when the difference between the effects makes the difference between the causes a causal power. I shall tell you in just a moment. But it may be worth emphasizing that the cases we are interested in are not ones where the property that distinguishes the causes is *itself* the property of having a certain causal power.

Consider the case where CP1 just is the property of having the causal power to produce events that have EP1. Then, of course, the difference between having CP1 and not having it is the difference between having a certain causal power and not having it. This sort of case is easy because *it is non-contingent* that having CP1 is having a causal power. There are other, slightly less transparent, cases of this kind. For example, it is non-contingent that *being soluble in water* is having a causal power, because it is non-contingent that things that have that property have the power of dissolving in water; and the property of *being a camshaft* is a causal power because it is non-contingent that things that have that property have the power to lift the valves in a certain kind of engine (given conditions of optimal functioning, etc.). There are, of course, scientifically interesting questions about properties that are non-contingently causal powers; for example, there are interesting questions about the supervenience bases of these properties and about their proper analysis into microfunctions. But there are not any interesting questions about whether things that have these properties have causal powers in virtue of having them. That question answers itself.

Compare, however, the properties of being a planet, being a meteor, and the like. These are causal powers in virtue of, for example, their respective abilities to produce Keplerian orbits and craters. But, in so far as being a planet is a causal power in virtue of the ability of planets to produce Keplerian orbits, it is contingent that being a planet is a causal power (for it is contingent that planets have Keplerian orbits); and in so far as being a meteor is a causal power in virtue of the ability of meteors to make craters, it is contingent that being a meteor is a causal power (for it is contingent that meteors make craters).

Notice that the broad content cases are like the meteor and planet cases and unlike the dispositional and functional cases. It may be that being connected to water that than twater (hence having water thoughts rather than twater thoughts) is having a causal power; but if it is, it is contingent that it is. The property of being connected to water is not *identical* to the property of having a certain causal power, though it may be that there are causal powers that one has if one is connected to water that one would not have if one were not.

I draw two morals. First (contrary to some suggestions of R. van Gulick's),[11] the fact that having a functional property is *ipso facto* having a certain causal power throws no particular light, one way or the other, on the question whether having a broad-content property is having a causal power. This conclusion may seem paradoxical since, after all, it is supposed to be that psychological properties *are* functional; so, if functional properties are non-contingently causal powers, and if psychological properties are functional, how could water thoughts and twater thoughts fail to be causal powers?

The answer is that it is actually not in dispute whether water thoughts and twater thoughts are causal powers. On the contrary, *of course* they are: my water thoughts are causally responsible for my reaching for water, my twin's twater thoughts are causally responsible for his reaching for twater . . ., and so on. The question on which local supervenience – hence individualism – turns, however, is whether the difference between water thoughts and twater thoughts is a *difference* in causal powers. The anti-individualist says 'yes, it is, in virtue of the intentional difference between the behaviors that water thoughts and twater thoughts cause'. The individualist says 'no it isn't. Water thoughts and twater thoughts are the same causal powers, only they're instantiated in people with different causal histories.' The idea that mental states are functional roles resolves this dispute only on the question-begging assumption that water behaviors and twater behaviors are behaviors of different kinds.

Imagine that we had different words for *being thirsty and born in the Bronx* and *being thirsty and born in Queens*. There would then be no question but that being Bronx-thirsty and being Queens-thirsty are causal powers; being Bronx-thirsty and being Queens-thirsty both make people drink, for example. But a question might arise whether being Bronx-thirsty and being Queens-thirsty are *different* causal powers.[12] My point is that this issue would still be open *even though* there is no question but that being Bronx-thirsty and being Queens-thirsty are causal powers.

A functionalist might undertake to argue that they are different causal powers because, on the one hand, psychological states are functionally individuated, and, on the other hand, Bronx thirst and Queens thirst lead to different behavioral consequences, namely, to Bronx thirst-quenching behaviors in the one case and Queens thirst-quenching behaviors on the other. But, clearly, to argue this way would be to beg the question. For, anybody who denies that Queens thirst and Bronx thirst are different causal powers, will also deny – and for the same reason – that Bronx thirst-quenching behavior and Queens thirst-quenching behavior are behaviors of different kinds. So, the principle that psychological states are functionally individuated does not settle questions about identity and difference of causal powers in this sort of case. And, of course, for an individualist, 'wants water' *is* this sort of case; for an individualist, 'wants water' means something like 'thirsty and born *here*'.

What distinguishes twins and threatens local supervenience is the property of *having water thoughts rather than twater thoughts*. No doubt, if functionalism is true, then mental states are one and all causal powers. But, of course, it does not follow from functionalism that differences between mental states are one and all functional differences; so it does not follow that differences between mental states are one and all differences of causal power. In fact, so far as I can tell, the only relevant connection between functionalism and the present issues about individualism is this: if, as I have claimed, the difference between the mental states of twins is at best *contingently* a difference of causal powers, it follows that it *cannot* be a difference of functional role, since differences of functional role are differences of causal powers *non*-contingently.[13] Compare being water soluble rather than twater soluble. It is *not* contingent that having *this* property is having a causal power; to be soluble in water but not in twater just is to have the power to dissolve in the first but not in the second. So it is all right to allow that *being water soluble rather than twater soluble* is a functional property, as, indeed, intuition demands.

My impression is that this is all reasonably untendentious. In general friends of broad content argue that it perfectly well *could turn out* – that there is no metaphysical reason why it should not turn out – that having mental states that differ in their broad content is having mental states that differ in their causal powers. (For example, it could turn out that there are causal laws that distinguish between twins.) But I do not remember hearing anyone argue that having mental states that differ in the way that the mental states of twins do *just is* having mental states that differ in their causal powers. On the contrary, according to the usual understanding, it is their causal *histories* that distinguish the mental states of twins. And the intuition about features of causal history is that some of them are causal powers (e.g. *having been dropped in transit; having been inoculated for smallpox*) and some of them are not (e.g. *having had a Bulgarian grandmother; having been born on a Tuesday*) and it is contingent which are which.

So, then, the second moral that I draw is that, in our hunt for a useful condition on what makes a difference in causal properties a difference in causal powers, we can restrict ourselves to cases where it is *contingent* whether the difference in the properties constitutes a difference between powers. We are, finally, getting to where you can smell blood.

I am now, at last, going to tell you a story about why being a planet (for example) is a causal power and having siblings (for example) is not. I propose to do this in two steps. First, I shall tell you a simplified version of the story; it has the virtue of making the basic idea relatively transparent, but it has the disadvantage that it does not work. I shall then make the technical moves required to plug the leak; the complicated version that emerges will be a motivated condition upon a property of a cause being a causal power; one which, I claim, broad-content properties fail to meet.[14]

So, then: here is me and here is my molecular twin; and I have siblings and he does not; and in virtue of my having siblings my sons are nephews, and in virtue of his not having siblings his sons are not nephews; and what we want to know is: why is *having siblings* not a causal power in virtue of its being responsible for this difference in our offspring? Here is a first fling at the answer: it is because having siblings is *conceptually* connected to having sons who are nephews; to be a nephew *just is* to be a son whose parents have siblings. And, to put it roughly, your causal powers are a function of your *contingent* connections, and not of your conceptual connections. As, indeed, Uncle Hume taught us.

Similarly: though it is a fact that all the world's particles become H-particles when my coin is heads up, that fact does not make being heads up a causal power of my coin. That is again because the connection between all the world's particles becoming H-particles at t and my coin's being heads up at t is conceptual. To be an H-particle at t *just is* to be a particle at a time when my coin is heads up.

Compare cases of relational properties that really are causal powers, like *being a planet*. Being a planet is a causal power in virtue of, for example, its contingent (*a fortiori*, non-conceptual) connection with having a Keplerian orbit. That is, being a planet is a causal power because it is true and contingent that, if you have molecularly identical chunks of rock, one of which is a planet and the other of which is not, then, *ceteris paribus*, the one which is a planet will have a Keplerian orbit, and *ceteris paribus*, the one which is not a planet will not.

Here is the general form of the proposed solution.[15] Consider an instance of schema S. C1 has CP1, C2 has CP2, E1 has EP1, E2 has EP2, and the difference between the causes is responsible for the difference between the effects in the sense that E1 would not have had EP1 (rather than EP2) but that C1 had CP1 (rather than CP2). And what we want to know is: when does the fact that this difference in the causes is responsible for this difference in the effects make CP1 and CP2 causal powers? The answer, which I shall call *condition C* is:

Only when it is not a conceptual truth that causes differ in that one has CP1 where the other has CP2 have effects that differ in that one has EP1 where the other has EP2.[16]

So, for example, it is all right with condition C for *being a meteor* to be a causal power in virtue of the fact that meteors are responsible for craters. Take a pair of rock-twins such that one is a meteor and the other is not. Then (*ceteris paribus*) craters will be among the effects of the first but not among the effects of the second. And the relation between the difference between the rock-twins and the difference between their effects is non-conceptual. So it is all right for being a meteor (rather than a meteor twin) to be a causal power in virtue of the fact that meteors cause craters and meteor twins do not.[17]

Notice that the moral is that it is all right for being a meteor to be a causal power in virtue of this fact; not that being a meteor *is* a causal power in virtue of this fact. Satisfying condition C is, I suppose, necessary but not sufficient for being a causal power. As we are about to see, however, broad-content properties *fail* to satisfy this necessary condition, and that is enough to vindicate individualism.

Consider, first, the property of having water in your history (the property of being connected to water in whatever way it is that I am and my twin is not). The difference between being so connected and not being so connected is responsible for a certain difference between the broad contents of my thoughts and the broad contents of my twin's, namely, that I have water thoughts and he has twater thoughts. What we want to know is: does this difference between our histories count as a causal power in virtue of the difference between the contents of our thoughts for which it is responsible. And the answer is: 'No, because it is *conceptually necessary* that if you are connected to water in the right way then you have water thoughts (rather than twater thoughts) and it is again conceptually necessary that if you are connected to twater in the right way then you have twater thoughts (rather than water thoughts).' To have a water thought *just is* to have a thought that is connected to water in the right way, and to have a twater thought *just is* to have a thought that is connected to twater in the right way.[18] So it is not the case that my being connected to water rather than to twater is a difference in my causal powers in virtue of its responsibility for my having water thoughts rather than twater thoughts.

Now consider the difference between having water thoughts and having twater thoughts. Water thoughts cause water behavior (drilling for water and the like); twater thoughts cause twater behavior (drilling for twater and the like). What we want to know is: does the difference between having water thoughts and having twater thoughts count as a causal power in virtue of the fact that it is responsible for this difference in the intentional properties of the behavior of the thinker? And the answer is: 'No, because it is conceptually necessary that people who have water thoughts (rather than twater thoughts) produce water behavior (rather than twater behavior).' Being water behavior (rather than twater behavior) *just is* being behavior that is caused by water thoughts (rather than twater thoughts). So, though it is true that water thoughts are responsible for water behavior and twater thoughts are not, it does not follow that water thoughts have a causal power that twater thoughts lack. On the contrary, being a water thinker is the same causal power as being a twater thinker, only instantiated in a person with a different causal history.

I have been saying that it is only when the difference between the causes is not conceptually connected to the corresponding differences in the effects that the difference in the causes counts as a difference in causal powers. I think this really is the heart of the matter; it is why being responsible for particles' being H-particles, being responsible for sons' being nephews, being responsible for behavior's being water behavior, and the like do not count as causal powers. But alas, the proposal does not work as stated and I shall have to do some patching.

Suppose that water is Bush's favorite thing to drink. Then, we have both:

1   If I am connected to water in the right way then my thoughts are water thoughts.
2   If I am connected to water in the right way, then my thoughts are thoughts about Bush's favorite drink.

Notice that both 1 and 2 distinguish me from my twin: because he is not connected to water in the right way, it is false of him that he has water thoughts, and it is also false of him that his thoughts are about B's favorite drink. And, though, 1 is conceptually necessary, 2 is contingent. That is, even though the difference between being water-connected and being twater-connected does not satisfy condition C in virtue of its being responsible for the difference between having water thoughts and having twater thoughts, it *does* satisfy condition C in virtue of its responsibility for the difference between having thoughts that are about Bush's favorite drink and having thoughts that are not. Hence, it satisfies condition C in virtue of making some *prima facie psychological* difference, some difference that is *prima facie* relevant to psychological taxonomy. So, even if, as I claim, condition C has its heart in the right place, still, as stated it has no teeth. Damn![19]

Everything is going to be all right, however. Let G be a property that nephews have, and let it be as contingent as you like that nephews have it. (G might be the property of glowing in the dark if it turns out that nephews do that.) Then the following is necessary:

3   If G is a property that nephews have, then if I have siblings then my sons have G.

So, for example, it is necessary that (if nephews glow in the dark, then if I have siblings, then my sons glow in the dark). The reason that this is necessary is, roughly, that it is conceptually necessary that the sons of people with siblings are nephews, so it is conceptually necessary that if you have a sibling then your sons have whatever properties nephews have. Notice, to repeat, that this is true even of properties that nephews have contingently: it is conceptually necessary that if P is a property that nephews have contingently then if you have siblings then your sons have P. (What *is not* true, of course, is 3′, the variant of 3 that has the model operator imported. 3′ is false in the cases where P is a property that nephews have contingently.)

3′ If P is a property of nephews, then if you have siblings then it is necessary that your sons have P.

Now compare 4, which I take to be clearly contingent.

4 If E is a property that Keplerian orbits have then, if I am a planet, then my orbit has E.

(You might wish to try out 4 reading E as the property of being elliptical.)

The reason that 4 is contingent is, roughly, that it is contingent that planets have Keplerian orbits, so it is contingent that if I am a planet then my orbit has whatever properties Keplerian orbits do. This is true even if E is a property that Keplerian orbits have necessarily (like being a Keplerian orbit).[20]

Now we can do the case that was bothering us before. Consider 5, where B might be the property of being a thought about Bush's favorite drink:

5 If B is a property that water thoughts have, then if I am connected to water in the right way, then B is a property that my thoughts have.

I take it that 5 is obviously conceptually necessary. The reason is, roughly, that it is conceptually necessary that if I am connected to water in the right way then my thoughts are water thoughts, and it is a truism that if something is a property of water thoughts then it is a property of my thoughts if my thoughts *are* water thoughts.[21] Similarly, *mutatis mutandis*, with 6.

6 If B is a property that water behaviors have, then if my thoughts are water thoughts then my behaviors have B.

Thus 6 is conceptually necessary because, roughly, it is conceptually necessary that the behaviors that water thoughts cause are water behaviors, so it is conceptually necessary that if something is a property of water behaviors then it is a property of the behaviors of water thinkers. This is true even if B is a property that water behaviors have contingently, like being behaviors that are concerned with Bush's favorite drink.

Compare these cases with ones where thoughts have *bona fide* causal powers. Suppose that thinking about topology gives one headaches. Then we have 7:

7 If B is a property of headaches then if I have topology thoughts then my mental state has B.

Clearly, 7 is contingent, and it is so because of the contingency of the (putative) relation between something's being a topology thought and its having head-aches among its effects. Notice that 7 is contingent even if B is a property that headaches have necessarily (like being headaches).

So, here is the story. For the difference between being CP1 and being CP2 to be a difference of causal powers, it must at least be that the effects of being CP1 differ from the effects of being CP2. But, I claim, it is further required that this difference between the effects be *non-conceptually* related to the difference between the causes. This further condition is motivated both by our intuitions about the examples and by the Humean consideration that causal powers are, after all, powers to enter into non-conceptual relations. Broad content differences, *per se*, do not satisfy this condition, however. There are differences between my behavior and my twin's which are due, in the first instance, to the diference between the intentional contents of our thoughts, and, in the second instance, to my being connected to water in a way that he is not. But these differences among the effects are conceptually related to the differences between the causes; it is conceptually necessary that being con-nected to water rather than twater leads to water thinking rather than twater thinking; and it is again conceptually necessary that water thinking leads to water behavior and twater thinking does not.

So, then, the difference between the mental states of twins does not count as a difference in causal power in virtue of its responsibility for the intentional differences among twin behaviors. So argument B is no good; what is wrong with it is that the inference from 2′ to 3′ is unsound.[22] Finally, since it is assumed that the effects of mental states that differ only in broad content are (relevantly) different *only* under intentional description, it follows that there are *no* taxonomically relevant differences consequent upon broad content differences as such. From the point of view of psychological taxonomy, my mental states must therefore belong to the same natural kind as those of my molecular twin. So individualism is true and local supervenience is preserved. End of story.

> Oi! Halt thief! Stop that person.
> What's the matter?
> You promised me an argument *for* narrow content. But all you've given me is an argument *against* arguments against individualism. I want my money back.
> Sorry.

We have seen that twater thoughts and water thoughts are not different causal powers. So, for the psychologist's purposes, they are the same intentional state.[23] But they cannot be the same intentional state unless they have the same intentional content. And they cannot have the same intentional content unless intentional content is individuated narrowly. Now it is an argument for narrow content.

Much obliged.

My pleasure.

Appendix: A Note on the Cross-context Test for Identity of Causal Powers

Suppose that my twin and I are both green, but I live in red world (where everything except me is red) and he lives in green world (where everything including him is green). So then, he has a property of *being adapted to the color of his environment* which I lack. And, intuitively, this property is a causal power: because he has it, he can sneak up on things; because I lack it, I cannot. But this appears to make trouble for the idea that identity of causal powers has to be assessed *across* contexts. The cross-context test implies that there cannot be a difference in our causal powers unless there are counterfactuals that are true of one of us but not of the other; but, in the present case, it looks like the counterfactuals come out the same for him as they do for me. If he were in my world, he could not sneak up on things; if I were in his world, I could. So our causal powers are the same according to the cross-context test. So there must be something wrong with the idea that identity of causal powers should be assessed across contexts. (For elaboration of what I take to be essentially this line of argument, see van Gulick, 'Metaphysical arguments for internalism'.)

But this argument is fallacious; it rests on a confusion between, to put it roughly, an attributive and referential way of reading the definite description in 'the color of his environment', with a consequent confusion about how the cross-context test applies. This will only take a minute to sort out. If you read 'the color of his environment' referentially, then my twin's being adapted to the color of his environment is his being green. Read that way, then, *I too am adapted to the color of his environment* (I am green, too); so being adapted to the color of his environment is a causal power that we *share*. As, indeed, the cross-context test for causal powers properly predicts: if I were in his environment, I would be able to sneak up on things; if he were in mine, he would not. It is just that, since I am *not* in his environment and he is, being adapted to the color of his environment does him a lot more good than it does me.

If, however, you read 'the color of his environment' attributively, then his being adapted to the color of his environment consists in his being the *same color as the environment that he is in*. So, if you move *that* property across contexts, then when he is in *my* environment his being adapted to the color of his environment consists in his being (not green like me but) *red*. So, if he is adapted to the color of his environment in *that* sense, then when we are both in my environment, he can sneak up on things and I cannot. So, according to the cross-context test, being adapted to the color of his environment is a causal power that my twin has and I lack, which is, again, the intuitively correct result.

So there is nothing wrong with the test.

Question: But what about the property of *being-adapted-to-the-color-of-red-world-and-in-red-world*. Is *that* not a causal power that defies the cross-context test?

Answer: It does not *defy* the cross-context test; it merely satisfies it trivially. Red-world is the only context in which one *can* have that property.

Acknowledgements

This chapter is deeply indebted to conversations with Georges Rey and Steve Stich. Help from Ned Block, Anne Jacobson, Tim Maudlin, Colin McGinn, Brian McLaughlin and Stephen Schiffer is also gratefully acknowledged, as are edifying emails from Fred Adams, Joe Levine and David Rosenthal.

Notes

1   J.A. Fodor, *Psychosemantics* (Cambridge, Mass., MIT Press, 1987).
2   S. Stich, *From Folk Psychology to Cognitive Science* (Cambridge, Mass., MIT Press 1983).
3   Here is a related case, suggested by an example of Colin McGinn's, that I take to be susceptible to the same sort of treatment. Suppose on earth$_2$ there is not only twin-water, but also twin-salt (it is LCaN rather than NaC1). And suppose the fact is that thinking about salt makes you want water (whereas thinking about LCaN makes your twin want XYZ. So, would there not then be a difference between the causal powers of salt thoughts and twin-salt thoughts in virtue of these differences between the contents of the wants that they cause? No, because salt thoughts do not have the power to cause water wants *come what may*; what they have is the power to cause water wants *in somebody who has the concept water*. (That is, in somebody who has the appropriate causal/historical, or whatever, connections to H$_2$O.) But, of course, twin-salt thoughts have *that* power too (just as salt thoughts have the power to cause twater wants in somebody who has the appropriate causal/historical connections to XYZ. Here as elsewhere, one applies the cross-context test by asking whether A would have the same effects as B does have if A were to interact with the same things (in the present case, with the same *mental* things) with which B does interact. The box score is: the cross-context test shows that *certain differences that their effects have under intentional description* (namely, causing NaC1 wants versus causing LCaN wants) and *certain differences that their effects have under non-intentional description* (see text) do *not* make the difference between having water thoughts and having twater thoughts a difference of causal power. We are about to see, however, that there are differences between the effects that twin mental states exhibit under intentional description which *survive* the cross-context test. These are the ones that, *prima facie*, make trouble for individualism.
4   This, surely, is the intuitively natural way to compare causal powers. Consider:

> 'Cats raised in Manhattan unable to climb trees', top scientist says.
> 'Why, that's rather disturbing. How do you explain it?'

'There aren't any trees in Manhattan for them to climb.'
'Oh.'

(For more on this, see the Appendix.)

5   It is important, in order that relevant questions not be begged, that this is *all* that is required for the fact that C1 has CP1 to be 'responsible for' the fact that E1 has EP1 (and similarly, *mutatis mutandis*, for the fact that C2 has CP2 to be responsible for the fact that E2 has EP2.) In like spirit, nothing in the examples will depend on stressing the requirement that the Cs and the Es be related as causes and effects, so long as it is assumed that the difference between the Cs is responsible for the difference between Es in the sense just specified.

6   It will ease the exposition if we think of schema S sometimes as relating events and sometimes as relating event types. I shall exploit this ambiguity in what follows; but nothing in the argument turns on it.

7   Reminder: 'water behavior' means not *behavior that has to do with water* but *behavior that has a reference to water in its intentional description*. We are assuming (see above) that the only relevant descriptions under which the behaviors of twins differ are intentional.

8   'Individuation and causation in psychology', *Pacific Philosophical Quarterly* 70 (1989), 303–22.

9   Another *a priori* taxonomic intuition that cries out to be taken seriously; it is (as *Psychosemantics* urged) preposterous to suggest that neurological (or biochemical or molecular) states should be taxonomized by reference to the sorts of properties that distinguish twins in the standard examples – by whether there is water or twater in the local puddles, for example. Burge remarks that perhaps all this shows is that psychological taxonomy is more contextually sensitive than neurological taxonomy. But surely that will not run: if someone were to discover (for example) that living near high-tension wires turns your dendrites green, you can bet the neurologists would pay attention. So: what is the difference between living near high-tension wires and living near puddles of twater such that one, but not the other, is a candidate for a neurological causal power? (See below.)

10 Even being an H-particle would be a causal power in virtue of the nomological possibility of building H-particle detectors. Particle detecting is notoriously expensive and tricky; but once you have got a particle detector, it is trivial to convert it to detect H-particles. An H-particle detector is a particle detector that is hooked up to any gadget that is sensitive to which face of my coin is up. A particle detector that is hooked up to a Bulgarian grandmother would do.

11 'Metaphysical arguments for internalism and why they don't work', in S. Silvers (ed.) *Representation*, Philosophical Studies Series, no. 40 (Boston, Kluwer, 1989).

12 This might well turn out to be the same question as whether 'is Bronx-thirsty' and 'is Queens-thirsty' are projectible; whether, for example, psychological generalizations about Bronx-thirsty people as such are confirmed by their instances.

13 This comports with the idea that, whereas *having a belief* (desire, whatever) is being in the right functional state, having a belief *that P* is a matter of having the right head-to-world relations. So the difference between having a belief that P and a belief that Q *is not* a functional difference. For more on this, see *Psychosemantics*.

14 Perhaps I had best reiterate that this is short for: 'a motivated condition for a difference between properties of causes being a difference in their causal powers' and that the claim is not that being a water (/twater) thought is not a causal power,

but rather that the difference between having a water thought and having a twater thought is not a difference in causal power. More generally, the claim is that no two states differ in their causal powers *just* in virtue of differing in their broad contents.

15   But please, *please* keep it in mind that this solution applies in cases where, if the properties under consideration are causal powers, then they are causal powers contingently. In particular, it is *not* supposed to apply to properties that are causal powers necessarily, like dispositions (see above).

16   I want to emphasize that condition C does not impugn the Davidsonian doctrine that the necessity/contingency of relations among *events* is description-relative. Suppose $e1$ causes $e2$, so that '$e1$ causes $e2$' is contingently true. Still, there will be descriptions satisfied by $e1$ which entail (/presuppose) that $e1$ causes $e2$ (for example, such descriptions as 'the cause of $e2$'; 'the cause of $e2$ caused $e2$' is, of course, necessarily true). But none of this implies that there is anything description-relative about whether the instantiation of one property entails the instantiation of another (about whether, for example, it is conceptually necessary that whatever instantiates bacherlorhood instantiates unmarriedness; or whether it is conceptually necessary that whatever instantiates *water-thinker-hood* instantiates *causally-connected-to-water-hood*. It is these latter sort of claims, not the former sort, which are at issue in respect of condition C.

17   By contrast, I take it that their ability to produce *meteor* craters (where a meteor crater just is a crater that is caused by a meteor) is not a causal power that meteors have over and above their power to produce craters *tout court*. This is for the now familiar sort of reason: it is conceptually necessary that, whereas a crater caused (in the right way) by a meteor is a meteor crater, a crater caused (in whatever way) by a molecularly identical non-meteor is not. Analogously, its ability to produce sunburns is not a casual power that the sun has over and above its power to produce burns.

18   More precisely (and assuming that functionalism is right about what beliefs, desires, and the like are) to have a water thought is to have a thought that (a) is connected to water in the right way; and (b) has whatever functional properties water thoughts and twater thoughts share. I leave out (b) in the text to simplify the exposition. No doubt the exposition could do with some of that.

19   I am indebted to Stich for this line of argument. I suppose he thinks I should be grateful.

20   4 is necessary, however, if you choose E as some property that *everything* has necessarily; like being self-identical. This does not, of course, prejudice the present point.

21   For those following the technicalities: in effect, my original line of argument depended on there being a conceptual relation between water connectedness and water thoughts construed *de dicto*. Stich gets a *contingent* relation between water connectedness and water thoughts *de re* by invoking such contingent premises as, for example, that water is Bush's favorite drink; and thus trivially satisfies condition C. In effect, 5 provides a substantive version of C by conditionalizing on these contingent premises.

22   I can imagine that someone might now want to say: 'All this follows from my conceding that the intentional properties that distinguish twins are causal powers contingently if they're causal powers at all. Well, I was wrong; those sorts of differences among broad content states are *non*-contingently differences of causal

powers. For example, the property of having water thoughts (rather than twater thoughts) is *identical* to the property of being able to produce water behaviors (rather than twater behaviors); the property of being connected to water (rather than twater) is *identical* to the property of being able to have water thoughts (rather than twater thoughts), etc. Notice that being soluble is a causal power even though the difference between being soluble and not is conceptually connected to the difference between dissolving and not.' All right, but it really does not help; if having water thoughts (rather than twater thoughts) is identical to having (*inter alia* the power to drill for water (rather than twater), then the broad content psychological generalizations that distinguish twins (like, 'if you have water wants [rather than twater wants] then you drill for water [rather than twater]') themselves all come out conceptually necessary (a kind of point to which Ryleans were, of course, entirely alert). So, if the assumption is that intentional states are non-contingently causal powers, then the appropriate form for the individualist's supervenience claim is that no *contingent* intentional generalization can distinguish twins (no contingent intentional generalization can be such that one but not the other of the twins satisfies its antecedent or consequent). The moral would then be: no causal laws about broad intentional states as such (in fact, just the sort of moral that Ryleans used to draw). It is true that being soluble is a causal power even though it is conceptually connected to dissolving. But the price for thus evading condition C is the 'quasi-logical' status of 'if soluble then dissolves'.

23 But why can this putative psychologist not allow them to be *different* states but with the *same* causal powers? Because, if he does, his theory misses generalizations, namely, all the generalizations that subsume me and my twin. Good taxonomy is about *not* missing generalizations.

12

Reply: Intentional Properties and Causation

Tyler Burge

In 'A modal argument for narrow content' (Chapter 11), Jerry Fodor tries to show that psychological properties typed by ordinary intentional propositional content (which he calls 'broad content') cannot be associated with distinctive causal powers for purposes of psychological taxonomizing. Causal powers are relevantly distinctive in so far as they are distinguished from 'twin earth' psychological properties. Thus Fodor attempts to show that ordinary intentional propositional content cannot be basic for taxonomizing causal powers in psychology. I think that he does not succeed.

Before discussing his argument, I want to remark on his methodology. Fodor calls his argument '*a priori*'. He seems to mean by this only that it is the sort of argument that could be given from an armchair (Chapter 11, p. 211). Certainly, most of his claims (for example, the claim about H and T-particles) do not seem to be *a priori* in any traditional sense. Something is a T-particle at time *t* if it is a physical particle and the coin in Fodor's hand at time *t* is tails up. Our knowledge that being a T-particle is not having any particular causal power is perfectly obvious apart from any particular investigation; but it clearly relies broadly on our empirical experience.

Fodor takes his proposal to be justified by its sorting examples, like the T-particle example, and by its respecting 'Humean intuitions' about causation. It seems to me that he is simply attempting to generalize about causal explanation in the empirical sciences. This is certainly a philosophically valuable enterprise. But I think that it is treacherous when its conclusions appear to be in opposition to actual scientific practice.

Fodor's conclusion does appear to be in opposition to the actual practice of psychological explanation. Psychologists use ordinary content in many of their causal explanations. There is no wholesale movement in intentional psychology to make its explanations more 'general', or more in accord with Fodor's conception of causally relevant kinds, by replacing ordinary content attributions with attributions of another sort of content (which he calls 'narrow content'). Narrow content seems to play no explicit role that would replace that of ordinary content. So I think that there is strong armchair reason to think that Fodor's argument will not establish its conclusion. I think that it is another in a long line of philosophical proposals to revise science. Such proposals have a poor track record; they have given philosophy a bad name. Fodor is advocating a change in the formulation of scientific generalizations rather than a flat-out denial of scientific claims. But I think that it is no more likely to be scientifically useful than its more notorious ancestors. Let us consider the argument itself.

Fodor begins by assuming that differences in intentional properties are the only relevant differences between the behaviour of a person and a twin earth twin (Chapter 11, p. 208). I think that this is a mistake. Non-intentional descriptions of behavioral relations between an individual and specific kinds in his/her environment seem to be a significant part of what psychology is interested in.

Fodor dismisses non-intentionally and relationally described behavior (for example, getting water) by reference to his 'cross-context' test. He maintains, 'you have to judge identity and difference of causal powers in a way that bears the counterfactuals in mind, namely, *across* contexts rather than *within* contexts' (Chapter 11, p. 208). The idea is that a twin would get water if placed on earth, and an earthling would get twater if placed on twin earth, given that they made the same requesting sounds in their respective languages. Fodor concludes that the behavior of the two protagonists, on earth and twin earth, is the same as far as psychological taxonomy and causal power are concerned.

Fodor is certainly right that causal power is a counterfactual notion. But his test, at least in the way he applies it, is useless for individuating causal powers. The trouble is that deciding which contexts are relevant for determining and distinguishing causal powers is not independent of assumptions about how to individuate explanatory kinds.[1]

Imagine that a heart and an organ that pumps digestive waste (from a completely different evolutionary scheme) were physically indistinguishable up to their boundaries. Clearly they would be of two different biological kinds, with different causal powers, on any conception of causal power that would be relevant to biological taxonomy. Judging the heart's causal powers presupposes that it is connected to a particular type of bodily environment, with a particular sort of function in that environment. One cannot count being connected to such a body to pump blood as just one of many contexts that the heart might be in, if one wants to understand the range of its biologically relevant causal powers. It would show a serious misconception of biological kinds to argue that the causal powers and taxonomically relevant effects of the heart and its physical twin are the same because if one hooked up the waste pump to the heart's body, it would pump blood and cause the blood vessels to dilate; and that if one hooked the heart to the waste pump's body, it would move waste.

But that is how Fodor argues regarding relational behavioral effects of psychological states. The argument ignores the fact that specific relations between an entity and its normal environment may be of interest to a special science, and fundamental to its causal taxonomy. Causal power is judged against background assumptions about what kind of thing is being evaluated. And kinds are sometimes what they are because of their relations to, and functions within, a specific environment. Fodor's treatment of any environment as being on a par with other 'contexts' for testing causal powers is in effect an assimilation of the special sciences to physics. It certainly begs the question against my view.

The test gives no reason to think that psychology should not be, or is not, interested in explaining non-intentional behavioral relations between an individual and specific sorts of things in his/her environment. In fact, psychology is engaged in explaining many successes and failures that relate an individual's intentional states to kinds of things in the individual's environment: specific successes or failures in perception, in knowledge, in action. I see no good reason to think that psychology does or should gloss these explanations of success or adaptation in environmentally neutral ways (as Fodor attempts to do in his Appendix).

Fodor concentrates his discussion on intentionally described behavior. He does so because he thinks that such descriptions pass his cross-context test (Chapter 11, p. 208). He therefore devises a further condition which is supposed to show that ordinary intentional psychological states are not distinctive causal powers with respect to intentionally described behavior.

Fodor offers a necessary condition for when a difference between having causal properties CP1 and CP2 is a difference in 'causal powers' in virtue of the difference's being responsible for a certain difference between effect properties EP1 and EP2. (The difference in causal properties CP1 and CP2 is said to be responsible for the difference between the effect properties in the same sense that if CP2 had been instantiated instead of CP1, the effect would have had property EP2 instead of EP1; and if CP1 had been instantiated instead of CP2, the effect would have had EP1 instead of EP2; (Chapter 11, p. 209).

Fodor never formulates his condition in final form. But his core answer is:

(C): Only when it is not a conceptual truth that causes that differ in that one has CP1 where the other has CP2 have effects that differ in that one has EP1 where the other has EP2 (Chapter 11, p. 217).

The idea is that being a meteor can be a causal power in virtue of the fact that meteors are responsible for craters because the relation between the difference between meteors and rock-twins-of-meteors which are not meteors and their respective effects (the effects: making craters and whatever effects the rock-twins have) is 'non-conceptual' (Chapter 11, p. 217). By contrast, Fodor says, 'it is conceptually necessary that people who have water thoughts (rather than twater thoughts) produce water behavior (rather than twater behavior)' (Chapter 11, p. 217). So being a water thought (a thought that involves the concept *water*) cannot be a distinctive causal power in virtue of the fact that water thoughts are responsible for water behavior. Fodor thinks that his condition is a necessary condition on causal properties' being 'psychological natural kinds ' (Chapter 11, p. 213).

Fodor stipulates that condition C is not to apply to causal properties that are individuated *as* causal powers with certain specific sorts of effects. He cites being a camshaft and being soluble in water as properties that are non-contingently causal powers of their characteristic effects. The problem Fodor anticipates is that characteristic camshaft effects (lifting valves of certain sorts) necessarily have the effect properties which the property of being a camshaft is conceptually associated with. And any such effects will be different, on conceptual grounds, from characteristic effects of physical-camshaft-twins that have different functions. Yet it would seem that being a camshaft is a distinctive causal power in good standing. So condition C should not apply to such causal properties, canonically described.

By contrast, Fodor assumes that being a meteor is only contingently a causal power with respect to such effects as making craters. And he explicitly says that being a water thought is contingently a distinctive causal power with respect to its effects on behavior characterized, intentionally, in terms of the concept *water*. More generally, he believes that specific propositional attitudes characterized in the usual way are only contingently causal powers with respect to intentionally described behavior characterized in terms that indicate intentional elements in the propositional attitudes (Chapter 11, p. 216). So Condition C is applicable to them.

Since Fodor believes that propositional attitudes characterized in the usual way fail condition C, he concludes that they are not causal powers in virtue of their characteristic intentionally described effect properties: they do not differ in their causal power from propositional attitudes of twin earth counterparts. That is, it is a conceptual truth that 'broad content' propositional attitudes differ in their characteristic intentionally described effect properties from those of their 'broad content' twins. So condition C is violated. So 'broad content' propositional attitudes do not differ in causal power from their twins. I find the complexity of these formulations unappealing, and less than immediately intuitive. I characterize Fodor's position to have it on the table for discussion.

There's more complexity than I have so far mentioned. Fodor has to do some patching of his core answer (Chapter 11, p. 218). For by redescribing causal properties or effect properties, one can produce a non-conceptual relation between concepts of any given pair of properties. Fodor does not make fully clear what his patch is to be, but as Ned Block has pointed out, it appears that the line of response that he proposes cannot solve the problem. For in all the examples he gives (pp. 218–20) the properties he cites could still be redescribed to produce statements that are about the same properties but that are not conceptually necessary. The problem is that conceptual necessity is (if anything) a property of relations between concepts of properties, not of relations between properties.

In my view, however, this is not a fundamental problem for Fodor. I think that he can and should speak of canonical descriptions (or canonical conceptions) of properties – descriptions (or conceptions) that are candidates for use in explanatory theories. 'Being a meteor', 'being a water thought', 'being phlogiston', and so on are of this sort. 'Being Harry's favorite property' is not. At least I am willing to accept this emendation, despite its vagueness. I agree also not to cavil over the notion of conceptual necessity. Given that we assume that we are testing canonical descriptions (or conceptions) of the property of being a water thought, I think Fodor need not do any patching on his original proposal at all.

I want now to return to Fodor's assumption that having thoughts involving the concept *water* are not themselves necessarily distinctive causal powers with respect to behavioral effects intentionally described in terms of the concept *water*. To put it another way, Fodor assumes that it is contingent that 'having mental states that differ in their broad content is having mental states that differ in their causal powers' (Chapter 11, p. 214,220).

As noted, he contrasts the property of having thoughts whose intentional content involves the concept of water with the property of being water soluble. He observes that it is not contingent that having this latter property is having a distinctive causal power (Chapter 11, p. 215). And he thinks that it is 'reasonably untendentious' to assume that having intentional thoughts are different in this regard:

> friends of broad content argue that it perfectly well *could turn out* – that there is no metaphysical reason why it should not turn out – that having mental states that differ in their broad content is having mental states that differ in their causal powers. (For example, it could turn out that there are causal laws that distinguish between twins). But I do not remember hearing anyone argue that having mental states that differ in the way that the mental states of twins do *just is* having mental states that differ in their causal powers. On the contrary, according to the usual understanding, it is their causal *histories* that distinguish the mental states of twins. And the intuition about features of causal history is that some of them are causal powers (e.g. *having been dropped in transit* . . .) and some of them are not (e.g. . . . *having been born on a Tuesday*) and it is contingent which are which. (Chapter 11, p. 215)

I cannot speak for others. But this articulation of Fodor's assumption contains several misunderstandings of the point of view that has motivated my anti-individualism. I will discuss some of them as a preliminary to discussing the assumption.

What distinguishes the twins is not confined to their causal histories. Their propositional attitudes themselves differ. Their intentionally described behavior differs. Their interactions with their environments, including their effects on their environments, differ. I believe that intentional ascriptions of psychological states and specific relational behavioral descriptions are taxonomically primitive: they characterize psychological kinds. Some of the other properties of a person not shared with the person's twin are *not* psychological kinds. In particular, I think it highly unlikely that the historical individuating conditions of specific psychological states will be psychological kinds.

It is for psychology and other scientific enterprises an empirical question whether and to what extent they will make use of ordinary propositional attitude ascriptions in their explanations. I believe that the question whether they will use ordinary propositional attitude ascriptions is already settled for psychology and a wide range of other explanatory endeavors. But perhaps in some cases it could, in principle, 'turn out' otherwise.

An analogous epistemological point applies to the property of being water soluble. Water solubility is in itself a causal notion. Let us suppose that it serves some explanatory enterprises (though it may in fact be explicable in more general terms). It could have 'turned out' that there was no such property or that it had no distinctive explanatory role.

We can also say about water solubility that it is necessarily a causal notion, and that it is individuated partly in terms of its effects. So its canonical description implies necessary or conceptual relations between the causal property and appropriately described effects. On the supposition that it is an explanatorily useful property, anything that has it is taxonomically or explanatorily distinct from anything that lacks it.

I think that in these respects intentional psychological properties are similar. They necessarily have causal implications as such. They are scientifically and causally relevant kinds.[2] And many of them bear a conceptual relation to standard conceptions of the properties that are causally effected by them. (I shall return to the sense in which this is so.) Given, as I think, that ordinary intentional properties are causally relevant kinds, they are necessarily distinct from other causally relevant properties, including twin earth analogues.

Fodor is right that much of the focus of the discussion of anti-individualism has been on the role of causal-historical antecedents in concept individuation. One reason for this focus is that the arguments for anti-individualism grew out of previous work on reference in the philosophy of language.[3] Another reason, at least for me, is that in view of the failure of behaviorism and the programmatic, almost empty, character of all the sorts of functionalist reductionism that I know of, it is difficult to state in an illuminating, even sketchy, way what causal relations most psychological states bear to behavior (intentionally characterized or otherwise). It is approximately as difficult as psychology is.

Nevertheless, I think that it is probably a fault of some expositions within this tradition (a fault I myself am guilty of) that there has been so much more emphasis, in the account of attitude individuation, on historical chains leading up to employment of a concept, than on the individual's activity in interacting with an environment. Still, even causal-historical antecedents have consistently been said to involve *interaction* between individuals and their environments. Interaction is not passive reception of input.

In any case, it seems to me clearly true that specific actions by individuals on their environment are part of what is involved in individuating ordinary intentional contents. This is what underlies the conceptual relation between certain sorts of behavior and intentional psychological states. For example, what an individual perceives is not independent of what the individual or conspecifics can discriminate.[4]

The theory of perception takes for granted that among the things that in a patterned way cause perceptual representations, the kinds of things that are represented can, in most cases, only be those that the creature's perceptual apparatus can function, under appropriate conditions, to discriminate. Discrimination here is a behavioral as well as teleological notion. But it is a notion whose application is circumscribed by the possibilities for discrimination in the individual's normal environment. Necessarily, things perceived, in optimum or normal conditions, function in some way not only in a species' or individual's causal history but in the species' members' actions on the world. The individuation of various beliefs about macro-objects and properties also depend on looser but still significant relations to the individual's acting on the relevant objects or properties.

Despite the relative concentration on historical antecedents in parts of the anti-individualist tradition, it is strange that Fodor regards his assumption as untendentious. Fodor would be begging the question to assume that ordinary intentional psychological properties, standardly conceived, are not distinctive causal and explanatory kinds. But it is obvious that if they have causal implications, some ordinary intentional properties, under their standard conceptions, bear conceptual relations to some of the properties that are causally effected by them, standardly conceived. These effect-properties include both intentionally described behavior and behavior described in terms of relations to specific kinds of things in the environment. That ordinary intentional properties are necessarily distinct from twin analogs in their causal implications follows from the anti-individualist view that they are taxonomically relevant kinds. It is not an independent question.

Fodor's attribution of the view that it could 'turn out' that there are ordinary intentional causal laws (or causal law-like generalizations) is at best misleading. He purports to be talking about necessity. But 'could turn out' talk is epistemic, not modal in the ordinary senses. Epistemic contingency is irrelevant to the application of condition C. It may well be that Fodor has confused an epistemic view with a metaphysical or causal-taxonomical view.

Fodor's main argument rests on the assumption that ordinary intentional psychological states are unlike being a camshaft and water solubility in that they are not necessarily causal powers and are not necessarily distinct in their causal implications from twin earth analogs. Since this assumption is mistaken, the argument is inapplicable.

In a brief note, Fodor anticipates this response late in his chapter, (n. 22). He claims that if ordinary intentional states are like water solubility in being both conceptually and causally connected to their behavioral effects – and in a way that distinguishes them from their twin analogs – then there is even less reason to think them causally and taxonomically significant:

> the broad content psychological generalizations that distinguish twins (like, 'if you have water wants [rather than twater wants] then you drill for water [rather than twater]') themselves all come out conceptually necessary ... The moral

would then be: no causal laws about broad intentional states as such . . . It is true that being soluble is a causal power even though it is conceptually connected to dissolving. But the price for thus evading condition C is the 'quasi-logical' status of 'if soluble then dissolves'. (Chapter 11, n.22)[5]

But this point contains a simple fallacy. The fact that there is some conceptual connection between explanans and explanandum (or antecedent and consequent) does not mean that the psychological generalizations come out to be conceptually necessary. It does not preclude their being interesting causal law-like statements. The conceptual link between antecedent and consequent may be merely that 'water' occurs in both (intensionally in the former, either intensionally or extensionally in the latter), and that being a thought about water has some causal implications or other, with respect to water.[6] It does not follow that the consequent follows conceptually from the antecedent.

In fact, psychological law-like generalizations do sometimes have such conceptual links between statements about psychological antecedents and statements about behavior. And if they amounted to no more than 'if something is a water-type thought, it tends under optimal circumstances to cause water-related or water-conceived behavior', they would yield no real insight into causal relations.[7] But such generalizations in intentional psychology presuppose or contain existence assumptions that are contingent. For example, some generalizations presuppose or entail that water thoughts exist. They also contain detailed specifications of conditions in their antecedents and consequents. The detail makes the generalizations scientifically interesting, as well as contingent.[8]

One can see this by thinking about the heart case again. One could plausibly claim that it is conceptual truth that hearts differ from twin waste-pumps in that they pump blood. One could plausibly claim that it is conceptually necessary that if something is a heart, then when functioning normally, it pumps blood. Although these are true statements, they do not provide deep insight into causal relations. If physiology contented itself with such statements, it would certainly be remiss. But these points do nothing to show that hearts are not taxonomically significant kinds.

The interest for physiology lies first in the existence of hearts and blood. This is both contingent and empirically known. Interest lies second and more richly in the account of how much blood a given type of heart pumps, in what particular ways it pumps it, in what ways pumping action causes blood vessels to dilate, and so on. Answers to these questions are non-trivial, contingent causal truths, even though 'heart' and 'blood' are conceptually connected.

Psychology is broadly like that. Many of its intentional notions are individuated partly in terms of very broadly described cause – effect relations. This form of individuation insures some conceptual relations between taxonomically relevant descriptions of causes and taxonomically relevant descriptions of effects. This is one of the grains of truth in functionalism. But these conceptual relations provide only a broad frame for psychological theorizing. They do not make intentional psychology anything like trivial.

Fodor's main argument does not succeed because it fails to apply to the cases at issue. His subsidiary argument that typical statements about causal properties that are individuated partly in terms of effect properties are 'quasi-logical' and useless for science is based on a fallacy.

The difficulty with Fodor's attempt to apply Humean and Rylean intuitions about causation is that the conceptual relations between descriptions of causes and effects occur at a very high level of abstraction. The relevant propositional attitude concepts have causal implications. But the implications are very general. They are at the level: something is not a perception unless it functions in a system for causing discriminative behavior; one cannot attribute perception of rough texturedness to an organism unless its perceptual system functions to cause it to respond to or otherwise discriminate rough texturedness under environmentally normal circumstances; water thoughts enter in some way, under some appropriate conditions, into causing behavior having to do with water, or at least behavior whose intentional description involves the concept of water. Some intentional psychological properties have even looser causal implications than these. Psychological law-like generalizations, by contrast, are much more specific. They involve statements of specific, contingent conditions that must be satisfied for the causal relations to occur.

Arguments against the scientific relevance of intentional notions that invoke Humean principles or Rylean intuitions are likely to gloss over (as Fodor's does) the enormous difficulty and complexity of stating a true, interesting law-like generalization in psychology. In my view, such arguments tend to carry on bad habits of behaviorism and physics-worship. The habits can remain even in those who are to be admired for what they have done to undermine behaviorism and over-simple pictures of the special sciences.

Acknowledgment

I am indebted to Ned Block for several very valuable criticisms.

Notes

1 I have made this point with essentially the example that follows in 'Individuation and causation in psychology', *Pacific Philosophical Quarterly* 70 (1989), 303–22.
2 Cf. my 'Mind-body causation and explanatory practice' in J.Heil and A.Mele (eds), *Mental Causation* (Oxford, Oxford University Press 1993).
3 Cf. my 'Philosophy of language and mind: 1950–1990', *Philosophical Review* 101 (1992), esp. pp. 45ff.
4 B.O'Shaughnessy, *The Will* (Cambridge, Cambridge University Press, 1980), vol. 2, ch. 8; M.Davies, 'Individualism and perceptual content', *Mind* 100 (1991), 461–84;

M.Davies, 'Perceptual content and local supervenience', *Proceedings of the Aristotelian Society* 92 (1992), 21–45. I think that by concentrating on the role of behavior in perceptual-state individuation, one can produce a simpler, stronger argument for anti-individualism than the general philosophical one I give in 'Individualism and psychology' (chapter 10 of this volume).

5   I am sure that Fodor knows that nothing about twater would occur in a psychological generalization about water. His point must be that 'water' really occurs primitively in the generalization. I must also point out that Fodor's idea that 'wants water' means something like 'thirsty and born here' (Chapter 11, pp. 214–15) is wildly inaccurate. As I have shown, 'water' contains no indexical element. Cf. my 'Other bodies', in A.Woodfield (ed.), *Thought and Object* (Oxford, Oxford University Press, 1982). At best he is proposing some replacement for the ordinary use of 'water' in psychological discourse.

6   It is important not to oversimplify here. Having water thoughts does not necessitate the existence of water. One can imagine a chemist who has theorized about the existence of H_2O and has imagined and visualized the macro-properties of H_2O. Such a being could have water thoughts but lack any causal relations to water. So having water thoughts cannot necessitate having causal relations to water, except relative to fairly strong parameters stating optimal conditions. In cases where a thinker has water thoughts but there is no water, the water thoughts will necessitate causal relations to instances of other physical kinds in the thinker's environment. And there will be necessary causal relations to acts or actions intentionally characterized in terms of the concept *water*. But the causal relations to actual entities in the thinker's environment that are necessitated by having the concept *water* are quite complicated and merely bring in relations to and concepts of *some* kinds in the thinker's actual environment. (I made this point years ago in 'Other bodies'). None of this constitutes the slightest concession to the idea that beings on twin earth, in the relevant thought experiments, have the concept *water*.

7   Fodor describes the relevant necessary statements in rather puzzling ways. 'If soluble then dissolves' and 'Having water thoughts is identical to having (*inter alia*) the power to drill for water' and 'if you have water wants … then you drill for water' are obviously not necessary. I have done the best I can on Fodor's behalf in formulating rough necessities of the sort he seems to be gesturing toward. I think that when one fills out what the necessities really are – involving as they do terms like 'normally', 'in appropriate circumstances' – they come to seem familiar and harmless. Filling them out by determining relevant circumstances both produces contingent statements and illustrates how hard and complex causal generalizations in intentional psychology are.

8   Fodor's mistake here seems to me to infect his main condition on being a causal power, even if one waives the point that Fodor's mistaken presupposition about intentional psychological properties makes the condition irrelevant. The idea of the condition (Chapter 11, p. 217) seems to be that if a conceptual connection between properties of a cause and properties of its effect is not based on individuating the cause as a causal power, then the conceptual connection prevents a causal relation between those properties from being of any taxonomical interest. But this seems to me to be a more subtle form of the same fallacy I have just criticized. The conceptual connection between the properties need not be so full that it allows no room for a taxonomically interesting connection.

Biopsychology

13

Introduction: The Biological Turn

Graham Macdonald

Psychology's struggle for scientific recognition has a long history. One aspect of this struggle has been the belief that intentional terms are inherently unsuited to scientific explanatory tasks. The strategy often invoked to deal with this is to replace or reduce such terms to those used in natural science. Clearly much depends upon what is considered to be a 'natural science'. During the heyday of positivism, physics was the paradigm, and it was argued that reducibility to physics was required. This was usually construed as a reduction of the mental to the neurophysiological, with the explanations conforming to something like the deductive nomological model.

The latest turn the strategy takes involves a turn to biology as the relevant natural science. The reasons for this change are both empirical and conceptual. On the empirical side the required reductions to neurophysiology did not seem to be forthcoming. If anything, the empirical evidence tended to go against proposed reductions, as it appeared that mental capacities could not be aligned with neurophysiological capacities in the manner required for a reduction. The conceptual reasons stemmed from the desire to retain, in the reducing science, the element of normativity which was, and is, thought essential to mental activity. For instance, it is essential to our conception of the intentional (broadly construed, so as to include all propositional attitudes) that cognitive agents have the ability to make mistakes: we can have false beliefs about the world, we can misrepresent it to ourselves, we can make invalid inferences, and so on. To identify a state as *mis*representing the world, it is necessary to identify that state independently of the (piece of) environment which might have caused it to occur. We must be able to say that, despite being caused to occur by this aspect of the world, the state is *meant to* depict some other aspect. It is this normativity which any straightforward causal-correlational account of representation will have difficulty in capturing, and which the biological accounts claim as their strength.[1]

Central to an account of our intentional mental states, then, must be a notion of what the state *is meant to do*. If, as seems plausible, some of our representational mental states are inherently fallible, then that fallibility must be captured in any reducing theory of those states. The distinctive claim of the bio-naturalists is that biological theory is better suited to this task than either physics or chemistry, it being irreducible to physics and chemistry. This irreducibility stems from the use in biology of functional explanations. Biologists are wont to talk of the *function* of the body's organs: of the function of the heart to pump blood around the body, of the function of the eyes to provide information about the environment to the brain, of the function of genes to programme for the production of proteins, of the function of the immune system to rid the body of unhealthy cells. Talk of functions both prevents reduction to physics and chemistry and provides normativity, since a bodily part may *malfunction*. In order to identify such a malfunction, we need to be able to identify the function independently of what the organ is actually doing. A 'straight' causal explanation of what an organ is doing must take its actual effects into account, so a causal explanation of what a malfunctioning organ is doing will simply give us an explanation of what is happening. It is difficult to see how such an explanation can provide the basis for an account of what the organ is meant to be doing. It is this independence from actual processes which makes functionality the key to the irreducibility of biology.

How is this independence achieved? It is crucial to the bio-naturalists that 'function' be defined so that one can identify malfunctions in a way in which causal accounts seem to fail. Although there is no definition of 'function' which is universally recognized as correct, most of the bio-naturalists adopt an aetiological account of function.[2] This relies upon the operation of natural selection on the variation within a species to produce, within members of that species, adaptations to their environment. It is natural to see such adaptations as functional: the long neck of the Giraffe, to take a standard example, is an adaptation and has the function of enabling giraffes to eat the leaves at the top of tall trees. On the aetiological account, this capacity is the *function* of the long neck because previous giraffes whose genes produced longer necks than their contemporaries were better producers of offspring, and were so just because of the advantage conferred on those giraffes in the food wars. This results, in the long run, in more long-necked giraffes, until the giraffe is a long-necked species. Put as briefly and generally as possible, the aetiological account says that functionality arises because some variants within a group (a mutant gene, for example) have novel features with capacities which are favourable to their possessors' ability to reproduce (i.e. more favourable than the non-possession of those features by the other members of the group). Such features are transmitted to their descendants, proliferating within the group in the process. The feature of the organism will then, and only then, have as its function the exercise of the favourable capacity.

This account of functionality is very general: it applies not just to biological entities, but to all units which have the required characteristics of:

1 Variation of features within a group.
2 Selection of some of the variants.
3 Variable transmission of the selected features to descendants.

In the biological case, variation is caused by mutation, selection involves the differing interactions between the environment and both mutant and non-mutant members of the group, and transmission is the (differential) reproduction of the genetic material. Given this general account, we can now answer the question about a function's independence from actual causal processes, and so see how malfunctions can occur.

Suppose that we have established the functionality of a particular feature possessed by members of a group. Say that we have established that the heart's function is to pump blood around the body. Then *provided that we can identify hearts independently of their actually performing this task to the required standard,* we can check whether a specific heart is performing its function adequately. If not, it is malfunctioning – not doing what it is meant to do. Applied to the case of intentional states, if mental representations have the function of accurately representing their environment, we can tell when they are misrepresenting because we know what the function of such a representation is.

This is one way of seeing the connection between representation and function, one which identifies the content of the representation with its function to accurately represent the world. However, there are variations of the biopsychological approach which make the connection between function and representation less direct. The most sophisticated biopsychological theory, one developed by Ruth Garrett Millikan, takes the indirect route, and we turn now to an outline of her theory.

Beginner's Guide to Millikan

In her seminal book, *Language, Thought, and Other Biological Categories* (1984) Ruth Millikan introduces a detailed and novel way of looking at intentional phenomena. The first sections of the book provide a general theory of a variety of functions and, as Millikan's terminology is specialized, it will be useful to have at hand a number of her definitions. For ease of exposition, I will concentrate on the definitions as they apply to linguistic categories, giving as brief an outline as possible.

According to Millikan, organs such as kidneys and hearts, *and* semantic items such as words, are assigned to their biological categories in terms of their *proper functions.* Having a proper function has to do with the history of an item, and not with its causal powers. *Direct proper functions* are functions of devices that are members of families of devices similar to one another, such families being *reproductively established families* (refs). Individual A is a reproduction of individual B if and only if B has some determinate properties in common with A and this can be explained by a natural law operating in that environment. These common properties are the reproductively established properties of B. Now only first-order refs reproduce in this manner. *Higher-order refs* (horefs) are produced by first-order refs. My own and my ancestors' two-leggedness is the result of common genes, such genes being first-order refs. They have certain properties in common, this being ensured by the laws of genetic inheritance. Not everything produced by first-order refs is a higher-order ref; only those items produced by the same first-order ref when it is a direct proper function of that family to produce such items, and these are all produced in accordance with a *normal explanation*. So, for example, hearts are not reproductions of each other (and so not members of a ref); but hearts produced in *normal conditions* according to the proper functioning of genes that are copies of one another form higher-order refs. That is, these hearts are produced in normal conditions according to a normal explanation.

> A *Normal Explanation* is a preponderant explanation for those historical cases where a proper function was performed. Similarly, *Normal Conditions* to which a Normal Explanation makes reference are preponderant explanatory conditions under which that function has historically been performed. (Millikan, 1984, p. 34)

It is important to note that Normal Conditions may not be 'normal' in the sense of 'usual' or 'average'; very few sperm exist under conditions Normal for the performance of their proper function, as very few actually find an ovum to fertilize.

It is worth anticipating one aspect of the later discussion to note one consequence of this approach to biological categorization, and that is that if one considers my possible world twin, composed of molecules accidentally type-identical to those which compose me, then my twin will lack a heart, liver, kidneys, etc., since these would not have been reproduced in the manner necessary to fit into the relevant biological category. Given the lack of relevant history, there would not be a Normal Explanation of the production of these pseudo-hearts. According to Millikan, my twin will also lack my beliefs.

Now it looks as though all members of refs will have to be normally functioning members. However, Millikan produces the following caveat: a *malfunctioning* member of a ref can be produced provided it has been produced by a device the proper function of which is to produce members of the ref in question, that it is in some aspects similar to other members of the ref, and that its production has an explanation which *approximates* (in some undefined degree) to a Normal Explanation for the production of members of the ref. Millikan calls the properties common to all members of a ref the *Normal Character* of the ref. A member, m, of a ref, R, has the function F as a direct proper function if and only if (some of) its ancestors performed F, F correlates positively with the Normal Character, C, of R, and one of the explanations as to why m exists refers to this positive correlation, either by directly causing reproduction of m or by explaining the existence of m as a result of the proliferation of members of R, such proliferation being due to the possession of C (and its positive correlation with F). For example, the long necks of giraffes have the function of helping giraffes reach high leaves; their long necks correlate positively with this function, and so the possession of long necks is partially explanatory of the proliferation of more long-necked giraffes. This last feature allows for *m* to have a function even when it cannot perform the function, its having that function being derived from its being a member of a ref which has that function. This ensures the autonomy of possession of a function from the actual performance of that function, such independence being required for the possibility of malfunctioning organs. It is (selectionist) ancestry, not, for instance, physical constitution, that determines whether or not a device has a function. Because functions require such a history, the first member of a ref cannot have a function specific to that ref.

The ability to perform a proper function may often depend upon there being a suitable environment, and this environment may include the proper functioning of members of other refs. The pollen of certain flowers has the function of aiding the propagation of those flowers; it does this by combining with the activity of bees, this activity serving a different function. If language devices have proper functions these will depend upon co-operation between speaker and hearer. As Millikan says, if all our utterances were responded to in a totally haphazard fashion, then they would not be systematically reproduced. Now in the bee/flower case, pollination is achieved by the combination of the different functions of the pollen and the bees' activity. In the case of language devices, it is more likely that some of the functions of such devices is geared to both speaker's and listener's goals. This type of function is called a *stabilizing function*, which keeps speakers using the device in standard ways, and keeps hearers responding in standard ways. Linguistic change is allowed for by allowing a member of a ref to have both a historically remote and historically proximate function. Etymological research often produces the remote functions of the ref, functions which are no longer performed by present members of the ref. They are still functions of the ref since the present members of the ref would not have existed had these functions not been performed by remote ancestors of the present members. So, for each ref there may be historically remote or historically proximate explanations of the presence of a function, depending upon which function is being invoked in the explanation. Obviously refs may have a variety of proper functions which may either be alternatives or performed simultaneously. For example, the circulation of the blood performs a number of simultaneous functions, transporting oxygen, nutrients etc.

There can also be *serial proper functions*, as for example when the heart's pumping blood causes oxygen to circulate, which in turn causes brain cells to live, which in turn causes neuro-transmitters to function, and so on. This raises the question: why is 'pumping blood' *the* function of the heart? Millikan suggests that this decision is determined by explanatory proximity. Sometimes serial functions are performed without any alternative additional functions (conjunctive or disjunctive) being performed: the last member of such a series is the *focused function* of the device initiating the series. For example, the receptors at the end of the afferent nerves have focused functions; they cause impulses to cause impulses up the nerve, to eventuate in inputs into the brain. The focused function of the eye is to cause visual representations, which themselves have diverse functions. Because the visual representations have a variety of functions, no one of these can be singled out as the focused function of the eye.

An extremely important definition for the debate which follows is that of *a relational proper function*, which is a function to do something bearing a certain relation to something else. The chameleon's skin-colour mechanism has the relational function of making the chameleon's skin match that of its environment (whatever that colour may be). Given a specific colour to adapt to, the mechanism then acquires an *adapted proper function*. So when it is sitting on a brown plant the adapted proper function of the device is to produce brown skin. Crucial here is that the brown skin may never have been produced before, so it is not a member of a ref, and the production of it is not a direct proper function of the device. That to which an adapted device adapts is its adaptor (the brown plant being the adaptor in this case). Consider the dance of the bees which acts as a signal to other bees, 'telling' them to go south-east, where the nectar is to be found. This dance is adapted to the location of the nectar, so has an adapted function. The flight of the bees to the south-east is adapted to this adapted function. The proper functions of adapted devices are *derived proper functions*, derived from the proper functions of the devices that produce them. But the specific bee dance, having a derived proper function, is also a member of a horef since it displays the abstract character of conforming to an abstract description common to every well-formed dance, say, the description 'being in a figure of eight, with a definite, discernible, orientation and energy level' (these being the features 'read' by the bees as informative). As a member of this horef, the bee dance's most immediate direct proper function is relational, to move the bees in a direction bearing a certain relation to the more exact form of the dance, whatever that form may be. So in this case there are two sources of proper function, derived and direct. In mistakes there may be maladaptation of the adapted device if, for example, it does not bear the right relation to its adaptor (the nectar is in the north-east). The same device can acquire conflicting proper functions *via* maladaption. The nectar is seen in the south-east but due to maladaptation the dance conforms to the rules for 'nectar north-west'. The dance has the derived adapted function to move the bees to the nectar (south-east), and it has the adapted proper function (*qua* its membership of the ref containing members of syntactically correct bee dances) to move the bees north-west. The interpreter's mechanisms acquire the adapted proper function to move the bee north-west but also the opposing function to move the bee toward the nectar (south-east).

A crucial question arises in this confusion: what is being represented in the dance? This, says Millikan, depends upon the dance's direct proper function, a function it can only have *qua* member of ref. It is this to which the interpreters adapt. The direct proper function is to move the bees in a direction having a specific relation to its concrete form.

The most dominant notion of what is signed by signs is derived by reference to direct proper functions of the signs themselves – not by reference to adapted functions of the signs' producing devices. (Millikan, 1984, p. 43)

To apply some of the above to the case of linguistic representation is fairly straightforward. Language devices (words, sentences) have direct proper functions *qua* members of refs. They also have derived proper functions, derived from, for example, the speaker's intentions. When the two come into conflict it is the direct proper function which dominates the decision as to what is being represented, and misrepresentation, misunderstanding, irony, and so on, can result,

In this account it is assumed that words and synactic forms have stabilizing functions, such functions being direct proper functions of the first-order refs, of which these devices are members. The performance of the stabilizing (or standardizing) functions must then account for the proliferation of these members, and it does this by accounting for the proliferation of speakers' utterances and hearers' responses. It is because the words have such functions that they continue to be used and responded to in standard ways.[3] The stabilizing function of the indicative mood is to convey information (true belief). The performance of this function can be frustrated, as when the speaker lies. It can also be frustrated when neither the speaker nor hearer realizes it, when the indicative conveys misinformation. Note that if true belief transmission falls below a certain frequency level then sentences in the indicative mood cease to have a stabilizing function, and will either change or disappear altogether.

A word will belong to a ref in virtue of its history (even if the Martian 'Es regnet' means the same as the German, it will belong to a different ref), so these are called genetic types. Within genetic types there may well be the historically remote stabilizing funtions and the more proximate. When tokens of these refs are classified as having the same sense, they share the same independent stabilizing function, each such function being capable by itself of explaining the proliferation of the word's tokens. Such 'same sense' classifications are called *least types*, being the smallest sub-division of the refs. There may be several such least types for any word. Suppose that there are twenty Australian philosophers called 'Bruce'. Then there will be twenty different least types, as their tokens proliferate independently of each other. To talk about a person one need only acquire knowledge of their name on the model of members of the least type that has him or her as referent. Again the first use of a name (where there is no naming ceremony) will have no function independent of speaker's intentions. That will come only when it is being reproduced as a member of a ref, due to its correlation with a particular function. It is this stabilizing function that is the word's public sense, and it is only when it has such a function that there can be a divorce between private intention and public sense. It is also by being a member of a ref with such a sense that a token of the ref can misrepresent, by being produced on the model of other members of the ref, but in a situation where some of the normal conditions for the performance of the function are not satisfied. In this case the stabilizing function is not being performed. The word still has that stabilizing function *qua* member of its ref even when it malfunctions.

Representation

The foregoing account is an outline of an extremely detailed and ambitious theory. For our purposes, the interest is that one of the stated aims of the theory is to give a naturalisic account of representation and intentionality. In Chapter 14 Millikan expands on how she sees biosemantics and biopsychology developing.

A number of features of her discussion are worth noting. The first is the importance attached to the role of the consumer (user) of the representation, rather than the producer. The correspondence relation between representation and the world is required for the performance of the consumer's functions, it being a normal condition for the proper performance of those functions, *whatever those functions might be*.[4] The producer and the representation are, however, also important. As Millikan puts it:

> a *full* explanation of how the consumer has historically managed to perform its function or functions ... would include that the *producer* first performed *its* function properly, and it would include an explanation of *how* the producer's function has, historically, been accomplished. (Millikan, 1990, p. 154)

The producer's function is not just to produce a representation, but to produce one which corresponds to a state of the world, and a full explanation of past performances of the consumer's function will have to explain how this correspondence has been effected in the past.[5] However, a *proximal* explanation of how the consumer (successfully) performed its function would not need this detail, and would not need to go so far back in time. Given the variety and abundance of initial conditions, conditions which actually obtain when a function is performed, a proximal explanation would need to pick out those obtaining conditions which are necessary for successful performance, and one of these will be a relation of *coincidence* between the representation and a state of the environment, that state being the one it is said to represent.

Now any representation will have many relations to many states of the environment: this is the heart of the 'indeterminacy of content' which haunts attempts at naturalizing content, including the causal – correlational accounts mentioned earlier. Can biopsychology provide determinate content? Consider the case of the frog whose ability to stay alive crucially depends upon its perceiving, and consequently catching, food. We note that the frog's tongue lashes out when flies fly in front of its eyes (except, perhaps, when it is fly-replete). It also lashes out when black spots, fly look-alikes from the frog's perspective, float across its visual field. How should we describe what the frog sees: what is the content of its perceptual state? On Millikan's account, a Normal Condition for the proper performance of the tongue's function is that the environment should contain an edible bug, so the frog's detection system is designed to detect such edible bugs, and not black spots. Remember that this will hold even if the frog, or all frogs, strike out at black spots in the majority of cases. These will not be *successful* performances of the frog's food-gathering function, and so will not be included as a normal condition for the proper performance of successful functioning.

Further threats of indeterminacy of content are avoided by bringing in the producer. While it is true that other states of the environment are essential to the proper performance of the frog's tongue, most of these states (the presence of oxygen, for example) are not ones to which the frog responds, in the sense that there is no mechanism in the frog geared to making the frog's tongue react to oxygen on those occasions when oxygen is present. It is the job of the producer of representations to see that it produces representations which correlate with items which are useful to interpreters of those representations. So the frog's bug-detecting device should, occasion by occasion, produce a representation which stimulates the eating mechanism into action. This may give rise to faulty tongue-firings (when there are black spots and not bugs present), but this does not disturb the account of what the producer's function is.

A second important feature of Millikan's discussion is that, although there is no necessity that the representation is always accurate, there is a principle of minimal charity involved. Unless the consumer can use the representations as a guide to the world in enough cases – unless, to take one case of representations, there are sufficient true beliefs – there would be no representation, and no beliefs. 'Sufficient' here does not mean 'most'; it is not required that the majority of my beliefs must be true. As Millikan notes biological advantage can accrue from a feature which only performs its function on very few occasions. From the biopsychological perspective, we may well more often breach rational norms than conform to them, consistent with reason involving norms which we ought to obey.

A third feature of Millikan's position is that, because the functions determining semantic categorization arise historically, the historical origin of a function cannot confer causal power on the functional item. Thus, according to Millikan, it is not *because* a thing has a function that it does anything. Further, it is implausible to hold that there are going to be any interesting, strict or loose, laws forthcoming in a future cognitive science, this lack of causal law further undermining the case for causal efficacy of reasons.[6] The main consequence of these claims is that one should not expect biological, or psychological, explanations to be predictive in the manner of explanation *via* causal laws.

A fourth point that emerges from Millikan's discussion is the distinctiveness of the theory in its insistence on the possibility of what is known as 'external' content (see 'Anti-individualism and Psyhological Explanation', also in Part II of this volume). A problem facing any account of intentional content which focuses on the way the content-state is causally produced is to decide upon which cause determines the content. In many cases we would want to say that the content of a belief, say the belief that there is a cat in the garden, is determined by a distal cause, the cat in the garden. The problem is to say why it is the cat which determines the content, rather than a more proximate cause, such as the sensory stimulation caused by the presence of the cat. On Millikan's account, the belief corresponds to the presence of the cat if and only if that correspondence is a normal condition for the proper functions of the consumer of the belief. If pseudo-cats and images of cats do not fulfil this role then they are not what is represented in the belief that there is a cat out there, even when the cat-image, say, produces identical behaviour (cat-chasing behaviour) to the behaviour produced by the presence of a cat. It will be a real state of the environment (usually) to which representations correspond.

This strong externalism, with its commitment to realism, is allied to doubts about self-knowledge. On Millikan's account, it may be the case that we are thoroughly confused about what we believe. Our beliefs about our beliefs may be just wrong. The environment may trick us into thinking that our beliefs are of one type when, in fact, they are not. The idea that our self-knowledge is infallible or transparent to us in any way is rejected by Millikan as a remnant of a non-naturalistic Cartesian epistemology.

A final point worth noting is that an essential property of Millikan-style biopsychology is that it allows for the possibility of novel beliefs, beliefs whose content has never been entertained before. This is impossible on some naturalistic theories of psychological processes which make use of the input from biological natural selection.[7] If function determines content, and function-ality only arises *after* a process of natural selection, then the state or feature which is the origin of the process will not have a function and so, on these accounts, will not have any intentional content. This is a problem because it seems clear that we do have novel beliefs, minimally exemplified in our ability to learn about our environment.[8] Some functional theories go non-biological at this stage, relying on a selection process occurring within the person during trial and error learning.[9] Millikan does not need to go non-biological to generate new content: given the above characterization of adapted and derived functions and their application to the bee-dance case, it is easy to see how novel beliefs may occur. In these cases no additional selection processes are needed for new biological 'purposes' to emerge.

Critical Responses

The theory put forward by Millikan is ambitious and detailed. Needless to say, there have been several critical responses, mainly dealing with the foundations of the approach. I will briefly comment on the two worries that are raised by Christopher Peacocke in Chapter 15. First, does selection give us the *right* content for intentional states? Secondly, is it right to assume that, because 'having a mind' (possessing intentional states) is an adaptation, and so is something for which a natural selection explanation is appropriate, we must therefore give what Peacocke calls a *constitutive* account of the intentional states in biological (functional) terms? Must we give an account of the nature of what is produced by evolution in biological terms?

The first problem puts in question the relation between natural selection and the content of a representation, such as a belief. One aspect of this problem, one not raised by Peacocke, concerns the connection between truthful representation and natural selection. Call this 'the truth problem'. We usually think that beliefs must aim to be true. The paradox in saying 'I believe that the cat is in the garden, but the cat is not in the garden' indicates the intimate connection between believing and aiming at the truth. However, there is no necessity for natural selection to select beliefs on account of their truth; false beliefs may on many occasions be more advantageous for biological purposes. One example is that of animals whose continued existence depends upon immediate detection of predators. Given the necessity for quick evasive action, it is likely to be a good survival strategy for the animals to take flight whenever they see something like a predator. In the majority of cases they may misidentify and run from innocuous shadows, but in doing this their interests may be better served, despite energy costs, than if they were to wait around for a closer inspection of the suspicious shape. Now the type of theory put forward by Millikan seems able to meet this objection, given that content is determined by *successful* performance of the interpreter's (of that content) functions. Successful performance of predator evasion will be just that – evasion of a predator, and not flight from a predator-shaped shadow.

A different example might, however, prove more troublesome. It has been discovered that it is functional (in the sense of promoting well-being and welfare) for us to overestimate our own abilities. Those with a slightly higher opinion of themselves than the facts allow perform better in a number of important respects than those who have an accurate self-portrayal.[10] *If* this inaccurate self-estimation leads to better biological functioning (which it appears to do), then it would appear that the mechanism producing the false beliefs can be selected for without the saving grace of it being due to the truth of some of the beliefs being produced. In particular, successful performance of the representation-user's functions appears in this case to require falsity of the representation.

We mention the truth problem to highlight the role played by selection in the determination of content. In his comments in Chapter 15 Peacocke concentrates on a different aspect of the worry about the connection between content and selection. He thinks that concentration on selection will lead to an impoverished content in certain crucial cases. He calls this 'the problem of reduced content', which shows itself most clearly in cases such as those accidental generalizations which are believed by us. Say we believe that all Londoners are friendly, on the basis of contact with some Londoners. On the biopsychological account, so the criticism contends, what explains the persistence of the belief, and the mechanism by whose means it is produced, is just the true consequences of those beliefs which causally impact on the thinker. The reason for this is that selection works via causal interaction with the environment; non-actual consequences of beliefs (hypothetical consequences) cannot be part of the selectionist explanation of the persistence of the belief. If only actual consequences are required for the persistence of the belief, then only these will figure in the content of the belief. But, so the objection goes, the content of such beliefs (beliefs having accidental generalizations as their content) is not restricted to just those causally impacting true consequences of the beliefs. The content will include commitments to consequences that play no part in the selectionist explanation. The content of the belief about Londoners generates a commitment to believe that the next Londoner we meet will be friendly, even if the next Londoner has played no part in the selection of either the belief or the mechanism which produced it. If these consequences are not included in the content of a believed generalization, then that content will be 'reduced' – more restricted than we would normally take it to be.

The second objection raised by Peacocke relates to what might be called the 'reach' of a biological explanation of the existence and persistence of an organ. We can agree that having mental states, say intentional states such as beliefs, is biologically desirable, and that their presence is explained by this fact. One can still resist the move which makes biological functionality *determine* the content of the mental state. In Peacocke's terms, the constitutive account of the state, one which gives its essential nature, may not be a functional account even though the state is functional for the organism. The significance of this is that it permits rejection of the following exclusive disjunction suggested by some biopsychologists: either content is constituted by biological function or our 'mindedness' is, from the biological point of view, a sheer accident.

In her response to Peacocke, (Chapter 16) Millikan concentrates on the issue of reduced content, noting the importance in her account of an invariant relational function which underlies variation in adapted functions. The adapted function (see above) gives a fixed reading for a specific state of the environment, as in the case of a chameleon's skin turning brown. What underlies this adaptation (which may be novel) is the invariant relational function of matching its skin colour to the colour of what it is lying on, whatever that colour may be.[11] The semantic rules that apply to a mental representation are relevant to the invariant relational explanation for the performance of the representation and of the consumers of the representation. The truth condition of the mental representation derives from this invariant relational function, and so may not match the environment in any particular case. Millikan goes so far as to say that it may well be logically impossible for the truth condition to be met with in some particular cases. Crucially, it is the invariant relational explanation (say the relational explanation of what the different bee dances have in common when they point the worker bees to different nectar locations) which is selected for in ancestors of the present producer of the representations.

A second point made by Millikan relates to the *systematic* way producers of representations function in producing representations which correspond to a varying environment. A systematic mechanism for the production of representations must have actually produced the 'right' representations in the past for the mechanism to have been selected. (Such 'right' representations are ones where the consumers of the representations can make use of the correspondence between representation and environment.) The important point here is that the representation is produced by a mechanism which produces it systematically, according to rules for the proper production of representations in such-and-such circumstances.

Millikan uses these points to suggest that Peacocke's criticism is directed at too specific a target, at how particular representations, such as beliefs, function. Her interest is in relational descriptions and explanations of function, and these underly the production of a great many particular beliefs. The systematic production of these beliefs is what makes it possible to produce beliefs with a content which transcends the particular causal interactions between that belief, or even ancestors of that belief, and the environment. With the case of universal beliefs, Millikan makes the suggestion that there could be a mechanism which produced beliefs that mapped onto a 'universal state of affairs'. It will be this mechanism which will have been selected for, and selection could have been assisted when the mechanism worked to produce a belief which had a restricted domain, such as 'All people in this room are philosophers.' Given the restricted domain, all members (or parts) of the domain may have made a difference to the user of the universal belief, and so explained the selection of the mechanism. In other cases, the mechanism may produce a universal belief which, as it happens, has a much larger domain. It will be the rules for the generation of universal belief-contents which determine the assignment of content to this belief, and those rules will be relevant even if the domain is unsurveyable.

What will be crucial in this debate is how one describes the mechanism for the production of particular beliefs. Or, to put it another way, how the rules by which the mechanism *systematically* produces the varied beliefs are specified. Peacocke may well think that to specify the rules in a way that allows for universal generalization over an unrestricted domain is already to favour one description of the belief – producing mechanism over another, the favoured description being that which is contested. In the background here is the general issue of the determinate, or indeterminate, nature of the function which can be attributed on the basis of the historical evidence. Does the selectionist history of the development of a trait provide sufficient evidence to unambiguously assign a function to that trait, to distinguish one such function – attribution from another which may be extensionally equivalent as far as selectionist history goes, or does that history leave it open as to which of several specifications of function is apt? This problem becomes particularly acute when the distinctions required are distinctions of intentional content.[12]

Notes

1 A simple causal-correlational account makes the representational content of the representing state depend on what caused that state to occur. Misrepresentation is impossible, given that whatever caused the state to occur is the represented state.

2 For further discussion of functionality see Karen Neander (1991). Neander raises interesting questions concerning Millikan's 'layered' approach to functions, especially the derived functions. See n. 10 p. 461, and her discussion of the difference between natural selection and intentional design, pp. 460–3. The connection between functionality and the irreducibility of biology is argued for in Graham Macdonald (1992).

3 Millikan suggests that the utterances of a parrot will also have a direct proper function, being a member of the relevant ref. It may be, however, that we could claim that the Normal Explanation for the production of members of these refs is that they are produced by intentional agents, which may rule out parrots. For Millikan herself notes that the stabilizing function is not independent of intentions in general; there must be a certain number of occasions on which the use of the words is such that they perform their function in accordance with speakers' and hearers' purposes.

4 This aspect of the theory leads Andrew Woodfield (1990) to query whether it is, in fact, a functional theory of representational content. It is one in virtue of the crucial role played by the proper performance of functions of both producers and consumers of representations.

5 'Correspondence' here relies on the representation being an articulated sign, one with a structure whose elements can vary with variation in what is represented. The timing of a signal, say the time during which a warning red flag flies on a beach, will be part of its structure, co-varying with the time that danger is present.

6 See Chapter 3 for a different perspective.

7 David Papineau's theory makes it impossible for the first occurrence of a belief state to have any content (see Papineau, 1987).

8 That one must allow for the acquisition of novel beliefs is to be distinguished from another more controversial claim, that a physical duplicate of yourself created a minute ago would have exactly the same beliefs which you have. *No* teleo-functionalist account of belief can allow this latter claim, given that the duplicate's states have no relevant biological history. As noted above, the new twin will not have any biological states. Whether this is a problem for biopsychology is unclear; there may be perfectly good reasons to deny that the duplicates share the same psychological states. Certainly those states whose content requires causal contact

with the environment in the past (for example, any state involving or presupposing memory) will not be found in the new twin.

9   See Millikan's (1990) discussion of Dretske, and Woodfield's (1990) interesting variant, which uses sub-personal selection processes to generate new representations.

10   See Roy Baumeister (1989, p. 182): 'nondepressed people tend to overestimate their success, efficacy, and good qualities. Seeing self and world accurately is associated with depression.'

11   This is a bit ambitious for chameleons, as they cannot adapt to many colours, these not being found in the environment of their ancestors when the relational function was fixed. We ignore this complication.

12   This problem is stressed by Jerry Fodor (1991).

References

Baumeister,R. (1989) 'The optimal margin of illusion'. *Journal of Social and Clinical Psychology* 8 (2) 176–89

Fodor,J. (1991) 'Reply' to Millikan's 'Speaking up for Darwin'. In B.Loewer and G.Rey (eds), *Meaning and Mind: Fodor and his Critics*, pp. 293–6. Oxford, Basil Blackwell.

Macdonald,G. (1992) 'Reduction and evolutionary biology'. In D. Charles and K.Lennon (eds), *Reduction, Explanation, and Realism*, pp. 69–96. Oxford, Oxford University Press.

Millikan,R.G. (1984) *Language, Thought, and other Biological Categories*. Cambridge, Mass., MIT Press.

Millikan,R.G.(1990) 'Compare and contrast Dretske, Fodor, and Millikan on teleosemantics'. *Philosophical Topics* 18 (2), 151–62.

Neander,K. (1991) 'The teleological notion of function'. *Australasian Journal of Philosophy* 69 (4) 454–68.

Papineau,D. (1987) *Representation and Reality*. Oxford, Basil Blackwell.

Woodfield,A. (1990) 'The emergence of natural representations'. *Philosophical Topics* 18 (2), 187–213.

14

Biosemantics
Explanation in Biopsychology

Ruth Garrett Millikan

BIOSEMANTICS

Causal or informational theories of the semantic content of mental states which have had an eye on the problem of false representations have characteristically begun with something like this intuition. There are some circumstances under which an inner representation has its represented as a necessary and/or sufficient cause or condition of production. That is how the content of the representation is fixed. False representations are to be explained as tokens that are produced under other circumstances. The challenge, then, is to tell what defines certain circumstances as the content-fixing ones.

I

Note that the answer cannot be just that these circumstances are *statistically* normal conditions. To gather such statistics, one would need to delimit a reference class of occasions, know how to count its members, and specify description categories. It would not do, for example, just to average over conditions-in-the-universe-any-place-any-time. Nor is it given how to carve out relevant description categories for conditions on occasions. Is it 'average' in the summer for it to be (precisely) between 80° and 80.5° Fahrenheit with humidity 87 per cent? And are average conditions those which obtain on at least 50 per cent of the occasions, or is it 90 per cent? Depending on how one sets these parameters, radically different conditions are 'statistically normal'. But the notion of semantic content clearly is not relative, in this manner, to arbitrary parameters. The content-fixing circumstances must be *non-arbitrarily* determined.

A number of writers have made an appeal to teleology here, specifically to conditions of normal function or well-functioning of the systems that produce inner representations. Where the represented is R and its representation is 'R', under conditions of well-functioning, we might suppose, only Rs can or are likely to produce 'R's. Or perhaps 'R' is a representation of R just in case the system was designed to react to Rs by producing 'R's. But this sort of move yields too many representations. Every state of every functional system has normal causes, things that it is a response to in accordance with design. These causes may be proximate or remote, and many are disjunctive. Thus, a proximate normal cause of dilation of the skin capillaries is certain substances in the blood, more remote causes include muscular effort, sunburn, and being in an overheated environment. To each of these causes the vascular system responds by design, yet the response (a red face), though it may be a natural sign of burn or exertion or overheating, certainly is not a representation of that. If not every state of a system represents its normal causes, which are the states that do?

Jerry Fodor[1] has said that, whereas the content of an inner representation is determined by some sort of causal story, its status *as* a representation is determined by the functional organization of the part of the system which uses it. There is such a thing, it seems, as behaving like a representation without behaving like a representation of anything in particular. What the thing is a representation of is then determined by its cause under content-fixing conditions. It would be interesting to have the character of universal I-am-a-representation behavior spelled out for us. Yet, as Fodor well knows, there would still be the problem of demonstrating that there was only one normal cause per representation type.

A number of writers, including Dennis Stampe,[2] Fred Dretske,[3] and Mohan Matthen,[4] have suggested that what is different about effects that are representations is that their function is, precisely, to represent, 'indicate' or 'detect'. For example, Matthen says of (full-fledged) perceptual states that they are 'state[s] that [have] the function of *detecting* the presence of things of a certain type'.[5] It does not help to be told that inner representations are things that have representing (indicating, detecting) as their function, however, unless we are also told what kind of activity representing (indicating, detecting) is. Matthen does not tell us how to naturalize the notion 'detecting'. If 'detecting' is a function of a representational state, it must be something that the state effects or produces. For example, it cannot be the function of a state to have been produced in response to something. Or does Matthen mean that it is not the representational states themselves, but the part of the system which produces them, which has the function of detecting? It has the function, say, of producing states that correspond to or co-vary with something in the outside world? But, unfortunately, not every device whose job description includes producing items that vary with the world is a representation producer. The devices in me that produce calluses are supposed to vary their placement according to where the friction is, but calluses are not representations. The pigment arrangers in the skin of a chameleon, the function of which is to vary the chameleon's color with what it sits on, are not representation producers.

Stampe and Dretske do address the question of what representing or (Dretske) 'detecting' is. Each brings in his own description of what a natural sign or natural representation is, then assimilates *having the function of representing R* to being a natural sign of representer of *R* when the system functions normally. Now, the production of natural signs is undoubtedly an accidental side-effect of normal operation of many systems. From my red face you can tell that either I have been exerting myself, or I have been in the heat, or I am burned. But the production of an accidental side-effect, no matter how regular, is not one of a system's functions; that goes by definition. More damaging, however, it simply is not true that representations must carry natural information. Consider the signals with which various animals signal danger. Nature knows that it is better to err on the side of caution, and it is likely that many of these signs occur more often in the absence than in the presence of any real danger. Certainly there is nothing incoherent in the idea that this might be so, hence that many of these signals do not carry natural information concerning the dangers they signal.

II

I fully agree, however, that an appeal to teleology, to function, is what is needed to fly a naturalist theory of content. Moreover, what makes a thing into an inner representation is, near enough, that its function is to represent. But, I shall argue, the way to unpack this insight is to focus on representation *consumption*, rather than representation production. It is the devices that *use* representations which determine these to be representations and, at the same time (*contra* Fodor), determine their content. If it really is the function of an inner representation to indicate its represented, clearly it is not just a natural sign, a sign that you or I looking on might interpret. It must be one that functions as a sign or representation *for the system itself*. What is it then for a system to use a representation *as* a representation?

The conception of function on which I shall rely was defined in my *Language, Thought, and Other Biological Categories*[6] and defended in 'In defense of proper functions'[7] under the label of 'proper function'. Proper functions are determined by the histories of the items possessing them; functions that were 'selected for' are paradigm cases.[8] The notions 'function' and 'design' should not be read, however, as referring only to origin. Natural selection does not slack after the emergence of a structure but actively preserves it by acting against the later emergence of less fit structures. And structures can be preserved due to performance of new functions unrelated to the forces that originaly shaped them. Such functions are 'proper functions', too, and are 'performed in accordance with design'.

The notion 'design' should not be read – and this is very important – as a reference to innateness. A system may have been designed to be altered by its experience, perhaps to learn from its experience in a prescribed manner. Doing what it has learned to do in this manner is then 'behaving in accordance with design' or 'functioning properly'.[9]

My term 'normal' should be read normatively, historically, and relative to specific function. In the first instance, 'normal' applies to explanations. A 'normal explanation' explains the performance of a particular function, telling how it was (typically) historically performed on those (perhaps rare) occasions when it was properly performed. Normal explanations do not tell, say, why it has been common for a function to be performed; they are not statistical explanations. They cover only past times of actual performance, showing how these performances were entailed by natural law, given certain conditions, coupled with the dispositions and structures of the relevant functional devices.[10] In the second instance, 'normal' applies to conditions. A 'normal condition for performance of a function' is a condition, the presence of which must be mentioned in giving a full normal explanation for performance of that function. Other functions of the same organism or system may have other normal conditions. For example, normal conditions for discriminating tastes, and normal conditions for seeing very large objects are not the same as for seeing very small ones. It follows that 'normal conditions' must not be read as having anything to do with what is typical or average or even, in many cases, at all common. First, many functions are performed only rarely. For example, very few wild seeds land in conditions normal for their growth and development, and the protective colorings of caterpillars seldom actually succeed in preventing them from being eaten. Indeed, normal conditions might almost better be called 'historically optimal' conditions. (If normal conditions for proper functioning, hence survival and proliferation, were a statistical norm, imagine how many rabbits there would be in the world.) Secondly, many proper functions only need to be performed under rare conditions. Consider, for example, the vomiting reflex, the function of which is to prevent (further) toxification of the body. A normal condition for performance of this function is presence, specifically, of poison in the stomach, for (I am guessing) it is only under that condition that this reflex has historically had beneficial effects. But poison in the stomach certainly is not an average condition. (Nor, of course, is it a normal condition for other functions of the digestive system.)[11]

If it is actually one of a system's functions to produce representations, as we have said, these representations must function as representations for the system itself. Let us view the system, then, as divided into two parts or two aspects, one of which produces representations for the other to consume. What we need to look at is the consumer part, at what it is to use a thing *as* a representation. Indeed, a good look at the consumer part of the system ought to be all that is needed to determine not only representational status but representational content. We argue this as follows. First, the part of the system which consumes representations must understand the representations proffered to it. Suppose, for example, that there were abundant 'natural information' (in Dretske's sense)[12] contained in numerous natural signs all present in a certain state of a system. This information could still not serve the system *as* information, unless the signs were understood by the system, and, further-more, understood as bearers of whatever specific information they, in fact, do bear. (Contrast Fodor's notion that something could function like a represen-tation without functioning like a representation of anything in particular.) So there must be something about the consumer that *constitutes* its taking the signs to indicate, say, *p*, *q* and *r* rather than *s*, *t* and *u*. But, if we know what constitutes the consumer's *taking* a sign to indicate *p*, what *q*, what *r*, etc., then, granted that the consumer's takings are in some way systematically derived from the structures of the signs so taken, we can construct a semantics for the consumer's language. Anything the signs may indicate *qua* natural signs or natural information carriers then drops out as entirely irrelevant; the represen-tation-producing side of the system had better pay undivided attention to the language of its consumer. The sign producer's function will be to produce signs that are true *as the consumer reads the language*.

The problem for the naturalist bent on describing intentionality, then, does not concern representation production at all. Although a representation always is something that is produced by a system whose proper function is to make that representation correspond by rule to the world, what the rule of correspon-dence is, what gives definition to this function, is determined entirely by the representation's consumers.

For a system to use an inner item as a representation, I propose, is for the following two conditions to be met. First, unless the representation accords, *so* (by a certain rule), with a represented, the consumer's normal use of, or response to, the representation will not be able to fulfill all of the consumer's proper functions in so responding – not, at least, in accordance with a normal explanation. (Of course, it might still fulfill these functions by freak accident, but not in the historically normal way.) Putting this more formally, that the representation and the represented accord with one another, so, is a normal condition for proper functioning of the consumer device as it reacts to the representation.[13] Note that the proposal is not that the content of the representation rests on the function of the representation or of the consumer, on what these do. The idea is not that there is such a thing as behaving like a representation of X or as being treated like a representation of X. The content hangs only on there being a certain condition that would be *normal* for performance of the consumer's functions – namely, that a certain correspon-dence relation hold between sign and world – whatever those functions may happen to be. For example, suppose the semantic rules for my belief representations are determined by the fact that belief tokens in me will aid the devices that use them to perform certain of their tasks in accordance with a normal explanation for success only under the condition that the forms or 'shapes' of these belief tokens correspond, in accordance with the said rules, to conditions in the world. Just what these user tasks are need not be mentioned.[14]

Secondly, represented conditions are conditions that vary, depending on the *form* of the representation, in accordance with specifiable correspondence rules that give the semantics for the relevant *system* of representation. More precisely, representations always admit of significant transformations (in the mathematical sense), which accord with transformations of their corresponding representeds, thus displaying significant articulation into variant and invariant aspects. If an item considered as compounded of certain variant and invariant aspects can be said to be 'composed' of these, then we can also say that every representation is, as such, a member of a representational system having a 'compositional semantics'. For it is not that the represented condition is itself a normal condition for proper operation of the representation consumer. A certain correspondence between the representation and the world is what is normal. Coordinately, there is no such thing as a representation consumer that can understand only one representation. There are always other representations, composed other ways, saying other things, which it could have understood as well, in accordance with the same principles of operation. A couple of very elementary examples should make this clear.[15]

First, consider beavers, who splash the water smartly with their tails to signal danger. This instinctive behavior has the function of causing other beavers to take cover. The splash means danger, because only when it corresponds to danger does the instinctive response to the splash on the part of the interpreter beavers, the consumers, serve a purpose. If there is no danger present, the interpreter beavers interrupt their activities uselessly. Hence, that the splash corresponds to danger is a normal condition for proper functioning of the interpreter beavers' instinctive reaction to the splash. (It does not follow, of course, that it is a usual condition. Beavers being skittish, most beaver splashes possibly occur in response to things not in fact endangering the beaver.) In the beaver splash semantic system, the time and place of the splash varies with, 'corresponds to', the time and place of danger. The representation is articulate: properly speaking, it is not a splash but a splash-at-a-time-and-a-place. Other representations in the same system, splashes at other times and places, indicate other danger locations.

Secondly, consider honey bees, which perform 'dances' to indicate the location of sources of nectar they have discovered. Variations in the tempo of the dance and in the angle of its long axis vary with the distance and direction of the nectar. The interpreter mechanisms in the watching bees – these are the representation consumers – will not perform their full proper functions of aiding the process of nectar collection in accordance with a normal explanation, unless the location of nectar corresponds correctly to the dance. So, the dances are representations of the location of nectar. The full representation here is a dance-at-a-time-in-a-place-at-a-tempo-with-an-orientation.

Notice that, on this account, it is not necessary to assume that most representations are true. Many biological devices perform their proper functions not on the average, but just often enough. The protective coloring of the juveniles of many animal species, for example, is an adaptation passed on because *occasionally* it prevents a juvenile from being eaten, though most of the juveniles of these species get eaten anyway. Similarly, it is conceivable that the devices that fix human beliefs fix true ones not on the average, but just often enough. If the true beliefs are functional and the false beliefs are, for the most part, no worse than having an empty mind, then even very fallible belief-fixing devices might be better than no belief-fixing devices at all. These devices might even be, in a sense, 'designed to deliver some falsehoods'. Perhaps, given the difficulty of designing highly accurate belief-fixing mechanisms, it is actually advantageous to fix too many beliefs, letting some of these be false, rather than fix too few beliefs. Coordinately, perhaps our belief-consuming mechanisms are carefully designed to tolerate a large proportion of false beliefs. It would not follow, of course, that the belief consumers are designed to *use* false beliefs, certainly not that false beliefs can serve all of the functions that true ones can. Indeed, surely if none of the mechanisms that used beliefs ever cared at all how or whether these beliefs corresponded to anything in the world, beliefs would not be functioning as representations, but in some other capacity.

Shifting our focus from producing devices to consuming devices in our search for naturalized semantic content is important. But the shift from the *function* of consumers to *normal conditions* for proper operation is equally important. Matthen, for example, characterizes what he calls a 'quasi-perceptual state' as, roughly, one whose job is to cause the system to do what it must do to perform its function, given that it is in certain circumstances, which are what it represents. Matthen is thus looking pretty squarely at the representation consumers, but at what it is the representation's job to get these consumers to do, rather than at normal conditions for their proper operation. As a result, Matthen now retreats. The description he has given of quasi-perceptual states, he says, cannot cover 'real perception such as that which we humans experience. Quite simply, there is no such thing as *the* proper response, or even a range of functionally appropriate responses, to what perception tells us'.[16] On the contrary, representational content rests not on univocity of consumer function but on sameness of normal conditions for those functions. The same percept of the world may be used to guide any of very many and diverse activities, practical or theoretical. What stays the same is that the percept must correspond to environmental configurations in accordance with the same correspondence rules for each of these activities. For example, if the position of the chair in the room does not correspond, so, to my visual representation of its position, that will hinder me equally in my attempts to avoid the chair when passing through the room, to move the chair, to sit in it, to remove the cat from it, to make judgments about it, etc. Similarly, my belief that New York is large may be turned to any of diverse purposes, but those which require it to be a *representation* require also that New York indeed be large if these purposes are to succeed in accordance with a normal explanation for functioning of my cognitive systems.

III

We have just cleanly by-passed the whole genre of casual/informational accounts of mental content. To illustrate this, we consider an example of Dretske's. Dretske tells of a certain species of northern hemisphere bacteria which orient themselves away from toxic oxygen-rich surface water by attending to their magnetosomes, tiny inner magnets, which pull toward the magnetic north pole, hence pull down.[17] (Southern hemisphere bacteria have their magnetosomes reversed.) The function of the magnetosome thus appears to be to effect that the bacterium moves into oxygen-free water. Correlatively, intuition tells us that what the pull of the magnetosome represents is the whereabouts of oxygen-free water. The direction of oxygen-free water is not, however, a factor in *causing* the direction of pull of the magnetosome. And the most reliable natural information that the magnetosome carries is surely not about oxygen-free water but about distal and proximal causes of the pull, about the direction of geomagnetic or better, just plain magnetic, north. One can, after all, easily deflect the magnetosome away from the direction of lesser oxygen merely by holding a bar magnet overhead. Moreover, it is surely a function of the magnetosome to respond to that magnetic field, that is part of its normal mechanism of operation, whereas responding to oxygen density is not. None of this makes any sense on a causal or informational approach.

But on the biosemantic theory it does make sense. What the magnetosome represents is only what its *consumers* require that it correspond to in order to perform *their* tasks. Ignore, then, how the representation (a pull-in-a-direction-at-a-time) is normally produced. Concentrate, instead, on how the systems that react to the representation work, on what these systems need in order to do their job. What they need is only that the pull be in the direction of oxygen-free water at the time. For example, they care not at all how it came about that the pull is in that direction; the magnetosome that points toward oxygen-free water quite by accident and not in accordance with any normal explanation will do just as well as one that points that way for the normal reasons. (As Socrates concedes in the *Meno*, true opinion is just as good as knowledge so long as it stays put.) What the magnetosome represents then is univocal; it represents only the direction of oxygen-free water. For that is the only thing that corresponds (by a compositional rule) to it, the absence of which would matter: the absence of which would disrupt the function of those mechanisms which rely on the magnetosome for guidance.

It is worth noting that what is represented by the magnetosome is not proximal but distal; no proximal stimulus is represented at all. Nor, of course, does the bacterium perform an inference from the existence of the proximal stimulus (the magnetic field) to the existence of the represented. These are good results for a theory of content to have, for otherwise one needs to introduce a derivative theory of content for mental representations that do not refer, say, to sensory stimulations, and also a foundationalist account of belief fixation. Note also that, on the present view, representations manufactured in identical ways by different species of animal might have different contents. Thus, a certain kind of small swift image on the toad's retina, manufactured by his eye lens, represents a bug, for that is what it must correspond to if the reflex it (invariably) triggers is to perform its proper functions normally, while exactly the same kind of small swift image on the retina of a male hoverfly, manufactured, let us suppose, by a nearly identical lens, represents a passing female hoverfly, for that is what it must correspond to if the female-chasing reflex it (invariably) triggers is to perform its proper functions normally. Turning the coin over, representations with the same content may be normally manufactured in a diversity of ways, even in the same species. How many different ways do you have, for example, of telling a lemon or your spouse? Nor is it necessary that any of the ways one has of manufacturing a given representation be especially reliable ways in order for the representation to have determinate content. These various results cut the biosemantic approach off from all varieties of verificationism and foundationalism with a clean, sharp knife.

IV

But perhaps it will be thought that belief fixation and consumption are not biologically proper activities, hence that there are no normal explanations, in our defined sense, for proper performances of human beliefs. Unlike bee dances, which are all variations on the same simple theme, beliefs in dinosaurs, in quarks and in the instability of the dollar are recent, novel and innumerably diverse, as are their possible uses. How could there be anything *biologically* normal or abnormal about the details of the consumption of such beliefs?

But what an organism does in accordance with evolutionary design can be very novel and surprising, for the more complex of nature's creatures are designed to learn. Unlike evolutionary adaptation, learning is not accomplished by *random* generate-and-test procedures. Even when learning involves trial and error (probably the exception rather than the rule), there are principles in accordance with which responses are selected by the system to try, and there are specific principles of generalization and discrimination etc. which have been built into the system by natural selection. How these principles normally work, that is, how they work given normal (i.e. historically optimal) environments, to produce changes in the learner's nervous system which will effect the furthering of ends of the system has, of course, an explanation: the normal explanation for proper performance of the learning mechanism and of the states of the nervous system it produces.

Using a worn-out comparison, there is an infinity of functions which a modern computer mainframe is capable of performing, depending upon its input and on the program it is running. Each of these things it can do, so long as it is not damaged or broken, 'in accordance with design', and to each of these capacities there corresponds an explanation of how it would be activated or fulfilled normally. The human's mainframe takes, roughly, stimulations of the afferent nerves as input, both to program and to run it.[18] It responds, in part, by developing concepts, by acquiring beliefs and desires in accordance with these concepts, by engaging in practical inference leading ultimately to action. Each of these activities may, of course, involve circumscribed sorts of trial and error learning. When conditions are optimal, all this aids survival and proliferation in accordance with a historically normal explanation – one of high generality, of course. When conditions are not optimal, it may yield, among other things, empty or confused concepts, biologically useless desires, and false beliefs. But, even when the desires are biologically useless (though probably not when the concepts expressed in them are empty or confused), there are still biologically normal ways for them to get fulfilled, the most obvious of which require reliance on true beliefs.[19]

Yet how do we know that our contemporary ways of forming concepts, desires and beliefs do occur in accordance with evolutionary design? Fodor, for example, is ready with the labels 'pop Darwinism' and 'naive adaptationism' to abuse anyone who supposes that our cognitive systems were actually selected for their belief and desire using capacities.[20] Clearly, to believe that every structure must have a function would be naive. Nor is it wise uncritically to adopt hypotheses about the functions of structures when these functions are obscure. It does not follow that we should balk at the sort of adaptationist who, having found a highly complex structure that quite evidently is currently and effectively performing a highly complex and obviously indispensable function, then concludes, *ceteris paribus*, that this function has been the most recent historical task stabilizing the structure. To suspect that the brain has not been preserved for thinking with or that the eye has not been preserved for seeing with – to suspect this, moreover, in the absence of any alternative hypotheses about causes of the stability of these structures – would be totally irresponsible. Consider: nearly every human behavior is bound up with intentional action. Are we really to suppose that the degree to which our behaviors help to fulfill intentions, and the degree to which intentions result from logically related desires plus beliefs, is a sheer coincidence – that these patterns are irrelevant to survival and proliferation or, though relevant, have had no stabilizing effect on the gene pool? But the only alternative to biological design, in our sense of 'design', is sheer coincidence, freak accident – unless there is a ghost running the machine!

Indeed, it is reasonable to suppose that the brain structures we have recently been using in developing space technology and elementary particle physics have been operating in accordance with the very same general principles as when prehistoric man used them for more primitive ventures. They are no more performing new and different functions or operating in accordance with new and different principles nowadays than are the eyes when what they see is television screens and space shuttles. Compare: the wheel was invented for the purpose of rolling ox carts, and did not come into its own (pulleys, gears, etc.) for several thousand years thereafter, during the industrial revolution. Similarly, it is reasonable that the cognitive structures with which man is endowed were originally nature's solution to some very simple demands made by man's evolutionary niche. But the solution nature stumbled on was elegant, supremely general, and powerful, indeed; I believe it was a solution that cut to the very bone of the ontological structure of the world. That solution involved the introduction of representations, inner and/or outer, having a subject/predicate structure, and subject to a negation transformation. (Why I believe that that particular development was so radical and so powerful has been explained in depth in *LTOBC*, chs 14–19. But see also the section on 'Negation and Propositional Content' below.)

V

One last worry about our sort of position is voiced by Daniel Dennett[21] and discussed at length by Fodor.[22] Is it really plausible that bacteria and paramecia, or even birds and bees, have inner representations in the same sense that we do? Am I really prepared to say that these creatures, too, have mental states, that they think? I am not prepared to say that. On the contrary, the representations that they have must differ from human beliefs in at least six very fundamental ways.[23]

1 *Self-representing elements* The representations that the magnetosome produces have three significant variables, each of which refers to itself. The time of the pull refers to the time of the oxygen-free water, the locale of the pull refers to the locale of the oxygen-free water, and the direction of pull refers to the direction of oxygen-free water. The beaver's splash has two self-referring variables: a splash at a certain time and place indicates that there is danger at that same time and place. (There is nothing necessary about this. It might have meant that there would be danger at the nearest beaver dam in five minutes.) Compare the standard color coding on the outsides of colored markers: each color stands for itself. True, it may be that sophisticated indexical representations such as percepts and indexical beliefs also have their time or place or both as significant self-representing elements, but they also have other significant variables that are not self-representing. The magnetosome does not.

2 *Storing representations* Any representation the time or place of which is a significant variable obviously cannot be stored away, carried about with the organism for use on future occasions. Most beliefs are representations that can be stored away. Clearly this is an important difference.

3 *Indicative and imperative representations* The theory I have sketched here of the content of inner representations applies only to indicative representations, representations which are supposed to be determined by the facts, which tell what is the case. It does not apply to imperative representations,

representations which are supposed to determine the facts, which tell the interpreter what to do. Neither do causal – informational theories of content apply to the contents of imperative representations. True, some philosophers seem to have assumed that having defined the content of various mental symbols by reference to what causes them to enter the 'belief box', then when one finds these same symbols in, say, the 'desire box' or the 'intention box', one already knows what they mean. But how do we know that the desire box or the intention box uses the same representational system as the belief box? To answer that question we would have to know what constitutes a desire box's or an intention box's using one representational system rather than another which, turned around, is the very question at issue. In *LTOBC* and 'Thoughts without laws: cognitive science with content',[24] I developed a parallel theory of the content of imperative representations. Very roughly, one of the proper functions of the consumer system for an imperative representation is to help *produce* a correspondence between the representation and the world. (Of course, this proper function often is not performed.) I also argued that desires and intentions are imperative representations.

Consider, then, the beaver's splash. It tells that there is danger here now. Or why not say, instead, that it tells other nearby beavers what to do now, namely, to seek cover? Consider the magnetosome. It tells which is the direction of oxygen-free water. Or why not say, instead, that it tells the bacterium which way to go? Simple animal signals are invariably both indicative and imperative. Even the dance of the honey bee, which is certainly no simple signal, is both indicative and imperative. It tells the worker bees where the nectar is; equally, it tells them where to go. The step from these primitive representations to human beliefs is an enormous one, for it involves the separation of indicative from imperative functions of the representational system. Representations that are undifferentiated between indicative and imperative connect states of affairs directly to actions, to specific things to be done in the face of those states of affairs. Human beliefs are not tied directly to actions. Unless combined with appropriate desires, human beliefs are impotent. And human desires are equally impotent unless combined with suitable beliefs.[25]

4 *Inference*   As indicative and imperative functions are separated in the central inner representational systems of humans, they need to be reintegrated. Thus, humans engage in practical inference, combining beliefs and desires in novel ways to yield first intentions and then action. Humans also combined beliefs with beliefs to yield new beliefs. Surely nothing remotely like this takes place inside the bacterium.

5 *Acts of identifying*   Mediate inferences always turn on something like a middle term, which must have the same representational value in both premises for the inference to go through. Indeed, the representation consumers in us perform many functions that require them to use two or more overlapping representations together, and in such a manner that, unless the representeds corresponding to these indeed have a common element, these functions will

not be properly performed. Put informally, the consumer device *takes* these represented elements to be the same, thus identifying their representational values. Suppose, for example, that you intend to speak to Henry about something. In order to carry out this intention you must, when the time comes, be able to recognize Henry in perception as the person to whom you intend to speak. You must identify Henry as represented in perception with Henry as represented in your intention. Activities that involve the coordinated use of representations from different sensory modalities, as in the case of eye – hand coordination, visual – tactile coordination, also require that certain objects, contours, places or directions etc. be identified as the same through the two modalities. Now, the foundation upon which modern representational theories of thought are built depends upon a denial that was is thought of is ever placed before a naked mind. Clearly, we can never know what an inner representation represents by a direct comparison of representation to represented. Rather, acts of identifying are our ways of 'knowing what our representations represent'. The bacterium is quite incapable of knowing, in this sense, what its representations are about. This might be a reason to say that it does not understand its own representations, not really.

6 *Negation and propositional content* The representational system to which the magnetosome pull belongs does not contain negation. Indeed, it does not even contain contrary representations, for the magnetosome cannot pull in two directions at once. Similarly, if two beavers splash at different times or places, or if two bees dance different dances at the same time, it may well be that there is indeed beaver danger two times or two places and that there is indeed nectar in two different locations.[26] Without contrariety, no conflict, of course and more specifically, no contradiction. If the law of non-contradiction plays as significant a role in the development of human concepts and knowledge as has traditionally been supposed, this is a large difference between us and the bacterium indeed.[27] In LTOBC, I argued that negation, hence explicit contradiction, is dependent upon subject – predicate, that is, propositional, structure and vice versa. Thus, representations that are simpler also do not have propositional content.

In sum, these six differences between our representations and those of the bacterium, or Fodor's paramecia, ought to be enough amply to secure our superiority, to make us feel comfortably more endowed with mind.

EXPLANATION IN BIOPSYCHOLOGY

The theory of mental representation proposed in 'Biosemantics' (above) invites a traditional question about the status of psychological explanation. According to the biosemantic theory, both the fact that a belief is a belief at all, and the fact that it has a certain semantic content, rest directly on the history of the belief. Nothing in the belief's current dispositions, hence nothing about its causal potencies, makes it be the belief that it is. How then can the fact that a person has certain beliefs help to causally explain how that person acts?

Biopsychology is a Predictive Science if at all, then only Accidentally

These reflections on the nature of intentional psychology entail that, as a *biological* science, it does not aspire to be predictive. Biopsychology studies what happens when biological processes proceed normally, but the normal is neither the necessary nor always the statistically average. Prediction and control do, of course, play an important role under parts of the wide umbrella called psychology – for example, psychological testing, human engineering, psycho-therapy etc. – but prediction and control are not required by-products of intentional psychology. Indeed, intentional attitude psychology is a rather unlikely candidate to aspire to the detailed prediction of individual human behaviors.

This is true for at least two reasons. The first is diversity among individual constitutions. For psychology to predict individual behaviors, just as a starter, babies would have to be born cognitively and affectively, indeed also physically, alike. But it is abundantly clear that different newborns, inserted into identical environments, would not behave at all alike, unless under the most general and vacuous of descriptions. People are born with predispositions to different cognitive and affective styles, with different cognitive strengths and weaknesses. Non-psychological factors such as body-build, reaction time, energy level and health also play a large role in determining behavior. Further, it is likely that many aspects of our cognitive processes are partly stochastic, hence that which, among many possible solutions to a given problem, an individual discovers and executes is often not governed by well-defined psychological principles at all. Surely nothing short of complete physical and chemical analysis could, in fact, predict the detailed behaviors of any individual. The individual is not a replica of its ancestors or of its friends. It is a bundle of heavily redundant unfolding sub-systems adapted each to the others' concrete peculiarities to form coordi-nated larger units, this in accordance with principles of coordination and development all of which are, as yet, subject to merest speculation. We are still trying to find out how an individual's muscles and tendons grow the right length to fit the individual's bones, let alone how the various facets of individual cognitive development and function grow into a coherent unit. But there is no reason to suppose that exactly how an individual thinks is any more governed by laws quantifying over individuals than, say, now he/she walks or plays tennis, or how he/she reacts to allergens.

The second reason that intentional psychology cannot be required to predict individual behaviors is that there is no compelling reason to suppose that all or even most of the norms that it describes are usually fulfilled. Most obvious is that the *environment* cannot always be relied upon to do its part in completing the functions of the cognitive systems. Because this is so obvious, it has been equally apparent to all that there could not possibly be any reliable laws of organism–distal environment interaction, certainly not for the case of humans. Hence theorists who take it that psychology's main business is to deal in laws have found it necessary to insist that a scientific intentional psychology would have to be 'narrow', that it would have to ignore the environment. But it is also likely that those portions of the cognitive functions that are carried out *inside* the organism are abundantly vulnerable to failure. The cognitive mechanisms seem to be paradigms of functional redundancy and layered back-up systems, commanding a variety of means to the accomplishment of the same or functionally equivalent projects. If at first you don't succeed, try another way, is a fundamental heuristic for our cognitive functions. Witness, for example, the well-documented variety of forms of compensation employed by those with brain damage. This redundancy strongly suggests the vulnerability of various cognitive techniques taken separately. It follows that there is little reason to suppose that the exact progression of anyone's inner cognitive systems could be predicted on the basis of even the most exact understanding of all types of human cognitive teleo-function, an understanding of all the biological *norms* involved.

Suppose, for example, that man is indeed a *rational* animal; that conformity to certain logical principles is a biological norm for human thought processes. It would not strictly *follow* that conformity to reason was so much as a common occurrence. Reasoning could be one among other functions of the behavior-controlling systems, one that sometimes worked and was then to the organism's advantage. It could also be one that seldom caused irreparable damage when it failed, due to redundancy and to backing by various cruder behavior-controlling devices such as those found in the lesser animals. Indeed, remembering the way evolution works, it seems that there must at least have been a *time* when human reason had exactly this tentative status. It is not likely that the ability to reason well or to learn to reason well arrived all at once in a single lucky mutation. And we can raise the question of how well, in fact, the average *modern* human reasons. Clearly, from the fact that drawing rational inferences may be a *norm* for human cognitive systems, it does not follow that any reliable predictions about inference patterns can be made. Even though man is a rational animal, rational psychology could remain very far from a reliable predictive science.

But a strong contemporary tradition has it that rational psychology *must* be a predictive science if it is to be a science at all, and that its central job is exactly to predict *individual* humans' behaviors. It is claimed, further, that our layman's way of thinking about intentional mental states constitutes a 'folk psychological theory', the *central employment* of which is to effect prediction of the behaviors of our fellows, for this is necessary in order to project our own paths through the tangle of other folks' actions. Do I maintain that it is mere illusion that we thus predict the actions of others?

No, it certainly is not an illusion that we do a lot of correct predicting concerning the behaviors of others. Most ordinary forms of social intercourse and social cooperation would be impossible if we could not. But there may be a misunderstanding over the *methods* that we typically employ for prediction. The tool that we most commonly use, I suggest, is not a theory of the inner *mechanisms* that lie behind predicted behaviors. The tool is not, for example, belief – desire theory. Most of our predictions are done with a much blunter tool: the method of brute correlation. In many cases there is, of course, some understanding of the outlines of the psychological mechanisms lying behind predicted behaviors, but our predictions do not usually rest on this understanding, either at all, or at least very deeply. They rest mainly on observations of past behavioral regularities for the individual and for the group(s) to which the individual belongs. Within fairly well-defined limits, people, especially people from the same culture, just *do* behave uniformly in a theatre, on the road, at the grocer's, even in the park. Most people are more likely than not to meet what others consider to be their business and social obligations, to conform to general expectations concerning what is appropriate or seemly and, very important, to do the things they have *said* they will do. Beyond this, we project ahead patterns observed in the past for particular individuals. Known personality traits, character traits and habits serve as our guides. Of course, such knowledge merely *limits* the boundaries of people's likely behavior. It does little or nothing towards actually *determining* behavior in its variety. But seldom do we make an attempt to predict others' behaviors in much more detail than this. How inept we actually are at predicting behaviors, even of our best friends and family members, when these behaviors are not covered by known regularities, may be illustrated by friends who become separated in a large crowd, say at a fair, each trying in vain to outguess what the other will do in an attempt at reunion.

Reasons and Causes

If we are rational, what that means is that rationality is a biological *norm* for humans, not that rationality is necessitated by special causal laws of human psychology. Compatibly, it is standard nowadays to claim (though on somewhat different grounds) that thoughts categorized in accordance with their semantics are not the sort of things that could, even in principle, fall under causal laws. On the account of this chapter, the semantic category of a thought is determined relative to its biological functions, which depend in turn upon its history, upon its place relative to certain prior events. But having a certain history is not, of course, an attribute that has 'causal powers'. Hence reasons cannot be, as such, causes. More generally, that a thing has a teleo-function is a causally impotent fact about it. Especially, it is never directly *because* a thing *has* a certain function that it performs that function or any other function.

More nearly the reverse is true. The thing exists and has a certain function because things homologous to it have performed that function (better, had that effect) in the past. Moreover, here the 'because' is only partly causal, the other part is constitutive or logical.

But perhaps it will be thought that although things that have functions cannot be supposed to perform these functions either *on account* of having these functions or in accordance with *strict* causal laws, still they must perform them in accordance with *ceteris paribus* laws. Roughly, there have to be conditions under which the functional item *would* perform its functions since there have to have *been* conditions under which its ancestors *did* perform these functions, and the same kind of item in the same kind of conditions would do the same kind of thing again. This ignores defective members of function categories: diseased hearts, injured limbs etc. It also ignores the fact that performance of their functions is, for many items, a relatively rare occurrence. Would we really wish to speak of *ceteris paribus* laws in cases where *ceteris* are not *paribus* most of the time? And it ignores also a third point.

Characteristically, the same function could, at least in principle, be performed by many differently constituted items. But if these items are differently constituted, if they operate in accordance with different principles, then the supporting conditions required for them to effect this function must differ as well. Brain cells performing the division algorithm require oxygen, whereas computer chips require electric currents, and so forth. Similarly, the outer world conditions that support the bat's mosquito-locating abilities and those that support its mosquito-catching abilities are different from those that support the same abilities in humans. (The bat can perform in the dark on silent mosquitoes, humans cannot.) The result is that there are no *ceteris paribus* laws covering all items having a certain function. For *ceteris paribus* conditions are unspecified conditions that must remain the *same* from case to case for the law to hold, whereas here the necessary conditions would have, precisely, to *vary* from case to case. A 'law' applying to all such cases could say no more than that the items falling under the law could be *made*, by adding different circumstances tailored specifically to each case, to perform the function. But surely anything can be made to effect anything if one adds the right intervening media, if one adds enough special enough circumstances. So any such 'law' would be empty. There are no causal laws of any kind, then, that directly concern the causal efficacy of reasons *as such*. The closest we could get would be *ceteris paribus* laws for human reasons, other *ceteris paribus* laws for dolphin reasons, still others for Martian reasons, and so forth.

Normalizing Explanations

Our argument suggests that explanation of an agent's behavior by reference to reasons for acting is not best analyzed as explanation by subsumption under causal laws. The question that arises then is what kind of explanation the citing of reasons for acting *is*, and how it can still be causal-order explanation. Intentional attitude explanations of behaviors proceed, I will argue, by subsumption of behaviors under biological *norms* rather than laws, and/or by noting departures from these norms and, perhaps, causes of these departures. Following Philip Pettit,[28] to whose views mine run parallel here, I call such explanations 'normalizing explanations'. The status of explanations of individual behaviors by reference to reasons concerns the relation of normalizing explanations to other forms of causal-order explanation that are, perhaps, better understood.

To explain a phenomenon by subsuming it under norms is to exhibit it as an instance of conformity to or departure from proper operation of some teleological system. A very simple form of normalizing explanation explains the occurrence of a phenomenon by reference, merely, to something whose function it was to produce that phenomenon. For example, the dishes are clean because they have been put through the dishwasher; the washing machine door is locked because the washer has not finished spinning and the door is designed not to unlock until it has finished spinning; the bear is asleep because it is winter and it is (biologically) normal for bears to sleep through the winter.

In order to explain a phenomenon this way it is necessary, of course, to classify it appropriately *as* the outcome of a teleo-functional process, and this classifying may itself count as a simple form of explanation. What is happening? What is it doing? It's washing dishes, not making soup or just dirtying the water; it's winding a magnetic coil, not storing wire on a spool; it's resting, cooling its motor between cycles, not playing dead, or broken; and so forth.

More complex normalizing explanations tell or implicitly refer to the place an event has in a series or interdependent pattern of functions, or tell where, and perhaps why, malfunction occurred within such a series or pattern. Thus, that cog-wheel's turning in the calculator is its carrying one in a certain addition algorithm; the car went through the lights because its brakes failed; the outboard stalls because there's dirt in the carburetor that gets into the needle-valve. Normalizing explanations often make reference to conditions that must be presupposed for normal operation of a device or system. Thus the outboard won't start because the spark-plugs are wet or because there's no gas in the tank, the scuba-diver passed out because it was too cold or because his tank ran out of oxygen, and so forth.

Finally, the relation between certain conditions of the functional system itself or of the environment and certain states of the system that normally adapt the system's progress to those conditions may be targeted in a normalizing explanation. Thus, the motor is racing because the heavy-load switch is on but the load is not heavy; the washer failed to fill properly because the soap was put into the tub rather than into the dispenser so that the rising suds tripped the water cut-off before the tub was full; the animal's winter-approaching detectors failed because it was kept indoors, which is why it is attired inappropriately or is behaving inappropriately for the season.

Normal Roles of Beliefs and Desires

Notice how natural it would be to say in the last two of these cases that the washer *thought* it was full when it wasn't and that the animal's system didn't *know* it was winter. This is because a belief or a bit of knowledge is likewise a teleo-functional item, one whose function is to adapt the containing system so that it can perform its functions under certain conditions, namely, those conditions which the belief is about. Or, being a little more precise, it is the belief-*forming* mechanisms that produce the adaptations, the adjustments of the organism to the environment, the beliefs. Beliefs themselves are functionally classified, are 'individuated', not directly by function but according to the special conditions corresponding to them that must be met in the world if it is to be possible for them to contribute to proper functioning of the larger system in a historically normal way. Somewhat similarly, the water switch's being off will promote the washer's tasks normally only if the condition is fulfilled that the washer is full. And the animal's winter detectors' being off will effect appropriate functioning of the animal in accordance with historically normal reasons only if winter is not yet approaching.

Explicit human beliefs, however, are much more than just biological adapters to certain environmental conditions. They are adapters that perform their tasks in a certain *sort* of way, namely, through participation in inference processes. A picture that I advocate[29] but will not try to defend here shows beliefs and desires as working for the organism by *modelling* (in accordance with very abstract mathematical mapping functions) the environment, modeling the organism's goals, and modeling types of environmental transitions that the organism knows how to bring about. Normal practical thinking then involves tinkering with these models until solutions are found that will effect transitions from the present state of the environment to various desired states. On this picture the teleo-functions of desires (which they may not very often perform), like those of blueprints, are to effect what they model, to get themselves realized. When everything goes according to norm, action guided by the models inside is action conformed to the outside world so as to issue in productive loops through the environment. This happens in accordance with explanations that, made fully general, that is fully spelled out relationally, apply perfectly generally to all successful uses of the (same capacities of the) species' cognitive systems, historical and current. *Theoretical* inference is then interpreted as a process whereby the internal model of the environment grows or extends itself in accordance with principles that model various logical, geometrical and causal necessities or regularities or dependencies in the environment.

Be all this as it may, what seems quite certain is that there must exist some sort of systematic teleo-functional organization of the human cognitive systems whereby the making of good practical and theoretical inferences corresponds to normal (but perhaps not average) functioning for beliefs and desires, and whereby it is biologically normal (not average) for desires to be fulfilled, at least under certain conditions. (Why else the capacity to have desires?) Accordingly, explanations of behaviors by reference to reasons for action are normalizing explanations.

How Normalizing Explanations Circumscribe Causes

Why it is that normalizing explanations explain, how it is that they fall under a general theory of explanation, is too large a question for this chapter. Our question here is only how such explanations connect with simpler kinds of causal explanation. One connecting link is that whatever has a teleo-function has a normal *way* of operating, a normal *way* of performing its function. For functional artifacts this may be, in part, the way the designer proposed that the function be performed, for biological devices, it is the way the function has been performed historically. An exhaustive analysis of the way, given its history, that any functional item operates when operating normally, arrives eventually at a description of normal *physical* structure for such a device and normal *physical* conditions for its operation, such that physical laws generate performance of this function given this structure and these conditions. By making implicit reference to such causal explanations, normalizing explanations may thus circumscribe quite specific physical explanations without detailing them.

Guided by Cummins,[30] we notice that the analysis of how a system normally functions may have several parts. First, the larger function or functions of the system may be analyzed into sub-functions that are performed either serially or simultaneously or in some more complicated pattern of interaction. This kind of analysis Cummins calls 'functional analysis'. Cummins suggests that a functional analysis may generally be represented by a flow-chart, but of course highly parallel processes, especially those that interact to some degree stochastically, must be represented otherwise. Secondly, the system may be analyzed into sub-systems, which may or may not correspond to discrete physical parts, each of which is responsible for a designated set of sub-functions. This kind of analysis Cummins calls 'compositional analysis'. Compositional analysis results in a description of the *normal* (not necessarily actual) constitution of the system by reference to parts described *teleo-functionally*, that is, normatively rather than dispositionally. (Here I depart from Cummins, who equates functions with dispositions.) Finally, the normal *physical* constitutions of the elements normally composing the system may be described, along with the surrounding physical conditions required for normal functioning, and it may be shown how these descriptions together account, in accordance with physical law, for cases of normal operation. That is, the system may ultimately be analyzed into a set of physical parts and physical dispositions rather than, merely, functionally categorized parts and normal functions.[31]

By reference to the possiblity of this kind of physical analysis, explanations of behaviors according to reasons for action may circumscribe physical causes. Compare explaining why a man shakes by saying that he suffers from Brown's syndrome, even though the etiology of Brown's syndrome may not be known. Or compare explaining why a man has brown hair by saying he has genes for brown hair rather than, say, having dyed his hair, though no one knows the constitution of the gene or how it produces brown hair.[32]

That this is not the complete answer to how reasons circumscribe causes becomes evident, however, when we remember that devices falling in the same function category can have widely varying constitutions. For example, we do sometimes explain, say, how John managed to get the can open by noting that he finally found a can-opener, but given the enormous variety among can-openers, the various different principles on which they may work, how could such an explanation possibly do anything towards circumscribing physical causes or types of physical processes lying behind the can's having come open? Similarly, if there really were various other creatures designed quite differently from humans and made of quite different stuffs but who still have beliefs and desires, then explanation of actions by reference to beliefs and desires without mention of the species of creature involved would seem not to circumscribe any particular *kind* of physical process at all (cf. Block, chapter 2).

But, looking more closely, whether it circumscribes a kind of process depends on how you *type* your kinds. Behind every normalizing explanation is a device or system with teleo-functions, and an item acquires a teleo-function only by having a very special sort of causal history. For example, if the cat's purr is explained as produced by a purr-box, an organ especially designed, in the smaller cats, to produce purrs, then we know that the purr-box itself has resulted, ultimately, from the operation of prior purr-boxes in ancestor cats which produced purrs, these purrs somehow having survival value, contributing an essential link, at least occasionally, to the historic cat-chain. Thus a salient cause of the purr is a series of prior purrs. Of course, when the functions referred to by normalizing explanations are described categorially though they are actually derived from *relational* functions, no such simple analysis applies. Still, to assign to any phenomenon a place in a functional system is to claim that it has emerged from a very special kind of causal-historical process, a kind that defines functionality. It is to distinguish its particular type of causal origin quite sharply from other etiological patterns.

Notes

1 'Banish discontent', in J. Butterfield (ed.), *Language, Mind and Logic* pp. 1–23; (New York, Cambridge, 1986), *Psychosemantics* (Cambridge, Mass., MIT Press, 1987).

2 'Toward a causal theory of representation', in P. French, T. Uehling Jr and H. Wettstein (eds) *Contemporary Perspectives in the Philosophy of Language*, pp. 81–102 (Minneapolis, Minnesota University Press, 1979).

3 'Misrepresentation', in R. Bogdan (ed.), *Belief: Form, Content, and Function* pp. 17–36 (New York, Oxford University Press, 1986).

4 'Biological functions and perceptual content', *Journal of Philosophy* 85 (1) (1988), 5–27.

5 Ibid., p. 20.

6 Cambridge, Mass., MIT Press, 1984 (hereafter *LTOBC*).

7 *Philosophy of Science*, 61 (2) (1989), 288–302.

8 An odd custom exists of identifying this sort of view with Larry Wright, who does not hold it. See my 'In defense of proper function'. Natural selection is not the only source of proper functions (see *LTOBC*, chs 1 and 2).

9 See *LTOBC*; and 'Truth rules, hoverflies, and the Kripke – Wittgenstein paradox', *Philosophical Review* 99 (1990), 323–53.

10 This last clarification is offered to aid Fodor ('On there not being an evolutionary theory of content' [hereafter *NETC*], unpublished, who uses my term 'Normal' (here I am not capitalizing it but the idea has not changed) in a multiply confused way, making a parody of my views on representation. In this connection, see also notes 14 and 19.

11 'Normal explanation' and 'normal condition for performance of a function', along with 'proper function', are defined with considerable detail in *LTOBC*. The reader may wish, in particular, to consult the discussion of normal explanations for performance of 'adapted and derived proper functions' in ch. 2, for these functions cover the functions of states of the nervous system which result in part from learning, such as states of human belief and desire.

12 *Knowledge and the Flow of Information* (Cambridge, Mass., MIT Press, 1981).

13 Strictly, this normal condition must derive from a 'most proximate normal explanation' of the consumer's proper functioning. See *LTOBC*, ch. 6, where a more precise account of what I am here calling 'representations' is given under the heading 'intentional icons'.

14 In this particular case, one task is, surely, contributing, in conformity with certain general principles or rules, to practical inference processes, hence to the fulfillment of current desires. So, if you like, all beliefs have the *same* proper function. Or, since the rules or principles that govern practical inference dictate that a belief's 'shape' determines what other inner representations it may properly be combined with to form what products, we could say that each belief has a *different* range of proper functions. Take your pick. Cf. Fodor, 'Information and representation', in P. Hanson (ed.), *Information, Language, and Cognition* (Vancouver, British Columbia University Press, 1989); and *NETC*.

15 These examples are of representations that are not 'inner' but out in the open. As in the case of inner representations, however, they are produced and consumed by mechanisms designed to cooperate with one another; each such representation stands intermediate between two parts of a single biological system.

16 Matthen, 'Biological functions and perceptual content', p. 20. Dretske in 'Misrepresentation', p. 28, and D. Papineau in *Reality and Representation* p. 67ff, (New York, Blackwell, 1987), have similar concerns.

17 Dretske, 'Misrepresentation', p. 28.

18 This is a broad metaphor. I am not advocating computationalism.

19 A word of caution. The normal conditions for a desire's fulfillment are not necessarily fulfillable conditions. In general, normal conditions for fulfillment of a function are not quite the same as conditions which, when you add them and stir, always effect proper function, because they may well be impossible conditions. For example, Fodor, in 'Information and representation' and *NETC*, has questioned me about the normal conditions under which his desire that it should rain tomorrow will perform its proper function of *getting* it to rain. Now, the biologically normal way for such a desire to be fulfilled is exactly the same as for any other desire: one has or acquires true beliefs about how to effect the fulfillment of the desire and acts on them. Biologically normal conditions for fulfillment of the desire for rain thus include the condition that one has true beliefs about how to make it rain. Clearly this is an example in which the biological norm fails to accord with the statistical norm: most desires about the weather are fulfilled, if at all, by biological accident. It may even be that the laws of nature, coupled with my situation, prohibit my having any true beliefs about how to make it rain; the needed general condition cannot be realized in the particular case. Similarly, normal conditions for proper function of beliefs in impossible things are, of course, impossible conditions: these beliefs are such that they cannot correspond, in accordance with the rules of mentalese, to conditions in the world.

20 *Psychosemantics* and *NETC*.

21 *Brainstorms* (Montgomery, VT, Bradford Books, 1978).

22 'Why paramecia don't have mental representations', in P. French, T. Uehling Jr and H. Wettstein (eds.), *Midwest Studies in Philosophy* 10 pp. 3–23. (Minneapolis, Minnesota University Press, 1986).

23 Accordingly, in *LTOBC* I did not call these primitive forms 'representations' but 'intentional signals' and, for items like bee dances, 'intentional icons', reserving the term 'representation' for those icons, the representational values of which must be identified if their consumers are to function properly (see the section on 'Acts of Identifying' below).

24 *Philosophical Review* 95 (1) (1986), 47–80.

25 Possibly human intentions are in both indicative and imperative mood, however, functioning simultaneously to represent settled facts about one's future and to direct one's action.

26 On the other hand, the bees cannot go two places at once.

27 In *LTOBC*, I defend the position that the law of non-contradiction plays a crucial role in allowing us to develop new methods of mapping the world with representations.

28 Philip Pettit, 'Broad-minded explanation and psychology', in P. Pettit and J. McDowell (eds), *Subject, Thought and Context*, pp. 17–58 (Oxford, Clarendon Press, 1986).

29 See *LTOBC*; 'Thoughts without laws'; 'Compare and Contrast Dretske, Fodor, and Millikan on teleosemantics', *Philosophical Topics* 18(2) (1990), 151–62.

30 R. Cummins, 'Functional Analysis', *Journal of Philosophy* 72 (1975), 741–65; *The Nature of Psychological Explanation* (Cambridge, Mass., MIT Press, 1983).

31 This does not imply that, given a certain species, there is a classically understood type – type identity relation between, say, normally constituted and normally functioning beliefs and desires about *x*, on the one hand, and certain physiological structures, on the other. Certainly, if the physical constitution of human beliefs are typed categorially there is no reason at all to suppose that any such identity holds.

If there are bridge laws for humans that map the semantics of thoughts onto physiological structures, surely what these laws map is certain semantic *relations* among beliefs and desires onto physical *relations* among these, hence *principles* of logical interaction onto *principles* of causal interaction, not categorial meanings onto categorial physiological 'shapes'.

32   Compare Ned Block in chapter 2 of this volume.

15

Concepts and Norms in a Natural World

Christopher Peacocke

The Challenge

Is it consistent for a theory to mention concepts in describing mental phenomena while also adhering to a naturalistic worldview? That is the question I will be addressing in this chapter.

Why should anyone think that there is prima facie a problem in reconciling the use of concepts in the description of mental phenomena with a naturalistic worldview? One reason lies in the ontology of concepts itself. The reference of a concept need not be naturalistically problematic, nor need some mental representation with that concept in its content. But what, naturalistically, are these *ways* in which the referent is thought about? And if there is a problem about concepts as entities from a naturalistic point of view, there is all the more of a problem about the relation of grasping a concept, relied upon by Fregean theorists.

In chapters 1 to 4 of *A Study of Concepts* (1992), I attempted to provide the materials for answering these sorts of naturalistic concerns about a theory of concepts. In chapter 4 I attempted to show how the description of a belief by mentioning its conceptual content is a way of characterizing a complex, empirical, relational property of that state. In chapter 2, I also tried to explain ways in which a thinker's satisfaction of a possession condition – his 'grasping the sense', as Frege would say – can be explanatory. The properties of a mental state in virtue of which it has a particular conceptual content involve a complex of relations to other mental states and, arguably, to the subject's environment. It is certainly a live issue how, if at all, these highly relational properties can themselves be explanatory, but what I want to address in this chapter is another source of concern.

This second source of concern about reconciling naturalism with the mention of concepts in describing mental phenomena lies in the essentially normative character of concepts. These normative characteristics fall into two sorts. Those of the first sort are not specific to concepts but rather are present for any notion of content. Any notion of content will somehow or other, perhaps with various relativizations and qualifications, bring with it a distinction between correctness and incorrectness. This property of correctness depends upon the way the world is. It is a normative property: we aim at such correctness in forming beliefs. This property is one that applies as much to propositions built to Russell's specifications, with objects and properties as constituents, as to those built to Frege's. The question of how normative properties of this first sort are naturalistically possible obviously has to be addressed. But the problems in answering it are ones that arise even if the notion of a concept is rejected.[1]

The second sort of normative property covers those specific to concepts. These include what I call the 'normative liaisons' of a specific concept or type of concepts. Certain circumstances in which a thinker may find himself can give him good reasons for taking particular attitudes to thoughts built up from given constituent concepts. In some cases the status of the reasons as good reasons is dependent upon the identity of one of the constituents of the complete content in question. When it is, we can count the triple of circumstance, attitude and thought as among the normative liaisons of the constituent in question. Descartes could plausibly halt the progress of doubt with the thought 'I think'; he could hardly have done so with 'Descartes thinks.' Again, seeing a man to be bald can give a thinker good reason to judge the perceptual-demonstrative thought 'That man is bald'; it gives no such reason to judge 'The spy is bald.'

For many theorists, the notion of rationality plays a crucial role in explaining the nature of content-involving psychological explanation. For these theorists, normative liaisons must be taken as equally essential to content-involving psychological explanation. As all the examples above illustrate, rationality requirements on what attitudes should be taken in given circumstances are requirements that operate at the level of concepts (as I am using the term), rather than at the level of reference. It seems that one cannot formulate such requirements wihout use of a notion of a concept, with its normative dimension.

These two reasons – one relating to the ontology of concepts, the other to norms – do not exhaust the reasons why concepts might be thought to be naturalistically problematic. Another is the nature of the distinction between those liaisons that are supposed to be constitutive of a concept and those that depend upon collateral information. Yet another is the notion, apparently essential to content-involving, personal-level psychological explanation, of acting for a reason. But the issue of normative characteristics seems to be fundamental. If we had a naturalistic resolution of that issue, these others would fall into place.

What, then, is naturalism? The doctrine I mean has two parts, one about explanation and one about truth. The naturalistic claim about explanation is that any explanation of an event or temporal state of affairs is a causal explanation. Here the underlying intuition is that a treatment of an area is naturalistic only if it counts explanations within that area as fundamentally of the same kind as those that apply to the natural world, namely as causal explanations. This is compatible with acknowledging that there are many distinctions to be drawn within the class of causal explanations.[2] A conception that violates this first component of naturalism is found in Descartes. He appears to have held that when a person makes a judgment, this is sometimes a free act of the will that cannot be explained causally at all.[3]

The naturalistic doctrine about truth is that any truth is supervenient on purely descriptive truths. We can distinguish a moderate from a radical form of the doctrine. The moderate form allows that the supervenience of any truth upon descriptive truths may in some cases hold only when we take into account other possible worlds as well as the actual world. For purposes of the moderate version, these other worlds may be what David Lewis calls *ersatz* worlds: they do not have to be concrete, non-actual objects. This moderate naturalism about truth opposes, for instance, the claim that there are evaluative truths not supervenient on descriptive truths about this and other worlds.

The radical form of the naturalistic doctrine about truth holds that all truths supervene on descriptive truths about the actual world. Hume, on the reading that was until recently standard, was a radical naturalist about truths involving the relation of causation (as it is in this world). Radical naturalism is manifestly a challenging and controversial doctrine. There is, for instance, a question of whether it is consistent with any plausible account of truths involving necessity. The radical naturalist may either reject discourse about necessity as unintelligible or attempt some positive account of it consistent with his doctrine. If he rejects it as unintelligible, he should not, of course, formulate his position with use of the notion of supervenience, which is normally elucidated using modal terms. This radical naturalist would do better to characterize his position in terms of the reducibility of all truths to descriptive truths about the actual world, and to try to state the requirements on reduction in non-modal terms. It is also an issue whether there can be a coherent rationale for being a radical naturalist about some kinds of truths but not about others.

In this general characterization of naturalism, neither the component about explanation nor the component about truth, whether moderate or radical, seems dispensable in favor of the other. If we omit the part about explanation and leave only the part about truth, we are left with a position that could more appropriately be called descriptivism, actualist descriptivism in the case of the radical position. Descriptivism alone would not rule our Descartes's views on the explanation of human thought, or indeed anything, however bizarre, provided it was regarded as captured by descriptive truths. On the other hand, if we omit the naturalism about truth and leave only that about explanation, we leave entirely open the nature of causation (and many other relations). Such a position would not exclude radically non-naturalistic views of causation itself, or of any other relation.

Even if the doctrine about truth is endorsed only in its moderate form, this specification of naturalism leaves the challenge of reconciling naturalism with the mention of concepts firmly in place. The naturalistic claim about truth implies that there can be no concepts with normative dimensions unless the norms are supervenient on descriptive truths. The naturalist has at a minimum to show how this is possible.

Though the homeland of concepts is folk psychology, it is not only folk psychology that makes use of the notion. In one way or another it features frequently and essentially in theories in cognitive psychology. Any connectionist model given a 'conceptual' interpretation in Paul Smolensky's (1986) terminology will be one in which concepts or hypotheses built up using concepts are assigned to nodes or assemblies. If the assignments were merely at the level of reference, these models could not explain the phenomena they set out to explain, for instance, the perception of an array not just as a shape but as falling under a concept, as an instance of a certain word type. For similar reasons, the labeling of nodes in a network of the sort employed in 'spreading activation' models of memory (Anderson, 1983) has to be taken as a labeling with concepts. The point also holds for cognitive-psychological models of the processes underlying understanding a perceived utterance.

It has become common recently to compare the relation between folk psychology and cognitive psychology to that between folk physics and a serious scientific physics. Suppose that we accept this analogy. Then to hold that the notion of a concept is unsound or irremediably confused because it is coeval with a questionable folk psychology is analogous to holding that we can expect a scientific physics to contain no refined versions of folk ideas of force, momentum or friction. No doubt there is indeed much in folk psychology that is confused, erroneous or inconsistent. But the challenge of reconciling the notion of a concept with a naturalistic worldview will disappear only if a scientific psychology makes no use at all of the idea of the way in which an object or property is represented in thought. It seems to me that there is little prospect of the challenge evaporating from such a cause.

A Teleological Solution?

Among the many things done by a state or a device, we can pick out some as its *natural function(s)*. These are the things it does that, when done by similar states or devices in ancestors containing them, contribute to the survival and proliferation of the ancestors. Thus the heart does many things, but its natural function is, by this test, to pump the blood (Wright, 1976). More generally, we can classify states and what they do into types. Even if a state occurs for the first time ever in the history of a species, perhaps it has a certain function if it is a member of a more general type that includes states having a suitably corresponding natural function by this criterion. The idea is that for an attitude to have a certain content is for it to have a certain natural function in this sense. This idea has been in the air for some time and has been developed in detail by Ruth Millikan (1984, 1986) and David Papineau (1987, ch. 4). Millikan writes, 'The entities that folk psychology postulates are indeed defined by their proper function [natural functions, in my terminology]' (1986, p. 57). I will call such theories of content 'teleological theories'. Can teleological theories reconcile mentioning concepts with naturalism?

In two respects, teleological theories are initially promising for accomplishing this task. They clearly use notions that are as naturalistic as the concept of explanation they employ. They also introduce, and in a naturalistic fashion, a simple normative notion: that of something performing properly or not, according to whether it is performing its natural function or not. So it is important to see whether the initial promise is fulfilled.

Millikan develops the idea that 'apparently beliefs are named or described (typed) in accordance with certain of their Normal conditions for functioning properly' (1986, p. 69). A Normal condition for a device or state functioning properly is, in outline, a condition that is part of full explanations of the sort that historically accounted for the existence of such a device or state in organisms. More specifically, Millikan suggests, 'Presumably it is a proper function of the belief-manufacturing mechanisms in John to produce beliefs-that-p only if and when p' (1986, p. 69).[4] Similarly, Papineau's formulation, later qualified in his text, is that 'the truth condition of the belief is the "normal" circumstance in which, given the learning process, it is biologically supposed to be present' (1987, p. 67). The difficulty I want to raise for this idea I will call the 'problem of reduced content'.

What explains the proliferation and survival of the belief-producing mechanisms and the organisms containing them when p is believed, p is true, and all is working properly is the truth of all the (logical) consequences of p that have a causal impact on the organism.[5] Now the truth of all such consequences in some cases falls short of the truth of p. Take universal quantification, for instance, the belief that all Londoners are under seven feet tall. It is only the truth of instances of this quantification for objects that come into some sort of causal contact with the thinker that contribute to the explanation of the persistence of the belief-producing mechanisms and organisms containing them. In a nutshell, the problem of reduced content is this: how is the teleological theorist to block an incorrect assignment of content to beliefs, namely one that requires for its truth merely the truth of all the logical consequences of p that have a causal impact on the thinker, rather than the stronger condition of the truth of p itself?

How might the teleological theorist respond? One reply is this: she may say, 'The truth of all the consequences of p that have a causal impact on the thinker is itself explained by the truth of p. So there is no real gap here. The explanation of the persistence of the belief-producing mechanisms when all is working properly is that the belief that p is produced only when p is the case.' But it is not true for every type of content that the truth of all its consequences that have a causal impact on the thinker is explained by the truth of p. Maybe that is so for certain observational contents, but it is not so for all universal quantifications. This seems particularly clear for accidental, contingent generalizations. If it is true that all Londoners are under seven feet tall, that fact does not *explain* the singular instance about some particular Londoner (whether the thinker has causal contact with the particular Londoner or not).

By way of another reply, the teleological theorist may say, 'The commitments incurred in believing a content, including commitments about objects that have no causal impact on the thinker, are reflected in his inferential dispositions involving the content. These inferential dispositions are produced by his belief-manufacturing mechanisms and are subject to testing by natural selection, like everything else.' All this is true, but the truth (if they are true) of the commitments of a content that have no causal impact on the thinker remain unabsorbed into its content on the teleological theory as currently formulated. They do not contribute in the appropriate way to the explanation of the survival of the mechanisms and of members of the species. We should perhaps recall that in the case of absolutely unrestricted universal generalizations over space and time, these commitments will include those about objects outside the thinker's light cone, objects that could not have any causal impact on him. In discussing the correct characterization of the biological purposes of a particular ability, theorists like Millikan have very properly insisted that we should be careful not to include anything as a biological purpose that has not contributed in the required way to the explanation of the proliferation of organisms that exercise the ability: 'A complexity that can simply be dropped from the explanans without affecting the tightness of the relation of explanans to explanandum is not a *functioning* part of the explanation' (Millikan, 1990, p. 334). The objector who presses the problem of reduced content will emphasize that his or her objection rests precisely on this requirement.

The teleological theorist might try simply to incorporate such commitments as manifested in inferential dispositions, into the truth conditions. The theory would not then be a purely teleological one, since the notion of a commitment is not teleological. But, more important, this modification also seems to make the teleological apparatus redundant. For the appeal to commitments can be used to capture the right truth conditions even in cases where the consequences of p do have a causal impact on the thinker (for further discussion, see Peacocke 1986, ch. 3).

I have made the point with universal quantification, but other examples are available too. We could develop similar arguments for undecidable contents about the past. What explains the persistence of the belief-producing mechanisms concerned with past-tense contents is the truth of those consequences of believed past-tense contents that have a causal impact on the thinker. What is undetectably the case can have no such effects.

It is no accident that in developing the problem of reduced content, I consider contents for which a realistic, verification-transcendent account of meaning is most plausible. In these cases we always have the clearest divergence between the truth of a content and the truth of its consequences that have a causal impact on an individual. There is a certain irony here. Some teleological theorists like Millikan have aimed to use their ideas in support for forms for realism.[6] The problem of reduced content suggests that teleological theories of content will support only contents of a more constructivist stripe.[7]

To reject teleological theories because of the problem of reduced content is compatible with insisting that we build theories of why it is adaptive for organisms to have states with representational contents concerning the world. All that we are rejecting is teleology as a *constitutive* account of what it is to enjoy content-involving states. There is much that can be explained in terms of natural selection without it being the case that what is to be explained can itself be elucidated only in teleological terms. Natural selection can plausibly explain why we have eyes sensitive to just a certain range of wavelengths. What it is for eyes to be sensitive to that range should not itself be elucidated in teleological terms.[8]

Notes

1 Though, of course, the normative character of concepts is likely to be the ultimate source of these problems, according to a theorist who believes in senses.

2 Compare the many sub-varieties of causal explanation compatible with David Lewis's view (1986) that to give a causal explanation of an event is to give some information about its causal history.

3 For emphasis on the non-naturalistic character of this part of Descartes's thought, see Stroud (1977).

4 At a similar point in my exposition in Peacocke, (1990, p. 61), quotation marks came to be placed around a characterization of Millikan's position, even though the contained material is not from any of her texts. I apologize and hope that the characterization in the text here is more accurate.

5 Strictly, I should also take into account objects on which the thinker has a causal impact but that need not causally affect him. This addition is needed throughout the arguments below. I do not include it, because it complicates them but does not alter their conclusions.

6 See the later chapters of Millikan (1984). The problem of reduced content developed here for mental states can equally be developed for the theory of linguistic meaning that Millikan develops in that book.

7 In their formulations, neither Millikan nor Papineau is explicitly concerned with the level of sense. Indeed, Millikan is explicitly concerned with the level of reference (1986, p. 66). But the problem of reduced content still arises if we consider only the level of reference. In brief, the same arguments will show that 'all' (for instance) will have a narrower semantic value on the teleological account than it intuitively possesses or has on a realist's account; it will not involve objects (or a condition on first-level functions or properties that concerns objects) outside those having a causal impact on the thinker.

8 Though I have this disagreement with Millikan, I should emphasize a major point of agreement with her. In recent developments of her position (1990), Millikan appeals to facts about historical explanation to exclude Kripkean 'quus'-like descriptions of purpose and content. In the positive account I give later in *A Study*

of Concepts (1992), causal explanation also plays a crucial role in excluding such unwanted contents, but it does so in the context of a non-teleological theory.

References

Anderson, J. (1983) *The Architecture of Cognition*. Cambridge, Mass., Harvard University Press.

Lewis, D. (1986) Causal explanation. In his *Philosophical Papers*, vol. 2. New York, Oxford University Press.

Millikan, R.G. (1984) *Language, Thought, and Other Biological Categories*. Cambridge, Mass., MIT Press.

Millikan, R.G. (1986) Thoughts without laws: cognitive science with content. *Philosophical Review* 95, 47–80.

Millikan, R.G. (1990) Truth rules, hoverflies, and the Kripke – Wittgenstein Paradox. *Philosophical Review* 99, 323–53.

Papineau, D. (1987) *Reality and Representation*. Oxford, Blackwell.

Peacocke, C. (1986) *Thoughts: an Essay on Content*. Oxford, Blackwell.

Peacocke, C. (1990) Content and norms in a natural world. In E. Villanueva (ed.), *Information, Semantics, and Epistemology*. Oxford, Blackwell.

Peacocke, C. (1992) *A Study of Concepts*. Cambridge, Mass., MIT Press.

Smolensky, P. (1986) Neural and conceptual interpretation of PDP models. In J. McClelland, D. Rumelhart and the PDP Research Group (eds), *Parallel Distrubuted Processing*, vol. 2. Cambridge, Mass., MIT Press.

Stroud, B. (1977) *Hume*. London, Routledge.

Wright, L. (1976) *Teleological Explanation*. Berkeley, California, University of California Press.

16

Reply: A Bet With Peacocke

Ruth Garrett Millikan

Professor Peacocke's doubts (chapter 15) about the view of mental content offered in my 'Biosemantics' (see chapter 14) grow, I believe, from misunderstandings. So I shall try to make the relevant features of my position clearer. Especially, it may help to talk more about the nature of 'normal explanations' for cases of novel biological functions, and it may help to say more about the role that 'mapping' or 'picturing' plays in representing.

It takes many people by surprise that items uniquely associated with individual organisms, individual items quite new under the sun, can have biological functions in a sense defined by evolutionary history. As laymen, we tend to think of that which evolution 'designed' in us as being both inborn, and identical in all of us having the same responsible genes. We tend to contrast this with how the environment shapes us and, especially, with what we learn. But that view is not merely an oversimplification, it is faulty at the core. The environment is involved in the determination of every phenotypic trait right from the start, and the environment is highly variable from the start. The environment takes the form, first, of surrounding genes, then of egg or womb, and finally there is the world outside. Genes are selected only if they perform usefully, produce useful phenotypic properties, in a wide variety of environments, first genetic environments, and later external environments.

Sometimes genes are selected because they are capable of performing always the same function despite great variety in their environments. Sometimes, serendipitously, they perform a variety of different useful functions each in a different sort of environment. And sometimes, more systematically, they perform functions that vary in response to some kind of variation in the environment, such that they either utilize or compensate for that variation. In the latter case, and when the environment utilized is outer, we have adaptation of the individual animal to its individual environment. Each of various varieties of learning, such as imitation, conditioning, coming to know by perception, by inference, or by verbal communication, is an example. The expression of open instincts is a second, simpler example. The formation of calluses at the point of wear is a third, still simpler example.

One of a pair of identical twins, who plays the violin, has calluses on the left-hand finger-tips, while the other, who plays the clarinet, has a callus on the side of the right thumb. These different callous patterns have resulted from exactly the same genetic materials interacting in accordance with exactly the same biological 'plan' within different environments. The twins' calluses are not only in different places, they have different functions. Those on the finger-tips are there to prevent damage to the finger-tips, the one on the thumb is there to prevent damage to the thumb. Surely there is nothing mysterious about this, about the fact that though deriving their functions from the same selective history, these calluses have *different* biological functions. Because these different calluses have different functions, each must have a different normal explanation for proper performance of its function. The normal explanation for proper performance of the callus on the index finger begins with something persistently rubbing on the index finger but, because the callus is there, doing no tissue damage. The normal explanation for proper performance of the callus on the thumb begins with something persistently rubbing on the thumb.

But there is also a way of viewing the matter such that these calluses all have the same function, and the same normal explanation for proper performance. This way is to view the functions of the calluses as relational. Each of the calluses has the same function as each of the others, namely, preventing tissue damage to the site *just under it*. And the normal explanation for performance of this function is always the same. It begins with something's persisting in rubbing *where the callus is*, and ends with prevention of damage to the site just under where the callus is. This principle of substituting invariant relational descriptions for variant or novel categorial descriptions of functional items is completely generalizable. Take any variant part, state, aspect or activity of an individual organism that has resulted in accordance with a genetic biological 'plan' for producing such variants according to variation in the environment. Every such variant structure can be described relationally. It can be described as an invariant structure, one common to all individuals having (I am putting this too crudely) the same relevant genes. This description defines the structure as embedded in or relative to the individual animal's environment, rather than describing it in isolation or categorially. The structure is described as an invariant structure, exactly the same one as was present also in ancestors of the organism. This univocal relational structure has been systematically selected for over the generations on account of a relational function that it serves. And the way that this relational function is normally effected, the normal explanation for its performance, also has a univocal relational formulation. All novel responses to novel aspects of an individual organism's environment that are truly adaptive responses, that is, that are fitting in accordance with biological plan rather than by an accident of the moment, are responses that could also be described relationally. They could be described as invariant rather than as novel responses. The functions that these novel responses to a novel environment perform when they perform properly are also describable as invariant across the generations. And the *manners* in which these functions are performed, the normal explanations for their performances, are likewise invariant when described in relational terms.

Now consider the mapping rules that, according to 'Biosemantics', define the content of a mental representation. That is, consider the semantic rules that apply to it. Reference to these rules emerges when one gives an *invariant, relational* normal explanation for proper performance of the representation and of the consumers of the representation. This relational explanation may have quite a complex derivation. For example, if the representation embodies a particular propositional attitude of a particular human, the derivation will reach back at least to the evolutionary history of those human cognitive mechanisms that are responsible for concept formation, that is, roughly, for human capacities to learn how to learn. Involved will be normal explanations for how these prior learning mechanisms work, which will include as a part (doubly) relational explanations of how their products (the individual concepts formed) work, and ultimately of how particular propositional representations formed using these concepts work, when they work normally.

The truth condition for a mental representation is never, then, merely some novel condition that would be required in the particular case for proper performance. Indeed, the truth condition has nothing whatever to do with the particular case. The truth condition may not be met in the particular case; it may not even be logically possible that it be met in the particular case (compare chapter 14, n. 19). The truth condition is derived, rather, from an invariance in relational function and in the relational explanation for performance of that function applicable over a very long period of evolutionary history.

Any of a great number of combinations of ordinary or freakish circumstances might, in the particular case, suffice to combine with a mental representation to produce some kind of felicitous result. Similarly, worker bees reacting normally to a certain bee dance might succeed in finding nectar because there was nectar, not at the spot indicated, but somewhere (anywhere) on the path between the hive and that spot. Or they might succeed because there was nectar just so far west of the specified spot and a strong east wind was blowing, forcing them off course just enough to find it. Or they might succeed because there was nectar just so far east of the specified spot and a strong west wind was blowing, or because a bee trap was at the specified spot and the owner of the trap was waiting to transport the bees to a good nectar site, or for any of an uncountable number of other reasons. But, of course, none of these conditions, whether merely possible or actual, has any relevance to what counts as the semantic content of the bee dance. Nor would any such conditions be relevant just because there had in fact been ancestors of the bees who once got to nectar in similar accidental sorts of ways. The bee dance is a representation because there is, we take it, a univocal relational explanation that is invariant over the bulk of cases in which ancestors of our bees found nectar as a result of reacting as they do to bee dances. This explanation begins always in the same way, by pointing to the fact that the relational condition holds that there is nectar at a location projected in accordance with a certain mapping rule from the configuration of the dance, that is, that there is nectar that bears a certain set relation to the dance. This is a set or invariant normal condition for proper performance of all bee dances, or of all worker bee reactions to bee dances, for a given species of honey bee. Bee dances that lead worker bees to find nectar despite the fact that no nectar bears this set relation to the configuration of the dance do not perform properly *in accordance with a normal explanation*, but produce their proper effects for merely accidental reasons unrelated to the causes of the evolution of the dances.

Before bringing these observations directly to bear on Peacocke's remarks, there is a second point on the determination of the semantic rules for mental representations that we need also to have in mind. This is a point suppressed in 'Biosemantics', where the main task was to distinguish the biosemantic theory from causal/informational accounts, but it lay on the surface in Millikan (1984, ch. 6). (It is also implicit in Peacocke's own statement of the biosemantic theory in chapter 15 above.) It concerns normal explanations for production rather than for use or 'consumption' of mental representations.

An inner representation has semantic content only by reference to a normal process (or processes) of consumption and normal results or uses, more specifically, by reference to a normal *explanation* or *mechanism* for successful use. Equally, it has content only as having been produced by a mechanism that was designed to produce it. That is, the producer was designed to produce representations that map onto the world in accordance with the projection rules to which the normal consumer or normal process of consumption is adapted. The consuming and producing mechanisms must be biologically cooperating mechanisms. Roughly speaking, evolution has designed each such that proper performance of the other is a normal condition for performance of its own functions. The job of the producing mechanism or process is to produce representations that map onto environmental circumstances in accordance with a certain fixed set of semantic rules. That the representations do indeed map onto circumstances in accordance with these rules is a normal condition for the consuming mechanism's successful use(s) of them.

Now the proper functions of an item are defined as results or activities that a certain (typically very large) set of its ancestors once actually *effected*. So it could not possibly be a proper function of the representation producers to produce maps that map onto conditions by certain rules unless they have had an effective way of doing this. They must have had some way of systmatically producing the required relation between representation and represented. There must be a systematic way in which the makers produce these maps, making them vary as the mapped conditions vary. This does not mean that the producers are always, even usually, able to effect such mappings. But, at a minimum, there must have existed certain kinds of conditions under which they effected such mappings in the past, and thus enabled the representation consumers to perform in a manner that lead to the proliferation of the responsible genes. Nothing is represented by an inner representation without there being a systematic historically realized mechanism or system for getting representations of that type to map onto their representeds by the relevant rule, a system that has worked under at least some conditions. Further, these mechanisms must have produced past *effective* representations, ones that effectively guided the representation consumers in such a way as to help effect natural selection of the production – consumption system.

One final clarification needs to be made, perhaps, before looking at Peacocke's claims about 'reduced content'. The fact that a representation maps as it should onto environmental circumstances is, in general, only one of many normal conditions required for proper performance of its various functions. For the bee dance to make its proper contribution to the proliferation of the bees, the weather conditions must be moderate, the air must be pure enough, the sun must not be eclipsed, there must be no bee traps or bee eaters directly between the hive and the indicated nectar spot, a large variety of body parts of the worker bees must be normally constituted, and so forth. But the fact that many bee dances may not be able to perform their proper functions due to absence of various of these *other* conditions is not relevant to the question concerning the semantic content of the dances. This is because there is no produced and exploited *mapping* relation between the dances and these conditions. A representation represents only as a part of a system of representation. Where there is no systematic effective and designed way of varying the representation with the conditions to be represented, and no way of exploiting this systematic variance, there is no representing.

Thus there can be no question of interest concerning merely 'what explains the proliferation and survival of the belief-producing mechanisms and the organisms containing them when [some particular] p is believed, p is true, and all is working properly' (Peacocke, chapter 15, p. 000). First, we are not in any way interested in categorial descriptions of how particular beliefs function. We are interested only in relational descriptions and relational explanations of function. And we are interested in these only as they cover, univocally, very numerous exemplars of concepts and beliefs manufactured by ancestors of the general concept and belief-producing systems, ancestors numerous enough and ancient enough for natural selection to have effectively operated on them. Secondly, we are interested only in those conditions in the environment that the belief-producing systems have a way or ways, under certain ideal conditions, of *mapping* in a principled and effective way. The fact of actual correspondence of conditions by these mapping rules must figure in a uniform explanation of how very numerous past cases involving consumer uses of such maps happened to aid selection of the organisms harboring them. The form of the normal explanation sought, hence the description of the mapping rules sought, must be general enough to cover the bulk of effective past cases. It cannot possibly be derived by looking just for explanations that tightly cover this or that individual instance of usefulness. For every natural occurrence there exist innumerable correct explanations. The explanation we are seeking is one that covers the relevant past cases univocally, that shows how producer and consumer have historically cooperated with one another under ideal conditions, the one systematically producing certain mappings, the other systematically using them.

'In a nutshell', Peacocke tells us, 'the problem of reduced content is this: how is the teleological theorist to block an incorrect assignment of content to beliefs, namely one that requires for its truth merely the truth of all the logical consequences of p that have a causal impact on the thinker, rather than the stronger condition of the truth of p itself?' (chapter 15, p. 000). The assignment is blocked by the fact that it could not possibly accord with the requirements laid down, namely, that the mapping rules be a single set covering the majority of effective past representations produced by ancestor systems, a set mapping representations onto representeds such that the one varies systematically with the other, such that the representation producers have a systematic way of effecting this mapping, and such that the consuming mechanisms have a systematic way of using the maps that needs conformity to this mapping rule. How could the representation producers possibly manage in a principled way to vary the representations they produced depending upon which consequences were in fact destined at some future date to have an impact on the thinker? And how, if they could do this, would this sort of mapping be of any use to the consumer? We are talking here about a compositional semantics (broadly conceived, see chapter 14) for a historically effective representational system, not an accidental coincidence of two facts.

More specifically, consider first Peacocke's worry over beliefs about the past, then later his worries about universal beliefs. Concerning any kind of human beliefs we have the problem that we don't yet know much about the general principles governing normal conceptual development. We don't know, for instance, which kinds of cognitive skills have been selected to vary in individuals following variations in their individual environments, and which skills are, instead, fixed skills. We don't know, for example, whether the ability to have beliefs about the past is learned in accordance with some kind of very general principles governing the acquisition of concepts generally, or whether it merely matures in a roughly invariant way given a suitable internal and external environment. But let us suppose that for beliefs about the past to have semantic contents, there must have been prior beliefs, specifically about the past, that functioned so as to help preserve specialized 'belief-about-the-past' producing and comsuming mechanisms.[1]

Beliefs about the past can be very useful. The most obvious mechanism for this is that they combine with other beliefs to produce beliefs about the present or future, these latter beliefs having immediate utility. A normal explanation for this effectiveness makes reference, probably, to an isomorphism between the patterns by which beliefs about the present and future emerge from beliefs about the past, and patterns by which the corresponding present and future states of affairs emerge from past states of affairs. Peacocke apparently agrees that something like this can happen. I suggest that it not only can but does happen routinely. Most of our beliefs about the past are not about ancient history, after all, but about where we put the glue away yesterday, whether we remembered to pay the telephone bill, and whether the TV said it snowed yesterday on the ski slopes we wish to visit this weekend. Of course, when these beliefs find a normal use (one depending on their truth) it is usually because the conditions they map end up having some mediated effect upon the person who holds them.[2] Similarly, for a bee dance to find a normal use (one dependent upon its truth) it is required that the worker bees can get to the nectar mapped, that the bees are not somehow screened off from the nectar. We can conclude that surely many beliefs about the past, like some bee dances, never perform all of their proper functions – for beliefs, those functions beyond, say, participating in inferences – due to the fact that the conditions they map are screened off from having any impact on the believer. Similarly, to rehearse the Millikan litany, many sperm tails don't perform their proper functions, don't succeed in propelling their cargoes through the walls of ova, because most sperm don't land anywhere near ova, or are by some other means screened off from ova. All this is true. But none of it has any relevance to questions about the function of sperm tails or about the content of either bee dances or beliefs about the past. It is only the *past* successes of *some* bee dances and of *some* beliefs about the past that are relevant here – certain successes that actually had an effect on the constitution of the relevant gene pools. Surely most of the beliefs about the past that we acquire from history books, for example, are not destined to help preserve the species' general beliefs-about-the-past forming capacities, though they may, of course, help preserve the species' memorizing capacities, *via* unrelated (social) mechanisms.

Turn now to universal beliefs. As before, make the simplifying assumption that if universal beliefs have universal contents, there must be specialized genetically determined mechanisms that have historically made and used beliefs that mapped onto (don't hold me to this formulation) 'universal states of affairs'.[3] Certainly there are many true universal beliefs for which not all portions of the corresponding universal states of affairs do or even could have an impact upon the believer. For example, as Peacocke points out, if there are stars outside my light cone, their contribution to the truth of any universal propositions that I believe about stars can have no impact upon me. This is not to the point, however, so long as mapping rules for universal beliefs could be established through historic cases in which all portions of the relevant domain *did* make a difference and *did* help to explain how the belief's truth is needed for normal use. And, indeed, such cases are common. The overwhelming majority of our everyday universal beliefs concern very small domains, the exhaustion or lack of exhaustion of which is immediately relevant to our practical concerns. Thus the whole domain matters when I believe that all the cookies I made have been eaten, that all the students in Philosophy 102 showed up for their final examination, that none of the members of our philosophy department lives on campus, that all of the family bicycles are in use. Surely if we do have special mechanisms designed to make and use universal beliefs, these are the sorts of cases that historically put them in business.

Suppose that I make a million pound bet with Peacocke that I will get at least one legitimate reply when I place an add on the front page of the London *Times* offering his million to the first Londoner over seven feet tall to make himself known to us. If I lose this bet, my loss and Peacocke's gain will very likely be explainable by reference to the truth of his belief that all Londoners are under seven feet tall and the falsity of my belief to the contrary. Of course, it's possible that he will win not in this way, but only because all the Londoners seven feet or over neither read nor talk to anyone who reads – or because they are all locked in jail, or already have too many millions to care, or all get hit by trucks on the way to the post box. But these would not be biologically normal ways for his belief that all Londoners are under seven feet tall to help him to prosper.

Notes

1   In Millikan (1984, ch. 18) I suggested a different way that the mapping rules for beliefs about the past may be determined: through the mechanisms of public language taken with the law of contradiction.
2   It isn't in fact necessary in order that a belief about the past should find itself a normal use (one that requires its being true) that the condition it maps ends up having some eventual effect upon the person who holds it. For example, the belief might feed into an inductive inference yielding true belief in a natural law, and this latter belief might find a use, without the first belief having any independent impact on the thinker.
3   How universal representations map onto the world is discussed in Millikan (1984, ch. 14).

Reference

Millikan, R.G. (1984) *Language, Thought and Other Biological Categories*. Cambridge, Mass., MIT Press.

PART III

Tacit Knowledge, the Unconscious and Psychological Explanation

17

Introduction: Tacit Knowledge

Graham Macdonald

the rules of language are different from the rules of customary behaviour, in that they are in general not consciously or explicitly known. For this reason it is often said that the rules of a language are *tacitly* known to its speakers.

(Higginbotham, 'Philosophical issues in the study of language')

Background: Perception and Language

We can explain an enormous amount of what we do by citing rules or conventions that we follow. We stop at the red light because of a traffic rule, eat with a knife and fork because of local rules of etiquette, and sign our names on cheques because of banking rules. Most of the time we may well act as we do without having in mind the rule we nevertheless follow: having had the rule drummed into us, habit can take over, and we act unthinkingly. I cannot tell you how many red lights, if any, I stopped at on my way to work, but if I did stop at one it will be, partly at least, because of the rule ingrained in me. At some stage or other, knowledge of the rule will have been a causal factor in the production of the behaviour.

Because rule-following behaviour can become habitual it is tempting to place it in the category of merely regular behaviour, something done as a matter of course but for which there appears to be no guidance by a rule. There is, however, a crucial difference between rule-governed and merely regular behaviour, and that is that one can be criticized for failing to follow the rule, whereas with mere regularity our failure to conform is not in itself a matter for criticism. Higginbotham (1990) cites the example of stopping to admire the red sunset. This may be even more reliable as a regularity than stopping at red lights; we may be so enamoured of red sunsets that we can never just drive on by. Yet if we were to ignore the sunset, that itself would not be a cause for complaint. Somebody may berate us for our lack of aesthetic sensitivity, but that would not be a criticism directed at our failure to follow a rule. It is our aesthetic taste, not our non-conformity, which is being taken to task. An action performed in obedience to a rule is thereby open to criticism if it does not conform to the rule in the required way.

In the cases where many of the actions performed in accordance with a rule may be unthinkingly so done, the rule does not seem to lie very far beneath the surface of the mind. If asked why I stop at red lights, I can cite the relevant rule; similarly for rules of etiquette and banking. And an explanation can be given of why, on a particular occasion of rule-following, the rule was not consciously entertained by me. The explanation will be along the lines of the kind of instruction I have had, or the numerous repetitions of actions done consciously with the rule in mind, leading to the formation of a habit which short-circuits the conscious route to the action performed. Here the citation of a rule is not mysterious. We have evidence for the existence of the rule from what agents can say about why they performed a certain action. Conscious cognitive access to the rule is fairly straightforward.

This is not the case for a variety of other rules we are said to follow. Cognitive scientists are prone to model some mental capabilities in a manner which attributes to us unconscious rule-following, or which attributes to us the ability to arrive at certain judgements on the basis of making unconscious inferences. This is well illustrated by two phenomena, both discussed by Searle in chapter 19: that of visual illusions (the Ponzo illusion) and that of our supposed knowledge of the rules of grammar. These are just two examples of our possession of cognitive capabilities which seem to demand from us a different *kind* of knowledge of rules, a knowledge not immediately available to us as agents and only available to the theoretician in the field after long, hard study.

In the Ponzo illusion (chapter 19, p. 340)[1] our seeing the upper horizontal line as larger than the lower can be explained as an instance of (inappropriate) depth processing. We see one line as larger than another because we have made allowances for their perceived distance from us. Our perception of object size depends upon the visual angle subtended by an object at the eye and by the information we encode about the distance of the object from the eye. When the visual angle remains constant with variation of distance, the encoded information will be that the object is further away, so the object will appear larger. This account of perception of object size can be used to explain our tendency to see the moon as larger when it is closer to the horizon than when it is elevated: the explanation is that the horizon provides us with *clues* as to the large distance that the moon is from us, whereas when it is a lonely spot in the sky we have no such information. With the Ponzo illusion the explanation will only work if we can explain why the distance information is varied, why the upper line looks further away, and hence larger. An explanation of this is that we *use* perspective clues *to infer* depth, and so *take* the upper line to be farther away. This last move could also be described as *inferring* perceived size by *taking account* of distance. It is clear that such explanation is non-neurophysiological, and the italicized phrases used suggest some kind of intentionality at work. Rock (1991) suggests that they are perfectly legitimate functional explanations, even if they eventually yield to neurophysiological explanations.

The example of our knowledge of grammatical rules is slightly different from the cases of visual perception. Here there are two ways in which an explanatory problem is generated. One concentrates on our adult ability to differentiate between the grammatical and ungrammatical sentences of our language: we are able to do this without being able to articulate the grammatical principles which apparently underly the discriminative ability. It looks as though there is a set of rules which we use to detect ungrammaticality, but the rules are not consciously known. The second problem emerges when we consider how it is that children have acquired the rules in question. How do we learn the syntax of our language? The problem was once answered by saying that we learn these rules as we learn most others, either by explicit instruction, or by drill-type training, or by imitation when exposed to the necessary linguistic evidence.

The problem is that explicit instruction and drill-type training do not occur, or not in the way required. As children we are not told how pronominal co-reference works, yet we acquire knowledge of its functioning fairly uniformly and rapidly. Do we learn by generalizing on the basis of exposure to relevant utterances? The considered verdict is that the exposure provides evidence for the generalizations which is insufficient to account for the knowledge acquired. The evidence is deficient in so far as children are exposed to both grammatical and ungrammatical sentences, hindering the ability to make correct generalizations. There is also a problem in so far as the child acquires, on the basis of limited evidence, an ability to generate an infinite number of sentences. The conclusion is that the child acquires a sophisticated set of rules which enable him/her to speak grammatically even when he/she has never encountered the relevant sentence before.

The sophistication of the rules can be shown by the following examples, where one would expect the fourth sentence to be grammatical if the rules were formed by some 'straight' inductive generalization.

1a I expect the fur to fly.
 b I expect the fur will fly.
 c The fur is expected to fly.
 d *The fur is expected will fly.

2a Irv drove the car into the garage.
 b Irv drove the car.
 c Irv put the car into the garage.
 d *Irv put the car. (Pinker, 1990, p. 206)

In order to make the relevant discrimination, and so judge that 1(d) and 2(d) are ungrammatical, one must have acquired a fairly *abstract* set of rules which will generate the right consequences. If this were all acquired by usual inductive methods, we should detect considerable differences in the learning of the grammar between children of varying general intelligence, as we do in other inductively based abilities. But the evidence for the expected wide variation in ability does not exist.

The deficiency of the evidence available to the child, the rapidity of learning, the complexity of the ability acquired, and the uniformity of its acquisition despite differences in intelligence all suggest that there is an innate language-learning device. In addition, it suggests that what is innate must be common to all linguistic creatures: that our ability to speak grammatical French, English, German or Xhosa is a function of the innate grammar, this being appropriately called Universal Grammar, and a specific linguistic environment which adds variable detail to the invariant bare bones of the innate structure. On this view a grammar is the finite system describing an individual's linguistic capacities, a system which is *represented in the mind*.

> A grammar represents what a speaker comes to know, subconsciously for the most part, about his or her native language: it represents the fully developed linguistic capacity and is therefore part of an individual's phenotype. Speakers know that certain sentences (in fact, an infinite number) can occur in their speech and others cannot; they know what the occurring sentences mean and the various ways in which they can be pronounced and rephrased. Most of this largely subconscious knowledge is represented in a person's grammar. (Lightfoot, 1982, p. 22)

Tacit Knowledge

In the visual perception and language cases described above, the exercise of certain capacities seems to require a theoretician of the area to posit the existence of a set of rules which enable us to perform the task at hand (for example, to speak grammatically). The problem is that we, as non-theoreticians, do not know the rules we are said to follow. This is paradoxical: we follow the rules but do not know them, and yet what has distinguished rule-following from merely regular behaviour is our ability to act intentionally *in accordance* with the rule. So how can we say of a piece of behaviour that it involves the following of rules, but also that it is not known to the agent which rules, if any, are being followed? As indicated above, the common claim within cognitive science is that the rules are 'tacitly' known. The claim is that although we do not have explicit knowledge of the rules, we can still have the distinctive marks of a rule-following activity, as opposed to mere regularity, or mere physiological processes, since the knowledge is located at a deeper level, one that is not available to introspection. This kind of knowledge manifests itself in the actions we perform; for example, in those linguistic actions which are the uttering and understanding of a wide variety of sentences that are constructed in accordance with the rules of grammar. The cognitivist claim is that the *contents* of such rules are causally implicated in the production of such understanding, a claim validated, so it is claimed, by the specification of such contents' being a necessary feature of the best explanation of the actions available to us. If it is content that is relevant, then it seems as though it must be *represented* in us, without our consciously knowing the details of this representation.

But does this solve our problem? What exactly is 'tacit knowledge'? Any characterization of it involves (at least) two challenges. First, tacit knowledge needs to be distinguished from the everyday kind of knowledge we have, some of which is not consciously entertained by us. This requires giving a principled distinction between representational states which are tacitly known and those representational states which seem to be more of a surface affair, states whose contents are 'in principle' available to the consciousness of the agents who act on those contents. Secondly, the advocate of tacit knowledge must face a challenge from a different direction and say what distinguishes these representational states, and the relations between, them from 'brute' neurophysiological states and patterns. Why are *representational* states needed when consciousness of these is denied? In short, the advocate of tacit knowledge of representational states faces the problem that in so far as our cognitive relation to the contents of these states is in principle different from that relating us to ordinary beliefs, the question arises of why we need to characterize these states as representational at all. Is there this intermediate *psychological* level between full-blown propositional attitudes and neurophysiology?

The Debate

In 'Tacit Knowledge and Subdoxastic States' (chapter 18), Martin Davies is concerned more with the first than the second of the questions outlined above: what is the relation between the states whose content is tacitly known and the other intentional states? He puts the question in the context of our knowledge of the axioms and rules of a universal grammar, the grammar that underlies every person's syntactic abilities. There is a preliminary question to be faced: if there is more than one possible way of systematically representing the rules of such a grammar, then we face the question of *which* of the possible grammars it is that we are said to tacitly know. The epistemological position appears to be one in which the only evidence constraining the attribution of a particular version of universal grammar is the set of sentences produced and understood by the speakers of a language. This linguistic behaviour will be the only evidence we have for the postulation of grammatical knowledge, and the problem is that this evidence underdetermines the choice of a grammar. There will be more than one way of giving an axiomatic representation that will yield the linguistic behaviour. So if we are said to (tacitly) know a grammar, our preliminary problem is to decide which grammar it is we know. Which grammar is psychologically real?

Davies suggests that if the grammar is seen as neurophysiologically realized, then a requirement on the 'reality' of the grammar should be that the derivational structure of the theory be reflected in the causal structure in the speaker. If different theorems in the grammar make use of a single axiom, then at the causal level there must likewise be a common causal factor 'implicated in the explanations of the several corresponding pieces of knowledge about whole sentences' (chapter 18, p. 000). This increases the range of evidence available to the grammatical theorist, given that it is an empirical matter as to what the correct causal-explanatory account will be.

We remark on this aspect of Davies' paper for two reasons. It is important that Davies makes the consequences of the causal factor sensitive to the *semantic* content of the state. If it *is* sensitive, then this provides a compelling reason to think of the state as a representational state. In addition the 'common causal factor' strategy is used by Davies in his response to Searle's scepticism about our supposed tacit knowledge of rules. We will return to this issue when discussing Davies' response.

Secondly, if the proposal is to provide us with another source of evidence for the reality of grammar, then the causal factors have to be recognized independently of the grammar(s), and grammatical operations, in question. This poses a potential dilemma for Davies. The picture we get is one where a causal-explanatory structure is found to match a representational-explanatory structure, and this has a feel of reduction about it which the critics of tacit knowledge may use to their advantage.

Davies asks what the relation is between the person and the axioms and rules of grammar that he/she is said to know. Is it a belief-like relation? Are the states we are said to tacitly know just like belief states except that we are not conscious of them? This is a suggestion made by Chomsky (1991), who makes the difference simply a matter of inaccessibility to consciousness. The states which are tacitly known are like belief states except that they are inaccessible to consciousness. A second differentiating feature, suggested by Stich (1978), is that these states are not inferentially integrated with beliefs, and so are *subdoxastic*. Beliefs can be put to use by being the basis upon which we make inferences, thereby acquiring new beliefs. States of which we are only tacitly aware are not combined with beliefs to form new beliefs. Nor do beliefs combine with subdoxastic states to form new subdoxastic states. This inferential isolation suggests that the subdoxastic states exist in 'special purpose', separate sub-systems, a suggestion which brings to mind Jerry Fodor's account of modular systems. We leave the reader to ponder Davies' interesting discussion of the relation between inferential isolation and modularity.

Davies goes on to suggest a third differentiating feature of the states of which we have only tacit knowledge. With propositional states like beliefs we constrain the semantic contents of these states by using, in the description of the contents, only concepts available to (understood by) the believer. The concepts used must be grasped by the person to whom the state is attributed. Not so with states of tacit knowledge. With these the content is not so constrained. A believer is said to grasp a concept only if that person can use the concept in a variety of situations. More precisely, following Strawson's emphasis on the idea that a genuine predicate must be capable of being conjoined with a number of different subjects, we can say that grasp of a concept requires that the thinker be capable of applying that concept to different individuals. Concepts must have a general use-value. This generality constraint *necessarily* applies to the concepts employed in the attribution of propositional attitudes; it *may* be the case that in an information-processing sub-system we could have new informational states emerge on the basis of a recombination of the components of other states, but this ability to recombine is not essential to the information states. That it is possible for a pair of such states, say F(a) and G(b) to be followed by F(b) does not count against the proposal that the necessary generalizability of concepts distinguishes prop-ositional attitude content from the content of other representational states. The idea is that if we came across a person who appeared to believe both F(a) and G(b), but could not grasp (did not appear to understand) the proposition (Fb), then this would count as evidence against the attribution of the initial belief states, (Fa) and (Gb). On the other hand, if one found a person to whom one attributed information states (Fa) and (Gb), but found no reason to attribute the information state (Fb), then this would have no bearing on the initial assignment of information states.

Davies discusses each differentiating condition in turn. For the purposes of the present debate, it is the first of these conditions, that of inaccessibility to consciousness, that is of central importance, since it is this issue which perturbs Searle in his attack on the idea that there is such a thing as tacit knowledge. Searle thinks that there is an intimate connection between the mentality of a state and its availability to consciousness, a connection which makes the whole notion of an unconscious mental state problematic. One can only eliminate the problem if one ensures that any such unconscious mental state is *in principle* accessible to consciousness. This is Searle's 'connection principle'.

As mentioned, the inaccessibility to consciousness of subdoxastic states is the first differentiating condition discussed by Davies, and it is worth asking whether it or the third (graspability of concepts) is more foundational, or whether they may be just different formulations of the same condition. The latter thought is prompted by considering Searle's reasons for insisting on the mental's acccessibility to consciousness: it is essential to the *aspectual* feature of a mental state that it be so accessible. By this, Searle means that the content of a mental state must portray the subjective point of view of the person whose state it is, and this point of view just is that person's consciousness of the world. Similarly, that a person must grasp the concepts that are constituents of the contents of their mental states is explained by that person's (subjective) view of the world. We are constrained in our attributions of such contents to intentional states by the understanding the person has of the world around him/her. It is difficult to avoid the thought that the concepts must be available to the consciousness of that person. Davies allows that this may characterize belief as a conscious state, but he does not want to allow the difference between conscious belief and subdoxacity to depend upon potential access to consciousness: accesibility to consciousness does not, by itself, debar a state from being subdoxastic. The theorist who knows about the information-processing capacities of some sub-systems may well be in a position consciously to know what subdoxastic processes are going on when he or she is looking at a picture, one which requires perspectival information to be processed if the picture is to be accurately represented in consciousness. The theorist's conscious knowledge of the states should not rule them out as being subdoxastic, so 'accessibility to consciousness' is not sufficient to demarcate the belief states from the subdoxastic states.

This accessibility is, as Davies notes, not quite the same as the immediate *availability* to consciousness of ordinary belief states. The theoretician's knowledge seems essentially inferentially based, depending on prior knowledge of a theory, whereas our knowledge of the contents of our belief states is more immediate. Now Searle's target is the view that we, as theoreticians, are entitled to postulate such peculiar *mental* states at all, states whose content is not derived from the conscious awareness which subjects have of their world, such consciousness providing the aspectual feature of mentality. Note that on Davies' account, grasp of conceptual content is a constraint on the kind of content that can be attributed to a subject. If there are content-ful states (representational states) that are not so constrained, the question immediately arises: what does constrain the content of these states? Will it be a matter of 'anything goes'? Searle's accusation is that cognitive scientists have played fast and loose with the notion of the mental by postulating the existence of such strange states, given that it is essential to mental states that they be accessible to consciousness.

Searle distinguishes four types of mental states that may be said to be inaccessible to consciousness, and so 'unconsious'. The first two are unproblematic. In fact, the first is not really a mental state at all. It involves mentality only metaphorically, as when we attribute to a plant the desire to reach the sunlight. The second is familiar from everyday life, where we have beliefs, say, that are not occurrent, i.e. are not being consciously thought at a particular time, but which can be called into consciousness without effort. (These states form what Freud called the *descriptive* unconscious.) Thirdly, there are the deeper unconscious states postulated by psychoanalytic theory, which Searle prefers to call the repressed conscious states, since their inaccessibility to consciousness is dependent on their repression. For Freud, these states formed the *dynamic* unconscious, dynamic because the contents of these states had an effect in consciousness even though they were unconscious states. Given the way repression operates, such states are always potentially accessible to consciousness: eradicate the repression, and the content of the state will become manifest.[2] It is the fourth type of unconscious state that Searle decries: those 'deeply' unconscious states that are inaccessible in principle to consciousness. This inaccessibility deprives us of the means whereby we can determine the aspectual shape of the state.

The outline of Searle's argument can be briefly stated. If there is in principle inaccessibility to consciousness, then there is no aspectual shape. Without aspectual shape we do not have any mentality, no 'intrinsic intentionality'. Searle supports each stage of the argument, and provides an analysis of why it is that we make the mistake we do in thinking that it is necessary to posit such states. He suggests that we illegitimately anthropomorphize the brain much as pre-Darwinian biologists attributed purposes to the states of organisms. What Darwin taught us is that we can do without such purposes, so that what we need to do is to bring cognitive science into the post-Darwinian age by eliminating the states and rules which we are said to tacitly know. Such elimination would leave us with the simple account of what it is that we are conscious of, plus a 'hardware' explanation of what underlies our awareness. In visual illusion cases – for example, the Ponzo illusion discussed by Searle – it is said that our awareness of the the top line as being larger and farther away is partially due to the rules of perspective which we unconsciously follow. Searle replaces this by 'We consciously see the top line as farther away' – and that is all there is to the intentionalist account. Any additional explanation cannot be intentional; it must be functional or neurophysiological, or both. And as far as functional explanations go, Searle is resolutely instrumentalist about them: 'the actual facts of intentionality contain normative elements; but where functional explanations are concerned the only *facts* are brute, blind physical facts and the only norms are in us and exists only from our point of view'. (Chapter 19, p. 345). Searle takes a similar line with other 'tacit knowledge' explanations, as in the discussion of the vestibular ocular reflex (VOR). The proper explanation invokes only the physical mechanism which produces the required effect.

The elimination of the unconscious intentional level, plus the instrumentalism about functional explanation, makes it appear as though Searle believes there is only 'folk' (belief/desire) psychology and hard science; only the level of full intentionality that we use daily in explaining each others actions, and the level of neurophysiological explanation. Searle denies that this is his intention.[3] He claims that there can be different levels of explanation, and that the language of functionality can be employed. What he insists upon is that the functions are those of neurophysiology or of intentionality. It is often valuable to speculate about functional mechanisms in the brain prior to knowing how the functions are physically implemented. But this is functionality at the neurophysiological level. What Searle rejects is the possibility of a 'gap-filling' explanation, an intermediate level, which describes causal properties specified in neither intentionalist (in the sense of being accessible to consciousness) nor neurophysiological terms.

There is another important point in Searle's diagnosis of what goes wrong in cognitive science explanations. He suggests that the specific mistake we make as far as the unconscious following of rules is concerned is that we are prone to think that if two mental states are connected, then the connection must be meaningful. If we have an input and an output, both of which are mental states, then, Searle says, cognitive scientists succumb to the temptation to connect them *via* a process that is also described as mental. But there is no need to posit the meaningful connection: it could be a simple, non-meaningful, causal connection that does the required work.

The Response

Brief though Searle's argument is, it has, if sound, devastating consequences for cognitive science: many of the explanations favoured by cognitive scientists would be illegitimate explanations. Davies, in his response (chapter 20), notes these consequences, but thinks the position for cognitive scientists is not as problematic as Searle would have us believe. There are two central features in the case for cognitive science as made by Davies. The first involves an examination of the notion of 'accessibility to consciousness', and the second involves distinguishing different types of representational states, states that could be said to possess a content that is *about* something.

'In principle accessibility to consciousness', the mark of the mental favoured by Searle, is a phrase requiring considerable elucidation before it can do the work required of it by Searle. One needs to know considerably more both about the 'in principle' part of the phrase and the notion of consciousness that is being invoked. Davies concentrates some attention on the latter point, noting that there may be two types of consciousness involved in mentality: phenomenal consciousness and access consciousness. The former relates to our awareness of our experiences. It is connected with the idea that there is 'something that it is like' to be us, or more specifically, something that it is like for us to be in a particular type of mental state. This aspect of consciousness is directly connected to subjective awareness, so much so that for many of the states of which we are subjectively aware it is said that our being so conscious of them is both necessary and sufficient for us to be in those states. The necessary condition is relevant here: for example, with the experience of pain, it is often said that we are not in pain if we are not aware of being in pain. This would seem to give considerable support to Searle's position, in so far as this necessary awareness is a form of his 'connection principle', which requires accessibility to consciousness. The difference is that, as it is presently formulated, the necessary awareness only holds for some mental states, phenomenal states, whereas Searle makes accessibility to consciousness a mark of all mental states.

There is a different idea of consciousness, that associated with propositional attitudes, which Davies calls 'access consciousness'. It is typically exemplified in our ability to report what we are thinking. As Davies notes, *saying* what we are thinking may well be a feature of this type of consciousness, but is unlikely to be essential to it, given that we allow non-linguistic creatures to have states with content. The general idea of this type of consciousness harks back to Davies' earlier discussion, where a distinction is drawn between states whose content is graspable by a subject and those where this requirement is not met. With this type of consciousness it is at least a question as to how it relates to having content, or being a representational state. For 'full-blown' intentionality, that possessed by propositional attitudes, there does seem to be an intimate connection with access consciousness, but this immediately raises the question: are *all* representational states necessarily states with propositional attitude-type intentionality? Searle thinks that they are, but the argument connecting all mental content to in principle accessibility to consciousness could be equivocating on the kind of consciousness involved. It is plausible for some mental states that they be connected to an awareness of them, but these states are phenomenal states, ones without representational content. This necessary connection to consciousness is not so plausible, so Davies argues, when the states are representational and the consciousness is access consciousness. So could there not be a kind of intentionality, a kind of 'aboutness' which is not that exemplified in propositional states?

Davies argues for an affirmative answer, for the possibility that the notion of a representational state need not be as univocal as Searle makes it out to be. He distinguishes five types of 'aboutness', two of which may be used to plug the gap between neurophysiology and full-blown intentionality. One of these is 'indicator aboutness', which involves the notion of one thing or event being a sign for something else – clouds meaning rain – in virtue of some kind of causal correlation between the two. The importance of 'indicator aboutness' is that it can be argued that it exists independently of our interests, and that it is constrained by the requirement that there be a special type of causal correlation between the indicator state, say clouds, and the indicated state, say rain. The hope is that one will be able to specify the *type* of causal co-variation which will yield 'indicator aboutness' in a sufficiently rigorous way so that not just any two events will fit the co-variation requirement. Only if one can do this will 'indicator aboutness' avoid being trivialized. (For more on the indicator relation see chapter 5.)

If a robust account of 'indicator aboutness' is forthcoming, then there will be representational states that do not conform to Searle's accessibility to consciousness requirement. Davies suggests that the type of aboutness needed for cognitive science, 'subdoxastic aboutness', may well be constructable from 'indicator aboutness' and some idea of natural function. If so, then one will have the basis to use these representational states upon which to build an account of rule-following. A transition between states that exemplify rule-following will be distinct from a mere causal transition if the states in question are representational states. Davies concludes chapter 20 by examining two of the specific cases of 'malpractice' by cognitive scientists discussed by Searle, those of our knowledge of grammar and the processes involved in the vestibular occular reflex (VOR).

This response is a powerful plea for the practice of cognitive scientists. Representational states without in principle accessibility to consciousness will be vindicated if one can build on 'indicator aboutness' and natural functions. There are still some questions to ponder, however. Searle does formulate his argument against the idea of there being such representational states at all, and Davies' strategy may well work against this. The more limited claim that could be made is that these are not mental states, and Davies has not said much in defence of their mentality. 'Indicator aboutness' and natural functionality look more likely to yield biological states rather than anything distinctively mental.

This may appear to be nothing more than a fruitless boundary-drawing debate, but there could be ramificiations in the way in which the boundary skirmish is settled that are not trivial. In particular, the notion of tacit knowledge with which we started may be at risk if the controlling interest in the way representation is attributed to these states is a biological interest. We are less tempted to attribute to ourselves tacit knowledge of biological states, even when these are representational states. This is underlined by one way in which Davies defends sub-conscious rule-following: we have rule-following if the inputs and outputs of the processes are repesentational states and there is a particular mediating causal structure. Searle rejects this move. He thinks that the fact that the input and output are representational need make no difference: all that is required are causal processes, without any rule-following activity. What is needed is an in-depth investigation into the different types, and sources, of representation pointed to by Davies.

Notes

1 The explanation of what happens in the Ponzo illusion, and the extension to the moon 'illusion', is given by Irvin Rock (1991).
2 It seems as though Searle wants to make the aspectual shape of these unconscious states depend upon their potential availability to consciousness now or in the future. An alternative would be to make that shape dependent on their having been conscious, prior to repression.
3 This comes out clearly in Searle's (1991) response to Irvin Rock in LePore and van Gulick (1991).

References

Chomsky, N. (1991) *Knowledge of Language: its Nature, Origin, and Use.* New York, Praeger.
Higginbotham, J. (1990) Philosophical issues in the study of language. In D.N. Osherson and H. Lasnick (eds) (1990) *An Invitation to Cognitive Science, 1: Language,* pp. 243–57. Cambridge, Mass., MIT Press.

LePore, E. and van Gulick, R. (eds) (1991) *John Searle and his Critics*. Oxford, Basil Blackwell.

Lightfoot, D. (1982) *The Language Lottery: Toward a Biology of Grammars*. Cambridge, Mass., MIT Press.

Pinker, S. (1990) Language Acquisition. In D.N. Osherson and H. Lasnick (eds), *An Invitation to Cognitive Science, 1: Language,* pp. 199–242. Cambridge, Mass., MIT Press.

Rock, I. (1991) Psychological Explanation. In E. LePore and R. van Gulick (eds), *John Searle and his Critics*. Oxford, Basil Blackwell.

Searle, J. (1991) Reply to Irvin Rock. In E. LePore and R. van Gulick (eds), *John Searle and his Critics*, pp. 338–41. Oxford, Blackwell.

Stich, S. (1978) Beliefs and subdoxastic states. *Philosophy of Science.* 45, 499–518.

18

Tacit Knowledge and Subdoxastic States

Martin Davies

Two Questions about Tacit Knowledge

Fundamental to Chomsky's work in both linguistics and philosophy are these two claims. First, ordinary speakers of natural languages tacitly know a grammar – a set of rules or principles – for their language. Secondly, the acquisition of this attained grammar by an infant speaker depends upon a massive innate endowment; namely, innate knowledge of universal grammar. This chapter is about just the first of these claims; indeed, about just one aspect of that first claim.

Over the years, various terms have been used to elaborate the tacit knowledge claim. What the speaker tacitly knows is equated with the speaker's *competence* (Chomsky, 1965, p. 8; cf. 1980a, p. 39); and, in a further attempt to fend off what are argued to be irrelevant objections from terminologically fussy philosophers, the expression *'cognize'* is sometimes deployed. Thus, ordinary speakers know – in the familiar everyday sense – and also cognize facts about, for example, what various complete sentences mean. In addition, they cognize, even if they do not know in the ordinary sense, the facts from which those first facts follow (Chomsky, 1976, pp. 164–5; 1980a, pp. 69–70).

We might think of the first facts as stated by some of the theorems of a systematic theory. Then, the basic idea would be this. Ordinary speakers know and cognize the facts stated by these theorems. They also cognize – even if they do not know in the ordinary sense – the facts stated by the axioms from which the theorems are derived.

If we think of the issue in these terms, then it is easy to raise the first of two major questions that confront any friend of tacit knowledge. There will always be distinct sets of axioms from which we can derive the same theorems about, say, the meanings of whole sentences: extensionally equivalent sets of axioms. So, how can it make empirical sense to suppose that an ordinary speaker stands in any psychological relation to one set of axioms, rather than to an alternative extensionally equivalent set?

This is essentially *Quine's challenge* (Quine, 1972) to Chomsky's notion of tacit knowledge. A similar challenge about alternative axiomatizations arises when we consider theorems assigning more complex properties to sentences. I would aim to meet challenges of this form by construing tacit knowledge as a certain kind of causal-explanatory structure underlying – explanatorily antecedent to – the pieces of knowledge that a speaker has about the whole sentences. (See Evans, 1981; Davies, 1986, 1987.) The basic idea is that tacit knowledge of a particular systematic theory is constituted by a causal-explanatory structure in the speaker which mirrors the derivational structure in the theory. Where there is, in the theory, a common factor – for example, a common axiom – used in the derivations of several theorems, there should be, in the speaker, a causal common factor implicated in the explanations of the several corresponding pieces of knowledge about whole sentences.

Of course, not just any kind of causal common factor constitutes a state of tacit knowledge. Intuitively, we require that, if a state is to have semantic, as well as causal, properties, then its causal consequences should be sensitive to its semantic content. There are various ways of building this requirement of content sensitivity into an analytical account of tacit knowledge. For example, elsewhere (Davies, 1987), I have made use of the condition that, in order to constitute a state of tacit knowledge, a causal common factor should also be a locus of systematic revision – keeping the speaker's various beliefs about whole sentences in step with each other. The account of psychological reality for a grammar which Peacocke (1989) offers makes crucial use of the idea that the causal common factor should be a state of information that is drawn upon (see also Peacocke, 1986). This account is very much in the same spirit as the constitutive account of tacit knowledge that I would favour. (Indeed, under plausible assumptions about the notion of the information content of a state, the two accounts turn out to be equivalent.)

However exactly the details go, an account of tacit knowledge along these lines enables the theorist to meet Quine's challenge. For there can certainly be empirical evidence in favour of attributing to a speaker one underlying causal structure rather than another; and, as Chomsky often stresses (e.g. 1986, p. 250; 1987, p. 184), there is a no *a priori* limit to the kinds of evidence that might be relevant.

No doubt, this construal of tacit knowledge will fail to apply to many cases in which 'we can know more than we can tell' (Polanyi, 1967, p. 4). For example, if the proposal is to seem plausible at all, then the notion of tacit knowledge under scrutiny must be distinguished from what Lycan (1986) calls 'tacit belief'. Tacit beliefs are, roughly, the as yet undrawn consequences of what might be called, in contrast, 'explicit beliefs'. The construal in terms of a structure of causal-explanatory states is intended to be faithful to the fact that tacit knowledge, in Chomsky's sense, lies causally upstream, rather than downstream, of ordinary beliefs.

Dennett (1983) draws a distinction that is analogous to Lycan's; but he makes the contrast in terms of explicit versus implicit representation of information. He then constrasts both explicit and implicit representation with 'merely tacit knowhow' which is 'built into the system in some fashion that does not require it to be represented . . . in the system' (1983, p. 218), and goes on to categorize tacit knowledge in Chomsky's sense as a species of explicit representation, rather than merely tacit knowhow (pp. 218–19). Whether or not Dennett is right about Chomsky's commitments, the construal of tacit knowledge in terms of causal-explanatory structure is intended to group some cases of tacit knowhow together with certain cases of explicit representation of information; for cases of both kinds can exhibit the requisite pattern of causal common factors.

Supposing, then, that attributions of tacit knowledge are respectably empirical, and have a legitimate and specifiable role in psychological theory, we can turn to the second major question that confronts the friend of tacit knowledge: What is the best way of describing the psychological relation between a person – a thinker, a speaker – and the axioms or rules of the person's inernalized grammar. States of tacit knowledge are states that have semantic contents and figure in causal explanations. But are they like or unlike the more familiar psychological states which have those two properties; namely, propositional attitude states – beliefs, desires, intentions, hopes, wishes, and the rest? It is the second question that is addressed in what follows. I begin with Chomsky's own answer.

Chomsky's Answer and Three Intuitive Differences

Chomsky's answer to our question about tacit knowledge and propositional attitudes is not a simple one. There are several threads to be discerned. One line of thought (Chomsky, 1976. p. 163) leads to the idea that one 'might refer to the postulated cognitive structure as a "system of beliefs"'. 'Since the language has no objective existence apart from its mental representation, we need not distinguish between "system of beliefs" and "knowledge", in this case' (1972, p. 169). Another line culminates in the clear claim (1980a, p. 93) that 'we do not "believe" rules of grammar or other cognitive systems'. Chomsky attributes this claim to Fisher (1974), who stresses the distinction between knowledge *of* a rule and knowledge *about* à rule. And Chomsky (1986, p. 266) himself insists on the distinction between a speaker's knowing a rule R and knowing 'that R holds, obtains, is a rule of his language'.

Each of these threads deserves careful attention. But one dominant and recurrent component of Chomsky's position is the doctrine that what is cognized or tacitly known is something from which ordinary beliefs follow. The picture is of a complex cognitive structure, some parts of which happen to surface in consciousness as ordinary beliefs. Chomsky often suggests (e.g.

1986, p. 269) that the difference in point of accessibility to consciousness is all there is to the distinction between ordinary states of knowledge and belief, on the one hand, and states of tacit knowledge or mere cognizing, on the other. And he argues that the distinction between those states which are conscious and those which are not is of little significance. Thus, for example (1976, pp. 163, 165): 'It may be expected that conscious beliefs will form a scattered and probably uninteresting subpart of the full cognitive structure ... For psychology, the important notion will be "cognize", not "know"'. Thus, according to this dominant thread in the Chomskyan fabric, first, states of merely tacit knowledge differ from ordinary attitude states just in being inaccessible to consciousness, and secondly, the difference is of no theoretical importance.

Stich (1980) disputes both these claims. First, he argues that states of tacit knowledge are not only inaccessible to consciousness; they are also not inferentially integrated with beliefs. Then, secondly, he urges that this distinction between our beliefs and other psychological states does have theoretical significance. The latter states, which 'play a role in the proximate causal history of beliefs, though they are not beliefs themselves' Stich labels *subdoxastic* states (Stich, 1978, p. 499).

Chomsky himself finds Stich's suggestion problematic (Chomsky, 1980b, p. 57). For states of tacit knowledge certainly do combine with each other to yield consequences, which might be described as inferential consequences; and some of these consequences are ordinary beliefs. That is a crucial part of Chomsky's picture of a complex structure of states of cognizing. So we cannot say straightforwardly that states of tacit knowledge are inferentially isolated from beliefs.

But, despite this problem, it is very plausible that there is something right in the thought that inferential integration is a feature of beliefs that is not shared by states of mere cognizing. Certainly, this is a second intuitive difference which demands examination.

In a recent presentation, Chomsky says this (1986, p. 269; emphasis added):

> It has been argued that it is wrong, or even 'outrageous', to say that a person knows the rules of grammar, even in the sense of tacit or implicit knowledge. As a general statement, this cannot be correct. We do not hesitate to say that John knows, whereas Pierre does not know, that verbs cannot be separated from their objects by adverbs or that stops are aspirated except after/s/ – *assuming of course, that we know the meaning of the terms used in these ascriptions of knowledge.*

This passage alludes to one of several putative sources of philosophical hesitation about attributions of tacit knowledge; namely, that we have reservations about attributing knowledge in cases where we do not ourselves grasp the terms used in the attribution.

Chomsky rejects this putative source of hesitation (1986, pp. 266–7), on the grounds that it has nothing especially to do with knowledge about language –

let alone any special connection with tacit knowledge. For anyone making a claim about anything needs to know the meanings of the terms employed; otherwise he does not know what he is claiming.

Chomsky is surely right that this putative source of philosophical hesitation is spurious. But there is a rather similar point that is, in contrast, highly relevant. The question to focus on is not whether the person making the attribution needs to understand the terms used in the attribution; that is, needs to grasp the concepts involved in the contents of the states that are being attributed. Rather, the salient question is whether the person to whom the state is being attributed needs to grasp those concepts.

It is a familiar point (particularly stressed by neo-Fregeans, but not only by them) that no one can have a belief with a particular content – or entertain a thought with a particular content – without grasping the constituent concepts of that content; and Lycan extends this familiar point to cover his notion of tacit belief (1986, p. 78). But, if ordinary speakers are to be credited with tacit knowledge of linguistic rules, principles, or generalizations, then there can be no corresponding requirement relating to the contents of tacit knowledge states. For most ordinary speakers have no grasp at all upon the concepts of linguistic theory. The requirement of conceptualization by the thinking, speaking, person marks a third intuitive difference between ordinary propositional attitude states and states of merely tacit knowledge.

We need to explore in detail these three apparent differences between ordinary propositional attitude states and other cognitive psychological states, such as states of tacit knowledge of linguistic rules. The three intuitive differences add up to a prima facie case for a principled distinction between attitude states – particularly belief states – and subdoxastic states. And the aim of the current exploration is to discover whether a considered case for such a distinction can be made out. Such an exploration must presume upon some prima facie examples of subdoxastic states; but it must not begin by begging questions about how much falls within or without the domain of the common-sense scheme of attitude attribution and rational explanation.

The constitutive accounts of *tacit knowledge* that I mentioned at the beginning of this chapter (Evans, 1981; Davies, 1986, 1987; Peacocke, 1986, 1989) are all developed using the case of systematic semantic theories (in fact, theories of truth conditions) as a central example. This has the expository advantage that the derivational structure of such theories is very familiar. But the choice of example may give the impression that these accounts simply take for granted something that ought to be left as a matter for further arguement; namely, that states of an ordinary speaker which contain information about the semantic properties of words and constructions belong on the subdoxastic side of any principled divide.

This would, however, be a misleading impression. For all these accounts have the feature that their requirements for tacit knowledge could be met by an ordinary piece of conscious knowledge or a belief, provided that it served as a causal common factor in the right way. What these accounts really provide are conditions for *at least* tacit knowledge. Under certain empirical conditions, they license attribution, to an ordinary, unreflective speaker, of tacit knowledge of semantic rules. But it does not follow from such attributions that, if there is a principled distinction between attitude states and subdoxastic states, then knowledge of semantic rules or generalizations falls on the side of the subdoxastic – that is, of the *merely* tacit. These accounts of tacit knowledge are not guilty of begging delicate questions. Nor do they render redundant the present exploration of the differences between beliefs and subdoxastic states.

Accessibility to Consciousness

It is an appealing idea that, if there is a principled distinction between the domain of attitudes and the domain of mere information-processing, then accessibility to consciousness should mark the boundary. But the waters surrounding the notion of accessibility to consciousness can be muddied easily enough. It may be that, once the notion of consciousness is better understood, it can be employed as a basis for the distinction. But what I shall argue in this section is that the pre-theoretical and undifferentiated notion of consciousness cannot bear the required weight. To that extent, Chomsky's scepticism about the importance of any distinction between conscious knowledge and tacit knowledge will be vindicated.

There are at least three reasons why it is unwise to rest the weight of a principled distinction upon the contrast between accessibility and inaccessibility to consciousness. The first reason is simply that we do make use of – or at least psychoanalysts make use of – the notion of an unconscious belief. But these states are intuitively quite unlike the cognitive psychological states which we could take as prima facie examples of subdoxasticity. So, inaccessibility to consciousness had better not be a sufficient condition for a state to be subdoxastic.

It is certainly legitimate to respond to this example by noting that it is possible to protect the claim that states in a certain class are beliefs, even in the face of the fact that the states cannot be brought to conscious awareness. For the claim can be protected in the context of a psychological theory which postulates a mechanism blocking access to beliefs in the particular class (cf. Stich, 1978, p. 505). But that protective strategy must itself be constrained, on pain of a spurious defence of the claim that the prima facie examples of subdoxastic states are themselves beliefs. And it is difficult to escape the conviction that the required constraint will be furnished by some independent foundation for the distinction between beliefs and subdoxastic states.

The second reason is that there are features of the inferential web of beliefs of which we are typically unconscious. Fodor gives as an example (1983, p. 85) our unconscious 'acquiescence in the rule of *modus ponens*'. The idea behind the example is this. A thinker can systematically perform inferences which are, in fact, instances of *modus ponens*, can offer the premises of each such inference as reasons for accepting the conclusion, and can perform the inferences as a result of a single inferential disposition, without being able to frame the rule in its generality. The inferential rule is, in this sense, something of which the ordinary unreflective thinker is not conscious; in this respect, it is like a linguistic rule. But, for all that, our commitment to the rule of *modus ponens* is intuitively quite unlike the prima facie examples of subdoxastic states.

To this second reason for doubting that the notion of accessibility to consciousness can bear the weight of a principled distinction, there is a very natural response. For within information-processing psychology there is a distinction drawn between content-bearing, or representational, states on the one hand, and processes, or computations, over such states on the other. And the distinction is in many ways analogous to the distinction in logic between a formula and a rule of inference.

The natural response to the example of *modus ponens* would be this. The distinction between beliefs and subdoxastic state is, in the first instance, a distinction between belief states – over which inferences are performed – and other representational states – over which other computations are performed. Inaccessibility to consciousness is, in the first instance, to be taken as a mark of the subdoxastic for representational states. *Modus ponens* is a rule of inference, so our acquiescence in it can be thought of as the presence of a computational processor – what Peacocke (1989, p. 122) calls a transition mediator – rather than of a representational state. Consequently, the inaccessibility to consciousness of that inferential rule does not threaten its credentials as a feature of the web of beliefs.

The distinction on which this response depends is important. But the response does not constitute an effective defence of the claim that the notion of accessibility to consciousness can bear some theoretical weight. For, if inaccessibility to consciousness is only a mark of the subdoxastic in the case of representational states, then it follows that the inaccessibility to consciousness of linguistic rules is itself not directly relevant. For there is no reason to suppose that, in an information-processing model, an internalized linguistic rule must appear as a representational state rather than as a computational processor. The response thus undermines the significance of accessibility to consciousness still further.

Someone might seek to defend the theoretical significance of accessibility to consciousness, by pointing out that *if* accessibility to consciousness at least provides a clear distinction between beliefs and other representational states, then it also furnishes a derivative distinction between genuinely mental rules of inference and the computational processes of mere information-processing. For, given the initial distinction, it will be easy enough to classify a rule or process according as its domain is a class of beliefs, on the one hand, or a class containing subdoxastic representational states, on the other.

But, of course, the significance of this conditional claim depends upon whether accessibility to consciousness does provide for a clear and principled distinction among representational states. And the third reason why it is unwise to rest the weight of a principled distinction upon the undifferentiated notion of accessibility to consciousness concerns representational states directly.

This third reason is that there is a sense in which accessibility to consciousness is intuitively compatible with the classification of a state as subdoxastic; for there is more to conscious experience than propositional attitudes. Suppose, for example, that low-level representational states – prima facie examples of subdoxastic states – surfaced in conscious awareness, as distinctive itches or tickles, perhaps. That empirical difference from our actual situation would obviously not be enough to make those states into beliefs.

The idea behind this third challenge to the significance of accessibility to consciousness as such is that there might be an aspect of conscious experience whose cognitive psychological underpinning is the occurrence of a representational state, but which does not make a difference to what the experiencer would believe, taking the experience at fact value. We can suppose that a certain aspect of the phenomenological character of an experience might depend systematically upon the semantic content of the underlying representational state. That goes no way towards making that aspect of the experience into a candidate for belief. (On sensational properties of experience, see Peacocke, 1983; Sterelny, 1987.)

Someone might reply to this challenge as follows. We might allow that, in the imagined cases, the representational state is accessible to consciousness. But, even so, the content of the state is not accessible to consciousness; and it is this that matters for a principled distinction between beliefs and subdoxastic states. But this reply does not amount to a case for the load-bearing potential of the undifferentiated notion of accessibility to consciousness. What it amounts to is a suggestion for refining the undifferentiated notion into a notion of accessibility of content to consciousness. As we have just seen, this accessibility of content would need to be sharply distinguished from the mere systematic reflection of content in aspects of experience. It would also need to be distinguished from the kind of case where a person has beliefs about the contents of his or her own representational states. The fact that a theorist of vision, for example, may have beliefs about the representational states implicated in the information-processing that is going on within her or him does not render those states any less subdoxastic.

The intuitive basis for the distinction between accessibility of content and the possibility of beliefs about the content of a state might be this. If the content of a state is accessible to consciousness, in the required sense, then to be in that state is *ipso facto* to have the content available for report. (Cf. Fodor, 1983, p. 56: 'if we take the criterion of accessibility to be the availability for explicit report of the information that these representations encode'.) This condition is not met merely by the possibility of a belief about the content.

But the idea of actual verbal report seems inessential to this intuitive idea. What is more fundamental than availability for report is availability for thought. Consequently, what the suggestion for refining the undifferentiated notion of accessibility to consciousness ultimately provides is this. A representational state is subdoxastic if being in the state is not *ipso facto* to have the content of the state available as a content of thought, that is, of propositional attitudes. Arguably, this captures something of our idea of a belief as a conscious state. But – however compelling it may be – it cannot serve at this point as the basis for a principled distinction between subdoxastic states and attitude states. The third challenge to the significance of accessibility to consciousness as such remains unanswered.

For these three reasons, we should not presume upon the undifferentiated notion of accessibility to consciousness to ground a principled distinction between beliefs and subdoxastic states. If we set aside accessibility to consciousness, then two intuitive differences between beliefs and prima facie examples of subdoxastic states remain. One concerns inferential integration; the other concerns conceptualization.

Above, I remarked that the suggestion that subdoxastic states are not inferentially integrated with beliefs is plausible, despite the problem that Chomsky notes. It is time to explore the difference between inferential integration and isolation in more detail.

Inferential Isolation and the Modularity of Mind

The idea of the inferential integration of beliefs can be illustrated this way. A belief state is 'at the service of many distinct projects' (Evans, 1981, p. 337). The belief that these things before me are items of furry, purple footwear can combine with another belief – say, the belief that the only items of furry, purple footwear around here are Granny's slippers – and lead inferentially to a new belief – that these are Granny's slippers. That latter belief might, in its turn, combine with a desire – to pour champagne into Granny's slippers – to provide a reason for action. The original belief could also combine with quite different beliefs – say, that furry, purple things are liable to keep the cat amused – to yield different inferential consequences, and to contribute towards reasons for quite different actions.

In the familiar image, beliefs form a web, with inferential and evidential links. And part of what is involved in that image is that a new belief – that Granny has just entered wearing her slippers – may lead inferentially to the adjustment of previously held beliefs – those furry, purple things are not, after all, items of footwear.

Beliefs combine to yield inferential consequences; and beliefs are adjusted to avoid inconsistency. These are two aspects of the inferential integration of beliefs. But there is something else involved in the idea of a belief being at the service of many projects, but which is not immediately revealed by the image of a web of beliefs. For one belief can combine with many different desires to provide reasons for many different actions. This third property of beliefs is a striking feature of the domain of attitudes; and it is this feature that most directly blocks the reduction of statements about beliefs to statements about dispositions to behaviour (cf. Evans, 1981, p. 337).

Cognitive psychological states which are prima facie examples of subdoxastic states seem to lack these three properties of beliefs. For example, states of tacit knowledge of syntactic rules or principles, or the states implicated in early visual processing, do not directly combine with desires to provide reasons for action. It is only the distant consequences of those states that contribute to such reasons. These states thus seem to lack the third property of beliefs.

There is no intellectual discomfort over holding a belief which is incompatible with what is merely tacitly known (cf. Stich, 1980, p. 39). So states of tacit knowledge seem to lack the second property of beliefs; or rather, they lack that property relative to ordinary beliefs.

As Chomsky points out (1980b, p. 57), states of tacit knowledge do yield ordinary beliefs as (inferential) consequences. So we cannot say straightforwardly that subdoxastic states lack the first property of beliefs. But there is still a clear sense in which tacit knowledge states are inferentially isolated from the web of beliefs. This isolation has two aspects.

The first aspect is that prima facie examples of subdoxastic states do not combine inferentially with beliefs to yield further beliefs, even when their semantic content is closely related to the contents of the beliefs. For example, our identification of spoken words involves, at an early state, the registration of information about acoustic properties such as voice onset times. So a person who hears a word beginning with an unvoiced consonant will subdoxastically register the information that the voice onset time is, say, 25 milliseconds. Such a person might, for whatever inscrutable reason, have the belief that if the next syllable he hears has a voice onset time of 25 milliseconds, then it is time to prepare his lecture. But merely hearing the unvoiced consonant as such will not be enough to provide the person with a reason for starting his preparation.

The idea behind this example is that, if a thinker has two beliefs – one of the form *that if P then Q* and the other of the form *that P* – then the thinker will often draw the conclusion *that Q*. But if the two premises for *modus ponens* are divided – one the content of a belief and the other the content of a subdoxastic state – then the thinker typically does not come to believe the conclusion.

The second aspect of the inferential isolation of subdoxastic states is this. Ordinary beliefs usually – or at least often – do not combine with subdoxastic states to yield further subdoxastic states. Rather, the procedures that operate over states which are prima facie examples of subdoxastic states are to a considerable extent unaffected by what the person in question believes.

It is surely in virtue of this family of differences between the web of beliefs and prima facie examples of subdoxastic states that plausibility attaches to Stich's suggestion about inferential integration versus isolation, despite the problem that Chomsky notices.

Stich offers a picture of our mental and cognitive lives in which (1980, p. 39): 'Our mental apparatus is divided into a number of distinct components. Among these is a store of beliefs that are well integrated inferentially and generally accessible to consciousness.' Similarly: 'beliefs form a consciously accessible, inferentially integrated cognitive subsystem', while 'Subdoxastic states occur in a variety of separate, special purpose cognitive subsystems' (1978, pp. 507–8). This is a picture of the mind as modular; and, as such, it is welcomed by Chomsky (1980b, p. 57).

However, there are several different notions of modularity employed in psychological theory, and the proposal for a principled distinction between beliefs and subdoxastic states to be considered next concerns the specific idea of modularity elaborated by Fodor (1983). Before stating the proposal, I give some brief reminders of Fodor's thesis.

The major bifurcation within Fodor's schematic architecture of the mind is between the central cognitive system and input systems. An input system is an information-processing system which ultimately delivers information to the central cognitive system whose primary business, in turn, is the fixation of belief. In this model, the central cognitive system seems to correspond to the domain of propositional attitudes. Indeed, Fodor credits the central system with typical properties of the domain of the attitudes; in particular, with the property of evidential holism or isotropy (1983, p. 105).

Fodor's major thesis is that input systems are modules. This amounts, *inter alia*, to the claim that input systems are informationally encapsulated and domain specific, have their operation fast and mandatory and their interlevels relatively inaccessible to the central system, and exhibit a characteristic pace and sequencing of development and characteristic patterns of breakdown. For Fodor's modularity is defined in terms of these and other marks (1983, pp. 47–101).

The official definition of informational encapsulation is this. A system within an organism is informationally encapsulated if the information available to the system is considerably less than the totality of information represented in the organism (Fodor, 1983, p. 69). Informational encapsulation is 'what I take to be perhaps the most important aspect of modularity' (p. 37), and 'the essence of . . . modularity' (p. 71).

Given Stich's picture and Fodor's thesis, it is tempting to propose that the scientific pyschological category of modularity is what underlies the philosophical category of the subdoxastic. Several factors combine to reinforce this temptation. First, the apparent correspondence, in Fodor's model, between the central cognitive system and the domain of propositional attitudes suggestively leaves input systems corresponding to the domain (or domains) of subdoxastic states. Secondly, our prima facie examples of subdoxastic states are, indeed, states of Fodorian input systems: 'the perceptual systems *plus language*' (Fodor, 1983, p. 44). Thirdly, the property of informational encapsulation – which is the essence of modularity – is very reminiscent of one aspect of the inferential isolation of subdoxastic states. Fourthly, Fodor himself explicitly suggests

(p. 86) that it is the states of modules that exhibit the pair of features that Stich takes as characteristic of subdoxastic states.

This tempting proposal – that modularity is what underlies the subdoxastic domain – could be elaborated as a bolder or as a more cautious claim. In its boldest form, the proposal would be that modularity is the real essence of the subdoxastic. This would involve three substantial requirements upon modularity. First, the notion of modularity and its accompanying taxonomy should pull their weight in psychological theory. Secondly, the theory of modularity should furnish an explanation as to why the intuitive characteristics of subdoxastic states go together, to the extent that they do. Thirdly, the taxonomy should permit a principled classification of cases whose status is left indeterminate by the intuitive marks of the subdoxastic. The real essence proposal would also involve a controversial commitment to the possibility of fools' subdoxasticity: a commitment to refuse to classify a state as subdoxastic if it is not a state of a module, even if it exhibits all the philosophical characteristics of the subdoxastic domain.

A more cautious claim can retain much of the interest and appeal of the boldest form of the proposal, without the controversial commitment. According to the form of the proposal to be considered in the next section, modularity pulls its weight in psychological theory, explains – as things are – the co-occurrence of the intuitive marks of subdoxastic states, and assists in the classification of difficult borderline cases.

Assessing the Proposal: Explanation and Classification

This is not the place for a general evaluation of the explanatory credentials of Fodor's modularity thesis. I shall assess the proposal that modularity is what underlies the subdoxastic domain in terms of just two criteria. First, what are the prospects for a satisfying explanation, in terms of modularity, of the intuitive marks of subdoxastic states? Secondly, what are the prospects for using the notion of modularity to plot a boundary through border territory? In fact, I shall restrict the application of the first criterion to the explanation of the inferential isolation of subdoxastic states.

What kind of account of the inferential isolation of subdoxastic states can be extracted from Fodor's modularity thesis, if we take subdoxastic states to be states of input systems? Recall that this isolation has two aspects. One aspect is that beliefs do not combine with subdoxastic states to yield further subdoxastic states. This aspect, let us agree, is to be explained in terms of the informational encapsulation of modules. After all, the similarity between informational encapsulation and this aspect of inferential isolation was one of the factors that originally made the proposal tempting.

The other aspect of inferential isolation is that subdoxastic states do not combine with beliefs to yield further beliefs. This is not explained simply by informational encapsulation. The mark of modularity which is most closely related to this aspect of inferential isolation is, rather, the relative inaccessibility to the central system of the interlevels of a module (Fodor, 1983, pp. 55–60).

Our example of this aspect of the inferential isolation of subdoxastic states from beliefs concerned the early stages of identification of spoken words. A person may hear a word beginning with an unvoiced consonant, and register the information that the voice onset time is, say, 25 milliseconds; and may also believe that if the next syllable has a voice onset time of 25 milliseconds, then it is time to prepare his lecture. But merely hearing the unvoiced consonant will not be enough for the person to draw the consequence that it is time to prepare his lecture.

Is this aspect of inferential isolation well explained by the relative inaccessibility to the central system of a module's interlevels? There are reasons to think not. (The reasons are closely related to arguments towards the end of the section on 'Accessibility to Consciousness', concerning the third challenge to the significance of accessibility to consciousness.)

The interlevel that is relevant to our example is one at which acoustic analysis is complete, but phonetic analysis is not. This interlevel is inaccessible to the central sytem in quite a strong sense. For there are pairs of sounds which differ acoustically just as much as a pair comprising a voiced and an unvoiced consonant, yet which are heard as indistinguishable. Differences in voice onset time, as such, are not phenomenologically accessible. But this does not account for the inferential isolation of states which register such differences.

One reason (cf. Fodor, 1983, pp. 59–60) is that even phenomenologically inaccessible differences can affect reaction times, and can be the basis for a conditioned response. So we need a further explanation as to why such differences do not bring about systematic changes in the web of beliefs.

A further reason for doubting that this notion of inaccessibility can do the required explanatory work here is that there can be interlevels of input systems which are phenomenologically accessible – in the sense that information at this level is reflected in the character of experience – but which still do not interact inferentially with the web of beliefs.

An alternative explanation seems to be required for this aspect of the inferential isolation of subdoxastic states from beliefs. There is a kind of ancillary explanation that is certainly available to the friend of modularity. It begins from the idea of an information-processing system with its own proprietary code or format. According to this idea, the code of the central processing system is the language of thought (see Fodor, 1987, pp. 135–54). A domain-specific input system will have its own proprietary code; or rather, it will have a series of codes in use at its various interlevels. Given this, a representational state at an intermediate level of analysis does not combine inferentially with beliefs, simply because it is not in the code or format over which the inferential processors of the central system operate.

However, although this kind of explanation is available, it is not clear that there is any very close connection between the idea of a proprietary code, and the several marks of Fodorian modularity. So, the availability of this ancillary explanation does not count towards a positive assessment of the proposal.

Let us turn to the second criterion for assessing the proposal. In the case of our knowledge of language, it is plausible that our knowledge of syntactic rules or principles will be classified on the side of the subdoxastic. And it is plausible that our knowledge of pragmatic principles belongs in the domain of propositional attitudes. The difficult borderline case is provided by semantic rules. (For some inconclusive arguments about the status of semantic rules, see Evans, 1981; Campbell, 1982.)

What are the prospects for using the notion of modularity to plot a boundary through this border territory? Clearly this is an empirical issue, heavily dependent upon the results of work in experimental psycholinguistics. But the prospects are not enhanced by the fact that modularity is defined in terms of a large class of characteristic features. For different characteristic features of modules suggest different ways of locating the interface between input systems and the central system.

We can see this kind of conflict at work in the case of vision. On the one hand, consider informational encapsulation. Sometimes it seems prima facie that a psychological process does draw upon the wealth of background information available in the central cognitive system. In these circumstances we can still defend the claim that there is a modular process operating. We argue that the locus of interaction is not the process within the module, but rather the output of the module. That is to say, we draw the boundary of the modular input system earlier in the total process. The less processing that is assigned to the input system itself, the easier it is to maintain that the input system is informationally encapsulated.

It is not surprising, then, that in his discussion of informational encapsulation Fodor says this about the visual input system (1983, p. 74):

> There is a great deal of evidence for context effects upon certain aspects of visual object recognition. But such evidence counts for nothing in the present discussion unless there is independent reason to believe that these aspects of object recognition are part of visual input analysis. Perhaps the input system for vision specifies the stimulus only in terms of 'primal sketches' . . .

Since the primal sketch is a very early state of visual processing in Marr's model, this suggestion for drawing the boundary of the input system will leave a great deal of what might reasonably be called visual processing to be performed by the central system.

On the other hand, while the interlevels of a module are supposed to be relatively inacccessible to the central system, the outputs of a module are supposed to be 'phenomenologically salient' (p. 87): 'It seems to me that we want a notion of perceptual process that makes the deliverances of perception available as the premises of conscious decisions and inferences'. This sits very happily with the picture of the input systems as presenting to the thinking subject candidates for belief. Given this picture, we are to see context effects as just one aspect of the intelligent process of assessing a candidate for belief in the light of background knowledge, before going forward in judgement. It is in this spirit that Fodor says (p. 94):

> various candidates [for the output of the visual processor] ... must ... be rejected on the grounds of phenomenological inaccessibility. I am thinking of such representations as Marr's 'primal', '2.5D', and '3D' sketch ... Such representations ... would seem to be too shallow. If we accept them as defining visual processor outputs, we shall have to say that even object recognition is not, strictly speaking, a phenomenon of visual perception, since, at these levels of representations, only certain geometric properties are specified. But, surely, from the point of view of phenomenological accessibility, perception is above all the recognition of objects and events.

Here, in the interests of defending the phenomenological salience of a module's outputs, we find that very much more processing is being assigned to the input system.

These conflicting pressures upon the boundaries of modularity are generated by the competing claims of informational encapsulation of processing and phenomenological salience of output. The net result is that Marr's 2.5D sketch and 3D sketch are left as borderline cases. This does nothing to enhance the prospects for using the taxonomy generated by the modularity thesis to settle the classification of difficult borderline cases as belonging to the domain of the subdoxastic or the domain of the attitudes.

In the case of language processing, there is a similar indeterminancy created by the different characteristic features of modularity. On the one hand, the condition of informational encapsulation suggests that a great deal of what might reasonably be called language processing is not, in fact, performed by the language system at all. The detection of irony is evidently not an encapsulated process (Fodor, 1983, p. 88); that is hardly controversial. But Fodor suggests, more radically, that the task of the language system might just be to classify a presented token as being of a certain syntactic type, and perhaps to assign it a logical form (p. 89).

> In short, if you are looking for an interesting property of utterances that might be computed by rigidly encapsulated systems – indeed, a property that might even be computed by largely bottom-to-top processors – then the type-identity of the utterance, together, perhaps, with its logical form would seem to be a natural candidate.

This assigns comparatively little work to the language system.

On the other hand, the output of the language input system is supposed to be phenomenologically salient. And as Fodor points out, when you hear someone's utterance in a language that you understand, you quite literally cannot help hearing what the speaker said: 'and it is what is *said* that one can't help hearing, not just what is *uttered*' (p. 55). If the output of an input system is supposed to be phenomenologically salient, then it is not merely syntax and logical form that is computed by the language system, but also content or message.

In the case of visual processing, the conflicting pressures on the boundaries of modularity leave indeterminate the status of every component of visual object recognition after the primal sketch. Similarly, in the case of language processing, those same conflicting pressures leave indeterminate the status of every component of utterance comprehension after the assignment of logical form. In particular, the status of systematic semantic processing is left indeterminate by all this.

As things stand, then, the proposal that modularity is what underlies the subdoxastic does not measure up to the second criterion of assessment: the prospects are not good for using modularity to plot a boundary through philosophical border territory. It might seem that the way forward is to relieve the conflict of pressures by allowing the boundaries of modularity to be dictated by considerations of informational encapsulation, setting aside the requirement of phenomenological salience (cf. Fodor, 1983, p. 136,n. 31). But, there would be a price to be paid for that relief. For the requirement of phenomenological salience of the output of modules – of the interface between input system and the central system – is very closely related to the ideas that the business of the central system is the fixation of belief, and that the central system corresponds to the domain of propositional attitudes. To give up that requirement, and with it those ideas, is to give up a good deal of what made the proposal tempting in the first place. Indeed, it seems inevitable that, if the boundaries of modularity are dictated solely in terms of informational encapsulation, then very much more will be assigned to the central system than belongs in the domain of the propositional attitudes.

We cannot give a positive assessment to the proposal that Fodorian modularity is what underlies the subdoxastic domain. The failure of the proposal does not, of course, count against the significance of the difference that inspired it – the difference between inferential integration and isolation. But I shall not pursue the question whether it is possible to rest the weight of a principled distinction between beliefs and subdoxastic states directly upon that difference. Instead, I shall sketch a proposal drawing upon the third intuitive difference between beliefs and prima facie examples of subdoxastic states; namely, that beliefs have their semantic contents conceptualized by the person whose beliefs they are, while this is not so for the contents of subdoxastic states.

Conceptualization and the Generality Constraint

Strawson (1959, p. 99) says that 'the idea of a predicate is correlative with that of a *range* of distinguishable individuals of which the predicate can be significantly, though not necessarily truly, affirmed.' This truth about predicates has its echo in the domain of thought. For a thinker to have the concept of being F, the thinker must know what it is for an object to be F – that is, what it is for an arbitrary object to be F. And, taken together with the idea that having a belief – or in general, entertaining a thought – involves deploying concepts, this echo of the truth about predication has an important consequence.

To believe that *a* is F – or even to entertain the thought that *a* is F – a thinker must have the concept of being F. If a thinker has that concept, then the thinker knows what it is for an arbitrary object to be F. So, if a thinker believes that *a* is F and is able to think about the object *b*, then the thinker is able to entertain the thought that *b* is F. In particular, if a thinker can be credited with the thought that *a* is F and the thought that *b* is G, then the thinker has the conceptual resources for also entertaining the thought that *a* is G and the thought that *b* is F. Thus, one consequence of the conceptualization of the contents of propositional attitude states is that the domain of thought contents available to a thinker exhibits a kind of closure property. Thoughts are essentially structured; they have consituents that can be recombined in further thoughts.

Evans (1982, pp. 100–5; cf. 1981, p. 338) connects the idea of conceptualization with what he calls the *Generality Constraint* upon the contents of attitude states (1982, p. 104):

If a subject can be credited with the thought that *a* is *F*, then he must have the conceptual resources for entertaining the thought that *a* is *G*, for every property of being *G* of which he has a conception.

We thus see the thought that *a* is *F* as lying at the intersection of two series of thoughts: on the one hand, the series of thoughts that *a* is *F*, that *b* is *F*, that *c* is *F* . . . and, on the other hand, the series of thoughts that *a* is *F*, that *a* is *G* that *a* is *H*.

The proposal to be considered now is that the Generality Constraint – or rather, the extension of the constraint to cover more than just subject-predicate thoughts – can provide for a principled distinction between the domain of propositional attitudes and the subdoxastic domain. Indeed, Evans himself makes the suggestion that the Generality Constraint marks a distinction between the contents of propositional attitude states and the contents of states involved in 'the information-processing that takes place in our brains' (Evans, 1982, p. 104, n.22; cf. Davies, 1986, pp. 143–6).

The basic point here is that the following possibility is open. A thinker may be able to entertain the thought that a is F, and may be in a subdoxastic state which has the content that b is G. Yet it may be that the thinker cannot entertain the thought that a is G – because he lacks the concept of being G, and it may be that there is no actual or possible subdoxastic state whose content is that a is G, because the system which processes the information that b is G simply does not contain information about the object a. This basic point illustrates the way in which the total domain of attitude states and subdoxastic states taken together can easily infringe the Generality Constraint.

It does not follow from the basic point that, if we simply focus on a single information-processing system, then we shall find actual infringements of the Generality Constraint. On the contrary, it is possible to imagine systems whose states are prima facie examples of subdoxastic states, but for which the following is true. If there are actual or potential states of the system which have the contents that a is F and that b is G, then there are further actual or potential states of the system which have the contents that a is G and that b is F. So, given this possibility, does the Generality Constraint fail, after all, to capture any important difference between attitude states and subdoxastic states?

The answer to this question depends upon the way in which the Generality Constraint is supposed to ground the distinction between the two domains. Suppose that it is claimed simply that the contents of attitude states exhibit the closure property, while the contents of subdoxastic states fail to exhibit that property. Then the kind of example just imagined would show that claim to be false. But the claim on behalf of the Generality Constraint does not have to be quite so simple.

In the imagined system, the contents of the states do, in fact, meet the closure condition. But still, the assignment of contents to those states does not depend upon that fact. The states' having those contents is one thing; their meeting the closure condition is another. In contrast, the assignment of a semantic content to an attitude state is immediately answerable to the Generality Constraint. To believe that a is F is *ipso facto* to exercise mastery of the concept of being F; and that piece of concept mastery can be exercised by the thinker in thoughts about other objects. Meeting the closure condition is an essential, rather than a contingent, feature of the contents of attitude states.

What emerges from the proposal is that a principled distinction between attitude states and subdoxastic states is to be grounded in a distinction between two notions of content (cf. Woodfield, 1986). The Generality Constraint is partly constitutive of the notion of conceptualized content, which is applicable to attitude states. But it is only accidentally related to the notion of content applicable to subdoxastic states. This emergent idea keeps us close to the third of the original intuitive differences between beliefs and prima facie examples of subdoxastic states. The Generality Constraint can simply be viewed as making explicit part of what is involved in mastery of concepts or conceptualization.

However, since those intuitive differences were introduced in our section on Chomsky (above), we have acknowledged (in the following section) a distinction between, on the one hand, representational states and, on the other hand, computational processes or procedures that are performed over those states. One consequence of this refinement is that the present proposal for a principled distinction between belief states and subdoxastic states will not immediately confirm our intuitive judgement that tacit knowledge of syntactic rules falls on the side of subdoxasticity.

The distinction between conceptualized and unconceptualized semantic content yields, in the first instance, a distinction among representational states. In this respect, it is similar to the putative distinction in terms of accessibility to consciousness. Indeed, the idea of a distinction based upon the accessibility or inaccessibility of the content of a representational state might be regarded as an attempt in the direction of the present proposal.

But knowledge of syntactic rules might be realized by the presence of a computational processor, rather than by the presence of a collection of representational states over which processes are performed. So the fact that the semantic contents of certain states of (at least) tacit knowledge are not conceptualized by the person in question is not decisive in assigning that knowledge to one side of a binary divide rather than the other.

The classification of some pieces of (at least) tacit knowledge is a derivative matter. It answers to the prior classification of the representational states which serve as inputs and outputs of the processors which realize the tacit knowledge. In the case of tacit knowledge of linguistic rules and principles, the prior classification turns directly upon the question of whether the descriptions of sentences by which the sentences are brought within the scope of linguistic generalizations are descriptions that are conceptualized by the person in question. No doubt, this derivative classification will still result in many pieces of linguistic knowledge being assigned to the subdoxastic side of the divide.

The corresponding question about the rule of *modus ponens*, for example, is whether the descriptions of the world which serve as premises for inferences falling under the rule are themselves conceptualized by the person in question. Since the answer to this question is affirmative, a thinker's knowledge of that rule will be classified derivately as belonging in the domain of attitude states rather than in the domain of subdoxastic states. It is in the former domain, rather than the latter, that the rule operates.

Speculative Conclusion

The proposal that we have just considered is relatively philosophical and aprioristic in character. The earlier – ultimately unsatisfactory – proposal that modularity is what underlies the subdoxastic domain is, in contrast, based on empirical psychological theory. It is natural to speculate as to whether there is an alternative to Fodor's schematic architecture of the mind, which would cohere more or less happily with the philosophical distinction in terms of conceptualization.

Fodor's characterization of 'the perceptual systems *plus language*' (1983, p. 44) as input systems has struck many readers as odd; for knowledge of language is used in production as well as in comprehension. There are only relatively few aspects of language processing – computing phonetic descriptions from acoustic descriptions, for example – which are specific to linguistic input processes. So, if the choice is between knowledge of language being embodied in a module – that is, an input system – and being part of the central system, then – it seems – we should say that knowledge of language belongs in the central system (cf. Chomsky, 1986, p. 14, n. 10).

Now, this sits ill with the picture of the central system as engaged in the business of belief fixation, with candidates for belief being furnished by input systems. But perhaps we have to forsake that picture anyway. For that picture coheres with some of the marks of modularity, but not with others. In particular, it coheres with the phenomenological salience of the outputs of modules; but considerations of informational encapsulation – the essence of modularity – conspire to set the boundaries of modularity far nearer the sensory surfaces.

Suppose that we accept the apparent consequences of those more essential considerations. Then there is a new picture which can be sketched using materials that we have been obliged to use in earlier stages of this exploration. The new picture retains a division between informationally encapsulated modules and a central system; but the central system is engaged in more business than the fixation of belief.

Some of the representational states of the central system are attitude states, and some are not. As a philosopher would put it: some of the states of the central system have their contents conceptualized by the person in question, and some do not. A scientific psychological account will (partially) reconstruct the distinction as a difference between representational states in the language of thought, and states in other codes or formats. (As we noticed above, this difference is not essentially connected with Fodorian modularity.)

In this new picture, there are many different kinds of processes operating in the central system. There are ordinary inferential processes – such as *modus ponens* – which have sentences in the language of thought as both their inputs and their outputs. These processes link the representational states whose code is the language of thought into an integrated inferential web. There are other processes which effect transitions between formulas in one code and formulas in some other code. Some of these have as their input code, or as their output code, the language of thought. Some processes may be bi-directional.

There could be a processor which effects or constrains transitions back and forth between, say, representational states in a proprietary code for describing the syntactic properties of English sentences and representational states in the language of thought. The presence of such a processor could realize tacit knowledge of a particular set of linguistic rules, principles or generalizations.

In this way, according to the new picture, tacit knowlege of linguistic rules could be realized in the central system. The rules would not have to be explicitly represented in any representational state of the system. Still less would knowledge of the rules be realized in a state of the same kind as an attitude state. Nor would linguistic rules be indistinguishable, on this account, from ordinary rules of inference; for they would be differentiated by their characteristic input and output domains.

Such promise makes the picture initially attractive. Needless to say, its philosophical and empirical credentials will not be corroborated here.

References

Campbell, J. (1982). Knowledge and understanding. *Philosophical Quarterly* 32, 17–34.

Chomsky, N. (1965) *Aspects of the Theory of Syntax*.Cambridge, Mass., MIT Press.

Chomsky, N. (1972) *Language and Mind*. New York, Harcourt Brace Jovanovich.

Chomsky, N. (1976) *Reflections on Language*. London, Fontana/Collins.

Chomsky, N. (1980a) *Rules and Representations*. Oxford, Basil Blackwell.

Chomsky, N. (1980b) Rules and representations (with open peer commentary and author's response). *Behavioral and Brain Sciences* 13, 1–61.

Chomsky, N. (1986) *Knowledge of Language: Its Nature, Origin, and Use*. New York, Praeger.

Chomsky, N. (1987) Replies to Alexander George and Michael Brody. *Mind and Language* 2, 178–97.,

Davies, M. (1986) Tacit knowledge, and the structure of thought and language. In C.Travis (ed.), *Meaning and Interpretation*, pp. 127–58. Oxford, Basil Blackwell.

Davies, M. (1987) Tacit knowledge and semantic theory: can a five per cent difference matter?*Mind* 96, 441–62.

Dennett, D.C. (1983) Styles of mental representation. *Proceedings of the Aristotelian Society* 83, 213–26.

Evans G. (1981) Semantic theory and tacit knowledge. In S. Holtzmann and C. Leich (eds), *Wittgenstein: To Follow a Rule*. London, Routledge and Kegan Paul. Reprinted in *Collected Papers*, pp. 332–42. Oxford, Oxford University Press, 1985.

Evans, G. (1982) *The Varieties of Reference*. Oxford, Oxford University Press.

Fisher, J. (1974) Knowledge of rules. *Review of Metaphysics* 28, 237–60.

Fodor, J. (1983) *The Modularity of Mind*. Cambridge, Mass., MIT Press.

Fodor, J. (1987) *Psychosemantics*. Cambridge, Mass,. MIT Press.

Lycan, W.G. (1986) Tacit belief. In R. Bogdan (ed.), *Belief: Form, Content and Function*, pp. 61–82. Oxford, Oxford University Press.

Peacocke, C. (1983) *Sense and Content*. Oxford, Oxford University Press.

Peacocke, C. (1986) Explanation in computational psychology: language, perception and level 1.5. *Mind and Language* 1, 101–23.

Peacocke, C. (1989) When is a grammar psychologically real? In A. George (ed.), *Reflections on Chomsky*, pp. 111–30. Oxford, Basil Blackwell.

Polanyi, M. (1967) *The Tacit Dimension*. London, Routledge and Kegan Paul.

Quine, W.V.O. (1972) Methodological reflections on current linguistic theory. In D. Davidson and G. Harman (eds), *Semantics of Natural Language*, pp. 442–54. Dordrecht, D. Reidel.

Sterelny, K. (1987) Review of Peacocke, *Sense and Content. Philosophical Review* 96, 581–5.

Stich, S. (1978) Beliefs and subdoxastic states. *Philosophy of Science* 45, 499–518.

Stich, S. (1980) What every speaker cognizes. *Behavioral and Brain Sciences* 3, 39–40.

Strawson, P.F. (1959) *Individuals*. London, Methuen.

Woodfield, A. (1986) Two categories of content. *Mind and Language* 1, 319–54.

19

Consciousness, Explanatory Inversion and Cognitive Science

John R. Searle

Some years ago I wrote an article (Searle 1980a, b) criticizing what I call 'strong AI', the view that for a system to have mental states it is sufficient for the system to implement the right sort of program with the right inputs and outputs. Strong AI is rather easy to refute; the basic argument can be summarized in one sentence: a system, me for example, could implement a program for understanding Chinese, for example, without understanding any Chinese at all. This idea, when developed, became known as the Chinese Room Argument.

There is a lot more to be said, and I have tried to say some of it. The debate still continues. Though many interesting points have emerged, I think the original argument is quite decisive. In my view, 'weak AI', the use of computers to model or simulate mental processes, is untouched by this argument. Weak AI continues and, in its connectionist incarnation, at least, is flourishing. But strong AI is now primarily of historical interest, though it survives as a sociological phenomenon.

At the time I wrote that article, I thought the major mistake we were making in cognitive science was to think that the mind is a computer program implemented in the hardware of the brain. I now believe the underlying mistake is much deeper: we have neglected the centrality of consciousness to the study of the mind. In this chapter I will have nothing more to say about the Chinese Room Argument. I assume that it refutes strong AI, but nothing that follows depends on that assumption.

If you come to cognitive science, psychology or the philosophy of mind with an innocent eye, the first thing that strikes you is how little serious attention is paid to consciousness. Few people in cognitive science think that the study of the mind is essentially or in large part a matter of studying conscious phenomena; consciousness is rather a 'problem', a difficulty that functionalist or computationalist theories must somehow deal with. Now, how did we get into this mess? How can we have neglected the most important feature of the mind in those disciplines that are officially dedicated to its study? There are complicated historical reasons for this, but the basic reason is that since Descartes, we have, for the most part, thought that consciousness was not an appropriate subject for a serious science or scientific philosophy of mind. As recently as a few years ago, if one raised the subject of consciousness in cognitive science discussions, it was generally regarded as a form of bad taste, and graduate students, who are always attuned to the social mores of their disciplines, would roll their eyes at the ceiling and assume expressions of mild disgust.

When consciousness is no longer regarded as a suitable topic for scientific discussion, then something else must take its place and in this case that is obviously the *unconscious*. The idea is that there are unconscious processes, these account for our cognitive capacities, and the task of cognitive science is to lay bare their structure. But what exactly is the notion of the unconscious used in these discussions? Since Freud (1915) we have grown so used to talking about the unconscious that we have ceased to regard it as problematic. The naive notion of the unconscious that we have inherited from Freud is that unconscious mental states are just the same as conscious mental states only minus the consciousness. But what exactly is that supposed to mean? Pre-theoretically, I believe most people follow Freud in thinking that an unconscious mental state has exactly the same shape it has when conscious. Naively, we tend to think of unconscious mental states like furniture stored in the dark attic of the mind or like fish deep beneath the surface of the sea. The furniture and the fish have the same shape when invisible that they have when visible; it is just that it is impossible to see them in their unconscious form. Furthermore, somewhere between Freud and Chomsky an important shift took place: Freud apparently regarded unconscious mental states as at least potentially conscious. They may be, for one reason or another, too deeply repressed for the patient to bring them to consciousness without professional assistance, but there is nothing in principle inaccessible to consciousness about the Freudian unconscious. When we get to more recent writers, however, it turns out that many of the mental processes which their theories postulate are in principle inaccessible to consciousness.[1]And it is but a short step from the belief that we are dealing with unconscius mental processes to the belief that these processes are computational, and to the belief that the mind is a computer program operating in the hardware or wetware of the brain.

But, to repeat, what exactly is the conception of unconscious mental processes which is supposed to account for, say, visual information – processing or language – understanding? How, for example, are we to distinguish between *un*conscious *mental* phenomena in the brain and those *non*conscious phenomena in the brain which are not mental at all, but are just blind, brute, neurophysiological states and processes? How do we distinguish, for example, between my unconscious belief that Denver is the capital of Colorado when I am not thinking about it and the non-conscious myelination of my axons? Both are features of my brain, but one is in some sense mental and the other is not. The answer to the question is by no means obvious.

The Connection Principle

This chapter has two aims. First, I want to show that we have no notion of an unconscious mental state except in terms of its accessibility to consciousness. Secondly, I will attempt to lay bare some of the implications of this thesis for the study of the mind.

The first task is to demonstrate what I will call the 'Connection Principle'.[2] It can be stated in a preliminary fashion as follows. The ascription of an unconscious intentional phenomenon to a system implies that the phenomenon is in principle accessible to consciousness. I leave some of this deliberately vague, particularly what is meant by 'in principle', but I will try to transform this vagueness into clarity in the course of discussion. To substantiate this claim, I will also have to explore the notion of an unconscious mental state.

Before launching into the argument, I need to remind the reader of the distinctions between ontology, causation and epistemology. For any phenomenon, but for biological phenomena especially, we need to know:

1 What is its mode of existence? (ontology)
2 What does it do? (causation)
3 How do we find out about it? (epistemology)

So, for example, if we were examining the heart, the answer to our three questions would be (1) the heart is a large piece of muscle tissue located in the chest cavity (ontology); (2) the heart functions to pump blood throughout the body (causation); and (3) we find out about the heart indirectly through such methods as using stethoscopes, cardiograms and taking pulse, and directly by opening up the chest cavity and looking at the heart (epistemology). These distinctions also apply to both conscious and unconscious mental states.

The argument for the Connection Principle is in six steps.

Step 1 *There is a distinction between intrinsic and as-if intentionality*. We often make metaphorical attributions of intentionality to systems where the system does not literally have that intentional state or, indeed, any mental life at all. I can, for example, say of my lawn that it is thirsty, just as I can say of myself that I am thirsty. But it is obvious that my lawn has no mental states whatever. When I say that it is thirsty, this is simply a metaphorical way of describing its capacity to absorb water. Whereas when I say 'I am thirsty' I am describing an intrinsic mental state in me. We often make such metaphorical attributions of 'as-if' intentionality to artifacts: We say such things as, 'The carburetor of the car *knows* how rich to make the mixture'; 'The thermostat on the wall *perceives* changes in the temperature'; 'The calculator *follows rules* of arithmetic when it does addition'; and 'The Little Engine That Could is *trying very hard* to make it up the mountain.' None of these various attributions is meant to be taken literally, however. To mark this distinction, I say of my thirst that it is a form of intrinsic intentionality, but I say of the attribution of thirst to my lawn that it is only a metaphorical or *as-if* attribution. *As-if*, strictly speaking, is not a type of intentionality, but a type of attribution. (For an extended discussion of this issue see Searle, 1984b.)

I have seen efforts to deny this distinction, but it is very hard to take them seriously. If you think there is no principled difference, you might consider the following from the journal *Pharmacology*:

> Once the food is past the crico-pharyngus sphincter, its movement is almost entirely involuntary except for the final expulsion of feces during defecation. *The gastrointestinal tract is a highly intelligent organ that senses* not only the presence of food in the lumen but also its chemical composition, quantity, vicosity and adjusts the rate of propulsion and mixing by producing appropriate patterns of contractions. *Due to its highly developed decision making ability*, the gut wall comprised of the smooth muscle layers, the neuronal structures and paracrine-endocrine cells *is often called the gut brain*. (Sarna and Otterson, 1988, p. 8, my italics)[3]

This is clearly a case of as-if intentionality in the 'gut brain'. Now does anyone think that there is no principled difference between the gut brain and the brain brain? I have heard it said that both sorts of cases are the same; that it is all a matter of taking an 'intentional stance' towards a system. But just try in real life to suppose that the 'perception' and the 'decision-making' of the gut brain are no different from the real brain.

This example reveals, among other things, that any attempt to deny the distinction between intrinsic and as-if intentionality faces a general *reductio ad absurdum*. If you deny the distinction it turns out that everything in the universe has intentionality. Everything in the universe follows laws of nature, and for that reason everything behaves with a certain degree of regularity, and for that reason everything behaves *as-if* it were following a rule, trying to carry out a certain project, acting in accordance with certain desires, and so on. For example, suppose I drop a stone. The stone *tries* to reach the center of the earth, because it *wants* to reach the center of the earth, and in so doing it *follows the rule* $S = \frac{1}{2} g t^2$. The price of denying the distinction between intrinsic and as-if intentionality, in short, is absurdity, because it makes everything in the universe mental.

No doubt there are marginal cases. About grasshoppers or fleas, for example, we may not be quite sure what to say. And no doubt, even in some human cases we might be puzzled as to whether we should take the ascription of intentionality literally or metaphorically. But marginal cases do not alter the distinction between those facts corresponding to ascriptions of intrinsic intentionality and those corresponding to as-if, metaphorical ascriptions of intentionality. There is nothing harmful, misleading or philosophically mistaken about as-if metaphorical asscriptions. The only mistake is to take them literally.

Step 2. *Intrinsic intentional states, whether conscious or unconscious, always have aspectual shapes.* I am introducing the term of art, 'aspectual shape', to mark a universal feature of intentionality. It can be explained as follows: whenever we perceive anything or think about anything, it is always under some aspects and no others that we perceive or think about that thing. These aspectual features are essential to the intentional state; they are part of what makes it the mental state that it is. Aspectual shape is most obvious in the case of conscious perceptions; think of seeing a car, for example. When you see a car it is not simply a matter of an object being registered by your perceptual apparatus; rather you actually have a conscious experience of the object from a certain point of view and with certain features. You see the car as having a certain shape, as having a certain color, and so forth. And what is true of conscious perceptions is true of intentional states generally. A man may believe, for example, that the star in the sky is the Morning Star without believing that it is the Evening Star. A man may, for example, want to drink a glass of water without wanting to drink a glass of H_2O. There is strictly an infinite number of true descriptions of the Evening Star and of a glass of water, but something is believed or desired about them only under certain aspects and not under others. Every belief and every desire, and indeed every intentional phenomenon, has an aspectual shape.

Notice also that the aspectual shape must matter to the agent. It is, for example, from the agent's point of view that he can want water without wanting H_2O. In the case of conscious thoughts, the way the aspectual shape matters is that it constitutes the way the agent thinks about or experiences a subject matter. I can think about my thirst for a drink of water without thinking at all about its chemical composition. I can think of it *as* water without thinking of it *as* H_2O.

It is reasonably clear how this works for conscious thoughts and experiences, but how does it work for unconscious mental states? One way to get at our question is to ask what fact about an unconscious mental state makes it have the particular aspectual shape that it has, that is, what fact about it makes it the mental state that it is?

Step 3.   *The aspectual feature cannot be exhaustively or completely characterized solely in terms of third person, behavioral or even neurophysiological predicates. None of these is sufficient to give an exhaustive account of aspectual shape.* Behavioral evidence concerning the existence of mental states, including even evidence concerning the causation of a person's behavior, no matter how complete, always leaves the aspectual character of intentional states underdetermined. There will always be an inferential gulf between the behavioral *epistemic* grounds for the presence of the aspect and the *ontology* of the aspect itself.

A person may indeed exhibit water-seeking behavior, but any water-seeking behavior will also be H_2O – seeking behavior. So there is no way the behavior, construed without reference to a mental component, can constitute wanting water rather than wanting H_2O. Notice that it is not enough to suggest that we might get the person to respond affirmatively to the question. 'Do you want water?' and negatively to the question. 'Do you want H_2O?' because the affirmative and negative responses are themselves insufficient to fix the aspectual shape under which the person interprets the question and the answer. There is no way just from the behavior to determine whether the person means by 'H_2O' what I mean by 'H_2O' and whether the person means by 'water' what I mean by 'water'. No set of behavioral facts can constitute the fact that the person represents what he wants under one aspect and not under the other. This is not an epistemic point.

It is equally true, though less obvious, that no set of neurophysiological facts under neurophysiological descriptions constitutes aspectual facts. Even if we have a perfect science of the brain, and even if such a perfect science of the brain allowed us to put our brain-o-scope on the person's skull and see that he wanted water but not H_2O, all the same there would still be an inference, we would still have to have some law-like connection that would enable us to infer from our observations of the neural architecture and neuron firings that they were realizations of the desire for water and not of the desire for H_2O.

Since the neurophysiological facts are always causally sufficient for any set of mental facts,[4] someone with perfect causal knowledge might be able to make the inference from the neurophysiological to the intentional at least in those few cases where there is a law-like connection between the facts specified in neural terms and the facts specified in intentional terms. But even in these cases, if there are any, there is still an *inference*, and the specification of the neurophysiological in neurophysiological terms is not yet a specification of the intentional.

Step 4. *But the ontology of unconscious mental states, at the time they are unconscious, consists entirely in the existence of purely neurophysiological phenomena.* Imagine that a man is in a sound dreamless sleep. Now, while he is in such a state it is true to say of him that he has a number of unconscious mental states. For example, he believes that Denver is the capital of Colorado, Washington is the capital of the United States, and so on: but *what fact about him makes it the case that he has these unconscious beliefs?* Well, the only facts that could exist while he is completely unconscious are neurophysiological facts. The only things going on in his unconscious brain are sequences of neurophysiological events occurring in neuronal architectures. At the time when the states are totally unconscious there is simply nothing there except neurophysiological states and processes.

Now we seem to have a contradiction, however: the ontology of unconscious intentionality consists entirely in third person, objective, neurophysiological phenomena, but all the same states have an aspectual shape that cannot be constituted by such facts, because there is no aspectual shape at the level of neurons and synapses.

I believe there is only one solution to this puzzle. The apparent contradicition is resolved by pointing out that:

Step 5. *The notion of an unconscious intentional state is the notion of a state that is a possible conscious thought or experience.* There are plenty of unconscious mental phenomena, but to the extent that they are genuinely *intentional* they must in some sense preserve their aspectual shape even when unconscious; but the only sense we can give to the notion that they preserve their aspectual shape when unconscious is that they are possible contents of consciousness.

This is our first main conclusion. But the answer to our first question immediately gives rise to another question: What is meant by 'possible' in the previous two sentences? After all, it might be quite *impossible* for the state to occur consciously, because of brain lesion, repression or other causes. So in what sense exactly must it be a possible content of a thought or experience? This question leads to our next conclusion, which is really a further explanation of Step 5, and is implied by 4 and 5 together.

Step 6. *The ontology of the unconscious consists in objective features of the brain capable of causing subjective conscious thoughts.* When we describe something as an unconscious intentional state we are characterizing an objective *ontology* in virtue of its *causal* capacity to produce consciousness. But the existence of these causal features is consistent with the fact that in any given case their causal powers may be blocked by some other interfering causes, such as psychological repression or brain damage.

The possibility of interference by various forms of pathology does not alter the fact that any unconscious intentional state is the sort of thing that is in principle accessible to consciousness. It may be unconscious not only in the sense that it does not *happen* to be conscious then and there, but also in the sense that for one reason or another the agent simply *could not* bring it to consciousness; but it must be the *sort of thing* that can be brought to consciousness because its ontology is that of neurophysiology characterized in terms of its capacity to cause consciousness.

Paradoxically, the naive mentalism of my view of the mind leads to a kind of dispositional analysis of unconscious mental phenomena; only it is not a disposition to behavior, but a disposition – if that is really the right word – to conscious thoughts, including conscious thoughts manifested in behavior. This is paradoxical, even ironic, because the notion of a dispositional account of the mental was introduced precisely to get rid of the appeal to consciousness. I am, in effect, trying to turn this tradition on its head by arguing that unconscious beliefs are indeed dispositional states of the brain, but they are dispositions to produce conscious thoughts and conscious behavior. This sort of dispositional ascription of causal capacities is quite familiar to us from common sense. When, for example, we say of a substance that it is bleach or poison we are ascribing to a chemical ontology a dispositional causal capacity to produce certain effects. Similarly, when we say of the man who is unconcious that he believes that Clinton is president we are ascribing to a neurobiological ontology the dispositional causal capacity to produce conscious effects with specific aspectual shapes. The concept of unconscious intentionality is thus that of a *latency* relative to its *manifestation* in consciousness.

To summarize: the argument for the connection principle was somewhat complex but its underlying thrust was quite simple. Just ask yourself what fact about the world is supposed to correspond to your claims. Now when you make a claim about unconscious intentionality there are no facts that bear on the case except neurophysiological facts. There is nothing else there except neurophysiological states and processes describable in neurophysiological terms. But intentional states, conscious or unconscious, have aspectual shapes, and there is no aspectual shape at the level of the neurons. So the only fact about the neurophysiological structures that corresponds to the ascription of intrinsic aspectual shape is the fact that the system has the causal capacity to produce conscious states and processes where those specific aspectual shapes are manifest.

The overall picture that emerges is this: there is nothing going on in my brain but neurophysiological processes, some conscious, some unconscious. Of the unconscious neurophysiological processes, some are mental and some are not. The difference between them is not in consciousness, because, by hypothesis, neither is conscious; the difference is that the mental processes are candidates for consciousness, because they are capable of causing conscious states. But what in my brain is my 'mental life'? It is just two things: conscious states and those neurophysiological states and processes that – given the right circumstances – are capable of generating conscious states. Lets call those states that are in principle accessible to consciousness 'shallow unconscious' and those inaccessible even in principle 'deep unconscious'. Our first con- clusion is that there are no deep unconscious intentional states.

The Inversion of the Explanation

I believe that the Connection Principle has some quite striking consequences. To anticipate a bit, I will argue that many of our explanations in cognitive science lack the explanatory force we thought they had. To rescue what can be salvaged from them we will have to perform an inversion on their logical structure analogous to the inversion that Darwinian models of biological explanation forced on the old teleological biology which preceded Darwin. In our skulls there is just the brain with all of its intricacy, and consciousness with all its color and variety. The brain produces the conscious states that are occurring in you and me right now, and it has the capacity to produce lots more which are not occurring. But that is it. Where the mind is concerned that is the end of the story. There are brute, blind, neurophysiological processes and there is consciousness; but there is nothing else. If we are looking for phenomena which are intrinsically intentional but inaccessible in principle to consciousness there is nothing there: no rule-following, no mental information processing, no unconscious inferences, no mental models, no primal sketches, no $2\frac{1}{2}$D images, no three-dimensional descriptions, no language of thought and no universal grammar. In what follows, I will argue that the entire cognitivist story which postulates all these inaccessible mental phenomena is based on a pre-Darwinian conception of the function of the brain.

Consider the case of plants and the consequences of the Darwinian revolution for the explanatory apparatus we use to account for plant behavior. Prior to Darwin it was common to anthropomorphize plant behavior and say things such as the plant turns its leaves toward the sun in order to aid in its survival. The plant *wants* to survive and flourish, and in order *to do so* it follows the sun. On this pre-Darwinian conception there was supposed to be a level of intentionality in the behavior of the plant. But this level of supposed intentionality has been replaced by two other levels of explanation, a 'hardware' level and a 'functional' level. At the hardware level we have discovered that the actual movements of the plant's leaves in following the sun are caused by the secretion of a specific hormone, auxin. Variable secretions of auxin are quite sufficient to account for the plant's behavior, without any extra hypothesis of intentionality. Notice furthermore that this behavior plays a crucial role in the plant's survival, and at the functional level we can say things such as that the light-seeking behavior of the plant functions to help the plant survive and reproduce.

The original intentionalist explanation of the plant's behavior turned out to be false, but it was not just false. If we get rid of the intentionality and invert the order of the explanation, the intentionalistic claim emerges as trying to say something true. To be sure that what happened is absolutely clear, I want to show how in replacing the original intentionalistic explanation by a combination of the mechanical hardware explanation and a functional explanation, we are inverting the explanatory structure of the original intentionalistic explanation:

(a) The original intentionalists explanation: *because it wants to survive*, the plant turns its leaves towards the sun or *in order to survive* the plant turns its leaves towards the sun.

(b) The mechanical hardware explanation: variable secretions of auxin cause plants to turn their leaves toward the sun.

(c) The functional explanation: plants that are going to turn their leaves toward the sun anyway *are more likely to survive than plants that do not*.

In (a) the form of the explanation is teleological and the *representation* of the goal, survival, functions as the *cause* of the behavior, turning toward the sun. But in (c) the teleology is eliminated and the behavior that now, by (b) has a mechanical explanation, causes the brute fact of survival, which is now no longer a goal but just an effect that happens.

The moral I will later draw from the entire discussion can now be stated at least in a preliminary form: *where non-conscious processes are concerned we are still anthropomorphizing the brain in a way that we were anthropomorphizing plants before the Darwinian revolution*. It is easy to see why we make the mistake of anthropomorphizing the brain; it is after all the home of anthropods. But to ascribe a vast array of intentional phenomena to a system where the conditions on that ascription are being violated is still a mistake. Just as the plant has no intentional states because it does not meet the conditions for having intentional states, so those brain processes which are in principle inaccessible to consciousness have no intentionality, because they do not meet the conditions for having intentionality. The ascriptions of intentionality we make to processes in the

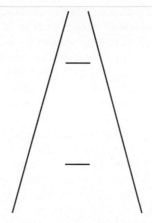

Figure 19.1.   The Ponzo illusion. The upper of the two equal and parallel lines is generally seen as longer.

brain which are in principle inaccessible to consciousness are either metaphorical, like metaphorical ascriptions of mental states to plants, or they are false, as our ascriptions to plants would be false if we tried to take them literally. Notice, however, that they are not *just* false; they are trying to say something true, and to get at what is true in them we have to do the same inversion of the explanation in cognitive science that we did for plant biology.

To work out this thesis in detail we will have to consider some specific cases. I will start with theories of perception and then proceed to theories of language in order to show what a cognitive science which respects the facts of the brain and the facts of consciousness might look like.

Irvin Rock concludes his excellent book on perception (Rock 1984) with the following observations:

> Although perception is autonomous with respect to such higher mental faculties as are exhibited in conscious thought and in the use of conscious knowledge, I would still argue that it is intelligent. By calling perception 'intelligent' I mean to say that it is based on such thoughtlike mental processes as description, inference, and problem solving, although these processes are rapid-fire, unconscious, and nonverbal . . . 'Inference' implies that certain perceptual properties are computed from given sensory information using unconsciously known rules. For example, perceived size is inferred from the object's visual angle, its perceived distance, and the law of geometrical optics relating the visual angle to object distance. (p. 234)

But now let us apply to this thesis to the explanation of the Ponzo illusion as an obvious example. Though the two parallel lines are equal in length, the top line looks longers (figure 19.1). Why? According to the standard explanation, the agent is unconsciously following two rules and making two unconscious inferences. The first rule is that converging lines from lower to higher in the visual field imply greater distance in the direction of the convergence and the second is that objects that occupy equal portions of the retinal image vary in perceived size depending on perceived distance from the observer (Emmert's Law). On this account, the agent unconsciously infers that the top parallel line is further away because of its position in relation to the converging lines; secondly, he or she infers that the top line is larger because it is further away. Thus there are two rules and two unconscious inferences, none of whose operations is accessible to consciousness, even in principle. It should be pointed out that this explanation is controversial and there are lots of objections to it (see Rock, 1984, pp. 156ff). But the point here is that the *form* of the explanation is not challenged and that is what I am challenging now. I am interested in this type of explanation, not just in the details of this example.

There is no way that this type of explanation can be made consistent with the Connection Principle. You can see this if you ask yourself which facts in the brain are supposed to correspond to the ascription of all these unconscious mental processes. We know that there are conscious visual experiences and we know that these are caused by brain processes, but where is the addiitonal mental level supposed to be in this case? Indeed, in this exam[ple it is very hard to interpret it literally at all without a homunculus; we are postulating logical operations performed over retinal images, but who is supposed to be performing these operations? Close inspection reveals that in its very form this explanation is anthropomorphizing the non-conscious processes in the brain in the same way that the pre-Darwinian explanations of plant behavior anthropo-morphized the non-conscious operations of the plant.

The problem is not, as is sometimes claimed, that we lack sufficient empirical evidence for the postulation of mental processes which are in principle inaccessible to consciousness; rather, it is not at all clear what the postulation is supposed to mean. We cannot make it coherent with what we know about the nature of mental states and the operation of the brain. We think, in our pathetic ignorance about brain functioning, that some day an advanced brain science will locate all these unconscious intelligent processes for us. But you only have to imagine the details of a perfect science of the brain to see that even if we had such a science there could be no place in it for the postulation of such processes. A perfect science of the brain would be stated in neurophysiological (i.e. hardware) vocabulary. There would be several hard-ware levels of description, and, as with the plant, there would also be functional levels of description. These functional levels would identify those features of the hardware that we find interesting in the same way that our functioning descriptions of the plant identify those hardware operations in which we take an interest. But just as the plant knows nothing of survival, so the non-conscious operations of the brain know nothing of inference, rule-following or size and distance judgments. We attribute these functions to the hardware relative to our interests, but there are no additional mental facts involved in the functional attributions.

The crucial difference between the brain on the one hand and the plant on the other is this: the brain has an intrinsically mental level of description because at any given point it is causing actual conscious events and is capable of causing further conscious events. Because the brain has both conscious and unconscious mental states we are also inclined to suppose that in the brain there are mental states which are intrinsically inaccessible to consciousness. But this thesis is incoherent, and we need to make the same inversion in these sorts of explanations that we made in the explanation of the plant's behavior. Instead of saying, 'We see the top line as larger because we are unconsciously following two rules and making two inferences', we should say: 'We consciously see the top line as farther away and larger.' Period. End of the intentionalistic story.

As with the plant there is also a functional story and a (largely unknown) mechanical hardware story. The brain functions in such a way that lines converging above appear to be going away from us in the direction of the convergence and objects which produce retinal images of the same size will appear to vary in size if they are perceived to be at different distances away from us. *But there is no mental content whatever at this functional level.* In such cases, the system functions to cause certain sorts of conscious intentionality, but the causing is not itself intentional. And the point, to repeat, is not that the ascription of deep unconscious intentionality is insufficiently supported by empirical evidence: It is incoherent, in the sense that it cannot be made to cohere with what we already know to be the case.

'Well,' you might say, 'the distinction does not really make much difference to cognitive science. We continue to say what we have always said and do what we have always done; we simply substitute the word 'functional' for the word 'mental' in these cases. And this is a substitution many of us have been doing unconsciously anyway since many of us tend to use these words interchangeably.'

I think the claim I am making does have important implications for cognitive science research, because by inverting the order of explanation we get a differenct account of cause-and-effect relations, and in so doing we radically alter the structure of psychological explanation. In what follows, I have two aims: I want to develop the original claim that cognitive science requires an inversion of the explanation comparable to the inversion achieved by evolutionary biology and I want to show some of the consequences that this inversion would have for the conduct of our research.

I believe the mistake persists largely because we lack hardware explanations of the auxin type. I want to explain the inversion in a case where we have something like a hardware explanation. Anyone who has seen home movies taken from a moving car is struck by how much more the world jumps around in the movie than it does in real life. Why? Imagine that you are driving on a bumpy road. You consciously keep your eyes fixed on the road and the other traffic even though the car and its contents, including your body, are bouncing around. In addition to your conscious efforts to keep your eye on the road something else is happening unconsciously; your eyeballs are constantly moving inside their sockets in such a way as to help you continue to focus on the road. You can try the experiment right now by simple focusing on the page in front of you and shaking your head from side to side and up and down.

Now in the car case it is tempting to think we are following an unconscious rule, as a first approximation: move the eyeballs in the eye sockets relative to the rest of the head in such a way as to keep vision focused on the intended object. Notice that the predicitions of this rule are non-trivial. Another way to do it would have been to keep the eyes fixed in their sockets and move the head, and in fact some birds keep retinal stability in this way. (If an owl could drive, this is how it would have to do it, since its eyeballs are fixed.) So we have two levels of intentionality:

A conscious intention: keep your visual attention on the road.

A deep unconscious rule: make eyeball movements in relation to the eye sockets that are equal and opposite to head movements in order to keep the retinal image stable.

In this case the result is conscious, though the means for achieving it are unconscious. But the unconscious aspect has all the earmarks of intelligent behavior. It is complex, flexible, goal-directed; it involves information-processing and has a potentially infinite generative capacity. That is, the system takes in information about body movements and prints out instructions for eyeball movements, and there is no limit on the number of possible combinations of eyeball movements the system can generate. Furthermore, the system can learn because the rule can be systematically modified by putting magnifying or miniaturizing spectacles on the agent. And without much difficulty one could tell any standard cognitive science story about the unconscious behavior: a story about information-processing, the language of thought and computer programs, just to mention obvious examples. I leave it to readers as a five-finger exercise to work out the story according to their favourite cognitive science paradigm.

The problem, however, is that all these stories are false. What actually happens is that fluid movements in the semi-circular canals of the inner ear trigger a sequence of neuron firings that enter the brain over the eighth cranial nerve. These signals follow two parallel pathways, one of which can 'learn' and one of which cannot. The pathways are in the brain stem and cerebellum and they transform the initial input signals to provide motor output 'commands', via motorneurons that connect to the eye muscles and cause eyeball movements. The whole system contains feedback mechanisms for error correction. It is called the vestibulo ocular reflex (VOR) (Lisberger, 1988; Lisberger and Pavelko, 1988). The actual hardware mechanism of the VOR has no more intentionality or intelligence than the movement of the plant's leaves due to the secretion of auxin. The appearance of an unconscious rule being followed, unconscious information-processing, and so on is an optical illusion. All the intentional ascriptions are *as-if*. So here is how the inversion of the explanation goes. Instead of saying:

Intentional: To keep my retinal image stable and thus improve my vision while my head is moving, I follow the deep unconscious rule of eyeball movement.

We should say:

Hardware: When I look at an object while my head is moving, the hardware mechanism of the VOR moves my eyeballs.

Functional: The VOR movement keeps the retinal image stable and this helps to improve my vision.

Now why is this shift so important? In any scientific explanation, among other things, we are trying to say exactly what causes what. In the traditional cognitive science paradigms there is supposed to be a deep unconscious mental cause and it is supposed to produce a desired effect, such as perceptual judgments, or grammatical sentences. But the inversion eliminates this mental cause altogether. There is nothing there except a brute physical mechanism that produces a brute physical effect. These mechanisms and effects are describable at different levels but none of them so far is mental. The apparatus of the VOR functions to improve visual efficiency, but the only intentionality is the conscious perception of the object. All the rest of the work is done by the brute physical mechanism of the VOR. So the inversion radically alters the ontology of cognitive science explanation by eliminating a whole level of deep unconscious psychological causes. The normative element that was supposed to be inside the system in virtue of its psychological content now comes back in when a conscious agent outside the mechanism makes judgements about its *functioning*. To clarify the last point I have to say more about functional explanations.

The Logic of Functional Explanations

It might appear that I am proposing that, unproblematically, there are three different levels of explanation: hardware, functional and intentional; and that where deep unconscious processes are concerned we should simply substitute hardware and functional explanations for intentional ones. But, in fact, the situation is a bit more complicated than that. Where functional explanations are concerned the metaphor of levels is somewhat misleading, because it suggests that there is a separate functional level different from the causal levels. That is not true. The so-called functional level is not a separate level at all, but simply one of the causal levels described in terms of our interests. Where artifacts and biological individuals are concerned, our interests are so obvious that they must seem inevitable and the functional level may seem intrinsic to the system. After all, who could deny, for example, that the heart *functions* to pump blood? But remember that when we say the heart functions to pump blood the only facts in question are that the heart does, in fact, pump blood; that fact is important to us, and it is causally related to a lot of other facts that also are important to us, such as the fact that the pumping of blood is necessary for staying alive. If the only things that interested us about the heart were that it made a thumping noise or that it exerted gravitational attraction on the moon we would have a completely different conception of its 'functioning' and correspondingly of, for example, heart disease. To put the point bluntly, in addition to its various causal relations the heart does not have any functions. When we speak of its functions we are talking about those of its causal relations to which we attach some *normative* importance. So the elimination of the deep unconscious level marks two major changes: it gets rid of a whole level of psychological causation and it shifts the normative component outside the mechanism to the eye of the beholder of the mechanism. Notice, for example, the normative vocabulary that Lisberger uses to characterize the function of the VOR. 'The function of the VOR is to stabilize retinal images by generating smooth eye movements that are equal and opposite to each head movement.' Furthermore, 'an accurate VOR is important because we require stable retinal images for good vision' (Lisberger, 1988, pp. 728–9).

The intentional level, on the other hand, differs from non-intentional functional levels. Though both are causal, the causal features of intrinsic intentionality combine the causal with the normative. Intentional phenomena such as rule-following and acting on desires and beliefs are genuinely causal phenomena; but as intentional phenomena they are essentially related to such normative phenomena as truth and falsity, success and failure, consistency, rationality, illusion and conditions of satisfaction generally (see Searle, 1983, esp. cha. 5, for an extended discussion). In short, the actual facts of intentionality contain normative elements; but where functional explanations are concerned the only *facts* are brute, blind, physical facts and the only norms are in us and exist only from our point of view.

The abandonment of the belief in a large class of mental phenomena which are in principle inaccessible to consciousness would therefore result in treating the brain as an organ like any other. Like any other organ the brain has a functional level – indeed many functional levels – of description; and like any other organ it *can be described as if it* were doing 'information-processing' and implementing any number of computer programs. But the truly special feature of the brain, the feature that makes it the organ of the mental, is its capacity to cause and sustain conscious thoughts, experiences, actions, memories and so forth.

The notion of an unconscious mental *process* and the correlated notion of the principles of unconscious mental processes are also sources of confusion. If we think of a conscious process which is *purely* mental we might think of something like humming a tune soundlessly to oneself in one's head. Here there is clearly a process and it has a mental content. But there is also a sense of *mental process* where it does not mean *process with mental content*, but rather *process by which mental phenomena are related*. Processes in this second sense may or may not have a mental content. For example, in the old associationist psychology there was supposed to be a process by which the perception of A reminds me of B, and that process works on the principle of resemblance. If one sees A, and A resembles B, then one will have a tendency to form an image of B. In this case the process by which one goes from the perception of A to the image of B does not necessarily involve any additional mental content at all. There is supposed to be a principle on which the process works, namely, resemblance, but the existence of the process according to the principle does not imply that there has to be any further mental content other than the perceptions of A and the thought of B or the thought of B as resembling A. In particular, it does not imply that when one sees A and is reminded of B one follows a rule whose content requires that if one sees A, and A resembles B, then one should think of B. In short, *a process by which mental contents are related need not have any mental content at all in addition to that of the relata;* even though, of course, our theoretical talk and thoughts of that principle will have a content referring to the principle. Now, this distinction is going to prove important, because many of the discussions in cognitive science move from the claim that there are processes which are *mental* in the sense of causing conscious phenomena (the processes in the brain which produce visual experiences, for example) to the claim that those processes are mental processes in the sense of having mental content, information, inference, and so on. The non-conscious processes in the brain that cause visual experiences are certainly mental in one sense, but they have no mental content at all and thus in that sense are not mental processes.

To make this distinction clear let us distinguish between those processes, such as rule-following, which have a mental content that functions causally in the production of behavior, and those processes which do not have a mental content but associate mental contents with input stimuli, output behavior, and other mental contents. The latter class I will call 'association patterns'. If, for example, whenever I eat too much pizza I get a stomach ache, there is definitely an association pattern, but no rule-following. I do not follow a rule: when you eat too much pizza get a stomach ache; it just happens that way.

Some Consequences: Universal Grammar, Association Patterns, and Connectionism

It is characteristic of intentionalistic explanations of human and animal behavior that *patterns* in the behavior are explained by the fact that the agent has a representation of that very pattern or a representation logically related to that very pattern in its intentional apparatus, and that representation functions causally in the production of the pattern of behavior. Thus, we say that people in Britain drive on the left; and that they do not drive on the right because they follow the same rule. The intentional content functions causally in producing the behavior it represents. There are two immediate qualifications. First, the intentional content of the rule does not produce the behavior all by itself. Nobody, for example, goes for a drive just to be following the rule; and nobody talks just for the sake of following the rules of English. And, secondly, the rules, principles, and so forth may be unconscious and for all practical purposes, they are often unavailable to consciousness even though, as we have seen, if there really are such rules they must be, at least in principle, accessible to consciousness.

A typical strategy in cognitive science has been to try to discover complex patterns such as those found in perception or language and then to postulate combinations of mental representations which will explain the pattern in the appropriate way. Where there is no conscious or shallow unconscious representation we postulate a deep unconscious mental representation. Epistemically, the existence of the patterns is taken as evidence for the existence of the representations. Causally, the existence of the representations is supposed to explain the existence of the patterns. But both the epistemic and causal claims presuppose that the ontology of deep unconscious rules is perfectly in order as it stands. I have tried to challenge the ontology of deep unconscious rules, and if that challenge is successful the epistemic and the causal claims collapse together. Epistemically, both the plant and the VOR exhibit systematic patterns, but that provides no evidence at all for the existence of deep unconscious rules; an obvious point in the case of the plant, less obvious but still true in the case of vision. Causally, the pattern of behavior plays a functional role in the overall behavior of the system, but the representation of the pattern in our theory does not identify a deep unconscious representation that plays a causal role in the production of the pattern of behavior, because there is no such deep unconscious representation. Again, this is an obvious point in the case of the plant, less obvious but still true in the case of vision.

Now, with this apparatus in hand, let us turn to a discussion of the status of the alleged rules of 'universal grammar'. I concentrate my attention on universal grammar, because grammars of particular languages, like French or English, whatever else they contain, obviously contain a large number of rules that are accessible to consciousness. The traditional argument for the existence of universal grammar can be stated quite simply: the fact that all normal children can readily acquire the language of the community in which they grow up without special instruction and on the basis of very imperfect and degenerate stimuli, and further that children can learn certain sorts of languages, exemplified by natural human languages, but cannot learn all sorts of other logically possible language systems, provides overwhelming evidence that normal children contain in some unknown way in their brains a special 'language acquisition device', and *this language acquisition device consists at least in part of a set of deep unconscious rules.*

With the exception of the last italicized clause, I agree entirely with the foregoing argument for a language acquisition device. The only problem is with the postulation of deep unconscious rules. That postulation is inconsistent with the connection principle. It is not surprising that there has been a great

348 JOHN R. SEARLE

deal of discussion about the sorts of evidence that one might have for the existence of these rules. And these discussions are always inconclusive, because the hypothesis is empty.

Years ago, I raised epistemic doubts about Chomsky's confident attribution of deep unconscious rules and suggested that any such attribution would require evidence that the specific content, the specific aspectual shape, of the rule was playing a causal role in the production of the behavior in question (Searle, 1976). I claimed that simply predicting the right patterns would not be enough to justify the claim that we are following deep unconscious rules; in addition, we would need evidence that the rule was 'causally efficacious' in the production of the pattern. With certain qualifications, Chomsky accepts the requirements. Since we are agreed on these requirements, it might be worth spelling them out:

1   The use of the word *rule* is not important. The phenomenon in question could be a principle, or a parameter, or a constraint, and so on. The point, however, is that it is at a level of intrinsic intentionality. For both Chomsky and me, it is not merely a matter of the system behaving *as if* it were following a rule. There must be a difference between the role of rules in the language faculty and, for example, the role of 'rules' in the behavior of plants and plants.

2   *Behavior* is not at issue, either. Understanding sentences, intuitions or grammaticality and manifestations of linguistic competence in general are what we are referring to by the use of the short-hand term 'behavior'. There is no behaviorism implicit in the use of this term and no confusion between competence and performance.

3   Neither of us supposes that all of the behavior (in the relevant sense) is caused by the rules (in the relevant sense). The point, however, is that in the best causal explanation of the phenomena, the rules 'enter into' (Chomsky's phrase) the theory that gives the explanation.

Now with these constraints in mind, what exactly was Chomsky's answer to the objection?

> Suppose that our most successful mode of explanation and description attributes to Jones an initial and attained state including certain rules (principles with parameters fixed or rules of other sorts) and explains Jones's behavior in these terms; that is, the rules form a central part of the best account of his use and understanding of language and are directly and crucially invoked in explaining it in the best theory we can devise ... I cannot see that anything is involved in attributing causal efficacy to rules beyond the claim that these rules are consistuent elements of the states postulated in an explanatory theory. (Chomsky, 1986, pp. 252–3)

In the same connection, Chomsky also quotes Demopoulos and Matthews (1983):

> As Demopoulos and Matthews (1983) observe, 'the apparent theoretical indispensability of appeals to grammatically characterized internal states in the

explanation of linguistic behavior is surely the best sort of reason for attributing to these states (and, we may add, to the relevant constituent elements) a causal role in the production of behavior'. (Chomsky, 1986. p. 257)

So the idea is this: the claim that the rules are causally efficacious is justified by the fact that the rules are constituent elements of the states postulated by the best causal theory of the behavior. The objection that I want to make to this account should by now be obvious: in stating that the 'best theory' requires the postulation of deep unconscious rules of universal grammar, all three authors are presupposing that the postulation of such rules is perfectly legitimate to begin with. Once we cast doubt on the legitimacy of that assumption, however, then it looks like the 'best theory' might just as well treat the evidence as association patterns that are not produced by mental representations that in some way reflect those patterns, but are produced by neurophysiological structures that need have no resemblance to the patterns at all. The hardware produces patterns of association, in the sense defined above, but the patterns of association play no causal role in the production of the patterns of behavior; they just are those patterns of behavior.

Specifically, the evidence for universal grammar is much more simply accounted for by the following hypothesis: there is, indeed, a language acquisition device innate in human brains, and this language acquisition device constrains the form of languages that human beings can learn. There is, thus, a hardware level of explanation in terms of the structure of the device, and there is a functional level of explanation, describing which sorts of languages can be acquired by the human infant in the application of this mechanism. Now, no further predictive or explanatory power is added by saying that there is in addition a level of deep unconscious rules of universal grammar, and indeed, I have tried to suggest that the postulation is incoherent anyway. For example, suppose children can only learn languages that contain some specific formal property F. Now that is evidence that the language acquisition device makes it possible to learn F languages and not possible to learn non-F languages. But that is it. There is no further evidence that the child has a deep unconscious rule representing F, and no sense has been given to that supposition anyway.

The situation is exactly analogous to the following: humans are able to perceive colors only within certain range of spectrum. Without formal training, they can see blue and red, for example, but they cannot see infrared or ultraviolet. This is overwhelming evidence that they have a 'vision faculty' that constrains what sorts of colors they can see. But now, is this because they are following the deep unconscious rules 'if it is infrared, don't see it' or 'if it is blue, it is ok to see it'? To my knowledge, no argument has ever been presented to show that the rules of universal *linguistic* grammar have any different status from the rules of universal *visual* grammar. Now ask yourself why exactly you are unwilling to say that there are such rules of universal visual grammar? After all, the evidence is just as good as, indeed it is in identical form with, the evidence for the rules of universal linguistic grammar. The answer, I believe, is that it is quite obvious to us from everything else we know that there is no such mental level. There is simply a hardware mechanism that functions in a cerain way and not others. I am suggesting here that there is no difference between the status of deep unconscious universal visual grammar and deep unconscious universal linguistic grammar: both are non-existent.

Notice that it is not enough to rescue the cognitive science paradigm to say that we can simply decide to treat the attribution of rules and principles as as-if intentionality; because as-if intentional states, not being real, have no causal powers whatever. They explain nothing. The problem with as-if intentionality is not merely that it is ubiquitous – which it is – but its identification does not give a causal explanation, it simply restates the problem which the attribution of real intentionality is supposed to solve. Let us see how this point applies in the present instance. We tried to explain the facts of language acquisition by postulating rules of universal grammar. If true, this would be a genuine causal explanation of language acquistion. But now suppose we abandon this form of explanation and say simply that the child acts *as if* he were following rules, but of course he is not really doing so. If we say that, we no longer have an explanation. The cause is now left open. We have converted a psychological explanation into speculative neurophysiology.

Now, if I am right we have been making some stunning mistakes. Why? I believe it is in part because we have been supposing that if the input to the system is meaningful and the output is meaningful then all the processes in between must be meaningful as well. And certainly there are many meaningful processes in cognition. But where we are unable to find meaningful conscious processes we postulate meaningful unconscious processes, even deep uncon-scious processes. And when challenged we invoke that most powerful of philosophical arguments: 'What else could it be?' 'How else could it work?' Deep unconscious rules satisfy our urge for meaning, and besides, what other theory is there? Any theory is better than none at all. Once we make these mistakes our theories of the deep unconscious are off and running. But it is simply false to assume that the meaningfulness of the input and output implies a set of meaningful processes in between and it is a violation of the Connection Principle to postulate in principle inaccessible unconscious processes.

One of the unexpected consequences of this whole investigation is that I have quite inadvertently arrived at a defense – if that is the right word – of connectionism (see Hanson and Burr, 1990). Among their other merits, at least some connectionist models show how a system might convert a meaningful input into a meaningful output without any rules, principles, inferences, or other sorts of meaningful phenomena in between. This is not to say that existing connectionist models are correct – perhaps they are all wrong. But they are not all obviously false or incoherent in the way that the traditional cognitivist models which violate the Connection Principle are.

Two Objections

I want to discuss two objections. One I thought of myself, though several other people[5] also gave me different versions of it; one is due to Ned Block (personal communication).

First objection: suppose we had a perfect science of the brain. Suppose, for example, that we could put our brain-o-scope on someone's skull and see that they wanted water. Now suppose that the 'I-want-water' configuration in the brain was universal. People want water if and only if they have the configuration. This is a total sci-fi fantasy, of course, but let's pretend. Now let's suppose that we found a sub-section of the population that had exactly that configuration but could not 'in principle' bring any desire for water to consciousness. They engage in water-seeking behavior but they are unable 'in principle' to become conscious of the desire for water. There is nothing pathological about them; that is just the way their brains are constructed. Now if this is possible – and why not? – then we have found a counter-example to the Connection Principle, because we have found an example of an unconscious desire for water which it is 'in principle' impossible to bring to consciousness.

I like the example, but I do not think it is a counter-example. Characteristically in the sciences we define surface phenomena in terms of their micro-causes; we can define red in terms of wavelengths of a certain number of nanometers, for example. If we had a perfect science of the brain of the sort imagined we would certainly identify mental states by their microcauses in the neurophysiology of the brain. But – and this is the crucial point – the redefinition works as an identification of an unconscious mental phenomenon only to the extent that we continue to suppose that the unconscious neurophysiology is still, so to speak, tracking the right conscious mental phenomenon with the right aspectual shape. So the difficulty is with the use of the expression 'in principle'. In the imagined case, the 'I-want-water' neurophysiology is indeed capable of causing the conscious experience. It was only on that supposition that we got the example going in the first place. The cases we have imagined are simply cases where there is a blockage of some sort. They are like Weiskrantz's (1982) 'blindsight' examples, only without the pathology (see also Champion et al., (1983)). But there is nothing 'in principle' inaccessible to consciousness about the phenomena in question, and that is why it is not a counter-example to the Connection Principle.

Second objection (due to Ned Block): the argument has the consequences that there could not be a totally unconscious intentional zombie. But why could there not be? If such a thing is possible – and why not? – then the Connection Principle entails a false proposition and is therefore false.

Actually, there could not be an intentional zombie and Quine's famous argument for the indeterminacy of translation (Quine, 1960, ch.2) has inadvertently supplied us with the proof: for a zombie, unlike a conscious agent, there simply is no fact of the matter as to exactly which aspectual shapes its alleged intentional states have. Suppose we built a 'water-seeking' zombie. Now, what fact about the zombie makes it the case that he, she or it is seeking the stuff under the aspect 'water' and not under the aspect 'H_2O'? Notice that it would not be enough to answer this question to claim that we could program the zombie to say, 'I sure do want water, but I do not want any H_2O' because that only forces the question back a step: what fact about the zombie makes it the case that by 'water' it means what we mean by 'water' and by 'H_2O' it means what we mean by 'H_2O'? And even if we complicate its behavior to try to answer the question there will always be alternative ways of interpreting its verbal behavior which are consistent with all the facts about verbal behavior but which give inconsistent attributions of meaning and intentionality to the zombie. And, as Quine has shown in laborious detail, the problem is not that we could not know for sure that the zombie meant, say, 'rabbit' as opposed to 'stage in the life history of a rabbit', or 'water' as opposed to 'H_2O'; there is simply no fact of the matter at all about which the zombie meant. But where there is no fact of the matter about aspectual shape there is no aspectual shape, and where there is no aspectual shape there is no intentionality. Quine, we might say, has a theory of meaning appropriate for verbally-behaving zombies. But we are not zombies and our utterances do, on occasion at least, have determinate meanings with determinate aspectual shapes, just as our intentional states often have determinate intentional contents with determinate aspectual shapes (Searle, 1987). But all of that presupposes consciousness.

The Unconscious

What is left of the unconscious? I said earlier that our naive pre-theoretical notion of the unconscious was like the notion of objects which, like the fish in the sea or furniture in the dark attic of the mind, keep their shapes even when unconscious. But now we can see that this notion is mistaken. It confuses the conscious form of an intentional state with a causal capacity to cause the state in that form, that is, it confuses the latency with its manifestation. It is as if we thought the bottle of poison on the shelf had to be poisoning something all the time in order really to be poison.

The final conclusion I want to draw from this discussion is that we have no unified notion of the unconscious. There are at least four different notions.

First, there are as-if metaphorical attributions of intentionality to the brain which are not to be taken literally. For example, we might say that the medulla wants to keep us alive so it keeps us breathing even while we are asleep.

Secondly, there are Freudian cases of shallow unconscious desires, beliefs, and so forth. It is best to think of these as cases of repressed consciousness, because they are always bubbling to the surface, though often in a disguised form. In its logical behavior the Freudian notion of the unconscious is quite unlike the cognitive science notion in the crucial respect that Freudian unconscious mental states are always potentially conscious. (I wish I had more time to discuss these in detail, but they are irrelevant to the main point of this dispute.)

Thirdly, there are the (relatively) unproblematic cases of shallow unconscious mental phenomena which just do not happen to form the content of my consciousness at any given point in time. Thus, most of my beliefs, desires, worries, and memories are not present to my consciousness at any given moment such as the present one. None the less, they are all *potentially* conscious in the sense I have explained (if I understand him correctly, these are what Freud meant by the 'preconscious' as opposed to the 'unconscious'; (Freud, 1949).

Fourthly, there is supposed to be a class of deep unconscious mental intentional phenomena which are not only unconscious but which are in principle inaccessible to consciousness. These, I have argued, do not exist. Not only is there no evidence for their existence, but the postulation of their existence violates a logical constraint on the notion of intentionality.

This discussion is the upshot of the application of two principles. Always ask yourself: what do you know for sure? And what facts are supposed to correspond to the claims you are making? Now, as far as the inside of the skull is concerned, we know for sure that there is a brain and that at least sometimes it is conscious. With respect to those two facts, if we apply the second principle to the discipline of cognitive science, we get the results I have tried to present.

Acknowledgement

I am indebted to a very large number of people for helpful comments and criticisms on the topics discussed in this chapter. I cannot thank all of them, but several deserve special mention; indeed many of these patiently worked through entire drafts and made detailed comments. I am especially grateful to David Armstrong, Ned Block, Francis Crick, Hubert Dreyfus, Vinod Goel, Stevan Harnad, Marti Hearst, Elisabeth Lloyd, Kirk Ludwig, Irvin Rock, Dagmar Searle, Nathalie van Bockstaele and Richard Wolheim.

Notes

1 Chomsky, (1976): 'Human action can be understood only on the assumption that first-order capacities and families of dispositions to behave involve the use of cognitive structures that express systems of (unconscious) knowledge, belief, expectation, evaluation, judgment, and the like. At least, so it seems to me' (p. 24). 'These systems may be unconscious for the most part and even beyond the reach of

conscious introspection' (p. 35). Among the elements that are beyond the reach of conscious introspection is 'universal grammar' and Chomsky says: 'Let us define universal grammar (UG) as the system of principles, conditions, and rules that are elements or properties of all human languages not merely by accident but by necessity – of course, I mean biological, not logical, necessity' (p. 29).

2   The argument here is a condensed version of a much longer development in Searle (1989). I have tried to keep its basic structure intact; I apologize for a certain amount of repetition.

3   I am indebted to Dan Rudermann for calling my attention to this article.

4   For these purposes I am contrasting 'neurophysiological' and 'mental', but in my view of mind/body relations, the mental simply is neurophysiological at a higher level (see Searle, 1984a). I contrast mental and neurophysiological as one might contrast humans and animals without thereby implying that the first class is not included in the second. There is no dualism implicit in my use of this contrast.

5   Specifically, David Armstrong, Alison Gopnik, and Pat Hayes.

References

Champion, J., Latto, R. and Smith, Y.M. (1983) Is blindsight an effect of scattered light, spared cortex and near-threshold vision. *Behavioral and Brain Sciences* 6 (3), 423–48.

Chomsky, N. (1976) *Reflections on Language*. London, Fontana/Collins.

Chomsky, N. (1986) *Knowledge of Language: Its Nature, Origin, and Use*. New York, Praeger.

Demopoulos, W. and Matthews, R.J. (1983) On the hypothesis that grammars are mentally represented. *Behavioral and Brain Sciences* 6 (3), 423–86.

Freud, S. (1915) *The Unconscious*. Reprinted in *Collected Papers*, vol. 4. New York, Basic Books, 1959.

Freud, S. (1949) *Outline of Psychoanalysis*, trans. James Strachey. London: Hogarth Press and the Institute of Psychoanalysis.

Hanson, S.J. and Burr, D.J. (1990) What connectionist models learn: learning and representation in connectionist networks. *Behavioral and Brain Sciences* 13 (3), 471–89.

Lisberger, S.G. (1988) The neural basis for learning simple motor skills. *Science* 242, 728–35.

Lisberger, S.G. and Pavelko, T.A. (1988) Brain stem neurons inmodified pathways for motor learning in the primate vestibulo-ocular reflex. *Science* 242, 771–3.

Quine, W.V.O. (1960) *Word and Object*. New York: Wiley.

Rock, I. (1984) *Perception*. New York: W. H. Freeman.

Sarna, S.K. and Otterson, M.F. (1988) Gastrointestinal motility: some basic concepts. *Pharmacology Supplement* 36, 7–14.

Searle, J.R. (1976) The rules of the language game (review of Noam Chomsky, *Reflections on Language. The Times Literary Supplement*, September 10).

Searle, J.R. (1980a) Minds, brains and programs. *Behavioral and Brain Sciences* 3, 417–57.

Searle, J.R. (1980b) Intrinsic intentionality. Reply to criticisms of 'Minds brains and programs'. *Behavioral and Brain Sciences* 3, 450–6.

Searle, J.R. (1983) *Intentionality: an Essay in the Philosophy of Mind*. Cambridge, Cambridge University Press.

Searle, J.R. (1984a) *Minds, Brains and Science* Cambridge, Mass. Harvard University Press.

Searle, J.R. (1984b) Intentionality and its place in nature. *Synthese* 61, 3–16.

Searle, J.R. (1987) Indeterminacy, empiricism and the first person. *Journal of Philosophy* March, 123–46.

Searle, J.R. (1989) Consciousness, unconsciousness, and intentionality. *Philosophical Topics* 17 (1), 193–209.

Weiskrantz, L. (1982) A follow-up study of blindsight. Paper presented at the Fifth INS European Conference, Deauville, France, June 16–18.

20

Reply: Consciousness and the Varieties of Aboutness

Martin Davies

Thinking is special. There is nothing quite like it. Thinking – judging, believing and inferring – occurs in the natural order; but, at least sometimes, it seems hard to accept that there could be a fully satisfying reconstruction of thought in the terms favoured by the natural sciences, particularly, the physical and biological sciences (Davies, 1990). Some of our intuitions about thought are, in this way, similar to intuitions about consciousness; for consciousness, too, strikes many as somehow defying scientific explanation (McGinn, 1988). So, what is the connection between thought and consciousness? Is it, for example, only conscious beings that can be thinking beings?

States and events of thinking are semantically evaluable. Acts of judging, states of believing and other propositional attitude states, such as states of desiring, or intending, have semantic content or aboutness. In virtue of their semantic content, belief states, for example, can be evaluated as true or false, correct or incorrect, depending upon how the world turns out to be. The aboutness that is characteristic of the domain of thinking is often known as intentionality. So, what is the connection between intentionality and consciousness? Does intentionality require consciousness?

In 'Consciousness, Explanatory Inversion and Cognitive Science' (Chapter 19), John Searle delivers a strong affirmative answer to this question. According to Searle, it is not just that a thinking being needs to be a conscious being. Rather, a requirement of consciousness – of accessibility to consciousness 'in principle' – applies thought by thought, intentional state by intentional state. Thus, Searle's 'Connection Principle': 'The ascription of an unconscious intentional phenomenon to a system implies that the phenomenon is in principle accessible to consciousness' (Chapter 19, p. 333). The Connection Principle plays a central role in Searle's chapter. Both the argumentative route leading up to it, and the route leading from the Connection Principle to the consequences that Searle draws, merit careful attention.

Contemporary cognitive science extends the notions of aboutness and semantic evaluability far beyond the domain of thinking, and far beyond what would ordinarily be regarded as the limits of accessibility to consciousness (even 'in principle'). Searle regards this as a major error, and moves from the Connection Principle to dramatic conclusions concerning cognitive science:

> If we are looking for phenomena which are intrinsically intentional but inaccessible in principle to consciousness there is nothing there: no rule-following, no mental information processing, no unconscious inferences, no mental models, no primal sketches, no 2½ D images, no three-dimensional descriptions, no language of thought and no universal grammar. (Chapter 19, p. 338)

The list includes many of the supposed glories of contemporary cognitive psychology and theoretical linguistics. So, it would seem that, if Searle is right, then the pretensions of those disciplines need to be re-evaluated quite radically.

These, then, are Searle's two aims: 'to show that we have no notion of an unconscious mental state except in terms of its accessibility to consciousness' – in short, to establish the Connection Principle – and 'to lay bare some of the implications of this thesis for the study of the mind' (Chapter 19, p. 333). There is a vast amount to be said about each of these aims. In its original publication, Searle's paper was accompanied by thirty-five commentaries, many – even most – of which were critical of one or another stage of his argument.

I agree with Searle that there is something special about intentionality, and that many of the states invoked in cognitive psychology and theoretical linguistics lack that special something. Indeed, the distinction to be recognized here is a deep one. We would fail to give the distinction its proper weight, if we said merely that intentional states and the states invoked in cognitive science are differing variations on the common theme of semantic evaluability. So far as his first aim goes, then, I am in substantial agreement with Searle. My disagreement with him is primarily over the *load-bearing* potential of the notion of accessibility to consciousness. I am not convinced that appealing to consciousness is the best way to make explicit what is distinctive about intentionality. Consciousness is the topic for the first section of this chapter.

But, even accepting that there is an important truth lying in the region of the Connection Principle, I disagree with Searle about the consequences of this truth for cognitive science. So far as his second aim goes, I claim that Searle's argument is undermined by the fact that he does not draw enough distinctions, at the outset, between different notions of aboutness. The varieties of aboutness provide the subject matter for the second section. The remaining two sections focus upon the Connection Principle and upon cognitive science.

Consciousness

Suppose that we were faced with the converse of the question to which the Connection Principle returns an answer. Suppose, that is to say, we were asked whether consciousness requires intentionality. Must a conscious being be a thinking being? Confronted by this question – whether intentionality is a necessary condition for consciousness – we are liable to find ourselves with conflicting intuitions. On the one hand, to the extent that consciousness is just a matter of undergoing sensations and other experiences, it does not seem to require the cognitive achievements of judgement, belief and inference – the achievements of conceptualized thought. And this first intuition is strengthened further if there is reckoned to be an essential connection between thought and language; for it is natural to attribute experiences to infants and to other animals that lack language. On the other hand, to the extent that consciousness is a matter of a subject being aware of, able to think about and ultimately to report upon, his or her own mental states, then of course consciousness requires all that thinking requires.

A plausible explanation for this conflict of intuitions is that we are actually making use of at least two different notions – or families of notions – of consciousness. Kathleen Wilkes remarks (1988, p. 38) that, 'it is improbable that something bunching together pains, and thoughts about mathematics, is going to be a reliable pointer to a legitimate natural kind', and Alan Allport is likewise sceptical that there is any such 'unitary phenomenon' as consciousness (1988, p. 162). These authors would, it is true, be almost as dubious about the idea that a mere binary distinction could bring order to this domain of enquiry. But let us, nevertheless, in a cautious and provisional spirit, begin by distinguishing between phenomenal consciousness and access consciousness (Block, 1990, 1991, 1992, 1993, 1995; Davies and Humphreys, 1993).

Phenomenal consciousness and access consciousness: the initial distinction

The idea of *phenomenal consciousness* is the idea of 'something that it is like' to which Thomas Nagel directed our attention (1979, p. 166): 'an organism has conscious mental states if and only if there is something that it is like to *be* that organism – something it is like *for* the organism.' We can say that a system is phenomenally conscious just in case there is something that it is like to be that system, and that a state of a system is a phenomenally conscious state if and only if there is something that it is like, for the system, to be in that state. Phenomenal consciousness, Ned Block (1995) tells us, is 'experience', and phenomenally conscious properties of states include'the experiential properties of sensations, feelings and perceptions'. There is something that it is like to undergo sensations – to feel an itch, or a pain, or a tickle. There is also something that it is like to have perceptual experiences – to feel for the alarm clock when it rings, to recognize the face of a friend, to see the planet Venus in the evening sky, to see, hear, taste and feel cool running water. It is this notion – phenomenal consciousness – that is seen by Nagel, and by other philosophers such as Frank Jackson (1982, 1986) and Colin McGinn (1989), as constituting a locus of mysteriousness, and as creating an 'explanatory gap'

(Levine, 1983, 1993) that cannot be bridged by the physical and biological sciences.

The idea of *access consciousness* is, to a very rough first approximation, the idea of availability for explicit verbal report (Fodor, 1983, p. 56). If a subject has a belief – say, the belief that the angle in a semi-circle is a right angle – then typically she can verbally express the content of that belief (by saying, 'The angle in a semi-circle is a right angle') and she can verbally report that she has that belief (by saying, 'I believe that the angle in a semi-circle is a right angle'). If she is unable to do these things, then we may well say that if she has the belief at all then it is an unconscious or tacit belief.

Something similar goes for a sensation, like pain. If a subject has a pain then typically she can verbally express the pain (by saying, 'Ouch') and she can verbally report that she has that pain (by saying, 'I am in pain'). But there are also differences between the case of pain and the case of belief. Pain has something that belief lacks: it is not very plausible that there is anything that it is like, in Nagel's sense, to believe that the angle in a semi-circle is a right angle. And belief has something that pain lacks: our subject can express the pain, but she cannot express the content of the pain, since pains plausibly do not have any semantic content. So, the notion of phenomenal consciousness applies only to the pain case, and one aspect of the notion of access consciousness applies only to the belief case. To the extent that it separates the pain case and the belief case, the distinction between phenomenal consciousness and access consciousness achieves some credibility as a response to Wilkes's remark about 'bunching together pains, and thoughts about mathematics'.

Access consciousness: some refinements

Access consciousness was introduced as availability for verbal report, but we need to refine that initial idea. Three different refinements will be considered.

Suppose that our subject verbally reports that she believes that the angle in a semi-circle is not always a right angle. Suppose that she says this, not on any introspective grounds but, rather, on the authority of her psychoanalyst. Her analyst credits her with this belief by way of interpreting a range of inappropriate behaviour, and she trusts her analyst even though at this stage of the analytical process she is not yet able to identify with that belief – to recognize it 'from the inside'. Intuitively, we do not want this kind of verbal report to be enough for access consciousness.

Similarly, suppose that our subject verbally reports that she tacitly knows that an anaphor is bound in its governing category while a pronominal is free in its governing category (Chomsky, 1986, p. 166). Suppose that she reports this on the authority of her linguistics professor, who has credited her with this piece of tacit knowledge by way of a partial explanation of her judgements about the grammaticality or otherwise of sentences such as:

I told them about each other.
I told them that Bill liked each other.

Then, once again, we would not want this to count as access consciousness of a state of tacit knowledge (cf. Searle, 1990, p. 634).

There are important differences between attributions of unconscious knowledge and belief in the case of psychoanalysis and in the case of theoretical linguistics. But the common feature that matters here is that, in each case, the subject's ability to make her report depends upon much more than just her being in the state that is reported upon. In each case, she relies on the authority of a third party. We do not want these cases to count as examples of access consciousness. So, we should say that a state that has semantic content is access conscious if *simply in virtue of being in that state* the subject is able to express verbally the content of the state, and to report verbally that she is in the state. This takes us closer to a sufficient condition for an intuitively recognizable notion of access consciousness. But the requirement of verbal report raises a question as to whether we have formulated a necessary condition. In order to move to the first refinement of the idea of access consciousness, we need to replace or dilute the requirement of verbal report.

First refinement: rational control of action   Allport, for example, having noted the consequences of the requirement of verbal report for a global aphasic (1988, p. 163), considers an alternative criterion of potential action (p. 165): 'In common usage, it seems, to be aware of something or conscious of something carries at least the implication that "something" can guide or control my choice of *action*.' But, the problem that Allport then raises is that this criterion trades upon the distinction between voluntary and involuntary actions, and 'there seems little distinction to be made between a "voluntary" action and one "consciously directed"' (1988, p. 167). In short, the criterion seems to reintroduce the very notion that it is intended to clarify.

The criterion that Allport discusses is similar in spirit to Block's (1995) account of access consciousness:

> A state is access-conscious if, in virtue of one's having the state, a representation of its content is (1) inferentially promiscuous, i.e. poised to be used as a premise in reasoning, and (2) poised for *rational* control of action and (3) poised for rational control of speech . . . I see [access consciousness] as a cluster concept, in which (3) – roughly, reportability – is the element in the cluster with the smallest weight, though (3) is often the best practical guide to [access consciousness].

We can take this – in which the verbal report requirement is heavily diluted – as our first refinement of the idea.

As the emphasis (in the original) indicates, the word 'rational' is not idle here. It is needed, rather as 'voluntary' is needed in the criterion discussed by Allport. In fact, whether or not there is a circularity in the offing, the appeal to reasoning and rational action in Block's account of access consciousness suggests that this first refinement of the idea is pointing us towards the notion of a state that inhabits the domain of thinking: the space of reasons. For what seems to be important is that the state should have the kind of content that fits it for the domain of judgement, belief, inference and intention – the conceptualized content of thoughts.

Second refinement: thought content   On many conceptions of the relationship between thought and language, the verbal expression or report of a psychological state is a relatively contingent effect of something more fundamental, namely, a judgement or, more generally, a piece of thinking. This reflection suggests a slightly different refinement of the idea of access consciousness, one that leads us even more rapidly to the notion of thought content. We might say that a state with semantic content is access conscious if, simply in virtue of being in that state, the subject is able to entertain in thought the content of the state.

So far as it applies to beliefs, there is something trivial about this refinement of the idea of access consciousness. Believing is a kind of thinking, along with framing a hypothesis, wondering whether it is so, doubting that it is so, wishing that it were so, and the like. So, of course, to be in a belief state is *ipso facto* to have the content of the belief available as a content of thought. But, suppose that there are also psychological states that have a different kind of semantic content from the contents of thought. Suppose, in particular, that there are psychological states whose content is not conceptualized.

Thought content is a kind of conceptualized content: no one can think a thought with a particular content without possessing the constituent concepts of that thought. No one can believe that – or wonder whether, or doubt that, or wish that – the angle in a semi-circle is a right angle, without possessing the concepts of angle, semi-circle, right angle, and so on. In contrast, psychological states with non-conceptualized content would be contentful states that a subject could be in even though he or she did not possess the concepts that we would use to specify the states' contents. Then clearly, to be in such a psychological state would not *ipso facto* be to have the content of the state available as a content of thought.

Thus, we are led by this second refinement of the idea of access consciousness to the distinction between states – principally, propositional attitude states – whose content is necessarily conceptualized by the subject, and states that have semantic content even though it need not be conceptualized by the subject.

Third refinement: higher-order thought   When we introduced the idea of access consciousness as availability for verbal report, we distinguished two components in the idea of verbal report. The subject can express verbally the content of the state, and can report verbally that she is in the state. When we strip away the requirement of verbal report, leaving just availability for thought, we can still retain two components. The first component now says that if a psychological state with semantic content is access conscious, then to be in the state is *ipso facto* to have the content of the state available as a content of thought. The second component says that if a psychological state is access conscious, then to be in the state is *ipso facto* to be in a position to judge that one is in that state. The refinement of the idea of access consciousness that we have just considered omits that second component. Let us now try adding it in.

The second component says that to be in an access conscious state is *ipso facto* to be in a position to judge that one is in that state. But there is a problem with that requirement. It is plausible that, for many psychological states, it is possible for a subject to be in the state without possessing the concept of that type of psychological state. Suppose, in particular, that it is possible to believe that the angle in a semi-circle is a right angle without having the concept of belief. Then clearly, just to have the belief is not yet to be in a position to judge that one has the belief. If we are going to add in the second component, then we shall get closer to an intuitive notion of accessibility to consciousness if we restrict attention to subjects who do possess the concept of the type of psychological state in question.

Given that restriction, what difference does it make if we add in the second component? Of course, if a state is classified as not access conscious by the lights of the first component in the idea of access consciousness, then it is likewise classified as not access consciousness when we add in the further requirement of the second component. But, in fact, the second component itself suffices for the negative verdict in these cases.

In order to judge that she is in a state of a certain type and with a certain content, a subject needs to possess the concept of that type of state, and also to possess the concepts that figure in the specification of the content. Let us suppose that a subject can be in a state of tacitly knowing that an anaphor is bound in its governing category while a pronominal is free in its governing category, without possessing the concepts of anaphor, governing category, and so on. Then to be in such a state of tacit knowledge is not *ipso facto* to be in a position to judge that one is in that state, even if one possesses the concept of tacit knowledge. This is simply because the content of the state is not *ipso facto* available as a content of thought. In effect, the second component contains the first component within it.

The difference that is made by adding in the second component becomes visible when we consider states with conceptualized content. If, for example, our subject has a belief then, trivially, the content of the belief is available as a content of thought. But intuitively, it is a further question whether the subject is, just in virtue of having the belief, in a position to judge that she has that belief. Indeed, intuitively this further question is very closely related to the question whether the belief is a conscious belief or not.

But, it is not clear that this third refinement of the idea of access consciousness quite captures the intuitive idea of a conscious belief. Suppose that the subject has a belief and is *ipso facto* in a position to judge that she has that belief. Then, it is very natural to suppose that there must be something about her belief state in virtue of which she is in a position to make that judgement. We might now ask which of two candidates it is that constitutes the belief's being a conscious belief. One candidate is the subject's being in a position to judge that she has that belief. The other candidate is the belief state's having the property – whatever property it is – that explains why the subject is placed in such a position. It is at least arguable that we should prefer the second candidate, rather than the first: the explanatory property, rather than the more dispositional property that it explains. But then, we must enter a reservation as to whether this notion of access consciousness, defined in terms of the more dispositional property, goes quite to the heart of the notion of a conscious belief.

Indeed, following this line of thought, we can even suggest that access consciousness, as it is defined in this third refinement, is not necessary for consciousness, as it applies to beliefs. For if what matters for conscious belief is the explanatory property, then we can envisage a belief state having that property, and so being a conscious belief, even though the subject lacks the concept of belief, so that this notion of access consciousness is not even applicable (Peacocke, 1992, pp. 152–3).

It should be acknowledged, though, that more work needs to be done if this appeal to an explanatory property of belief states is to be ultimately satisfying. A subject who is in pain is, we suppose, in a position to judge that she is in pain, provided only that she possesses the concept of pain. In this case, we may say that it is the pain state's being a phenomenally conscious state that explains why being in the state disposes the subject to judge that she is in pain. But, having denied that there is anything that it is like to believe, for example, that the angle in a semi-circle is a right angle, we cannot tell a parallel story about the grounds of the subject's dispositions to make judgements about her own beliefs.

However, whatever the complexities of that issue, there are other grounds for denying that this notion of access consciousness goes to the heart of consciousness as it applies to belief states. For access consciousness does not seem to be sufficient for consciousness as it applies to beliefs. There are imaginable cases in which a subject has a belief, and is thereby in a position to judge that she has that belief, and even does judge that she has that belief, but where both the first-order and the second-order beliefs would be intuitively reckoned as unconscious beliefs. An example could be based on unconscious guilt about an unconscious belief, since the most intelligible basis for the guilt would be recognition – also unconscious, of course – that one has that belief (cf. Peacocke, 1992, p. 154).

Adding the requirement that the subject be in a position to judge that she has a certain belief takes us close to an intuitive notion of consciousness – of conscious belief. But we have found reasons to doubt whether access consciousness, thus refined, is either necessary or sufficient for consciousness on the intuitive conception. To the extent that we doubt whether the third refinement of the idea of access consciousness captures the idea of a conscious belief, we shall also doubt that the so-called higher-order thought theories of consciousness are adequate. These are theories of consciousness that equate a psychological state's being a conscious state with the subject's actually having a thought about the state, to the effect that she is in that state (Nelkin, 1986, 1989a, b; Rosenthal, 1986, 1993). For exactly similar queries can be raised about both the necessity and the sufficiency of the higher-order thought theorist's conditions for being a conscious belief.

Does consciousness require intentionality?

After drawing a distinction between phenomenal consciousness and access consciousness, we have been considering three ways of refining the initial idea of access consciousness. The first and second refinements both point in the direction of conceptualized content as being the key notion. The third refinement goes further, but does not quite capture the intuitive notion of a conscious belief. These distinctions – introduced in a cautious and provisional spirit – may help us better to understand what is at issue in Searle's arguments. They may suggest a doubt, for example, as to whether the notion of accessibility to consciousness can bear the argumentative weight that Searle places upon it. We shall take up these matters below in the section on the Connection Principle.

Now, however, we can return to the question with which we began this section. Does consciousness require intentionality? If we consider access consciousness first, then the close tie with intentionality is immediately obvious. The first and second refinements point directly towards the notion of intentionality, and the third refinement clearly requires intentionality since the subject is said to be in a position to make a judgement, and so arrive at a belief, about her own mental state. Even when the mental state under consideration does not itself exhibit intentionality – a pain, for example – if the state is access conscious in virtue of the fact that the subject of the state, possessing the concept of pain, is in a position to judge that she is in pain, then the subject is capable of mental states that do have intentionality.

If we turn now to phenomenal consciousness, the plausible answer to the question, at least initially, is surely that phenomenal consciousness does not require intentionality. Suppose that a phenomenally conscious mental state, a pain, is also access conscious, in the sense that the subject of the pain, possessing the concept of pain, is able to judge that she is in pain. Then, as we have already noted, we may say that it is the pain state's being a phenomenally conscious state that explains the subject's disposition to judge that she is in pain. The pain's being a phenomenally conscious state is not itself dependent upon the subject's ability to make that judgement.

However, we should note two dissenting voices here. First, higher-order thought theories of consciousness treat phenomenal consciousness as a kind of access consciousness. So they return the verdict, across the board, that consciousness requires intentionality. We have, though, already noted reasons for querying the account of consciousness that these theories offer.

The other dissenting voice comes from Gareth Evans (1982). In a recommendation that is fundamental to his programme, Evans says that we should (1982, p. 123) 'take the notion of *being in an informational state with such-and-such a content* as a primitive notion for philosophy, rather than . . . attempt to characterize it in terms of belief'. He then deploys this notion of a state of information in his account of perceptual experience (1982, pp. 226–7):

> In general, we may regard a perceptual experience as an informational state of the subject: it has a certain *content* – the world is represented a certain way – and hence it permits of a non-derivative classification as *true* or *false*. . . The informational states which a subject acquires through perception are *non-conceptual*, or *non-conceptualized*.

However, in Evans's view, states of information are also implicated in unconscious processes that take place in our brains, and in the explanation of the correct 'guesses' of blindsight subjects, for example. So, what makes the difference between those informational states that constitute conscious perceptual experiences and mere unconscious informational states? Evans's answer is that (1982, p. 158) 'we arrive at conscious perceptual experience when sensory input is not only connected to behavioural dispositions . . . but also serves as the input to a *thinking, concept-applying, and reasoning system.*' It is only when we have a subject whose conceptualized judgements are appropriately sensitive to the non-conceptualized information content of perceptual states that we have a subject for whom those perceptual states amount to conscious experiences.

There is an important difference between this account and that of the higher-order thought theorists. The judgements mentioned in Evans's account are judgements about the world, rather than about mental states. But still, we might say that Evans treats phenomenal consciousness as something like access consciousness. Certainly for Evans, as for the higher-order thought theorists, consciousness – the phenomenal consciousness of perceptual experience – requires intentionality. An experiencing subject is also a thinking subject.

This is not the place to assess Evans's view about the link between consciousness and intentionality. But we should notice that his appeal to the notion of information, and to non-conceptualized content more generally, does not depend upon that link. (We shall mention Evans's view again below.)

The Varieties of Aboutness

Someone might point out that Searle's claim in the Connection Principle (Chapter 19, p. 333: 'The ascription of an unconscious intentional phenomenon to a system implies that the phenomenon is in principle accessible to consciousness') is subject to either a weaker or a stronger construal, and then seek to make peace between Searle and cognitive science by imposing just the weaker construal upon his words. On the weaker construal, Searle would merely be saying that psychological states that are inaccessible to consciousness have an importantly different kind of aboutness, or have aboutness in a different way, from conscious – or potentially conscious – psychological states, such as beliefs. On the stronger construal, he would be saying that the only genuine aboutness belongs to (at least potentially) conscious mental states; so that supposedly psychological states that are inaccessible to consciousness do not have genuine aboutness at all. On the weaker construal he would be allowing the possibility of a variety of grounds for non-derivative and non-trivial semantic evaluability, while on the stronger construal he would be ruling out that possibility.

Unfortunately for the peacemakers, Searle appears to intend the stronger construal of his conclusions. He does draw a distinction between genuine (or 'intrinsic') intentionality and mere 'as if' intentionality (pp. 333–4); and he allows that the unconscious states invoked in cognitive science participate in 'as if' intentionality. But this does not permit any kind of vindication of cognitive psychology and linguistics, since 'as if' intentionality is far too inclusive (p. 333):

> I can, for example, say of my lawn that it is thirsty, just as I can say of myself that I am thirsty. But it is obvious that my lawn has no mental states whatever. When I say that it is thirsty, this is simply a metaphorical way of describing its capacity to absorb water . . . We say, such things as, 'The carburetor of the car *knows* how rich to make the mixture'; 'The thermostat on the wall *perceives* the changes in the temperature'; 'The calculator *follows rules* of arithmetic when it does addition'; and 'The Little Engine That Could is *trying very hard* to make it up the mountain.' None of these attributions is meant to be taken literally, however.

And, likewise, in an earlier presentation of the position (1989, p. 198): 'water flowing downhill behaves *as if* it had intentionality. It *tries* to get to the bottom of the hill by ingeniously *seeking* the line of least resistance, it does *information processing* in order to *calculate* the size of rocks, the angle of the slope, the pull of gravity, etc.' If, as the Connection Principle states, genuine intentionality requires accessibility to consciousness and 'as if' intentionality is the only alternative, then trivialization is the fate that awaits great tracts of psychology and linguistics as those disciplines are currently conceived.

Still, the peacemaker's idea is not without relevance to the assessment of Searle's arguments. For it may be that, although Searle intends the stronger construal of his conclusions, it is only the weaker construal that is strictly licensed by the arguments that he gives. So, in the remainder of this section, I shall note – in as neutral a way as possible – a variety of kinds of aboutness, none of which appears to be as trivial as mere 'as if' intentionality. We begin with genuine, intrinsic intentionality.

Attitude aboutness

First, then, our belief states have aboutness. Suppose that Fiona believes that Venus is a planet. Her belief is about an object, Venus, and a property, being a planet: it is the belief that the former exemplifies the latter. More generally, beliefs, desires, hopes, fears, wishes and intentions – the propositional attitudes – have aboutness. We shall reserve the term 'intentionality' for this kind of aboutness: *attitude aboutness*.

We have already noted that attitude aboutness involves conceptualization. For present purposes, we can think of possessing a concept as having a particular cognitive ability; in the most basic cases, this is the ability to think of an object or a property in a certain way. Possessing a concept involves appreciating certain special, or canonical, rational connections between thoughts involving that concept and other thoughts or experiences. Thus, to pursue our well-worn example, Fiona might have a way of thinking of the planet Venus which we would describe as thinking of Venus as the first heavenly body to appear in the evening (whether or not Fiona could articulate that specification herself). Part of what is involved is that cognitive ability is appreciating that evidence that is made available by Venus's appearing in the evening sky is directly relevant to thoughts in which Venus is thought about in that way.

Clearly, Fiona could have other ways of thinking of the same planet Venus; for example, a way that would privilege evidence made available by Venus's appearance in the morning sky. In this neo-Fregean framework (Evans, 1982; Peacocke, 1986, 1992), ways of thinking, and equivalently concepts, are discriminated extremely finely, as finely as is required by differences in the cognitive significance of thoughts in which the same object or property is thought about. So, if Fiona has two thoughts which are about the same planet, to the effect that it exemplifies the same property, yet these thoughts differ in their cognitive significance for her, then the thoughts involve two different ways of thinking (of either the planet or the property).

Fine-grainedness is one characteristic of conceptualization, and so of intentionality, or attitude aboutness. Another characteristic is that the cognitive abilities that constitute possession of concepts, and are deployed together in one thought, can be recombined in countless other ways, enabling the thinking subject to entertain countless other thoughts. This is the characteristic of conceptualization that Evans spells out in the Generality Constraint (1982, p. 104). A third characteristic is that possession of any concepts of objects and properties at all seems to require possession of a range of spatial concepts and concepts for kinds of medium-sized material bodies, along with some appreciation of the fact, for example, that one way for a body to exist unperceived by a particular subject is for the body to exist at a place other than that at which the subject is located (Strawson, 1959; Evans, 1980).

On this kind of account, conceptualization – and so, intentionality – is a highly non-trivial cognitive achievement. Thinking is special.

Linguistic aboutness

Propositional attitude states are not the only things that have aboutness. A second clear example is provided by sentences – or utterances of sentences – of a public language. The English sentence 'Venus is a planet', like Fiona's belief, is about Venus and the property of being a planet. Also, like Fiona's belief, the sentence is true – or correct – if and only if Venus is indeed a planet. But arguably, the meanings of words in a public language cut less finely than ways of thinking do. Suppose that W is a word whose semantic value (reference) is an object or property V. Then it may be that two language users each count as understanding W as having the meaning that it does actually have, even though they think about V – the semantic value of W – in two quite different ways.

Belief states and utterances of sentences both have aboutness. But it would be wrong to assume that a philosophical account of the aboutness – or meaning – of sentences will take just the same form as an account of the aboutness – or intentionality – of beliefs. It is plausible that the meaning of public language sentences has something to do with the way that utterances of those sentences are conventionally used to communicate particular messages, to pass on beliefs from speaker to hearer. But that kind of account clearly cannot be applied to beliefs themselves. On the contrary, that kind of account of linguistic meaning seems to take the aboutness of beliefs and other propositional attitudes for granted. As Searle says (1983, p. 5), 'the direction of logical analysis is to explain language in terms of Intentionality'; and (1983, p. 27):

> An utterance can have Intentionality, just as a belief has Intentionality, but whereas the Intentionality of the belief is *intrinsic* the Intentionality of the utterance is *derived* . . . The mind imposes Intentionality on entities that are not intrinsically Intentional by intentionally conferring the conditions of satisfaction of the expressed psychological state upon the external physical entity.

So, as well as the *attitude aboutness* of beliefs and desires, we have the *linguistic aboutness* of sentences and utterances. To the extent that conventional signs, and perhaps also maps and pictures, inherit their aboutness from the intentionality of beliefs in a similar way, we might also call this *conventional aboutness*. But, whatever we call it, we should note that the aboutness of language is derived from the aboutness of propositional attitudes. It is a kind of derived intentionality: derived, rather than intrinsic, but still genuine, rather than merely 'as if'. Whatever we are doing when we say that a sentence or utterance has meaning or aboutness, we are not engaging in a pretence that the linguistic item is a bearer of mental states.

Indicator aboutness

At the beginning of Paul Grice's paper 'Meaning' (1957), we find the example, 'Those spots mean (meant) measles', along with the remark (1989, p. 213): 'I cannot say, "Those spots meant measles, but he hadn't got measles" . . . That is to say, in cases like the above, *x meant that p* and *x means that p* entail *p*.' Grice called this notion of meaning *natural meaning*, as opposed to non-natural meaning which is a matter of the speaker's intentions.

Other examples of this kind of meaning – phenomena that have meaning in the sense that they *indicate* something about the world – are not difficult to find. Thus, we say, 'Those spots mean – or indicate – measles', 'Those clouds mean – or indicate – rain', and 'The existence of thirty rings in that tree trunk means – or indicates – that the tree was thirty years old when it was cut down.'

This *indicator aboutness* is clearly distinct from the other two kinds that we have listed so far. As Grice points out, we cannot consistently say, 'Those clouds mean – or indicate – that it will rain, but in fact it will not rain.' But we can consistently say, 'The content of Fiona's belief is that it will rain, but in fact it will not rain.' And we can say, 'The meaning of (the utterance of) that sentence is that it will rain – that was the message that was communicated; but in fact it will not rain.' Indicator aboutness, at least in its simplest form, differs from attitude aboutness and linguistic aboutness in that it does not allow for the possibility of falsehood or misrepresentation.

There are broadly two views that a theorist might have concerning this kind of aboutness. On the one hand, a theorist might treat indicator aboutness as a further species of derived intentionality. The idea would be that the aboutness of the clouds – the clouds' meaning that it will rain – is inherited from the attitude aboutness of the belief that someone could form on the basis of observing the clouds. On the other hand, a theorist might regard indicator aboutness as a feature of the world that is not logically dependent upon the propositional attitudes of observers. On this second view, the fact that clouds in general, and those clouds in particular, mean that it will rain is something to be discovered, and then to be relied upon in forming beliefs. But the fact obtains, whether it is discovered or not.

As between these views, we can say that the second is more plausible as an explication of what Grice was pointing to with the notion of natural meaning. The first view makes indicator aboutness a highly relative notion, since different observers will arrive at different beliefs, depending upon their different bodies of background knowledge. There is such a notion – those clouds mean rain to me, but not to her – but it seems to be distinct from the notion of natural meaning. And the first view does not make it obvious why indicator aboutness closes off the possibility of falsehood. An aboutness that is derived from the intentionality of beliefs should allow for the same possibilities of error as does attitude aboutness.

The second view is to be preferred, then. As Fred Dretske says (1986,

p. 18): 'Naturally occurring signs mean something, and they do so without any assistance from us'. And we can take it that indicator aboutness is to be explicated in terms of reliable causal co-variation between events of two types. In the example of the clouds, the two types would be occurrences of a certain kind of cloud formation and occurrences of rain shortly afterwards.

Given this background, what should we say about the familiar example of the fuel gauge: 'The position of the fuel gauge means – or indicates – that the tank is almost empty'? Since the fuel gauge is an artefact, surely – it might seem – our intentions and beliefs enter into its aboutness. But it is important to distinguish indicator aboutness from a different notion here. If the states of the fuel gauge do reliably co-vary with the states of the fuel tank, then the position of the fuel gauge, towards the bottom of the scale, means or indicates that the tank is nearly empty, and it does so without any assistance from us. Suppose that the fuel gauge starts to malfunction, the co-variation becomes unreliable, and the needle takes up a position towards the bottom of the scale even when the tank is full. Then the position of the fuel gauge no longer indicates that the tank is almost empty, even though that is what it is supposed to indicate, and what the designer intended it to indicate. Upon this way of carving up the territory – in which, to be sure, there may be an element of stipulation – indicator aboutness is independent of the propositional attitudes of either observer or designer. But the function of the fuel gauge – what its purpose is, what it is for – is in this case a mind-dependent matter.

How does indicator aboutness fit into Searle's scheme? On the view that we are taking, indicator aboutness is not a kind of derived intentionality. So, according to Searle's taxonomy, it is either genuine, intrinsic intentionality, or else merely 'as if' intentionality. Since indicator aboutness extends to spots, clouds, tree rings and fuel gauges, things that have no mental life and are not conscious, indicator aboutness is not generally accessible to consciousness, even in principle. So, according to the Connection Principle, that would rule out genuine, intrinsic intentionality. Is indicator aboutness just 'as if' intentionality, then?

Searle certainly includes a room thermostat, which is relevantly similar to a fuel gauge, among his examples of 'as if' intentionality. But the classification is not entirely satisfying. I may say that it is as if my lawn is thirsty, as if the lawn wants it to rain, or even that it is as if the lawn believes that is going to rain soon. ('Brave lawn, refusing to die, and waiting for the rain that it believes will arrive shortly.') But these metaphorical attributions are not constrained by any requirement of a reliable causal co-variation, as attributions of indicator aboutness are.

On the other hand, a metaphorical attribution of intentionality carries with it a metaphorical attribution of all that is required for intentionality. So, it is said to be as if the lawn possesses concepts, as if the lawn has fine-grained ways of thinking about objects and properties, as if the lawn measures up to the Generality Constraint, and as if the lawn appreciates that an object may exist unperceived by the lawn in virtue of existing at a place different from where the lawn is located. It is not, of course, *very much* as if all these things are true; but then, some metaphors are better than others. However, there is nothing corresponding to any of this in the conditions for attribution of indicator aboutness. Indicator aboutness is not fine-grained, it is not subject to the Generality Constraint, and it does not carry with it any appreciation of objects existing unperceived.

The possible objection to Searle's scheme of things is thus that it involves the unsatisfying classification of central cases of indicator aboutness as examples of mere 'as if' intentionality on a par with the attribution of thirst, desire and belief to a lawn. A possible response is to say that nothing very much hangs on this classification since the notion of indicator aboutness can be of only limited theoretical interest. Two reasons could be given for not attaching great importance to indicator aboutness. The first is simply that it does not allow for the possibility of falsehood. The second is that, if indicator aboutness is just a matter of causal co-variation, then it is too cheap: too many things causally co-vary with each other.

This response has some force. But it still leaves a potential problem for Searle. For it is at least open that there may be a notion of aboutness that is just as independent of our intentions and beliefs as indicator aboutness, but which lacks the two features mentioned in the response. Any notion of aboutness which, like Dretske's functional meaning (1986, p. 22), combines the idea of causal co-variation with that of natural function (cashed out in terms of evolutionary selection) will be a candidate. However, rather than take that line of thought any further now, let us turn briefly to two further kinds of aboutness.

Experiential aboutness

Perceptual experiences present the world as being one way or another. They present objects as having certain properties. Thus, we may hear a sound as coming from the left; or we may see a box as being cubic and about four feet in front of us. This *experiential aboutness* is closely related to attitude aboutness; for we can form beliefs on the basis of experiences such as these. Thus we may have an auditory experience and come to believe that the sound is coming from the left; or we can have a visual experience and come to believe that the box is cubic and about four feet in front of us.

But still, it is worth distinguishing the content of experiences from the content of the beliefs that we form on the basis of those experiences. For, it is an important point about belief content that, in order to believe that the box is cubic, one has to possess the concept of a cube. But, it is arguable that merely having a box presented in experience as cubic does not, in the same way, require possession of that concept.

As we noted at the end of the section on 'Consciousness', this is Evans's (1982) view. Perceptual experiences have a kind of aboutness that does not require conceptualization by the subject of the experiences. Furthermore,

Evans recommended treating experiences as informational states, where the notion of such states is taken as a primitive and not explained in terms of belief. On this view, then, experiential aboutness is not a species of derived intentionality.

Experiential aboutness is clearly distinct from the other three notions that we have introduced. It is different from attitude aboutness in not requiring conceptualization. It is different from linguistic aboutness in not being derived. And it is different from indicator aboutness in permitting falsehood: perceptual experiences can present the world as being different from the way that it really is.

Subdoxastic aboutness

Finally, there are unconscious psychological states that have aboutness. At least such states are invoked throughout cognitive psychology and theoretical linguistics. In these disciplines, the unconscious processes that lead up to experience – and ultimately to belief – are certainly described in content-using, or semantic, terms. The very idea of information-processing psychology is committed to there being information in the visual system or the auditory system, for example: information about other states of the creature and also about states of the external world. The states that carry this information are often said to be mental representations.

Let us call this unconscious psychological aboutness *subdoxastic aboutness*, in line with Stephen Stich's (1978, p. 499) labelling of states which 'play a role in the proximate causal history of beliefs, though they are not beliefs themselves' as subdoxastic states. It is this notion of aboutness that is principally *sub judice* in the context of Searle's arguments leading up to, and onwards from, the Connection Principle.

But to the extent that this notion is legitimate at all, it is distinct from attitude aboutness, linguistic aboutness and indicator aboutness for the same reasons that experiential aboutness is different from those other three. Subdoxastic aboutness is distinct from attitude aboutness since, like experiential aboutness, it is a kind of non-conceptualized content. (Indeed, it is between those two kinds of non-conceptualized content that Evans, 1982, p. 158 distinguishes in terms of serving 'as the input to a thinking, concept-applying, and reasoning system'.) Subdoxastic aboutness is distinct from linguistic aboutness since it is not derived. Subdoxastic aboutness is also distinct from indicator aboutness, since it allows for the possibility of misrepresentation. We can say, for example, that a state of the auditory processing system represents the presence of a sound coming from the left even though there is not in fact any sound coming from the left. And finally, subdoxastic aboutness is quite unlike experiential aboutness, the fourth variety of aboutness, since it is not tied to consciousness.

Simplifications

Having distinguished five kinds of aboutness, we can simplify the discussion to follow by moving the notions of linguistic aboutness and experiential aboutness away from centre stage. In the case of linguistic aboutness, the reason is that there is nothing that is in dispute concerning this notion. In the case of experiential aboutness, it is not quite clear whether this notion is legitimate from Searle's point of view. Since it is the aboutness of perceptual experiences, it is closely tied to consciousness, so that is a point in its favour. On the other hand, Searle has not expressed any sympathy for the idea of non-conceptualized content. In any case, the issues are too complex to pursue here.

Then, we can achieve some further simplification by noting that, while the notions of indicator aboutness and subdoxastic aboutness are distinct, still a substantive theory of subdoxastic aboutness might well draw upon and refine the notion of indicator aboutness. In particular, it may be that a theory of subdoxastic aboutness will make use of the idea of co-variation on both the input side – causal antecedents – and the output side – causal consequences – along with the idea of natural function. It is plausible that, from these resources, we can construct a notion that allows for the possibility of misrepresentation, and is rather more expensive than indicator aboutness.

Classification of core cases of subdoxastic aboutness as examples of mere 'as if' intentionality will then be just as unsatisfying as the similar classification of cases of indicator aboutness. On the one hand, metaphorical attributions of 'as if' intentionality are not constrained by requirements of causal co-variation or of natural function. On the other hand, there is nothing in attributions of subdoxastic aboutness that corresponds to the heavy commitments of conceptualization. Subdoxastic aboutness presents itself, then, as a prima facie candidate for being a ground of non-derivative and non-trivial semantic evaluability, distinct from genuine, intrinsic intentionality.

With our attention focused now upon attitude aboutness and subdoxastic aboutness – upon genuine, intrinsic intentionality and the kind of semantic content that is widely invoked in cognitive science – we can consider Searle's arguments.

The Connection Principle

The Connection Principle plays a central role in Searle's argument. His twin aims are to establish the principle and then to draw out its consequences for the study of mind. One way to avoid the alleged consequences of the Connection Principle – 'no rule-following, no mental information-processing, no unconscious inferences, no . . .' – and defend cognitive science would be totally to reject the Connection Principle itself. Indeed, this would be the natural response from a friend of cognitive science who shared Searle's background assumption that aboutness is a roughly unitary phenomenon: that there is only one kind of non-derived, non-trivial aboutness. This kind of friend of cognitive science is likely to regard accessibility to consciousness as an optional extra, distinguishing a sub-class of semantically evaluable states with no scientific integrity, 'a scattered and probably uninteresting subpart of the full cognitive structure', as Chomsky puts it (1976, p. 163).

The position that I favour is intermediate between Searle and Chomsky. Thinking is special, as Searle says. Cognitive science is in good order, as Chomsky says. Crucially, I disagree with Searle about the Connection Principle's consequences for cognitive science. The first of three claims that I shall make in this section is that, if the notion of subdoxastic aboutness – as distinct from attitude aboutness – is so much as allowed to get to first base, the Connection Principle cannot then deliver a threat to its legitimacy.

On the other hand, I agree with Searle that there is something special about attitude aboutness, though I disagree with him about the *load-bearing* potential of the notion of accessibility to consciousness. The second claim in this section is that what is special about thinking is not best captured by the Connection Principle's criterion of accessibility to consciousness in principle.

The third claim in this section is simply that the argument for the Connection Principle is far from watertight. As Searle himself remarks (1990, p. 634): 'Many commentators point out ... that the argument does not demonstrate the Connection Principle with absolute certainty. They are right about that. The argument is explanatory though not demonstrative ....' To deny that the argument is watertight is not, however, to deny that there is an important truth lying in the region of the Connection Principle. Indeed, my view is that there is something true and important there, something that is not yet well understood.

The consequences of the Connection Principle

Let us allow, for the moment, that attitude aboutness – genuine, intrinsic intentionality – requires accessibility to consciousness, just as the Connection Principle says. And let us accept that many of the semantically evaluable states invoked in cognitive psychology and theoretical linguistics are not, in the relevant sense, accessible to consciousness. Still, this does nothing to threaten the legitimacy of the notion of subdoxastic aboutness. Certainly it does not suggest that the only thing to be said about subdoxastic aboutness is that it is mere 'as if' intentionality.

The first step in the argument for the Connection Principle is that 'There is a distinction between intrinsic and as-if intentionality' (Chapter 19, p. 333). The reason for insisting upon this distinction is that (1989, p. 198) 'the price of giving it up would be that everything becomes mental, because relative to some purpose or other anything can be treated *as if* it were mental'. We shall scarcely dispute this, any more than we should dispute the distinction between dogs and 'as if' dogs. The price of giving up that distinction would be that everything would be counted as a dog, since anything at all can be treated as if it were a dog. But it would be a mistake to move from the importance of this distinction to the idea that all that can relevantly be said about a cat is that it is an 'as if' dog. Similarly, it would be a mistake to think that all that can relevantly be said about a state that lacks genuine, intrinsic intentionality is that it is a case of 'as if' intentionality.

The friend of cognitive science wants to describe states as being non-derivatively and non-trivially semantically evaluable, as being assessable as correct or incorrect, true or false. In opposition, Searle argues that this talk of semantic evaluation should be replaced by talk about hardware and about function (pp. 341–2). But, in order not to be question-begging, Searle's argument must not simply build in an assumption saying that attitude aboutness is the only possible source of non-derived, non-trivial semantic evaluability. So, let us imagine that it is explicit that we start by allowing for the possibility of other kinds of aboutness.

It should be clear that, if that possibility is allowed at the beginning, the later stages of the argument cannot then close it off. Suppose that the argument establishes that attitude aboutness requires accessibility to consciousness. Then, whatever is in principle inaccessible to consciousness is not attitude aboutness. But it does not follow that it is not a source of semantic evaluability. The situation would remain the same if the Connection Principle were replaced by a principle linking intentionality to something other than accesibility to consciousness. If attitude aboutness requires X, and the states invoked in cognitive science lack X, then those states do not have attitude aboutness. But they may yet be semantically evaluable in virtue of having some other kind of aboutness.

There is a response that might be made, on Searle's side of the disagreement. It might be said that, while a state that is inaccessible to consciousness could be semantically evaluable, this would only be in some extended and trivial sense, since it would be a case of mere 'as if' intentionality. But there is a fallacy that must be avoided here. It is true that the state in question would lie within the domain of 'as if' intentionality, along with states of dry lawns and water flowing downhill. But the state in question may have genuine semantic properties of its own, semantic properties that are lacked by the states of lawns and streams. The state may have genuine aboutness; not genuine attitude aboutness or intentionality, of course, but genuine aboutness all the same.

It appears, then, that the argument for the Connection Principle could only have consequences threatening to cognitive science if it were to be augmented by the assumption that the only distinctions that are worth drawing, among kinds of aboutness, are those between genuine, intrinsic intentionality, derived intentionality, and 'as if' intensionality. But, so far, we have no good justification for that assumption. What is needed, if Searle's second aim is to be carried out, is an independent reason to cast doubt on the notion of subdoxastic aboutness and its cognitive science kin. We shall return to this point below.

The criterion in the Connection Principle

A theorist who maintains, against Searle, that there is a prima facie viable and explanatory notion of subdoxastic aboutness might still accept the Connection Principle as imposing a requirement upon attitude aboutness. For this theorist can allow for – may even insist upon – the importance of the difference between attitude aboutness and subdoxastic aboutness. This theorist is free to embrace the specialness of thinking – of concept possession, judgement, belief and inference – and might offer accessibility to consciousness as the distinctive mark of the domain of thinking. However, my own view is that what is special about thinking is not best captured by the Connection Principle's criterion of accessibility to consciousness in principle.

In 'Tacit knowledge and subdoxastic states' (Chapter 18), I addressed the question whether subdoxastic states – such as states of tacit knowledge – are like or unlike propositional attitude states. Chomsky says (1986, p. 269):

> Suppose that the facts were different, and that we could become conscious, by thought and introspection, that we do in fact make use of these rules and principles in our mental computations. Then, I think, one would have no hesitation in saying that we know them. If so, then cognizing would appear to have the properties of knowledge in the ordinary sense of the term, apart, perhaps, from accessibility to consciousness.

There are two claims in this strand of Chomsky's thought. One is that the difference between subdoxastic states and states of ordinary knowledge and belief is to be characterized in terms of accessibility to consciousness. The other is that the distinction is of no great importance for serious explanatory purposes.

I suggested, in contrast, that three intuitive differences between beliefs and subdoxastic states – accessibility to consciousness, inferential integration and conceptualization – add up to a prima facie case for a principled distinction. But, I also suggested that it is difficult to found the distinction upon the difference between accessibility and inaccessibility to consciousness, given our limited understanding of that notion.

One reason that I offered began from the fact that we do make use of the idea of unconscious beliefs (Chapter 18, p. 314). These states would have to be allowed to count as accessible, if the criterion were to be plausible. One way – the only obvious way – of protecting the idea that these belief states are accessible to consciousness is to introduce into the criterion the idea of being accessible save for the presence of a blocking mechanism. But then this strategy must itself be restricted, lest it be used to classify even paradigm cases of subdoxastic states as being accessible if only there were not a blocking mechanism. And whatever restriction we impose is likely to go more nearly to the heart of the distinction between beliefs and subdoxastic states than does the idea of accessibility to consciousness.

Searle allows that unconscious beliefs are accessible in principle (Chapter 19, p. 332): 'there is nothing in principle inaccessible to consciousness about the Freudian unconscious', and in response to an objection, he links the notion of accessibility in principle with that of a blocking mechanism. It is predictable, then, that many of his commentators (e.g. Block, 1990; Chomsky, 1990; Clark, 1990) object that relaxing the requirement of accessibility to accessibility 'in principle' risks obliterating the contrast between accessibility and inaccessibility altogether.

Another reason for not relying upon the notion of accessibility to consciousness to provide a criterion for the distinction between beliefs and subdoxastic states is that the notion is simply unclear. We can add some clarity by using the notions of phenomenal consciousness and access consciousness (cf. Block, 1990). But still we seem to be pointed elsewhere for the fundamental ground of the distinction. On the one hand, phenomenal consciousness is of no direct help here, for even if some kind of experience were to be associated with the occurrence of a state that had hitherto been classified as subdoxastic, that would not be enough to turn it into a belief state (Chapter 18, p. 316). Access consciousness, on the other hand, might seem more promising. Its title suggests as much. But we need to recall the various refinements of the idea.

The first two refinements that we considered point more or less directly in the direction of conceptualized content as providing a more fundamental criterion. We noted, for example, that Block's account of access consciousness suggests that what is important is that a state should have the kind of semantic content that fits it for the space of reasons, the domain of judgement, belief, inference and intention. As Block points out in his commentary on Searle (Block, 1990, p. 597), if there is not a more fundamental criterion in the offing, then it is difficult to see what interest could attach to the question whether a state is well situated with respect to reasoning and reporting processes.

The third refinement of the idea of access consciousness goes beyond the notion of conceptualized content by introducing the further requirement that the subject should be in a position to judge that she is in the state in question. But, as we noted, the effect of this requirement is only visible when it is used to distinguish between conscious and unconscious beliefs. And this means that the added requirement is no help for our present purposes, since accessibility in principle is supposed to include unconscious beliefs. Exactly the same reflections apply, of course, if we replace the subject's being in a position to judge that she has a certain belief by the belief state's having the property that explains why the subject is placed in such a position.

It seems, then, that the key to the distinction between beliefs and subdoxastic states is to be found, not in the notion of accessibility to consciousness, but in the idea of conceptualization. The content of beliefs and other propositional attitude states is necessarily conceptualized by the subject of those states, while the content of subdoxastic states does not require conceptualization by the subject of those states.

We can relate this proposal to the previous subsection, and to the next one. First, a principle linking intentionality and conceptualization has no dire consequences for cognitive science. If attitude aboutness requires conceptualization, and the states invoked in cognitive science have non-conceptualized content, then those states do not have attitude aboutness. But they may yet have some other kind of aboutness that constitutes a source of non-derived and non-trivial semantic evaluability. Secondly, even if accessibility to consciousness in principle is not a load-bearing notion, there may still be an important link between attitude aboutness and consciousness, mediated by the requirement of conceptualization. Indeed, conceptualization is a close relative of the notion that plays a pivotal role in Searle's argument for the Connection Principle, the notion of aspectual shape.

Aspectual shape and the Connection Principle

Searle's argument for the Connection Principle turns upon the claim (Step 2 of his argument) that 'Intrinsic intentional states . . . always have aspectual shapes' (Chapter 19, pp. 334–5). The notion of aspectual shape is explained: 'Whenever we perceive anything or think about anything, it is always under some aspects and not others that we perceive or think about that thing.' and then further elucidated by way of some examples:

> When you see a car it is not simply a matter of an object being registered by your perceptual apparatus; rather you actually have a conscious experience of the object from a certain point of view and with certain features . . . A man may believe . . . that the star in the sky is the Morning Star without believing that it is the Evening Star. A man may . . . want to drink a glass of water without wanting to drink a glass of H_2O.

What both the explanation and the examples suggest is that Searle's notion of aspectual shape is much the same as the Fregean notion of a mode of presentation. In the domain of judging, believing and inferring, objects and properties are always thought about under a mode of presentation; they are thought about in one way rather than another. And perceptual experiences make possible thoughts about objects and properties under perceptual demonstrative modes of presentation (Evans, 1982, ch. 6; Peacocke, 1983, ch. 5 and 6). So, the doctrine about aspectual shape is something to which we are committed, if we think that conceptualization is what is distinctive of attitude aboutness – or genuine, intrinsic intentionality – and if we have a neo-Fregean view of concepts. Let us agree: intentionality requires a Fregean sense-reference distinction.

The question now is whether there is a close link between conceptualization and consciousness, a link that would sustain the Searlean conclusion that a conceptualized state must be accessible to consciousness at least in principle. Although Searle himself does not make use of the distinction, we can consider this question for access consciousness and then for phenomenal consciousness.

The answer to the question whether there is a close link between conceptualization and access consciousness is that the connection is all too close. Searle's notion of accessibility to consciousness in principle is intended to apply to unconscious beliefs, and we have just noted, in the last section, that the notions of access consciousness that meet that requirement (the first and second refinements) are scarcely distinguishable from the notion of conceptualization. Interpreted in terms of access consciousness, the Connection Principle says that genuine, intrinsic intentionality involves a special kind of content: conceptualized content. By my lights, this is a correct principle. But it is surely less than Searle was seeking to establish.

The question whether there is a close link between conceptualization and phenomenal consciousness is much more difficult to answer. But Searle's argument – from pivotal point to conclusion – makes good sense when construed as directed towards a positive answer to this question. When Searle says (Step 3 of his argument): 'The aspectual feature cannot be exhaustively or completely characterized solely in terms of third person, behavioral or even neurophysiological predicates. None of these is sufficient to give an exhaustive account of aspectual shape.' (p. 335) it is impossible not to be reminded of Nagel on the elusiveness of phenomenal consciousness (Nagel, 1979, p. 167):

> If physicalism is to be defended, the phenomenological features must themselves be given a physical account. But when we examine their subjective character it seems that such a result is impossible. The reason is that every subjective phenomenon is essentially connected with a single point of view, and it seems inevitable that an objective, physical theory will abandon that point of view.

There is a complication to be dealt with in this construal of Searle, since we have said that there is nothing that it is like to have the belief, for example, that the angle in a semi-circle is a right angle. Phenomenal consciousness belongs to sensations and perceptual experiences (see above). But we can take it that Searle is using a notion of consciousness that is tied to Nagel's idea of 'something that it is like', but extends to what we would intuitively regard as conscious beliefs.

Against that background, suppose that we were to grant both that genuine, intrinsic intentionality involves aspectual shape (Step 2), and that the fundamental philosophical account of aspectual shape adverts to what it is like to be in the intentional state in question (something very like Step 3). Then it would be natural to argue from those two premises to the conclusion that there is something problematic about the notion of an intentional state for which there is nothing that it is like to be in that state. This is essentially the point Searle reaches at his Step 4: 'Now we seem to have a contradiction' (Chapter 19, p. 336). Furthermore, it would then be practically inevitable to suggest a particular way of resolving the apparent contradiction. A state to which the philosophically fundamental account of aspectual shape cannot apply directly could be credited with a aspectual shape derivatively from some other state to which it stands in an appropriately intimate relationship. One candidate for the required relationship would be causal antecedence. Thus, Searle (p. 338):

> [T]he only fact about the neurophysiological structures [realizing states that there is nothing that it is like to be in] that corresponds to the ascription of intrinsic aspectual shape is the fact that the system has the causal capacity to produce conscious states and processes where those specific aspectual shapes are manifest.

There would be a legitimate query to be raised as to whether the relationship of causal antecedence is quite intimate enough. After all, subdoxastic states, which are precisely not states with genuine, intrinsic intentionality, are defined by Stich (1978, p. 499) as states that 'play a role in the proximate causal history of beliefs'. But this is a matter of detail. It is clear enough how to proceed from premises corresponding to Steps 2 and 3 of Searle's argument to something very close to his conclusion.

Modulo the extension of the notion of phenomenal consciousness to encompass conscious beliefs, Searle's actual argument for the Connection Principle makes good sense when it is construed as an argument for a link between intentionality and phenomenal consciousness. But that is not yet to say that the argument is compelling.

The reconstructed argument begins from two premises. One premise is that genuine, intrinsic intentionality involves aspectual shape. To the extent that aspectual shape is equivalent to Fregean mode of presentation or sense, this premise is something to which we are committed by what we have said about conceptualization. The other premise is that the fundamental philosophical account of aspectual shape adverts to what it is like to be in the intentional state in question. This premise is controversial if aspectual shape is taken to be equivalent to Fregean mode of presentation or sense. There are at least two reasons for this. First, this premise depends crucially upon the extension of the notion of phenomenal consciousness from sensations and perceptual experiences to conscious beliefs. But that extension was entertained only in order to construe Searle's argument, and not as a positive recommendation. Secondly, this premise depends upon an extrapolation to all modes of presentation from the case of conscious perceptions: 'Aspectual shape is most obvious in the case of conscious perceptions' (Chapter 19, p. 335). This premise can, of course, be rendered uncontroversial by a stipulation about the way in which the notion of aspectual shape is to be taken. But then, the controversy is simply shifted to the other premise. For nothing that we have said about conceptualization leads to the view that there is always something that it is like to be in an intentional state.

As we are construing Searle's argument for the Connection Principle, then, the problem that it faces is this. The argument turns upon the claim that 'Intrinsic intentional states . . . always have aspectual shapes.' If a requirement of phenomenal consciousness is built into the notion of aspectual shape, then the argument onwards from the pivotal point is plausible, but the claim itself is controversial. If a requirement of phenomenal consciousness is not built into the notion of aspectual shape, then the claim itself is plausible, but the onward argument limps. (Some such dilemma as this seems to motivate a number of Searle's commentators: e.g. Lloyd, 1990; Rosenthal, 1990.)

But even if – as Searle himself accepts (1990, p. 634) – the argument for the Connection Principle is not absolutely compelling, still there may well be an important truth connecting intentionality and phenomenal consciousness. Genuine, intrinsic intentionality – attitude aboutness – involves conceptualization, and conceptualization involves senses or modes of presentation. Among modes of presentation, those demonstrative modes of presentation that are afforded by perceptual experience constitute particularly clear examples. Suppose now that we could argue that some theoretical primacy attaches to perceptual demonstrative modes of presentation. Suppose, even, that we could argue that in order to be able to think about objects at all, a subject needs to be able to think about objects under perceptual demonstrative modes of presentation. Then there would be a deep connection between intentionality and consciousness, just as Searle says, although not one that holds intentional state by intentional state.

Whether or not we can establish any theoretical primacy for perceptual demonstrative thoughts is not a topic for this chapter. Considerations in favour of such primacy would begin from the role of demonstrative thoughts in the explanation of a subject's actions upon objects in her environment (Perry, 1979). But, for now, it is enough to raise the question and to note that the issue is far from being well understood.

Cognitive Science

We have seen (in the section on the 'Consequences of the Connection Principle') that an attack on the legitimacy of subdoxastic aboutness must draw upon resources going beyond the Connection Principle. One possible line of objection to subdoxastic states, tacit knowledge of rules, information-processing and the rest of cognitive science's core notions, is generated by a threat of trivialization. Certainly, the need to avoid trivialization constitutes a challenge for any development of the notion of subdoxastic aboutness.

Concerning 'as if' intentionality, Searle says (Chapter 19, p. 334): 'Everything in the universe follows laws of nature, and for that reason everything behaves with a certain degree of regularity, and for that reason everything behaves *as if* it were following a rule . . . For example, suppose I drop a stone.

The stone . . . *follows the rule S* = $\frac{1}{2}g\ t^2$.' So, perhaps Searle would claim that, once we move away from conscious, conceptualized attitude aboutness, there is no way to prevent the notion of tacit knowledge of a rule from becoming utterly trivial, so that a wooden block sliding on a smooth surface would be credited with tacit knowledge of the rule $a = F/m$, for example. Certainly the block's motion conforms to that rule.

An initial reply to this worry is to say that, as the notion is used in information-processing psychology, a system that possesses knowledge of a rule is a system that has a resource enabling it to perform inference-like transitions between input and output states that are themselves states with aboutness, states that have semantic content. Knowledge of the rule $a = F/m$, for example, would permit the transition from an input state with the semantic content that the force is n units to an output state with the semantic content that the acceleration is n/m units. If we are asking about the presence or absence of that piece of knowledge, then the relevant input-output transitions are not from an input state that *is* a force to an output state that *is* an acceleration, but from an input state that *represents* a force to an output state that *represents* an acceleration. Likewise with Searle's example. Trivialization only threatens if we cannot block the attribution of tacit knowledge of the rule $S = \frac{1}{2}g\ t^2$ to the falling stone. And, on the face of it, we can block that attribution by pointing out that there are no plausible candidates for states of the stone that represent the elapsed time, or the distance travelled.

In fact, the notion of tacit knowledge that I sketched in chapter 18 (p. 310) is even further removed from the trivialization that might be suggested by Searle's remark. For attributions of tacit knowledge are not licensed simply by an input-output relation; they require, in addition, a particular causal-explanatory structure in the mechanisms that mediate between input representations and output representations (Evans, 1981; Davies, 1986, 1987, 1989, 1995).

It would be entirely fair to respond, on Searle's behalf, that this way of avoiding trivialization in the notion of tacit knowledge of rules is only as convincing as the idea that we can assign aboutness to the input and output states of these processing mechanisms. If the only notion of aboutness that is applicable to those states is 'as if' intentionality, then we have scarcely advanced the matter at all. But we should need to be given some good reason to suppose that this is so, in the context of our earlier discussion of indicator aboutness and subdoxastic aboutness, and particularly given the differences that we noted between those notions and mere 'as if' intentionality.

If the notion of tacit knowledge of rules as I have sketched it here, and developed it elsewhere, is at all close to the notion actually used in cognitive science, then Searle underdescribes the practice of cognitive science when he says:

> A typical strategy in cognitive science has been to try to discover complex patterns such as those found in perception or language and then to postulate combinations

of mental representations which will explain the pattern in the appropriate way
... Epistemically, the existence of the patterns is taken as evidence for the
existence of the representations. (p. 347)

We can see this underdescription in Searle's use of the examples of language
acquisition and the vestibulo-ocular reflex (VOR).

Language acquisition

In the case of language acquisition, the starting point of Chomsky's theory is
that the state attained by the normal adult language-user involves a body of
knowledge that is brought to bear – in ways that are not specified by Chomsky
– in both perception and production of sentences. A theory of how the
knowledge is used is a theory of performance; a theory of the body of
knowledge itself is a theory of competence. Given this starting point, there is
then an argument for postulating a substantial innate endowment that is
specific to the task of acquiring language.

In early versions of the theory – the Standard Theory (Chomsky, 1965) –
the attained body of knowledge is supposed to consist primarily of a set of rules
(a grammar). The innate endowment is then supposed to include at least two
components. There is a body of knowledge about the universal features of
humanly possible grammars. And there is an evaluation procedure for selecting
one grammar from among those that are both attainable and consistent with
the linguistic data that is available to the developing child.

In more recent versions – the Government-Binding Theory (Chomsky,
1986) – the attained body of knowledge and the innate endowment are more
closely related. Now, the innate endowment, or initial state of the language
faculty, is a body of knowledge that can be specified by a set of principles. In
these principles, the values of certain parameters have yet to be fixed; they are
like switches waiting to be set. The attained state is a body of knowledge
specified by those same principles, but now with the values of the parameters
set, in each case to one of finitely many possible values. The role of the
linguistic data available to the child is simply to enable the parameters to be set
to one of their possible combinations of positions.

There are powerful reasons for the changes in the theory over a period of
twenty-five years or so, but the whole story about language acquisition lapses if
the starting point is rejected; that is, if it is denied that the attained state is a
state of knowledge, a state with semantic content. The issue between Searle
and the explanatory practice of theoretical linguistics would be seen most
clearly if Searle were to reject this starting point; and, indeed, it would be
natural for him to do so. After all, at least so far as the attained state involves
knowledge of principles, the principles are typically quite inaccessible to
consciousness. But, in fact, Searle focuses the dispute on the innate endowment: knowledge of universal grammar.

The reason that he gives for not focusing on the attained state is that 'grammars of particular languages, like French and English, whatever else they contain, obviously contain a large number of rules that are accessible to consciousness' (p. 347). But this is not clearly a very good reason. At least three considerations are relevant here.

First, when Searle speaks of the rules of grammars of French or English, he is not using the term 'grammar' as it is used within the theory under discussion. Searle is using the term as roughly equivalent to what Chomsky calls 'pedagogical grammar' (1986, p. 6): 'a full list of exceptions (irregular verbs, etc.), paradigms and examples of regular constructions, and observations at various levels of detail and generality about the form and meaning of expressions.' But this is quite different from the body of knowledge that is reckoned to be the attained state of the language faculty.

Secondly, within Chomsky's theory there is a distinction between core grammar and periphery (1986, p. 147). The distinction is, as Chomsky remarks, theory internal: the differentiation within the attained state is dictated by the collection of principles that are included in the initial state of the language faculty. The core grammar is just that part of the attained grammar that is constituted by the collection of universal principles with their parameters now set. The periphery is 'whatever is added on in the system actually represented in the mind/brain of the speaker-hearer' (1986, p. 147). Now, it may be that some of what is in the periphery is accessible to consciousness. But, even so, the core grammar would have provided an example of aboutness without accessibility to consciousness, an example upon which to focus the issue.

Thirdly, we do, of course, have conscious access to many of the consequences of the body of knowledge in the attained state, and particularly to many of the consequences of core grammar. Thus, most English speakers are aware that there is 'something wrong' with the sentence:

John and Peter wanted me to vote for each other

even though it is clear how that sentence would have to be interpreted (as saying that John wanted me to vote for Peter and Peter wanted me to vote for John). But conscious access to consequences of the principles is not the same as conscious access to the principles themselves.

Concerning the attained state – particularly, core grammer as that is conceived in the principles and parameters framework – Searle could have made two claims exactly parallel to those he makes about universal grammar. The first claim is that, if the very idea of a body of knowledge that is inaccessible to consciousness is illegitimate and incoherent – if the hypothesis that there is such a body of knowledge is 'empty' (p. 348) – then it is futile to try to defend the idea on the grounds that it is invoked in the 'best theory'. Searle's second claim is this. If we have to live without the idea of unconscious knowledge, and to view the hypothesis that there is such a body of knowledge as empty, then that is really no great loss. For, Searle says, whatever evidence was supposed to favour the hypothesis can be 'much more simply accounted for' by alternative hypotheses about hardware and function (p. 349).

It is in this second claim that the underdescription of cognitive scientific practice can be seen. For the alternative hypotheses scarcely go beyond the evidence plus the assumption that the brain is somehow implicated in the causal history of that evidence. Thus, James Higginbotham says (1990, p. 609):

> No hint of theory is in sight here; rather, we have a replacement of explanations of the customary sort with sheer description of the facts that they were supposed to explain. It is thus highly misleading for Searle to say that the evidence for universal grammar is 'more simply' accounted for in his view, since the alleged account consists merely in stating the empirical facts.

Having to do without the idea of unconscious bodies of knowledge really would mean a diminution in explanatory power.

To the extent that Searle does not see this, it is presumably because he is already convinced that the notion of tacit knowledge of rules is trivial. If the friend of tacit knowledge cannot prevent the attribution of tacit knowledge of the rule $a = F/m$ to a body sliding on a smooth surface, then he is indeed open to an objection of the form that Searle envisages. For, whatever the attribution of tacit knowledge is supposed to explain can be 'much more simply accounted for' by the alternative (hardware) hypothesis that, for a body of a given mass, the acceleration produced is proportional to the net force applied. But what we have already argued is that the threat of trivialization can be blocked.

The second claim is not, then, a telling point against the practice of theoretical linguistics. The first claim, in contrast, is surely correct. If a notion is illegitimate, and hypotheses using the notion are empty, then it is pointless to insist that the theory in which these hypotheses figure is the best theory. But no dire consequences follow, unless it is shown that the notion of a body of knowledge that is inaccessible to consciousness *is* an illegitimate notion. It is not shown to be illegitimate by the argument for the Connection Principle, provided that we distinguish the aboutness of the body of knowledge from attitude aboutness. Nor has it been shown to be a trivial notion, yielding hypotheses that are devoid of empirical content.

The vestibulo-ocular reflex

The vestibulo-ocular reflex (VOR) generates eye movements that compensate for head movements in such a way as to keep stable the image of the world (or the image of a moving object that is being tracked) on the surface of the retina. It is a feedforward, rather than a feedback, system; the VOR does not operate by detecting visual errors. Indeed, (Churchland and Sejnowski, 1992, p. 356): 'The basic VOR circuit consists of detection [of head movements] by transducers, projection to the vestibular nucleus in the brain stem, and projection from there to cranial nerve nuclei, where motor neurons originate that project to the eyes muscles.' As a result of these very direct linkages, the VOR operates much more rapidly than the optokinetic system, which uses feedback from slippage of the retinal image, and the pursuit system, which is used for tracking small objects. Indeed, the VOR operates at extraordinarily high speeds: typically the compensating eye movements begin around 12–14 milliseconds after the onset of the head movement. By way of comparison, eye movements that are produced by the optokinetic and pursuit systems are delayed by more than 80 milliseconds (Miles and Lisberger, 1981, pp. 275–6; Churchland and Sejnowski, 1992, p. 353).

One way of describing the VOR, then, is simply as a system by means of which head movements cause equal and opposite eye movements. We might call this a mechanical input-output description. Another way to describe the VOR is as a system in which certain information-processing takes place. The starting point for this second kind of description is that transitions take place, not just from head movements of certain velocities to eye movements of certain velocities, but from representations of head movement velocities to representations of eye movement velocities (Churchland and Sejnowski, 1992, p. 357–8):

> If we assume that neurons projecting to the vestibular nuclei in the brain stem carry signals specifying head velocity, and that motor neurons carry signals specifying muscular contractions to produce an eye velocity, then the computational action, so to speak, is located between these two at the several vestibular nuclei, lumped together for convenience as 'VN'.

It is only against the background of this second kind of description that there is any question of crediting the system with tacit knowledge of rules relating head velocity and eye velocity. To invoke knowledge of such rules given only the first kind of description, the mechanical input-output description, would be to trivialize the notion. It would be like crediting a wooden block sliding on a smooth surface with knowledge of the rule $a = F/m$.

So, the assumption of input and output states that have semantic content is a necessary condition for a description of the intervening causal transitions in terms of knowledge of rules. But, it is not yet a sufficient condition for crediting the system with tacit knowledge of a rule or generalization relating head velocity to eye velocity. According to the notion of knowledge of rules that I favour, tacit knowledge of a rule in a processing system requires that the various input-output transitions that are in conformity with the rule should have the same causal explanation; roughly, should be mediated by the same component mechanism within the system (see again Evans, 1981; Davies, 1986, 1987, 1989, 1995). And that is not a completely trivial requirement.

A properly constrained information-processing account of the operation of the VOR in terms of 'a deep unconscious rule' cannot, then, simply be replaced by a hardware account as Searle suggests (p. 344): 'When I look at an object while my head is moving, the hardware mechanism of the VOR moves my eyeballs.' There would be a loss of explanatory power in that replacement. Someone who denies that there is any such loss is likely to be overlooking the necessary starting point for an information-processing account, and supposing instead that the account in terms of rules is set against the background of only the mechanical input-output description of the reflex.

The computational problem posed by the VOR is, in any case, rather more complex than the starting point for an information-processing account might suggest. For, as Churchland and Sejnowski go on the explain (1992, p. 358):

> VN is actually an area of convergence, receiving not only vestibular signals, but also signals from smooth-pursuit neurons and saccadic-burst neurons . . . The computational problem for the VN centers on what transformation should be applied to the input vector carrying the three kinds of information so as to solve the problem of how the eyes should move.

Searle appears to reject the whole idea of an exploration of the VOR in information-processing, or computational, terms, preferring some neurophysiological elaboration of this sketch (p. 343):

> What actually happens is that fluid movements in the semi-circular canals of the inner ear trigger a sequence of neuron firings that enter the brain over the eighth cranial nerve. These signals follow two parallel pathways . . . in the brain stem and cerebellum and they transform the initial input signals to provide motor output 'commands', via motorneurons that connect to the eye muscles and cause eyeball movements.

But against this we have to set the fact that, while there will surely be a neural account of the VOR, this is no reason to exclude other levels of explanation unless those other levels have been shown to be inevitably headed in the direction of triviality or incoherence. So, we should pay some heed to such a statement as this, from David Robinson (1981, p. 463):

> When we ask how the brain works, the question is perceived quite differently by people working at the many levels of the nervous system. Certainly it is necessary to know how the hardware of the nervous system works . . . but we all recognize that the solutions to these problems are not an end in themselves. They are the means that will enable us to understand how the brain processes information . . . .

Robinson's own work on the VOR (e.g. Robinson, 1981, 1987; Cannon et al., 1983; Cannon and Robinson, 1985) contains a fine example of the role of an information-processing description in neuroscientific research.

Robinson's research suggests that, in general, the firing rate, R, of the ocular motor neurons (responsible for initiating the muscle contractions that produce eye movement) is characterized by an equation:

$$R = b + kE + r(dE/dt)$$

where b is a constant – the background discharge rate of the neuron – and the other two terms are proportional to the eye displacement, E, and the eye velocity, dE/dt, respectively (1981, p. 467). Given that some muscle force is required just to maintain the eye in a position displaced from straight ahead, even if the eye is not moving, the presence of the kE term in the equation makes good sense. But the problem that it poses is that, while conversion of head-velocity information to an eye-velocity command is a simple, even trivial, computational matter, obtaining information about eye displacement from information about velocity requires integration. (This is not integration in the sense of bringing information together, as in cross-modal integration, but integration as in high school calculus.)

The project of devising a model of a neural integrator provides a classic example of interaction between levels of explanation. Very roughly, the idea that a neural integrator is needed comes from a high-level task analysis (Robinson, 1987, p. 1915): 'The need for a neural integrator was apparent as soon as anyone trained in systems analysis sat down and looked at this reflex.' An initial computational, in fact, neural network, model (Cannon et al., 1983) had some attractive features, and solved the problem of how to avoid integrating the background firing rate along with the velocity signal. But the units in the neural network model differed in important ways from the corresponding population of real neurons, believed to be in the vestibular nuclei. So, considerations from neurophysiology motivated a revised model, returning the research to the computational level (Cannon and Robinson, 1985).

Whether or not Robinson's story about the neural integrator is ultimately correct, the investigation, moving as it does among several levels of description, constitutes an episode of strikingly explanatory research in cognitive science. There is nothing in Searle's arguments that reveals a hitherto concealed vacuity in this research programme.

To be sure, there will be theorists who regard the use of a level of description at which neural firing rates are credited with semantic content as a level having primarily heuristic importance, guiding the development of detailed neurophysiological theories. These theorists will go beyond mere appreciation of interlevel interaction in the direction of more reductive aspirations, and to that extent they will regard descriptions in terms of aboutness, information and rules as having diminishing importance as science progresses. But even these reductionist theorists can still agree that the descriptions in terms of aboutness are far from trivial. They are certainly constrained more tightly than the mere 'as if' description of my lawn as thirsty, or as desiring or even believing that it will rain. So, even a reductionist theorist can reject Searle's claim that, in an information-processing account of the VOR, 'All the intentional ascriptions are *as-if* (p. 343).

Conclusion

The first two sections of this chapter were taken up with some distinctions. First, there was the distinction between two notions of consciousness – phenomenal consciousness and access consciousness – along with three refinements of the second of those notions. Next, there were distinctions between five different notions of aboutness that might plausibly find a place in our thinking about psychology and the mind. We then simplified the discussion by focusing on just two of those notions: attitude aboutness and subdoxastic aboutness.

With these distinctions in place, we have been concerned, in the last two sections of the chapter, with Searle's two aims: to establish the Connection Principle, and then to show that it has serious negative consequences – 'no . . ., no . . ., no . . .' – for cognitive science. I argued for three claims of my own. First, the Connection Principle does not, by itself, threaten the legitimacy of the notion of subdoxastic aboutness. If it appears to do so, then this is because a question-begging assumption has been used. This is the assumption that the only distinctions worth drawing in the area of aboutness are the distinctions among genuine, intrinsic intentionality, derived intentionality, and 'as if' intentionality. Secondly, what is special about thinking is best captured by a criterion of conceptualization rather than a criterion of accessibility to consciousness. Thirdly, although the argument for the Connection Principle is far from watertight, there may well be a link between intentionality and consciousness, mediated by the requirement of conceptualization and the idea of perceptual demonstrative modes of presentation. More work is needed to improve our understanding here.

Although the Connection Principle does not pose an independent threat to subdoxastic aboutness, information-processing, knowledge of rules, and the like, these notions do face a challenge. They must avoid the threat of trivialization. In the last section, I argued that this challenge can be met. Indeed, the appearance of a serious threat depends, to some extent, upon an underdescription of the practice of cognitive science.

Thinking – concept possession, judgement, belief, desire, inference, intention – is special. There is nothing quite like it. Certainly, unconscious information-processing and tacit knowledge of rules are not quite like it. But those explanatory resources deployed in cognitive psychology and theoretical linguistics still have their own integrity as involving non-derived and non-trivial semantic evaluability.

References

Allport, A. (1988) What concept of consciousness? In A.J. Marcel and E. Bisiach (eds), *Consciousness in Contemporary Science*, pp. 159–82. Oxford, Oxford University Press.

Block, N. (1990) Consciousness and accessibility. *Behavioral and Brain Sciences* 13, 596–8.

Block, N. (1991) Evidence against epiphenomenalism. *Behavioral and Brain Sciences* 14, 670–2.

Block, N. (1992) Begging the question against phenomenal consciousness. *Behavioral and Brain Sciences* 15, 205–6.

Block, N. (1993) Review of D.C. Dennett, *Consciousness Explained. Journal of Philosophy* 90, 181–93.

Block, N. (1995): On a confusion about a function of consciousness. *Behavioral and Brain Sciences* 18.

Cannon, S.C. and Robinson, D.A. (1985) An improved neural-network model for the neural integrator of the oculomotor system: more realistic neuron behavior. *Biological Cybernetics* 53, 93–108.

Cannon, S.C., Robinson, D.A. and Shamma, S. (1983) A proposed neural network for the integrator of the oculomotor system. *Biological Cybernetics* 49, 127–36.

Chomsky, N. (1965) *Aspects of the Theory of Syntax.* Cambridge, Mass., MIT Press.

Chomsky, N. (1976) *Reflections on Language.* London, Fontana/Collins.

Chomsky, N. (1986) *Knowledge of Language: Its Nature, Origin, and Use.* New York, Praegar.

Chomsky, N. (1990) Accessibility 'in principle'. *Behavioral and Brain Sciences* 13, 600–601.

Churchland, P.S. and Sejnowski, T.J. (1992) *The Computational Brain.* Cambridge, Mass., MIT Press.

Clark, A. (1990) Aspects and algorithms. *Behavioral and Brain Sciences* 13, 601–2.

Davies, M. (1986) Tacit knowledge, and the structure of thought and language. In C. Travis (ed.), *Meaning and Interpretation*, pp. 127–58. Oxford, Basil Blackwell.

Davies, M. (1987) Tacit knowledge and semantic theory: can a five per cent difference matter? *Mind*, 96, 441–62.

Davies, M. (1989) Connectionism, modularity, and tacit knowledge. *British Journal for the Philosophy of Science* 40, 541–55.

Davies, M. (1990) Thinking persons and cognitive science. *AI and Society* 4, 39–50. Reprinted in A. Clark and R. Lutz (eds), *Connectionism in Context.* London, Springer-Verlag.

Davies, M. (1995) Two notions of implicit rules. In J.E. Tomberlin (ed.), *Philosophical Perspectives 9: AI, Connectionism, and Philosophical Psychology.* Atascadero, California, Ridgeview.

Davies, M. and Humphreys, G.W. (1993) Editors' Introduction. In *Consciousness: Psychological and Philosophical Essays*, pp. 1–39. Oxford, Blackwell.

Dretske, F. (1986) Misrepresentation. In R. Bogdan (ed.), *Belief: Form, Content and Function*, pp. 17–36. Oxford, Oxford University Press. Reprinted in W.G. Lycan (ed.), *Mind and Cognition: A Reader.* Oxford, Basil Blackwell, 1990.

Evans, G. (1980) Things without the mind. In Z. van Straaten (ed.), *Philosophical Subjects*, pp. 76–116. Oxford, Oxford University Press. Reprinted in *Collected Papers.* Oxford, Oxford University Press, 1985.

Evans, G. (1981) Semantic theory and tacit knowledge. In S. Holtzman and C. Leich (eds), *Wittgenstein: To Follow A Rule*, pp. 118–37. London, Routledge and Kegan Paul. Reprinted in *Collected Papers*. Oxford, Oxford University Press, 1985.

Evans, G. (1982) *The Varieties of Reference*. Oxford, Oxford University Press.

Fodor, J. (1983) *The Modularity of Mind*. Cambridge, Mass., MIT Press.

Grice, H.P. (1959) Meaning. *Philosophical Review* 66, 377–88. Reprinted in *Studies in the Way of Words*. Cambridge, Mass., Harvard University Press, 1989.

Grice, H.P. (1989) *Studies in the Way of Words*. Cambridge, Mass., Harvard University Press.

Higginbotham, J. (1990) Searle's vision of psychology. *Behavioral and Brain Sciences* 13, 608–10.

Jackson, F. (1982) Epiphenomenal qualia. *American Philosophical Quarterly* 32, 127–36. Reprinted in W.G. Lycan (ed.), *Mind and Cognition: A Reader*. Oxford, Basil Blackwell, 1990.

Jackson, F. (1986) What Mary didn't know. *Journal of Philosophy* 83, 291–5. Reprinted in D.M. Rosenthal (ed.), *The Nature of Mind*. Oxford, Oxford University Press, 1991.

Levine, J. (1983) Materialism and qualia: the explanatory gap. *Pacific Philosophical quarterly* 64, 354–61.

Levine, J. (1993) On leaving out what it's like. In M. Davies and G.W. Humphreys (eds), *Consciousness: Psychological and Philosophical Essays*, pp. 121–36. Oxford, Blackwell.

Lloyd, D. (1990) Loose connections: four problems in Searle's argument for the 'Connection Principle'. *Behavioral and Brain Sciences* 13, 615–16.

McGinn, C. (1988) Consciousness and content. *Proceedings of the British Acadamy* 74, 219–39. Reprinted in *The Problem of Consciousness*. Oxford, Basil Blackwell, 1991.

McGinn, C. (1989) Can we solve the mind-body problem? *Mind* 98, 349–66. Reprinted in *The Problem of Consciousness*. Oxford, Basil Blackwell, 1991.

Miles, F.A. and Lisberger, S.G. (1981) Plasticity in the vestibulo-ocular reflex: a new hypothesis. *Annual Review of Neuroscience* 4, 273–99.

Nagel, T. (1979) What is it like to be a bat? In *Mortal Questions*, pp. 165–80. Cambridge, Cambridge University Press. Reprinted in D.M. Rosenthal (ed.), *The Nature of Mind*. Oxford, Oxford University Press, 1991.

Nelkin, N. (1986) Pains and pain sensations. *Journal of Philosophy* 83, 129–48.

Nelkin, N. (1989a) Propositional attitudes and consciousness. *Philosophy and Phenomenological Research* 49, 413–30.

Nelkin, N. (1989b) Unconscious sensations. *Philosophical Psychology* 2, 129–41.

Peacocke, C. (1983) *Sense and Content*. Oxford, Oxford University Press.

Peacocke, C. (1986) *Thoughts: An Essay on Content*. Oxford, Basil Blackwell.

Peacocke, C. (1992) *A Study of Concepts*. Cambridge, Mass., MIT Press.

Perry, J. (1979) The problem of the essential indexical. *Noûs* 13, 3–21. Reprinted in *The Problem of the Essential Indexical and Other Essays*. Oxford, Oxford University Press, 1993.

Robinson, D.A. (1981) The use of control systems analysis in the neurophysiology of eye movements. *Annual Review of Neuroscience* 4, 463–503.

Robinson, D.A. (1987) The windfalls of technology in the oculomotor system. *Investigative Ophthalmology and Visual Science* 28, 1912–24.

Rosenthal, D.M. (1986) Two concepts of consciousness. *Philosophical Studies* 49, 329–59.

Rosenthal, D.M. (1990) On being accessible to consciousness. *Behavioral and Brain Sciences* 13, 621–2.

Rosenthal, D.M. (1993) Thinking that one thinks. In M. Davies and G.W. Humphreys (eds), *Consciousness: Psychological and Philosophical Essays*, pp. 197–223. Oxford, Blackwell.

Searle, J.R. (1983) *Intentionality*. Cambridge, Cambridge University Press.

Searle, J.R. (1989) Consciousness, unconsciousness, and intentionality. *Philosophical Topics* 17, 193–209.

Searle, J.R. (1990) Who is computing with the brain? *Behavioral and Brain Sciences* 13, 632–40.

Stich, S.P. (1978) Beliefs and subdoxastic states. *Philosophy of Science* 45, 499–518.

Strawson, P.F. (1959) *Individuals*. London, Methuen.

Wilkes, K.V. (1988) ——, yìshì, duh, um, and consciousness. In A.J. Marcel and E. Bisiach (eds), *Consciousness in Contemporary Science*, pp. 16–41. Oxford, Oxford University Press.

Psychoanalytic Explanation

21

Introduction: Psychoanalytic Explanation

Graham Macdonald

Background

Since its inception over a century ago, psychoanalytic explanation has taken a hammering from an assortment of philosophers and psychologists. By 'psychoanalytic explanation' we mean the sort of explanation which is typified in the seminal work of Freud.[1] After the early stages of his career, Freud developed a view of the contents of the mind which credits a subject with a rich *unconscious* mental life in order to provide a mentalistic explanation of behaviour which would, without the unconscious element, be so irrational as to be inexplicable by normal means. To this general account, Freud added specific components as his theory developed; in particular, he attributed to the mind a certain structure (id, ego and super-ego), and mechanisms such as repression which serve to explain the contents of the unconscious.

The need to posit the existence of unconscious mental states arose within the context of Freud's analysis of women patients who suffered from hysteria. On Freud's early account, the symptoms associated with hysteria were caused by traumatic events experienced while the women were young children. On his initial account, these women had told him that they remembered being the victims of early seduction or rape.[2] It later occurred to Freud that the seduction/rape scenes were not real, but imagined; it also transpired that the women had not *told* him, in so many words, of the seductions. These had been inferred by Freud from what the women did tell him, and by his subsequent questioning of them. The evidence, as interpreted by Freud, provided the necessary ingredients for the positing of the unconscious: the imaginary scenes were the product of a desire, and the desire was of such a kind that it could not be presented 'straightforwardly' to consciousness. The presence of the desire in consciousness was only via certain of its effects, and these were suitably disguised so that the source of the effects could not be known. So dreams, for instance, are understood as being the expression of certain desires and wishes, but this expression being in a form whose manifest content, the way the dream appears, 'hides' the latent content, the deeper meaning of the dream content. An important further element is added when one sees the dream, or symptom, as affording some release from repression. In the symptoms of psycho-neurosis, Freud saw the *activity* of the sexual impulse, and so the symptom, or its counterpart, the dream, can afford a certain satisfaction of the repressed desire, a 'substitute' satisfaction.

Desires cannot be present in consciousness in undisguised form because of a conflict between it and other components of the psyche. In much of his work Freud concentrated on the desires that were derived from the sexual instinct, but it is important to the overall design of his theory that the sexual instinct is not the only instinct. It is essential to the dynamic character of psychoanalytic theory that there be a conflict between instincts, and most of this conflict was, at least initially, thought of as a conflict between sexual instinct and 'ego instincts', which included the formation of the superego at a crucial stage in the development of the child. (Later Freud came to attach some importance to the death instinct as a distinct source of conflict with the sexual instinct.) One function of the ego was to defend itself against the force of sexual desires, and so it formed the repressing agency which shut off the content of the desires from consciousness.

The complaints against the positing of such unconscious states are varied and of varying strength, and we will not survey all of them here. In particular, we are not going to explore one of the most difficult areas, that of the epistemology of psychoanalysis, although what is said below does have implications for this aspect of the debate. By the 'epistemology of psychoanalysis' we mean the controversies over whether specific psychoanalytic explanations are confirmed or falsified, and over the success, or otherwise, of the therapy(ies) associated with psychoanalytic diagnoses. These two aspects are often conflated; it is thought that one shows the truth of the diagnosis by successful treatment of the patient. In general, though, we do not presume such a tight epistemological connection between diagnosis and cure: it is usually possible for a specific diagnosis to be true (and shown to be true) together with the truth of the *inefficacy* of the putative cure associated with that diagnosis. One could correctly diagnose measles, say, and prescribe a 'cure' which happened to be the wrong medicine. In the Freudian case, it seems possible for the analyst's description and explanation of a psycho-neurosis, say, to be correct, but for the 'talking cure' – the cure associated with psychotherapy – to be ineffective. However, the discussion in the preceding section of Part III, on tacit knowledge, shows that there is an aspect of therapy which may be central to the legitimacy of the postulation of unconscious states. In that discussion Searle was happy to allow that unconscious states, as posited in psychoanalysis, were bona fide mental states, and this because they were 'in principle' accessible to consciousness. The 'in principle' in this case is justified by the thought that what prevents the conscious awareness of such states is a blocking mechanism – repression – which once removed would allow the awareness of the states. Bringing the state to consciousness is part of the purpose of therapy, so this aspect of therapy could be crucial to the validation of the existence of the unconscious mental life.

Unfalsifiability

The role of repression and resistance in psychoanalytic theory immediately leads to another topic related to the epistemological controversies which does spill over into debates about the nature of psychoanalytic explanation, and that is whether such explanations are falsifiable. The connection with the preceding topic is that Freud associated the therapist's attempt to lift the repression with resistance on the part of the subject. The subject's avoidance of the analyst's approach to, and uncovering of, the crucial desires which give rise to the symptoms, may well be understandable given the need for repression in the first place, but it allows for increased interpretive licence; it permits the analyst to use the subject's *rejection* of an interpretation of a symptom as further evidence that the interpretation is correct. The denial can be seen as just resistance to the unmasking of the hidden desire. The question arises that if this amount of leeway is allowed to the analyst, the interpreter of the symptom, then how can one know when an interpretation is false? Does the postulation of unconscious states and impulses become detached from any empirical base?

The charge of unfalsifiability was pressed by Karl Popper, who made falsifiability by 'basic statements' the criterion for the scientific status of a hypothesis. (Popper's basic statements, restricted existential statements about 'mascroscopic' objects, are his version of the positivists' observation statements. 'There is a table', not being restricted, is unfalsifiable and not a basic statement. 'There is a table in this room now' is falsifiable, so can serve as a basic statement.) In order for a theory or hypothesis to be falsifiable there must be some possible conflict between it and some basic statement, so that the hypothesis and that basic statement could not both be true. Popper's judgement was that Freudian explanations failed the test. In comparison to Einstein's Theory of Relativity:

> The two psychoanalytic theories [Freud's and Adler's] were in a different class. They were simply non-testable, irrefutable. There was no conceivable human behaviour which would contradict them ... These theories describe some facts, but in the manner of myths. (Popper, 1963, pp. 37–8)

Einstein's theory made precise predictions and so was falsifiable. In this it was different from both Marxist and Freudian theory, but these latter two theories differed in the manner of their unfalsifiability. Marx's theory of historical change had been falsifiable, according to Popper. It made specific predictions about the forthcoming socialist revolutions in advanced capitalist countries. It was only when these predictions turned out to be false that Marxists, by adjusting and modifying the original theory, rendered historical materialism unfalsifiable. With Freud it was different: his theory was unscientific from its inception, its unfalsifiability arising from the very nature of the proffered explanations. The source of the trouble was the essential role played by the mechanisms of repression and unconscious guilt. Faced with the example of an adolescent male exhibiting loving behaviour towards his father, the behaviour 'falsifying' the Oedipus complex hypothesis (that adolescent males wish to have sex with their mothers and kill their fathers), a psychoanalyst could invoke the repression of the murderous desire which, together with hypotheses about over-compensation due to the residual guilt, would explain the loving behaviour. So, claimed Popper, *no* behaviour could falsify the original psychoanalytic hypothesis. There was no basic statement about behaviour which could conflict with psychoanalytic theory.

The accusation of unfalsifiability has proved powerful. We cannot go into the details of the subsequent debate now, but we can relate it to the issues discussed below. The best way of skirting the complexities of the controversy is to admit that psychoanalytic explanations are not confirmable or falsifiable *in the same way* as are explanations in physics and chemistry. On this point Popper was right. The defender of psychoanalytic theory ought to respond by saying that this is true of other explanations as well.[3] In particular the counter-claim should be that all intentional explanations have built into them the potential for escaping refutation. Or, less ambitiously, the claim should be that all those intentional explanations that allow for the possibility that agents are unaware of their own motivations, so that the actions can have a meaning contrary to that conferred upon them by the subject (the agents), will have this potential for escaping refutation. The reason is that any such action will be able to be interpreted as having two meanings, that given it by the agent (the manifest meaning) and that ascribed to it by the deeper interpretation (a latent meaning), so the interpreter will have a great deal of flexibility available in order to make the facts fit the hypothesis.[4] If this is true it renders the scope of the unfalsifiability objection very large. It looks as though many of our everyday explanations will be rendered metaphysical by this criterion, since it is true that such explanations allow us to attribute to the agents motivations of which they are unaware. The defence will be: accept that psychoanalytical hypotheses are viable explanations (even if different), or eliminate mentalistic explanations entirely.[5]

This case rests essentially on the idea that ordinary intentional explanations will attribute motivations and desires of which agents are unaware. Freud himself pointed to the phenomena of post-hypnotic actions, where agents act under the instruction of a hypnotist but are unaware of so doing, in defence of the propriety of explanations averting to unconscious motivations. The usual way of dealing with such actions is to say that the agents were doing what they were told, even though this is not the story the agents themselves would tell. However, this case does not seem to possess the distinctive marks of a psychanalytic explanation. The post-hypnotic agent does not *need* to be unaware of the underlying motivation in the way that the neurotic needs to mask the real significance of the act. The latter, it is said, is 'deliberately' hiding from the truth in a way in which the former need not. There seems to be, in the case of the candidate for psychoanalytic explanation, the peculiar phenomenon of the agent both knowing what the real significance of the action is, and escaping from this knowledge at the same time. In the hypnosis case we have the hypnotist to blame for the state of unawareness of the agent; in the psychoanalytic case we have only the agent. In some way psychoanalytic agents (actively) suppress the information which is available to them, and this suggests that the appropriate analogy for psychoanalytic explanation is with explanations that appeal to self-deception. In cases of self-deception we have the phenomenon of agents deceiving themselves, hiding the truth from themselves.

The claim now is: we often use the notion of self-deception in attributing motives to others; it is a part of our everyday intentional idiom. Given this, there would appear to be a reason to use its features to cover the psychoanalytic case. If this can be done, psychoanalytic explanations will be seen to be not extraordinary, but an extension of the ordinary. The accusation of unfalsifiablity will be defused if it can be shown that this sort of unfalsifiablity is endemic to a general kind of explanation, and is not peculiar to psychoanalytic hypotheses.

Sartre and Self-deception

If the suggested tactic of defending psychoanalytic explanation by claiming it is similar to normal intentional explanation is to work, then we need to show not only that the similarities exist, but also that in those respects in which the two explanations are similar there is no problem lurking. It would be no good if the postulation of repressed unconscious desires conformed to an aspect of ordinary mentalistic explanation if this aspect were itself under suspicion. Likening repression to 'ordinary' self-deception will normalize repression only if self-deception is considered coherent. Unfortunately, there are many who think that the notion of self-deception is inherently problematic because it leads to the paradox of self-deception: that agents both know and do not know that they have a certain belief or desire. What has to be made clear is how it is that the paradox does not lead to real contradiction.

Before discussing the contributions to this section, it will be worthwhile to consider the argument of one vehement critic of psychoanalysis, Jean-Paul Sartre, precisely because the argument concentrates on the alleged incoherence of an agent both knowing and not knowing his or her own beliefs or desires. Sartre goes to the heart of the issue: he suggests that the problem arises because of the distinctiveness of the intentional. An intentional mental state is, he claims, one which points beyond itself, one which is essentially related to something other than itself. But it is not related to this other as things causally connected are related. This latter kind of relation is an external relation, whereas the connection between intentional state and its object is an internal, signifying relation. The connection between human beings' lighting a fire and the later effects, ashes, is a causal connection, so the presence of the human beings 'is not contained in the remaining cinders, but connected with them by a relation of causality: the relation is external, the ashes of the fire are passive considered in that causal relation, as every effect is in relation to its cause' (Sartre, 1962 pp. 51–2). With the signifying relation matters are different. 'To signify is to indicate something else; and to indicate in such a way that in developing the signification one finds precisely the thing signified' (Sartre, 1962, p. 27).

The intentional state must wear its meaning on its sleeve: its being is constituted by its appearance. *What* is being represented must be apparent from the content of the intentional state, and is not dependent on some hidden process. This does not mean that the meaning must be perfectly explicit, only that

> we should not interrogate the consciousness from outside, as one would study the remains of the fire or the encampment, but from within; that we should look into it for the signification . . . If symbolisation is constitutive [of the conscious phenomenon] it is legitimate to see an immanent bond of *comprehension* between the symbolisation and the symbol'. (Sartre, 1962, p. 53)

For Sartre, Freud made the mistake of treating the meaning of the mental state on the model of a cause-effect relation, making the meaning external to the state. Only it cannot consistently do this, since there is 'a difficulty of principle. If consciousness organises emotions as a special type of response adapted to an external situation, how does it manage to have no consciousness of this adaptation?' (Sartre, 1962, p. 55). Sartre's accusation is that psychoanalysis treats a mental state, such as an emotion, as a type of adaptational response, an adaptation chosen by the subject. The same point holds for neurotic symptoms, for example, since in so far as they afford some release from repression and some satisfaction of the repressed desires, they are also functional for the subject. They afford the subject a compromise between the conflicting impulses or desires which give rise to them.[6] The question Sartre poses is how the subject, the agent, has no consciousness of the desire to which the symptom is an adaptation. The problem would disappear if the relation between symptom and desire was treated as a biological adaptation, but Sartre's point is that, in so far as the symptom represents the desires, the two are *internally* related. The accusation is that psychoanalytic explanations treat the relation between the signifying and the signified as both an external causal relation and as a bond of comprehension, and if it stuck to the latter perspective it would not be able to locate the significance of the conscious state as residing in a prior experience which the agent no longer comprehends.

The importance of the Sartrean critique is that it locates the problem as one which emerges because of the nature of intentional conscious states: such states have a significance which is constituted by the agent, so this significance must be comprehended by the agent. Now one might think that any problem here resides in Sartre's view of the mental, perhaps it is 'Cartesian' in its insistence that the meaning of our intentional states must be transparent to the agents, or that agents do not have the meaning-conferring role Sartre thinks they do. However, the problem Sartre alludes to – the mixing of causal and intentional explanatory modes – can be seen to emerge within psychoanalytic explanation, with the way some states are deemed responsive to others in the causal order, and also to be responsive to the meaning, or symbolic, content, of those other intentional states. The tension between the two types of explanatory strategies, the causal and the intentional, can be seen in the way that symptoms, phenomena which at first sight appear to be simply part of causal processes in the sense that their appearance is beyond the control of the agent, acquire a sense, and so become part of the intentional. On one account symptoms which are beyond the control of agents – involuntary twitches or tics, say – become neurotic symptoms if they are used by the agent to express feelings or desire.[7] Such a use seems to presuppose that a choice has been made by the agent, and that the sense of the symptom, its representational or expressive character, relates to this choice. Sartre's question then returns: given this involvement of the agent, how is the agent unaware of what the symptom relates to?

One way of replying to Sartre's attack would be to reject the assumption that causal and intentional (reason-based) explanations are exclusive. This would involve rejecting his view that intentional states are not part of the causal order. Reflecting on this aspect, however, takes us back to the problem. Suppose that reasons and causes are related in the way Donald Davidson has claimed, i.e. that reasons are causes described in such a way as to make it *intelligible* why agents have acted as they have (Davidson, 1980). Rendering actions intelligible requires that their causes be viewed as reasons for those actions; in fact, treating behaviour as an *action* requires that its cause be a rationalizing cause. This leads to an agreement with Sartre on the first issue, that under its mental guise the cause must be related to its effect (the action) internally (there must be a description of the cause which is conceptually connected to a description of the action). Now obviously not just any old reason will be satisfactory; one only makes the action intelligible by seeing why it was that *the agent* had a reason to do it. One may see that the action had a rationale, but unless it is seen as a rationale for the agent, intelligibility will not have been achieved. Intentional explanations succeed in making actions intelligible in so far as they represent the agents epistemic and attitudinal position, portray the world from that point of view, and produce reasons within, or emanating from, that point of view.

Two aspects of this account lead us to the Sartrean problem. The first is the idea that the causes are mental only if they fit into a pattern of reasons: to be a mental phenomenon just is to fit into a rationalizing account of an agent's behaviour. The second aspect is the idea that it is necessary for an account to be a rationalizing one, that it describe the world from the agent's perspective, where this is taken to mean 'from the agent's mental perspective'. The relation between action and agent must, as Sartre says, be one of 'comprehension'. The upshot is that it is difficult to see how an action can have a meaning of which the agent is unaware – one which falls outside of that mental perspective. And the problem gets worse if our explanation of why the agent is unaware alludes to further mental processes of the agent, such as repression, which seem to require that the ignorance of the meaning of the action is the result of the agents own (inner) action of repression, of which the agent is also ignorant. The paradox of self-deception is there – the repressing agent needs to know what to repress – and it threatens to lead us to the conclusion that psychoanalytic explanation can take no comfort from the 'ordinary' mental phenomenon of self-deception, since this phenomenon is itself incoherent. And we seem driven to arrive at this conclusion because of the very nature of the mental.

The Davidsonian Solution and Split Minds

This account of the mental is Davidsonian, so it will be worth while to sketch Davidson's own solution to the problem of self-deception (Davidson, 1982). Going back to Freud's own justification for the idea that an agent can act from unconscious motives, that of the hypnotist causing an agent to act unaware of the instruction of the hypnotist, one can see that the problem need not arise if there are two agents, hypnotist and patient, since one mental cause of the action can be located in the hynotist's mind, while another can be located in the agent's mind. Here the unknown mental cause is unknown to the agent because of its separation from the agent's mind, it is mental because of its relation to other mental states in the mind of the hypnotist, and it is a cause of the agent's behaviour. The one intentional state causes the other without being a reason for it; we have the situation Sartre thought that Freud was committed to, that of *mental* states being related *only* causally, 'externally'. It is a short step from this picture to the position where the same external relation between two mental states is envisaged, but the states are located within one agent. It is clear that what is important in the hypnotism case is not physical separation of the mental states, but their functional separation. They can causally relate to each other without relating in the rational manner typical of the mental. If one partitions the mind of the agent, in particular if one detects a sub-system within the larger whole which appears to be operating with a certain degree of autonomy from the whole, it seems as though one can get the post-hypnotic effect, an action caused by an unknown 'reason'.

On this model a number of questions arises, some of which are discussed below. One acute question concerns the unity of the mind. Some explanation is required as to why the mind is thus partitioned, and what the epistemic relation is between the parts. Answers to the first question threaten to forge some kind of epistemic connection between the parts, especially if those answers make use of the Freudian device of repression, thus raising once again the peculiar nature of the 'known but unknown' mental cause. Again, we also need to know why the cause is deemed to be mental, why it has a 'reason' aspect at all. With two minds we can satisfy Sartrean demands by connecting the states to their different centres of consciousness, their different points of view. With the partitioned mind it is more difficult to do this, unless we take the radical step of postulating internal homunculi, each with its own centre of consciousness, making the individual into a society. This will transform the everyday phenomenon of self-deception into the much rarer complaint of multiple personality disorder. Underlying this worry is a concern which takes us back to the falsifiability debate; what restrains us from mentalizing any number of causal connections, once we are given the freedom to posit unknown reasons, and even to homuncularize to our hearts content? Will we be left with any sensible constraints upon explanation?

The Davidsonian response to all this is minimalist. The sub-system of the mind which is responsible for self-deception need not be a separate centre of fully fledged intentionality. It need not be a 'centre of agency'. It must, in order to be a mental sub-system, have its own internal consistency: there must be a 'constellation of beliefs, purposes and affects of the sort that . . . allow us to characterise certain thoughts as having a goal or intention' (Davidson, 1982, pp. 303–4). This need not, at least in some cases, require there to be an agent directing each sub-system, nor need there be a separate centre of awareness for the sub-system. The system may well have its own information-processor, one which monitors its own success in achieving its goals, but this need not involve full awareness (see the discussion of different types of intentionality by Martin Davies in chapter 20). Indeed, there is strong evidence to disallow full agency and awareness to the sub-system, and that is provided by the inability of the agent to provide a satisfying description of the intention by which the self-deception is produced: 'the concept of a self deceptive basic mental act lacks a feature of the concept of non-self deceptive basic mental act, like adding one to nine; the self deceiver cannot produce a description of it from the agent's point of view' (Pears, 1991, p. 401)[8].

How damaging this is depends upon our success at making sense of an intentional sub-system without a 'point of view' (see the discussion by and of Searle in chapters 17–20). From the vantage point of psychoanalytic theory, comfort can be gained by looking at how a Davidsonian could respond to a potential objector. Davidson's approach to mentality has been characterized as one in which the mental is constituted by its place in a system of rational thought, where the reasons are those given from the agent's perspective. It looks as though one could not make sense of an intentional system, with goals and purposes, without that system having a point of view. The objector may reinforce this by noting that it is also part of the Davidsonian approach to deny beliefs to animals, partly on the grounds that to have a belief is to be capable of having beliefs about those beliefs: one must, in order to be a believer, be capable of beliefs about one's beliefs, where this is plausibly construed as saying one must be able to be aware of those beliefs. Given that the sub-system lacks such awareness, it looks as though it must be denied beliefs, and the case for treating it as an intentional sub-system will be very weak.

However, the *capacity* to have beliefs about beliefs is not exercised all the time; one can have the capacity and be a fairly unreflective person most of the time. And it is part of psychoanalytic doctrine that (correct) awareness of the source of one's irrationality can be obtained, via suitable psychoanalytic therapy. Nor, as Pears notes, is it necessary in less serious cases of self-deception to see the agent as unaware of the motivation to form self-deceptive beliefs; it is only necessary when the motive is operative that the agent be unaware of its operation at that time. The epistemic barrier between sub-system and main system may be permeable. So it is open to the psychoanalytic theorist to resist the Sartrean demand for transparency of mental motivation at every turn in favour of a looser constraint which makes our awareness of our thoughts and motivations a capacity. Its not being exercised at every turn will be explained variously, from mere inattention to a trauma-induced block. And, in the end, there will be a point of view from which one can see the reason behind the irrationality: the perspective not just on the present portion of the agent's world, but on the history of that agent's relation to the world.

This still leaves unanswered a question posed by Sartre: if self-deception (or an emotional response) is an *adaptation* of the agent, how can it be that the agent is unaware that he or she is so adapting? Put in terms of sub-systems and main system, the question can be phrased in terms of what the main system makes of the sub-system's 'helpful' intrusion into its normal operation. What does it do with, say, the deceptive belief fed into it by the sub-system? It cannot recognize this belief under the description which identifies it in the constellation of beliefs and desires of the sub-system; to allow it to do so would render redundant the whole construction of a partitioned mind. How, then, does it characterize this belief? This is a question raised by Johnston (chapter 23) in order to discredit this type of solution to the paradox of self-deception, so we will return to it below.

The Debate

What has been sketched above is only an account of how self-deception, and analogous irrationality, is conceptually possible. The explanations of why the irrationalities occur on specific occasions will involve substantial theories of mental processes, and it is just such a substantial account that psychoanalytic theory hopes to provide. Against the background of the above discussion, we can see how Jim Hopkins (chapter 22) takes on the task of defending the thesis that psychoanalytic explanation is an extension of ordinary intentional explanation. He does this by using the Davidsonian approach to the mental in order to deflect some of the general question that have been raised concerning the 'scientific' status of psychoanalytic explanations. These explanations have the status and evidentiary backing which we allow to other mentalistic explanations; there is nothing *especially* troublesome about the use of the psychoanalytic posits. What troubles critics is that psychoanalytic accounts fail to conform to the model of physical science. Hopkins agrees, but claims that this just marks it off as being (an elaboration of) an intentional explanation. What one has to be careful about is one's choice of an aspect of normal intentionality to which to relate the psychoanalytic case. Hopkins takes as central that aspect of imagination associated with wishful thinking. Elaborating on this imaginative capacity will, he argues, illuminate the logic of psychoanalytic explanation.

In order to give backing to this claim, Hopkins discusses the problem raised by psychoanalytic accounts of those actions which contain a symbolic element, where there is supposed to be a deep significance attaching to the action. He looks at the hypothetical case of a man whose action of lunging at lampposts with his umbrella is explained as being the expression of his Oedipal desire to kill his father. Representing this on the model of rational action would attribute to the man the incredible belief that lunging at lampposts is a suitable way of killing one's father. Hopkins concludes that wish-fulfilment should not be described 'on the pattern of rational action but rather as activity of the imagination' (chapter 22, p. 412). The explanatory task is to show why wish-fulfilling thought was required in the first place, since in wish-fulfilment there is no real gratification of the desire which leads to wish-fulfilling phantasy or action. The move to wish-fulfilment is usually generated by the impossibility, for one reason or another, of straightforward satisfaction of desire in 'rational' action. Freud's theory is an attempt to show why and how this happens; the 'why' concerns the existence of desires and impulses which the subject cannot openly acknowledge, as such acknowledgement would induce immense guilt or anxiety. Hopkins shows, in his examination of the case of the Rat Man, how such a conflict is handled; how the desires are transformed in appearance by the mechanisms of defence, projection and transference. He goes on to sketch the source of these types of conflict in the handling by the ego and superego of the desires emanating from the id. The id is the source of erotic and aggressive impulses, the immediate gratification of which would lead to catastrophe for the individual. There has to be mediation, supplied by the ego, between these impulses and reality. There is also the necessity to control and suppress certain desires – a function performed by the superego, which is formed in the individual by parental and social training and education. The conflicts produced between these parts of the self is the material which generates the need for the disguise of the troublesome desires; such desires may only be satisfied, suitably disguised, via wish-fulfilment.

This subtly argued case requires the partitioning of the mind in the Davidsonian manner, and it is the necessity for such a divide that is contested by Mark Johnston's view of things (chapter 23). He takes the radical step of questioning the Davidsonian identification of the mental with the rationally interpretable. This identification makes the problems of irrationality and of self-deception particularly difficult, since it requires that the sub-system be seen as acting *intentionally*. A consequence is that it is difficult to resist the interpolation of 'little agents', homunculi, into each sub-division. Davidson resists this, but does insist that the sub-division has sufficient rational coherence to allow characterization of certain events as having intentions. Johnston thinks that this ends up attributing too much in the way of intentionality to the sub-system; it has to monitor its effect on the main system to make sure the intended effect is secured. Given that the effect is one which serves the main system, the sub-system has to be seen as acting protectively towards the main system. This picture also requires too much of the main system, says Johnston, but in the opposite direction. Whereas the sub-system has to be too clever, the main system has to be too stupid. In the case of self-deception, the sub-system produces a belief which it then inserts into the main system, a belief for which there is, at best, no evidence. What is the main system to do with this belief, asks Johnston? It has to be very gullible just to take it as an ordinary belief, and yet that seems to be what it proceeds to do.

In contrast to this 'over-rationalized' conception of the mental, Johnston suggests that there are mental processes which are purposive but not intentional. These sub-intentional processes are involved in non-accidental, purpose-serving, mental regularities, and it is these regularities, 'mental tropisms', which are involved in self-deception and the more complicated Freudian processes. A mental tropism involves a simple regularity in the sense that the cause of the belief that p (where this belief is not based on evidence, or is believed despite contrary evidence) is not a reason for believing that p; the link between cause and effect is established because it works, because believing (falsely) that p reduces anxiety. Johnston defends the anti-Sartrean thesis that such tropisms act blindly; there is no agency required, there is need for the cause of the belief to be taken to be intentional. The cause need not function as a reason for the belief. The further contention is that such tropisms are a pervasive part of the mental, underlying our everyday common-or-garden mental inferences.

Three aspects of this response merit attention. First, it is worth asking how different it is from the Hopkins – Davidson position. This position also insists that the mental cause is not a reason for its effect, and so could also explain the regularity in the functional manner proposed by Johnston. We say 'functional' because Johnston seems to give a selectionist twist to the establishment of the non-accidental regularity:

> processes of this kind [the mental process of self-deception] persist because they serve the end of reducing anxiety. Hence I speak of a mental tropism, a characteristic pattern of causation between types of mental states, a pattern whose existence within the mind is no more surprising, given what it does for us, than a plant's turning toward the sun. (Johnston, chapter 23, p. 455)

The second, related, aspect concerns the issue of intentionality versus sub-intentionality. Johnston resists the sub-dividing response, the partitioned mind, as he thinks that this drives one to postulate the intention of a sub-system to deceive the main system, and such a postulation, in itself implausible, over-sophisticates what is essentially a simple causal regularity. The partitioning account seems to attribute too much 'knowingness', too much sagacity, to the sub-system, and for this reason Johnston thinks that the account is implausible. Johnston's preferred alternative is to have the causes act in a sense blindly, without any intentional plan, and so the states are not intentional states. On the other hand, they do not act without *any* purpose, as the extract above implies. Such causes do serve a purpose: they reduce anxiety. The issues here revolve around what counts as intentionality (see chapters 17–20). Given that there are different types of intentionality, the differences here seem to be a matter of what type of intentionality to attribute to the cause. More precisely, it is a matter of what type of teleology is present, of how the 'purpose' of either the tropism or the sub-system is conceived. Johnston goes for a functional account; Hopkins for a mentalistic approach.

Connected to this is the third aspect. The partitioned mind was required in order to preserve the idea that the cause was a mental cause. The partition was effected by a part of the mind displaying a greater degree of coherence among its elements than it does with the elements of the main system. Being an element in a (rationally) cohering part of the mind ensured that the cause was a mental cause, providing scope for the postulation of unconscious states that are similar to conscious beliefs and desires, and so merit their classification as mental. The question raised by Johnston's rejection of the Davidsonian identification of the mental with the rational is what he would count as constitutive of the mental. Teleology, or 'purposiveness', seems to be part of the answer, but as there are biological purposes, these would need to be distinguished from the mental variety.[9]

In his response (chapter 24) Hopkins agrees with Johnston that there is more to the mental than rationality, but takes this to be consistent with a Davidsonian approach to the mental. He takes Davidson to be saying that (rational) interpretation is constrained by its relation to the physical. Supervenience requires identity of mental interpretation given identity of a suitably extended physical base. However, in the last resort interpretive results arrived at via the use of a *a priori* (in some sense) 'laws' of interpretation will be the final arbiter of the mental. Hopkins takes these laws to be *a priori* not in the sense that they are not amenable to any empirical confirmation, but in the sense that they are so well grounded, and applied so rapidly by ordinary interpreters in normal life, that they function at a deeper level than the empirical laws of other sciences. What psychoanalysis has achieved is an extension of these interpretive maxims. One such extension is

(1)   A's desire that P-[causes]$\rightarrow$A's *b*-rep that P

where 'A's b-rep that P' is a belief-like state in that it is a representational state caused by A's desire for P to be true. The idea here is that wish-fulfilling phantasy exemplifies this pattern, where our desire for P to be true causes in us a belief-like, or experience-like, representation of P.

The question arises as to what relation these 'laws' have to the non-accidental mental regularities invoked by Johnston. Are they mental tropisms? Hopkins sees no barrier to accepting them as such, not even on the Davidsonian account of the mental, given that this allows for mental generalizations to hold, where such generalizations are less strict than, say, the laws of physics. Critical to this debate will be how it is envisaged that these loose laws relate the mental antecedents to their effects. In Johnston's view the antecedent states are *mere* causes, in the sense of not being also reason-givers. Although he sees mental tropisms as pervasive in mental causation, Johnston's use of the tropisms here is primarily concerned with their role as non-rationalizing sub-intentional causes. They do accomplish a purpose, but they do so non-rationally. On the other hand, a central feature of the interpretative approach is that the mental antecedents are reason-givers for their effects, with the ensuing problem being that of accounting for mentally caused actions which are not rational. The question here is: does (1) give us rationalizing conections, or is it *just* a mental regularity?

Hopkins' argument locates (1), and its cognate laws, within the pattern established by reason-giving explanations. But, of course, the 'rationality' of desire-satisfaction via a *representation* of reality, rather than from reality itself, is at best partial. In the normal course of events wish-fulfilling phantasy can be mere day-dreaming, where the representation substitutes for the real thing because we know that the real thing is unobtainable. There is no irrationality here; imagined glory is better than none at all. The cases of self-deception, and the more complicated Freudian examples, require us to explain the source of the desire, the cause of its non-satisfaction and the manner of its appearance in the psyche.

Hopkins argues that Freudian theory, especially that version of it presented by Melanie Klein, has the resources to provide such explanations, explanations which extend our normal understanding of ourselves and that are well-grounded.

Notes

1   The concentration hereafter on Freudian-type explanations does not diminish the significance of the debate, since only the general features of his position, features shared by a variety of psychoanalytic approaches, are central to the discussion.

2   This phase of Freud's career has given rise to considerable controversy. For some critical views see the article, and books cited therein, by Frederick Crews (1993) in the *New York Review of Books*. For some responses, see the letters page of the ensuing *New York Review of Books*, December 1993. For an excellent sympathetic

account of the details and development of Freud's theory see Richard Wollheim (1971).

3 Note that Popper had misgivings about Darwinian 'theory' as well.

4 The differing perspectives afforded by first-and third-person views of an action may yield differing interpretations independently of hypotheses about unconscious motivation, but these hypotheses make the differing perspectives more intractably different.

5 Thus B.F. Skinner's critique of psychoanalysis was of a piece with his criticism of mentalistic idioms in general, and the treatment was the same: eliminate mental descriptions of behaviour in favour of 'responses and controlling variables'. The cogency of an environmental variable is simply obscured by the postulation of an intervening mental state. 'What has survived throughout the years is not aggression and guilt, later to be manifested in behaviour, but rather patterns of behaviour themselves' (Skinner, 1961, p. 117).

6 'Every symptom must therefore in some way comply with the demands of the ego which manipulates the repression; it must offer some advantage, it must admit of some useful application, or it would meet with the same fate as the original instinctual impulse itself which has been fended off' (Freud, 1953, vol. 14 p. 53).

7 See Richard Wollheim's discussion of the 'involuntary' nature of symptoms (Wollheim, 1971, p. 91).

8 Pears (1991) contains a lucid discussion of different approaches to self-deception, including that of Johnston.

9 For an illuminating discussion of the relation between Freud's work and his biological beliefs see Sulloway (1980).

References

Crews, F. (1993) 'The unknown Freud'. *New York Review of Books* November 18, 55–66.

Davidson, D. (1980) 'Actions, reasons, and causes'. In *Essays on Actions and Events*, pp. 3–19. Oxford, Oxford University Press.

Davidson, D. (1982) 'Paradoxes of irrationality'. In R. Wollheim and J. Hopkins (eds), *Philosophical Essays on Freud*, pp. 289–305. Cambridge, Cambridge University Press.

Freud, S. (1953) *The Complete Psychological Works of Sigmund Freud*, ed. J. Strachey. London, Hogarth Press.

Pears, D. (1991) Self deceptive belief formation, *Synthese* 89, 393–405.

Popper, K.R. (1963) *Conjectures and Refutations*. London, Routledge and Kegan Paul.

Sartre, J.P. (1962) *Sketch for a Theory of the Emotions*, trans. P. Mairet. London, Methuen.

Skinner, B.F. (1961) 'Critique of psychoanalytic concepts and theories'. In P.G. Frank (ed.), *The Validation of Scientific Theories*. New York, Collier.

Sulloway, F.J. (1980) *Freud, Biologist of the Mind*. Suffolk, Fontana.

Wollheim, R. (1971) *Freud*. Glasgow, Fontana.

22

Introduction to *Philosophical Essays on Freud*

James Hopkins

In his psychoanalytic work Freud characteristically found the meaning of a dream, symptom or other phenomenon by understanding it as a wish-fulfilment. What is meant by this can be seen in a simple example. Freud observed that frequently when he had eaten anchovies or some other salty food before sleeping he would dream that *he was drinking delicious cool water*. After some repetitions of the dream, he would wake up thirsty and get a drink of water. (This common dream has, of course, a counterpart concerning urination.)

In dreaming, Freud produced an imaginative representation of himself as doing and experiencing something, that is, drinking. Also it seems that while sleeping, Freud desired or wished to drink. He was in a state such that if he had been aware of it and able to describe it he would have recognized it as one of desiring or wishing to drink (as he did on waking).[1] So clearly the content of Freud's desire is related to that of his dream. Since the desire is to drink, and the dream is that he is drinking, the dream represents the gratification of the desire, or represents the desire as fulfilled.

Dreams and other imaginative representations involve something like experience, belief and feeling. In dreaming he is drinking the dreamer has an experience as of drinking, and in some sense believes this. Still, this experience of gratification or satisfaction must be regarded as imaginary or, as Freud says, hallucinatory. For no water was in fact drunk, and the dreamer's genuine thirst remains unsatisfied.

It seems that the content–content relation between desire and dream in this case is strong evidence that it is no accident that the dream accompanied the desire. Rather, it seems, we should suppose that the desire caused the dream. This consideration is evidently reinforced by what we know about the connection between content and causal role. The dream is thus an imaginative representation of the experience of the satisfaction of a desire, caused by that desire. These are, I think, the central features of a (Freudian) wish-fulfilment; the fulfilment in such cases being imaginary or hallucinatory.

Any structure with these features, it seems, will involve a twofold denial or falsification of reality – a falsification, in psychoanalytic terms, of inner and outer reality. In representing an unfulfilled desire or wish as gratified, a wish-fulfilment falsely represents the psychological state of the agent. Thus the dreamer, while thirsty, experiences himself as drinking. Further, in representing the agent as gratifying rather than suffering his unfulfilled desire or wish, a wish-fulfilment falsely represents the activity of the agent. The dreamer, asleep, takes himself to be active, drinking.

Although there are other cases of dreams in which the content of the representation and that of the desire represented as gratified are independently and easily determined, those with which Freud was mainly concerned are less easy. Most dreams can rightly be seen as wish-fulfilments only when their content is compared with desires inferred from the memories, ideas etc. which the dreamer associates with the content of the dream. These can be considered, moreover, only if the dreamer enters a frame of mind in which they can emerge, and pursues them and submits them to investigation.

So, for example, one of Freud's patients dreamt that she wanted to give a supper party but was unable to do so, since she had only a little smoked salmon and was unable to get anything else. The dream could be seen as wish-fulfilling only in light of the recollection that an underweight friend of whom she was jealous (and whose favourite food was smoked salmon) had the day before enquired when she was to be asked to another meal. Not giving a supper party with smoked salmon could thus be seen to fit, among other things, her desire not to feed her rival.[2]

Finally, and especially in cases of conflict, a dream may represent the gratification of a desire symbolically. Thus after a session in the back of a car during which – with some difficulty – she restrained herself, a girl dreamt that she was in the car with her boy friend; he took out his knife and cut an item of her clothing. Again, a man dreamt that a young girl closely related to him offered him a flower, and he took it – this seemed a beautiful dream; later he dreamt (as he put it) he was deflowering her, and awoke in anxiety.

Symptoms occasionally have a fairly obvious representational content. Freud describes an intelligent and unembarrassed-looking girl who came for examination with two buttons of her blouse undone and one of her stockings hanging down, and showed her calf without being asked. Her main complaint was that she had a feeling in her body as if there was something 'stuck into it' which was 'moving backwards and forwards' and was 'shaking' her through and through. Sometimes it made her whole body feel 'stiff'.[3] Generally, however, they can be treated as wish-fulfilling only where associations or other information make it plausible to assign to them both a content and an appropriate relation to a desire.

Consider, for example, the obsessional patient referred to as the table-cloth lady.[4] Many times a day she would run from her room into a neighboring one, stand beside a table, ring for the maid, and send her away again. The compulsion to repeat this apparently meaningless action was perplexing to the patient, and presumably wearing for the maid. Part of the significance of the symptom emerged with two observations. The patient recalled that on her wedding night her husband – from whom she had separated and who was much in her thoughts – had been impotent. Many times he had run from his room into hers to try to have intercourse, and finally, saying that he would feel ashamed before the maid when she came to make the bed, poured some red ink on the sheets – but in the wrong place. To this the patient could add that when she rang she stood in such a way that the maid should see a prominent stain on the tablecloth. So it appeared that the symptom was a representation of events on her wedding night, with the difference that she ensured that the maid should see the stain. It does not seem easy to determine the content of this represen-tation precisely. Freud remarks that the symptom shows wish-fulfilment (the husband is represented as potent), a sort of identification (with the absent husband, whose part the patient plays), and representation by means of a familiar symbolism (table and cloth for bed and sheet). Also, the activity of the maid – in service, as it were, to the patient's representing imagination – shows a way in which the production of wish-fulfilling representations can involve cooperative or coercive activities among persons. So far as living persons are used in representations which involve symbolism, metaphor or likeness to what they represent, wish-fulfilment is potentially an important social matter.

Finally, the role of wish-fulfilment as regards memory is exemplified in the following material from a young man who, despite a desire to settle down with a girl he loved, felt compelled to make other girls fall in love with him and to behave in what he considered an unduly seductive and promiscuous way. He began analysis by saying that being outside the consulting room door (while the analyst was with another patient) before his first session had reminded him of being outside the shut door to his parents' bedroom when he was little. Later he remembered something: he was very young, in his parents' bed (he could remember the pyjamas he was wearing, from early childhood) ... his mother seemed to be rolling back and forth against him, as if excited and yearning, almost in tears ... he too was excited. It could be ascertained fairly certainly that the memory related to a period when he used to cry at night and was sometimes allowed to come into his parents' bed. It was not his mother, however, but he who had rolled excitedly. The transformation in his memory was apparently wish-fulfilling.[5]

Now it is natural to suppose that the explanation of wish-fulfilment is the same kind as that of action. This seems to have been the assumption of most philosophers (and analysts) who have explicitly addressed the explanation of symptoms, etc. And this assumption seems to have engendered debate about the rationality or coherence of wish-fulfilment.

Thus Alexander and Mischel[6] have discussed a hypothetical case of wish-fulfilment in which someone's (Oedipal) wish to kill his father is expressed in his lunging at lampposts with his umbrella, this latter being, it seems, a representation of an attack. They disagree as to whether he can be said to have reason, or good reason, for doing this.

Alexander argues that 'if my wish to kill my father were conscious it would be obvious to me that it was not adequately satisfied by lunging at lampposts'. Hence, he says, 'these "reasons" can be reasons for this behaviour only if they are unconscious for they would not look like reasons if they were conscious.' This, he thinks, shows that in an ordinary sense they cannot be regarded as good reasons, or perhaps as reasons at all. Mischel replies that 'if I (unconsciously) want to kill my father and (unconsciously) identify lunging at lampposts with killing him, then, given this irrational starting point, I do have good reason for lunging at lampposts.' This, he thinks, shows that explanation in this case is analogous to explanation of action by a reason.

The argument seems to turn upon Alexander and Mischel's common assumption that the symptomatic action in question should be explained by the agent's desire to kill his father together with some such belief as, that lunging at lampposts would be a way of doing so. Such a belief would, as Mischel says, identify lunging with killing, and so would fulfil the condition, which Alexander mentions, of ensuring that the desire to kill can be taken as satisfied by lunging. On this reading, Alexander's point would be that the belief that lunging at lampposts is a way of killing one's father would not be credible as a conscious belief, and so cannot serve as a constituent of a reason in the ordinary sense; and Mischel's reply would be that still we have here the elements of a reason, a desire and an (irrational) belief, in the dim light of which the action to be explained would appear desirable.

It would be possible, although it does not seem plausible, to interpret each of the examples we have considered in this way. Thus the table-cloth lady's ritual might be explained by some such desire as to have her wedding night over again except with things right, and a belief that running to the table, etc., was a way of doing so. The dream of drinking could be explained by a desire to drink and some such belief as, that dreaming of drinking was a way of drinking. Perhaps even the analysand's memory could be explained by his desire to avoid recollection of unrequited desire and his belief that remembering wrongly in this way was a way of doing so. In these accounts, however, we encounter two difficulties. The first is that indicated by Alexander. Even if the desire to be linked to a wish-fulfilling representation is clear, and it seems reasonable to suppose that the representation is caused by that desire, still the belief required to explain the representation in accord with the pattern used to explain actions by reasons seems scarcely comprehensible or coherent.[7] The second, related to this, is that in many cases we cannot plausibly link the content of a wish-fulfilment directly with a desire for action. Thus it does not seem quite right to say that the table-cloth lady's ritual shows her desire to repeat her wedding night; rather, in so far as we link it to the past, it seems we should say that it expresses her wish that things had been different. These considerations both suggest that we should not describe wish-fulfilment on the pattern of rational action, but rather as activity of the imagination.

We imagine by representing things to ourselves. Since wish-fulfilling activities consist in the imaginative representation of the gratification of desires or wishes, it seems we can regard them simply as forms of imagining that things are as (in some way) we wish they were. Such imagining may be caused by a desire to perform a certain kind of action, but it does not seem to be undertaken because of a belief that it is a way of performing that kind of action. It seems natural, for example, that someone hungry should imagine eating; but this carries no suggestion that he supposes that the imagining is a way of eating. No more is this implied if he hallucinates, and so believes that he is eating. Again, his imagining, like his desire to eat, may show his belief that eating is a way of satisfying hunger; but this is a belief about eating, not imagining.

We can imagine things at will, and imagining may involve experiences of gratification. These facts may suggest that the imagining in wish-fulfilment is a kind of intentional action. In many central cases this does not seem to be so. Some cases, however, may involve a certain kind of primitive confusion about actions and events, or an exercise of will of a kind prior to that in intentional action. An adequate discussion of this would require detailed consideration of the psychoanalytic account of the development of the mind. Some arguments, however, may serve to indicate a line of thought.

Wish-fulfilment may seem most like action where it is effected by bodily or intentional activity, as in the *tableau vivant* of Freud's obsessional patient or the stabbing with an umbrella discussed above. Someone may indeed imagine himself to be performing one kind of action (attacking his father) by actually performing another (lunging with an umbrella); his imagining, that is, may consist partly in his doing something which symbolizes, resembles or otherwise represents (to him) what he imagines doing. That imagining may govern someone's intentional actions in this way, however, does not show that the imagining itself is intentional. Characteristically, it seems, the actions will be intentional but the imagining not. This is because imaginative activity seems not to be governed by desire and belief in the way intentional action is. It is not typically undertaken, for example, because of a desire to obtain an experience of gratification and a belief that imaging something would be a way of doing so. The variety of our imaginings seems to outrun any beliefs we might have on this score, and what we imagine, with its pleasures or pains, usually arises in us unbidden. Nor is the enaction of a live representation typically undertaken because of a desire to represent something and a belief that performing certain actions may be a way of doing so. Rather it seems that the mark of the imagination – in this or other forms – is the capacity to create representations which are unanticipated and new. Activity like this could not be governed by beliefs about how to represent things.

We can think of imagining as like breathing, which follows a natural course in adjustment to need unless intention or will intervenes. On such a view the natural activity of imagination would encompass the spontaneous production of images of gratified desire, while willed imagining might hold, recapture or elaborate these or others from perception or memory.[8] From the outside we can think of the aim of such imagining in terms of the production or alteration of images or experiences. A correct description of the intentions with which such imagining is done, however, must depend upon how the person himself regards his activity. He can be said to intend to imagine or represent only if he can think of his activity in that way. So far as he is unable to distinguish imagining from acting or altering the world, his intentions in imagining must likewise be regarded as confused, unformed or indeterminate.

We may speculate that in the first months of life, before an infant comes to think of the objective world and his activities in it as distinct from what he imagines, this indeterminacy is radical and pervasive. In particular, it seems that the infant may picture the world in ways systematically distorted by his wishes, and also as partly subject to his will in the way his imaginings are. In Freudian terms, this would be the period of the domination of the pleasure principle[9] and infantile omnipotence of thought, before the establishment of the reality principle. The willed imagining by which the child alters his world during this period can be regarded as a kind of proto-action; and so far as symptoms and dreams involve reversion to this way of thinking, they can be viewed in the same way.

Looking to Freud's theories in the terms we have been trying to clarify, we can see that one of his central claims was that a wide range of human activities involved the wish-fulfilling representation of certain themes in desire. These included not only dreams, symptoms, slips and transference, but also those of children at play and adults in serious pursuits (perhaps the table-cloth lady's serious symptomatic play with her maid suggests that these are not entirely distinct categories). This claim, as we can see from Freud's interpretive work, was meant to be supported by a systematic correlation and coherence among the results of the interpretation of wish-fulfilment and action.

Abstracting from the content of Freud's theory, we can think of such a correlation as built up as follows. We can interpret almost any action in terms of reasons which cohere with those for other actions. However, some activities which spring from the mind – dreams, symptoms, irrational actions – appear senseless or unmotivated in some respect. So far as these can cogently be interpreted as involving representation and wish-fulfilment, we can form hypotheses which partly explain them by relating them to desires or wishes. These hypotheses, in turn, can be tested through their coherence or dissonance with the results of interpreting both actions and other putative wish-fulfilments. In addition, they may lead to further interpretations of both actions and other wish-fulfilments. These may be tested as before; and so on. Such a process might lead by cogent interpretive steps to a theory which radically transcended common-sense psychology, and yet was strongly supported by interpretive coherence in the same way.

This extended psychology would supplement the assumption of the rationality of action with another concerning the ubiquity and connectedness of wishful imagining. As interpretive success in common-sense psychology sustains the strongly predictive guiding principle of interpretation that for almost any action reasons are to be found which cohere with those for many other actions, so success in the extended psychology might ultimately sustain the strongly predictive principle that for almost any wish-fulfilment desires are to be found which cohere with those for many actions and many other wish-fulfilments. This would mean that interpretations in the extended psychology could be strongly confirmed or disconfirmed, by very many instances of coherence or dissonance with others. So far as the ascription of new and definite patterns of desires was thus strongly and repeatedly confirmed, an extended psychology of determinate content would be strongly supported, and would itself contribute explanation and coherence to the common-sense psychology upon which it was based.

Also, still abstracting from the detail and content of Freud's theory, we can see how the interpretation of a wish-fulfilling structure in such a psychology may provide a condition for a sort of psychic development. An imaginary experience of gratification is precisely suited to preclude awareness of the desire which causes it, as an illusory experience of drinking may prevent awareness of thirst or a vivid phantasy of being desired may prevent awareness of unrequited desire. Now, for a desire or other mental item to be kept from awareness is partly for it to be kept from interacting – logically and causally – with other desires, beliefs etc. in thought and action. Hence the desire may remain both ungratified and unmodified, like the dreamer's thirst masked by his illusion of drinking.

Interpretation of such a structure may bring awareness of it, and hence the possibility that it should be changed. This, however, involves acknowledging both the internal and external falsification of reality in it – recognizing an unfulfilled desire together with the fact that a range of apparently gratifying experience was illusory. This is partly modelled in the way a dreamer becomes aware of his thirst, and that his recent experiences of drinking have been chimerical, in waking to get a drink; but the hostility of wishful thinking to awareness of real desire is familiar from other areas of life.

The role of awareness here merits further consideration. Wish-fulfilment involves a certain incoherence or irrationality – the persistence of a desire together with an imaginary belief in, or experience of, its gratification. Likewise unconscious motivation characteristically involves contradictory beliefs or desires, of which the agent is unaware. Suppose, for example, that someone is hypnotized and told that after the trance is over he will open an umbrella whenever the hypnotist gives some signal. He wakes up and seems to remember nothing about the trance, but ascertains where the umbrella is and keeps his attention on the hypnotist. Then at the signal he opens the umbrella, confusedly giving some excuse for doing so.

He is best understood as acting on the hypnotist's instructions. This implies that he believes that he was told to open an umbrella and in some sense desires to do as he was told. He may, however, sincerely deny that anyone has told him this, and he may be strongly opposed to any form of unthinking compliance with instructions. In this sense he has contradictory beliefs and desires. We may assume, as often happens, that if he learnt of the suggestion he would try hard to oppose it, and if he remembered being given it he would lose all desire to act accordingly. This means that a kind of memory and awareness would enable him to act more rationally; that is, to choose the course of action (refraining from opening an umbrella for no good reason) in best accord with his desires and beliefs, all things considered.[10]

This indicates how awareness is central to rationality. A person acts rationally when she acts best to satisfy all her own desires, obligations and so forth, as she sees things. To do so she must choose the most preferable – the most desirable, all things considered, or the best in light of her own motives, whatever they are – of the alternative actions she can perform. So far as her desires, beliefs or other motives are not adequately reflected in her choices, she may fail to act rationally. What a person is fully aware of, it seems, enters most completely into her processes of thought, and plays its proper role in determining her choices. Sometimes, as in the examples mentioned, awareness may lead to resolution of incoherence or contradiction and hence to a simple and rational change in action. Things are more complicated, however, as regards the kind of motives with which psychoanalysis is concerned.

There is no rational satisfaction for the desires Freud thought represented in the incest and parricide of Sophocles' *Oedipus Rex*, awareness of which could not be borne. In theory, so far as the boy explicitly represents such desires as gratified he feels unbearable anxiety and despair at the damage he has done his parents and also fear of retaliation from his father. Yet so far as he acknowledges his parents' love for one another he suffers unbearable jealousy. Hence, in one line of thought, he represents his mother as loving him rather than his father, and his father as jealous rather than himself. This, however, results in fear of his father's jealous hostility and also of the consequences of his own wishful retaliation. So this representation is replaced by one in which the relations between father and son are idealized.

The jealous hatred and desire for possession masked by this idealization may, partly because they are so masked, be rendered unmodifiable by experience. This otherwise enables the boy more fully to appreciate and accept his role as a child who is loved by parents who nurture and care for him, help him to grow up, and so forth; and hence to accept that the way they love him is quite different from the way they love each other. So far as the primitive emotions remain unmodified they may continue to be expressed in representations which cause anxiety (or actual damage), may be guarded against by inhibition, and so on.

The reasons for anxiety will include love and concern for the parents. Hence interpretation of these representations will not tend to bring action on the desires shown in them, but rather modification of these desires and their products through awareness and contact with others in thought. Knowledge that hostility and imagined hostility are based on misconception and wish-fulfilment, for example, may bring a lessening of fear and hatred, and awareness that imagined possession and destruction are illusory may bring relief from guilt. Such changes may in turn diminish the role of such motives in the imagination, and hence the intensity of anxiety and idealization consequent on them.

All this may enable the patient to appreciate and accept more fully his place in the family, and to understand what was done for him as a needful child (rather than an imperious little parent). If so, his representations of possession and damage may be replaced by others which express his desires – previously shown mainly in idealization – to make good the relations between and with his parents which were distorted by his own infantile feelings, and to do other things from love, care, gratitude and so on. Since these like other representations may involve activities which partly replicate or symbolize what they represent, this may mean an indirect but far-reaching change in action.[11]

According to this last part of the theory, the sublimation of primitive sexual and aggressive desires which follows upon awareness of them and their modification in thought leads to the inception of new desires and interests, and so to more deeply satisfying rational action. This part of the pattern of rational action, however, takes its form and capacity to satisfy partly from its role as benign wish-fulfilment. (So gardening might be thought a continuously satisfying activity because of what it represented as well as because of its instrumental function.) Hence on this view of the working of the mind, it might be said, reason is not so much the slave of the passions as the servant of the imagination.

As the remarks above suggest, the psychoanalytic conception of defence is partly to be understood in terms of the kind of representation we have been considering. For example, in using projection as a defence against feelings of frustration or aggression, a person represents and feels another, rather than him or herself, to be frustrated or aggressive. This can be a simple wish-fulfilling reversal, such as was to be seen in the memories of the analysand above, who represented his mother rather than himself as yearning for erotic contact. Again, transference, which Freud described from his early work as the patient's tendency to make the analyst the object of the thoughts and feelings involved in his or her symptoms, consists in the patient's unconsciously representing the analyst as a figure from his or her past. This is a source of one of the interpretive correlations mentioned above, since if the patient's symptoms arise, as Freud claimed, from the Oedipus complex, then he will unconsciously experience and represent the analyst in the Oedipal terms hypothesized in theory.

This can partly be illustrated by reference to Freud's patient called the Rat Man. He was a lawyer, described by Freud as a young man of value and promise, who suffered from a number of incapacitating obsessions and compulsions. Recently he had been particularly tormented by the thought and fear that a certain punishment, in which rats gnawed their way into the anus of the victim, should be applied to his lady and his father, whom he loved. Thoughts of aggression directed towards his lady and his father were a constant source of anxiety and guilt to him, and he employed special formulas and other means to protect the victims.

The idea of the rat punishment being applied in this way had occurred to him when a Captain (his father had been a soldier) had told him about it on manoeuvres. Also, when this Captain told him of a small debt (his father had incurred a debt while in the army which he had apparently failed to repay) he developed a confused obsession with repaying it, supposing that if he failed to do so the punishment would be applied. The Captain advocated corporal punishment, and seemed to him obviously fond of cruelty. As he told Freud the story of the punishment, the patient's face took on a strange, composite expression, which Freud interpreted as one of horror at pleasure of his own of which he was unaware. And while telling Freud of his attempts to pay the debt, the patient became confused, and repeatedly called him 'Captain'.[12]

His father was dead, but much in his thoughts. This had been evidenced not only by his anxiety, but also by his thinking when he heard a joke that he must tell it to his father, by studying to please his father (but not being able to carry his studies through), and by actually imagining, when he heard a knock at the door, that it might be his father. His relationship with his father had been, as he described it, almost ideal. He said he was his father's best friend, and his father his; and in many respects this seemed to be true.[13] There was only one subject of disagreement between them. His father had been the suitor of a poor girl before marrying the patient's wealthy mother. The son's lady was not rich, and his father had thought the connection imprudent. He seemed to remain poised between his dead father's will and his desire for the lady; and before he had broken down his mother and family had encouraged him to marry a wealthy girl. He had suicidal impulses, and was tormented with self-reproach, as if he were a criminal, for not being present at his father's death. Also, when he had visited his father's grave, he had seen a large beast which he took to be a rat gliding over the grave; he assumed it had been gnawing on the corpse.

Despite his love for his father there seemed in his mind to be a lethal opposition between his father and his own sexual or marital gratification. He remembered before his father died thinking that the death might make him rich enough to marry his lady, and he thought later that his marrying might harm his father in the next world. He had not copulated before his father's death, and had masturbated only a little. From after his father's death, however, he remembered occasions of this which seemed significant because of their connection with the idea of a prohibition being defied.

In response to an interpretation about masturbation and thoughts of death or castration by his father, he remembered a period when he was suffering from a desire to masturbate, but was also tormented with the idea of his penis being cut off. And in connection with this he remembered that on the occasion of his first copulation he had thought 'This is a glorious feeling! One might do anything for this – murder one's father, for instance.' (He also described a scene which he had been told of from his childhood, when he had been enraged with his father for punishing him, and had abused his father roundly. His father had apparently said that he would be either a great man or a criminal.)[14]

His sense of opposition between his father and his own gratification apparently went back into childhood. He could remember thinking at the age of twelve that a little girl with whom he was in love might be more kind to him if he should suffer some misfortune – such as the death of his father. And even from the age of six, as far back as he could remember things completely, he could recall wanting to see girls naked, but feeling that if he had such thoughts his father might die.

His symptoms and thoughts fairly explicitly represented his father as punitively tortured or killed. According to the fragment of psychoanalytic theory sketched above, these symptoms or thoughts would involve the imaginary fulfilment of hostile wishes which had arisen in childhood when he had perceived his father as prohibiting his possession and enjoyment of his mother and which had remained relatively unmodified by his subsequent experience. To represent these wishes as fulfilled would lead to anxiety or guilt, whereas to represent himself as in possession of his mother and hence prohibiting his father in this way would lead to fear of castration or death. To avoid such jealousy and hostility the relationship would have to be imagined as equal and friendly, or as one of admiration etc.

The hypothesis that such a complex of wishes and feelings was active would bear upon a number of features of the case. It would partly explain why, despite the genuine friendship between the patient and his father, the patient none the less also seemed to feel his father to be a barrier to his satisfaction which could be overcome only through harm or death. This was evidenced in his still hesitating in regard to the relationship of which his father had disapproved, and imagining that consummation of it might bring harm to his father in the afterlife; in his having thought that his father's death might enable him to marry the lady, or that one might murder one's father to enjoy the glorious feeling of sexual intercourse; in his having supposed that if his father died his childhood romance might prosper, or that his father might die as a result of his wishes to see girls naked. It would also partly explain his association of castration with masturbation, and his having begun to masturbate mainly after his father's death and then in connection with the idea of a prohibition being defied. It would explain his propensity to think of his father's death or torture, and his guilt and anxiety in doing so; his intensified guilt after his father's death; his suicidal impulses; and so on.

He was extremely reluctant to accept that he might harbour hostility towards his father. When Freud interpreted that there was a wish to kill his father in what he said he replied that he could not believe that he had ever entertained such a wish. Then, apparently disconnectedly, he remembered a story. It was about a woman who as she sat by her sister's sick bed felt a wish that her sister might die, so that she might marry her sister's husband. She thereupon committed suicide, thinking she was not fit to live. He said he could understand this, and it would be right if his thoughts were the death of him, for he deserved nothing less. The story repeated the themes which Freud was interpreting, in particular suicidal guilt because of a death wish consequent upon a desire to marry. Also, although the patient denied the wish he yet considered that he deserved to die because of his thoughts, as if they did reflect his desires or intentions. So despite the patient's denial, Freud could regard his response as partly confirming the correctness of his hypothesis.

Although he denied hostility towards his father, he later began showing hostility towards Freud. This intensified after analysis of a protective formula he used in masturbating.[15] In his deliberate actions he treated Freud with the greatest respect, but he attacked him in his thoughts, which as part of the treatment he put into words. He had phantasies of intercourse and fellatio with Freud's daughter; phantasies of Freud's mother naked, swords stuck into her breast and the lower part of her body and especially her genitals eaten up by Freud and his children (cf. the rats of the torture, and the rat seen in the graveyard);[16] of Freud's mother dead; and so on. These depressed him and also made him fearful.

While telling Freud of his phantasies he got up off the couch (as he had in first telling of the rat torture) and walked about the room. He said his reason for doing so was delicacy of feeling – he could not lie there comfortably while he was saying these things about Freud; and he kept hitting himself, as in self-punishment, while saying them.[17] But he agreed he was walking about the room not for this reason, but out of fear that Freud might beat him.

He imagined Freud and his wife with a dead child lying between them, and became particularly afraid that Freud would turn him out. He knew the origin of this – when he was a little boy he had been lying in bed between his father and his mother; he had wet the bed; and his father had beaten him and turned him out of bed.

His demeanour during all this was that of a man in desperation and one who was trying to save himself from blows of terrific violence. He buried his head in his hands, rushed away, covered his face with his arms, etc. He told Freud his father had a passionate temper, and did not know what he was doing. Later he said he had thought Freud might be murderous, and would fall on him like a beast of prey to search out what was evil in him.[18]

Now fairly clearly the patient's experiencing extreme fear that Freud would beat him and turn him out, while remembering his father's having beaten him up and turned him out (of bed),[19] instantiates the assumption that he was experiencing Freud as he had his father in the past. This experience was at first unconscious, then became conscious. That he was beaten and turned out as a result of what he did (with his penis) while lying between his parents is related to the Oedipal theme, and also to his symptoms.

He was lying between his parents, and so preventing his father having access to his mother. His father punished and displaced him, and so prohibited and barred his access. In his thoughts the father who had displaced him from the parental bed likewise stood between him and his lady or his gratification, and so might have to die or be murdered for him to marry to have sexual intercourse. (The symptoms would represent both the hatred of his father for this, and also his maintenance of the prohibition within himself, to avoid the terrible consequences of breaking it.) In his symptoms his father was also subjected to punishment, as in return.

Beneath the patient's attitude of respect and delicacy of feeling towards Freud were the unconscious hostility shown in his associations (for which he punished himself, and which depressed him) and the fear expressed at first in his walking about the room. This would cohere with the assumption that beneath his friendliness and respect for his father there was the hostility and consequent self-punishment and depression shown in his symptoms, and also a fear of his father. The ascription of fear would fit with the way his respect and delicacy of feeling gave way to fear of Freud as a murderer or wild beast, especially since he felt this while remembering and describing his father's (as he saw it) fearful violence. (This would be the coming to awareness, through reliving in the transference, of a repressed fear.)

He expressed his hostility towards Freud in part in the form of phantasies of Freud and his family behaving like the rats of his own symptomatic thoughts of the punitive torture of his lady and his father, and expected a reciprocal punitive hostility from Freud as a wild beast. This would cohere with the hypothesis that he had felt such hostilities towards his father in childhood – so that the thoughts of his symptoms were of infantile origin – and that he had expected a comparable hostility in return.

His fear surfaced in an image of a dead baby, lying between Freud and his wife. This would cohere with his thoughts of Freud as a murderer, and also with his memory of lying between his parents and being punished for what he did, as an image of what the terrifying and punitive father whom Freud now represented might do. Such a dreadful image, moreover, might still involve elements of wish-fulfilment. The child was between the parents, and Freud and his father were murderers, not himself. This image might thus represent the projection of the murderous impulses explicit in his symptoms on to Freud as on to his father. It seems to have been with the occurrence of this image that his greatest fear, and also his conscious remembering, began. An assumption of projection would cohere with his excessive fear of Freud, as well as the general tendency in his associations to present Freud (or his children) as possessing desires related in content to his symptoms. This might also be connected with his idea that he deserved death because of his thoughts about his father.[20]

Having illustrated some aspects of the Freudian concepts of transference, defence and the Oedipus complex, we can approach the more abstract theoretical notions of ego, super-ego and id.[21]

So far as the patient's present inner conflicts – like those of the Rat Man – reflect previous conflicts in the world between his own erotic and aggressive impulses and the parental authority which prohibits gratification of them, it seems we must regard the original sources of conflict as in some way replicated now within the patient's mind. We can do so by thinking of the mind as containing parts or agencies.

One part would be the locus of the erotic and aggressive impulses involved in such conflicts. These would appear to be present from infancy, and since they correspond, on the one hand, to the sexual and nurturing feelings involved in reproduction, and on the other to intense desires for killing and death, they can be taken as expressions of biologically grounded drives or instincts towards life and death respectively. Since the unrestrained and incoherent operation of these drives would be incompatible with individual survival and cooperative life, they require and receive parental and social control. The locus of these drives and impulses would be the id.

Another part of the mind would discharge in the adult those functions of encouragement and prohibition of instinctual impulse which the parent reforms in relation to the child. This part of the mind would be acquired during maturation, and would be modelled on the role of the parents. Among its functions, therefore, would be those of conscience. This part, the super-ego, would be fully established by the time the individual attains independence and maturity, and its proper functioning would be shown in his capacity to love and work cooperatively in family and society.

To a third part of the mind, the ego, is assigned the function of mediating between the external world and the desires of the id, and later between the id and the super-ego as well. Since the drives of the id are not sufficiently coherent to admit of satisfaction in reality, the ego must be assumed to have the capacities of perception etc. to learn about reality, and also to be capable of learning to act and to form and modify desires so as to obtain satisfaction in it. One way in which the ego may do this is by following the example provided by other persons.

The reality with which a very young child has contact is significantly constituted by his parents. Parental regulation – control of feeding, imposition of toilet training, encouragement to self-restraint, more grown-up ways, etc. – is in early life liable to be felt especially intolerable and frustrating, and so may be represented in the mind as incoherently demanding, prohibitive and punitive. Hence this kind of representation may be the basis for the development of the super-ego. The child may begin to achieve regulation of his own impulses, that is, by imagining himself as standing in relation to such a figure; and this kind of representation, in this role, may become a permanent feature of the mind.

Failure by the ego to obtain satisfaction for the desires of the id leads to frustration, whereas failure to act in accord with the demands of the super-ego leads to anxiety. Those desires which are felt most violently to conflict with parental regulation (in particular, those comprising the Oedipus complex) are the greatest source of anxiety, and so have to be kept from the attention of the super-ego. Although these cannot be represented or acted on straightforwardly, they may find expression in wish-fulfilment, provided they are suitably disguised or disowned.

The ego employs various mechanisms of defence to mask the representation of forbidden desires, including symbolism and projection. This latter allows desires which are subject to prohibition to be represented quite explicitly and openly, but as desires of another, and so without provoking anxiety from the super-ego. Indeed, projection can lead to a certain ratification of an otherwise forbidden desire: if the object of malevolent aggressive desires, for example, is represented as having these desires, he can then be thought of as a malevolent and aggressive enemy, and so regarded as a legitimate object of hatred and aggression. (In such a case, as it were, the super-ego joins with the id in aggressive hatred of the object.)

The super-ego is part of the ego, and the development and functioning of the one is bound up with that of the other. Their proper establishment in the young man is achieved through his identification with his father – that is, through his taking as his own a regulative image derived from that of his father as a paternal figure whose encouragements and prohibitions he can accept and on whose model he can love and act. This formative change in his ego and super-ego ensures that his desires and ways of satisfying them no longer require external regulation, and so renders him capable of the autonomous and rational pursuit of his own ends. His incorporating his father's prohibition against incest and correlatively following his father's example in choosing non-incestuous sexual love means that while he becomes like his father in type of sexual love he becomes different from his father in the object of it, so that the sources of Oedipal rivalry between father and son are removed. Thus the final development of the ego and super-ego through identification coincides with the dissolution of the Oedipus complex.

The relative functioning of these parts of the mind, however, may go wrong in a number of ways which impede development. For example, a child's intolerance of the frustrations imposed upon his early desires through his relations with his parents might lead to the formation of a severe super-ego. The anxiety generated by this might lead to a correspondingly severe masking and isolation of the aggressive desires of his id. These in turn could obtain representation as gratified, or legitimate gratification, only through projection. The projection of hostility aroused by frustration or prohibition, however, would serve to reinforce the infantile distortion of the parental images involved in his super-ego. Thus both the severity of the super-ego and the aggression of the id would remain in part unmodified by thought, and hence infantile.

For the boy this would mean that the unconscious images of his father related to the Oedipal period would be hostile and punitive in the extreme, and his own Oedipal desires and hatreds liable to correspondingly severe repression and projection. This in turn would continue to reinforce the distortion of the images of his father involved in his early super-ego. In these circumstances he might be unable to form an integral image of his father as a paternal figure whose encouragements and prohibitions he could make his own, and so be unable to accomplish the complete identification with his father required for the dissolution of his Oedipus complex.

In his failure to love on the model of his father he would neither become like his father in choosing non-incestuous love nor become entirely different from him in his object of sexual love, so that together with his childhood super-ego his early Oedipal emotions would remain partly intact. In his failure to act on the model of his father he would remain subject to unintegrated and archaic desires and demands which he could neither assume as his own nor renounce on the basis of an alternative identification. As his super-ego would retain its immature severity, so the unmodified desires of his id would remain unsatisfied, while his weak or incompletely developed ego could have recourse only to projection, wish-fulfilment which would cause anxiety, and so on.

Such theoretical considerations might cast further light on features of the case already discussed. If the Rat Man's impulses were regulated through his representing himself as in relation to a disciplining paternal figure, it would be intelligible that he should feel such a figure to be opposed to his gratification and so forth. Hence we might better be able to understand the correlative role in the Rat Man of unconscious hostility to his father for prohibiting sexual gratification, images from his childhood of his father as particularly frightening and punitive, a severe conscience resulting in anxiety and suicidal guilt, and also a conscious image, which remained quite disparate from the others, of his father as a close friend. These ideals also might bear on explaining why the Rat Man fell ill when confronted with a choice between being unlike his father (and subject to his father's disapproval) in marrying a poor girl, or like his father (of whom he disapproved in this respect) in marrying a rich girl, as his rich mother encouraged him to do; or again why he developed an obsession over paying a debt, as his father had once failed to do. Here illness seems to be bound up with the kind of identification which is supposed to be formative for the ego and super-ego.

These considerations may also serve to explain something of the Rat Man's behaviour in Freud's consulting room, and perhaps something of the earlier disturbing influence of the Captain with whom he first identified Freud. In the terms under discussion we can say that the Rat Man's terror when his repressions began to lift was at confrontation with an image of his own super-ego, which had been turned by projection, as Freud said in another context, into a pure culture of the death instinct. A link with the super-ego is suggested by the way, as the image became externalized, the Rat Man ceased to inflict upon himself punishment motivated from within as by his conscience, and started rather to fear punishment from without. This punishment was to come from something with murderous impulses, which would fall on him like a beast of prey, so as – and here there is another link with conscience – *to search out what was evil in him*.

The Captain who advocated corporal punishment and spoke of the punish-ment of criminals by other searching animals may also have been significant because he realized a paternal figure of the Rat Man's imagination. On this assumption the Captain's fondness for cruelty would have been significant precisely because it mirrored cruelty of his own of which the Rat Man was unaware. Some such mirroring is suggested by the fact that the Rat Man followed the example of the Captain in expressing cruelty through the thought of the rat punishment, and also took pleasure in thinking of the punishment being applied. In the case of the Rat Man, however, this was a pleasure of which he was unaware, and which horrified him.

In these theoretical terms the changes in desire, belief, imaginative representation etc. pursued in psychoanalysis are described as involving modifications in structural features of the mind. Where internal conflicts can be externalized, understood and worked through in transference, or where episodes in which the super-ego took shape can be re-experienced and so considered again, the ego and super-ego admit of change. Ideally such development will facilitate belated completion of the identification required for the dissolution of the Oedipus complex. Any change of this kind, however, will mean an increase in satisfaction (or diminution in frustration) for the desires associated with the id.

I do not wish to suggest that this is the best way to describe these matters, but rather to indicate some of the point of doing so. Even if this is not an ultimately satisfactory way of representing things – and it is worth noting that there is no incoherence in supposing that parts of the mind should do some of the things done by the mind, or that functioning within the mind is in some ways comparable to that among persons – it apparently serves to describe important phenomena, and so deserves continued use until a better description is formulated.

When Freud arrived at his theories of dreams and symptoms he wrote to his friend Wilhelm Fliess 'Reality–wish-fulfilment: it is from this contrasting pair that our mental life springs.'[22] The aspects of the contrast discussed so far do not exhaust its role in Freud's work. It is found also, as noted above, in his idea of primary and wish-fulfilling processes of thought, operating in accord with a pleasure principle, as opposed to secondary, rational processes, devoted to taking account of reality; or again in his remarks about the unconscious being contradictory, unchanging, but subject to wish-fulfilment. As the contrast seemed to Freud to fill our mental life, so it seems to pervade his thought.

The examples given above have been meant to illustrate, not to produce theoretical conviction. Even supposing that psychoanalytic theory were true, it would not be possible to demonstrate it in this way. This is not because psychoanalysis is unscientific or incapable of confirmation. We saw above that just as in common-sense psychology interpretation and verification and falsification are guided and sustained by underlying predictions about reasons and their relations, so in psychoanlysis they can be regarded as guided and sustained by underlying predictions about wish-fulfilments, desires, reasons and their relations. This renders judgments in psychoanalysis, and the theoretical framework itself, verifiable or falsifiable in the same way as those of common-sense psychology. Although this seems as much as could be expected in principle, in practice it does not suffice to produce agreement.

Psychoanalytic, like physical, theory ranges holistically over a vast number of instances and cases. Although a certain amount of theory may be seen to be applicable in a given case, its justification consists in the way it serves to order and explain the whole field. In the case of psychoanalytic theory, the field is particularly difficult to survey.

Accurate assessment of the explanatory scope and power of a theory can be made only by those who know how to use it. Although ability to interpret in common-sense terms comes naturally, a capacity to interpret in psychoanalytic terms (in any serious way) must be acquired through fairly extensive work and thought, and is therefore relatively rare. The material to which the theory has its central applications, moreover, is mainly outside the public domain. The psychoanalytic interpretation of the unconscious content shown in free associations takes place in conditions of privacy, and the more dramatic and unmistakable manifestations of content typically arise only after interpretation of the right themes has eased repression sufficiently for what is beneath to surface and be expressed.[23] (It is true that everyone can read case material, and also try to interpret his own dreams, slips, etc. Since, however, the grounds for interpretive judgments cannot be represented adequately or extensively in print, and self-analysis is difficult to carry far, the bearing of evidence gained in this way is generally relatively limited.) Hence even if we should accept that analysts who regularly observe behaviour which strikingly exemplifies psychoanalytic concepts have good grounds for theoretical conviction, still there would seem to be no generally available and compelling reasons for others to agree with them.

It may also be, as Freud thought, that there is resistance to the theory. Psychoanalysis is partly concerned with the representation in imagination and thought of activities involving biologically significant organs by which we pass things in and out of our bodies and exchange them with those of others. Since we nourish, live and reproduce through cycles of activity involving these organs, it is not implausible *a priori* that the mental representation of them should be of great psychological importance. Nevertheless we know that many people find the contemplation of such things either fascinating or repulsive or both. Also, if psychoanalysis were, as presented here, a theory of wish-fulfilment, it would be resisted whatever its content. It would be in the nature of any such theory to threaten to awaken people to the content of their unfulfilled wishes and the illusory nature of the gratifications which mask but do not finally satisfy them. Any such theory would spawn alternatives which again represented the wishes as gratified and allowed people to sleep on, and so forth. It is possible that this has happened.

Empiricist psychologists have tried to test psychoanalytic theory without relying on the extensive use of interpretive explanations by which it has been built up and is sustained in use. Many results seem to have been vaguely favourable to Freud, but complete agreement has not been achieved.[24] One reason for this comes from the nature of indirect statistical testing itself, and so may be worth noting here.

Suppose a theory postulates that something unobservable or resistant to a favoured means of observation occurs, so that the theory cannot be tested directly.[25] Still it can be tested indirectly, if we can formulate some testing hypothesis to the effect that if the theory is true certain observable correlations may be expected to obtain, say in how people will answer questions when shown pictures or in taking standardized tests, or among customs in a number of societies.

Now clearly the presence or absence of a hypothesized correlation will bear upon the testing hypothesis as well as upon the theory itself. The presence of a correlation can confirm only both together, whereas absence can disconfirm either one or the other, but not both. Hence assessment of the outcome of tests will depend partly upon prior attitudes to both theory and hypothesis. A psychologist who regards the theory as more plausible than an individual testing hypothesis will tend to view absence of correlation as casting doubt on the putative test, whereas one who thinks the hypothesis superior will count the result against the theory. Clearly, there is room for the operation of prejudice here.

Further, a theory and its associated testing hypotheses will differ in character. The testing hypotheses will link parts of the theory either to behaviour which is directly observable or to some other correlations which are, in a way that the theory itself does not. (If the theory did so, it would not require this kind of indirect testing.) So the testing hypotheses will be more operational or behavioural than the theory itself, and consequently may misrepresent the content of meaning of the theory. For this reason no serious assessment of a theory will involve a general preference for testing hypotheses; any such preference risks implicit systematic distortion of the theory under test.

This means that the evaluation of results may be influenced not only by prior attitude towards theory, but also by general psychological outlook. Someone who favoured a theory and found irrelevant correlations might wrongly claim support from them. But also, someone who was prejudiced against a theory, or again was unduly influenced by behaviourism or operationalism, might systematically favour testing hypotheses at the expense of the theory,[26] thus at once distorting it and representing it as refuted or disconfirmed. It appears that objectivity in this area may be difficult to attain.

Notes

1 Desires seem more closely related to possibilities of action than wishes, in the sense (for example) that a person is better said to wish than to desire that his past life had been different. Desires clearly go together with related wishes, and both involve unfulfilment or frustration which we may imagine away. So I shall use either notion as required to facilitate discussion.

2   S. Freud, *The Standard Edition of the Complete Psychological Works*, ed. J. Strachey, vol. 4, p. 147. London: Hogarth Press and the Institute of Psychoanalysis. Subsequent references to Freud will be to this edition, giving date, volume and page number only.

3   Freud, 1900, vol. 5, p. 618.

4   Freud, 1916, vol. 16, p. 263.

5   On this topic Eysenck and Wilson write that 'Certainly Freud's choice of words is often curiously indecisive, as if he were afraid to say something that could be tested in any rigorous way. Cioffi urges us to "consider the idioms in which Freud's interpretations are typically phrased. Symptoms, errors, etc. are not simply *caused* by but they 'announce', 'proclaim', 'express', 'realize', 'fulfil', 'gratify', 'represent', 'imitate', or 'allude to' this or that repressed impulse, thought, memory, etc." . . . these phrases may have been used to avoid refutation, as Cioffi suggests.' (*The Experimental Study of Freudian Theories*, p. 11 (London, 1973). The reference is to F. Cioffi, 'Freud and the idea of a pseudo-science', in R. Borger and F. Cioffi (eds), *Explanation in the Behavioural Sciences*, p. 496, (Cambridge, 1970)). The suggested criticism seems based upon misunderstanding of Freudian theory. Freud uses 'express', 'represent', 'fulfil', 'realize', and 'gratify' as well as 'cause' in connection with wish-fulfilments not to avoid refutation but because he holds that wish-fulfilments which express wishes are not simply caused by them but also represent them as fulfilled, realized or gratified. He uses 'imitate' because representation may involve an element of imitation, as in the table-cloth lady's imitation of her husband's running. Similarly, because of their role and content, wish-fulfilling representations can be said to announce, allude, etc. The girl's dream above alluded to events in the back of the car, as did the lady's symptom to her wedding night. The analysand's first statement on the couch – about being outside the shut door – both alluded to the past and announced (as first communications in analysis often do) a theme which was to dominate his analysis: his inability to tolerate the exclusivity of his parent's relations in their bedroom. And in connection with this his recall of a distorted memory of being in their bed gave a presumably early example of the defensive *motif* already proclaimed in his symptoms, namely that of representing the others as desiring and frustrated rather than himself. (The transposition of this theme on to the analytical situation, also announced in the first communication, continued with his coming to believe that the analyst envied and admired him, perhaps secretly loved and depended on him, preferred him to all other patients, etc.) On the importance of first communications in analysis see Freud's note at the beginning of the case of the Rat Man, discussed below (1909, vol. 10, 160n, p. 200). For description of some of Cioffi's misunderstandings see V.L. Jupp, 'Freud and pseudo-science' *Philosophy*, October (1977) 441–53. An aspect of the account of Freud given by Eysenck et al. is discussed in A.V. Conway, 'Little Hans: misrepresentation of the evidence', *Bulletin of the British Psychological Society* 31 (1978), 385–7; and N.M. Cheshire, 'A big hand for Little Hans', the same *Bulletin* 32 (1979), 320–3.

6   P. Alexander, 'Rational behaviour and psychoanalytic explanation', *Mind* (1962), 326–41 and a reply by T. Mischel, *Mind* (1965), 71–8. On this topic see also R. Audi, *The Monist* (1972), 444–64. An attempt to reformulate psychoanalytic theory in terms relating to action is in Schafer, *A New Language for Psychoanalysis* (New Haven, Yale, 1976).

7   Reflecting on this same difficulty W. Alston refers to the possibility 'that the

unconscious is quite illogical' ('Psychoanalytic theories, logical status of', *Encyclopaedia of Philosophy*, vol. 6, pp. 512–16, New York, 1967). This particular illogicality, if I am right, is simply the result of the imposition of an inappropriate pattern of explanation. See also F. Cioffi, 'Wishes, symptoms, and actions', *Proceedings of the Aristotelian Society Supplementary Volume* (1974), 97ff, and the reply of P. Alexander.

8 See Freud's abstract and simplified account of this in vol. 5, p. 565 (1910) and elsewhere.

9 See Freud, 1911b, vol. 12, p. 215ff, 'Formulations on the two principles of mental functioning'. For more on the role of imagination in psychoanalytic theory see R. Wollheim, 'Identification and imagination' in *On Art and the Mind* (London, 1973), and 'Wish-fulfilment', in R. Harrison (ed.), *Rational Action* (Cambridge, 1979). Wollheim's account of omnipotence of thought is slightly different from that indicated here.

10 Logical consistency figures at two levels – often not grammatically distinguished – in our description of a person. If we take a person as an object which satisfies psychological predicates, then of course the predicates a person satisfies must be consistent. Also, we regard one another as rational, and so generally consistent in belief. This means that the contents of the beliefs we ascribe to one another will generally be consistent. These are, however, distinct matters. We can, as above, give a consistent description of an imperfectly consistent agent. It may be tempting to think that such a description leads to contradiction. For, one may say, if he believes that it is not the case that the hypnotist told him to open an umbrella, then he doesn't believe that the hypnotist told him. So it seems that it is the case that he believes this, and also that it is not the case that he believes this; which is a contradiction. Such reasoning is, however, invalid; it requires us to assume the agent's consistency at just the point at which we know it to fail.

11 I should make clear that this sketch of theory is extremely incomplete, and is meant for illustration. Also, the emphasis on reparation and gratitude in sublimation is taken from Melanie Klein; see Hanna Segal, *Klein* (London, 1980).

12 Freud, 1909, vol. 10, pp. 155–320. I have made use of Freud's case notes from the time, appended as 'Original record of the case', pp. 253ff, and especially pp. 263–4 and 281–5. The patient's inability quite to distinguish his thoughts of punishment from the occurrence of punishment itself, and his connected belief in the power of his own thoughts may exemplify the kind of omnipotence of thought mentioned above. The 'Captain' parapraxis is an early indication of the transference which emerges fairly clearly at pp. 283–5 and is discussed below.

13 It may be important that the relationship is represented as one in which there is no disproportion between father and son.

14 Here interpretation of a theme in the patient's associations had apparently enabled further associations to arise, in which the theme was represented more explicitly. See Freud, vol. 10, p. 263 for the interpretation, pp. 264–5 for the associations it released.

15 The emergence of hostility seems to begin with the completion of the *Glejisamen* work on p. 281.

16 Later associations had Freud's son eating excrement, and Freud himself eating his mother's excrement. Those familiar with psychoanalytic theory will recognize the connection with the patient's attitude towards the lady (who was to be tortured by the rats as well) and to his mother, who was condemned because of her money.

And it should be pointed out that although the Rat Man was neurotic, the patterns and phantasies in his associations – including those of attacking the mother's breast and eating into her body – are found in the material of normal adults and children as well. Freud remarked that the Rat Man's recognition of his identification with rats – and so those of the cemetery and the torture – was part of the analytic work which relieved his symptoms. Elsewhere Freud links the themes found here – of killing and eating a prohibiting and castrating father – with the setting up of the super-ego and the acquisition of guilt. He does not, however, relate this in detail to individual development, but rather (and quite implausibly) ascribes it to events which happened in the prehistory of mankind, of which he supposed we have phylogenetic memories. Thus he cites a child who wanted to eat some 'fricassee of mother' in connection with the eating of the primal father (1912–13, vol. 13, p. 131). Melanie Klein found such oral themes to be very prominent in the play and speech of children in analysis. Thus a patient 'phantasied about a woman in the circus who was sawn in pieces, and then nevertheless comes to life again, and now he asked me if this were possible. He then related . . . that actually every child wants to have a bit of his mother, who is to be cut in four pieces . . . first across the width of the breast, and then of the belly, then lengthwise so that the *pipi* [penis] the face and the head were cut exactly through the middle . . . he constantly bit at his hand and said that he bit his sister too for fun, but certainly not for love . . . every child took the piece of his mother that it wanted, and [he] agreed that the cut up mother was then also eaten' (*Love, Guilt and Reparation* pp. 70, London, 1975). She was able to place this material in a theoretical framework which coheres with Freud's work but supplements it with an account, among other things, of the role of cannibalistic, coprophagous, and other oral phantasies in early development.

17   Compare the boy in note 16 biting himself as he describes his phantasy.

18   Someone he knew to be constantly making things up had told him Freud's brother was a murderer. Also, he later remembered his sister having remarked that one of Freud's brothers would be the right husband for his lady, and took this as a further cause for jealous hostility to Freud's family. What he had been told does not seem to go far in explaining this scene, since he had been aware of it all along, and it only became important in the context of his transference and emerging parallel memory. Jealousy provoked by his sister's remark would fit in with his transference feelings, but would not itself explain them. Representation of the analyst or father as a biting or devouring beast occurs elsewhere in the material of Freud's patients, as in other psychoanalyses which reach a certain depth. Little Hans' fear was of being bitten by a horse, which animal Freud took to represent his father (1909, vol. 10, p. 5ff). Freud's patient called the Wolf Man represented his father and related figures by fearful devouring wolves. He repeatedly dreamt of six or seven wolves staring at him, riveting their attention on him; as a child he awoke screaming in fear that the wolves might eat him. He linked this with the story of 'The Wolf and the Seven Little Goats', of whom six were eaten. In early sessions he would look towards Freud in a very friendly way, as if to propitiate him, then look away to a large grandfather clock opposite. He was able to explain this to Freud when he recalled that the youngest of the little goats had hidden in such a clock while his brothers were eaten by the wolf. Apparently he was representing himself as the youngest little goat, and Freud as the wolf who might eat him (1918, vol. 17, p. 9ff). The representation of the parent or analyst as such a beast would be a

mirror image (projection) of the desires to devour or attack with the mouth and teeth mentioned in the note above.

19   There may be an identification of the scene of the analysis here with the parental bedroom comparable to that in the case mentioned above.

20   Although I think transference and projection are to be seen in this material, these interpretive remarks are not so much meant to convince on particular points as to indicate the presence of a field of imaginative representation related to Oedipal themes. This material could be linked with many other theoretical considerations, for example Freud's hypothesis that a boy's urination may be an expression of sexual excitement, ambition and aggression, or the idea that mental projection may go together with bodily evacuation.

21   See Freud, 1933, vol. 22, pp. 57–80, 'The dissection of the psychical personality'. The discussion which follows is both selective and supplemented by post-Freudian work.

22   *The Origins of Psycho-Analysis*, p. 277 (Imago, London, 1954).

23   Hence these may be missed by psychotherapists who do not give such interpetations, or again by other observers who attend only to material in which the unconscious is not particularly manifest. There is no reason to suppose that the Rat Man's transference or memories of pp. 283–4 would ever have emerged clearly had Freud not given him such interpretations as that of p. 263 and others later. In trying to assess the cogency of interpretation by reference to case material, B.A. Farrell considers an earlier interpretation given the Rat Man (that which led to his remembering the story of the woman who wished her sister would die) and says that although it may have 'produced some movement' this 'could be explained by an Adlerian theory according to which (as we have seen) L. had feelings of inferiority and resentment at the father, not feelings of an Oedipal character.' In this he follows Popper's claim that every conceivable case of human behaviour could as well be explained by Adler's theory as by Freud's, which he cites with some approval (*The Standing of Psychoanalysis*, pp. 62, 72, Oxford, 1981). Farrell omits to consider the interpretation of p. 263, to which the Rat Man responded by reporting that the idea of his penis being cut off had troubled him intolerably at a time when he had desired to masturbate, that he remembered thinking that one might murder one's father for sexual intercourse, and that he was reminded of a scene in which he had been punished and had abused his father – which scene was connected in content with, and led to, that discussed above, in which his memory of being taken from between his parents in bed and punished had surfaced together with an image of a dead baby, his feeling Freud to be murderous, and so on. Since the feelings in this material seem to be fairly specifically Oedipal, it is difficult to see how it could be equally well explained by a theory according to which, as Farrell says, the Rat Man did not have feelings of an Oedipal character towards his father. Vague reference to feelings of inferiority and resentment has no specific explanatory purchase here at all.

The Popperian claim that non-Freudian theories can equally well or easily explain the responses above, or the oral and anal material with which they are interwoven, or many other aspects of this case, seems utterly implausible. Theories qualify as non-Freudian partly through their denial of such Freudian factors as oral sadism, castration anxiety, Oedipal sexual rivalry, transference of early childhood conflicts, and so on. They consequently lack resources for explaining material which is plausibly taken as manifesting these factors.

In this connection it should be remembered that Popper simply made up the examples he used to support and illustrate his claim. Even followers of Popper should agree that this is not an adequate substitute for the consideration of such real and testing examples of behaviour as are provided by the Rat Man. Such examples, however, seem to disconfirm Popper's claim. Farrell tries to support similar claims by examining a transcript of some exchanges in analytically oriented psychotherapy. The material to which he devotes his careful scrutiny, however, contains no distinctively Freudian interpretations, nor any directed to what is repressed or unconscious. So consideration of it is irrelevant to the present point, as is Farrell's invention of an Adlerian version of the same material.

24   Thus P. Kline (*Fact and Fantasy in Freudian Theory*, Edinburgh, 1972) says in his survey of the literature that so much 'that is distinctively Freudian has been verified' that 'any blanket rejection of Freudian theory as a whole (e.g. Eysenck, 1952) simply flies in the face of the evidence' (pp. 346, 350), while Fischer and Greenberg, in a more recent survey, remark that they were generally impressed with how often the results of tests had borne out Freudian expectations (*The Scientific Credibility of Freud's Theories and Therapy*, p. 393, New York and Sussex, 1977). Eysenck and Wilson, however, in *The Experimental Study of Freudian Theories*, continued to regard Freudian theory as disconfirmed or entirely unsupported. For discussion of the outcome of psychotherapy influenced by psychoanalysis see R.B. Sloane et al., *Psychotherapy versus Behavior Therapy*, (Harvard, 1975), and for discussion of the outcome of various kinds of psychotherapy see Shapiro in the *British Journal of Medical Psychology* 53, (1980) 1–10.

25   Thus an academic psychologist might consider that events like the Rat Man's rushing away, covering his face with his hands, and so forth, *in fear of Freud as representing his father*, were improperly observable, either because they could normally be observed by only one person, or because they had to be interpreted in terms of theoretical concepts to be seen as an instance of the theory. This latter objection would apparently hold for any interpretive judgment whatever.

26   In this context note Eysenck and Wilson's remarks about how unjustly favourable to Freud it might be to concentrate on positive rather than negative results, *The Experimental Study of Freudian Theories*, p. xii.

23

Self-Deception and the Nature of Mind

Mark Johnston

When paradox dominates the description of a widespread phenomenon, dubious presuppositions usually lurk. Paradox dominates the philosophical treatment of bad faith or self-deception.[1] Part of the explanation is that the descriptive content of any claim that someone has deceived himself can be made to seem paradoxical. Such paradox mongering is not a fetish found only among analytic philosophers. Here is J.P. Sartre:

> One does not undergo one's bad faith; one is not infected with it ... but consciousness affects itself with bad faith. There must be an original intention and a project of bad faith: this project implies a comprehension of bad faith as such and a pre-reflective apprehension of consciousness as affecting itself with bad faith. It follows first that the one to whom the lie is told and the one who lies are one and the same person, which means that I must know in my capacity as deceiver the truth which is hidden from me in my capacity as the one deceived.[2]

This suggests *the surface paradox of self-deception*. If bad faith or self-deception is lying to oneself then a self-deceiver must stand to himself as liar to liar's victim. As liar he knew or strongly suspected that, as it might be, he was too drunk to drive home safely; as victim of the lie he did not know or strongly suspect this. If the same subject of belief or knowledge is both liar and liar's victim, we have a simple contradiction in *our* description of his condition: he both knew and did not know that he was too drunk to drive home safely.

There is a natural homuncularist response to this surface paradox of self-deception.[3] Distinct sub-systems that play the distinct roles of deceiver and deceived are located within the self-deceiver. So no single subject of belief is required to both believe (know) a proposition and not believe (know) it.

The homuncularist picture has some independent appeal. For there is another sort of epistemic duality in self-deception which the homuncularist picture can capture. There is a sense in which the self-deceiving drunkard who believes and claims he will make it home safely also knows he may very

well not, but this latter knowledge is suppressed, unacknowledged or inoperative. When he is drunk it does not find useful expression in his thought or
speech. When he sobers up or comes out of his self-deception he might
plausibly say that he knew all along that it would be disastrous for him to drive.
The self-deceptive belief that he will make it home safely can be located in the
deceived system, and the knowledge that he probably won't can be located in
the deceiving system. One snag remains. If the deceiving system is actively to
deceive, then its knowledge of the facts must be operative and available to it.
But then the homuncularist must also find a privileged sense in which
knowledge is inoperative in self-deception. A strategy suggests itself. Let the
deceived system be the analogue of the Freudian ego – the locus of the
person's conscious thought, perception, decision and voluntary control of the
body. What is stored in the deceiving system is then hypothesized as not
accessible to consciousness and so inoperative and inaccessible from the point
of view of the ego or main system. So the homuncularist not only avoids
contradiction in his description of the self-deceiver but also appears to be able
to explain, in terms of mental compartmentalization, how it is that the self-
deceiver could believe propositions that are contradictory.

If another model of self-deception were produced then this account of the
duality involved in self-deception might seem forced. One can make perfectly
good sense of conscious belief that p and unacknowledged knowledge of the
contrary without thinking that there are particular loci within the mind which
are the respective subjects of attitudes of these sorts, as if 'consciousness',
'preconsciousness', and 'unconsciousness' were names for layers or compart-
ments of the mind.

One reason for thinking that another model should be produced is that the
homuncular explanation replaces a contradictory description of the self-
deceiver with a host of psychological puzzles. How could the deceiving sub-
system have the capacities required to perpetrate the deception? For example,
do such deceiving sub-systems have a much higher alcohol tolerance than their
hosts? Is that why they seem particularly active when one is drunk? Why should
the deceiving sub-system be interested in the deception? Does it like lying for
its own sake? Or does it suppose that it knows what is best for the deceived
system to believe?

Again, how does the deceiving system engage in an extended campaign of
deception, employing various stratagems to alter the beliefs of the deceived
system, without the deceived system's somehow noticing? If the deceived
system somehow notices, then the deception cannot succeed without the
collusion of the deceived system. However, to speak of the collusion of the
deceived system in its own deception simply reintroduces the original problem.
The deceived system is now both (partial) agent and patient in the deception.
Must we now recognize within the deceived system a deceiving sub-system
and a deceived sub-system? If so, we face a dilemma: either a completely
unexplanatory regress of sub-systems of sub-systems or the termination of the
regress with a deceived sub-system stupid enough not to notice the strategies

of deception and so one for which the question of collusion does not arise. The latter may always seem to be the way out until we reflect on the fact that the knowing, *complex*, and deceiving sub-system must have a curious kind of self-effacing motivation both to deceive the stupid and *simple* sub-system *and* to let it speak for and guide the whole person on the issue in question. Often self-deception involves a matter vital to the self as a whole, for example whether one will survive the drive home tonight. It is hard then to see why the wiser, deceiving sub-system should stand aside and let its foolish victim's belief control subsequent inference and action.

In fact, homuncularism is a premature response to the surface paradox of self-deception. A dubious presupposition does lurk behind the familiar construal of the paradox. To be deceived is sometimes just to be *misled* without being *intentionally* misled or lied to. The self-deceiver is a self-misleader. As a result of her own activity she gets into a state in which she is misled, at least at the level of conscious belief. But the presupposition that generates the paradox is that this activity must be thought of as the intentional act of lying to oneself so that self-deception is just the reflexive case of lying. Evidently, *as the surface paradox shows*, nothing could be *that*. The homuncularist holds to the presupposition that the intentional act of lying is involved but drops the strict reflexive condition. If self-misleading is to be lying then the best one can do is to have parts of the self play the roles of liar and liar's victim. (Some have suggested that temporal parts of the self over time could play this role, but as we shall see this will not provide a general account.)[4]

The suggestion I wish to explore is that the surface paradox and deeper paradoxes of self-deception (i.e. those developed by Bernard Williams, by Sartre in a different passage, and by Donald Davidson)[5] arise because as theorists of self-deception we tend to over-rationalize mental processes that are purposive but not intentional. These are processes that serve some interests of the self-deceiver, processes whose existence within the self-deceiver's psychic economy depends upon this fact, but processes that are not necessarily initiated by the self-deceiver for the sake of those interests or for any other reason. If we call mental processes that are purposive but not initiated for and from a reason *sub-intentional* processes then we can say that our over-rationalization of self-deception consists in assimilating sub-intentional processes to intentional acts, where an intentional act is a process initiated and directed by an agent because he or she recognizes that it serves a specific interest of his or hers.[6] Faced with the sub-intentional processes of division, denial, repression, removal of appropriate affect, wishful perception, wishful memory and wishful thought, the theorist whose only model for things done by an agent is that of the intentional act will multiply sub-agents complete with their own interests and action plans. Self-deception is an important test case for such a theorist since the very characterization of someone as self-deceived suggests both mental division and self-directed agency. If the sub-agency or homuncularist picture applies anywhere it should apply here. However, as I shall argue, little in the way of plausible interests and action plans can be constructed in order to carry out the program of representing self-deception as an intentional act of a lying sub-agency. In any case, this would misrepresent what we are censuring when we censure someone for self-deception. For in censuring the self-deceiver we do not blame any sub-agency for simply lying, nor are we mixing such blame with sympathy for an innocent victim of the lying sub-agency.

The recognition of sub-intentional mental processes points the way out of the so-called paradoxes of self-deception and avoids an implausible homuncularism. The sub-intentional mental process involved in wishful thinking and self-deception is an instance of a non-accidental mental regularity: anxious desire that p, or more generally anxiety concerning p, generates the belief that p. Deeper morals about the nature of the mind emerge from the recognition of such non-accidental, purpose-serving, mental regularities – mental tropisms, as I shall call them.

The existence and ubiquity of mental tropisms whose relata do not stand in any rational relation falsifies a certain view of the mental which is gaining currency. This *interpretive view* of mental states and events has it that there is nothing more to being in a mental state or undergoing a mental change than being apt to have that state or change attributed to one within an adequate interpretive theory, i.e. a theory that takes one's behavior (including speech behavior) as evidence and develops under the holistic constraint of construing much of that behavior as intentional action caused by rationalizing beliefs and desires that it is reasonable to suppose the subject has, given his environment and basic drives. On this conception, when we attribute a mental state to another, we are not locating within him an instance of a mental natural kind or property that as such enters into characteristic causal relations in accord with non-accidental psychological or psycho-physical regularities. On the view in question there are no natural mental properties and so no law-like psychological or psycho-physical regularities. Instead, attributions of mental states and changes have a point only within a whole pattern of potential reason-explanations, i.e. explanations that exhibit the subject as a rational agent pursuing what is reasonable from his or her point of view. Fitting into a pattern of reason-explanations that serve to interpret their subject is thus a constitutive condition of something's being a mental attribution. More, there can be no other content to the idea that something is a *mental* attribution. In this sense, rationality is constitutive and exhaustive of the mental.

Donald Davidson has done the most to promote this conception of mental attributions.[7] Armed with it he is able to show in a relatively *a priori* fashion that mental vocabulary needs no special ontology of its own, i.e. that the intentional mental descriptions of an adequate interpretive theory pick out physical event tokens.[8] But, as Davidson recognizes, both mere wishful thinking and self-deception provide prima facie counter-examples to the interpretive view of mental states and events.[9] For they seem to be cases in which desire brings about belief in a characteristic way which on the face of it is not subject to rational explanation. The generated belief could not be the outcome of any practical syllogism with the desire as premise. My suggestion is that the appearances are correct and point to a characteristic, non-accidental and non-rational connection between desire and belief – a *mental tropism* or purpose-serving mental mechanism. Finally, it will emerge that such mental tropisms are not peripheral pathologies but are central bases of rational and irrational connections alike.

Wishful Thought

The accusation of self-deception is related to the charge of wishful thinking, a charge that points to motivated belief, i.e.: belief adopted not in response to the available evidence but in conformity with what one wants to be the case. Whereas the wishful thinker accepts a proposition without possessing sufficient evidence, or at least without relying upon sufficient evidence that is in his possession, the self-deceiver accepts a proposition against what he at some level recognizes to be the implications of the evidence. Hence it is sometimes said that, whereas the mere wishful thinker is only self-indulgent, the self-deceiver is perverse and duplicitous. He resists the natural implications of the evidence, and in order to do this he employs certain stratagems of denial. A self-deceiver is properly charged with wishful thinking. But to leave the charge at that is to be much less informative and disdainfully self-righteous than one could be.

Self-deception is then a *species* of wishful thought: it is motivated belief in the face of contrary evidence. There is, however, a way of thinking about belief which makes nonsense of the very idea of purely motivated belief, i.e. belief generated from desire and not formed in response to evidence. Thus H.H. Price writes, '[We] cannot strictly be said to believe without evidence, what is so described is not belief but something else.'[10] Price's remark suggests an easy way out. Concede the term 'belief' to those who wish to tie belief essentially to responses to evidence and recognize a range of attitudes that share the action- and inference-guiding role of belief but not necessarily its (conceded) relation to evidence, so that these attitudes can be generated by desire or, more generally, be under the control of the will.

At this stage this quick dismissal of the worry is too facile. If wishful or self-deceptive thought is to serve its characteristic purpose of reducing anxiety that one's desires will not be satisfied, it must result in one's adopting a cognitive attitude, i.e. an attitude that involves one's taking the world to be a certain way, namely, in accord with or soon to be in accord with one's desires. The doubts about the coherence of talk of a belief's having its origin not in response to evidence but in the will, extend to any sort of attitude that is cognitive, i.e. that involves its subject in taking the world to be a certain way. So for example, when Bernard Williams argues that necessarily I cannot bring it about, just like that, that I believe something independently of the evidence, he gives an argument that would apply to any cognitive attitude, i.e. any attitude that purports to represent reality. Williams writes:

> If I could acquire a belief at will, I could acquire it whether it was true or not; moreover I would know that I could acquire it whether it was true or not. If in full consciousness I could will to acquire a 'belief' irrespective of its truth, it is unclear that before the event I could seriously think of it as a belief, *i.e. as something purporting to represent reality*. At the very least, there must be a restriction on what is the case after the event; since I could not then, in full consciousness, regard this as a belief of mine, i.e. something I take to be true, and also know that I acquired it at will. With regard to no belief could I know – or, if all this is to be done in full consciousness, even suspect – that I had acquired it at will. But if I can acquire beliefs at will, I must know that I am able to do this; and could I know that I was capable of this feat, if with regard to every feat of this kind which I had performed I necessarily had to believe that it had not taken place?[11] (emphasis added)

The crucial claim in this passage is that I cannot take something to be a belief of mine *and* believe that I acquired it at will. The idea seems to be that, in the simplest case, if I recognize that I have just acquired a 'belief' at will, have just conjured up a representation and assented to it, I thereby recognize that I possess no evidence in favor of the truth of that representation so that I cannot then take it to be a true representation of the way reality is. This needs amendment. If someone offers me a million dollars if I can get myself to believe that I will be a millionaire, and I succeed and am about to be given the money, then although I know I acquired the belief at will, I have come to possess sufficient evidence in favor of its truth. I had evidence that if I acquired the belief at will then it would be a true belief. By acquiring the belief at will I simultaneously come to have evidence of its truth. This sort of complication can arise in any case in which acquiring a belief makes it more likely that the believed proposition is true. (See the discussion of positive thinking below.)

What might seem odd is any conscious state that involves one's intentionally coming to believe some proposition p while recognizing that one neither presently possesses nor will possess evidence for p, so that one has no evidential basis for thinking p true. For then we have an intentional act, e.g. assenting to some representation that p, done without its typical and particularly appropriate reason, namely, that there is evidence for p. However, the atypical is possible, and we should allow for the possibility of one's intentionally coming to believe p out of a desire to believe p which is not itself the result of any sensitivity to the evidence for p – for example, a desire springing from an interest in the causal consequences of one's doxastic states, as opposed to an interest in the truth-values of the propositions one's doxastic states are beliefs in. The appeal of Pascal's wager crucially depends upon the cultivation of such an interest. (See also the discussion of the sophisticate below.) But intentionally coming to believe that p neither out of such interests nor from any evidential reason for p is a contradiction in terms – an intentional act done from and for no reason.

How does this bear on the possibility of intentional and immediate wishful thought, i.e. intending to adopt the belief that p, just like that and just because one wants p to be the case?

Any intentional act can be described *as if* it were the outcome of a stretch of practical reasoning from reasons that the agent can be said to have and to have acted because of. This is not to say that prior to each intentional act some reasoning must occur. However, even if practical reasoning did not actually take place prior to some intentional act, our claim that it was an intentional act commits us to the claim that it is possible to *construct* a plausible practical syllogism from beliefs and desires of the agent to the intention to carry out the act. This much follows from the assumption that the agent acted for and from a reason. When the purported intentional act is wishfully acquiring the belief that p or, more generally, wishfully taking p to be the case, what could the associated practical syllogism be? What beliefs in conjunction with the wish or desire that p could rationalize or provide the practical premises for the intention to adopt the attitude of taking p to be the case?

It seems that the relevant belief will have to be some conviction that the acquisition of the belief that p will make p more likely to be true. How otherwise could the acquisition of the belief that p be thought to serve the desire that p? There are cases in which such a conviction is reasonably attributed to the agent, cases in which the belief figures in making itself true. Thus the advocates of auto-suggestion think that if they can only believe that they will succeed then they will be more likely to succeed. So they set about trying to inculcate such potentially self-fulfilling beliefs in themselves. William James gives the example of a person who must leap across a deep crevasse.[12] His chance of a successful leap in part depends upon his allaying his own anxiety by convincing himself that he will make a successful leap. So he has reason to try to acquire a belief that cool weighing of the evidence would not support. In some quarters this sort of potentially self-fulfilling wishful thinking is called 'positive thinking', and a whole industry of self-help books is built around its advocacy. Whatever its drawbacks and lack of appeal to those of us who are less upbeat in temperament, positive thinking, even when intentionally pursued, is not incoherent.

It would, however, be implausible to suppose that all wishful thinking is some kind of positive thinking. This might be more plausible as a claim about members of a community in which beliefs were thought to be generally self-fulfilling, for example, a community in which ritual magic or voodoo permeated everyday life so that quite generally the symbolic representation of the desired outcome is taken to be efficacious. Even here, if all wishful thought was to be positive thought, it would have to be true that *whenever* someone's desire generated a wishful belief, he or she had a collateral belief that the generated belief would play some role in the satisfaction of his or her desire. This is not our situation; we are not *that* superstitious, and our particular superstitions are not perfectly tailored to our wishful thoughts. There is then a residual class of cases of wishful thoughts that are not positive thoughts. Concerning them,

Williams seems largely vindicated. Cases of positive thinking apart, nothing could be an intentional act of immediately coming to wishfully believe in the recognized absence of supporting evidence. We could call this the *paradox of wishful thinking or believing* if we liked, but the way out is too obvious to linger long with paradox. Wishful thought, the process that leads from anxious desire that *p* to belief that *p*, is not something done as an intentional act.

A complication arising from Freud's work remains. Consider someone apprised of the existence and function of what Freud called primary process thinking, a representational process that manifests itself in daydreaming and more directed phantasy and which provides a surrogate satisfaction for frustrated desire.[13] Such a person might reason as follows: 'I have the unsatisfied desire that *p*. Primary process thought provides a surrogate satisfaction for unsatisfied desire, so I will engage in primary process thought that *p*.' This is of course absurdly over-explicit. But that cannot be an objection, since we are simply exploring the *possibility* of constructing a practical syllogism from beliefs and desires of the agent to the act of adopting a wishful belief. The real objection is that even if someone could bring herself to be concerned with assuaging her unsatisfied desires with the appropriate doses of phantasy, as if her own desires were for her mitigatable conditions, the outcome of such practical reasoning would not be wishful thinking. The intentional act prompted by these reasons, the act of engaging in the phantasy that *p*, does not involve one in taking *p* to be the case, any more than pretending that *p* does. One can, of course, get lost in a phantasy or a pretense, that is, cease to realize that it is such and come to believe that what one was phantasizing or pretending to be the case is the case. This further step would be wishful thinking, but it would not itself be rationalized by any practical reasoning, any more than someone's falling asleep while pretending to be asleep would be rationalized by his reasons for pretending to be asleep.

Consider this example. A non-superstitious gambler who wants blackjack (an ace and a ten or a face card) on the hand being dealt to him may find himself phantasizing that a ten or a face card will follow the ace that he has been dealt, but he may have no reason to believe this and is likely not to believe it. If the dealing was interrupted and he was asked to bet a further substantial sum at even money on his getting blackjack, he would typically refuse, knowing that the odds are roughly nine to four against. He has no superstitious belief about the effect of his anticipatory phantasies, but he has anticipatory phantasies none the less. Yet they do not in themselves involve him in believing that he will be dealt a ten or a face card next.

Still, all too rapidly even the non-superstitious gambler can lose himself in such hopeful phantasies, coming thereby to believe that he will get blackjack on the next hand and betting accordingly. Getting lost in a phantasy in this way is just another name for wishful thinking, and so presents the same problem. Certainly the gambler's desire to be dealt blackjack gives him no reason to believe that he will. The gambler wants blackjack; his coming to believe that he will get blackjack is not something that has any independent or supplementary appeal for him. His interest is in the cards and the pay-off, not in some doxastic state he might come to be in. We do not understand his getting lost in his phantasy by treating it as an intentional or rationalizable act. But how then should we understand it?

The gambling example is not peripheral. Repetitive gambling is an arena of action in which wishful thinking is rife. The anxious desire that prompts wishful thought easily arises because there is so much eventful giving of hostages to fortune in relatively short periods of time.[14] Casino proprietors know that the selective reinforcement of anticipatory phantasies of winning can solidify them into the belief that one will win. (Slot machines with their fixed pay-off percentages are built around this psycho-physical law.) In such a setting the phenomenology of holding out against wishful thinking, in particular resisting the dangerous conviction that one will certainy win in the short run, is the phenomenology of resistance to conditioning or the manipulation of one's attitudes by internal and external rewards. But there is a problem with the simple conditioning model of wishful thinking which has the wishful belief that one will win figure as a rewarding response to one's desire to win. The model I have in mind treats the desire to win as a potentiality to be rewarded by winning. Winning is correlated with the belief that one has won, and we may expect that this belief will acquire some of the rewarding significance of winning itself. In so far as a belief of the appropriate sort can arise spon- taneously (has a certain operant level) its arising in the presence of the appropriate desire will be rewarding, and so beliefs of this sort will tend to arise in the presence of the desire to win. In the jargon of conditioning theorists, the event of a wishful belief's arising or coming about is a reinforced because rewarding operant.

Compare David Pears's account of the functional role of the wishful belief in his book *Motivated Irrationality*. Pears writes:

> the explanation must start from the fact that achievement of the real thing would not produce any satisfaction if [one] were unaware of it. The belief is the intermediary, the messenger with the good news, and, when actual achievement causes satisfaction, it is the belief in the achievement that is the immediate cause. The causal linkage makes it possible for [one] to take a short cut to satisfaction: [one] simply manufactures the belief without the real thing.[15]

Such an explanation is not in general adequate. For example, the belief that is correlated with or brings the good news of winning is the belief that one *has* won, whereas the wishful belief correlated with the desire to win is typically anticipatory. It is the belief that one *will* win. Nor is the difficulty to be got around by the Freudian suggestion that primary process thought and hence wishful thought is not significantly tensed but represents a kind of 'dream time' that is not determinately past, present or future. For after all, it is the quite determinately tensed and wishful belief that one *will* win which leads one to bet so recklessly on the *next* hand rather than reach out for one's imagined winnings or do something, whatever it might be, that is intermediate between the two.

No, if we are to understand anticipatory belief as a reinforced operant, we must explain why the arising of a future-tensed belief can be rewarding. The explanation tells us something important about the etiology of wishful thinking and hence of self-deception. A future-tensed belief can reduce anxiety about the future. If this is the rewarding role of anticipatory wishful thought – the reduction of anxiety about a desired outcome – then we should expect anticipatory wishful thought in the presence of the desire that p coupled with the fear that not-p. This speculation finds some confirmation in the wisdom of those who aim to fight wishful thought. Thus it is said that the gambler who does not want to get carried away with his phantasies must not play with 'scared' money (money that he cannot afford to lose) and that he must remind himself that he is in a positive expectation game (otherwise he has no business playing) and has only to make the correct plays and bet well within his bankroll in order to win in the long run. These are, *inter alia*, practical defenses against anxiety and the wishful thought that anxiety generates. Moreover, much of the efficacy of what is presented as positive thinking, i.e. exhortations to believe that one will succeed with the accompanying suggestion that this will make success more likely, derives from the fact that such beliefs tend to reduce debilitating anxiety about the desired outcome. So it is in James's case of the crevasse jumper.

The suggestion is then that we should understand wishful thinking, not as the actual or potential outcome of practical reasoning occurring in the unconscious or in some homuncular part of the mind, but as a mental mechanism or tropism by which a desire that p and accompanying anxiety that not-p set the conditions for the rewarding (because anxiety-reducing) response of coming to believe that p. And now, having properly located and sidestepped the deeper worry about the very possiblility of a cognitive attitude like belief being generated by the will, we can deal summarily with Price's objection that such purely motivated belief that p does not really deserve the name of 'belief' because it is neither grounded in what one takes to be evidence for p nor reliably connected to the state of affairs that p. Granted, its claims to the title of belief that p do not lie there but in its being a disposition to the occurrent thought that p, in its action-guiding potential, and in its potential to allay anxiety that not-p. Call it 'quasi-belief' if you must, but recognize its similarity on the output side to the best-grounded beliefs.

The treatment of wishful thought and, by implication, self-deception as the non-intentional outcome of a mental tropism is a rebuff to those who would represent such phenomena as intentional. But knowledge of the existence of a mental mechanism allows one to form plans that intentionally duplicate its typical benefits. A sophisticate could reason that since she wants to reduce her anxiety that not-p she should think that p and dispose herself so to think, i.e. try to believe that p and *not* fear the worst. This would be a case of intentionally aiming at the wishful belief that p for the very reason that it reduces one's anxiety that not-p. It is precisely an interest in the causal consequences of her own doxastic states which is characteristic of our sophisticate. But to regard the sophisticate's reasoning as representing what is essential (if implicit) in every case of wishful thinking is to massively over-rationalize a more primitive phenomenon. The unsophisticated need not be relying upon any beliefs about the relation between belief and anxiety in order to accept the soothing balm of wishful thought. Indeed, in the more virulent cases of wishful thought, one is incapable of distancing oneself from one's present anxiety and considering it as an unwanted state of oneself to be treated with the right dose of belief.

Furthermore, there seems to be a conceptual condition on the sophisticate's intentional wishful thinking, a condition that is not satisfied in the ordinary case. The sophisticate engages in or is disposed to engage in the following train of thought:

I anxiously fear that not-p.

I do not want to anxiously fear that not-p.

If I were to come to believe that p then I would not anxiously fear that not-p.

So I will believe that p.

Drawing the conclusion of this train of thought involves the sophisticate's thinking of her believing that p as not prompted by evidential considerations but only by the hope for its soothing balm. Assuming the sophisticate does not pursue belief that p in a way that allows her to forget her reasons for pursuing it, she must recognize that her coming to believe p does not in any way reflect the truth of the matter as to p.[16] But then it is entirely mysterious how one could think that adopting an attitude that one recognized as not in any way reflecting the truth of the matter as to p could help to allay the anxiety that not-p. The sophisticate's practical reasoning is comprehensible only if she believes that her believeing that p will make p more likely to be true, e.g. by reducing debilitating anxiety that not-p. Once again, as in James's case, the only kind of rationalizable step from desire that p to belief that p involves positive thinking about p, i.e. thinking in which, for one or another reason, the thinker holds that the desired outcome is made more likely if she believes in it. In other cases there is simply no plausible way to rationalize wishful thinking. The sub-intentionalist account seems forced upon us.

Self-Deception

Our tentative conclusion is that wishful thought that is not positive thought is not rationalizable and so not intentional. But it does serve a purpose in that it reduces anxiety about the desired outcome. It is reasonable to be less anxious that not-p if one comes to believe that p. So although the efficacy of the wishful thought or belief is intelligible only in terms of a rational connection between the attitudes involved, the generation of the wishful thought is not mediated by any rational connection.

In wishful thought there need not be any appearance of a split within the agent. Someone may simply exploit the slack between inductive evidence and conclusion and wishfully think that the evidence that his wife is unfaithful to him is misleading and is to be otherwise explained. That this was wishful thought on his part rather than conservative thought need not be shown by the existence of some unacknowledged recognition in him that the evidence more or less establishes her infidelity. It can be shown by the fact that when presented with corresponding evidence about other married women he makes the judgment of infidelity.

Once one is no longer theoretically committed to understanding wishful thought as something intentionally done, one need not postulate some degree of recognition in the wishful thinker of what he or she has done, recognition that then has to be taken as somehow dissociated or sequestered from the mainstream of consciousness in order to avoid having the mainstream entertain what seems an impossible combination, i.e. both the wishful belief and the belief that this belief is wishful and so is not supported by anything that would suggest that it is true. Here we have a prima facie theoretical advantage of the sub-intentionalist treatment of wishful thought, since there is no direct implication of mental division in the accusation of mere wishful thought.

Things seem otherwise with self-deception strictly so-called. To the extent that the self-deceiver is to be distinguished from the mere wishful thinker by his perversely adopting the wishful belief *despite* his recognition at some level that the evidence is to the contrary, we have reason to regard the self-deceiver as divided. For it is hard to see how anxiety could be reduced by a wishful belief if the wishful belief is co-present in consciousness with the recognition that the evidence is strongly against it. Indeed, it is hard to see how the wishful belief could persist in consciousness under these conditions. So it seems that some play must be given to the concept of *repression* in discussing self-deception. If anxiety that not-p produced by recognition of telling evidence for not-p is to be reduced, not only must the wishful belief that p arise, but the recognition of the evidence as more or less establishing the contrary must also be repressed, i.e. the subject must cease consciously acknowledging it. The strategies by which one ceases consciously to acknowledge that one recognizes the evidence to be against one's wishful belief are manifold. One may selectively reappraise and explain away the evidence (rationalization). One may simply avoid thinking about the touchy subject (evasion). One may focus one's attention on invented reasons for p and spring to the advocacy of p whenever opportunity presents itself (overcompensation). Where repressive strategies abound, it is plausible to postulate a repressive strategist. But the strategist cannot be the main system, in which the wishful belief allays anxiety. For then the main system would have to aim to put down the threatening belief or recognition of the import of the contrary evidence *in order* that it should cease to be aware of the threatening belief. Consciousness of its reason for repression makes the main system's task of forgetting impossible. Ignorance of its reason makes the task uninteresting. So we seem driven to recognize a sub-agency distinct from the main system, a sub-agency that, like Freud's censor or super-ego, is active in repression.

However, as Sartre maintained in his attack on Freud, it can appear that the Freudian account of repression in self-deception, e.g. the account of repression in self-deceptive resistance to the probings of the analyst, represents no advance over having the main system play the role of repressive agency.[17] If the censor who controls the border traffic between unconsciousness and consciousness is to successfully repress condemned drives and so resist the analyst, it must be aware of the drive to be repressed in order not to be conscious of these repressed drives. So it seems that the censor's putative project or intention is an impossible one – at the same time to be aware and not to be aware of the repressed desire. Now even if there is reason to doubt this objection of Sartre's to Freud's resort to the censor, say because it is unclear why the *censor* should have to be unaware of the repressed material, Sartre has still highlighted a real difficulty about repression. And this difficulty generalizes, so that we may speak of *a paradox of repression*. No project or action plan can satisfy the condition of simultaneously including awareness and ignorance of the repressed material. Given Sartre's ambition to use the paradox of repression to undermine Freudian pessimism about the scope of conscious choice in our mental life, it is ironic that the way out of the paradox seems to be the same as the way out of the paradox of wishful thought and the surface paradox of self-deception. We should not treat repression, even in its complex manifestations, as an intentional act of some sub-agency guided by its awareness of its desire to forget. On the contrary, we should understand repression as sub-intentional, i.e. not guided by reasons but operating for the purpose of reducing anxiety. For where we can find neither a coherent intention in acting nor a coherent intention to be acted upon we cannot discern intentional action. But before we take this way out of the paradox of repression we must deal with an alternative solution and then (in the next section) with an alternative account of the role of the censor or protective system in self-deception, an account developed by David Pears.

First, why should the condition of *simultaneously* including awareness and ignorance of the repressed material be a natural condition to impose on any repressor's action plan? Surely there are cases of deceiving oneself in which the shadow of forgetfulness falls between the intention and the act.

Forgetfulness can sometimes be planned around. Certain powerful sleeping pills cause retroactive amnesia. One's memory of what one did in the hour or so before taking the pill is very indistinct and sometimes apparently erased completely. Knowing this, one could get up to mischief during such a period and avoid the guilt of the morning after by taking the precaution of rearranging things so that in the morning one will be misled about what one did the night before. This is certainly intentional activity, and if it succeeds it results in the deception of one's later self by an earlier self. Similarly, taking to holy water and rosary beads, i.e. acting as if one accepted the tenets of Catholicism, was Pascal's suggested method of bringing about the belief in those tenets. This is certainly intentional activity, and it can result in the production of a desired belief in one's later self, presumably because it gradually inclines one to view the favorable evidence more sympathetically and not attend to the countervailing evidence. Here we have self-deceptive action plans involving repression and forgetting, and yet nothing paradoxical.

Indeed, it has been suggested[18] that in general the way to avoid the surface paradox of knowing deceiver and unknowing victim's being embodied in the one agent is to exploit the fact that self-deception takes time: in the interim the deceiver can forget what he knew and forget that he set out to mislead himself. This time-lag strategy, however, not only leaves the most puzzling cases of self-deception untreated but also leaves unexplained the most puzzling features of many of the cases it seems to render unparadoxical.

Not all self-deception takes a form in which stages of the self-deceiver's history are successively stages of deceiving, forgetting and being the victim of deceit. One can simultaneously develop as deceiver and deceived. A case of progressive and self-deceptive alcoholism might be of this sort. As the alcoholic's case worsens and more evidence accumulates, his self-deceptive denials develop concurrently.

Moreover, it cannot be the mere fact that self-deception takes time (if it does take time) that allows the self-deceiver to forget what she knew and forget that she set out to mislead herself. Rather, what is crucial to the cases in which the time delay seems to allow a non-paradoxical description is that the self-deceiver explicitly employs a means to achieve her motivated belief, a means whose operation does not require that the self-deceiver attend to it under the description 'means of producing in me the desired belief' or something equivalent. Let us call a means that does not require this kind of monitoring, an *autonomous* means. In the case of nocturnal mischief, the autonomous means is a combination of a process in the external world, the persistence of misleading evidence, and the intended outcome of a drug-induced process of forgetting, a process that is not itself an intentional act and so does not require directive monitoring after the taking of the pill. In the case of Pascal's method, the means is the adoption of a practice itself sufficiently engaging so that past a certain point one need not think of one's participation under the description 'means of getting me to believe in the tenets of Catholicism in the absence of sufficient evidence' in order to intend to participate. Past a certain point one just gets carried along.

The phrase 'past a certain point' itself masks a puzzling feature of the case. Around the point in question there must be a transition from intending one's participation in the practice under the description 'means of getting me to believe in the tenets of Catholicism in the absence of sufficient evidence' to doing it habitually and perhaps under more particular descriptions internal to the practice, e.g. 'asking for God's forgiveness'. This very transition, which might be called 'falling in with the practice', may be compared to getting lost in a phantasy or a pretense, not in order to belittle it but in order to point out that the transition in question involves a kind of forgetfulness that cannot itself be represented as an intentional act, something done from and for a reason. For this forgetfulness simply *occurs* at a certain point, and to represent it as something done for a reason is to allow that it could be monitored as something tending to satisfy and ultimately satisfying an intention. The intention would have to be something like 'to forget that my only reason for engaging in this practice is as a means of producing in me belief in the tenets of Catholicism'. The paradox of repression simply recrystallizes at the point at which I recognize that this intention is satisfied. I would have to recognize some concurrent act of mine as forgetting that my only reason for engaging in the practice is as a means to produce in me belief in the tenets of Catholicism. That is, I would have to be lucidly aware of what I am supposed to be concurrently forgetting.

The time-lag theory does not illuminate the nature of self-deception, and when it provides a way out of the surface paradox of self-deception it does this by admitting that only sub-intentional forgettings could produce the intended or desired outcome of having forgotten. But it might be thought that the theory at least has served dialectically to force us to formulate the concept of an autonomous means, which now allows us to qualify our main thesis appropriately. That is, we should say that motivated believings and cessations of conscious belief *that do not employ autonomous means* are not intentional acts but are non-intentional outcomes of mental tropisms.

The restriction does not render the main thesis uninteresting, since it points to a large class of cases that cannot be explained in a certain way. More important, the cases omitted are those in which the means of producing the desired belief operates without one's attending to it. Indeed, it is important that one does not intend or monitor the process throughout. But then the operation of the means, although intended to occur, is not itself an intentional act, and neither is the outcome produced by the means, although it is an intended outcome of a process one set in motion. One can describe what one does in the case of nocturnal mischief as 'deceiving oneself by arranging misleading evidence and taking the amnesic drug'. The description corresponds to a statement of intention that captures one's reason for arranging the misleading evidence and taking the amnesic drug. One intended to deceive oneself by arranging misleading evidence and taking the amnesic drug. But what one *did* in arranging the evidence and taking the drug did not itself constitute self-deception. Only the cooperation of future events made what one did deserve the name of *deceiving oneself* by arranging misleading evidence and taking the amnesic drug. So the main thesis can be stated without restriction: nothing that itself constitutes motivated believing or motivated cessation of (conscious) belief is an intentional act. In the cases of self-deception and repression in which autonomous means are employed, the motivated believing and accompanying repression are constituted by the intentional acts of setting the means in motion *plus* the brute operations of those means culminating in the belief and the forgetting. And this captures the peculiar opacity to intention that self-deception and its associated repressions exhibit. Even when there is a self-deceptive or repressive action plan, no intentional act is *intrinsically* a self-deception or a forgetting. So at least things currently seem to stand.

Homuncularism Revisited

David Pears has recently offered a response to Sartre's paradox of repression by way of providing a new model of the role of the censor or protective system in self-deception.[19] Pears offers a model in which self-deception is constituted by an intentional act of a lying sub-agency.

Sartre's mistake, according to Pears, is to suppose that the sub-agency that does the deceiving and repressing and monitors its success in these projects needs itself to be deceived. Instead, Pears proposes that we should take quite literally a model that locates a protective system as the agent in self-deception, a protective system that operates like a paternalistic liar, protecting the main system or ego for what the protective system takes to be the ego's good. The lying protective system need never deceive itself and so need never be engaged in the contradictory project of trying to believe what it knows to be false. The lying protective system need never produce forgetfulness in itself and so need never aim at forgetting something that having this aim forces it to keep in mind.

Donald Davidson has articulated still another paradox that he takes to show that something like this sub-system model must be the right account of what is going on in all cases of self-deception and wishful thinking.[20] Davidson writes:

> In standard reason explanations, as we have seen, not only do the propositional contents of various beliefs and desires bear appropriate logical relations to one another and to the contents of the belief, attitude or intention they help explain; the actual states of belief and desire cause the explained state or event. In the case of irrationality, the causal relation remains, while the logical relation is missing or distorted. In the cases of irrationality we have been discussing, there is a mental cause that is not a reason for what it causes. So in wishful thinking, a desire causes a belief. But the judgment that a state of affairs is, or would be, desirable, is not a reason to believe that it exists . . .
>
> If events are related as cause and effect, they remain so no matter in what vocabulary we choose to describe them. Mental or psychological events are such only under a manner of description, for these very events surely are at the same time neurophysiological, and ultimately physical, events, though recognizable and identifiable within these realms only when given neurophysiological or physical descriptions. As we have seen, there is no difficulty in general in explaining

mental events by appeal to neurophysiological or physical causes: this is central to the analysis of perception or memory, for example. But when the cause is described in non-mental terms, we necessarily lose touch with what is needed to explain the element of irrationality. For *irrationality* appears only when rationality is evidently appropriate: where both cause and effect have contents that have the sort of logical relations that make for reason or its failure. Events conceived solely in terms of their physical or physiological properties cannot be judged as reasons, or as in conflict, or as concerned with a subject matter. So we face the following dilemma: if we think of the cause in a neutral mode, disregarding its mental status as a belief or other attitude – if we think of it merely as a force that works on the mind without being identified as part of it – then we fail to explain, or even describe, irrationality. Blind forces are in the category of the non-rational, not the irrational. So, we introduce a mental description of the cause, which thus makes it a candidate for being a reason. *But we still remain outside the only clear pattern of explanation that applies to the mental, for that pattern demands that the cause be more than a candidate for being a reason; it must be a reason, which in the present case it cannot be.* For an explanation of a mental effect we need a mental cause that is also a reason for this effect, but, if we have it, the effect cannot be a case of irrationality. Or so it seems.[21] (emphasis added)

The pivotal claim driving Davidson's *paradox of irrationality* is that the only clear pattern of explanation in which mental events or states so described can figure requires those mental events or states to be rational causes, i.e. to rationalize what they cause. This is a consequence of the interpretive view of mental states and events. The problem is that wishful and self-deceptive thought seems to involve a characteristic and explanatory causal connection between the desire that p and the belief that p, but an explanatory connection that is not a rational connection. The anxious desire that p is not a reason to believe that p. Because the interpretive view counts rationality as both constitutive and exhaustive of the mental, it has trouble finding a place for the very possibility of a *mental* state, anxious desire, which characteristically has irrational *mental* consequences. Nor can the idea of *irrational* (as opposed to arational) consequences be captured if anxious desire and wishful belief are considered as mere physical states.

In fact Davidson seems to back away from the pivotal claim, but in doing so he suggests a way in which it might be defended.

There is, however, a way one mental event can cause another mental event without being a reason for it, and where there is no puzzle and not necessarily any irrationality. This can happen when cause and effect occur in different minds. For example, wishing to have you enter my garden, I grow a beautiful flower there. You crave a look at my flower and enter my garden. My desire caused your craving and action, but my desire was not a reason for your craving, nor a reason on which you acted. (Perhaps you did not even know about my wish.) Mental phenomena may cause other mental phenomena *without being reasons for them, then, and still keep their character as mental, provided cause and effect are adequately segregated. The obvious and clear cases are those of social interaction. But*

I suggest that the idea can be applied to a single mind and person. Indeed, if we are going to explain irrationality at all, it seems we must assume that the mind can be partitioned into quasi-independent structures.[22] (emphasis added)

There is a difficulty here. The desire caused the craving and action via a system of intermediate causes that involved the bringing about of an enticing state of affairs, a perception of it, and a subsequent comprehensible desire to explore the enticing state of affairs. In such a case we have a rational connection in the sense of a matching of the salient state of affairs before the eyes and the content of perception, and a subsequent rational connection between the perception of an enticing state of affairs, a standing interest in such states of affairs, and a desire to explore the state of affairs. This is why there is no puzzle in this case as to how one person's desire can cause another's. We have not a mysterious sort of telepathy but a chain of rational causes. This leaves two questions. What is the analogue of such a chain of rational causes in the case of self-deception and wishful thinking? And how does the resort to sub-systems within the agent help us to find it?

I suggest that if the segregation, within distinct sub-systems, of the relevant mental cause and effect is to do anything to resolve the alleged paradox of irrationality associated with wishful thinking and self-deception, then one must follow Pears and understand these processes as the suggestive implantation of belief in the main system by a protective system. Only then will one have an appropriate analogue of the perceptual link, namely, one person saying something to another who hears what he said and believes it. (The analogy has some appeal. Thomas Reid actually took the receiving of testimony to be a sort of perception via conversation.)[23] In this way the theoretical division of a person into a protective, lying system and a main system that is its gullible victim allows us to re-establish a chain of rational causes. The main system is aware of and reasonably accepts the testimony of the protective system. The protective system's reason for offering this testimony is to allay the anxiety of the main system. So also the protective system may go in for distracting the main system from its anxiety-producing beliefs.

Here we have a homuncularism that solves all the paradoxes of self-deception we have encountered and which seems to represent self-deception (and wishful thinking) as constituted by intentional acts of protective systems. The surface paradox is solved by having distinct sub-systems play the respective roles of liar and victim of the lie. The paradox of wishful thinking is solved by having the protective system altruistically set out to allay the main system's anxiety that not-p by inculcating the belief that p in the main system. The paradox of repression is solved by having the protective system altruistically set out to allay the main system's anxiety that p by distracting it from its anxiety-producing belief that not-p. The paradox of irrationality is solved by modeling self-deception (and wishful thought) on interpersonal testimony. If the main strategy of this chapter is to work, that is, if we are to use the paradoxes of self-deception to support a tropistic and anti-intentionalist account of the processes involved, then we must discredit the account of self-deception in terms of protective and main sub-systems.

This account can be discredited so long as we do not allow its advocates the luxury of hovering non-committally between the horns of a dilemma: either take the sub-system account literally, in which case it implausibly represents the ordinary self-deceiver as a victim of something like multiple personality, or take it as a metaphor, in which case it provides no way to evade the paradoxes while maintaining that intentional acts constitute self-deception and wishful thinking.

The several difficulties for the sub-agency account literally construed may be stated as objections to Pears's explicitly worked-out model of a protective system influencing a main system. (It should be emphasized that Pears is not committed to the *general* applicability of this model.)

The main system may be thought of as having the desire for some outcome p and the anxiety that p will not occur. Somehow, as a result of these conditions, a protective system is either generated or set into operation, a protective system that has its own internal rationality directed toward the quasi-altruistic manipulation of the main system. Whereas the inferential processes of the main system are typically introspectable by the self-deceiving person and thereby constitute *his* conscious feelings, thoughts, memories etc., those in the protective system are not, so that the self-deceiver is not aware of the protective system's manipulation of his beliefs.

Although the system's operations are not introspectable by the self-deceiver and so are not in that sense part of his consciousness, they are not mere instinctual drives, like hunger and thirst, unconsciously pushing the self-deceiver toward outcomes that in fact constitute their satisfaction. The protective system has rather complex beliefs and desires about the main system. In the light of these the protective system acts on the main system by means of various stratagems until it produces the protective belief. That is, the protective system has to have the capacity to manipulate its representations of the main system in practical inference that issues in action on the main system, action that the protective system monitors for its effectiveness. This is Pears's motive for referring to the protective system's operations as *preconscious*, i.e. as involving complex manipulations of representations, manipulations that are not introspectable to the main system and so not part of the self-deceiver's conscious life. The question arises how the protective system could do all this without being conscious of (introspecting) its own operations. After all, it has to compare the outcome it is producing with the outcome it aimed for and act or cease to act accordingly. Any consciousness by the protective system of its own operation is 'buried alive', i.e. is not accessible to the consiousness of the main system.

Pears suggests that in wishful and self-deceptive thought such a protective system is either generated or set into operation by the main system's desire for some outcome. The protective system 'crystallizes around' the main system's desire. This is puzzling. For it is unclear how the main system's desire that p

could give the protective system any reason to produce in the main system the belief that p. The belief that p does not satisfy the desire that p. At most it can reduce the concurrent disturbing anxiety that not-p will obtain. So if any desire of the main system gives the quasi-altruistic protective system a reason to aim to produce in the main system the belief that p, it is the main system's understandable desire to be rid of its anxiety that not-p.

This desire of the main system gives the protective system a reason to aim to produce the wishful belief in the main system only if the protective system is altruistically disposed to the main system. But whence this altruism? Surely *not* from a history of sympathetic identification born of recognition of likeness and fellow feeling. Pears calls it quasi-altruism, thereby suggesting that this is the altruism of concern for the larger unit – the self-deceiver – which includes both the protective, deceiving altruist and the deceived sub-system. But then it must be objected that in many cases of self-deception all but the self-deceived person can see that he would be better off without the protective belief. In such cases the putative actions of the protective system cannot be represented as the outcome of lucid concern for the whole system, which includes it and the main system as parts. Indeed, in many such cases the main system and the person as a whole suffer considerably as a result of the putative actions of the protective system, so that the protective system must have a curiously narrowed focus of quasi-altruistic concern.

Take, for example the sort of case Freud discusses in the essay 'Mourning and melancholia'.[24] One very much wants to love one's mother, and yet one feels hostility toward her for the pain she has caused. This conflict generates anxiety that is relieved by the repression of one's hostility toward one's mother. Such repression can be seen as self-deceptive blocking of thought. One ceases to acknowledge or actively entertain one's hostile beliefs, and perhaps one comes to believe that one simply loves one's mother. But as Freud points out, the repressed or unacknowledged hostile beliefs can none the less operate to produce unacknowledged guilt experienced as objectless depression and a desire for self-punishment which prompts self-destructive behavior. Here we have a familiar case of self-deceptive resolution of conscious ambivalence and associated anxiety by repression of one's hostile attitudes, with subsequent hell to pay. If a protective system is intentionally repressing the hostile, anxiety-generating belief, and if the effects of repression are often considerably worse than the anxiety produced by the original conflict in the main system, then either the protective system must have a curiously sadistic concern for the main system, involving a readiness to get the main system out of the psychic frying pan and into the fire, or the protective system, despite its otherwise excellent monitoring of the main system, must itself have a curious blind spot that prevents it from seeing the destructive effects of its own characteristic way of reducing anxiety in the main system.

Suppose somehow that these difficulties are solved without making the protective system so limited that it collapses into a tropistic anxiety-reducer, too simple to have motives or intentions.[25] So somehow the protective system's motives are plausibly made to mesh with what it is supposed to do. Concentrate instead on what it is supposed to do, i.e. get the main system to adopt the protective belief. Notice that we invite a regress if we say what is nevertheless plausible, namely, that this is all too easy because the main system is all too ready to accept the protective belief. Such collusion by the main system would itself be wishful acceptance of belief, reproducing within the main system the kind of duality that the intentionalist-gone-homuncularist is trying to keep outside. Instead it must be that the protective system somehow slips the protective belief into the main system, even though the main system's acquiring that belief does not satisfy the main system's ordinary standards of belief acquisition. After all, the main system must be inclined to recognize that the belief does not come from the main system's perceptual input or from its memory or from inference from its other beliefs. The protective belief just pops up. Why does the main system so happily tolerate this?

Moreover, it is clear that getting the main system to adopt the protective belief cannot be something the protective system does directly without employing any particular means. One agency cannot will as a *basic* act of its own that another adopt a belief or ignore evidence or not acknowledge its beliefs. Given this, it is hard to see how wishful thought that involves wishfully exploiting the slack between inductive evidence and conclusion could be brought about simply by the protective system. For the crucial move in such a process is the main system's failing to see that the evidence is sufficient to make the anxiety-provoking conclusion believable. How is this act of the main system explained by anything that the protective system could intentionally do? Well, we may allow for purposes of argument that the protective system can distract, suggest and cajole, but this leaves the worrying question why the main system is so distractable, suggestable and biddable in this matter. At a certain point, the protective system's suggestions to the effect that, despite the evidence, p, are supposed to be accepted by the main system as sufficient to believe p. Why? The main system has no reason to regard these suggestions as reliable testimony. So why does it accept them? The tempting answer is: because it wants to believe p and so is all too ready to collude in its own deception. But 'collude' is an intentionalist idiom that raises the very difficulties the protective system was postulated to deal with. Should we then postulate within what we were taking to be the main system a second protective system and a more primary system? This would be to make any explanation of self-deceptive and wishful thought forever recede as we try to grasp it. For the very same problems would arise for the actions of the second protective system. We can take as many turns as we want on the intentionalist roundabout, but we will still be left with our original problem: how is it that some main or primary system's desire to believe p leads it to accept suggestions that p as grounds for believing p even though that system has no reason to believe that they are reliable indications that p is true? In short, how could the desire that p lead the main or primary system to be favorably disposed toward believing p? And there seems no other answer but the anti-intentionalist and tropistic one: this is the way our minds work; anxious desire that p simply leads one to be disposed to believe that p.

Finally, the anti-intentionalist and tropistic account does better than the homuncularist account in enabling us to explain the kind of censure involved in accusations of self-deception. On the homuncularist account the deceived and non-colluding main system, a system that has good claim to be the analogue of the Freudian ego, the active controller of the person's conscious thought, speech and bodily action, is an innocent victim of deception. It is simply lied to. Correspondingly, the protective system is a straightforward, albeit paternalistic, liar. But our accusations of self-deception seem to be accusations of a sort of failure not unlike that involved in cowardly flight from the frightening. For example, in that part of Augustine's orgy of self-accusation in which he confesses his past self-deceptions, he explicitly employs the metaphor of mental flight from horrific features of himself.

> Ponticianus told us this story [of a conversion] and as he spoke, you, O Lord, turned me back upon myself. You took me from behind my own back, where I had placed myself because I did not wish to look upon myself. You stood me face to face with myself, so I might see how foul I was, how deformed and defiled, how covered with stains and sores. I looked, and I was filled with horror but there was no place for me to flee from myself. If I tried to turn my gaze from myself, he still went on with the story that he was telling, and once again you placed me in front of myself and thrust me before my own eyes, so that I might find out my iniquity and hate it. I knew what it was, but I pretended not to; I refused to look at it and put it out of my memory.[26]

Here the self-directed accusation of self-deception is an accusation of mental cowardice, of flight from anxiety (or angst), a failure to contain one's anxiety, a lack of courage in matters epistemic. The homuncularist picture of the self-deceiver prevents us from rationally reconstructing a fitting subject for this sort of censure. The protective system is simply lying. The main system is simply the victim of a paternalistic liar. This does not add up to anything like mental cowardice.

The anti-intentionalist and tropistic account does better. Though mental flight, like physical flight, is typically sub-intentional, one can still be held responsible for lacking the ability to contain one's anxiety and face the anxiety-provoking or the terrible. The accusation of self-deception is a familiar case of being held responsible for an episode that evidences a defect of character, in this case a lack of the negative power that is reason, i.e. the capacity to inhibit changes in beliefs when those changes are not well grounded in reasons.

Tropisms and Reason

The presupposition that drives the paradoxes of self-deception or bad faith is succinctly expressed by Sartre at the beginning of his statement of the surface paradox: 'one does not undergo one's bad faith, one is not infected with it . . . But consciousness affects itself with bad faith. There must be an original intention and a project of bad faith.'[27] This is to assume that if self-deception is something *done* rather than merely undergone it must be something intentionally done. We know already from the case of bodily activity that this assumption is false. For example, running our eyes predominantly over the tops and not the bottoms of printed words is something many of us do, since many of us read *by* running our eyes predominantly over the tops of printed words. A way to make this vivid to oneself is to cover the bottom half of a line of print and try to read it and then cover the top half of a similar line of print and try to read it. Now it would be absurd to suggest that using our eyes this way must be something we do intentionally, e.g. for and from the reason that this makes it possible to read more quickly. For many of us, performing the little experiment just outlined gives us the first inkling of what we were up to. But, of course, the explanation of why this method of reading is unwittingly used by many of us has to do with the fact that it helps us to read faster. The method, once hit upon, persists because it serves a purpose; it is not intentionally employed for that purpose.

Similar things need to be said about the mental process of self-deception by which anxiety that one's desire that p will not be satisfied is reduced by one's acquisition of the belief that p (wishful thinking) and one's ceasing to acknowledge one's recognition of the evidence that not-p (repression). This process is not mediated by intention; rather, processes of this kind persist because they serve the end of reducing anxiety. Hence I speak of a mental tropism, a characteristic pattern of causation between types of mental states, a pattern whose existence within the mind is no more surprising, given what it does for us, than a plant's turning toward the sun.

In fact mental tropisms abound. When the victim of Korsakoff's syndrome confabulates or spontaneously and without deceptive intent fills in the considerable gaps in his memory, we see in operation a process that produces a needed coherence in the patient's remembering of his past, but a process that is not carried on for and from this reason.[28] When we encounter an instance of the phenomenon of so-called 'sour grapes', in which the subject's desires are tailored to what he can get in an *ad hoc* way that reduces the chances of frustration, we see the securing of a comprehensible goal but not intentional activity.[29] When at a reception one's attention suddenly and automatically shifts from the weary discussion of comparative mustards in which one has been idly involved to the nearby conversational group that happens to be discussing one's secret passion, one need not be intentionally turning one's attention to the more interesting exchange. More typically, one has been served by an automatic filtering process that is ordinarily inaccessible to introspection and which determines that what is salient in perception will be what answers to one's interests.

Dogmas die hard, so it is natural to suppose that such tropisms either are peripheral to the mind or represent breakdowns in the otherwise smooth working of the reason machine, the movements of which are properly mediated or guided by reason and are *therefore* different in nature from irrational processes. But this too can be made to seem like a quaint phantasy.

What is it for the normal operations of the mind to be mediated by reason? I suggest that it is just for causal relations to hold between mental states one of which in fact is a reason for another. What is it for mental operations to be *guided* by reason? Just for the reasoner to employ a certain inhibitory capacity – the capacity to inhibit conscious changes in attitude when he recognizes that those changes are not well grounded in reason. Here too we have mental tropisms, characteristic causal processes leading from one kind of attitude to another, tropisms that qualify as rational processes not because of some *sui generis* manner – rational causation – in which the one attitude causes another but because the one attitude is in fact a reason for the other.

Consider a case of intentional and rational belief change. I explicitly reason from my belief that p and my belief that if p then q to a belief that q. Thanks to my good schooling there takes place in me a causal process the terms of which are mental states whose contents, taken together, conform to *modus ponens*. Indeed, I might have explicitly aimed to guide my thought in accord with *modus ponens*. Then, thanks to my good schooling, there takes place in me a causal process leading *from* my desire so to guide my thought, my belief that p, my belief that if p then q, and my belief that *modus ponens* prescribes that I come to believe q, *to* my coming to believe q. This causal process is relevantly different from the mental tropisms we have been discussing only in involving as antecedent causes mental states that are reasons for my coming to believe q. Given this fact about the terms of the causal process, that causal process *constitutes* my explicitly guiding my thoughts in accord with *modus ponens*. No special kind of event intervening between reasons and my response to them, no special kind of intrinsically rational causation, is needed to make a causal process between mental states a case of rational, and intentional, belief change. Wayward causal cases aside,[30] the existence of a causal process connecting mental states that conform to a rational pattern can itself constitute rational and intentional belief change.

For suppose that what is required over and above causation by states that are in fact reasons for the states or changes they cause is as follows. First, the agent must recognize that he or she has reasons that support the drawing of a certain conclusion or the performance of an intentional act; secondly, the agent must will the drawing of the conclusion or will the performance of the act; and, thirdly, as a result of the willing, draw the conclusion or perform the act. The special something extra distinguishing rational causal processes from the mere mental tropisms that constitute irrational changes in belief is then supposed to be an intervening act of will rationalized by recognition of sufficient reason. This *could* on occasion go on in a person – she recognizes that she has sufficient reason for an act and she wills that she perform the act in question and she does perform it. But it cannot capture a general condition on rational inference or intentional action. For now we have a causal connection between someone's recognizing that she has reasons to perform a certain act and her willing or coming to intend to perform that act. This is a rational connection – the recognition of reasons rationalizes or gives a point to the willing or the forming of an intention to act. But if a condition on its being a rational connection is its including an intermediate forming of an intention to intend or a willing to will, we are launched on a regress we can never stop without at some point abandoning the general demand for an intervening willing to constitute a rational connection. At some point we must recognize an intentional act that is constituted merely by attitudes causing activity that they rationalize. So in particular, the case of intentionally drawing the logical conclusion from one's beliefs must ultimately turn on the operation of tropisms connecting the attitudes in question. Thanks to innate dispositions, training and employment of the capacity to inhibit competing irrational operations, certain mental operations conform to good inferential rules but are as blind as the operations of the tropisms that do not conform. If we are to be able to draw any conclusions at all we must in the relevant sense draw some conclusions blindly, which is not to say unintentionally but rather to say without there occurring in us anything more than an automatic response to those reasons, a response that is in fact rationalized by them.

Just as a condition of understanding is that one must at some point respond appropriately to representations without interpreting them in terms of further representations,[31] a condition of reasoning is that one must at some point allow one's reasons to work on one in the appropriate fashion. Better, one's allowing them to work on one in accord with reason is one's reasoning from them, just as responding to one's representations in accord with convention constitutes one's understanding of them.

If this is the truth about rational connections among mental states, then the operations of mental tropisms (blind but purpose-serving connections between mental state types) are not peripheral phenomena but are the basic connections that constitute rationality and irrationality alike. Rational connections are not constitutive and exhaustive of the mental. Rationality could hardly be constitutive and exhaustive, given that minds evolved under conditions in which rational mental tropisms conferred only limited advantages. That a creature whose environment is too complicated for it to get by on the strength of its instincts does better in some ways if it can monitor its desires and rationally exploit means to their satisfaction is no surprise. But it should be no more surprising that such a creature, fallen from simple harmony with nature, does better in other ways if its frequent and debilitating anxieties that its desires will not be satisfied are regularly dealt with by doses of hopeful belief.

Though we specially prize reason, it is just one adaptive form mental processes can take.

Acknowledgments

In writing this chapter I have been helped by John Cooper, Raymond Guess, Gilbert Harman, Richard Jeffrey, David Lewis, Alison McIntyre, Michael Smith and Bas van Fraassen.

Notes

1 See R. Demos, 'Lying to Oneself', *Journal of Philosophy* 57 (1960), 588–95; J. Canfield and P. McNally, 'Paradoxes of self-deception', *Analysis* 21 (1961), 140–4; H. Fingarette, *Self-Deception* (New York, Humanities Press, 1969); D. Pears, 'The paradoxes of self-deception', *Theorema* 1 (1974). J.T. Saunders, 'The paradox of self-deception', *Philosophy and Phenomenological Research* 35 (1975), 559–70; R. Reilly, 'Self-deception: resolving the epistemological paradox', *Personalist* 57 (1976), 391–4; J. Foss, 'Rethinking self-deception', *American Philosphical Quarterly* 17 (1980), 237–43; D. Kipp, 'On self-deception', *Philosophical Quarterly* 30 (1980), 305–17; M. Haight, *A Study of Self-Deception* (London, Harvester Press, 1980).

2 JP Sartre, *Being and Nothingness*, trans. H. Barnes (New York, Philosophical Library, 1956), ch. 2.

3 The *loci classici* of the resort to homuncularist models to explain irrational mental processes are S. Freud, 'Repression' (1915), *The Ego and the Id* (1923), and 'Splitting of the ego in the process of defence' (1938), all in *The Standard Edition of the Complete Psychological Works*, ed. J. Strachey, A. Freud, A. Strachey, and A. Tyson (London, Hogarth Press and The Institute of Psycholanalysis, 1954–1974). David Pears develops a homuncularism specifically tailored to deal with self-deception in *Motivated Irrationality* (Oxford, Oxford University Press, 1985). Both Fingarette and Haight consider the homuncularist response to the surface paradox.

4 R.A. Sorenson, 'Self-deception and scattered events', *Mind* 94 (1985), 64–9

5 B. Williams, 'Deciding to believe', reprinted in *Problems of the Self* (Cambridge, Cambridge University Press, 1973); Sartre, *Being and Nothingness* ch. 2; D. Davidson, 'Paradoxes of irrationality', in R. Wollheim and J. Hopkins (eds), *Philosophical Essays on Freud* (Cambridge, Cambridge University Press, 1982).

6 For discussion of sub-intentional bodily processes and their significance for a theory of the will, see B. O'Shaughnessy, *The Will* (Cambridge, Cambridge University Press, 1981), vol. 2, ch. 10.

7 See 'Mental events', 'Psychology as philosophy', and 'The material mind', all reprinted in Davidson's collection of papers, *Essays on Actions and Events* (Oxford, Oxford University Press, 1980). And see 'Belief and the basis of meaning', and 'Radical interpretation', both reprinted in Davidson's *Truth and Interpretation* (Oxford, Clarendon Press, 1984). Colin McGinn endorses something like the interpretive view in 'Philosophical materialism', *Synthese* (1980), Daniel Dennett, in 'Intentional systems', reprinted in *Brainstorms* (Cambridge, Mass., MIT Press, 1978) argues that there is no more to one's being in a belief or desire state than

it's being the case that the state is attributed to one within an adequate interpretive theory.

8   Davidson, 'Mental events' and 'Psychology as philosophy'. I explore this argument and its relations to the interpretive view in 'Why having a mind matters', in E. LePore and B. McLaughlin (eds), *The Philosophy of Donald Davidson* (New York, Blackwell, 1985).

9   Davidson, 'Paradoxes of irrationality', p. 289. 'An aura of rationality is thus inseparable from these [mental] phenomena, at least as long as they are described in psychological terms. How can we explain or even tolerate as possible, irrational thoughts, actions or emotions?' The phenomenon of wishful thinking prompts Davidson to modify the interpretive view. It would be interesting to explore whether his argument for token physicalism can survive the modification. In any case, I shall suggest that no mere modification of the interpretive view is adequate. Rationality is not constitutive and exhaustive of the mental.

10 H.H. Price, *Perception* (London, Methuen, 1973), p. 140.

11 Williams, 'Deciding to believe', p. 148.

12 W. James, 'The will to believe', in A. Cashell (ed.), *Essays in Pragmatism* (New York, Hafner, 1948).

13 For Freud's discussion of primary process thought se 'The unconscious' (1915), in *The Standard Edition of the Complete Psychological Works*.

14 For a penetrating analysis of eventfulness and its role in the appeal of gambling, see Erving Goffman's essay 'Where the action is', in *Interaction Ritual* (Harmondsworth, Penguin, 1967). Goffman's essay betrays considerable inside knowledge of what is going on in gambling.

15 Pears, *Motivated Irrationality*, p. 11.

16 The need for the assumption will become evident in the next section, where the notion of an autonomous means is introduced.

17 Sartre, *Being and Nothingness*, ch. 2.

18 Sorensen, 'Self-deception and scattered events', and D.W. Hamlyn, 'Self-deception', *Proceedings of the Aristotelian Society* 45 (1971), 45–60.

19 Pears, *Motivated Irrationality* ch. 6.

20 Davidson, 'Paradoxes of irrationality'.

21 Ibid., pp. 298–300.

22 Ibid. p. 300.

23 T. Reid, 'Of social operations of mind', essay 1, ch. 8 in *Essays on the Powers of the Human Mind*.

24 Freud, 'Mourning and melancholia' (1915), in *The Standard Edition of the Complete Psychological Works*.

25 When is a system too simple to have intentions, in particular the intention to deceive? This is a complicated matter, but I think that if a system is to be correctly ascribed intentions then the system should have some capacity for practical reasoning and have a means of representing its own desires and beliefs, a means of representing possible outcomes of action and the extent to which they serve its desires, and a capacity to act upon what it has judged to be the best alternative. Call such a system a *primary homunculus*. Now Daniel Dennett, among others, has suggested that we might take the intentional stance even towards things that are not primary homunculi, e.g. plants. That is to say we might explain the plant's turning toward the sun by attributing to it a desire for sunlight on its leaves and a belief that turning will make this more likely (see his 'Intentional systems'). In

some quarters this is called 'homuncular explanation'. Evidently, this sort of homuncular explanation is not at issue in this chapter. If any explanatory end is served by understanding a plant as if it has beliefs and desires, as much could be done by so understanding a tropistic anxiety-reducer. However, it is obvious that those who invite the paradoxes of self-deception by explaining self-deception on the model of other-deception are driven to postulate *primary* homunculi, i.e. systems that are rich enough to have intentions, in particular the intention to deceive. In 'Machines and the mental', *Proceedings and Addresses of the American Philosophical Association* 59 (1985), Fred Dretske presents what amounts to an argument that the attributions of beliefs and desires to systems that lack internal representation cannot be literally true. So there may well be problems with taking the intentional stance toward plants or tropistic anxiety-reducers.

26   St Augustine, *Confessions* VIII, 7–16. I thank Bas van Fraassen for drawing my attention to this passage. It is quoted and discussed in his 'The peculiar effects of love and desire', chap. 5 in B. McLaughlin and A. Rorty (eds), *Perspectives on Self-Deception* (California, University of California Press, 1988).

27   Sartre, *Being and Nothingness*, ch. 2.

28   See N. Butters and L.S. Cermak, *Korsakoff's Syndrome* (New York, Academic Press, 1980).

29   This is effectively argued in J Elster, *Sour Grapes* (Cambridge, Cambridge University Press, 1983).

30   In wayward causal cases, states that rationalize other states or events cause them, but cause them by a tortuous route employing processes not typical of willing (i.e. that do not typically constitute willing). See D. Davidson, 'Freedom to act', in *Essays on Actions and Events*.

31   This is surely part of the lesson of Wittgenstein's *Philosophical Investigations*, section 201, though I shy away from saying what else is going on there.

24

Reply: Irrationality, Interpretation and Division

James Hopkins

The Introduction to *Philosophical Essays on Freud* (chapter 22) was written to deadline over a decade ago, and the flaws in my statements of both philosophical ideas and clinical descriptions are more glaring with time. Still, the account seems worth going on with, and the essay remains the only short philosophical introduction to these topics. I have revised and extended a number of points in subsequent articles, and also written a separate discussion of the work of Melanie Klein, which was treated mainly in footnotes. These developments flow fairly naturally from the Introduction (chapter 22), and are noted in the comments on Johnston (chapter 23) which follow.[1]

I

A main theme of the Introduction (chapter 22) was that a significant part of Freud's thinking could be understood in terms of the notion of wish-fulfilment, or wish-fulfilling phantasy; and that this should be regarded not as intentional action, but rather as a form of wishful thinking or imagining, in which a wish or desire causes an imaginative representation of its fulfilment, which is experience- or belief-like. Such a causal sequence has a pattern, which it will be useful to set out more explicitly, so that it can be compared with others. Letting the agent be A, and abbreviating the notion of belief- or experience-like representation to 'b-rep', we can write the pattern as

(1)   A's desire that P -[causes]$\rightarrow$ A's b-rep that P

Simple instances of this pattern were the case in which (as we can put it) Freud's desire that he drink causes his dream that he is drinking and also the symptom of the unembarrassed girl, caused, there seems reason to say, by an underlying desire which was sexual. In these cases the imaginative representation has a content which is easy to grasp. Hence the content of the underlying causally active desire (or wish) can be read from its effect in accord with (1), which serves as a sort of template for interpretation.

In more complex instances – such as the dream of not giving a supper party with smoked salmon[2] or again the obsessional symptom of the table-cloth lady showing the maid the spot – the representational content is less manifest. Where this is so the content must be brought more fully to light, by way of the free associations of the patient or dreamer, before the pattern can be applied.[3] Still the pattern of even very complex examples remains simple in form, and has been traced in empirical material in a vast range of instances and cases, often in remarkable detail. So (1) can be seen as having a pervasive role in psychology, despite both its internal simplicity and the interpretive complexity by which some of its instances are disclosed.

Although Mark Johnston's 'Self-deception and the Nature of the Mind' (chapter 23) was not written with these claims in mind, it seems at least in part to accord with them. In particular, Johnston independently emphasizes the role of wishful thought, and also argues that this should be understood as involving causation which is non-rational and non-intentional, and which holds between desire and something like belief. He describes the causal role of desire in such cases in terms of 'mental tropism', and speaks of the result as 'quasi-belief', which seems close to the idea of belief-like representation above; and he also takes the tropistic causation of quasi-belief to be very common. Johnston also indicates in passing that he too applies, or would apply, this account, not only to self-deception, but also to a number of phenomena described in psychoanalysis: division, denial, repression, removal of affect, and wishful perception and memory.[4] Thus we seem to agree on these main points, and also to share a common perspective on the philosophical exposition of psychoanalytic theory.

Johnston also sets out a number of other lines of argument. He holds, for example, that the commonness of wishful tropism contradicts Davidson's intepretive approach to the mind; and he argues as against both Davidson and Pears, that a tropistic account of self-deception avoids difficulties inherent in their homuncular ones. Despite the interest and force of the arguments which Jonston puts foreward, these conclusions seem to me premature, and to require serious qualification. In what follows I will concentrate on these points of disagreement, and especially as they bear on the philosophical understanding of psychoanalysis, which I shall discuss in as much detail as space permits. The reader should bear in mind, however, that this was *not* Johnston's main topic, and hence that emphases and additions in my discussion are not meant to indicate shortcomings in his.

II

Let us first take Johnston's critique of Davidson, whose approach to common-sense psychology I was attempting to extend to psychoanalysis. As Johnston observes (p. 449), Davidson says in 'Paradoxes of Irrationality' that: 'the only clear pattern of explanation that applies to the mental ... demands that [a] cause be more than a candidate for being a reason; it must be a reason [for what it causes].' Now plainly Johnston and I disagree with Davidson on this point, since we both take the causal pattern of wish-fulfilment above to be clear, explanatory and widely applicable to the mental. Since Davidson is also well aware of this pattern, and indeed calls it 'a model for the simplest form of irrationality' (Davidson, 1982, p. 298), I have thought the statement above a slip, with little bearing on his main views. Johnston, however, regards it as more consequential. He writes that:

> The existence and ubiquity of mental tropisms whose relata do not stand in any rational relation falsifies a view of the mental which is gaining currency. This *interpretive view* of mental states and events has it that there is nothing more to being in a mental state or undergoing a mental change than being apt to have that state or change attributed to one within an adequate interpretive theory, i.e. a theory that take's one's behavior (including speech behavior) as evidence and develops under the holistic constraint of construing much of that behaviour as intentional action caused by rationalizing beliefs and desires that it is reasonable to suppose the subject has, given his invironment and basic drives. (chapter 23, p. 436)

Davidson's approach can rightly be called interpretive, but this description does not do it justice. Thus it is doubtful that according to Davidson there is 'nothing more to being in a mental state or undergoing a mental change' than being apt to have that state or change interpretively ascribed. For Davidson holds that mental events are identical with physcial events, that mental properties (predicates) supervene on physical ones, and that a person's psychological dispositions and abilities, which include desires, beliefs and the capacity to speak and act intentionally, are realized or 'constituted' by 'physical state[s], largely centered in the brain'. In consequence, Davidson notes that in identifying a physical event with an action, say, we must 'be sure that the causal history of the physical event includes events or states identical with the desires and cognitive states that yield a psychological explanation of the action' (Davidson, 1973/1980, p. 256).[5] Davidson therefore explicitly constrains the role of interpretation in his account of the mental by a series of notions – identity, supervenience, and constitution or realization – which relate the mental to the physical, and so as to ensure that all causal relations of the mental have an appropriate physical realization 'centred in the brain'. The role of these physical constraints has not been fully articulated,[6] but their existence contradicts a literal reading of Johnston's 'nothing more' above.

Davidson also argues that no strict law – no law which is sharp and exceptionless, and which contains no ineliminable caveats, *ceteris paribus* clauses or the like – holds between a particular type of desire and any type of constituting state or mechanism in the brain. Thus, for example, the type *desire to have coffee with milk* cannot be strictly connected with any neural mechanism which can be precisely specified in physical terms. This can be seen as a consequence of his emphasis on interpretation. The idea would be that if we hold that the ascription of a desire is ultimately answerable to the interpretive explanation of behaviour, then we cannot at the same time hold that the desire is related by a strict law to some well-defined physical mechanism. For the presence or absence of such a mechanism would be a clear physiological fact, and this, by the strict law, would fix the presence or absence of the desire in all nomologically possible circumstances. So to hold that there is such a mechanism-specifying law would be (implicitly) to take the ascription of the desire as answerable to a specific mechanism rather than to the explanation of behaviour.

In envisaging the existence of psycho-physical laws we tend to assume that everything will come out in perfect harmony: that there will be no conflict between ascribing the desire on the basis of its supposedly lawfully constituting physical state or mechanism, and ascribing it on the basis of interpretation, nor any uncertainty, given the mechanism, as to whether the desire is actually there. This, however, misses the point of the argument, which is that the existence of strict law should actually preclude the empirical possibility of this kind of disharmony. In holding that ascriptions are ultimately answerable to considerations of interpretive psychological explanation we show that we do not assume that this possibility is foreclosed, and hold that the final verdict lies with interpretation. This, however, is the position for which Davidson argues.

Another argument may bring out the nature and plausibility of this position, and will also serve to introduce some further matters relevant to the discussion. Let us reflect on our practice of describing motives, which we schematize by speaking of the desire that P, the belief that Q, and so forth. In this, 'P' and 'Q' stand for, or can be replaced by, sentences of natural language. We understand these sentences, in turn, as true in the worldly conditions or situations which they specify, and hence in accord with a semantic pattern which we can indicate by

(2)   'P' is true just if P

This schematic pattern[7] is supposed to cover our systematic understanding of the truth-conditions of indefinitely many sentences of our language, and hence to describe a vast amount of information relating language and the world, which, of course, it does only very roughly indeed. Equally schematically, the conditions in which we take the sentence 'P' to be true are also those in which we take the desire that P to be satisfied, the belief that P to be verified, the hope or fear that P to be realized, and so on. Thus to take our example: when we say that Freud desired that he (Freud) drink, we use the sentence 'he (Freud) drink[s]' to describe Freud's desire; in accord with pattern (2) we take 'he (Freud) drinks' to be true just if Freud drinks; this, therefore, we also take as the situation in which Freud's desire would be satisfied. So in accord with (1), this is the situation which Freud b-reps as obtaining, in dreaming that he (Freud) drinks. The artificiality in these phrasings reflects something of the roughness in our specification of the relevant patterns; but the existence of such patterns seems clear.

Our commonsense practice is thus to recycle our worldly sentences, to describe the mind in its engagement with the world; and we do this in such a way as to enable us to understand this engagement in accord with our understanding of the sentences themselves. This mode of description is at once semantic and causal: for in employing it we use the semantic relations of our motive-describing sentences to map causal relations between motive and motive, and motives and the world. We take it, for example, that desires serve to bring about (cause) the semantically specified conditions in which they are satisfied. This shows in a further pattern, which we can write as follows:

(3)   A's desire that P -[causes]→P

This is a pattern we find in successful rational action, such as that in which Freud desires that he drink, and this brings it about (causes) that he drinks. This form, incidentally, is common to other kinds of teleological explanation, which postulate representations of goals which operate within the systems of which they are part to bring about (cause) those goals.[8] What is unique about explanation by desires is not this basic teleological form, but rather that the system in which goals (desires) are represented has the expressive and computational power of human language (cf. the pervasive role of (2) above). Also, of course, this pattern can still be applied when the connection between desire and situation is mediated by further desires and beliefs, as in (5) below.

Similarly, we hold that beliefs serve to register (be caused by) the situations which verify them. This gives the pattern

(4)   P -[causes]→A's belief that P

This pattern is also widespread: we take it for example, that when Freud drinks, this brings it about that Freud believes that he drinks, and something like this is characteristic of intentional action. It is also rational, since it is that of belief which is both true and justified by the presence of a kind of causal relation which makes for knowledge. Like (3), this pattern extends to cases in which the connection between belief and situation is mediated: for example, by further belief or theory. Indeed it might be said that the point of theory is to make our beliefs sensitive to the world as in (4), so that our desires can work in it as in (3).

We also use deductive semantic relations between sentence and sentence to map causal relations between motive and motive. In general, we take it that beliefs cause beliefs in accord with patterns of logic, which we will not specify separately here. Also, we apply such patterns to desires, for example in holding that an agent who desires that Q and believes that if P then Q thereby has reason to desire that P. This gives the causal pattern of practial reason:

(5) A's desire that Q and belief that if P then Q -[causes]→ A's desire
that P

Here the pattern of motive-specifying sentences, read from right to left, is that
of *modus ponens*. This shows that if the belief in the pattern is true, then
satisfying the derived desire must also satisfy the initial one, so that an agent
who forms or modifies motives in accord with the pattern is thus far rational.[9]

(3) and (4) relate motives described by sentences to the worldly situations in
which those sentences are true, and so in effect incorporate (2); so the patterns
with which we are dealing are at once semantic, rational and causal. They
illustrate how our common-sense system of understanding persons coordinates
norms of language, as partly specified in (2), with norms for the working of
motive, as specified in (3)–(5); so that the understanding of language, and that
of motive in rational action, form a hermeneutic and causal unity. Hence,
arguably, the basic form of application of this system is in the interpretation of
persons as rational, i.e. as thinking, acting and speaking in accord with such
norms, and thus in accord with schema like (2)–(5).

Such interpretation can be represented as a process in which an interpreter
explains sequences of an interpretee's bodily movements as intentional actions,
motivated by desires and beliefs with appropriate environmental conditions of
truth, satisfaction and the rest, where this includes interpreting the making of
strings of sounds as the utterance of sentences with particular environmental
conditions of truth.[10] In this the interpreter in effect maps sentences of his or
her own language on to both the behaviour of the interpreter and the
environment shared by them both, and thereby systematically links the
interpretee's behaviour with their common environment.

In the simplest case, in which the interpretee happens to use the same words
and sentences as the interpreter, and in the same way, interpretation can at
least partly be understood in terms of the repeated application of patterns like
(2)–(5); for in the idealized situation in which the interpretee judges accurately
and so acts successfully, the interpreter can always use a single sentence, or
closely related sentences, to characterize both the interpretee's belief and its
object, both his/her desire and its satisfaction, and both his/her sentence and
its meaning. Such overlapping characterization, in turn, registers that the
causal relations which hold among the interpretee's motives and the environment generally are as they should be, and this is the simplest case of the kind
of pattern of coherence which marks successful psychological explanation. The
interpreter's own use of language, including that in interpretation, are also to
be understood as construable by interpretation, and hence answerable to the
norms imposed in the course of it, in the same way as the interpretee's. So an
interpretive view offers us an account of the content and causal role of both
motives and sentences, as fixed in harmony through the applicability of
interpretive teleological (and causal) explanation of behaviour.

It seems, therefore, that interpretive patterns such as are roughly indicated in
(2)–(5) have an epistemic status which is worth noting. We interpret behaviour

in accord with them naturally, and hence spontaneously, rapidly and continu-
ally. In this sense we use them more frequently, and rely on them more deeply,
than any generalizations of science. (But, of course, we have no need to realize
that this is so.) We learn such patterns together with language, so that their use
is in a sense *a priori*. Also, however, we find them instantiated, and hence
supported in a way which is both empirical and *a posteriori*, in instances of
successful interpretive understanding too dense and numerous to register.

Patterns of this kind are also predictive. For example when an interpreter
takes it that an interpretee is acting, or is going to act, on a certain desire, the
interpreter's description of the desire by a sentence 'P' constitutes a prediction
in accord with (3). The interpreter's description, that is, can be regarded as a
hypothesis, which is framed and tested by successive uses of the same sentence:
the first use describes the motive, and the second the action or situation which
this motive should bring about. (Roughly, the hypothesis is confirmed if the
sentence used to describe the desire also serves to describe the action or
situation caused by the desire, and disconfirmed if not; hence, as stressed in
the introduction, the hypothesis tends to be confirmed by sentential coherence,
and disconfirmed by its absence.) Something analogous also holds in instances
of (1), (4) and (5); so that uses of these patterns constitute a system which is
subject to a variety of predictive tests, each framed by the use of a single
sentence and confirmed or disconfirmed by further uses of that sentence, and
hence by instances of descriptive (interpretive) coherence, or lack of it.[11] More
generally, success in interpretation enables us to achieve and predict further
success of the same kind. So past use of such patterns gives us good reason to
count on finding them instantiated in the future, and on their continuing to
locate the same sorts of motives that they have consistently specified so far.

Part of the argument of the introduction – that involving the 'strongly
predictive guiding principle[s] of interpretation' of action and wishfulfilment –
can be represented (charitably) as claiming that (1) has acquired an empirical
status akin to that of (3), through the psychoanalytic interpretation of episodes
in behaviour which had not previously been observed or understood; and that
in this use (1) and (3) tend in fact to home in on the same recently discovered
but basic motives. Uses of (1) and (3) thus interact in psychoanalytic practice
to support one another in an extension of commonsense psychology which is
potentially sound, cumulative and radical. Sound, because the extending
interpretations cohere both with the basic patterns, and also with one another
in locating very many supporting instances for the relevant values of P;
cumulative, because each discovery of the operation of new motives naturally
facilitates the discovery of others, and radical, because the extension offers
significantly deeper, fuller, and more coherent explanations of actions and
wishfulfilments generally, and by reference to motives which, in the main, had
not previously been contemplated. This view still seems to me to be mainly
correct, but will receive some revision in what follows.

We have seen that (2)–(5) can be taken to indicate patterns of psychological
dispositions – to link sentence with situation, situation with motive, and motive

with motive – which accord with causal and semantic norms. Hence, interpretation in accord with such patterns represents the mind of the interpretee as rational, and as a semantic engine, whose inputs, working, and output are registered in terms of belief, reason, and the satisfaction of desire (Hopkins, 1992, 1994b, forthcoming). The mechanism which realizes such dispositions, and hence the engine which we thus indirectly describe, is the nervous system, and in particular the brain. Patricia Churchland takes the aim of research in computational neurophysiology to be that of mapping the 'phase-spaces', the 'as the world presents itself' space, and the 'as my body should be' space, which the working brain relates.[12] This, it seems, is also the task which common-sense psychology already partly performs, via the use of language, in describing persons in terms of patterns like (2)–(5).

Such causal-semantic description of motives is like our commonsense description of a photograph, which doesn't describe the picture chemically, say, but rather in terms of the objects or persons in the environment which are represented in it, and which played a certain causal role in its production. We assume that the look of a photograph supervenes on its intrinsic physical state, and also that this state can be explained causally, by reference to the objects or situations specified in an environmental description and the physical processes involved in photography. Environmental and intrinsic descriptions of photographs are in a clear sense descriptions of the same things (the same representations). They are both useful, and further scientific inquiry can specify them further and relate them in greater detail; and since they are not competitors, no sensible person who knew their uses could want to eliminate either. Also we know that the same environment can photograph in different ways, and different environments in the same way, so we take it that such descriptions will not be strictly related type by type.

This situation seems entirely unproblematic in the case of representations like photographs. So if we take the desire or belief that P to involve a neural representation of the situation P, the parallel claim should be equally acceptable. This, however, is the claim that there is no strict correlation between psychological descriptions (*that P* descriptions) and intrinsic physical descriptions of representational mental states. We can be sure that an environmental description of a representation will be systematically connected with intrinsic descriptions of the same representation, when we can frame them. But describing representations in terms of a complex causal role vis-à-vis the environment is very different from describing them intrinsically. Knowing the working of these two forms of description – and in particular knowing that description via causal connection with the environment invariably introduces a degree of slack – we can see that their correlation should not be strict.

Both this argument and that derived from Davidson above turn on the notions of interpretation and strictness. States which are described by the interpretive specification of environmental conditions of truth, satisfaction, and the like will not be strictly related to specific internal mechanisms. As the analogy with photographs suggests, however, the slack need not be great.[13]

Thus it is consistent with the letter of such arguments that there should be something like a language of thought, with a specific 'syntactic' neural mechanism for each desire or belief – so long as this syntax was, say, ineliminably rough, or susceptible to ambiguity, local variation, or the like. Still acknowledgment of the role of interpretation suggests something more radical. As a connectionist might put the point, it seems that we should take desires and beliefs as realized by neural networks which may vary from person to person, or, even in the same person, from time to time. This also allows that the network realizing one desire or ability can realize others, so that there would be no strict pairing of distinct parts of the network, or of distinct neural structures, with distinct desires or beliefs. This is not part of Davidson's argument, but fits with his emphasis on the interconnection of beliefs and other attitudes with content. For on this picture the agent's system of motives and their neural realization would match not item by item but rather only net by net. [14]

Johnston goes on to claim that:

> On this conception, when we attribute a mental state to another, we are not locating within him an instance of a mental natural kind or property that as such enters into characteristic causal relations in accord with non-accidental psychological or psycho-physical regularities. On the view in question there are no natural mental properties and so no law-like psychological or psycho-physical regularities. Instead, attributions of mental states and changes have a point only within a whole pattern of potential reason-explanations, i.e. explanations that exhibit the subject as a rational agent pursuing what is reasonable from his or her point of view. Fitting into a pattern of reason-explanations that serve to interpret their subject is thus a constitutive condition of something's being a mental attribution. More, there can be no other content to the idea that something is a *mental* attribution. In this sense, rationality is constitutive and exhaustive of the mental. (chapter 23, p. 436)

Thus, as Johnston spells out his refutation of Davidson's view:

> wishful and self-deceptive thought seems to involve a characteristic and explanatory causal connection between the desire that *p* and the belief that *p*, but an explanatory connection that is not a rational connection. The anxious desire that *p* is not a reason to believe that *p*. Because the interpretive view counts rationality as both constitutive and exhaustive of the mental, it has trouble finding a place for the very possibility of a *mental* state, anxious desire, which characteristically has irrational *mental* consequences. (chapter 23, p. 449)

Again, however, Johnston's remarks do not characterize Davidson's view correctly. Since Davidson's argument is directed only against strict laws, it is consistent with a range of claims about realization. And even if we take the radical alternative sketched above, it remains false to say that we are not, in attributing a mental state to another, locating within that other something which 'as such enters into characteristic causal relations in accord with non-accidental psychological or psychophysical regularities.' For on any such view mental states like desires and beliefs still enter 'as such' into characteristic causal relations, and in accord with non-accidental psychological regularities. Such states involve dispositions and Davidson suggests that 'the laws implicit in reason explanations are simply the generalizations implied by the attributions of dispositions' of this kind.[15] The attribution of dispositions (or causal powers, capacities, etc.) is clearly that of non-accidental generalizations. To ascribe a desire is to attribute, among other things, a disposition to produce a situation in which the desire is satisfied. So here the relevant non-accidental psychological regularity is that specified in (3) above. (And of course we also locate the mechanism which realizes the disposition :'within' the person to whom we ascribe the desire.) This, however, seems a companion pattern to the version of (1) which Johnston also describes. Davidson's slip apart, these patterns seem too alike in role and content to be distinguished further to his disadvantage, despite the fact that (3) is rational while (1) is not.

As noted, Davidson has stressed that such generalization over desire and action as we find in (3) is not strict. The predictive use of (3) considered above, for example, involves a claim that an agent is acting, or will act, on a specified desire. But the mere fact that someone has a desire, even a strong desire, does not itself render action on that desire interestingly probable. Countervailing desires may usually or invariably, be stronger, and for many desires we may know this in advance. Davidson gives the example of 'the ratio of actual adulteries to the adulteries which the Bible says are committed in the heart' (Davidson, 1976/1980, p. 264), and despite their strength, persistence and pervasive influence, the ratio for intentional action on Oedipal desires is more infinitesimal yet. In these cases we both accept that the desires involve dispositions specified in terms of action and also hold that such action is very unlikely; that is, we take the desires to show themselves via (1) rather than (3). Also, as Davidson emphasizes, we generally have no way of specifying in advance of action which desires – which values for P in (3) – will be strongest at a given time, or which will get acted in accord with. This point also holds for (1); and the fact that both generalizations have the same antecedent, desire, suggests that their lack of strictness is comparable.

This lack is no sign that we cannot interpret actions and wish-fulfilments in accord with these patterns with accuracy and efficiency. Our natural interpretive abilities would seem to have arisen because they enable us to extract information from the behaviour of others (see chapter 22), and hence to have evolved together with the forms of behaviour which they enable us to understand.[16] The patterns are thus made for the sequences of behaviour on which they operate, and vice versa. The cognitive task of extracting information from such behaviour is not solely that of saying ahead of time what the sequences will be; the point is not just to *predict* the information-bearing specifics, but rather to *use* them, and hence the information they carry, for further purposes, which may include prediction of other things. Hence the lack of predictive strictness in the patterns is no fault, but rather a mark of their fitness to the task we perform in accord with them.

Moreover, the pattern of the working of desire in successful action should not be seen as distinct from that shown in wish-fulfilment. Both, rather, are implicit together in rational action itself. To bring this out, let us distinguish between the *satisfaction* and the *pacification* of a desire, as follows. A desire is *satisfied* just if it operates to secure its conditions of satisfaction in successful action; and a desire is *pacified* if it is caused to cease to operate, or to alter in its operation, in certain normal ways. In terms of this distinction, we can say that in the everyday explanation of action, we assume that satisfaction characteristically causes pacification, and at least partly by way of belief. Thus Freud desires that he drink, and as a result he drinks, so that his desire is satisfied; and as a further result he believes that he has drunk, and this belief, perhaps together with the drink itself, pacifies his desire to drink, so that it ceases to govern his actions.[17] In wish-fulfilment, by contrast, we take desire to cause satisfaction-like experience and quasi-belief directly, and so to yield pacification without satisfaction. Thus Freud desires to drink, and as a result dreams that he is drinking, and this, as it seems, pacifies his desire, at least temporarily.

The phenomenon of pacification as distinct from satisfaction plays a salient role in interpretive practice. One of our principal ways of verifying hypotheses about the desires upon which we presume people to be acting is through observing that they cease to act as on a particular desire precisely when that desire should be pacified; that is, when the relevant conditions of satisfaction obtain, *and* the agents become aware of this. We thus implicitly interpret action by reference to the content of pacifying belief, just as we explicitly interpret wish-fulfilment by reference to the content of pacifying quasi-belief; and interpretation in both cases consists in taking the believed content as derived from a desire which the action or wish-fulfilment serves to pacify. In light of the phenomenon of pacification, we must note that action and representation are fundamentally interwoven; action and phantasy are both aimed at the production of pacifying representation, and interpreted by reference to the content of this.

Taking pacification explicitly into account, we can say that our understanding of the causal pattern in even the simplest successful action involves a fuller pattern than that which appears in (3), which we can write as:

(3)* A's desire that P -[causes]→ P -[causes]→ A's belief that P -[causes]→ A's desire that P is pacified.

As before, this can serve as a predictive pattern, in which we frame a hypothesis by the use of the sentence which describes the desire, and test this hypothesis by further uses of that same sentence, to characterize not only the action or situation which the desire brings about, but also a belief which the agent forms as a result of this, and the consequent inner process, in which the belief causes the initial desire to cease to operate. (This cycle, again, is found in other forms of teleological explanation, in which a representation causes a system to attain a goal and this in turn causes a further representation which operates to curtail or alter the activity of the first.) In the case of human motive, the pattern includes within that of veridical belief, specified in (4) above; and in this it particularly contrasts with wishfulfilment. (1) can likewise be filled out to

(1)* A's desire that P -[causes]→ A's b-rep that P -[causes]→ A's desire that P is pacified.

This makes it clear that we can regard wish-fulfilment as a kind of short-circuiting of a path from desire through reality to belief to pacification which is at every step rational, and which we find in successful action. For we can see (1)* is obtained from (3)* precisely by omission of the causal role in the latter of the situation that P, which is real and satisfying, and which distinguishes veridical belief from mere belief-like representation. This emerges again if we note that (3)* is cast in terms of belief, and (1)* in terms of belief-like representation. Since belief can be treated as the limiting case of belief-like representation, we can rewrite (3)* in a more general form as

(3)** A's desire that P -[causes]→ P -[causes]→ A's b-rep that P -[causes]→ A's desire that P is pacified.

Again, omitting the causal role of the real situation that P yields (1)*, the pattern of pacifying wish-fulfilment.

It thus appears that, contrary to Johnston's statement above, an interpretive view of the mind – even one which places particular emphasis on the 'pattern of reason-explanations' – need have no trouble in finding a place for the pattern relating desire to quasi-belief. For both this latter pattern and that relating desire to satisfaction now appear as partial sub-patterns in the overarching and representation-mediated connection between desire and pacification characteristic of rational action itself. In this perspective, the interpretation of rational action and wish-fulfilment are naturally inter-related. In common-sense psychology we interpret actions in accord with the basic generalization that the role of a desire that P is to produce a situation that P, which in turn should produce a belief that P which (perhaps together with the situation) pacifies the desire. In understanding persons we both tacitly use this generalization, and also sustain it inductively, as noted above. Since this generalization already includes the idea that representation (belief) that P serves to pacify the desire that P, we also take it as an intelligible, and indeed common, phenomenon that a desire that P should play a role in causing a belief-like representation that P, which tends to pacify the desire.

This is another generalization we already both use and sustain, in understanding many forms of pacifying representation with which we are familiar. These include not only the instances mentioned above, but also children's play, and adult forms of representation from traditional song or story through drama and art, and such related recent achievements as advertising. We know, of course, that pacification consequent on real satisfaction and veridical belief is, among other things, more thorough and lasting than that obtained through representation or phantasy. But we also know that desire far outruns the possibilities of satisfying action, so that attempts at pacification by representation alone are common.

Thus I think we already understand, say, that a child may represent itself as a hero in play, or that we repeatedly represent certain situations in fiction, film, etc. because these situations seem desirable, and their representation therefore provides opportunity for the pacification of desire, via one form or another of quasi-belief (cf. the notion of make-belief, suspension of disbelief, etc.). We are aware, for example, that someone playing a video game in which he mutilates a variety of enemies may not only be satisfying his desire to play an exciting game, but also pacifying other desires which the game represents as fulfilled, and that the arousal and pacification of these desires may be a source of the excitement of the game. Understanding of this common-sense kind is continuous with the psychoanalytic interpretation of a dream or symptom. Compare, for example, Freud's interpretation of the Rat Man's recurrent symptom of imagining his father being punished by the rats, and feeling anxiety and depression as a result. In accord with (1)* we can see this as expressing a desire that his father be punished, repeatedly represented as satisfied, and therefore repeatedly temporarily pacified, in the virtual reality of his own phantasy, whose boundaries he could not keep distinct from everyday belief.[18] The patterns with which we began can thus be regarded as implicit and interwoven in pre-theoretical common-sense understanding of action and representation, and hence also as capable of interacting to extend common-sense psychology, in something like the way indicated above.[19]

III

Let us now turn to the division of the mind, as this appears in Davidson and Freud. Here I think we encounter what can be seen as two distinct tendencies of thought. Davidson's divisions in the self are 'overlapping territories' in the field of an agent's motives: they are 'constellations of beliefs, purposes, affects' which cooperate rationally with one another in producing intentions; and they can conflict with other such constellations, or motives in these, and in this act 'in the modality of non-rational causality'. Strictly speaking, such constellations do not *have* motives; rather they *are* (groups of) motives, many of which have a role in more than one constellation, and all of which are had by one and the same agent. So they are not really distinct agents, but at best analogous to these. Davidson stresses explicitly that 'The analogy does not have to be carried so far as to demand that we speak of parts of the mind as independent agents . . . the idea of quasi-autonomous division is not one that demands a little agent in the division (Davidson, 1982, pp. 300–304). His idea thus seems to be to stop short of the postulation of homunculi, and make do with cohesive groups of motives instead. And it is difficult to see how the explanation of irrationality might proceed without reference to such groups in any case: how, for example, might the wish not to know cause one to avoid relevant evidence, except via the web of belief?

Freud's ego, super-ego and id, by contrast, can certainly be regarded as distinct and autonomous 'agencies'. In so far as this is so, however, they seem not best thought of as agents which have desires, beliefs and practical reason, but rather as functional systems, which we describe in a teleologial way, that is, in terms of the goals which we take them to operate to secure, and the information they use in doing so. This seems the way to interpret, for example, Freud's description of the ego as 'a special organization . . . which acts as an intermediary between the id and the external world', and which also 'makes far-reaching changes in its organization' in the state of sleep; or again his description of the super-ego as 'a special agency [in the ego] in which . . . parental influence is prolonged' (Freud, vol. 23, pp. 145–146).[19] Teleological description of this kind is closely related to that in terms of beliefs and desires; but the two have differences which are relevant to the present discussion.

As noted above, when we describe people in terms of desires and beliefs, we can also be regarded as indirectly describing a neural system (the human brain) in a teleological way, in terms of the environmental goals of the system and information upon which it operates. In this, however, we represent the goals and information in terms of human language, and thereby imply that the system (person) we are describing represents goals and information in a comparably subtle and powerful way. We take it that a person to whom we ascribe a desire for Scotch whisky, for example, has the concept of Scotch whisky, and therefore has many beliefs about Scotch whisky and can readily compute many more; and we make constant tacit use of this in interpretation, for example in our applications of logical principles such as (5). Where we give teleological explanations of the behaviour of animals and artifacts, however, we relax this implication. We take it that a rat whose goal is to get Scotch whisky – say, by pressing a bar – has some representation of this outcome, otherwise we would not ascribe this goal. But we do not assume that the rat has our representation of Scotch whisky, and so we do not regard the ascription of the goal as having the same consequences as in the case of a person. The point is the same in the case of the ego, super-ego and id. We may describe such systems as if they had motives, in describing their goals, and information on which we take them to operate; but we do not take these descriptions to have the same consequences as in the case of the desires and beliefs of persons. And since the motives of persons are the basic paradigms of desire and belief, we might do better to follow Wittgenstein and Davidson, and say that other animals (or artifacts, or systems of neurons) do *not* have desires and beliefs, although they may embody representations which operate in a similar way.

The situation is particularly complicated in the case of Freud's agencies.

While the ego and super-ego are clearly meant to be functional neural systems, teleologically described, these systems are also understood as embodying neural prototypes of actual persons in the environment. Freud's mode of explanation combines the idea of functional systems with the observation that the way persons actually function depends upon the prototypes by which they represent themselves and their relations to others. The ego thus embodies the prototypes which the child forms of the parents in their role as agents acting to satisfy desires, and the super-ego still earlier prototypes ('the earliest parental imagos') of regulating and controlling figures, laid down in relation to the infant's own basic impulses, such as those to eat and defecate, and severely distorted by early emotion and projection. Hence Freud describes the operation of these systems in terms of the motives of the basic prototypes which the systems embody. The super-ego is thus, for example, 'an agency . . . which observes and threatens to punish' and which in some cases of disturbance becomes 'sharply divided from [the] ego and mistakenly displaced into external reality' (Freud, vol. 31, pp. 59, 64).

Such descriptions are likely to seem at once mistakenly abstract and anthropomorphic; but in fact they serve to generalize over clinical data. Recall the Rat Man, who cowered in terror of Freud, feeling him as someone who would give him a savage punishment, at the same time as he began to recover repressed memories of his father as actually punishing him, and seeming just such a savage and terrifying figure as he had been feeling Freud to be. This is one of many cases which fits Freud's description: a part of the ego, which observes and threatens to punish, is here seen to be split off and displaced into the external world (in this case into the figure of the analyst). This part, in turn, is evidently related to a distorted prototype of the patient's punishing father, as emerged in conscious memory; and there is reason to suppose that the activation of a similar prototype, in the encounter with the captain fond of cruelty and physical punishment, precipitated his breakdown in the first place.

So Freud and Davidson divide the self in contrasting ways: Freud postulates partly distinct agencies which we describe in terms of figures with desires and beliefs, but which are ascribed these in what is ultimately a metaphorical way; and Davidson postulates partly distinct groups of desires and beliefs, which we may describe as agents, but only metaphorically. Johnston, by contrast, discusses the same topic in terms of the postulation of 'primary homunculi', which are real agents, with real motives (see his note 25). These are, therefore, clearly *not* the same as Freud's real agencies with only metaphorical motives, or Davidson's real motives which are only metaphorical agents. (Johnston also considers explanations which take 'the intentional stance' to things like plants, but these are not representation-ascribing teleological explanations at all.)

Since Johnston's criticisms are directed at a conception of division distinct from that of both Freud and Davidson, they apply to neither. This is clear from Johnston's own account of his critique. After describing 'a homuncularism which solves all the paradoxes of self-deception we have encountered' Johnston urges that

This account can be discredited so long as we do not allow its advocates the luxury of hovering non-committally between the horns of a dilemma: either take the sub-system account literally, in which case it implausibly represents the ordinary self-deceiver as a victim of something like multiple personality, or take it as a metaphor, in which case it provides no way to evade the paradoxes while maintaining that intentional acts constitute self-deception . . . (chapter 23, p. 451)

Johnston's arguments enlarge on this claim, and also enforce his earlier remarks about the 'puzzles' inherent in homuncular explanation. But while an account of division in terms of 'primary homunculi' might well be impaled on this dilemma, those of Freud and Davidson clearly avoid both horns, and in different ways; so neither is in the least discredited. Freud's distinct systems constitute one person, and the way these are ascribed motives, although metaphorical, is nonetheless genuinely explanatory, as far as it goes. Davidson's 'constellations' contain genuine motives, which serve to explain in the usual intentional way, except that their working is in some respects abridged; and they are not distinct agents at all. So in neither case is there a threat of multiple personality, nor of the substitution for intentional explanation of unacceptable metaphor. Davidson can avoid the paradoxes by reference to cohesive motives and intentional acts, and Freud by reference to agencies and their goals; and these kinds of explanation are coherent, both internally and with one another.

We can indicate this by starting with Davidson's account of akrasia, and moving from it towards the kind of description in terms of the super-ego which we have already considered. Davidson gives the following example, taken from a note in Freud's case history of the Rat Man:

A man walking in a park stumbles on a branch in the path. Thinking the branch may endanger others, he picks it up and throws it in a hedge beside the path. On his way home it occurs to him that the branch may be projecting from the hedge and so still be a threat to unwary walkers. He gets off the tram he is on, returns to the park, and restores the branch to its original position . . . It is easy to imagine that [he] realizes that his action is not sensible. He has a motive for removing the stick, namely that it may endanger a passer-by. But he also has a motive for not returning, which is the time and trouble it costs. In his own judgment, the latter consideration outweighs the former; yet he acts on the former. In short, he goes against his own best judgment. (Davidson, 1982, p. 294; cf. Freud, vol. 10, p. 192).

Davidson explains how this example fits his account of akrasia, and also indicates how it might be deepened, through exploring his conception of a divided mind:

Recall the analysis of akrasia. There I mentioned no partitioning of the mind because the analysis was at that point more descriptive than explanatory. But the way would be cleared for explanation if we were to suppose two semi-autonomous departments of the mind, one that finds a certain course of action to be, all things considered, best, and another that prompts another course of action. On each side, the side of sober judgment and the side of incontinent intent and action, there is a supporting structure of reasons, of interlocking beliefs, expectations, assumptions, attitudes and desires. To set the scene this way still leaves much unexplained, for we want to know why this double structure developed, how it accounts for the action taken, and also, no doubt, its psychic consequences and cure. What I stress here is that the partitioned mind leaves the field open to such further explanations . . .

To think about further explanations it will be useful to replace Davidson's example from Freud with another to which it is closely related. In the original example it was plain that the branch was more dangerous in its original position, so that the incontinent intent was also hostile. In this Freud took the example to be similar to many from the Rat Man's own behaviour. Thus once when his lady was leaving. 'He found a stone lying in the roadway and had a phantasy that her carriage might hit up against it and she might come to grief. He therefore put it out of the way, but twenty minutes later it occurred to him that this was absurd and he went back in order to replace the stone in its position' (Freud, vol. 10, p. 307). It is easy to imagine that the Rat Man also thought it would be best, all things considered, to let the stone remain in the safe place to which he had moved it, so that his action in moving it again was akratic. Here, however, we know something further about 'two semi-autonomous departments of the mind' each with many cooperating motives, one of which was for, and the other against, the akratic act. The Rat Man's attitude towards his lady was marked by the same deep ambivalence and conflict as that towards his father, as shown in the fact that he also frequently wished the rats on her, and suffered as a result, particularly, it seems, when she vexed him by doing things like going away from him, as in the example above. On the side of moving the stone again, then, were arrayed a group of motives hostile to the lady, and shown also in the original phantasy that she might come to grief on it; while good sense (as well, perhaps, as the constellation involving the desire to protect her in accord with which he first moved the stone) would council letting it lie in its safe new place.

The Rat Man was often ready to acknowledge his 'vindictive impulses' (vol. 10. p. 185) towards his lady, so the episode as described might not have involved even ordinary self-deception. Still we can easily imagine that it did, and that this can be explained in Davidson's way. Suppose, having told Freud of the episode, the Rat Man had tried to explain his bothering to return – to put the rock in what had originally struck him as a dangerous position – by saying 'I did it to adhere to the ideal of rationality.' There might be a good deal behind this: as he walked along the road, say, he muttered rhythmically to himself 'I *must* be rational, I *shall* be rational, I *shall* leave things as they were.' And acting rationally, we might suppose, was one of his ideals, and one he took Freud and himself to share, but which he knew he often fell short of.

We can imagine that this made him more comfortable, but that it was self-deception. For he recalls, say, that – although he was scarcely aware of it, and did not think about it at the time – he was in fact feeling angrier with his lady with each step he took along the road, and hence with each rhythmic muttering about doing what was rational; and as he walked away he imagined her carriage smashed to bits on the stone he had put back, and thought '*That* will serve her right, for having dared to abandon me!' Material like this might lead us to judge that he had moved the stone as a result of an impulse to harm his lady, but that (in accord with a cohesive constellation of motives aimed at) wanting to look better in his own eyes, he had made himself think that he was doing it to adhere to an ideal of rationality, and had done so partly by talking to himself.[21]

Such an explanation would presuppose that the agent's motives fell into groups partly comparable to those of a deceiver and a deceived, and also that he was not fully aware of their operation in these constellations at the time. Ascribing this lack of connecting awareness, however, would not be treating him as two distinct agents: for the motives were all his, and he was more or less aware of the thoughts and feelings connected with their operation, and clearly relevant to their ascription, all the time. Hence also he might readily acknowledge in retrospect that he had been deceiving himself with his talk of rationality, and that this had involved something like the 'flight from anxiety' which Johnston emphasizes: and in this he might also appreciate that the 'protective' constellation of motives on which he had acted in stressing rationality was a natural concomitant of his ambivalence, which required him to be more or less unaware of his real motives so as to act in accord with his hatred without suffering guilt. And we might know, and he might be able to acknowledge, that in deceiving himself in this way he had chosen his means well, because he knew his man: the line he fed himself worked because it was flattering, and it was one he could be depended on to fall for.

Some divided constellations of motives thus are, or might be, clear enough; and these might serve to explain instances of akrasia and self-deception in considerable detail. Still, as Davidson says, this leaves much unexplained, for we want to know about the causes of these divisions, and where relevant their cure. This is what Freud's account tells us. Division or fragmentation in the self goes with division or fragmentation in (the representation of) those to whom the self has been most fundamentally related. The 'double structure' of love and hate is ultimately built around disparate 'imagos' or prototypes of the parents, which were the earliest objects of these emotions, and hence the objects towards which they were directed in their most primitive forms. These early prototypes remain active in us, and shape our representations of ourselves and of subsequent objects of thought and feeling, and so partly determine the thoughts and feelings themselves. In this they contribute to the forming of what Freud called the ego and super-ego, so that the image of a prohibiting and punitive father can both cause a rebellious and resentful desire to punish, and also be incorporated in a conscience whose punitive severity renders its possessor suicidally depressed; and such images can emerge in analysis, as indicated in chapter 22, and hence be modified by further experience and thought. Still, the altering of basic psychic prototypes is a far more difficult matter than unravelling a piece of self-deception. Such change requires what Freud called working through, and this can be a time-consuming process; but the psychic consequences are accordingly more far reaching.

The understanding of such early prototypes, and hence of division in the mind more generally, was significantly advanced by the work of Melanie Klein. She was able to extend Freud's methods to the analysis of even very young children, by allowing them free and uninhibited play as well as free association; and she observed that in these conditions children not only played out the satisfaction of the childhood desires which Freud had hypothesized, but also others, which were more extreme, and which allowed her to extend his theories in a systematic way (cf. notes 11, 16 and 18 in chapter 22). She found that very disparate images of the parents, and hence of the self, seemed operative in disturbed children from early in life; and that the earliest prototypes, which lay at the root of all others, were the most fragmented, incoherent and extreme of all. Hence she hypothesized that the original conflict-engendering images were laid down in early infancy, before the baby developed a working grasp of the concept of identity. The infant liable to violent emotion and excessive projection could not, in Hume's phrase, 'unite the broken appearances' of the parents, by synthesizing them into coherent wholes; and this incoherence was reflected back in its infantile experience and image of itself. Thus, on Klein's account, a fundamental task of infancy is that of integrating our experience, including that of persons, by means of the concept of an enduring and spatio-temporally coherent object. Psychoanalysis traces divisions in the self to failures in this original synthesis, and so provides an explanation of the 'double structure' which is both conceptually and empirically deep. And in the case of the self, the understanding of the broken images which are the causes of its division tends also to knit these images together, and so provide the means of its cure.

Notes

1 In what follows, references to Freud (1956) will be by volume and page number in parentheses. The topics of irrationality and the division of the self are also discussed in relation to psychoanalytic theory in Gardener (1993).

2 This particular dream is discussed more fully, and Freud's interpretation defended against criticisms advanced by Clark Glymour and Adolf Grunbaum, in Hopkins (1988, p. 45 ff). Methodological issues connected with psychoanalysis and interpretation more generally are considered in Hopkins (1992, 1994b, forthcoming).

3 The role of free association is considered in more detail in Hopkins (1992).

4 The material from the case of the Rat Man in chapter 22 illustrates a number of these phenomena. Thus, for example, he appears to have repressed his fear of his father (and of Freud in the transference) by wishfully representing their relations as ideal, and in ways which involved wishful memory and perhaps perception (that

his father never punished him, that his relations with Freud and his father were marked by delicacy of feeling on his own part). Again, his thought during his first intercourse – 'This is a glorious feeling; one might do anything for this – murder one's father, for instance' – was not felt to be hostile, and so would seem to have had some of its affect removed or denied. This was true also of his other symptomatic thoughts: in a number of cases, for example, he wished the rats on people in hostility, and knew that he was doing so; in the case of his father, however, he was aware neither of the hostility nor the wishing, but only the resulting phantasy. The topic of division is discussed in some detail below.

5   Davidson has not sought to clarify the notion of identity of state he here seems to draw upon, and it is unclear that he either needs or is entitled to it.

6   But see the use of supervenience to rebut charges that anomalous monism makes the mental causally irrelevant in Davidson (1993).

7   Tarski (1956) criticized and replaced the use of quotation marks in this schema. I trust the displaced use will serve for purposes of illustration here.

8   Compare the more detailed treatment of teleological explanation in Bennett (1982).

9   Note that when the desire that Q and the (true) belief that if P then Q cause the desire that P and hence P, this will in turn cause Q. So the overall pattern will be one in which the desire that Q causes Q, that is, a further instance of (3). Specifications like this fail to bring out the comprehensive way in which our explanations by reasons reach from overarching goals through the plans by which we pursue them to the sequential bodily movements by which we effect these plans. This is relevant to the interpretive coherence stressed in chapter 22, and is discussed in more detail in Hopkins (1994b) (forthcoming).

10 An interpreter faced with an utterance of some sentence 'S' can be thought of as trying to find an explanation of this speech act along the lines of (5) and (3), and hence by fitting it into some such pattern as:

A's desire that he says that p and belief that if he utters 'S' then he says that p - [causes]→A's desire that he utters 'S' -[causes]→A's utterance of 'S'

This involves a schema in the form of (5), in which the fillings for Q and if P then Q are 'A says that p' and 'If A utters "S" then A says that p' respectively. The interpreter thus represents the semantic beliefs in accord with which the interpretee says things by instances of the pattern 'If A utters "S" then A says that p.' To specify these beliefs, therefore, the interpreter must be able to map indefinitely many values for 'S' on to values for p in accord with this pattern. If interpreter and interpretee speak the same language, the interpreter's own correlation (2) suffices; if not the interpreter must find the relevant correlation, by constucting something like a theory of truth for the interpretee's language.

11 The notions of interpretive coherence and dissonance are discussed more fully in Hopkins (1994b, forthcoming); the notion of an interpretative correlation or regularity is related to Wittgenstein in Hopkins (forthcoming).

12 See Churchland (1986, ch. 10; the quoted phrases are from p. 428). For a more recent account of research of this kind see Churchland and Seznowski (1992), and for reference to its relation to Freud see note 18 below.

13 Davidson holds that we know many non-strict psychological generalizations – one example he gives is 'The burnt child fears the fire' – which support counterfactuals but 'unlike those of physics, cannot be sharpened without limit, cannot be turned

into the strict laws of a science closed within its area of application' (1973, 1980, p. 250). His negative argument thus turns on his conception of strictness and his example of strictness is physics. The required interpretive slack emerges only as difference from generalizations which can be reduced to, or sharpened like, those of physics; and it seems likely that very many useful generalizations will, by this criterion, remain forever slack. Hence Davidson speculates that analogous claims may hold for other sciences, such as biology, and stresses also that some sciences use generalizations which are less strict than many in psychology (1974, 1980, p. 240; and cf. 1993, pp. 8–9). Fodor (1981) discusses a range of analogous cases. In giving his argument, Davidson points out that many of our psychological generalizations have surprisingly little strictness; they contain tacit circularities, the *ceteris paribus* clauses implicit in their use are generous and open-ended, and so on. What he actually seeks to prove, however, is less dramatic. Still, Johnston seems to provide no objection to Davidson's argument, nor to the view of the psychological which it is meant to reinforce; and what I take to be the errors in Johnston's characterization of Davidson's position would be explicable on the assumption that he has overlooked Davidson's emphasis on strictness.

14   On this account neural structures would stand in a one–many relation to the psychological states (dispositions) which they realize, just as molecular structures stand in a one–many relation to the manifest properties and dispositions of material objects. This claim seems also supported by commonsense considerations: events of perception, or change of mind, seems always to involve many beliefs together, rather than a single belief.

15   cf. Davidson (1976, 1980, p. 265: 'the line I have been developing suggests that the laws implicit in reason explanations are simply the generalizations implied by the attributions of dispositions'.

16   Millikan (1984) contains a most interesting discussion of common-sense psychology from an evolutionary perspective.

17   There are, of course, also other cases: e.g. that in which a desire is satisfied but not pacified: the agent doesn't think that the conditions of satisfaction obtain, and so keeps trying; or again that in which there is an equivalent of pacification, but without belief-like representation, as when someone ceases to want to drink because unknown to him he has been given water intravenously.

18   This interpretation coheres with so much in the case, including his repeatedly 'wishing the rats' on people who annoyed him, and as an expression of hostility, that it seems hard to regard it as unsupported. Thus compare his 'for every copulation a rat' at p. 296; 'for each *krone* a rat' and 'for each florin a rat for the children' at p. 288; 'so many *kreutzers*, so many rats' at p. 307; and 'he wished the rats on her' at p. 308.

19   The notion of pacification on which these remarks turn seems closely related to what Pears (1985) says about the role of belief as the 'messinger' and hence 'immediate cause' of the gratification consequent on success, in the paragraph quoted by Johnston on p. 441. In reply to this Johnston points out, in effect, that the pacificatory role of belief does not itself explain the role of anticipatory wishful thought, which is directed specifically to the future, and which he illustrates by the case of the gambler who risks getting lost in phantasies of winning, and so betting irrationally.

It is unclear that this does need separate explanation, since even in the case of belief about the future, wishful phantasy still represents satisfaction as if it were present. The gambler who loses himself in anticipatory wishful phantasies surely imagines himself as *winning*, as watching the longed-for face card turn up, or as triumphantly raking in the pot, cutting a grand figure with the winnings, or whatever. So although his wishful belief is that he *will* win, the phantasies that prompt and accompany this belief may still occupy the causal role which Pears describes as that of messinger, and this seems the paradigmatic case. Johnston rightly objects to the idea of 'a kind of "dream time" which is not determinately past, present or future'. The fact remains, however, that anticipatory phantasy does involve a sort of temporal dislocation. We are dealing, as we can say, with cases of counting one's chickens before they are hatched; and counting before they are hatched really is different from believing that once hatched they *will be* numerous, with a clear eye to the future. Hence the day-dreaming gambler may try to bring himself back by concentrating on real temporal relations, by saying things like 'Nothing of the kind has so far happened, and it will not happen unless you keep your head.'

Still Johnston's demand for explanation at a deeper level, such as that of conditioning which he explores, is certainly relevant in general. The place to look, however, would now seem to be recent work on connectionism, which Freud anticipated in some detail. Thus, as sketched in Hopkins (1994a), in his early *Project for a Scientific Psychology* (Freud, vol. 1, p. 283 ff), Freud hypothesized that the working of the brain could be understood as the passage of some form of excitation by way of connections among neurons. On this view information was stored in the brain in the form of alterations – facilitations or inhibitions – of these connections, and was processed in the course of passing through, and thus again altering, the interconnected neurons themselves. Hence, as Freud put it, 'psychic acquisition generally', including memory, was '*represented by the differences in the facilitations*' of neural connections. (Freud, vol. 1, p. 300).

Accordingly, Freud sought to explain the tropism involved in wish-fulfilment in terms of a conception of neural prototype activation similar to that recently developed in Churchland (1989, chs. 9 and 10), and via Hebbian mechanisms which would also explain conditioning; and many other instances of non-rational causality in his work are either implicitly or naturally treated in the same terms. Thus transference can be seen in terms of the activation of prototypes of the parents; for example, that of the punishing father shown in the episode discussed at chapter 22, p. 420 and following. Likewise, condensation in dreams can be seen in terms of the simultaneous activation of emotionally related prototypes, and so forth. At a more abstract level Freud attempted to treat the ego as a system of interconnected neurons which had the power to alter facilitations and levels of excitation elsewhere in the brain, and this has similarities to ideas in recent work on evolved teaching networks, e.g. in Nolfi and Parisi (1991) and discussed in Clark (1993).

Freud's *Project* and its relation to connectionism is discussed in Glymour (1991); an interesting previous discussion is Gill and Pribram (1976). There is a recent overview of connectionist work in relation to neuroscience in Churchland and Sejnowski (1992).

20 It is worth noting that these descriptions seem clearly compatible with Freud's first account of the ego as a special system of interconnected neurons capable of exciting, inhibiting, and facilitating others, as mentioned in footnote 21 above, and discussed in some detail in Pribram and Gill 1976.

21 As regards the role of talking to oneself, cf. Johnston on the 'perceptual link' (chapter 23, p. 450), and note Davidson's use of the same sort of link, in the example of the mirror, or the testimony of a flatterer, in Davidson (1985, p. 144). Despite Davidson's apparent objection, it seems that people commonly lie to themselves by talking to themselves; it is just that they are characteristically unaware of their intentions in doing so.

22 Something of this development is noted in Hopkins (1994a); and Klein's work is discussed in some detail, and compared with that of Piaget, in Hopkins (1987). The notes in this article also relate Klein's theories to the Rat Man: cf. for example, the particularly clear projection of his early oral impulses on to Freud and his children, as shown in his phantasy of them gnawing away, like the rats of his other phantasies, at Freud's mother's body. This indicates a deeper level of oral phantasy, directed towards the mother, which Freud did not take up in his analysis.

References

Bennett, J. (1982) *Linguistic Behaviour*. Cambridge, Cambridge University Press.

Clark, A. (1993) *Associative Engines: Connectionism, Concepts and Representational Change*. Cambridge, Mass., MIT Press.

Churchland P.A. (1986) *Neurophilosophy*. Cambridge, Mass., MIT Press.

Churchland, P.A. and Sejnowski, T. (1992) *The Computational Brain*. Cambridge, Mass., MIT Press.

Churchland, P.M. (1989) *A Neurocomputational Perspective*. Cambridge, Mass., MIT Press.

Davidson, D. (1963) Actions, reasons and causes. *Journal of Philosophy* 60, 685–700. Reprinted in *Essays on Actions and Events*, pp. 3–19. Oxford, Oxford University Press, 1980.

Davidson, D. (1973) The material mind. In P. Suppes, L. Henkin, G. Moisil and A. Joja (eds), *Proceedings of the Fourth International Congress for Logic, Methodology and Philosophy of Science*. Amsterdam: North Holland. Reprinted in *Essays on Actions and Events*, pp. 245–59. Oxford, Oxford University Press, 1980.

Davidson, D. (1974) Comments and replies to 'Philosophy as Psychology'. In S.C. Brown (ed.), *Philosophy of Psychology*. London, Macmillan. Reprinted in *Essays on Actions and Events*, pp. 229–44. Oxford, Oxford University Press, 1980.

Davidson, D. (1976) Hempel on explaining action. *Erkenntnis* 10, 239–53. Reprinted in *Essays on Actions and Events*, pp. 261–75. Oxford, Oxford University Press, 1980.

Davidson, D. (1980) *Essays on Actions and Events*. Oxford, Oxford University Press.

Davidson, D. (1982) Paradoxes of irrationality. In R. Wollheim and J. Hopkins (eds), *Philosophical Essays on Freud*, pp. 289–305. Cambridge, Cambridge University Press.

Davidson, D. (1985) Deception and division. In E. LePore and B. McLaughlin (eds), *Actions and Events: Perspectives on the Philosophy of Donald Davidson*. Oxford, Basil Blackwell.

Davidson, D. (1993) Thinking causes. In J. Heil and A. Mele (eds), *Mental Causation*. Oxford, Clarendon Press.

Fodor, J. (1981) Special sciences. In *Representations: Philosophical Essays on the Foundations of Cognitive Science*. Brighton, Harvester Press.

Freud, S. (1956) *The Standard Edition of the Complete Psychological Works*, ed. J. Strachey. London, Hogarth Press and the Institute of Psychoanalysis.

Gardener, S. (1993) *Irrationality and the Philosophy of Psychoanalysis*. Cambridge, Cambridge University Press.

Gill, M. and Pribram, K. (1976) *Freud's Project Re-assessed*. London, Hutchinson.

Glymour, C. (1991) Freud's androids. In J. Neu (ed.), *The Cambridge Companion to Freud*. Cambridge, Cambridge University Press.

Hopkins, J. (1987) Synthesis in the imagination: psychoanalysis, infantile experience, and the concept of an object. In J. Russell (ed.), *Philosophical Perspectives on Developmental Psychology*. Oxford, Basil Blackwell.

Hopkins, J. (1988) Epistemology and depth psychology. In S. Clark and C. Wright (eds), *Psychoanalysis, Mind and Science*, pp. 33–60. Oxford, Basil Blackwell.

Hopkins, J. (1991) The interpretation of dreams. In J. Neu (ed.), *The Cambridge Companion to Freud*. Cambridge, Cambridge University Press.

Hopkins, J. (1992) Psychoanalysis, interpretation and science. In J. Hopkins and A. Savile (eds), *Psychoanalysis, Mind and Art: Perspectives on Richard Wollheim*, pp. 3–35. Oxford, Basil Blackwell.

Hopkins, J. (1994a) The unconscious. In S. Guttenplan (ed.), *A Companion to the Philosophy of Mind*. Oxford, Basil Blackwell.

Hopkins, J. (1994b) Patterns of Interpretation. In L. Marcus (ed.), *Cultural Documents: the Interpretation of Dreams*. Manchester, Manchester University Press.

Hopkins, J. (forthcoming) Wittgenstein, Davidson, and the methodology of interpretation.

Millikan, R.G. (1984) *Language, Thought, and Other Biological Categories*. Cambridge, Mass., MIT Press.

Nolfi, S. and Parisi, D. (1991) Auto-teaching: networks that develop their own teaching input. Institute of Psychology, CNR, Rome, Technical report PCIA91–03.

Pears, D. (1985) *Motivated Irrationality*. Oxford, Oxford University Press.

Tarski, A. (1956) The concept of truth in formalized languages. In A. Tarski (ed.), *Logic, Semantics, and Metamathematics*. Oxford, Oxford University Press.

Index